Introduction to Philosophy of Religion

3rd Edition

Ted M. Preston, Ph.D.
Rio Hondo College

A Local Source Textbook™ Company

Introduction to Philosophy of Religion

Preface to the Third Edition

The third edition of this text corrects minor errors from the previous edition, and offers a substantially revised and expanded chapter on critical thinking. The chapter on the problem of evil has been expanded to incorporate some of the "soul making" theodicy of John Hick. I have also added an entirely new chapter on the alleged tension between divine foreknowledge and human free will. These changes and additions are the product of the "living laboratory" provided by my students, for whom I am grateful.

Acknowledgments

The motivation for this textbook is both personal and professional. Professionally, my desire for this book is the same as that of my others: that it provides an engaging, accessible, affordable, and possibly even enjoyable introduction to difficult (but fascinating) philosophical ideas and themes. Personally, I am myself intrigued by the questions explored in the philosophy of religion, and this journey is as much my own as I hope it will be for those who read these pages.

I would once again like to thank my colleague Dr. Adam Wetsman for his vision of Gnutext, and for knowing how to make it all happen. I continue to be in debt to my colleague and friend, Professor Scott Dixon, for not only reviewing portions of this book, but also for the countless (fruitful) conversations we've had on the topics addressed herein. I owe an intellectual debt to Professor Steven Davis for being my first instructor in the philosophy of religion, and whose clear analytical prose I hope to have modeled in my own writing. Last, but not least, I would like to thank my students, for whom I write.

Table of Contents

Introduction

Despite its title, this is not a book about "religion." It might not even be a book about "God," despite its best efforts. Indeed, one of the issues addressed in this book is the extent to which philosophical arguments for, against, or about God are meaningful and useful.

I hope I haven't poisoned my own well with that introduction! Given that the topic of this book is the "philosophy of religion," though, a confession (of sorts) seemed appropriate. If all goes according to plan, you will be able to discern for yourself whether or not arguments for (or against) God's existence are convincing or useful, and to what extent philosophy may be of service to the legitimately important questions to which the philosophy of religion is devoted.

Let there be no misunderstanding: the fundamental issue addressed in this book (and others like it)—the existence of God—is arguably the most important issue with which any of us might grapple. If classical logic has any role to play in this conversation, then either there *is* something "divine" (somehow conceived) about Reality, or there is *not*. Either way, it would seem that the answer to that most fundamental of questions should be of monumental importance to the way we understand the world and how it works, human nature and identity, the purpose and value of existence, the nature of goodness (and evil) and moral obligation, the nature of death, and numerous other *really important and interesting things.* Blaise Pascal expressed something similar in his *Pensées*:

"Among those who do not believe, I make a vast difference between those who strive with all their power to inform themselves, and those who live without troubling or thinking about it.... And how can it happen that the following argument occurs to a reasonable man?

'I know not who put me into the world, nor what the world is, nor what I myself am. I am in terrible ignorance of everything. I know not what my body is, nor my senses, nor my soul, not even that part of me which thinks what I say, which reflects on all and on itself, and knows itself no more than the rest. I see those frightful spaces of the universe which surround me, and I find myself tied to one corner of this vast expanse, without knowing why I am put in this place rather than in another, nor why the short time which is given me to live is assigned to me at this point rather than at another of the whole eternity which was before me or which shall come after me. I see nothing but infinities on all sides, which surround me as an atom, and as a shadow which endures only for an instant and returns no more. All I know is that I must soon die, but what I know least is this very death which I cannot escape.

As I know not whence I come, so I know not whither I go. I know only that, in leaving this world, I fall for ever either into annihilation or into the hands of an angry God, without knowing to which of these two states I shall be forever assigned. Such is my state, full of weakness and uncertainty. And from all this I conclude that I ought to spend all the days of my life without caring to inquire into what must happen to me. Perhaps I might find some solution to my doubts, but I will not take the trouble, nor take a step to seek it; and after treating with scorn those who are concerned with this care, I will go without foresight and without fear to try this great event, and let myself be led carelessly to death, uncertain of the eternity of my future state.'[1]

Who would desire to have for a friend a man who talks in this fashion? Who would choose him out from others to tell him of his affairs? Who would have recourse to him in affliction? And indeed to what use in life could one put him?"

In other words, the sorts of questions we explore are really important questions that ought to be explored (regardless of the particular conclusions one might reach). Legitimate debate is not only possible, but actual, with regard to how best to address those questions (including "the big one"), and even whether or not the question *can* be (intelligibly) addressed. The primary purpose of this book is to explore ways in which we can use the tools of philosophy to think about the existence (or non-existence) of God. Be forewarned: this is not a book aimed at Evangelism. Although I have my own view, of course, about the issues we will explore, I will not attempt to convert any of you to any particular position, or persuade you of the merits of any particular argument (with a few exceptions, perhaps). To that end, I hope to mask my own point of view as much as I am able, though, being all-too-human, it's possible that I will fail to do so. Any such failure is an accident.

Before going any further, I want to attempt to distinguish the philosophy of religion from theology and religious studies. This is important because the distinctions are admittedly fuzzy, easily confused, and can generate a lot of misunderstanding and false expectations with regard to the philosophy of religion.

The philosophy of religion is a prominent and thriving aspect of philosophy in general. It tends to be popular because religion is popular (even for those hostile to it). As one might expect, philosophy of religion is simply an examination of religious issues using the tools of philosophy. As such, a great many topics fall into its domain. A very incomplete list might include the following:

- Arguments for or against the existence of God
- Examining the relationship between omniscience and human free will
- Examining the relationship between Providence or predestination and free will
- Examining the problem of evil
- Examining whether the alleged properties of God are internally consistent
- Examining the epistemological properties of faith

---

[1] Pascal, Blaise. *Pensées*. Translated by W.F. Trotter (1910). Section 3, #194.

The list can go on and on, but this is sufficient to get a crude idea of what we talk about when doing philosophy of religion. You might have noticed something conspicuous in the list: it was all very "generic." That is, there were no obvious references to particular religious traditions. No mention of Jesus, or Moses, or Allah, for example. There's a reason for that. Although there are always exceptions, and although the lines are often blurred, and although not everyone always plays by these rules, there is a difference between philosophy and theology.

Theology, in general, is usually an examination of religious issues from within the perspective of a particular religious tradition. This is why we have Christian theology, Jewish theology, Muslim theology, etc. We even have further divisions within the same religion: Protestant theology, Catholic theology, etc. Some of you might have noticed that I've not mentioned Buddhism, Hinduism, or any other non-Western religious tradition. There's a reason for that. I'm a Western philosopher, and my expertise is in the Western philosophical tradition. The concept of God that is usually addressed in Western philosophy is drawn from the great religions of the West: Christianity, Judaism, and Islam. This is not to say that there is no such thing as philosophy of Buddhism. It is to say that such a focus is an uncommon specialty in the West—though quite common in the East! In other words, don't read too much into the selectivity of the traditions we're addressing. It's simply a culturally-contingent outcome.

As mentioned, theology usually works from within a particular religious tradition. Though this is certainly not a requirement, it is often the case that theologians are themselves a member of that same religious tradition. A great many Christian theologians are priests or pastors, or at least consider themselves Christians. A great many Jewish theologians are rabbis, or are, at the very least, Jewish. And so on. What's more, theology can take for granted what philosophy must put to the question. What do I mean by that?

Christian theologians don't tend to spend very much time trying to convince their readers that God exists, or that the Christian experience of God is the correct one. It's taken as a "given."

They're preaching to the choir, in that respect. There are always exceptions, but for the most part, theologians take for granted the most basic assumptions of their religion and use those foundational assumptions to explore more minute, and subtle aspects of the religion.

Philosophers of religion, on the other hand, will often focus on those very same foundational issues, trying, for example, to prove the existence of God. Consider the different ways a Christian theologian and a philosopher might explore various issues concerning "prophecy."

Theologian (Christian)	Philosopher of Religion
What is the best interpretation of the Book of Revelation?	To what extent is belief in prophetic claims epistemically warranted?
Who is the Church and what will happen to it during "end times"?	Is prophecy compatible with personal freedom and responsibility?

Don't get hung up on trying to discern the precise differences between theology and philosophy. That's not the point, and it's bound to be a frustrating exercise. The point in mentioning this contrast is mainly to provide for appropriate expectations of what's to come. Most people taking introductory level philosophy classes are not exactly experts in philosophy (if they were, I'm puzzled as to why they would be taking an introductory philosophy class!), and misunderstandings of what philosophy is, and is not, abound. Students enrolling in a philosophy of religion course, or upon noting that there will be a unit on philosophy of religion in a general introductory course, will often misinterpret what that means, and will anticipate something akin to a Bible study class. This misunderstanding is exacerbated by at least two additional factors.

First, in popular book stores (e.g., Walden Books, Barnes & Noble), the philosophy section is often next to (or mixed in with) the religious studies section, or even the "new age" section. Plato's *Republic* sits next to a book on the use of healing crystals, and Nietzsche's *Beyond Good and Evil* sits next to a concordance to the Bible.

Second, at the community college level, there is usually no distinct religious studies department, and religious studies courses are actually labeled "philosophy courses." At my own college, for example, we used to offer an introduction to world religions course. This course was, in essence, an introduction to the concept of religion, a general overview of the historical development of religions, and a basic survey of the major religious traditions of the world. The course was part history, part anthropology, part literature, and part comparative religion. If any philosophy was done in the course, it was incidental to the actual goal and methods of the course. Yet, this course was named "Philosophy 150."[2]

Again, let's not dwell overmuch on this issue. For our purposes, understand that philosophy and theology (or religious studies) are two distinct (equally legitimate and impressive) disciplines, each with their own methods and foci. Understand, too, that because we are approaching religious issues from the perspective of philosophy, the sorts of questions we will ask, and answers we will seek, will tend to be abstracted

---

[2] You might have noted the use of the past tense in my mention of that course. My colleague and I decided to no longer offer the course based on just the reasons I mentioned: it was a course in religious studies, and both of us are philosophers. There is nothing wrong with such a course. Indeed, the history and comparison of the world's religious traditions is fascinating and worthy of study—and therefore worthy of being taught by people who have devoted their academic and professional life to religious studies.

away from the more specific historical and doctrinal elements of any particular (Western) religious tradition.

Now that we have a rough sense of what the philosophy of religion is, we can actually do some of it. Chapter 1 will provide an introduction to some basic aspects of critical thinking. This might be review for some of you—especially if you are already students of philosophy—but it's important to have some shared vocabulary and ways of thinking in place before tackling particular arguments. Chapters 2 and 3 will consider the role and value of theistic arguments. Chapters 4-7 will be devoted to the most prominent (general) arguments for God's existence in the Western philosophical tradition: the ontological, cosmological, design, and moral arguments. Within each of those chapters, we will also consider the more prominent criticisms of each argument. Chapter 8 will be devoted to an argument *against* God's existence— arguably the most common and visceral of such arguments: the problem of evil. Of course, we will consider criticism of the problem of evil as well. Chapter 9 will consider the alleged tension between omniscience and free will. Chapter 10 will turn to the epistemic status of miracles, and chapter 11 will consider issues of religious pluralism/universalism versus exclusivism.

Each chapter will begin with a few comprehension questions. These are questions that you should be able to answer once you have read that chapter, and digested the information you read. They are also, therefore, indicators of key ideas from each chapter—especially important things that I think you should know. The questions are there for your benefit, so I encourage you to use them. Read the questions before reading the chapter, so as to give yourself a preview of the especially important ideas on which to focus. Then, when you have finished a chapter, see if you can answer those questions, with confidence. They are meant to provide a means of self-assessment, a way for you to gauge how well you understood the material.

Finally, at the end of nearly every chapter you will find one or more reading selections pertaining to the main topic of that chapter. These are excerpts from some of the larger works of some of the finest minds from Western philosophy of religion. Although I like to think that my own summaries and introductions are illuminating, engaging primary source materials is an essential part of studying philosophy. You will discover that (with a few exceptions), I have not provided specific summaries or explanations of the text selections themselves. There is a reason for that. Engaging the readings yourself, grappling with the arguments, and coming to your own understanding—even if initially hesitant—is one of the primary tasks of philosophy. Your instructor will undoubtedly offer assistance along the way, but it's important to meet with these thinkers, your mind to their minds, and participate in the great conversation that we call philosophy. It's also important to remember that we all stand on the shoulders of those who came before us. To remain ignorant of their ideas and achievements, and to attempt to "reinvent the wheel" ourselves, is inefficient at best, and intellectually dishonest and disrespectful, at worst.

Chapter 1: Critical Thinking

Comprehension questions you should be able to answer after reading this chapter:

1. What is "epistemology?"

2. What is the definition of "knowledge?"

3. What is a "claim?" What does it mean to say that a claim has a "truth-value?"

4. What is an argument?

5. What is meant by a "relevance-relationship" between premises and a conclusion? What does it mean for a deductive argument to be "valid?"

6. What does it mean for a deductive argument to be "sound?"

7. Why is the soundness of arguments often difficult to establish?

8. What is the principle of charity?

9. What is a "worldview?" What do we usually do (in general) when a claim fits with our worldview? What about when it conflicts with it? If a claim that conflicts with our worldview is proven to be true, what should we do with our worldview?

10. What are the four conditions under which it is reasonable to accept an unsupported claim as true?

11. What are the ways in which we establish the expertise of sources?

12. What are the two justification questions we ask when presented with a new piece of information?

13. What are the different meanings of "fake news?" Why is "fake news" a problem?

14. When should we suspend judgment concerning the truth or falsity of a claim?

15. How is "truth" understood by epistemic relativism and by the correspondence theory?

Argument

When one thinks of "religion," including "philosophy of religion," the word "argument" probably comes to mind—though probably for the wrong reason. It's an old cliché that one doesn't talk about politics or religion at parties, and ethical issues are often regarded in the same way. For most of us, if you want to start an "argument" at a family dinner, we should bring up either politics or religion or some sort of moral issue. That is not usually, however, what an "argument" means in the context of philosophy.

Before delving into the nuances of arguments, though, we need to back up and develop a basic understanding of epistemology, so that we *know* what we're talking about.

Epistemology, the focus of this chapter, is the study of knowledge. Believe it or not, there's some pretty serious debate concerning how best to understand "knowledge." Some, for example, believe that we can never possess knowledge. Classical skeptics fit this description. Others believe that "knowledge" is never more than personal perspective. Despite the plurality of views, there is a generally accepted definition of knowledge that seems to work for most people, in most cases. There are some complications, of course, and some disagreements here and there, but, for the most part, Plato's understanding of knowledge is pretty good. In his dialogue, the *Theaetetus*, Plato has the character Socrates (his real life mentor and friend) explore the proper definition of knowledge. The most promising candidate that emerges is that knowledge is "justified, true belief." Or, as Plato puts it, "true belief with an account."

Why should we accept Plato's definition? Plato is a giant in Western Philosophy, to say the least. A student of Socrates himself, Plato (428/427 BCE—348/347 BCE) founded the first institution of higher education (an "Academy") in the Western world. He also developed very impressive accounts of virtually every major topic of philosophical interest. Indeed, the 20th century philosopher Alfred North Whitehead said of Plato and Philosophy:

> *The safest general characterization of the European philosophical tradition is that it consists of a series of footnotes to Plato. I do not mean the systematic scheme of thought which scholars have doubtfully extracted from his writings. I allude to the wealth of general ideas scattered through them...*

Still, just because a definition comes from Plato doesn't *automatically* make it correct. To assume so is a fallacy—an "appeal to authority." The reason why (most of us) use this definition is because it seems like a pretty good one! You'll soon see why.

Knowledge: justified, true belief

Plato's definition has three components, each of which requires a little bit of explanation.

1. Belief

It is generally accepted that in order to know something, one must also believe it. It seems odd to say that I know Donald Trump is the current U.S. President, but that I don't believe that he is. Note that the reverse is not also true. We are quite comfortable with the idea that someone can believe something without also knowing it. For example, at the moment I'm writing this sentence, I believe my mother is at her home, but I wouldn't claim to *know* that she is. It's entirely possible that I'm not remembering her schedule accurately, and that she's volunteering somewhere. Or, perhaps she's on an errand? As we can see, to know something, one must also believe it, but one can believe without knowing.

An easy way to think of the relationship between belief and knowledge, in this sense, is with the language of a "promotion." We believe all kinds of things, but some of the things we believe have a special quality to them. These beliefs earn a "promotion," and a new title: knowledge. What is this quality that earns the belief a promotion to knowledge? As it turns out, this quality is the other two parts of our definition of knowledge: justification, and truth.

Before delving into justification, we'll spend a little more time on belief and complicate matters by asking what a belief *is*. A good chunk of my doctoral dissertation was devoted to just that question, but, once again, that level of analysis and expertise is not needed for our own purposes right now. At the minimum, we can simply talk about what form beliefs take in our language, so that we may easily identify them in speech and writing.

Very simply, beliefs appear in the form of "claims." *Claims* are statements, assertions, or propositions (different terms meaning roughly the same thing), and, due to that fact, have what is called a *"truth-value."* To say that a claim has a truth-value is simply to say that it must be either true or false (if true, then its truth-value is true; if false, then its truth-value is false). Note that we do not need to know *which* truth-value applies to a claim to know that it is a claim. Consider the examples below.

Claims	Not Claims
You are reading this sentence right now.	What time is it?
Barack Obama is the current U.S. president.	Please shut the door.
There is intelligent life elsewhere in the universe.	Ouch.

Remember, a claim is a statement that has to be either true or false (even if we're not sure which it is). You either are, or you are not, reading this book right now. Barack Obama either is, or is not, the current U.S. President. You're probably pretty confident about those two. What about life elsewhere in the universe? Well, you probably aren't certain either way. But (and this is the important part), we know that there either is, or there is not, intelligent life elsewhere in the universe. In other words, that claim has a truth-value, even though we don't know (for sure, right now) if that value is "true" or if it is "false."

Now, consider the other column of examples. What time is it? True or false? You probably had to reread those sentences just now, and my question probably still doesn't make any sense. There's a reason for that. "What time is it?" is not the sort of thing that can be either true or false. Neither is "Please shut the door." Neither is "ouch." None of those has a truth-value, because none is a claim, and therefore none is a belief. Why does this matter? Because claims are the building blocks of arguments, and arguments form the core of what we study and what we do in philosophy.

For most of us, if you want to start an "argument" at a family dinner, we should bring up either politics or religion or some sort of moral issue. That is not usually, however, what an "argument" means in the context of philosophy.

An argument is an attempt to establish the truth of a claim (the conclusion) by offering evidence (premises) in support of that claim. No name-calling, no chair-throwing, no raised voices—not even any presumption of disagreement. In a philosophical context, an argument is not a fight, but simply an attempt to make a point, using evidence, and following certain rules of reason.

Although we don't usually encounter arguments in the following format (except in philosophy courses), all arguments at least implicitly have the same general form:

Premise$_1$
Premise$_2$
Conclusion

Please note that we have not yet specified any particular content for that argument. That is because arguments can be about *anything*. Any time you try to persuade someone to believe anything at all, on the basis of some kind of reason/evidence, you are offering an argument. Also note that although there were two premises in the generic argument above, there is nothing special about that number. You might have only a single premise (piece of evidence), or you might have a hundred premises, or any other number whatsoever. So long as you have at least one piece of evidence, at least one reason to believe that the conclusion is true, you have provided an argument.

Every philosophical essay that you read in this book (or any other) is an argument, or at least contains arguments. What all arguments have in common is that they are attempts to prove that a claim (the conclusion) is true, by offering other claims (premises) as evidence. Note that both the conclusion of an argument and all the premises in an argument, are *claims*. This is not a trivial observation! Every (proper) piece of every argument is a claim. Therefore, every (proper) piece of every argument has a truth-value—which is what makes argument evaluation possible.

However, although some professional philosophers will sometimes write out their arguments in obvious "premise$_1$, premise$_2$, therefore conclusion" format, most philosophical readings are not so blatantly reader-friendly. Philosophical arguments will be made in the context of paragraphs, essays, chapters, or even entire books. As we read, then, our job is to identify the main point the author seems to be trying to make. This is the conclusion. Then, we must try to identify all of the supporting points the author provides in defense of that conclusion. These are the premises. Once we have identified the conclusion and premises, we are prepared to evaluate the argument.

I hope it's obvious that not all arguments are created equal. Just because you have offered a reason to believe something is true doesn't mean you have provided a *good* reason, or even a relevant one. Consider the following example:

Argument (A)
1.   Egg yolks are high in cholesterol.
2.   High cholesterol is associated with increased risk of heart disease.
3.   Therefore, God exists.

Argument (A) is laughably bad, and I'm sure you realize that, but it's important to recognize *why*. It doesn't take much reflection, or any fancy vocabulary, to describe what's going "wrong" with that argument: the premises don't have anything to do with the conclusion! You might rightfully be wondering what the heck eggs and cholesterol have to do with whether or not God exists! Clearly, the premises aren't *relevant* to the conclusion.

Relevance-relationships are an important initial way to evaluate the quality of an argument. In general, if the premises aren't "relevant," then we would say that little (if any) support has been provided for the conclusion—and that doesn't make for a very good argument! One specific example of this relevance relationship occurs with deductive arguments

Deductive arguments are constructed with the intent to provide for the certainty of the conclusion, on the assumption that the premises are true. Such arguments are (generally) evaluated in terms of their validity, and soundness. Both of those words (valid, sound) have specific meaning in the context of argument, and both (especially validity) have different uses in everyday speech. For example, you might hear someone say "that's a valid point." What that person means is that you have made a good point. In that usage, valid means something like "good," or "apt," or "true." That is not what "valid" means for our purposes, though.

Validity

A deductive argument is <u>valid</u> if the conclusion necessarily follows (logically) from the premises. Another way of putting that idea is that an argument is valid when, *if* the premises are true, the conclusion must also be true. Or, an argument is valid if it's impossible for the conclusion to be false, *if* all the premises are true. To repeat: validity indicates the right kind of "relevance-relationship" between the premises and the conclusion.

You might have noticed that I italicized the word "if" in a couple of places in the previous paragraph. There's a good reason for that. When we assess an argument's validity, it's a hypothetical exercise. We're not making any claim that the premises are, in fact, true—we're just asking what would happen *if* the premises are true. Consider the following:

1. All humans are mortal.
2. Preston is a human.
3. Therefore, Preston is mortal.

Is this argument "valid," according to our definition? To find out if it is, ask yourself the following: *if* all the premises are true, must the conclusion also be true? *If* it's true that all humans are mortal, and *if* it's true that Preston is a human, then, must it also be true that Preston is mortal? The answer, of course, is "yes." Therefore, this is a valid argument. This indicates that there is the right kind of logical relationship between the premises and conclusion, there is a relationship of structural relevance between them. We haven't yet established that the premises are, in fact, true (that's a later step), but we have established that if they are true, the conclusion is as well. That is very important. Let's reconsider example (A) from above:

Argument (A)
1. Egg yolks are high in cholesterol.
2. High cholesterol is associated with increased risk of heart disease.
3. Therefore, God exists.

Just a few paragraphs ago, we articulated the "badness" of this argument using ordinary language. Presumably, you recognized that eggs, cholesterol, and heart disease risks have nothing to do with whether or not God exists. There isn't the right kind of relationship between those premises, and the conclusion. If we consider this in terms of validity, the problem becomes clear.

Is it possible for it to be true that egg yolks are high in cholesterol, and true that high cholesterol is associated with increased risk of heart disease, and yet for it to be false that God exists? Of course that's possible! So, if, for some weird reason, you try to prove God's existence by appealing to the cholesterol content of eggs, you will fail in grand, embarrassing fashion. Even if all your evidence is proven to be true, you still will not have proven that your conclusion ("God exists") is true.

Soundness

If validity appeals to the hypothetical truth of the premises, soundness refers to their actual truth. *A deductive argument is "sound" when it is both valid and all its premises are, in fact, true.* Notice that in order for an argument to be sound, it must first already be valid. You can imagine an implicit checklist for argument evaluation:

☐   Is the argument valid?
☐   Is the argument sound?

Only if we can "check the first box" do we bother to consider whether the argument is sound. Let's go back to one of our earlier examples:

1. All humans are mortal.
2. Preston is a human.
3. Therefore, Preston is mortal.

Is the argument valid? Yes, it is (as established above).

✓   Is the argument valid?
☐   Is the argument sound?

Since it's valid, we can now move on to consider its soundness. Are all of the premises, in fact, true? To be honest, the question of "truth" opens Pandora's proverbial box. What does "truth" mean? What does it take for something to be true, let alone known to be true? You could spend an entire career as a philosophy professor focusing solely on the concept of "truth," and still have plenty of questions remaining. We will not spend entire careers on the concept of truth, but we will spend some time later in this chapter on several different interpretations of what it means for a claim to be true. For now, however, let's set aside the murky notion of "truth" and assume (for the sake of argument) that we know what it means for a claim to be true. Even so, how can we tell if a particular claim is, in fact, true?

Obviously, not all claims will be easily verifiable as true. While we might be fairly confident that it is true that egg yolks are high in cholesterol, some truth-values (unfortunately, probably the ones we tend to care the most about—truth-values for claims about morality, religion, politics, etc.), might be especially difficult to establish.

Do aliens exist, or not? Hard to say, since we haven't explored the entire universe just yet. Is abortion immoral? Hard to say, since there's so much disagreement, and so many compelling arguments that can be given on both sides. Does God exist? Hard to say, since there are compelling arguments on both sides of the debate, and legitimate debate as to what does or could count as evidence for God's existence in the first place....

Recognizing that some claims will be difficult to establish, let us return to a relatively easy argument just to complete our discussion of "soundness."

1. All humans are mortal.
2. Preston is a human.
3. Therefore, Preston is mortal.

In order for this argument to be sound, it has to be valid, and all of its premises must be true. We've already established that it's valid. Are its premises, in fact, true? Does the claim that "all humans are mortal" seem to be true? If we interpret "mortal" in its usual sense ("liable or subject to death"), then it does, in fact, appear to be true. That all humans are subject to death seems to be true, like it or not. What about the second premise? Is it, in fact, true that Preston (the author of this book) is a human? Again, if we're assuming the usual sense of "human" ("a member of the genus *Homo* and especially of the species *H. sapiens*"), then it would appear that Preston being human is true as well. Given that both premises are, in fact, true, we have established that the argument is not only valid, but sound.

✓ Is the argument valid?
✓ Is the argument sound?

If you have established that an argument is sound, you have proven that the conclusion is true. It doesn't get any better than that! Unfortunately, whenever we're dealing with serious, important arguments, it's usually pretty challenging to establish that the argument is sound. Consider another argument for God's existence:

(B)
1. The Bible proclaims that God exists.
2. The Bible is the true, inspired Word of God.
3. Therefore, God exists.

You should know the routine by now:

☐   Is the argument valid?
☐   Is the argument sound?

If it's true that the Bible proclaims that God exists, and it's also true that the Bible is the true, inspired Word of God, must it also be true that God exists? Yes. Technically, this is a valid argument. However, in this case, before even addressing the soundness of the argument, we have to address a sneaky little problem with its validity. This requires us to consider the strategy used by the person making this argument. This person is using the testimony of the Bible (premise 1) as support for the claim that God exists (conclusion). Why should we take the testimony of the Bible as good evidence? Because the Bible isn't just any ordinary book; it is a special book whose testimony is truthful because it is the inspired Word of God (premise 2). Of course, in order for the Bible to be the inspired Word of God, God would have to exist. So, implicit in the second premise is the claim that God exists. To be transparent, we would need to fill out the argument so as to reveal the implied (suppressed) premises, in which case the argument (now considerably longer and restructured) would look something like this:

1.   God exists.
2.   God's Word is always true.
3.   The Bible is the true, inspired Word of God
4.   The Bible proclaims that God exists.
5.   Therefore, God exists.

Really, this argument is much more complicated than it needs to be. We can simplify it by cutting out some (ultimately) unnecessary premises:

1.   God exists.
2.   Therefore, God exists.

If the premise (God exists) is true, must it be the case that the conclusion (God exists) is also true? You bet! If it is true that God exists, then it is also true that God exists. However, as I'm sure you've figured out, while this argument is valid, there is nothing impressive about it, even before considering issues of soundness. This argument is "question begging." An argument "begs the question" (or is question begging) when it assumes, in a premise, the very thing it is attempting to prove (the conclusion). Assuming what you are trying to prove is not really an argument anymore, but simply an assertion. Using less formal vocabulary, many of you probably figured out that the argument was problematic because only people who already believe that God exists would accept that the Bible is the Word of God. Please note that recognizing that argument (B) is question-begging, and therefore a flawed argument (in spite of its validity) does *not* indicate that any of its premises are, in fact, false, let alone that its conclusion is false. Just because the argument is (informally) fallacious doesn't somehow mean that the Bible is *not* the Word of God, or that God does *not* exist—it just means that this argument doesn't effectively *establish* God's existence.

Let's take a moment to summarize the ground we've covered so far. An argument is an attempt to prove some point by appealing to reasons that support that point. In order for an argument to be a good argument, it needs to at least be valid, and preferably sound as well. For an argument to be valid, it needs to be the case that if all the premises are true, the conclusion has to be true as well. For it to be sound, all the premises must, in fact, be true.

Some of you might have wondered about one of the sentences in that previous paragraph: "in order for an argument to be a good argument, it needs to at least be valid, and preferably sound as well." Perhaps that sentence made you pause, and ask something like "why only *preferably* sound? Why doesn't the argument have to be both valid and sound in order to be good?" If you wondered about that, good for you!

Ideally, of course, good arguments *will* be *both* valid and sound. But, if we insist that an argument be sound in order to be "good," we might be setting the bar so high that few, if any, arguments are "good." This is because, as we have already seen, soundness can be difficult and controversial to establish. Consider one more argument:

Argument (C)

1. If God does not exist, objective moral values and duties do not exist.
2. Objective moral values and duties do exist.
3. Therefore, God exists.

This is actually one of the more famous arguments for God's existence known as the "moral argument." We will consider the moral argument (MA) in a later chapter. For now, though, let's consider our checklist:

☐   Is the argument valid?
☐   Is the argument sound?

If both premises are true, must the conclusion also be true? Yes—and this shouldn't be surprising. Any of the "major" arguments for God's existence, the arguments that have withstood the test of time (often centuries, if not millennia), are presumably going to be valid—otherwise they would have been abandoned long ago.

✓   Is the argument valid?
☐   Is the argument sound?

Now that we know it's valid, is it sound? Is it, in fact, true that if God does not exist, objective moral values and duties do not exist? Is it, in fact, true that objective moral values and duties do exist? Those who use the moral argument for God's existence will offer reasons to accept both premises as true. If you find those reasons compelling, you will presumably conclude that both premises are, in fact, true—in which case you will conclude that the argument is sound. But, if you think the reasons are not compelling, you will instead conclude that the premises are not true—in which case you will conclude that the argument is not sound. Or, perhaps some of you, even after considering the MA in our later chapter, will come to the honest conclusion that you're just not sure if those premises are true, or not—in which case you will conclude that you don't know whether the argument is sound.

✓   Is the argument valid?
?   Is the argument sound?

That the soundness of this (or any other of the major arguments for, *or against*, God's existence) is in question should not be surprising. Remember: if an argument is sound, its conclusion *is, in fact, true*. So, if an argument for God's existence can be shown to be sound, that would mean that it is, in fact, true that God exists—and that this has been proven! Conversely, if an argument against God's existence were shown to be sound, it would mean that God has been proven not to exist. Had either of these events occurred, you probably would have heard about it! The fact that people still passionately debate these issues should tell us something about the difficulty in establishing the soundness of those sorts of arguments. Don't be discouraged, though. Just because it's difficult to establish the soundness of these sorts of arguments doesn't mean that there's no point in evaluating them, nor does it mean that we will be unable to say anything evaluative or interesting about them. Even if we're not *sure* if the MA (example C) is sound, it's clearly a better argument for God's existence than the one referencing the risks of high cholesterol (example A)!

It's important to point out that it's not very common, in everyday life, to encounter deductive arguments—let alone ones that are presented in such user-friendly formats as a clearly-indicated series of promises with an easily identifiable conclusion. Most people, most of the time, experience (and offer) arguments in far less formal terms. Accordingly, I think it's important to recognize the importance of concepts like validity and soundness, but not to get fixated on them. Recognize that they are examples of broader concepts of argument evaluation.

When someone is trying to convince you of something, the first thing to ask is whether or not any support is being offered. If the answer is "no," then that person is just making a statement, and we will consider how to evaluate unsupported claims a little later in this chapter. If, however, support is being offered, then you have been presented with an *argument*.

If someone is presenting you with an argument, you need to determine whether that support is relevant to the conclusion. With deductive arguments, this is a question of *validity*—but generally speaking you can just ask whether the premises are "relevant." If they are not relevant, that doesn't mean their conclusion is false, but it does mean their evidence doesn't really count as support, and you should treat the conclusion as an unsupported claim. If the premises are relevant, then the next step is to determine if they are true.

When relevant premises are not actually true, then they don't properly support their conclusion, and you should treat the conclusion as an unsupported claim. If the premises are true, however, then the argument is in pretty good shape. After all, we already determined they were relevant, and now we've determined they're also true. With deductive arguments, that means the argument is *sound*, and the conclusion has been *proven* to be true. Even if the argument isn't deductive, though, there is still probably some very impressive support for the conclusion such that it's at least likely to be true. In that case, you should consider how well that newly-proven conclusion fits with your worldview.

We will discuss worldviews in greater detail later in this chapter, but, for now, just know that your worldview is your basic understanding of the world and how it works. When claims fit with our worldview, they don't tend to surprise us, and we usually presume they are true (even though they might not be). When they conflict with our worldviews, however, we tend to be skeptical and presume they are false (even though they might be true). When a conclusion has been proven to be true, though, that should make a difference to your worldview. If, for example, my current worldview includes a general skepticism about the existence of aliens, but I then see live footage of an alien spacecraft on every major news network, and I am personally abducted by aliens and experimented upon, you better believe that I will revise my worldview to now include the existence of aliens!

Whatever the content of the argument, and perhaps especially when the conclusion conflicts with our own worldview, we need to be self-aware when we are evaluating it. One important element of (honest) argument evaluation is what's known as the *"principle of charity."* Basically, we want to be "charitable" when evaluating arguments—especially if we're inclined to disagree with them.

It's all too easy to develop a "straw man" interpretation of someone else's position, and then dismiss it as foolish, fallacious, or misguided. The fact of the matter is that people don't tend to view their own arguments as foolish. This doesn't mean they aren't, but in order to perform an honest evaluation of an argument, we need to present it in its best possible light. We must put ourselves in the position of the person who presented the argument, consider the argument in the strongest possible way (given the original author's intentions), and then evaluate the argument, so charitably constructed. This is a good approach to evaluating arguments, in general, but it's especially apt in the context of considering formal philosophical arguments in a book like this one.

The sorts of theistic arguments we will consider (both positive and negative) have stood the test of time. They're considered in this book for a reason. No matter what your personal views happen to be (e.g., theist, atheist, agnostic, etc.), it's uncharitable to casually dismiss "the other side" as fools offering lousy arguments. You might well conclude that "their" arguments fail, but to be justified in that conclusion you need to consider those arguments charitably, in their best light.

2. Justification

Having just spent a lot of time on arguments, and determining their relevance-relationship and truth of their premises, let us now turn to (perhaps) the most critical component of argument evaluation: justification.

Justification is probably the most critical aspect of this process because it is the process by which we attempt to determine whether claims (e.g., premises or conclusions) are (in fact) true, and therefore whether arguments are good arguments, and therefore whether or not we can "know" whether the conclusion of an argument is true. Justification is crucially involved in determining the truth of the premises in argument (once relevance has been established), and in evaluating the truth of an unsupported claim when no proper argument is present at all.

Justification is probably the most controversial element of our definition of knowledge, primarily because we can bicker over what, exactly, counts as sufficient justification. Again, this is a very complicated subject, but this is not an extended treatment of epistemology, so we can get by with a basic understanding of the key ideas.

To say that knowledge requires justification is simply to say that you can only "know" something on the basis of good reasons. If I present you with a jar filled with marbles, and you guess there are 457 marbles in the jar (just pulling a number "out of the air," at random), and, with a startled look on my face, I tell you that there are, in fact, 457 marbles in the jar, we wouldn't want to say that you *knew* the number of marbles in the jar at the time you guessed. We call it a guess for a reason! You didn't know, but you took a shot at it, and happened to get lucky. That's not knowledge; it's a lucky guess.

Sometimes, we like to distinguish "believing" from "knowing" by making explicit appeals to how much justification we have for the belief in question. I claimed to believe that my mother was at home, because I have reason to think that she is. However, my confidence in those reasons is pretty low, so I don't think I have sufficient justification to claim to *know* that she's at home.

As I mentioned, justification can be a thorny issue. How can we tell when we have enough justification to claim that we know something, as opposed to merely believing it? As with many questions in philosophy, there's no obvious, uncontroversial answer to that question. We can, however, talk about ways in which our beliefs are justified, and the degree to which our beliefs are supported by evidence.

When we are presented with an unsupported claim (including the premises of an argument), our three basic options are to accept it as true, reject it as false, or to suspend judgment because we're not sure either way. How do we know which one of those three options is the right one to exercise?

Generally speaking, it is reasonable to *accept* an unsupported claim if the claim:

1. Does not conflict with our own observations
2. Does not conflict with other credible claims
3. Comes from a credible source that offers us no compelling reason to expect bias
4. Does not conflict with our background information/worldview

1)   The Claim does not Conflict with our own Observations

We are justifiably skeptical about claims that directly contradict what we have personally observed! If you're texting with a friend, and he is telling you that he's in his car and on the way to meet you at Starbuck's, but you are personally observing him (in secret), right then and there, standing outside the Apple Store talking to your girlfriend, then either your friend is saying something false or you are hallucinating (or something else equally unlikely). Not surprisingly, in such a case you would be inclined to reject his claim as false. On the other hand, if you just came in from the rain and are shaking off your umbrella, and your friend calls and tells you he's running late because it's raining out, you're probably going to accept his claim as true. After all, you personally witnessed the rain too.

2)   The Claim does not Conflict with other Credible Claims

In courtroom settings, one of the best ways for an attorney to undermine the evidence offered by a witness or expert is to provide another witness or expert who will contradict that evidence. This is often very successful in creating "reasonable doubt" in jurors. So, for example, if one blood-splatter expert testifies that the spray patterns suggest the killer was at least six feet tall (which is bad news for the 6-foot-tall defendant), that claim is undermined if another, equally respectable, blood splatter expert says the patterns are inconclusive. In the context of philosophy, this is a notorious experience for philosophy students. One philosopher offers a compelling case that we have no free will, but then another equally impressive philosopher says the opposite. In such cases, we often must suspend judgment, even if we don't outright reject the original claim. If, on the other hand, there is no such conflict, if the claim is not being contradicted by other (credible) claims—let alone if there is consensus from a variety of sources—then we are likely to accept the claim as true.

3)   The Claim comes from a Credible Source that Offers Us no Compelling Reason to Expect Bias

This criterion actually has two elements: bias, and credibility. "Bias" is an issue when the person making the claim is suspected to have an ulterior motive. For example, if someone is trying to sell you their used car, they have a personal incentive for you to buy it, and they might be inclined to be less than completely honest about the condition of the vehicle. This doesn't mean they're automatically lying, of course, but careful car buyers will inspect the vehicle, and even enlist the help of someone who knows a thing or two about cars (e.g., an automotive mechanic) to confirm the car really is in good condition. Similarly, when the Tobacco industry spent decades deny the link between smoking and cancer, a clear case can be made that they had an ulterior motive to make that claim.[3] After all, if they admitted smoking caused cancer, it might reduce the number of people who smoke, and therefore their profits. Similarly, we might be reasonably skeptical when the petroleum industry funds lobbying groups denying the link between automobile emissions and climate change.[4] The possibility of bias doesn't demonstrate the *falsity* of the claim, of course. To presume so would actually be an example of what is called the "genetic fallacy"— denying (or accepting) the truth of a claim *solely* because of its source. However, while a possibly-biased source doesn't necessarily indicate their claim is false, it should inspire us to be especially vigilant when evaluating the evidence (if any) that they

---

[3] http://www.who.int/tobacco/media/en/TobaccoExplained.pdf
[4] https://www.theguardian.com/environment/2015/jul/15/exxon-mobil-gave-millions-climate-denying-lawmakers

provide in support of their claim.

Setting aside issues of bias, we can now turn to credibility. Unless one is a radical epistemic relativist, we recognize that not all sources are equally credible. When evaluating a claim, the source matters—especially if the subject matter is significant or if the claim conflicts with our own worldview. I should hope that you trust the testimony of your medical doctor more than you trust the testimony of your neighbor when it comes to your health—unless of course your neighbor also happens to be a medical doctor!

If someone is especially knowledgeable about a particular topic, we tend to give extra "weight" to their claims made about that topic. Sometimes, we consider such persons "experts."

We establish expertise, generally, by considering the following criteria:

1) Education
2) Experience
3) Accomplishments

Education is just what you think it is. Generally speaking, the more educated someone is on a topic, the more likely we are to (reasonably) take him or her to be an expert on that topic. Someone who majored in chemistry as an undergraduate probably knows a lot more about chemistry than someone who majored in something else—let alone someone who has never studied chemistry at all. Someone who has a Master's degree (M.S.) in chemistry probably knows even more, and someone with a doctorate (Ph.D.) probably knows even more than that. To be skeptical of this would require you to be profoundly skeptical of the effectiveness of our education system, in general! Keep in mind, of course, that expertise based on education is limited to the focus of one's education. That Ph.D. in chemistry doesn't mean the chemist is also an expert on criminal law!

Experience is also just what you think it is. While education is terribly valuable, relevant experience is valuable as well. *All else being equal*, a medical doctor who has been in practice for 20 years is probably more knowledgeable than a first-year M.D. Once again, we have to be careful of relevance. The fact that I have been a philosophy professor for fifteen years doesn't mean that I "know better" than a first year lawyer when it comes to legal issues. Despite the fact that President Donald Trump has been a successful business man for decades, his claim that he "knows more about ISIS than the generals" is dubious on its surface.[5] For all his business acumen, and despite his clear mastery of the media, then-candidate Trump had literally *no* experience relevant to ISIS, in contrast to "the Generals" and their combined decades of military experience, including years of recent experience specifically opposing ISIS.

Accomplishments often (though not always) come from education and experience, as well as merit. If a cancer researcher, for example, has won a Nobel Prize for her research, that scientist is probably pretty knowledgeable! Sometimes, some awards or "achievements" are questionable, and serve primarily to stoke the vanity of their recipients. For example, I get solicitations every year to be an "invited

---

[5] https://www.youtube.com/watch?v=kul34O_yMLs

speaker" at a conference called the Oxford Round Table. It is held at the very prestigious Oxford University, and being able to put "invited speaker" on your résumé is usually a respectable achievement, for a professor like myself. However, the Oxford Round Table has no affiliation with Oxford University at all (they just rent space!), "invited speakers" (or their campuses) must pay several thousand dollars for the privilege to attend, and whether or not one is invited seems to be much about whether you're on the email mailing list rather than actual achievements or status on the field. In other words, this conference is largely a scam designed to make money for the organizers of the event. Today, with the increasing influence of social media, we have to be careful not to confuse "notoriety" with being "accomplished." As of 2017, Katy Perry has over 95 *million* twitter followers compared to only 45 million for CNN. It would be absurd to think that somehow Katy Perry is a more credible source of information, however, based solely on her superior popularity.

Putting all these ideas together, we can consider a "real-life" example of two experts.

Richard Dawkins:
BA, Ph.D.: Oxford University Professor (emeritus) Oxford
Specialization: evolutionary biology
Achievements: numerous awards and publications

William Lane Craig:
BA (Wheaton College),
MA Phil of Religion & History of Christian Thought (Trinity Evangelical Divinity
   School), Ph.D. in PHIL (University of Birmingham),
Ph.D. in Theology (University of Munich).
Professor: Trinity Evangelical school and Talbot School of Theology
Specialization: Philosophy of religion & Christian doctrine
Achievements: numerous awards and publications

A legitimate evaluation of these two scholars recognizes that they are both very well educated and accomplished in their respective fields. Both are undoubtedly intelligent persons who deserve respect. This doesn't mean they are always correct, of course—but it does mean we should take them seriously when they offer claims concerning their areas of expertise.

An interesting application that applies to these two, specifically, is that they are considered "rivals." Craig is an outspoken Christian who debates prominent atheists around the world, trying to demonstrate the rationality of Christian faith. Dawkins, on the other hand, is a notorious critic of religion, and the author of such books as "The God Delusion."

While both men are credible experts, even legitimate experts can be guilty of stepping outside their areas of genuine expertise. Dawkins, for example, while unquestionably one of the finest scholars on evolution living today, is *not* an expert on Western philosophy—let alone the philosophy of religion. Not surprisingly, when he writes a book like "The God Delusion" that deals with philosophy, rather than evolution, his credibility is strained. His critiques of the most famous arguments for

God's existence in the Western tradition are undeniably outdated, and rely heavily on the criticisms offered by David Hume—written some two and a half centuries ago. What's worse, is that what he calls his "central argument" is demonstrably invalid (according to the very standards we have addressed earlier in this chapter). Indeed, Craig has described the argument as "the worst atheistic argument in the history of Western thought."[6] In fairness, Craig should be equally cautious about extending his own expertise into the realm of biology. . . .

4) The Claim does not Conflict with our own Worldview

We each have, at our disposal, what we may call our "background knowledge," or "background information, or our "worldview." Whatever we want to call it, it is that vast collection of everything we have heard, seen, read, and otherwise learned, throughout our lives. This collection is everything we know (or think we know) about the world and how it works. It includes your understanding of hugely important questions such as whether or not God (somehow conceived) exists, to your understanding of human psychology, world history, economics, State capitals, and even sports statistics. If you have learned about it, it is part of your worldview.

When presented with a claim, we all immediately evaluate that claim not only in terms of evidence, source, and our own observations, but also with respect to how well it "fits" with our worldview. We can summarize and simplify this process by asking two general questions about that claim.

1. *To what extent is the belief supported by good reasons and compelling evidence from reliable sources?*

Is the belief in question supported by your own first-hand observations? Or, is it in conflict with your own observations? If you're receiving your evidence from another source, how reliable is that source? How credible is the source? Does the source have any relevant expertise? Is there any reason to be biased?

2. *To what extent is the belief consistent with my worldview?*

Every time we are confronted with a piece of information, we automatically and instantly evaluate it against our background knowledge. If the new information seems to "fit" with our background knowledge, we're likely to accept it as true. If it does not fit, however, if the claim is surprising to us, we're likely to hesitate and to demand more justification before accepting it as true. For example, if I were to claim that I drove home on the Southbound 605 freeway at 5 PM on a Thursday afternoon, and the freeway was wide open, with hardly any cars on it at all, anyone living in Southern California (that is, anyone for whom the 605 freeway, on a weekday, at 5 PM, is part of their background knowledge/worldview) would immediately doubt what I'm saying. Why? Because her understanding of the world and how it works is that

---

6 http://www.reasonablefaith.org/dawkins-delusion

Southern California freeways are jammed at that time of day.

When it comes to justification, then, we'll want to know if the belief is consistent with other things that we know about the world and how it works. If the belief is consistent, so far, so good. If it is not, then we'll naturally be skeptical, and we'll require further evidence before accepting the belief.

We always need to be aware, however, that our own background knowledge can be flawed. For example, it used to be part of most people's worldview that the Sun revolved around the Earth. Now, it's part of our worldview that it's the Earth that moves relative to the Sun. Background knowledge is subject to revision. So, *the mere fact that a piece of information conflicts with your understanding of the world does not automatically mean that the claim is false. It's possible that it's true, and that it's your understanding that needs revision.*

Whenever you get presented with a claim (including the conclusion of an argument) that conflicts with your worldview, but for which you're confident it's true, the reasonable thing to do is to revise your worldview accordingly. Obviously, the more you know, the better equipped you are to evaluate claims, and to be accurate in your evaluations.

It is also important to be honest about the threat of bias posed by our worldviews when evaluating information—a bias that we are *all* subject to. Thus far, I have casually commented on our tendency to accept claims that fit with our worldview, and to be skeptical of those that clash with it. This is a well-known and studied psychological tendency known as the "confirmation bias." What makes the confirmation bias dangerous, though, is that it distorts our ability to honestly and objectively evaluate claims. This is not merely some anecdotal complaint about the state of debate today. There is scientific evidence to suggest that our brains are "wired" to be resistant to change with respect to "firmly held beliefs."

A study published in 2016 showed, via neuroimaging, that when subjects were presented with arguments that contradicted their strongly held political views, they experienced "increased activity in the default mode network—a set of interconnected structures associated with self-representation and disengagement from the external world."[7] The default mode network is normally shown to active during such states as daydreaming and mind-wandering. It is labeled "default" because the network activates "by default" when the person is not engaged in a task requiring attention. This is fascinating, if true! It suggests that when our firmly-held political beliefs are challenged, our brains "check out" in ways analogous to daydreaming. How responsive to evidence and argument are we likely to be if our brains are in a "day-dreaming" state when evidence contrary to our firmly held beliefs is presented? Our resistance to counterevidence to our "political" beliefs is likely to be at least *similar* to our resistance to counterevidence to our "religious" beliefs....

In the final speech President Obama gave as President, he warned against our increasing tendency to operate within our own ideological "bubbles."

---

[7] Kaplan, J. T. et al. Neural correlates of maintaining one's political beliefs in the face of counterevidence. Sci. Rep. 6, 39589; doi: 10.1038/srep39589 (2016). Available at http://www.nature.com/articles/srep39589

For too many of us, it's become safer to retreat into our own bubbles, whether in our neighborhoods or college campuses or places of worship or our social media feeds, surrounded by people who look like us and share the same political outlook and never challenge our assumptions. The rise of naked partisanship, increasing economic and regional stratification, the splintering of our media into a channel for every taste – all this makes this great sorting seem natural, even inevitable. And increasingly, we become so secure in our bubbles that we accept only information, whether true or not, that fits our opinions, instead of basing our opinions on the evidence that's out there.[8]

This isn't merely some anecdotal cautionary tale about the liberals only watching MSNBC and conservatives only watching Fox news. A study published in the "Proceedings of the National Academy of Sciences of the United States of America" concluded that "selective exposure to content is the primary driver of content diffusion and generates the formation of homogeneous clusters, i.e., 'echo chambers.' Indeed, homogeneity appears to be the primary driver for the diffusion of contents and each echo chamber has its own cascade dynamics.[9] In other words, people on Facebook mostly share news that they already agree with, that is consistent with their worldview, and they don't share information that challenges it. As the researchers put it: "users show a tendency to search for, interpret, and recall information that confirm their pre-existing beliefs." Combine this tendency with the fact that Facebook has nearly 2 billion users (out of roughly 7 billion people on the planet), and reaches 67% of U.S. adults, and that 62% of Americans get their news mainly from social media sites such as Facebook and Twitter.[10] A majority of Americans get their news primarily from social media, and research confirms the application of the confirmation bias to social media platforms. It should go without saying that these trends seriously compromise our ability to think critically, and to responsibly accept or reject claims.

A recent and ominous development of this trend has inspired me to add an entire subsection to this chapter for the first time: "Fake News."

"Fake News"

As of 2017, "Fake News" has entered into the American vocabulary, initially and specifically in the realm of politics—though the phrase is likely to "trend" and apply to other contexts as well. Initially used by liberals to describe right-wing "conspiracy theories," the phrase expanded in use just as did the frequency of fake news itself. Conservatives then adopted the phrase themselves, and the phrase now

---

[8] http://www.latimes.com/politics/la-pol-obama-farewell-speech-transcript-20170110-story.html

[9] http://www.pnas.org/content/113/3/554.full

[10] http://www.journalism.org/2016/05/26/news-use-across-social-media-platforms-2016/?utm_content=bufferae870&utm_medium=social&utm_source=twitter.com&utm_campaign=buffer

gets used to describe multiple, significantly different things. This is where philosophy has a chance to shine, considering the experience philosophers have with conceptual analysis. The primary meanings of "fake news" seems to be the following:

- *A work of fiction, known to be so by the author, but presented as real/true for personal, political, or financial motives.* This is the original meaning of fake news, and all other meanings are a departure from this. Another word to describe this kind of fake news is a "lie." A clear illustration of this kind of fake news is the example of Cameron Harris. As reported in an interview with Harris by the New York Times, he admitted to writing multiple completely fabricated stories that he thought would be effective "click-bait" for Trump supporters.[11] He claimed to have done so for financial reasons, citing that he made $22,000 in ad-revenue from his stories, though it was later revealed that he also worked as an aide to a Maryland Republican lawmaker.[12] Eight of his fake news stories were popular enough to attract the attention of (and debunking by) Snopes.com.[13] His most "effective" story claimed "Tens of thousands of fraudulent Clinton votes found in Ohio warehouse." By his own admission, he invented an imaginary electrical worker and named him "Randall Prince." He copied and pasted a screen shot of man standing in front of ballot boxes using a google image search. He also identified the motive for the imaginary ballot-tampering: "the Clinton campaign's likely goal was to slip the fake ballot boxes in with the real ballot boxes when they went to official election judges on November 8th." The fact that the story was a complete *lie* did nothing to stop it from being shared with 6 million people. The fake news story went sufficiently viral that the Franklin County (Ohio) board of elections was forced to investigate—after which they confirmed the story had no basis in reality.[14]

- Satire: while also a work of fiction (and known to be so by the author), the work is presented as fiction for the sake of entertainment or to make a point. Satire is a long-practiced means of both entertainment and persuasion. "The Onion" is perhaps the most famous satirical website today, and it makes no pretense that its stories are true. When The Onion runs the headline, "Trump Calms Nerves Before Inaugural Address By Reminding Himself He's The Only Person Who Actually Exists," it is presumed that the reader will know that are only trying to be funny.[15] Similarly, when Jonathan Swift famously argued that a solution to Irish poverty was for Irish parents to sell their children as food to wealthy Englishmen, he wasn't being serious! Despite eating children being presented as

---

[11] https://www.nytimes.com/2017/01/18/us/fake-news-hillary-clinton-cameron -harris.html?_r=0

[12] http://www.inquisitr.com/3901102/cameron-harris-fake-news-writer-bought-christian-times-newspaper-for-5-made-22000-and-got-fired/

[13] http://www.snopes.com/tag/christian-times-newspaper/

[14] http://files.constantcontact.com/b01249ec501/58eeb35a-7d61-4807-b168-765d27ca11cf.pdf

[15] http://www.theonion.com/article/trump-calms-nerves-inaugural-address-reminding-him-55095

his "Modest Proposal," his actual proposals were much more serious:

Therefore let no man talk to me of other expedients: Of taxing our absentees at five shillings a pound: Of using neither clothes, nor household furniture, except what is of our own growth and manufacture: Of utterly rejecting the materials and instruments that promote foreign luxury: Of curing the expensiveness of pride, vanity, idleness, and gaming in our women: Of introducing a vein of parsimony, prudence and temperance:...Of teaching landlords to have at least one degree of mercy towards their tenants. Lastly, of putting a spirit of honesty, industry, and skill into our shop-keepers, who, if a resolution could now be taken to buy only our native goods, would immediately unite to cheat and exact upon us in the price, the measure, and the goodness, nor could ever yet be brought to make one fair proposal of just dealing, though often and earnestly invited to it.

Satire is "fake news" in the sense that it is not *real*, but nor is it intended to be— and that is a significant difference

- *A work thought to be true and intended to be true by the author, but mistaken in one or more significant details.* In another words, a mistake. An example of a mistake in reporting that was, nevertheless, denounced as "fake news" occurred on the day Donald Trump was inaugurated as President. A White House pool reporter tweeted that a bust of Martin Luther King Jr. had been removed from the Oval Office.[16] In fact, the bust had simply been moved to a different part of the office, and the reporter hasn't seen it—something the reporter later acknowledged and for which he apologized. Nevertheless, the initial report was called "fake news" by detractors all the same.[17] At the risk of editorializing: honest mistakes, while bad, are not properly "fake news." A relevant indicator of intent is whether or not the person who made the initial claim is willing to admit (and correct) the mistake, and apologize.
- *A news story deemed "irrelevant" or unimportant or distracting from "real" news* (according to the reader). An example of this might be when reporters comment on the fashion choices of a politician, rather than the substance of her policies. As another example, when Senator Jeff Sessions was nominated to be U.S. Attorney General by President Trump, some reporters (and Democratic politicians) pointed to allegations of racism from his point as a potential disqualifier for confirmation. This was labeled by some as "fake news."
- *A news story disliked by the reader.* This is perhaps the most disturbing usage of "fake news" of them all, in my opinion. This usage occurs when information is dismissed as "fake" simply because it conflicts with the reader's worldview, or because it would be distressing, if accepted as true. To be blunt: not liking a piece of information doesn't mean that it's false. If your medical doctor tells you that

---

[16] https://twitter.com/philipindc/status/822603029950173187
[17] http://www.thegatewaypundit.com/2017/01/fakenews-media-falsely-reports-trump-removed-mlk-bust-oval-office/

you have cancer, dismissing it as "fake news" is of no help.

The problem with the varied and inconsistent usage of the phrase "fake news" isn't just an issue of conceptual fussiness from overly-picky philosophers. Words have meaning. When President Trump refused to take questions from a CNN reporter, and dismissed the network as "fake news," it's likely that what he really meant is something like "I don't like CNN."[18] However, people who listen to and respect President Trump might take his words to mean that CNN intentionally prints stories they know to be false for ulterior motives, and thereby lose confidence in the network as a reliable news source. This isn't just bad news for CNN's viewership or profit margins, but if confidence in mainstream media sources is undermined, people will retreat even *further* into their ideological bubbles, and their critical thinking skills will be even further compromised. President Trump later again labeled major media sources (viz., the New York Times, NBC, ABC, CBS, and CNN) as "fake news," but when further by denouncing them as the "enemy of the American People."

Cognitive linguist George Lakoff finds this strategy to be both intentional and dangerous. The adjective "fake" modifies the function of "news." The primary purpose of "news" is to pass along factual information in service to the public good. If "news" is modified with the term "fake," it implies that the basic function of "news" has been compromised.

> It is done to serve interests at odds with the public good. It also undermines the credibility of real news sources, that is, the press. Therefore it makes it harder for the press to serve the public good by revealing truths. And it threatens democracy, which requires that the press function to reveal real truths.[19]

Perhaps we would be better and more accurately served by refraining from using the phrase "fake news" entirely? When Hillary Clinton claimed in 2008 to have run from sniper fire in Bosnia, and her claim was proven to be false, the best-case scenario is that her memory was "mistaken," and the worst-case is that she intentionally lied

---

[18] http://www.cnn.com/videos/politics/2017/01/11/donald-trump-jim-acosta-cnn-fake-news.cnn

[19] http://www.npr.org/2017/02/17/515630467/with-fake-news-trump-moves-from-alternative-facts-to-alternative-language

for some reason.[20] Why bother calling it "fake news" when a "lie" or "mistake" more accurately conveys what occurred? When President Trump's press secretary, Sean Spicer, in his very first press briefing, not only claimed that President Trump's inauguration audience was the largest ever, but also condemned journalists for writing "fake news" downplaying the size of the crowds, several troubling things occurred. For one, his claim about viewership was demonstrably false. President Trump's Nielson television ratings were the fifth highest since President Richard Nixon—lower than President Obama's first inauguration, for example, but higher than the inaugurations of both Presidents Clinton and George W. Bush.[21] It's likely that President Trump and his staff would have liked it if their inauguration attendance and Nielson ratings had been the highest, but that preference doesn't mean that reporters who provide the factual numbers, in contrast, are disseminating "fake news." To suggest that they are is, again, to undermine confidence in the press, in general. It also seems unlikely to be helpful when President Trump's counselor, Kellyanne Conway described Spicer's actions in the following way: "You're saying it's a falsehood, and they're giving- Sean Spicer, our press secretary, gave alternative facts to that."[22]

For the sake of conceptual clarity: facts are objective, and are, by definition, true. An "alternative fact," therefore, is a clever term for something that is false—either a mistake, or a lie. If it is a fact that 2+2 = 4, it is silly to label 2+2 = 5 as an "alternative fact." If it is a fact that Donald Trump is the 45th President of the United States, to claim that Bernie Sanders is the 45th President is not to offer an "alternative fact," but is simply to claim something that *is not true*. That President Trump's Nielson ratings for his inauguration were not the highest ever is a *fact*. To assert otherwise is not to provide an "alternative fact," but is simply to be either mistaken, or lying.

If you agree that "fake news" is troubling, and if you are motivated to be a good critical thinker, what can you do to be more wary when it comes to the news stories you accept or reject? The good news is that you have already learned how, earlier in this chapter! All of our previous discussion of justification, and how we should evaluate claims, is directly relevant to discerning whether a claim is "fake news," a lie, a mistake, or just simply true or false.

First of all, is the claim supported by evidence? In other words, is it an argument? Press Secretary Spicer didn't offer any evidence in support of his claim about the inauguration Nielson ratings—he just made an assertion. If he had offered an argument, you could try to determine whether his premises were relevant to the conclusion, and ultimately whether they were true. Had he cited Nielson numbers, you could easily fact-them—probably on your phone!

Don't forget the general process of evaluating unsupported claims. It's generally

---

[20] https://www.washingtonpost.com/news/fact-checker/wp/2016/05/23/recalling-hillary-clintons-claim-of-landing-under-sniper-fire-in-bosnia/?utm_term=.e6222cd61035

[21] http://www.washingtonexaminer.com/trump-inaugurations-nielsen-ratings-fourth-highest-since-nixon/article/2612602

[22] http://time.com/4642689/kellyanne-conway-sean-spicer-donald-trump-alternative-facts/

reasonably to accept an unsupported claim if it:

1. Does not conflict with our own observations
2. Does not conflict with other credible claims
3. Comes from a credible source that offers us no compelling reason to expect bias
4. Does not conflict with our background information/worldview

While it might not always be practical for you to investigate the source, at the very least you can try to be aware of the influence of your own worldview. If you know you are firm Trump supporter, then be aware that you are especially vulnerable to believing negative stories about Hillary Clinton—just as Hillary supporters would be especially vulnerable to believing negative stories about President Trump. Before getting indignant (and retweeting or sharing) an incendiary piece of news, try taking a few moments to carefully reflect on the claims being made, and maybe even do some fact-checking before taking a stance. Snopes.com is as very helpful resource in this regard. Another very simple tip is to initially skeptical about any stories riddled with spelling or grammar problems, or that use lots of CAPS or exclamation marks!!! Actual, serious journalists are usually pretty good writers, and poor writing can be a sign of an amateur blogger or internet troll.

You might be wondering why we just spent so much time on "fake news" and examples that were obviously political in nature, considering that this is a philosophy of religion text book. The explanation for that is because of the common overlap between "religion" and "politics." Our religious views inform our political views (and vice versa!). Most of us don't read articles or books on the philosophy of religion (present company excluded, of course!), but most of us *do* engage with books, articles, television broadcasts, radio programs (etc.,) that deal with politics. The strategy is the same in any case. The very same precautions we should take when evaluating "political" claims will apply to claims made in the context of the philosophy of religion.

Thus far, we've only seriously addressed the conditions under which we accept or reject a claim, but there is a third alternative that requires some attention as well: *suspending judgment*. Basically, to accept a claim means you think it's true, to reject it means you think it's false, and to suspend judgment means you're just not sure either way.

It is OK to suspend judgment.

Let me repeat that: it is OK to suspend judgment. You certainly don't want to spend your life shrugging your shoulders and pleading ignorance, but nor should you pretend to know the truth value of a claim if you honestly don't. Far too often, people accept or reject claims, and take stances on issues, when they know little, if anything, about the subject in question. Pardon my coarse language, but when people do so they are engaging in "bullshit."

Believe it not, "bullshit" is officially a philosophical term, thanks to the philosopher Harry Frankfurt. Is his aptly title book, "On Bullshit," he discusses this tendency in human behavior, and distinguishes it from lying. According to Frankfurt, "bullshit" occurs when "a person's obligations or opportunities to speak about some topic exceed his or her knowledge of the facts that are relevant to the topic."

In other words, if you ask me what I think about President Trump's choice for Secretary of the Interior, and I have no idea who that is (or even what he or she does), and instead of admitting "I don't know" I instead say that I don't approve of the choice, I have engaged in some "bullshit."[23] The claim I have made exceeds the relevant knowledge I actually have on that topic.

It's clear, I hope, that the proper thing to do in a situation like that is to suspend judgment. Yet, all kinds of people "bullshit" all the time. Why? According to Frankfurt: "Closely related instances arise from the widespread conviction that it is the responsibility of a citizen in democracy to have opinions about everything, or at least everything that pertains to the conduct of his country's affairs."

In other words, there is a perceived social expectation that everyone is supposed to have (and be ready to provide) an opinion about everything. When this is combined with a crude presumption of epistemic relativism (according to which all opinions are equally legitimate), then we get an especially troubling situation: everyone feels obliged to opine about everything, and no matter how uninformed they might be, somehow their own opinion is just as good as anyone else's, and therefore worth sharing.

An intellectually honest alternative to "bullshitting," and one that, frankly, requires both self-awareness and some courage, is to be willing to suspend judgment if you honestly don't know whether a claim is true or false.

We can put all these considerations together by comparing two claims.

1. "I believe that, someday, my body will die, because (bodily) death is the natural end of living."
    - Question: To what extent is the belief supported by good reasons and compelling evidence from reliable sources?
    - Answer: Ample evidence is supplied every day, every time someone dies. Obituaries, news stories about deaths, and personal experiences and memories of people (and every other animal on Earth) dying all serve as evidence.

    - Question: To what extent is the belief consistent with my worldview?
    - Answer: The claim is consistent with the complex web of our beliefs involving the natural sciences. Biology and history both inform our worldview, and our worldview certainly includes bodily death.

2. "I believe that I will win the lottery this week."
    - Question: To what extent is the belief supported by good reasons and compelling evidence from reliable sources?

---

[23] In case you are curious, President Trump's Secretary of the Interior is Ryan Zinke (as of the time of this writing), and the Secretary's job is to manage the Department of the Interior, which is the government department that oversees federal land, natural resources, and the administration of programs relating to Native Americans, Alaskans, and Hawaiians.

- Answer: Excluding the possibility of cheating, there is no compelling evidence to indicate I will win. Indeed, it's unclear what could possibly count as evidence of this in the first place.

- Question: To what extent is the belief consistent with other my worldview?
- Answer: The claim that I will win the lottery conflicts with our understanding of probability in general, and with our experience of lotteries, in particular.

When we compare these examples, we can detect a sharp contrast. In both cases, you probably (rightfully) think you do not have to suspend judgment, but can actually take a stance. The first claim (concerning bodily death) is so strongly justified that you probably not only accept it as true, but with sufficient justification to constitute knowledge. If you disagree with this, and deny that you know that your body will die someday, you probably think it's impossible to know anything. That's not necessarily a bad thing. There is a respectable and ancient school of thought called "Skepticism" that regards knowledge as impossible to obtain. You'll learn more about skepticism later. The second example (me winning the lottery) is so poorly justified as to be little better than wishful thinking—certainly not knowledge. In fairness, the lottery claim is about the future, and many epistemologists would say that future-indexed claims have an indeterminate truth-value, since they haven't happened yet. For that reason, you might be inclined to suspend judgment-and that is a fair position to take. However, even if you're suspending judgment for that reason, you probably think the claim is very likely to turn out to be false.

3. Truth

Having discussed beliefs and justification, what about truth? It is generally accepted that one can't know something that is false. I can't know (as of 2017) that George Washington is the current U.S. President—because he isn't!

Note that we can *think* that we know all kinds of things, and then discover that we were mistaken. In those cases, we never *really* knew what we believed we knew at all. This is complicated, but only a very basic understanding is needed for our purposes. In summary, if we really do know something, it must be something that is true.

What does it mean for something to be true? Once again, this is a complicated issue, but, once again, we can avoid needless complications by focusing just on some key concepts. Though there are several ways of understanding truth, we can focus on just a few that seem useful.

Epistemic Relativism

Epistemic relativism claims that truth is "relative" to the observer. Or, to put it a bit more famously, truth is a matter of perspective. Truth depends on one's point of view.

Now, at a certain level, this is obvious and unobjectionable. Most everyone would agree that there are certain kinds of claims we can make, certain kinds of judgments, which are merely expressions of personal opinion, or personal taste. One's favorite color, or whether or not one likes a band, or whether or not one likes spicy food—all such things seem to be matters of perspective. I like spicy food. My mother doesn't. She's not "wrong" or "mistaken" about spicy food—she just has different taste preferences. I really like the band "Switchfoot." I'm sure some people couldn't bear them (as hard as that is for me to believe). Again, no one is in error over such matters.

We call these sorts of claims "subjective claims." When we're dealing with subjective claims, there is no one right point of view, no single correct answer to the questions involving subjective claims. In cases of disagreement, it's not the case that someone must be wrong. Also, in cases of disagreement, there's little that can be accomplished from debate. I can sing the praises of spicy food for hours, but my mother will never be convinced of the truth of my claims and change her mind. This isn't because she's stubborn, it's because she just doesn't like spicy food! Her opinion on this matter is no better, or worse, than my own. It's just different.

Think about this, briefly, in the context of ethics. To apply epistemic relativism to religion would mean believing that claims about religious matters are simply matters of opinion. Such claims that would be opinions (as opposed to facts) might include the following:

- God exists.
- God does not exist.
- Several gods exist.
- God has foreknowledge of every "choice" we make.
- God is the morally perfect source of objective moral values.

For some of you, to say that such claims are matters of personal opinion only might be "common sense," or perhaps terribly controversial. Where epistemic relativism likely becomes controversial for almost anyone is when we realize that the theory claims that *all* truths are relative in the way that subjective claims are.

If you stop to reflect on that for a moment, you can start to see how extraordinary that claim really is (whether true, or not). If all "truths" are matters of perspective, and if no perspective is inherently any more privileged than any other, then everyone is always "right" about everything.

You believe the Earth is a sphere. I believe it's flat (I don't, really). Assuming each claim represents our own respective opinions, why would your opinion be any more "right" than mine? In a sense, we're both right—even though we're making mutually exclusive claims. I think George W. Bush is the current U.S. President (I don't believe that either). That's my opinion, and I'm entitled to it, and your opinion isn't any more accurate than mine. "But," you might counter, "no one else shares your opinion, while lots of people share mine." Fine. That just means your opinion is more popular—it doesn't mean it's more accurate.

If all truth is subjective, then all truth is like my taste in music. If 99% of the world population couldn't stand Country music, but I loved it, my opinion that Country music is great would be no less legitimate than the nearly six billion who disagree— it would just be a lot less popular. If this sounds counter-intuitive to you, this idea that there are no "right answers" and that *all* truth is merely a matter of perspective, then I think you're on to something....[24]

To make matters even more interesting, consider this: "all truth is relative" is a claim. That means it's either true, or it's false. If it's false, then we obviously have no good reason to entertain it any further. If, on the other hand, it's true that all truth is relative, then that very claim is itself only relatively true. That is, it's just a matter of opinion, a matter of perspective. In that case, if I disagree, then my opinion is no worse, no less correct, than that of those who embrace epistemic relativism. To sum this up, either "all truth is relative" is a relative truth, or it's not-relative. If it's relative, then it's merely an opinion that is no "more true" than an opposing opinion. If it's not-relative, then not all truth is relative, and the claim refutes itself. That's usually a bad thing, when a claim refutes itself.

There is something seemingly self-refuting, or internally inconsistent, with epistemic relativism. Since all opinions are equally true, it is simultaneously and equally true that epistemic relativism is, itself, both true and false.

Beyond this conceptual puzzle, a figure no less than Socrates himself points out that we do not, in fact, regard all opinions as equally true. Consider the following examples:

Subject	Expert
Medicine	Medical Doctor
Nutrition	Nutritionist
Carpentry	Carpenter
Botany	Botanist
Chemistry	Chemist
Physics	Physicist
Philosophy	Philosopher

I'll start with a deeply personal example. If you don't believe that my understanding of philosophy, on the basis of my several degrees (B.A., M.A., and Ph.D.), years of experience (more than 20 years at the time of this writing), and "accolades" (e.g., being a tenured professor, and having published multiple articles and textbooks, etc.), is any more informed than your own, why on Earth are you bothering to read this book, or take my class? What is the point of education, in general, if every student is equally informed as his or her teacher?

Let's make it more absurd. Why bother going to the doctor when you are sick and injured? If all opinions are equal, your own opinion about your medical condition is just as good as that doctor's!

Those astrophysicists who have spent studying the universe and who are debating whether or not this universe is situated within a broader multiverse? Their views are no better informed than the random person who has never studied that stuff a day in his or her life. Equally true opinions?

You don't accept that as true, of course—and this is the critic's point. In actual practice, we don't really believe that "all opinions are equal," but instead recognize

---

[24] Or, at least that's *my* perspective.

that some people know what they're talking about, and others don't. Socrates himself criticized epistemic relativism (and moral subjectivism) thousands of years ago:

> *Why, that all those mercenary individuals, whom the many call Sophists and whom they deem to be their adversaries, do, in fact, teach nothing but the opinion of the many, that is to say, the opinions of their assemblies; and this is their wisdom. I might compare them to a man who should study the tempers and desires of a mighty strong beast who is fed by him—he would learn how to approach and handle him, also at what times and from what causes he is dangerous or the reverse, and what is the meaning of his several cries, and by what sounds, when another utters them, he is soothed or infuriated; and you may suppose further, that when, by continually attending upon him, he has become perfect in all this, he calls his knowledge wisdom, and makes of it a system or art, which he proceeds to teach, although he has no real notion of what he means by the principles or passions of which he is speaking, but calls this honourable and that dishonourable, or good or evil, or just or unjust, all in accordance with the tastes and tempers of the great brute. Good he pronounces to be that in which the beast delights and evil to be that which he dislikes; and he can give no other account of them except that the just and noble are the necessary, having never himself seen, and having no power of explaining to others the nature of either, or the difference between them, which is immense (Republic, 493a-c).*

In other words, those intellectual mercenaries know nothing of good or evil, justice or injustice. Instead, they merely *observe* what actually happens in the world, what people seem to like and dislike, and *proclaim* those things to be good or bad, just or unjust.

If we recognize that this sort of relativism is rife with problems in other contexts (e.g., think about what it would mean for it to be "just a matter of opinion" that humans require oxygen to survive), why should we entertain the notion religious contexts? Does it seem plausible that every person's perspective is equally informed and "true" as any other person's when it comes to theology, and the philosophy of religion? To the various arguments and evidence concerning God's existence (or non-existence)? Do we *really* think that someone who has truly never pondered such issues a day in his life is as equally informed and authoritative as a scholar who has dedicated decades to research, debate, and thought on the subject?

The question we must now consider is whether religious claims concern a matter of possible expertise, in which case we would presumably recognize that some people are better informed than others, and that not all views are equally good. Or, if we reject that, then we are presumably treating religious claims as mere indicators of personal taste. I might recognize that some people might be experts at "baking," and are certainly better informed than I am when it comes to how best to bake a cake, but I don't recognize that anyone else is somehow more informed than I am about what sort of cake I like! If you've gone to culinary school, your understanding of how to bake a red velvet cake is probably better informed than my own, but it makes no sense to suggest that you know better than I do regarding whether or not I *like* red velvet cake. Is the philosophy of religion more like baking, or more like the kind of cake you like?

Consider the following examples and inferences:

- Two people taste the same chocolate cake. One thinks it's overly sweet. The other thinks it could stand to be sweeter. Therefore, the sweetness of the chocolate is merely a matter of individual perspective. There is no "Truth" regarding its sweetness.
- I look at a flower and perceive it to be yellow. A bee looks at the same flower and perceives it to be blue with a red center. Therefore, the appearance of the flower is a matter of individual perspective. There is no "Truth" regarding the appearance of the flower.

Such common sense differences in perspective seem to suggest that epistemic relativism might be the correct way to understand truth. However, if one considers carefully these examples, it will soon be clear that these examples do *not* imply that "*all*" truth is relative"—indeed they presuppose something very different. Epistemic relativism is driven by the force of the relativity of perception. That is, because it is such a common experience for people to perceive "the same thing" in very different ways, it's easy to conclude that truth is relative. Be careful, though! The relativity of perception, even if true, doesn't imply that *all* truth is relative. Some truths must be held absolute in order for the relativity to make any sense.

Reconsider the chocolate cake. Two people taste the same cake with different results. Therefore, perception is relative. What is not thought relative in this example, however, is the existence of the cake, the tasters, and the world in which both cake and tasters exist. The same sorts of presuppositions apply to the flower example.

The bee and I perceive the flower with different results, but what is *not* thought relative is the existence of the flower itself, the bee, myself, and the reality in which all three of us reside.

In order to even make sense of the relativity of perception, one must presuppose that it is "True" that observers exist, and that a reality exists that may be perceived differently. The commonsense observation that initially gives rise to relativism is that the "real world" exists, that perceivers (such as you, me, and the bee) exist, but that we experience the "real world" in different ways.

Even if it's true that perceptions vary, that perceptions are relative, that certainly doesn't entail that *all truth* is relative. Indeed, it's arguable that it *cannot* entail that conclusion, if one accepts that relativity of perception implies absoluteness of perceivers and the world that is being perceived.

Correspondence Theory

Consider the following statements:

- The claim that George W. Bush is the current U.S. President is true if and only if he really is the current U.S. President.
- The claim that there are exactly 457 marbles in the jar is true if and only if there

really are exactly that many marbles (457) in the jar.
- The claim that there is life on Mars is true if and only if there really is life on Mars.

Are these statements reasonable? If you think so, you're probably sympathetic to what is known as the correspondence theory of truth.

According to correspondence theory, a claim is true if it "corresponds" to the way things really are in the world, if the claim "matches up" with reality, if it "maps on" to how the world actually is. This is the most stringent of all the approaches to understanding truth because it claims that there is a way that the universe "really is," and our claims are true, or not, depending on whether they match up with the world. This is the approach implicitly employed by most people, whether they realize it or not.

Imagine that you intercept a fellow student on the way to class, and she tells you that the class has been cancelled. Has she told you the truth? What would you need to know in order to make that assessment? Simply this: you would need to know if the class really had been cancelled. If it had, her statement was true. If it had not, her statement was false. Her claim either "corresponded" to the world, or it didn't.

Obviously, not all of our claims will be so easily verifiable. Some truth claims (unfortunately, probably the ones we tend to care the most about—claims about morality, religion, politics, etc.), might be especially difficult to establish because we might not know how "the world is" concerning that particular subject. Do aliens exist, or not? Hard to say, since we haven't explored the entire universe just yet. Is abortion immoral? Hard to say, since there's so much disagreement, and so many compelling arguments that can be given on both sides. Should governments promote a strong middle class, primarily promote the interests of the working class, or sit back and let "the Market" decide? Hard to say, since there's so much disagreement, and so many compelling arguments that can be given on both sides.

What correspondence theorists *will* claim is that even if we're not sure what the answers to some of these difficult questions are, we nevertheless can be confident that there *are* answers—not merely opinions—out there for us to discover.

Conclusion

The purpose of this introductory chapter is to provide a basic overview of arguments, as understood in philosophy, provide a few key vocabulary terms (e.g., validity, soundness, claim, premise, etc.), and provide a framework within which to understood how we evaluate arguments. This will serve us for the remainder of this book.

Every chapter that follows this one will be offering one or more perspectives from across the history of Western philosophical thought. Each of these famous philosophers will be offering *arguments*—which is just to say that they will be defending their positions, offering reasons for what they believe. Your task (with me as your assistant) is to:

1. Using the Principle of Charity, identity the main points (conclusions) being made by these philosophers.

2. Using the Principle of Charity, identity the reasons/evidences (premises) being offered in support of those main points.

3. As best you can, and when possible, determine whether their arguments are valid. In other words, *if* the evidence they are offering is true, does it mean that their conclusions are true as well?

4. As best you can, and when possible, using the process of justification discussed in this chapter (i.e., considering evidence, source, and fit with your worldview), determine whether the argument is also sound. In other words, are their premises, and therefore their main points, in fact, *true*.

5. Determine your own degree of agreement or disagreement. Presumably, if you have concluded that their arguments are sound, you should agree! Conversely, if you still disagree, that should indicate that their arguments are *not* sound.

With this foundation in place, we will move on, in the next chapter, to consider a specific kind of argument: theistic arguments (TAs). A theistic argument (TA) is simply an argument concerning God's existence. Most of the chapters of this book consider specific examples of TAs, such as the ontological argument (OA), cosmological argument (CA), design argument (DA), moral argument (MA), and even arguments *against* God's existence such as the problem of evil (POE). In the next chapter, however, we will consider the status and value of TAs in general. What can they accomplish? What is their value? Are they even necessary?

Chapter 2:
The Role and Value of Theistic Arguments

> *Comprehension questions you should be able to answer after reading this chapter:*
>
> 1. What is a theistic argument (TA)?
> 2. Why are TAs unlikely to "work?"
> 3. What is the "myth of neutrality," and how does it apply to TAs?
> 4. What is "warrant?"
> 5. How can a successful TA contribute to "warrant"?

Though argument does not create conviction, the lack of it destroys belief. What seemed to be proved may not be embraced, but what no one shows the ability to defend is quickly abandoned. Rational argument does not create belief, but it maintains a climate in which belief may flourish.[25]

In the previous chapter, we introduced important concepts such as "argument," "validity," and "soundness." All of this was done in the context of theistic arguments (TAs). In this chapter, we will consider the possible purposes and value of a TA.

In general, I don't think the arguments work.

Now that I have possibly poisoned my own well, allow me to explain. In order for me to justify my claim that TAs (generally) don't "work," we need to understand what is meant by "work." There are several different possible interpretations. For a TA to "work" might mean:

a) The TA convinces someone of the truth of its conclusion, regardless of what they believed prior to being exposed to the TA.
b) The TA reinforces or strengthens the epistemic confidence for those who already accept its conclusion.
c) The TA demonstrates the rationality of those who accept its conclusion, even to those who do not accept the truth of its conclusion.

If, in order for a TA to "work," it must accomplish (a), then I think most TAs fail most of the time. That is, they don't "work." If, on the other hand, for a TA to "work" just means that it accomplish (b) or (c) (or both), then I think many TAs can, and do, "work."

Why do I think that TAs (generally) fail to convince people that their conclusions

[25] Austin Farrer, "The Christian Apologist," in Jocelyn Gibb, ed., *Light on C.S. Lewis* (New York: Harcourt Brace Jovanovich, 1965), p. 26.

are true regardless of what they already previously believed? Because, like it or not, most (if not all) of us are rather stubbornly committed to our understanding of the world and how it works, our "worldview." When we are confronted with a piece of information that harmonizes with our worldview, we're inclined to accept it as true. When we are confronted with a piece of information that clashes with our worldview, we are inclined to reject it as false. We are all, as psychologists might put it, "cognitive misers." That is, we rely on "cognitive shortcuts" (such as drawing on what we think we already know about the world and how it works) to filter new information and arrive at conclusions. I do it. So do you. So does everyone else. At its worst, this is the sort of pernicious intellectual laziness that results in dangerous and harmful prejudices and stereotypes. In its normal operation, however, it often results in efficient and generally reliable interpretations of reality.

When applied to the context of TAs, our cognitive miserliness simply means that we are predisposed to interpret and judge TAs through the filter we already have in place. For theists, that means a worldview that includes God. For atheists, that means a worldview that does not include God. Not surprisingly, then, a theist is predisposed to find TAs for God's existence more persuasive than would atheists. At the same time, atheists are predisposed to find fault with TAs that argue in favor of God's existence. In both cases, the tendency is the same: preserve and protect one's worldview.

Don't be tempted to divide up into partisan camps at this point and think (let alone say) anything along the following lines:

- "See? Those superstitious zealots are blinded by their misguided faith! They're deaf to reason and refuse to accept anything that contradicts their fairy tales!"
- "See? Those hard-hearted atheists have blocked their ears and minds to the Word of God! They refuse to be open to anything that might save them from their tragically misguided views!"

Both camps are equally "guilty" of this tendency. No matter how open-minded you might think you are, or I might think I am, we are naturally (and understandably) predisposed to filter information using the lenses we have in place. The ideal of a cold, calm, rational and objective evaluation of TAs solely on the merits of their content and form is a lovely ideal, but is found rarely, if ever, in "real life." In a 1985 debate at UC Irvine concerning God's existence, between a Christian theist (Dr. Greg Bahnsen) and an atheist (Dr. Gordon Stein), Bahnsen attempted to dispel what he regards as the "myth of neutrality."

> *I take it he wishes to judge hypotheses in the common sense - by tests of logical coherence and empirical observation. The problem arises when Dr. Stein elsewhere insists that every claim that someone makes must be treated as a hypothesis which must be tested by such evidence before accepting it. "There is to be nothing," he says, "which smacks of begging the question or circular reasoning."*

> *This, I think, is oversimplified thinking and again misleading, what we might*

call the Pretended Neutrality fallacy. One can see this by considering the following quotation from Dr. Stein: "The use of logic or reason is the only valid way to examine the truth or falsity of any statement which claims to be factual."

One must eventually ask Dr. Stein, then, how he proves this statement itself. That is, how does he prove that logic or reason is the only way to prove factual statements? He is now on the horns of a real epistemological dilemma. If he says that the statement is true by logic or reason, then he is engaging in circular reasoning; and he's begging the question which he [supposedly] forbids. If he says that the statement is proven in some other fashion, then he refutes the statement itself, that logic or reason is the only way to prove things.

Now my point is not to fault Dr. Stein's commitment to logic or reason, but to observe that it actually has the nature of a pre commitment or a presupposition. It is not something that he has proven by empirical experience or logic, but it is rather that by which he proceeds to prove everything else. He is not presuppositionally neutral in his approach to factual questions and disputes. He does not avoid begging crucial questions, rather than proving them in what we might call the garden variety, ordinary way.... He writes, " Supernatural explanations are not allowed in science. The theist is hard put to document his claims for the existence of the supernatural if he is in effect forbidden from evoking the supernatural as a part of his explanation. Of course, this is entirely fair; as it would be begging the question to use what has to be proved as a part of the explanation."

In advance, you see, Dr. Stein is committed to disallowing any theistic interpretation of nature, history or experience. What he seems to overlook is that this is just as much begging the question on his own part as it is on the part of the theist who appeal to such evidence. He has not at all proven by empirical observation and logic his pre-commitment to Naturalism. He has assumed it in advance, accepting and rejecting all further factual claims in terms of that controlling and unproved assumption.

Now the theist does the very same thing, don't get me wrong. When certain empirical evidences are put forth as likely disproving the existence of God, the theist regiments his commitments in terms of his presuppositions, as well.... They both have their governing presuppositions by which the facts of experience are interpreted, even as all philosophical systems, all world views do.

At the most fundamental level of everyone's thinking and beliefs there are primary convictions about reality, man, the world, knowledge, truth, behavior, and such things. Convictions about which all other experience is organized, interpreted, and applied. Dr. Stein has such presuppositions, so do I, and so do all of you. And it is these presuppositions which determine what we accept by ordinary reasoning and evidence, for they are assumed in all of our reasoning - even about reasoning itself.

Please reread those last two paragraphs above, as they are very important for the point I'm trying to make. Bahnsen has pointed out that Stein is employing a naturalistic/empiricist bias in what he is willing to consider as evidence. He is not willing to acknowledge, as legitimate, kinds of evidence that his own filter rejects—but then Bahnsen points out that theists (such as himself) engage in the very same sorts of filtering. In other words, there is no "neutral" stance from which to judge TAs. Neutrality is a myth.

I believe Bahnsen is right about that not only because I tend to agree with the epistemic and psychological theories that promote that view, but also on the basis of my own experience. I have taught courses in the philosophy of religion numerous times, and even a course in contemporary Christian apologetics. Although there were some exceptional cases in which a theistic student judged a TA for God's existence to be ineffective, or an atheist student acknowledging the cleverness of that same TA, in the overwhelming majority of cases the single greatest predictor of whether or not a student would find an argument compelling, or unconvincing, was whether that student already agreed with its conclusion. Those who already agreed with its conclusion tended to think the argument was "good," those who disagreed tended to think it "bad." As far as I know, not a single theist had her faith shaken by an argument against God's existence, and not a single atheist was converted by virtue of an argument for God's existence.[26]

You might recall from the previous chapter that I pointed out that the soundness of an argument is often difficult to establish, even if its validity can be granted. This is so in part because premises can be controversial and difficult to verify, in part because there can be disagreement as to what even counts as "verification" with regard to premises (just review Bahnsen's point above!), and in part because of our tendency to "do what is necessary" to preserve what we already believe. Consider a non-religious example: imagine that I am presented with what appears to be footage from a security camera showing my own mother murdering dozens of infants at a day care center. Even if presented with such footage, I assure you that my immediate reaction would be to question the footage. Why would I doubt the evidence before me? Because it's inconceivable to me that my mother would murder infants! Given my predisposition to reject the claim that she's an infant-killer, I'm likely to question any premises that suggest otherwise. A more formal presentation of this tendency follows:

---

[26] There are exceptions, of course. Some of you might already know the somewhat famous story of the philosopher Anthony Flew. An outspoken and dedicated atheistic philosopher of religion, he later "converted" to a version of theism. To be fair, though, this was a modest concession since, as he put it, "the God in whose existence I have belatedly come to believe" is "most emphatically not the eternally rewarding and eternally torturing God of either Christianity or Islam but the God of Aristotle that he would have defined — had Aristotle actually produced a definition of his (and my) God — as the first initiating and sustaining cause of the universe." (http://www.nytimes.com/2010/04/17/arts/17flew.html?_r=0)

1. Surveillance footage shows Preston's mother slaughtering dozens of infants.
2. If the footage is accurate, then she is a spree killer (of infants).
3. However, it's utterly implausible that she is a spree killer (of infants).
4. Therefore, the surveillance footage is not accurate.

A relatively recent non-hypothetical example reveals this sort of tendency in even more stark fashion. On April 15th, 2013, two home-made bombs exploded at the Boston Marathon, killing 3 and injuring more than two hundred more. Just days later, two suspects were identified: Dzhokhar and Tamerlan Tsarnaev. Tamerlan was killed during a confrontation with police, and Dzokhar was later captured and charged with numerous crimes. Their mother, Zubeidat Tsarnaeva, made headlines when she claimed (despite an abundance of evidence, including, it would seem, a confession from Dzokhar) that her sons were being framed for an attack that didn't actually happen, as it was instead a "really big play" with "paint instead of blood." Oddly enough, despite having claimed that there hadn't actually been a deadly attack, she also said that "what happened is a terrible thing but I know my kids have nothing to do with this. I know it, I am mother." She *knows* they're innocent, because she's their mother. . . So, rather than accept the conclusion that her sons perpetrated a deadly terrorist attack, she instead rejects the evidence, requiring that she deny the event took place at all, and that the police conspired to frame her sons for the non-event. "You know what I think? I think now they will try to make my Dzhokhar guilty because they took away his voice, his ability to talk to the world... They did not want the truth to come out."

1. Evidence from a variety of sources indicates that the Tsarnaev brothers planned and executed a deadly terrorist attack on the Boston Marathon.
2. However, it's impossible that they would do such a thing.
3. Therefore, the evidence is in some way false.

You might think that Zubeidat is an extreme and non-representative example. After all, she was a grieving mother of questionable mental and emotional stability whose world view was being challenged in profound ways. Are people who evaluate TAs really cut from that same cloth? Perhaps not exactly, but the idea that people have pre-commitments that they seek to preserve in the context of TAs seems clear. Theists not only do believe in God, but *want* that belief to be true. Atheists not only don't believe in God, but (arguably) want *that* belief (i.e., that God does not exist) to be true. The famous philosopher Thomas Nagel said, of his atheism: "I want atheism to be true and am made uneasy by the fact that some of the most intelligent and well-informed people I know are religious believers. It isn't just that I don't believe in God and naturally, hope there is no God! I don't want there to be a God; I don't want the universe to be like that."

Think of how these tendencies might apply to an actual TA. In a later chapter we will consider the status of miracles and how they might (or might not) be useful as a TA, or in support of TAs. Now imagine that someone points to the occurrence of miracles (past and/or present) as proof of God's existence. Now imagine that a sincere atheist is presented with the following argument:

1. If miracles occur, then God exists.
2. Miracles occur.
3. Therefore, God exists.

☐   Is the argument valid?
☐   Is the argument sound?

Let's assume for the sake of argument that we can agree on what would count as a miracle, and what is meant by "God" in this context. Is this argument valid? Absolutely! In fact, it's a "textbook" illustration of one of the most famous inference rules in logic known as "modus ponens."

✓   Is the argument valid?
☐   Is the argument sound?

Is the argument sound, however? Is it, in fact, true that miracles occur? Surely there are arguments available both for and against the truth of that claim (and we will consider them in that later chapter), but I'm going to be so bold as to reassert my previous point: the single greatest predictor of whether or not you believe miracles occur is whether or not you already believe that God exists. If you believe that God exists, presumably you believe that miracles have at least occurred in the past (and possibly still occur today). If you do not believe God exists, then it's a safe bet that you don't believe miracles exist either. If you are an atheist, then, the implicit tendency you will have when confronted with the "argument from miracles" is to construct a variant of the argument, as follows:

1. If miracles occur, then God exists.
2. However, God does not exist.
3. Therefore, no miracles occur.

Let's turn the tables. Is *this* argument valid? Yes! In fact, it's a "textbook example" of another famous inference rule known as "modus tollens." Is the argument sound? Once again, your assessment of its soundness is likely to be thoroughly influenced by the worldview you already possess. Atheists are unlikely to find the argument from miracles to be sound because they are unlikely to believe that miracles occur—their naturalism predisposes them to seek alternative explanations for alleged miracles. Theists, on the other hand, already predisposed to believe in the "supernatural" are likely to be sympathetic to the possibility of miracles, and likely to think that miracles would, indeed, be evidence of God's existence.[27] Unless an atheist personally

---

[27] This is not to suggest that theists always believe that every miracle story involved a genuine miracle! It is simply to say that those who believe in God are a

witnesses or experiences a "miraculous" event that resists any possible naturalistic explanation,[28] atheists are unlikely to be persuaded that the argument from miracles is sound.

If TAs don't "work," are they then useless? Are you wasting your time reading this book? Am I wasting my time writing it? I don't think so. Remember, there were several possible interpretations of what it would mean for a TA to "work."

a)   The TA convinces someone of the truth of its conclusion, regardless of what they believed prior to being exposed to the TA.

b)   The TA reinforces or strengthens the epistemic confidence for those who already accept its conclusion.

c)   The TA demonstrates the rationality of those who accept its conclusion, even to those who do not accept the truth of its conclusion.

I have claimed that TAs don't work given the standard supplied by (a), but I think they *can* and often *do* work with regards to the standards set by both (b) and (c)— and they might even have *some* effectiveness with regard to (a). Although it is always possible to resist the conclusion of a TA by denying one or more of its premises (such that one's worldview is preserved), William Lane Craig (a prominent contemporary Christian philosopher of religion) claims that a good TA can "raise the price of rejecting the conclusion by giving good evidence for the truth of the premises." In other words, although one always retains the ability to reject a conclusion despite whatever evidence is presented, at a certain point it becomes less an issue of being a "cognitive miser" and more an issue of being shamefully stubborn. At a certain point, I imagine even Mrs. Tsarnaev will be compelled to accept the painful truth about who her sons became, and what they did. Much more accessible than "conversion," however, is either of the goals set by (b) or (c) above.

Something that we haven't discussed yet is what philosophers call "warrant." *Warrant refers to the justification we have (or don't have) for something we believe.[29]* Now consider "warrant" in the context of the ability of a TA to satisfy (b)(the TA reinforces or strengthens the epistemic confidence for those who already accept its conclusion).

Imagine that someone believes that God exists, and does so for one, and only one reason: because that's what his parents taught him as a child. Now, the epistemic status of "testimony" is actually a fascinating and complicated philosophical issue, and there's genuine debate on the topic of "warrant transfer" (i.e., whether one person can transfer her warrant for a belief to another person by means of testimony), but I suspect that most of us would acknowledge that as far as warrant goes, someone who believes in God solely because that's what he has been told by his

---

neck of a lot more likely to believe that miracles (at least sometimes) occur than are people who don't believe in God.

[28] In which case, his or her worldview might be radically changed!

[29] For a review of how we establish degrees of justification, please review chapter 1 of this book.

parents as a child is either lacking in warrant, or at least has *less* warrant than a believer who believes not merely because of testimony as a childhood, but also by virtue of various TAs such as the OA, CA, DA, MA, etc. Compare the following:

I believe there are 457 marbles in the jar because:
1. I guessed.
2. I counted them.

I believe God exists because:
1. Mom says so.
2. The OA, CA, DA, and MA are each both valid and sound.

In both cases, there is surely more warrant for (2) than for (1). For believers, TAs for God's existence can provide warrant, or increase warrant—literally providing more or better reasons to believe what the theist already believes. As Craig puts it:

> One can envision great benefits of having such a dual warrant of one's Christian beliefs. Having sound arguments for the existence of a Creator and Designer of the universe or evidence for the historical credibility of the New Testament records of the life of Jesus in addition to the inner witness of the Spirit could increase one's confidence in the veracity of Christian truth claims. On Plantinga's epistemological model, at least, one would then have greater warrant for believing such claims. Greater warrant could in turn lead an unbeliever to come to faith more readily or inspire a believer to share his faith more boldly. Moreover, the availability of independent warrant for Christian truth claims apart from the Spirit's witness could help predispose an unbeliever to respond to the drawing of the Holy Spirit when he hears the Gospel and could provide the believer with epistemic support in times of spiritual dryness or doubt when the Spirit's witness seems eclipsed. One could doubtless think of many other ways in which the possession of such dual warrant for Christian beliefs would be beneficial.[30]

So too, of course, for the atheist. Atheists are just as subject to a "because Mom says so" scenario as are theists, and a TA against God's existence could similarly provide, or increase, warrant for the atheist's worldview.

Very much related to the ability of a TA to increase warrant is its ability to satisfy (c): demonstrating the rationality of those who accept its conclusion, even to those who do not accept the truth of its conclusion. Appealing once again to our (inevitable) tendency to interpret information and experience through the lens/filter provided by our worldview, it is all too easy for theists to dismiss atheists' views as the "tragically misguided product of our secular culture," or for atheists to dismiss the views of theists as "superstitious fantasies." It's more difficult (though still possible) to be so

[30] http://www.reasonablefaith.org/christian-apologetics-who-needs-it#ixzz2b1q3xpIi

dismissive when one (truly) realizes that there are intelligent, well-educated people on both sides of the debate, and intelligent, well-formed, and thoughtful TAs both for and against God's existence.

Imagine how differently a theist would be (or at least should be) perceived when that theist defends her belief by appealing to the fine-tuning necessary for life, the impossibility an actually infinite sequence of past events, as opposed to a "first cause," and perhaps the historical evidence for the accuracy of the Gospels, as opposed to a theist who defends her belief by appealing to her desire to go to Heaven. Imagine how differently an atheist would be (or should be) perceived when that atheist defends her belief by appealing to the evidential version of the problem of evil (POE), and the multi-verse model of cosmology (as an alternative to a model in which the universe has an absolute "beginning"), compared to an atheist who defends her belief by proclaiming her desire to not be subject to the moral requirements of "religion."

Well-constructed TAs (both for and against) can go a long way towards *demonstrating* the possible warrant of the believers (or non-believers) in question, towards *demonstrating* that such views, whether true or false, can be (and often are) seriously considered and thoughtfully held. Depending on what you, yourself, believe, you will necessarily conclude that people who disagree with you are mistaken, but that doesn't mean that you must also conclude that they are fools, or ignorant, or irrational.

I have thus far made a case for the possible value and effectiveness of TAs. My own view is that TAs can most certainly be useful and valuable, although I personally doubt that they often result in any sort of radical revision of one's worldview. In the next chapter, we will consider several additional views as regards belief and evidence in general, and belief in God in particular. We will start with Clifford's very stringent demand for evidence, and then we will consider Pascal's famous "wager." Finally, we will consider both James and Plantinga (in rebuttal, at times).

Chapter 3: Do We Need "Proof"?

Comprehension questions you should be able to answer after reading this chapter:

1. When does Clifford think we are justified in believing a claim to be true?

2. What are "*de jure*" objections to theistic belief?

3. What are "*de facto*" objections to theistic belief?

4. What is Pascal's Wager? How is it supposed to work, and for whom is it intended?

5. What are James' objections to Pascal's wager (there are several!), and how might a defender of Pascal respond?

6. What are James' objections to Clifford's standards for belief (i.e., your answer to question #1 above)? What four conditions does James offer that would justify belief without "sufficient evidence?"

7. What is classical foundationalism (CF)? What is a "noetic structure" (NS)? What is a basic belief?

8. What conditions must be met for a belief to be properly basic?

9. Why does Plantinga reject the CF demands for properly basic beliefs?

10. What is the "sensus divinitatis" and how could it render theistic beliefs "properly basic"?

11. What is the "Great Pumpkin" objection to Plantinga's "reformed epistemology," and how does he respond to it?

12. What is a "defeater?" An undercutting defeater? A rebutting defeater?

The previous chapter addressed the possible roles, value, and limitations of TAs. I argued that although it is difficult (and unlikely) for a TA to "convert" someone, TAs nevertheless are valuable by virtue of their ability to provide and increase warrant, as well as to display the rationality of believers (on both sides of the debate). But are TAs even necessary? With regard to theistic (or atheistic) beliefs, or belief in general, why would we think that proof and argument is needed?

Clifford

Part of the previous chapter presupposed the need for evidence. The entire discussion of warrant rests upon the assumption that beliefs require justification, that we shouldn't just believe something for "no reason." William Clifford went so far as to say that "it is wrong always, everywhere, and for anyone, to believe anything upon insufficient evidence."

Clifford is using "wrong" in the moral sense here—he's not merely saying it's incorrect, or imprudent, to believe upon insufficient evidence, but wrong. According to Clifford (and like-minded thinkers), we have an epistemic duty to be responsible with our beliefs, and part of that responsibility is only to believe when we have warrant. We shouldn't believe something for just any old reason, but only if there is sufficient evidence. In our current context, that would clearly mean that one should only believe in God on the basis of sufficient evidence (or, conversely, to believe that there is no God only on sufficient evidence of that).

Why does Clifford have such stringent demands for belief? In fairness, he's not just being obsessive about evidence, but is convinced that our beliefs have consequences—sometimes very serious ones. His opening example is that of a ship owner who convinces himself that his ship is sea-worthy, despite his reservations, and despite not bothering to have it inspected. It turns out that he was wrong, and the ship was lost at sea with no survivors. This ship owner believing that the ship was safe to sail, not on the basis of evidence, but on the basis of wishful thinking, cost men their lives.

> What shall we say of him? Surely this, that he was verily guilty of the death of those men. It is admitted that he did sincerely believe in the soundness of his ship; but the sincerity of his conviction can in no wise help him, because he had no right to believe on such evidence as was before him. He had acquired his belief not by honestly earning it in patient investigation, but by stifling his doubts. And although in the end he may have felt so sure about it that he could not think otherwise, yet inasmuch as he had knowingly and willingly worked himself into that frame of mind, he must be held responsible for it.[31]

Even if the owner turned out to have been correct, and the ship was indeed safe, and it never sank, it would make no difference (epistemically) to Clifford. His belief was still unwarranted, and he was still guilty of shirking his epistemic responsibilities. Note that warrant is not to be confused with truth. Clifford does a good job of explaining this: "the question is not whether their belief was true or false, but whether they entertained it on wrong grounds." Imagine someone working at an airport tasked with refueling planes. He doesn't bother to check if there's enough fuel in the plane for it to reach its destination, but just assumes that there probably is. Now imagine that there is, in fact, enough fuel, and the plane arrives safely. The employee got lucky (and so did everyone on the plane!). He was correct, but he wasn't warranted in his belief—he was still guilty of failing in his epistemic duty to believe only on good evidence, and this is another clear case where our beliefs can have potentially life-changing consequences not just for ourselves, but for others.

Clifford describes this duty to believe only on sufficient evidence as a (literally) *sacred* duty to humanity. What one person believes is transmitted to others. Beliefs inspire actions. There are *consequences* for what we believe, and how we believe.

---

[31] Clifford, William Kingdon. *The Ethics of Belief.* 1877. Section 1. [See the excerpt at the end of this chapter for a larger portion of the original text.]

... if I let myself believe anything on insufficient evidence, there may be no great harm done by the mere belief; it may be true after all, or I may never have occasion to exhibit it in outward acts. But I cannot help doing this great wrong towards Man, that I make myself credulous. The danger to society is not merely that it should believe wrong things, though that is great enough; but that it should become credulous, and lose the habit of testing things and inquiring into them; for then it must sink back into savagery.

The harm which is done by credulity in a man is not confined to the fostering of a credulous character in others, and consequent support of false beliefs. Habitual want of care about what I believe leads to habitual want of care in others about the truth of what is told to me. Men speak the truth to one another when each reveres the truth in his own mind and in the other's mind; but how shall my friend revere the truth in my mind when I myself am careless about it, when I believe things because I want to believe them, and because they are comforting and pleasant? Will he not learn to cry, "Peace," to me, when there is no peace? By such a course I shall surround myself with a thick atmosphere of falsehood and fraud, and in that I must live. It may matter little to me, in my cloud-castle of sweet illusions and darling lies; but it matters much to Man that I have made my neighbours ready to deceive. The credulous man is father to the liar and the cheat; he lives in the bosom of this his family, and it is no marvel if he should become even as they are. So closely are our duties knit together, that whoso shall keep the whole law, and yet offend in one point, he is guilty of all.[32]

Clifford seems to think that when we allow ourselves, on occasion, to believe without sufficient evidence, we are, in effect, training ourselves to be sloppy critical thinkers. We will be unable to restrict this intellectual laziness to only specific cases of belief, but will become "credulous"—gullible, too ready to believe what we are told.

Once again returning to our own context, the obvious application of Clifford's standard is that what we believe about God's existence or non-existence should not be the product of some casual, lazy, or unthinking process; it should not be the result of wishful thinking, peer-pressure, or any other illegitimate means of belief formation. If you believe in God, you should have good *reasons* for that belief. If you believe there is no God, you should have good reasons for that. It is sometimes pointed out that geography is the best predictor of one's religious beliefs. "If you were born in Baghdad, you can pretty much predict what religion that person will have. If you were born in Tennessee, you can pretty much predict what kind of person you are going to be with your religion, generally. It's the highest predictor."[33] This is sometimes used by atheists to challenge the warrant of theists' beliefs. "The only reason you believe in God is because you were born in the Bible-belt!" Sometimes theists will flip this around and (with some measure of irony) reply that "the only reason you're an atheist

---

[32] Ibid.

[33] Butt, Kyle and Dan Barker (2009), *Butt/Barker Debate: Does the God of the Bible Exist?* (Montgomery, AL: Apologetics Press).

is because of the contingent circumstances of *your* birth and life." Ultimately, either accusation is an example of the "genetic fallacy" *if* either party is suggesting that the belief is false simply because of its origin. The origin of a belief has no bearing on its truth or falsity, but it *could* (arguably) have some bearing on its *warrant*. Clifford would claim that both the theist and the atheist had better have better reasons for believing what they do than the circumstances of their birth and the community in which they were raised.

> *If a man, holding a belief which he was taught in childhood or persuaded of afterwards, keeps down and pushes away any doubts which arise about it in his mind, purposely avoids the reading of books and the company of men that call in question or discuss it, and regards as impious those questions which cannot easily be asked without disturbing it — the life of that man is one long sin against mankind.[34]*

Clifford's condemnation (while a bit melodramatic) has special relevance given what we're doing in this book. One condemnation, in particular, is worth repeating: one who "purposely avoids the reading of books and the company of men that call in question or discuss it, and regards as impious those questions which cannot easily be asked without disturbing it..." A theist who believes, on questionable (or no) evidence, and who purposely avoids contact with books, people, and conversations that might challenge his beliefs (and vice versa, for the atheist) is living a life that is "one long sin against mankind." That's a powerful condemnation! Fortunately, we can be reasonably confident that Clifford is not talking about any of *us*. After all, by virtue of reading this book, you *are* engaging evidence and arguments both for and against the existence of God. You're (at least partially) doing your due diligence. In theory, then, at the end of this process your beliefs (whatever they happen to be) will be warranted, or at least more warranted, than they once were.

One final note before moving on to our next philosopher: Clifford is addressing what is sometimes called the "*de jure*" problem of theistic belief. This is as opposed to the "*de facto*" problem. Briefly, the *de facto* problem concerns whether or not a claim is true. *De facto* objections to theistic belief amount to the assertion that such claims are just plain false. For example, if someone believes that life is the result of an supernatural act of special Creation approximately six thousand years ago, over the course of six twenty-four hour periods, and a naturalist offers geological and biological evidence that life is actually much older than six thousand years, that naturalist would be making a *de facto* objection to that particular belief. Perhaps interestingly, most objections to theistic belief that arise in philosophy are not *de facto* objections.[35] Instead, philosophers (on both sides of the debate) tend to grapple with *de jure* concerns.

A *de jure* objection isn't an assertion that a particular theistic claim is false, but

---

[34]Cllifford, Ibid.

[35] *De facto* objections are much more common in theological/religious studies contexts, where specific Biblical or doctrinal claims, for example, might be subjected to scrutiny.

rather, independently of its truth or falsity, that one is not rationally justified in believing it to be true. The allegation, ultimately, is that the believer is doing something intellectually embarrassing in believing as he does, that some sort of epistemic responsibility has been violated. Some examples of *de jure* objections to theistic belief include Freud's psychoanalytic interpretation of the origin of theistic belief, Feuerbach's theory of projection, Nietzsche's theory of "resentment," and some versions of the "problem of evil."

Let there be no confusion: *this chapter is concerned solely with de jure issues*, with whether or not one can be *rationally justified* in holding theistic beliefs. As has been mentioned, Clifford has offered one answer: one is rationally justified with regard to a theistic belief only if there is "sufficient evidence" for that belief. We will now consider a very different sort of answer.

Pascal

Clifford has told us that we should only believe on the basis of sufficient evidence, but what happens when evidence is questionable, or mixed—in other words, what happens when the evidence, by itself, isn't enough to let reason decide what to believe?

Blaise Pascal thought that belief in God provoked exactly that sort of dilemma. Pascal claimed that God is so transcendent, so "infinitely incomprehensible" that we are "incapable of knowing either what He is or if He is." This is a controversial view, of course, and while many theists will certainly agree that God cannot be fully comprehended by human reason, they will claim that we are, nevertheless, capable of *some* understanding of God. In fairness to Pascal, he wasn't claiming that humans can have no intelligible sense of God at all—just that our understanding is not supplied by reason, but instead by Revelation, and believed by faith. Using the vocabulary of his "wager," when he imagines being asked "is there no means of seeing the faces of the cards?" (in other words: is there no way of gaining insight into God?), his answer is "Yes, Scripture and the rest, etc."

Even if you don't agree with Pascal with regard to God being "infinitely incomprehensible," there is a more practical and less abstract application of the dilemma he's describing: for some, there is equally compelling evidence both for and against God's existence. For such persons, reason is not capable of making an informed choice between the two. We can imagine such persons to be either sincere agnostics, or either theists or atheists plagued by doubt. What can such persons believe? What *should* such persons believe?

Pascal encourages us to make his (now infamous) "wager."

Which will you choose then? Let us see. Since you must choose, let us see which interests you least. You have two things to lose, the true and the good; and two things to stake, your reason and your will, your knowledge and your happiness; and your nature has two things to shun, error and misery. Your reason is no more shocked in choosing one rather than the other, since you must of necessity choose. This is one point settled. But your happiness? Let us weigh the gain and the loss in wagering that God is. Let us estimate these two chances. If you gain, you gain all; if you lose, you lose nothing. Wager, then, without hesitation that He is.[36]

The table below illustrates the "decision matrix" Pascal is describing.

	God Exists	God does NOT exist
Believe in God	"Infinite" gain	"finite" gain
Don't believe in God	"Infinite" loss	"nothing"

The idea seems to be this: either God exists, or God does not. If God does exist, and you believe in God, you acquire an "infinite" gain (presumably in the form of Salvation). If God exists, and you don't believe in God, then you acquire an "infinite" loss (presumably in the form of Damnation). On the other hand, if God does not exist, and you do *not* believe, you have gained nothing, whereas if God doesn't exist and you *do* believe, you still gain *something*. What is this "something?" Pascal explains:

Now, what harm will befall you in taking this side? You will be faithful, humble, grateful, generous, a sincere friend, truthful. Certainly you will not have those poisonous pleasures, glory and luxury; but will you not have others? I will tell you that you will thereby gain in this life, and that, at each step you take on this road, you will see so great certainty of gain, so much nothingness in what you risk, that you will at last recognize that you have wagered for something certain and infinite, for which you have given nothing.[37]

For Pascal, the math is easy and obvious: when the stakes on one side are infinite loss or gain, and only gain (or nothing) on the other side, the prudent wager is to "bet on God."

James

Pascal's wager is very well-known, and not merely famous, but infamous. Perhaps equally famous are criticisms of the wager. We will now consider several of them—most being supplied by William James—and try to anticipate how Pascal would (or could) respond to them.

   i.   Belief isn't "voluntary"

To some, Pascal seems to be proposing something that is either impossible, or at least inadvisable: *choosing* to believe something. "But," the objector might protest, "belief doesn't work like that. I can't just choose to believe something if I don't have reasons to do so. Belief is more passive than that. We simply find ourselves believing things on the basis of evidence and reasons."

---

[36] Pascal, Blaise. *Pensées*. Translated by W. F. Trotter. 1910. [See the excerpt at the end of this chapter for more.]
[37] Ibid.

As James puts it:

Does it not seem preposterous on the very face of it to talk of our opinions being modifiable at will? Can our will either help or hinder our intellect in its perceptions of truth? Can we, by just willing it, believe that Abraham Lincoln's existence is a myth, and that the portraits of him in McClure's Magazine are all of someone else? Can we, by any effort of our will, or by any strength of wish that it were true, believe ourselves well and about when we are roaring with rheumatism in bed, or feel certain that the sum of the two one-dollar bills in our pocket must be a hundred dollars? We can say any of these things, but we are absolutely impotent to believe them;...[38]

There seems to be something legitimate about this concern. After all, try to believe that you have six arms right now. Try really, really hard to believe that you have six arms. You have failed. It does seem to be the case that we can't just make ourselves believe just anything. Moreover, even if we could, imagine what Clifford would say about that effort! Willfully trying to believe something, not on the basis of evidence, but on the basis of a cost-benefit analysis?

Imagine that you are a hard-core, devoted atheist, utterly convinced that God does not exist. Now try to believe that God does exist, for the possible "infinite" gain. Seems implausible, right?

But, Pascal would reply, such examples are misleading and fail to capture the situation described in the wager. Remember, Pascal has declared that *reason can't decide whether God exists, or does not.* In that scenario only, he's proposing that we use the wager. Neither of the examples that we considered satisfy the "reason can't decide" condition. Regarding the first example, I would dare say that reason *can* help you decide whether or not you have six arms! Open your eyes and look, use one of your hands to feel around to see if there are several more arms to be found—or simply consult your basic understanding of human anatomy and extrapolate to your own case. Regarding the second example, we clearly have someone who disagrees with Pascal that reason "can't decide" the God question. After all, if you are "utterly convinced" that God does not exist, then, presumably, your use of reason has produced that conclusion.

Pascal's wager applies only to a very specific subset of person: people who agree that reason can't decide whether or not God exists. That's it. If you think that reason *can* decide that question, the wager is not for you. If you think, for example, that any or all of the various TAs we will consider throughout this book can help to decide that issue, then the wager is not for you. Only if you agree (for whatever reason), that God's existence is not capable of being established by reason, does the wager apply to you.

---

[38]This, and other, quotations from James are all taken from his "Will to Believe." A larger excerpt is available at the end of this chapter, and a fuller version may be retrieved here: http://www.booksshouldbefree.com/download/text/Will-to-Believe-and-Other-Essays-in-Popular.txt.

ii.   The wager produces insincere belief, at best

A second objection to the wager (very much related to the first) is that the so-called belief it produces is insincere. Someone who takes Pascal's advice and "bets on God" might *say* they believe in God, or go through the motions of imitating someone who believes in God, but they won't *really* believe in God. In effect, Pascal is encouraging people to live a lie.

Pascal's reply is that there *is* something valuable about "going through the motions."

> *You would like to attain faith and do not know the way; you would like to cure yourself of unbelief and ask the remedy for it. Learn of those who have been bound like you, and who now stake all their possessions. These are people who know the way which you would follow, and who are cured of an ill of which you would be cured. Follow the way by which they began; by acting as if they believed, taking the holy water, having masses said, etc. Even this will naturally make you believe, and deaden your acuteness.*[39]

Remember Pascal's view on this: *reason can't decide* whether God exists, but such belief *can* be produced by Revelation and affirmed by faith. The wager is just the start of a process, intended for those for whom no other source of belief has manifested. Even James, in a moment of philosophical charity, grants this point.

> *Surely Pascal's own personal belief in masses and holy water had far other springs; and this celebrated page of his is but an argument for others, a last desperate snatch at a weapon against the hardness of the unbelieving heart.*[40]

By "betting on God," you are committing yourself to actions that will open you up to Revelation. This is why he gives specific advice that one go to Mass, receive Sacraments, spend time with people of faith, etc. In so doing, *sincere* belief in God will be formed (via Revelation). Stopping at the wager would indeed result in insincerity, but that's not what Pascal is proposing.

iii.   The wager wouldn't "work," even if God really does exist

This third objection is related to the second. The concern seems to be that if there really is an all-knowing God, God will see right through the people who profess belief not because they actually believe, but just for the hope of "infinite gain." In which case (presumably), that God would not actually dole out the infinite gain after all. Even if you make bet the Pascal recommends, you'll still "lose."

Once again appealing to James:

> *We feel that a faith in masses and holy water adopted wilfully after such a*

---

[39] Pascal, Ibid.
[40] James, Ibid.

mechanical calculation would lack the inner soul of faith's reality; and if we were ourselves in the place of the Deity, we should probably take particular pleasure in cutting off believers of this pattern from their infinite reward.[41]

Pascal's reply to this objection will largely be repetitive. Remember, the wager applies not to *everyone*, but only to those people who do not already believe in God by faith, and for whom no other appeal has been effective. Even for those people, the wager is intended as, at most, the *beginning* of faith. As said above, having made the wager, one should then attend church, read the Bible, pray, etc. Even if one is initially "faking it," the idea is that faith will eventually take over and the belief will become sincere.

iv.   Which "god" do we wager on?

This is, arguably, the most powerful objection to the wager. Pascal seems to be assuming that, as far as the "God question" is concerned, there are only two possibilities: either the Christian God exists, or else no God (of any kind) exists—but surely there are many other possibilities. Christianity is obviously one religion among many, contemporary and historical. Many believe in the Christian God, but many others are Jews, Muslims, Hindus, or Sikhs. Still others have a Buddhist worldview, or are Wiccan, or are Ásatrú, and so forth. Some (in satirical fashion) even worship a "flying spaghetti monster!"

The cost-benefit analysis that is supposed to drive someone (initially) to "bet on God" relies on the compelling nature of the choice: two options only, and one of them generates infinite gain or loss. But, given religious pluralism, a more realistic decision matrix would require us to have columns representing all those other religious possibilities as well—in which case it's no longer obvious which bet is the smart one. We will appeal to James one more time against Pascal:

It is evident that unless there be some pre-existing tendency to believe in masses and holy water, the option offered to the will by Pascal is not a living option. Certainly no Turk ever took to masses and holy water on its account; and even to us Protestants these means of salvation seem such foregone impossibilities that Pascal's logic, invoked for them specifically, leaves us unmoved. As well might the Mahdi write to us, saying, "I am the Expected One whom God has created in his effulgence. You shall be infinitely happy if you confess me; otherwise you shall be cut off from the light of the sun. Weigh, then, your infinite gain if I am genuine against your finite sacrifice if I am not!" His logic would be that of Pascal; but he would vainly use it on us, for the hypothesis he offers us is dead. No tendency to act on it exists in us to any degree.[42]

I have to admit that I find this to be a persuasive objection (though it's perfectly acceptable if you don't). Let's be fair to Pascal, though, and imagine how he might

---

[41] Ibid.
[42] Ibid.

respond. Remember that Pascal thinks the proper source of religious belief is Revelation (as opposed to reason). Revelation (in general) is the revealing of knowledge through communication (in some fashion) with a supernatural source (e.g., a deity). For a Christian like Pascal, Revelation is knowledge received from God via various media such as the Bible, the internal testimony of the Holy Spirit, etc. Part of that (Christian) Revelation has been that there is only one God (i.e., the Christian God). Accordingly, any other religious belief would not be the result of Revelation, but would instead be the erroneous product of myth or other cultural forces. Revelation reveals which God goes into the decision matrix, for Pascal. Is this a potentially controversial position to take? You bet! But, it's also one that we will explore later on in this chapter when we consider Alvin Plantinga's views on warrant, and in a later chapter when we consider the issue of religious pluralism in general.

Part of the point of James' last objection is that some hypotheses will have no persuasive force for us. In his cultural and historical context, appeals to the truth of Hindu or Muslim claims were not "live" possibilities for him or his contemporaries. This is not to say that such claims are, therefore, *false*—just that they will not (generally) be regarded as serious epistemic options.

On a personal note, I have several friends who are Ásatrú. I suspect many of you do not know what that means, so allow me to explain in very brief fashion. Ásatrú refers to a variety of pagan beliefs and practices derived from old Nordic religion. For many, the holy symbol of that faith is the Hammer of Thor. Some celebrate various cultural values, and others believe that the Norse pantheon (e.g., Odin, Thor, Loki, etc.) are real, and worship them. Although not widely known as a religious tradition, in May of 2013 the Hammer of Thor was added to the list of U.S. Department of Veteran's Affairs symbols for grave markers. Some veterans might get a cross on their tombstone, and others might opt for Thor's Hammer. My point in mentioning Ásatrú and my friends is that, although I like and respect them as persons, as a result of a variety of factors I just can't take seriously their claim that Thor really exists as the God of Thunder and that Valhalla awaits the valorous dead. They might as well try to get me to worship Zeus. Once again, my inability to take seriously their religious claims is *not* somehow proof that those claims are false. Instead, as James would say, it "shows that deadness and liveness in an hypothesis are not intrinsic properties, but relations to the individual thinker."

Why does this matter? Thus far, it seems that James disagrees with Pascal, and would therefore (perhaps) *agree* with Clifford, but this would be an overly hasty assumption to make. In fact, he disagrees (in part), with both.

In the first paragraph of "The Will to Believe," James introduces his essay as "a defence of our right to adopt a believing attitude in religious matters, in spite of the fact that our merely logical intellect may not have been coerced." This is in direct opposition to Clifford. He mentions Clifford several times by name, and quotes some of the very same lines from Clifford that we have reviewed above. He takes issue, however, with the suggestion (implied or outright stated) that Clifford's enthusiastic imperative that we believe nothing without sufficient evidence is somehow a dispassionate, objective approach to inquiry, and ultimately to belief and knowledge. Instead, he claims that Clifford's (zealous) desire to avoid error, which motivates his imperative, is just a *different* "passion" directing us what to believe.

Believe truth! Shun error!--these, we see, are two materially different laws; and by choosing between them we may end by coloring differently our whole intellectual life. We may regard the chase for truth as paramount, and the avoidance of error as secondary; or we may, on the other hand, treat the avoidance of error as more imperative, and let truth take its chance. Clifford, in the instructive passage which I have quoted, exhorts us to the latter course. Believe nothing, he tells us, keep your mind in suspense forever, rather than by closing it on insufficient evidence incur the awful risk of believing lies. You, on the other hand, may think that the risk of being in error is a very small matter when compared with the blessings of real knowledge, and be ready to be duped many times in your investigation rather than postpone indefinitely the chance of guessing true. I myself find it impossible to go with Clifford. We must remember that these feelings of our duty about either truth or error are in any case only expressions of our passional life. Biologically considered, our minds are as ready to grind out falsehood as veracity, and he who says, "Better go without belief forever than believe a lie!" merely shows his own preponderant private horror of becoming a dupe. He may be critical of many of his desires and fears, but this fear he slavishly obeys. He cannot imagine any one questioning its binding force. For my own part, I have also a horror of being duped; but I can believe that worse things than being duped may happen to a man in this world: so Clifford's exhortation has to my ears a thoroughly fantastic sound. It is like a general informing his soldiers that it is better to keep out of battle forever than to risk a single wound. Not so are victories either over enemies or over nature gained. Our errors are surely not such awfully solemn things. In a world where we are so certain to incur them in spite of all our caution, a certain lightness of heart seems healthier than this excessive nervousness on their behalf.[43]

James agrees that with respect to a great many subjects, it does indeed seem appropriate to suspend judgment, if necessary, unless and until sufficient evidence can direct our beliefs. If we're trying to determine what causes (or cures) cancer, for example, or why our car won't start, it's appropriate to draw conclusions (e.g., in those examples, diagnostic beliefs) solely on the basis of sufficient evidence.

… in our dealings with objective nature we obviously are recorders, not makers, of the truth; and decisions for the mere sake of deciding promptly and getting on to the next business would be wholly out of place. Throughout the breadth of physical nature facts are what they are quite independently of us, and seldom is there any such hurry about them that the risks of being duped by believing a premature theory need be faced. The questions here are always trivial options, the hypotheses are hardly living (at any rate not living for us spectators), the choice between believing truth or falsehood is seldom forced. The attitude of sceptical balance is therefore the absolutely wise one if we would escape mistakes. What difference, indeed, does it make to most of us whether we have

---

[43]Ibid.

or have not a theory of the Röntgen rays, whether we believe or not in mind-stuff, or have a conviction about the causality of conscious states? It makes no difference. Such options are not forced on us. On every account it is better not to make them, but still keep weighing reasons pro et contra with an indifferent hand.[44]

The relevant feature of these sorts of examples is that reason is equipped to gather evidence and weigh it in pursuit of the most well-supported conclusion.

There are some sorts of cases, though, that have different features, and in those sorts of cases, James thinks that Clifford's demands are inappropriate. The general features of those sorts of cases are that they demand a choice, and that the choice has the following properties:

1. <u>Live</u>: the choice must appeal to you as a distinct possibility. This is, admittedly, somewhat subjective. Believing in Thor is no more a live option for me than believing in Allah was a live option for James. The possibility that I actually have six arms is not a serious, distinct possibility, for me.

2. <u>Momentous</u>: something important will be irrevocably lost, on the basis of your choice. This, too, is a bit subjective. James' example is that of a Polar expedition, but I'll adapt one of my own. There is probably nothing "momentous" about whether or not you accept my offer to get a cup of coffee. Missing out on coffee is not a huge deal (in most cases), and the experience can probably be replicated or replaced. If someone from NASA made you a one-time offer to go into space, however, that is a "momentous" choice. If you turn it down, it's unlikely you'll get another chance to say "yes."

3. <u>Forced</u>: the two options are mutually exclusive, and exhaustive. One of James' examples is that of either going out with your umbrella, or without it. This is not a forced option, as described, because it offers a false dilemma. There's always the option of not going out at all! When offered "Coke or Pepsi," you can (presumably) have neither, or maybe a Mountain Dew instead. Some options are forced, though. You have only two choices, and you must pick one of the two.

4. <u>Intellectually ambiguous</u>: evidence is ambiguous with regard to the truth or falsity of the claim. In other words, the option is not decidable according to Clifford's standards of evidence. Like it or not, some ambiguity remains.

As you probably anticipated, James thinks that religious belief is a good candidate for satisfying these conditions.

Now, let us consider what the logical elements of this situation are in case the religious hypothesis in both its branches be really true. (Of course, we must

---

[44] Ibid.

admit that possibility at the outset. If we are to discuss the question at all, it must involve a living option. If for any of you religion be a hypothesis that cannot, by any living possibility be true, then you need go no farther. I speak to the 'saving remnant' alone.) So proceeding, we see, first, that religion offers itself as a momentous option. We are supposed to gain, even now, by our belief, and to lose by our non-belief, a certain vital good. Secondly, religion is a forced option, so far as that good goes. We cannot escape the issue by remaining sceptical and waiting for more light, because, although we do avoid error in that way if religion be untrue, we lose the good, if it be true, just as certainly as if we positively chose to disbelieve. It is as if a man should hesitate indefinitely to ask a certain woman to marry him because he was not perfectly sure that she would prove an angel after he brought her home. Would he not cut himself off from that particular angel-possibility as decisively as if he went and married some one else? Scepticism, then, is not avoidance of option; it is option of a certain particular kind of risk. Better risk loss of truth than chance of error,--that is your faith-vetoer's exact position. He is actively playing his stake as much as the believer is; he is backing the field against the religious hypothesis, just as the believer is backing the religious hypothesis against the field. To preach scepticism to us as a duty until 'sufficient evidence' for religion be found, is tantamount therefore to telling us, when in presence of the religious hypothesis, that to yield to our fear of its being error is wiser and better than to yield to our hope that it may be true. It is not intellect against all passions, then; it is only intellect with one passion laying down its law. And by what, forsooth, is the supreme wisdom of this passion warranted? Dupery for dupery, what proof is there that dupery through hope is so much worse than dupery through fear? I, for one, can see no proof; and I simply refuse obedience to the scientist's command to imitate his kind of option, in a case where my own stake is important enough to give me the right to choose my own form of risk. If religion be true and the evidence for it be still insufficient, I do not wish, by putting your extinguisher upon my nature (which feels to me as if it had after all some business in this matter), to forfeit my sole chance in life of getting upon the winning side,--that chance depending, of course, on my willingness to run the risk of acting as if my passional need of taking the world religiously might be prophetic and right.[45]

Notice several important details from this section:

1. The religious hypothesis has to be "live" for you, or else "you need go no further." For some of you, it's possible that the prospect of any sort of divinity is about as "live" as is the prospect of Odin for me. If so, James admits that something like Clifford's standards might best apply for you, in this case.

2. If we grant that the religious hypothesis is "live," it is clearly "momentous." It makes a big difference what stance we take with regard to God's existence

---

[45]Ibid.

(if, in fact, God does exist). In this, at least, Pascal was certainly right.

3.   The religious hypothesis is a "forced option." So long as the religious hypothesis is "live" for you, Clifford's demand that we defer belief until "sufficient evidence" presents itself is unrealistic because, "although we do avoid error in that way if religion be untrue, we lose the good, if it be true, just as certainly as if we positively chose to disbelieve." If God exists, and demands that we choose God, then there is no option of "wait and see." Not choosing is the same as choosing "no."

4.   Finally, given (1-3) above, given a certain intellectual ambiguity and given that a choice must be made, then "faith based on desire is certainly a lawful and possibly an indispensable thing."

"Faith based on desire?" one might ask. "Isn't that just wishful thinking?" Perhaps, James might allow—but if so, then no more so, and no more perniciously, than Clifford's own passion-driven demand that we never believe on insufficient evidence. What's more, there seem to be cases where desire and commitment are constructive elements in the belief being true in the first place.

Do you like me or not?-for example. Whether you do or not depends, in countless instances, on whether I meet you half-way, am willing to assume that you must like me, and show you trust and expectation. The previous faith on my part in your liking's existence is in such cases what makes your liking come. But if I stand aloof, and refuse to budge an inch until I have objective evidence, until you shall have done something apt, as the absolutists say, ad extorquendum assensum meum ["to force my unqualified assent"], ten to one your liking never comes.[46]

Here, James is clearly appealing to an example from personal relationships. There is (at times) a curious, synchronous relationship between the truth of a claim ("you like me") and belief in that claim. If I remain wary until convinced you like me, you might never come to like me. But, if I take a leap of faith (as it were), that might be the very condition needed to bring about your fondness for me in the first place. How is this relevant to the God question? Certainly not in the sense that belief in God somehow makes God exist—as if God's existence depends on whether or not I (or you, or whoever) believes in God. But (and here James sounds a bit like Pascal), believing in God (despite a lack of "sufficient evidence") might very well be the precondition for the experiences that validate that choice as accurate.

James ends his essay by quoting Fitz James Stephen, and I'm going to end this chapter's section on James in the same way.

In all important transactions of life we have to take a leap in the dark.... If we decide to leave the riddles unanswered, that is a choice; if we waver in our

---

[46]Ibid.

answer, that, too, is a choice: but whatever choice we make, we make it at our peril. If a man chooses to turn his back altogether on God and the future, no one can prevent him; no one can show beyond reasonable doubt that he is mistaken. If a man thinks otherwise and acts as he thinks, I do not see that any one can prove that he is mistaken. Each must act as he thinks best; and if he is wrong, so much the worse for him. We stand on a mountain pass in the midst of whirling snow and blinding mist, through which we get glimpses now and then of paths which may be deceptive. If we stand still we shall be frozen to death. If we take the wrong road we shall be dashed to pieces. We do not certainly know whether there is any right one. What must we do? 'Be strong and of a good courage.' Act for the best, hope for the best, and take what comes.... If death ends all, we cannot meet death better.[47]

Thus far, in this admittedly long chapter, we have discussed several interpretations of the requirements for (rational) belief in general, and in God, in particular. Clifford's rigorous requirement is that we never believe anything absent "sufficient evidence." Pascal, in contrast, argued that the intellect is incapable of deciding the issue and encouraged that we "bet on God" (and allow Revelation to do its work). James disagreed with both, in part; critiquing Pascal's wager while also claiming, contrary to Clifford, that religious belief may "lawfully" be decided by factors other than "evidence," under the right circumstances.

What we haven't discussed, yet, is what would even count as evidence in the first place, and why some might think that evidence of a certain sort (e.g., empirically verifiable evidence) is the only kind of evidence that "counts."

Part of this explanation is historical. It would be easy (and a mistake) to think that such emphasis on reason and evidence is a contemporary fetish, inaugurated, perhaps, by Clifford himself in the late 19th century. The emphasis on reason and evidence, though, is centuries older than Clifford. The "Enlightenment" Era of the 17th and 18th centuries generated, among other things, a mistrust in religious authority and an emphasis on human experience and reason as the only reliable guides to truth. One of the major philosophical figures of this period, John Locke (1632-1704), though a person of faith, nevertheless argues that reason has an important role to play with regard to theistic beliefs.

For where the principles of reason have not evidenced a proposition to be certainly true or false, there clear revelation, as another principle of truth and ground of assent, may determine; and so it may be matter of faith, and be also above reason. Because reason, in that particular matter, being able to reach no higher than probability, faith gave the determination where reason came short; and revelation discovered on which side the truth lay.

In matters where reason can afford certain knowledge, that is to be hearkened to. Thus far the dominion of faith reaches, and that without any violence or hindrance to reason; which is not injured or disturbed, but assisted and

---

[47]Ibid.

improved by new discoveries of truth, coming from the eternal fountain of all knowledge. Whatever God hath revealed is certainly true: no doubt can be made of it. This is the proper object of faith: but whether it be a divine revelation or no, reason must judge; which can never permit the mind to reject a greater evidence to embrace what is less evident, nor allow it to entertain probability in opposition to knowledge and certainty. There can be no evidence that any traditional revelation is of divine original, in the words we receive it, and in the sense we understand it, so clear and so certain as that of the principles of reason: and therefore Nothing that is contrary to, and inconsistent with, the clear and self-evident dictates of reason, has a right to be urged or assented to as a matter of faith, wherein reason hath nothing to do.[48]

In a fashion slightly reminiscent of Pascal's, Locke is acknowledging the role of Revelation in belief in (and about) God. Note, however, the boundaries Locke seems to be setting. If the claim involves something for which reason can reach "no higher than probability," then it is appropriate to allow Revelation and faith to carry the burden. But, in all other cases, we may "never permit the mind to reject a greater evidence to embrace what is less evident, nor allow it to entertain probability in opposition to knowledge and certainty." What's more, it seems that in the event of conflict between the conclusions of reason and the claims of faith, reason is (or ought to be) to the clear victor: "nothing that is contrary to, and inconsistent with, the clear and self-evident dictates of reason, has a right to be urged or assented to as a matter of faith, wherein reason hath nothing to do."

In an anticipation of Clifford, perhaps, Locke's motivation in proposing such standards seems also to be a concern about the consequences of too-readily believing claims in the absence of sufficient evidence, let alone when contrary to reason.

If the provinces of faith and reason are not kept distinct by these boundaries, there will, in matters of religion, be no room for reason at all; and those extravagant opinions and ceremonies that are to be found in the several religions of the world will not deserve to be blamed. For, to this crying up of faith in opposition to reason, we may, I think, in good measure ascribe those absurdities that fill almost all the religions which possess and divide mankind. For men having been principled with an opinion that they must not consult reason in the things of religion, however apparently contradictory to common sense and the very principles of all their knowledge, have let loose their fancies and natural superstition; and have been by them led into so strange opinions, and extravagant practices in religion, that a considerate man cannot but stand amazed at their follies, and judge them so far from being acceptable to the great and wise God, that he cannot avoid thinking them ridiculous and offensive to a sober good man. So that, in effect, religion, which should most distinguish us from beasts, and ought most peculiarly to elevate us, as rational creatures, above brutes, is that wherein men often appear most irrational, and more

---

[48] John Locke, "Essay Concerning Human Understanding," Book IV, chapter xviii, paragraphs 9-10.

senseless than beasts themselves.[49]

This side trip into the history of philosophy is more than sufficient for our purposes. The key "take away" from the last few paragraphs is the cultural/historical expectation that *all* beliefs, including the previously sacrosanct religious beliefs, be subjected to Reason and demands for evidence. In Epistemology, we can understand this trend as a feature of a theory of epistemic justification known as "Classical Foundationalism."

Classical Foundationalism

According to *Classical Foundationalism* (CF), we do (or at least ought to) believe claims on the evidential basis of other claims. This is just a fancy way of saying that we believe certain claims (e.g., my cat is awake), because of the evidence supplied by other claims (e.g., my cat's eyes are open, and she is stretching and meowing in my general direction). However, we do not believe all of the things we believe on the basis of evidence supplied by other beliefs, as this would involve an endless regress. Instead, there are "stopping points" at which we believe certain claims not on the basis of other claims, but because we "see that they [the claims] are true, and accept them."[50] These "stopping points" are called *"basic beliefs."* Perceptual beliefs are commonly employed examples of basic beliefs. As I'm writing this sentence, I'm looking at my aforementioned cat. I now believe that she is sleeping on my bed. I did not come to that belief by virtue of some argument—not even an implied argument. I didn't see my cat, and then infer that she is sleeping on my bed. Instead, I just came, immediately and directly, to believe that she is sleeping on my bed. Memory beliefs are also generally regarded as "basic." I remember having French toast for breakfast. I didn't deduce what I had for breakfast, or infer it on the basis of evidence—I just remember what I ate! My belief about my breakfast, then, is just something that I "see" and "accept."

Basic beliefs form the foundation of your "noetic structure (NS)." That is just another fancy term referring to your structure of beliefs. We might also call it your "worldview"—your basic understanding of the world and how it works. According to CF, every belief in your NS is either foundational ("basic"), or believed on the basis of other beliefs (which, themselves, eventually terminate in a basic belief). Not all basic beliefs are of equal standing, however. Some beliefs are "basic," and some are *"properly* basic."

Just because someone believes something "directly," and not on the basis of evidence, doesn't somehow guarantee that the belief in question is rationally justified. A gambler, for example, might "just believe" that he's bound to win big if he just stays at the poker table a little longer. He has no evidence for this. He's not coming to that belief as a conclusion derived from premises. He "just believes" he's going to win— and he's irrational for so believing. It's a form of wishful thinking. According to CF,

---

[49] Ibid., paragraph 11.

[50] Plantinga, Alvin. *Warranted Christian Belief*, Oxford University Press, 2000, 83.

what makes a belief *properly basic* is if it is any of the following:

- Self-evident
- Incorrigible
- Evident to the senses

Self-evident beliefs (though occasionally controversial) are claims that are just "obviously" true—so much so that you can't really even understand what the claim means without also recognizing its truth. Analytic claims are often taken to be self-evident. For example: "bachelors are unmarried men." If you understand what a bachelor is, then you can't help but recognize the truth of that claim. It's "self-evident." Other examples might include mathematical claims such as "2 + 2 = 4," or "a whole is greater than, or equal to, any of its parts." The deliverances of logic are also sometimes regarded as self-evident. Famously: "All men are mortal. Socrates is a man. Therefore Socrates is mortal."

Incorrigible beliefs are claims that are true just by virtue of being believed. They can't be "corrected," and we can't be mistaken about them. For example, if I say that "I seem to be hungry right now," that is an incorrigible claim. How could I possibly be mistaken about that? I'm not making any biological claims, or nutritional pronouncements. All I'm saying is that I *seem* to be hungry. If I seem to be hungry, then it is true that I *seem* to be hungry. Don't get too excited about incorrigible beliefs. As you might infer from my example, they don't tend to deal with anything momentous. For example, if I seem to believe that God exists, that doesn't mean that it's necessarily true that God exists—just that it's true that I *believe* God exists.

Evident to the senses refers to perceptual beliefs. I believe my cat is on my bed right now. I believe that because I'm looking right at her, this very moment. This belief is basic because I believe my cat is on my bed not on the basis of an argument, but simply because my perceptual experience "occasioned" the formation of that belief. According to Classical Foundationalism (CF), it's properly basic given the context: a continuous visual experience of my cat that is repeatable (e.g., I can close my eyes or look away, and when I look back to my bed, I still see my cat) and in a setting in which I have no reason to doubt the general reliability of my senses (e.g., there aren't any weird sensory conditions, I don't believe myself to be chemically impaired, I don't have a neighbor with a reputation for perpetrating cat look-alike practical jokes, etc.). Is it possible that I'm mistaken about any or all of those things, or about my cat being on the bed? Sure. Maybe I have a brain tumor that causes visual hallucinations. Maybe a neighborhood stray infiltrated my house, replacing my cat, and I never noticed. We can entertain all kinds of amusing (and implausible) "philosophy 101" scenarios—and none of them matters. Remember: we're dealing with justification, not truth. That my cat is on the bed is evident to my senses doesn't mean that it's true that my cat is on my bed, just that I'm justified in *believing* that she is.

Now, let's put all this together and refocus. Remember, we're dealing with CF, according to which, in order to be rationally (justifiably) held, our beliefs need to be either properly basic, or believed on the basis of other beliefs which are themselves properly basic. Here comes the application: *theistic beliefs do not appear to be properly basic.* That is, theistic beliefs do not appear to be self-evident, incorrigible, or evident to the senses. If theistic beliefs are not themselves properly basic, then, in order for them to be held rationally/justifiably, they must be supported by other beliefs which are properly basic—and now we can understand the emphasis on all the various versions of TAs for the past few centuries. Because theistic belief is not properly basic, a believer is obliged to demonstrate that her beliefs in (and about) God are held on the basis of other beliefs (evidence). In other words, a TA is needed— or else the believer has abdicated rationality.

Plantinga

Alvin Plantinga[51] flatly disagrees with the CF assumption that, in order to be held rationally, theistic beliefs must be based on a TA. To begin with, he argues that the demands of CF show themselves to be self-referentially inconsistent. He will then argue that theistic belief (or, at least specifically Christian belief) can receive its warrant by other means. First, let us consider the charge of inconsistency.

To review, according to CF, a claim is properly basic if and only if the claim is self-evident, incorrigible, or evident to the senses. Let us state this officially, and formally, and call the "classical picture" of what's needed for a belief to be properly basic "CP."

CP: <u>A proposition p is properly basic for a person S if and only if p is either self-evident to S or incorrigible for S or evident to the senses for S.</u>

Suppose, for the sake of the argument, that we accept those standards. If we do, then a (rational) subscriber to CF must himself or herself believe CP either because it's properly basic, or else on the basis of other properly basic propositions which support CP. If on the basis of other properly basic beliefs, then a good argument should be available with CP as its conclusion--but Plantinga claims he's aware of no such argument. If, however, CP is believed *not* on the basis of other, properly basic beliefs, then it's either irrational to believe CP, or else CP must itself be properly basic.

So, is CP properly basic? It does not appear to be self-evident, incorrigible, or evident to the senses. Therefore, it's *not* properly basic. Accordingly, CP requires those who believe it to violate their own standards, to be self-referentially inconsistent. What's more, Plantinga argues that if we take such standards seriously, most of our beliefs would fail to satisfy them!

I believe that I had cornflakes for breakfast, that my wife was amused at some little stupidity of mine, that there really are such 'external objects' as trees and squirrels, and that the world was not created ten minutes ago with all its dusty books, apparent memories, crumbling mountains, and deeply carved canyons.

---

[51] Although most of the philosophers mentioned (in detail) in this book benefit from their own primary source excerpts at the end of their respective chapters, Plantinga is one of a few for whom I offer no such reading selection. The reason is simple, and entirely cost-related. I have only included selections that are in in the public domain in order to preserve the low cost of this book.

These things, according to classical foundationalism, are not properly basic; they must be believed on the evidential basis of propositions that are self-evident or evident to the senses (in Locke's restricted sense) or incorrigible for me. Furthermore, they must be probable and seen to be probable with respect to propositions of that sort: there must be good arguments, deductive, inductive, or abductive to these conclusions from those kinds of propositions.

If there is any lesson at all to be learned from the history of modern philosophy from Descartes through Hume (and Reid), it is that such beliefs cannot be seen to be supported by, to be probable with respect to beliefs that meet the classical conditions for being properly basic. So either most of our beliefs are such that we are going contrary to epistemic obligations in holding them, or (CP) is false. It certainly doesn't seem that we must be flouting duty in holding these beliefs in the way we do. I believe in the basic way that there is a lot of snow in the backyard just now and that I met my class yesterday; I don't believe either of these things on the basis of propositions that meet the classical conditions for proper basicality; I do not believe there are any propositions of that sort with respect to which they are probable. Of course I realize I could be mistaken; but am I flouting duty in so believing? I reflect on the matter as carefully as I can; I simply see no duty here—and not because I doubt the existence of duties generally, or of epistemic duties specifically. Indeed there are duties of that sort: but is there a duty to conform belief to (CP)? I don't think so. But then how can I be guilty, blameworthy, for believing in this way?[52]

Given the inconsistency issues, as well as the counter-intuitiveness of most of our beliefs failing to be held rationally, given CP, Plantinga proposes that there are other ways in which a belief can be properly basic. We will focus exclusively on the "other way" that might apply to theistic beliefs.

Before delving into his proposal, however, I want to stress one more time that what we are dealing with here is not truth, but justification. Plantinga is not making claims about which of our beliefs are true, or what would make them true. He is simply offering an account of what would make our beliefs rational for us to hold. Whether they are, in fact, true is a different issue altogether.

To help set the stage for Plantinga's approach, consider the following quotations from some rather important thinkers in the history of the Christian tradition.

To know in a general and confused way that God exists is implanted in us by nature...."--Thomas Aquinas (Summa Theologica, First Part, Question 2, Reply to Objection 1)

For since the creation of the world God's invisible qualities--his eternal power and divine nature--have been clearly seen, being understood from what has been made, so that people are without excuse...."—The Apostle Paul (Romans 1:20)

---

[52] Ibid., 98.

There is within the human mind, and indeed by natural instinct, an awareness of divinity.... To prevent anyone from taking refuge in the pretense of ignorance, God himself has implanted in all men a certain understanding of his divine majesty.... Since, therefore, men one and all perceive that there is a God and that he is their maker, they are condemned by their own testimony because they have failed to honor him and to consecrate their lives to his will. . . there is, as the eminent pagan says, no nation so barbarous, no people so savage, that they have not a deep seated conviction that there is a God.... Therefore, since from the beginning of the world there has been no region, no city, in short, no household, that could do without religion, there lies in this a tacit confession of a sense of deity inscribed in the hearts of all.--Calvin (Institutes I, iii, 1)

The theme shared by all three quotations is that humans have an innate capacity to sense God's existence, to "perceive" God. According to all three (Paul, Aquinas, Calvin), all humans have an implanted capacity to know that God exists. Calvin calls this faculty for perceiving that God exists the "sensus divnitatis (SD)" Plantinga described the SD as *"a disposition or set of dispositions to form theistic beliefs in various circumstances, in response to the sorts of conditions or stimuli that trigger the working of this sense of divinity."*[53]

According to this model (what Plantinga refers to as the "Aquinas/Calvin," or "A/C" model), the SD is one of the cognitive faculties that humans possess. Analogous to other faculties, such as our sense faculties, the SD is "triggered" by various stimuli to produce belief. The visual experience of a large, black, furry creature sleeping on my bed is the occasion by which I form a belief about my cat and where she is sleeping. *Other* sorts of experiences are occasions for the SD to form beliefs in and about God. The sorts of examples Plantinga provide are as follows: majestic and awe-inspiring natural settings (e.g., mountain peaks, deserts, the roiling ocean, the "infinite" stars above), the "subtle play of sunlight on a field in spring," the awareness of divine disapproval that we experience as guilt and shame, the perception of forgiveness upon repentance, the instinctive turning to God (even by some atheists) in times of mortal danger or crisis.... Other possible examples are abundant, such as the sense of a "miracle" having occurred at the birth of your child, or the inarticulate sense that "something" must have made the universe, or an experience of "Truth" upon reading the Bible, or being deeply moved by a sermon.

Plantinga's point is that when and if belief in God is formed in such (or other) circumstances, it is not by virtue of some sort of TA. "It isn't that one beholds the night sky, notes that it is grand, and concludes that there must be such a person as God: an argument like that would be ridiculously weak."[54] Instead, the perception or experience is *the occasion by which* the beliefs "just arise within us." In this fashion, the beliefs formed by virtue of the SD are similar to perceptual and memory beliefs.

Recall from our earlier discussion: I don't believe my cat is sleeping on my bed by means of an argument with that belief as its conclusion. I just perceive my cat, and that experience "occasions" the belief. My memory of a French toast breakfast is not

---

[53] Ibid., 173.
[54] Ibid., 175.

the conclusion of an argument, but my memory "occasions" the belief that I had French toast. In both cases, the beliefs are basic. Immanuel Kant reflects, in his *Critique of Pure Reason*, on the two things that inspire him to "awe:" "the starry heavens above and the moral universe within." Plantinga might add that the occasion of beholding the "starry heavens above" and/or the occasion of sensing the "moral universe within" can trigger a basic belief in God.

Suppose that Plantinga is right, and that it's possible to believe in God not on the basis of a TA but as a basic belief. Is the belief *properly* basic? This is an important distinction, after all. It presumably means quite a bit whether someone's belief in God is like my belief in my sleeping cat, as opposed to a gambler's belief that he's bound to win eventually.

On the A/C model, then, theistic belief as produced by the sensus divinitatis is basic. It is also properly basic, and that in at least two senses. On the one hand, a belief can be properly basic for a person in the sense that it is indeed basic for him (he doesn't accept it on the evidential basis of other propositions) and, furthermore, he is justified in holding it in the basic way: he is within his epistemic rights, is not irresponsible, is violating no epistemic or other duties in holding that belief in that way.... There is another sense in which a belief can be properly or improperly basic: p is properly basic for S in this sense if and only if S accepts p in the basic way, and furthermore p has warrant for S, accepted in that way. Perceptual beliefs are properly basic in this sense: such beliefs are typically accepted in the basic way, and they often have warrant. (They are often produced by cognitive faculties functioning properly in a congenial epistemic environment according to a design plan successfully aimed at truth.) The same goes for memory beliefs, some a priori beliefs, and many other beliefs. I suppose the fact is most of our beliefs that have warrant, have it in this basic way; it is only in a smallish area of our cognitive life that the warrant a belief has for us derives from the fact that it is accepted on the evidential basis of other beliefs....

According to the A/C model I am presenting here, theistic belief produced by the sensus divinitatis can also be properly basic with respect to warrant. It isn't just that the believer in God is within her epistemic rights in accepting theistic belief in the basic way. That is indeed so; more than that, however, this belief can have warrant for the person in question, warrant that is often sufficient for knowledge. The sensus divinitatis is a belief-producing faculty (or power, or mechanism) that under the right conditions produces belief that isn't evidentially based on other beliefs. On this model, our cognitive faculties have been designed and created by God; the design plan, therefore, is a design plan in the literal and paradigmatic sense. It is a blueprint or plan for our ways of functioning, and it has been developed and instituted by a conscious, intelligent agent. The purpose of the sensus divinitatis is to enable us to have true beliefs about God; when it functions properly, it ordinarily does produce true beliefs about God. These beliefs therefore meet the conditions for warrant; if the beliefs produced are strong enough, then they constitute knowledge.[55]

Plantinga claims that theistic beliefs are not only basic, given the A/C model, but can be properly basic—if the model is true. The "if" in that last statement is very important. One last time, please recall that the focus of this section of this chapter is warrant: whether or not theistic beliefs are rationally/justifiably held. Plantinga's point is a surprisingly simple one: *if* God exists and *if* God has created humans with some sort of faculty for detecting God's existence (e.g., the SD), then theistic beliefs formed by those sorts of occasions are warranted, and they are *properly* basic. In that case, it is possible for someone to believe in God (and, in the scenario we're considering, that belief is true), and for her believing to be rational, even though she hasn't come to that belief by virtue of a TA. If, however, there is no God, and if there is no such thing as the SD, then clearly theistic beliefs are not warranted! In that scenario, someone who believes in God believes in something false, and has come to a false conclusion in an unwarranted fashion.

Don't be misled by the hypothetical nature of Plantinga's position into thinking that his accomplishments, if genuine, are somehow not significant. Recall that the theme of this entire chapter has been whether, and under what circumstances, we are justified in believing in God. Clifford claimed that we were so justified only given "sufficient evidence." Pascal claimed that reason (by itself) was incapable of deciding, but argued that we were justified in believing in, and even encouraged to believe in, God anyway. James took issue with Pascal's wager, but also with Clifford's stringent standards, and claimed that, under certain circumstances, we are justified in believing in God even if the evidence hasn't established it. This treatment of Plantinga has been part of that same conversation. Plantinga rejects the standards demanded by CF (a tradition of which Clifford is a part), and proposes a different scenario in which theistic beliefs *could* have warrant: given something like the A/C model and the SD. Plantinga, no more than Clifford, Pascal, or James, has argued (in this context) that it is *true* that God exists, but only that believing that God exists can be warranted, under certain conditions, even in the absence of a persuasive TA.

As I'm sure you've anticipated, Plantinga's position invites criticism, and we will consider two of the more famous and common objections.

Objection 1: Given this hypothetical SD, why doesn't everyone believe in (the same) God?

According to the A/C model Plantinga proposes, every single human being comes equipped with a SD, an innate capacity to detect God's existence and form beliefs (including that God exists) accordingly. And yet, there are still lots of atheists and agnostics in the world, as there have been throughout history. And, even among people who do seem to have "detected" God, not everyone has detected the same one! Many different experiences and interpretations of the divine exist, and have existed throughout history. If we all come equipped with the same "God-detector," why wouldn't it function the same for each of us?

---

[55] Ibid., 178-179.

Plantinga's reply involves at least two steps. The first concerns the problem of pluralism: the fact that there are many different, sometimes competing experiences of the divine. It's important to point out that the SD described in the A/C model isn't alleged to produce the specific doctrinal claims of Christianity—at least not in just any context. Aquinas acknowledges, for example, in that same section of the *Summa Theologica* quoted above, that such "knowledge" of God "is not to know absolutely that God exists; just as to know that someone is approaching is not the same as to know that Peter is approaching, even though it is Peter who is approaching,..." In other words, the SD, by virtue of an occasion of beholding the majesty of the night sky, might produce belief like "the universe has been created by something powerful and glorious," but it wouldn't produce the rather-specific belief that the Creator in question is a triune God: Father, Son, and Holy Spirit in one. Pangs of conscience might trigger the SD to recognize that we are bound by an objective moral law by which we will be judged, but those pangs of conscience aren't going to be the occasion for a belief that we ought not to eat shellfish! For the SD to "authenticate" those very specific beliefs, other occasions will be needed, such as reading the Bible, listening to a sermon, speaking with a missionary, etc.

The second step of Plantinga's reply needs to address those who don't form belief in any sort of divinity at all. Although it might be a controversial response, his answer, in a word, is "malfunction."

Before dealing with the more controversial theistic beliefs, consider "ordinary" beliefs instead. Certainly our cognitive faculties responsible for producing all our other sorts of beliefs are subject to malfunction, and thereby can produce false or unwarranted beliefs.

> *Of course, sometimes beliefs are accepted in the basic way but do not have warrant.... this can be due to cognitive malfunction, or to a cognitive faculty's being impeded by such conditions as rage, lust, ambition, grief, and the like; it can also be because the bit of the design plan governing the production of the belief is aimed not at truth but at something else (survival, e.g.), or because something in the testimonial chain has gone wrong (one of your friends has lied to you), or for still other reasons.*[56]

Think of how easily and often we might leap to judgment about something because of our moods. A grief-stricken mother believes her child survived a plane crash due to her desperate hope that he did. A jealous boyfriend believes that his girlfriend is lying to him about her whereabouts despite the evidence she presents. A gambler believes it's his lucky day because he really needs the money. In ordinary contexts, our cognitive faculties can malfunction and produce beliefs (or fail to produce them) on the basis of emotions, desires/will, or other influences.

According to the A/C model, the same sort of malfunction occurs with regard to the SD, and it is the result of "sin."

> *...we human beings have fallen into sin, a calamitous condition from which we*

---

[56] Ibid., 178.

require salvation—a salvation we are unable to accomplish by our own efforts. This sin alienates us from God and makes us unfit for communion with him. Our fall into sin has had cataclysmic consequences, both affective and cognitive. As to affective consequences, our affections are skewed and our hearts now harbor deep and radical evil: we love ourselves above all, rather than God. There were also ruinous cognitive consequences. Our original knowledge of God and of his marvelous beauty, glory, and loveliness has been severely compromised; in this way the narrow image of God in us was destroyed and the broad image damaged, distorted. In particular, the sensus divinitatis has been damaged and deformed; because of the fall, we no longer know God in the same natural and un-problematic way in which we know each other and the world around us. Still further, sin induces in us a resistance to the deliverances of the sensus divinitatis, muted as they are by the first factor; we don't want to pay attention to its deliverances. We are unable by our own efforts to extricate ourselves from this quagmire; God himself, however, has provided a remedy for sin and its ruinous effects, a means of salvation from sin and restoration to his favor and fellowship. This remedy is made available in the life, atoning suffering and death, and resurrection of his divine Son, Jesus Christ. Salvation involves among other things rebirth and regeneration, a process (beginning in the present life and reaching fruition in the next) that involves a restoration and repair of the image of God in us.[57]

Why doesn't everyone perceive that God exists? Because of the cognitive consequences of sin. Part of Salvation involves the repair of the SD so that the truths of God become more clear, and more readily known to be true.

"But all of that presupposes that God does exist, and a particular version of God at that!" Correct. But remember: this chapter isn't addressing *de facto* concerns, only *de jure* concerns—and also remember that Plantinga has only claimed that such beliefs have warrant *if* the core claims of Christianity are true. Plantinga has offered a worldview in which theistic beliefs can be properly basic, even in the absence of a compelling TA, and an explanation for why not everyone would arrive at those same properly basic beliefs. If we grant his success in so doing, we find ourselves facing the second objection.

Objection 2: If Plantinga can use the SD to provide warrant for Christian belief, then couldn't *any* belief be warranted?

So, let's say we acknowledge that Plantinga is addressing *de jure* objections to theistic belief, and not *de facto* objections, and that all he's trying to prove (in this context) is that theists (specifically, Christians) can be warranted in believing as they do, even in the absence of a compelling TA, and that the warrant is obtained by virtue of the details of the A/C model, including the SD. If we're willing to grant all of that, couldn't any of the following have warrant, and therefore be rational/justifiable to believe as well?

---

[57] Ibid., 205.

- A Muslim's belief in Allah
- A Hindu's belief in Vishnu
- Linus' belief in the Great Pumpkin
- A Pastafarian's belief in the Flying Spaghetti Monster[58]

Please note that the lumping together of Christianity, Islam, Hinduism, and belief in the Great Pumpkin or Flying Spaghetti Monster is *intentional* on the part of the critic. Supporters of Plantinga are presumed to think that belief in the Great Pumpkin is silly, and certainly unwarranted. But, if it can be shown that the same sort of story that provides warrant for Christian belief could be modified to provide warrant for the Great Pumpkin, then, by means of a *reductio ad absurdum* argument, it would demonstrate that there is likely something wrong with the warrant-granting notion of the SD as well.

In the spirit of parody: the Great Pumpkin (GP) created humanity with an innate capacity to detect his existence and form beliefs about him. We may call this the *"sensus magna cucurbita* (SMC)." Certain occasions (e.g., spending the night in a "sincere" pumpkin patch) trigger belief-formation with regard to the GP. However, clearly not everyone believes in the GP. This is because the commercialization of Halloween has produced "insincerity" in the hearts of most people, causing the SMC to malfunction. With the right amount of sincerity, however, the SMC can be repaired and belief in the GP will manifest.

I assume that none of you believes that there really is a magical GP that appears in the most sincere pumpkin patch each Halloween. I also assume that most (if not all) of you would doubt whether anyone could rationally/justifiably believe otherwise. I also assume that some of you believe that God exists (while others of you do not), and that some of you believe that such belief is warranted (while others of you do not). What difference is there, if any, between belief in the GP and belief in God?

Plantinga addresses this objection directly, in at least two ways. The first concerns that all-important distinction between *de facto* and *de jure* issues.

> the Reformed epistemologist (this Reformed epistemologist, anyway) doesn't claim as part of his philosophical position that belief in God and the deliverances of IIHS ["internal instigations of the Holy Spirit"] do have warrant. That is because... in all likelihood they have warrant only if they are true, and I am not arguing that these beliefs are in fact true. No doubt the Reformed epistemologist does believe that they are true, and is prepared to claim that they are, even if he doesn't propose to argue for that claim.[59]

That is, Plantinga has claimed that the beliefs in question have warrant *if* the Christian story (in general) is true. If false, however, then they don't have warrant. Similarly, if the GP really does exist, and has created humanity with a SMC, then belief

---

[58] This is an actual "thing." Sort of... http://www.venganza.org/
[59] Plantinga, Ibid., 347.

in the GP would presumably be warranted. But, if there is no GP, then believing in the GP probably isn't warranted. Although Plantinga uses the example of belief in voodoo rather than belief in the GP, he addresses this point below:

> It doesn't follow, of course, that the voodoo epistemologist is also warranted in claiming that voodoo belief is properly basic with respect to warrant. For suppose voodoo belief is in fact false, and suppose further that it arose originally in some kind of mistake or confusion, or out of a fearful reaction to natural phenomena of one sort or another, or in the mind of some group hoping to gain or perpetuate personal political power. If so, then those original voodoo beliefs did not possess warrant. Suppose still further that these voodoo beliefs were passed on to subsequent generations by way of testimony and teaching. Now if a testifier testifies to some belief p that has no warrant for her, then p will also have no warrant for anyone believing it on just the basis of her testimony. If p has no warrant for the testifier, then it has none for the testifiee either—even if the latter's faculties are working perfectly properly. I am taught a lot of garbage by my parents (out of profound ignorance, they teach me that the stars are really pinholes in a giant canvass stretched over the earth each night in order to give humankind a good night's sleep, or that Frisians are politically inferior and should not be allowed to vote); then, even if my own cognitive faculties are functioning properly in the conditions propitious for warrant, my beliefs acquired by way of this testimony lack warrant.[60]

Plantinga would acknowledge that both beliefs in voodoo and Christianity (or the GP, for that matter) can easily lack warrant, under the "wrong conditions" (e.g., their basic "stories" are false, the chain of testimony leading to belief contains a warrantless belief, etc.). Plantinga has also claimed that Christian belief can be warranted *under the right conditions*. These conditions include, importantly, that the basic Christian story is true, and also that the believer experience the right "occasions" to trigger theistic belief via the SD. Ultimately, Plantinga would argue that an important difference between Christian belief and belief in the GP is that there are grounds (even if not universally compelling) for believing the former, but none for the latter. There exists both evidence and arguments for God's existence, even if the evidence is debatable and the arguments are not universally compelling. Such belief also enjoys widespread and historical acceptance, as well as a coherent "story." None of this demonstrates that the beliefs are true, of course, but it does suggest (according to Plantinga) that there are important differences (with regard to warrant, in this context) between a belief in God and belief in just *anything*. To be blunt, not every "religious" tradition is epistemically equal. The Flying Spaghetti Monster is *intended* as satire. The GP is a feature of a comic strip. Without provoking too much controversy, or inciting holy wars, some major religious traditions have sophisticated arguments in their support, and others appear to be vulnerable to charges of internal

---

[60] Ibid., 348-349.

inconsistency or other "defeaters."[61]

Defeaters

I will end this lengthy chapter with a discussion of defeaters, as they ultimately represent the possible role of a TA with regard to warrant. I have previously argued that TAs have limited (though not non-existent) value in that they tend not to "convert" anyone from their position, nor do they successfully "prove" either that God exists, or that God does not. What they are far more likely to do is impact the warrant you have for your beliefs, whether that belief is that God exists, or that God does not exist.

This entire chapter has been about warrant, starting with Clifford's rigorous standards for warrant for any belief, moving through Pascal's and James' respective disagreements, and ending with Plantinga's claim that theistic belief can be warranted in a properly basic way (under the right conditions).

When a TA provides support for your belief, it increases your warrant for that belief. If nothing else, a TA can be valuable in just that respect: it can help you to be (justifiably) more confident that what you believe is true, and that you have good reason to believe it true. On the other hand, when a TA undermines your belief, it acts as a "*defeater*," and can *reduce* your warrant for that belief.

Generally, a defeater is simply a piece of information (e.g., evidence, an argument, etc.) that works against something that you already believe. Defeaters can be classified as "rebutting defeaters" and "undercutting defeaters."

A rebutting defeater is a piece of information that is just plain inconsistent with your belief. For example, suppose I believe that my cat is sleeping on my bed, but then I look down and see her at my feet, and feel her rubbing against my leg as I type. My cat rubbing against my leg is inconsistent with my belief that she is on my bed, so that new piece of information is a reason to conclude that my belief that she is on the bed is false.

An undercutting defeater does not directly contradict a belief, but does diminish your confidence in its truth. I believe my cat is sleeping on the bed, but then I realize that I have ingested a powerful hallucinogen and that I'm seeing all kinds of "interesting" things all over my house, including multiple versions of my cat. This information does not directly refute that my cat is sleeping on the bed, but it does undermine my confidence that my belief is accurate—after all, it could very well be one of my many hallucinations! The warrant for my belief has been diminished.

If you are an atheist, a TA in support of God's existence could serve as a defeater for your atheism, just as a TA against God's existence could serve as a defeater for a person of faith. Although some TAs appear to be intended as rebutting defeaters, in practice, they are more likely to work as undercutting defeaters, if anything. An atheist believes that there is no God, but struggles to come up with a persuasive counter to the cosmological argument (CA). As a result, her confidence in atheism is

---

[61] The Christian philosopher of religion William Lane Craig tackles this thorny issue on his website: http://www.reasonablefaith.org/is-uncertainty-a-sound-foundation-for-religious-tolerance

undermined, and her warrant for it decreases. A theist believes in God, but struggles with the problem of evil (POE). Her confidence in her belief is undermined, and her warrant for it decreases.

In the absolute best of scenarios, one or more of the TAs we will consider in the next several chapters will constitute a "proof" of God's existence (or non-existence), and therefore a rebutting defeater for the opposite view. Much more likely, though, I suspect that the TAs will instead work to increase warrant (at best) and thereby serve as undercutting defeaters for the opposite view.

As we consider these arguments, your first responsibility is to *understand* them. You are in no position to agree or disagree with the conclusions of these arguments, let alone evaluate them or critique them, if you have not first understood them. Determine what they are meant to prove, and how they attempt to do so. Then, with that understanding in place, assess their effectiveness. Do they increase warrant for their conclusion? Why, or why not? Do they serve as a defeater for the opposite view? Why, or why not?

Finally, be self-aware. Understand that if you already believe that God exists, you are going to be predisposed to find favor with the positive TAs and fault with the negative TAs (and vice versa, if you are an atheist). This is inevitable. But, by being aware of that fact, you can make a conscious effort to be as objective as is possible as you work through each argument. Make a conscious effort to be charitable (for the sake of argument) with those arguments with which you are predisposed to disagree, and to be honestly critical of those arguments with which you are predisposed to agree. In so doing, you will increase your understanding of both, better your understanding of your own view, and have increased confidence in the warrant of whatever position you settle on.

William Kingdon Clifford (4 May 1845 – 3 March 1879) was both an accomplished mathematician and a philosopher. In philosophical circles, he is most well-known for his position on evidentialism and belief. In "The Ethics of Belief" he makes his famous claim that "it is wrong always, everywhere, and for anyone, to believe anything upon insufficient evidence."

The Ethics of Belief[62]
William Kingdon Clifford

I.—THE DUTY OF INQUIRY

A SHIPOWNER was about to send to sea an emigrant-ship. He knew that she was old, and not over-well built at the first; that she had seen many seas and climes, and often had needed repairs. Doubts had been suggested to him that possibly she was not seaworthy. These doubts preyed upon his mind and made him unhappy; he thought that perhaps he ought to have her thoroughly overhauled and refitted, even though this should put him to great expense. Before the ship sailed, however, he succeeded in overcoming these melancholy reflections. He said to himself that she had gone safely through so many voyages and weathered so many storms that it was idle to suppose she would not come safely home from this trip also. He would put his trust in Providence, which could hardly fail to protect all these unhappy families that were leaving their fatherland to seek for better times elsewhere. He would dismiss from his mind all ungenerous suspicions about the honesty of builders and contractors. In such ways he acquired a sincere and comfortable conviction that his vessel was thoroughly safe and seaworthy; he watched her departure with a light heart, and benevolent wishes for the success of the exiles in their strange new home that was to be; and he got his insurance-money when she went down in mid-ocean and told no tales.

What shall we say of him? Surely this, that he was verily guilty of the death of those men. It is admitted that he did sincerely believe in the soundness of his ship; but the sincerity of his conviction can in no wise help him, because *he had no right to believe on such evidence as was before him.* He had acquired his belief not by honestly earning it in patient investigation, but by stifling his doubts. And although in the end he may have felt so sure about it that he could not think otherwise, yet inasmuch as he had knowingly and willingly worked himself into that frame of mind, he must be held responsible for it.

Let us alter the case a little, and suppose that the ship was not unsound after all; that she made her voyage safely, and many others after it. Will that diminish the guilt of her owner? Not one jot. When an action is once done, it is right or wrong for ever; no accidental failure of its good or evil fruits can possibly alter that. The man would not have been innocent, he would only have been not found out. The question of right

[62] Clifford, William Kingdon <1845 - 1879>: The Ethics of Belief. -- 1877. -- Fassung vom 2005-03-04. http://www.payer.de/religionskritik/clifford01.htm

or wrong has to do with the origin of his belief, not the matter of it; not what it was, but how he got it; not whether it turned out to be true or false, but whether he had a right to believe on such evidence as was before him.

There was once an island in which some of the inhabitants professed a religion teaching neither the doctrine of original sin nor that of eternal punishment. A suspicion got abroad that the professors of this religion had made use of unfair means to get their doctrines taught to children. They were accused of wresting the laws of their country in such a way as to remove children from the care of their natural and legal guardians; and even of stealing them away and keeping them concealed from their friends and relations. A certain number of men formed themselves into a society for the purpose of agitating the public about this matter. They published grave accusations against individual citizens of the highest position and character, and did all in their power to injure these citizens in their exercise of their professions. So great was the noise they made, that a Commission was appointed to investigate the facts; but after the Commission had carefully inquired into all the evidence that could be got, it appeared that the accused were innocent. Not only had they been accused on insufficient evidence, but the evidence of their innocence was such as the agitators might easily have obtained, if they had attempted a fair inquiry. After these disclosures the inhabitants of that country looked upon the members of the agitating society, not only as persons whose judgment was to be distrusted, but also as no longer to be counted honourable men. For although they had sincerely and conscientiously believed in the charges they had made, *yet they had no right to believe on such evidence as was before them*. Their sincere convictions, instead of being honestly earned by patient inquiring, were stolen by listening to the voice of prejudice and passion.

Let us vary this case also, and suppose, other things remaining as before, that a still more accurate investigation proved the accused to have been really guilty. Would this make any difference in the guilt of the accusers? Clearly not; the question is not whether their belief was true or false, but whether they entertained it on wrong grounds. They would no doubt say, "Now you see that we were right after all; next time perhaps you will believe us." And they might be believed, but they would not thereby become honourable men. They would not be innocent, they would only be not found out. Every one of them, if he chose to examine himself *in foro conscientiae*[1], would know that he had acquired and nourished a belief, when he had no right to believe on such evidence as was before him; and therein he would know that he had done a wrong thing.

It may be said, however, that in both of these supposed cases it is not the belief which is judged to be wrong, but the action following upon it. The shipowner might say, "I am perfectly certain that my ship is sound, but still I feel it my duty to have her examined, before trusting the lives of so many people to her." And it might be said to the agitator, "However convinced you were of the justice of your cause and the truth of your convictions, you ought not to have made a public attack upon any man's character until you had examined the evidence on both sides with the utmost patience and care."

In the first place, let us admit that, so far as it goes, this view of the case is right and necessary; right, because even when a man's belief is so fixed that he cannot think otherwise, he still has a choice in regard to the action suggested by it, and so cannot escape the duty of investigating on the ground of the strength of his convictions; and necessary, because those who are not yet capable of controlling their feelings and thoughts must have a plain rule dealing with overt acts.

But this being premised as necessary, it becomes clear that it is not sufficient, and that our previous judgment is required to supplement it. For it is not possible so to sever the belief from the action it suggests as to condemn the one without condemning the other. No man holding a strong belief on one side of a question, or even wishing to hold a belief on one side, can investigate it with such fairness and completeness as if he were really in doubt and unbiassed; so that the existence of a belief not founded on fair inquiry unfits a man for the performance of this necessary duty.

Nor is it that truly a belief at all which has not some influence upon the actions of him who holds it. He who truly believes that which prompts him to an action has looked upon the action to lust after it, he has committed it already in his heart. If a belief is not realized immediately in open deeds, it is stored up for the guidance of the future. It goes to make a part of that aggregate of beliefs which is the link between sensation and action at every moment of all our lives, and which is so organized and compacted together that no part of it can be isolated from the rest, but every new addition modifies the structure of the whole. No real belief, however trifling and fragmentary it may seem, is ever truly insignificant; it prepares us to receive more of its like, confirms those which resembled it before, and weakens others; and so gradually it lays a stealthy train in our inmost thoughts, which may some day explode into overt action, and leave its stamp upon our character for ever.

And no one man's belief is in any case a private matter which concerns himself alone. Our lives are guided by that general conception of the course of things which has been created by society for social purposes. Our words, our phrases, our forms and processes and modes of thought, are common property, fashioned and perfected from age to age; an heirloom which every succeeding generation inherits as a precious deposit and a sacred trust to be handed on to the next one, not unchanged but enlarged and purified, with some clear marks of its proper handiwork. Into this, for good or ill, is woven every belief of every man who has speech of his fellows. An awful privilege, and an awful responsibility, that we should help to create the world in which posterity will live.

In the two supposed cases which have been considered, it has been judged wrong to believe on insufficient evidence, or to nourish belief by suppressing doubts and avoiding investigation. The reason of this judgment is not far to seek: it is that in both these cases the belief held by one man was of great importance to other men. But forasmuch as no belief held by one man, however seemingly trivial the belief, and however obscure the believer, is ever actually insignificant or without its effect on the fate of mankind, we have no choice but to extend our judgment to all cases of belief whatever. Belief, that sacred faculty which prompts the decisions of our will, and knits into harmonious working all the compacted energies of our being, is ours not for ourselves, but for humanity. It is rightly used on truths which have been established by long experience and waiting toil, and which have stood in the fierce light of free and fearless questioning. Then it helps to bind men together, and to strengthen and direct their common action. It is desecrated when given to unproved and unquestioned statements, for the solace and private pleasure of the believer; to add a tinsel splendour to the plain straight road of our life and display a bright mirage beyond it; or even to drown the common sorrows of our kind by a self-deception which allows them not only to cast down, but also to degrade us. Whoso would deserve well of his fellows in this matter will guard the purity of his belief with a very fanaticism of jealous care, lest at any time it should rest on an unworthy object, and catch a stain which can never be wiped away.

It is not only the leader of men, statesmen, philosopher, or poet, that owes this bounden duty to mankind. Every rustic who delivers in the village alehouse his slow, infrequent sentences, may help to kill or keep alive the fatal superstitions which clog his race. Every hard-worked wife of an artisan may transmit to her children beliefs which shall knit society together, or rend it in pieces. No simplicity of mind, no obscurity of station, can escape the universal duty of questioning all that we believe.

It is true that this duty is a hard one, and the doubt which comes out of it is often a very bitter thing. It leaves us bare and powerless where we thought that we were safe and strong. To know all about anything is to know how to deal with it under all circumstances. We feel much happier and more secure when we think we know precisely what to do, no matter what happens, then when we have lost our way and do not know where to turn. And if we have supposed ourselves to know all about anything, and to be capable of doing what is fit in regard to it, we naturally do not like to find that we are really ignorant and powerless, that we have to begin again at the beginning, and try to learn what the thing is and how it is to be dealt with—if indeed anything can be learnt about it. It is the sense of power attached to a sense of knowledge that makes men desirous of believing, and afraid of doubting.

This sense of power is the highest and best of pleasures when the belief on which it is founded is a true belief, and has been fairly earned by investigation. For then we may justly feel that it is common property, and holds good for others as well as for ourselves. Then we may be glad, not that I have learned secrets by which I am safer and stronger, but that *we men* have got mastery over more of the world; and we shall be strong, not for ourselves, but in the name of Man and his strength. But if the belief has been accepted on insufficient evidence, the pleasure is a stolen one. Not only does it deceive ourselves by giving us a sense of power which we do not really possess, but it is sinful, because it is stolen in defiance of our duty to mankind. That duty is to guard ourselves from such beliefs as from a pestilence, which may shortly master our own body and then spread to the rest of the town. What would be thought of one who, for the sake of a sweet fruit, should deliberately run the risk of bringing a plague upon his family and his neighbours?

And, as in other such cases, it is not the risk only which has to be considered; for a bad action is always bad at the time when it is done, no matter what happens afterwards. Every time we let ourselves believe for unworthy reasons, we weaken our powers of self-control, of doubting, of judicially and fairly weighing evidence. We all suffer severely enough from the maintenance and support of false beliefs and the fatally wrong actions which they lead to, and the evil born when one such belief is entertained is great and wide. But a greater and wider evil arises when the credulous character is maintained and supported, when a habit of believing for unworthy reasons is fostered and made permanent. If I steal money from any person, there may be no harm done by the mere transfer of possession; he may not feel the loss, or it may prevent him from using the money badly. But I cannot help doing this great wrong towards Man, that I make myself dishonest. What hurts society is not that it should lose its property, but that it should become a den of thieves; for then it must cease to be society. This is why we ought not to do evil that good may come; for at any rate this great evil has come, that we have done evil and are made wicked thereby. In like manner, if I let myself believe anything on insufficient evidence, there may be no great harm done by the mere belief; it may be true after all, or I may never have occasion to exhibit it in outward acts. But I cannot help doing this great wrong towards Man, that I make myself credulous. The danger to society is not merely that it should believe wrong things, though that is great enough; but that it should become credulous, and lose the habit of testing things and inquiring into them; for then it must sink back into savagery.

The harm which is done by credulity in a man is not confined to the fostering of a credulous character in others, and consequent support of false beliefs. Habitual want of care about what I believe leads to habitual want of care in others about the truth of what is told to me. Men speak the truth to one another when each reveres the truth in his own mind and in the other's mind; but how shall my friend revere the truth in my mind when I myself am careless about it, when I believe things because I want to believe them, and because they are comforting and pleasant? Will he not learn to cry, "Peace," to me, when there is no peace? By such a course I shall surround myself with

a thick atmosphere of falsehood and fraud, and in that I must live. It may matter little to me, in my cloud-castle of sweet illusions and darling lies; but it matters much to Man that I have made my neighbours ready to deceive. The credulous man is father to the liar and the cheat; he lives in the bosom of this his family, and it is no marvel if he should become even as they are. So closely are our duties knit together, that whoso shall keep the whole law, and yet offend in one point, he is guilty of all.

To sum up: it is wrong always, everywhere, and for anyone, to believe anything upon insufficient evidence.

If a man, holding a belief which he was taught in childhood or persuaded of afterwards, keeps down and pushes away any doubts which arise about it in his mind,

William Hogarth (1697 - 1764): Credulity, superstition and fanaticism. 1762.

purposely avoids the reading of books and the company of men that call in question or discuss it, and regards as impious those questions which cannot easily be asked without disturbing it — the life of that man is one long sin against mankind.

Blaise Pascal (19 June 1623 – 19 August 1662) was a mathematician, scientist, and philosopher. His most famous philosophical work, the "Pensées"("Thoughts"), was published posthumously, and was originally to be titled "Apologie de la religion Chrétienne ("Defense of the Christian Religion"). Within this work we find the infamous "Wager."

Pascal's Wager[63]
A Selection from *Pensées*
Blaise Pascal

If there is a God, He is infinitely incomprehensible, since, having neither parts nor limits, He has no affinity to us. We are then incapable of knowing either what He is or if He is. This being so, who will dare to undertake the decision of the question? Not we, who have no affinity to Him.

Who then will blame Christians for not being able to give a reason for their belief, since they profess a religion for which they cannot give a reason? They declare, in expounding it to the world, that it is a foolishness, I Cor. 1. 21. ["For after that in the wisdom of God the world by wisdom knew not God, it pleased God by the foolishness of preaching to save them that believe."]; and then you complain that they do not prove it! If they proved it, they would not keep their word; it is in lacking proofs that they are not lacking in sense. "Yes, but although this excuses those who offer it as such and takes away from them the blame of putting it forward without reason, it does not excuse those who receive it." Let us then examine this point, and say, "God is, or He is not." But to which side shall we incline? Reason can decide nothing here. There is an infinite chaos which separated us. A game is being played at the extremity of this infinite distance where heads or tails will turn up. What will you wager? According to reason, you can do neither the one thing nor the other; according to reason, you can defend neither of the propositions.

Do not, then, reprove for error those who have made a choice; for you know nothing about it. "No, but I blame them for having made, not this choice, but a choice; for again both he who chooses heads and he who chooses tails are equally at fault, they are both in the wrong. The true course is not to wager at all."

Yes; but you must wager. It is not optional. You are embarked. Which will you choose then? Let us see. Since you must choose, let us see which interests you least. You have two things to lose, the true and the good; and two things to stake, your reason and your will, your knowledge and your happiness; and your nature has two things to shun, error and misery. Your reason is no more shocked in choosing one rather than the other, since you must of necessity choose. This is one point settled. But your happiness? Let us weigh the gain and the loss in wagering that God is. Let us estimate these two chances. If you gain, you gain all; if you lose, you lose nothing.

---

[63] This is a selection from Pascal's *Pensées*, translated by W. F. Trotter in 1910. http://philosophy.eserver.org/pascal-pensees.txt

Wager, then, without hesitation that He is. "That is very fine. Yes, I must wager; but I may perhaps wager too much." Let us see. Since there is an equal risk of gain and of loss, if you had only to gain two lives, instead of one, you might still wager. But if there were three lives to gain, you would have to play (since you are under the necessity of playing), and you would be imprudent, when you are forced to play, not to chance your life to gain three at a game where there is an equal risk of loss and gain. But there is an eternity of life and happiness. And this being so, if there were an infinity of chances, of which one only would be for you, you would still be right in wagering one to win two, and you would act stupidly, being obliged to play, by refusing to stake one life against three at a game in which out of an infinity of chances there is one for you, if there were an infinity of an infinitely happy life to gain. But there is here an infinity of an infinitely happy life to gain, a chance of gain against a finite number of chances of loss, and what you stake is finite. It is all divided; where-ever the infinite is and there is not an infinity of chances of loss against that of gain, there is no time to hesitate, you must give all. And thus, when one is forced to play, he must renounce reason to preserve his life, rather than risk it for infinite gain, as likely to happen as the loss of nothingness.

For it is no use to say it is uncertain if we will gain, and it is certain that we risk, and that the infinite distance between the certainly of what is staked and the uncertainty of what will be gained, equals the finite good which is certainly staked against the uncertain infinite. It is not so, as every player stakes a certainty to gain an uncertainty, and yet he stakes a finite certainty to gain a finite uncertainty, without transgressing against reason. There is not an infinite distance between the certainty staked and the uncertainty of the gain; that is untrue. In truth, there is an infinity between the certainty of gain and the certainty of loss. But the uncertainty of the gain is proportioned to the certainty of the stake according to the proportion of the chances of gain and loss. Hence it comes that, if there are as many risks on one side as on the other, the course is to play even; and then the certainty of the stake is equal to the uncertainty of the gain, so far is it from fact that there is an infinite distance between them. And so our proposition is of infinite force, when there is the finite to stake in a game where there are equal risks of gain and of loss, and the infinite to gain. This is demonstrable; and if men are capable of any truths, this is one.

"I confess it, I admit it. But, still, is there no means of seeing the faces of the cards?" Yes, Scripture and the rest, etc. "Yes, but I have my hands tied and my mouth closed; I am forced to wager, and am not free. I am not released, and am so made that I cannot believe. What, then, would you have me do?"

True. But at least learn your inability to believe, since reason brings you to this, and yet you cannot believe. Endeavor, then, to convince yourself, not by increase of proofs of God, but by the abatement of your passions. You would like to attain faith and do not know the way; you would like to cure yourself of unbelief and ask the remedy for it. Learn of those who have been bound like you, and who now stake all their possessions. These are people who know the way which you would follow, and who are cured of an ill of which you would be cured. Follow the way by which they began; by acting as if they believed, taking the holy water, having masses said, etc. Even this will naturally make you believe, and deaden your acuteness. "But this is what I am afraid of." And why? What have you to lose?

But to show you that this leads you there, it is this which will lessen the passions, which are your stumbling-blocks.

The end of this discourse.-- Now, what harm will befall you in taking this side? You will be faithful, humble, grateful, generous, a sincere friend, truthful. Certainly you will not have those poisonous pleasures, glory and luxury; but will you not have others? I will tell you that you will thereby gain in this life, and that, at each step you take on this road, you will see so great certainty of gain, so much nothingness in what you risk, that you will at last recognize that you have wagered for something certain and infinite, for which you have given nothing.

William James (January 11, 1842 – August 26, 1910) is arguably the most famous American philosopher (thus far). Trained as a medical doctor, he was also both a philosopher and a psychologist, at a time when psychology was first emerging as a distinct discipline from philosophy. He wrote and spoke extensively on both psychological and philosophical issues, and these disciplines come together in "The Will to Believe," where he criticizes both the evidentialist standards of William Clifford as well as the "Wager" of Blaise Pascal. [Editorial note: there are several latin phrases in this selection. For your convenience, I have provided translations as footnotes, when possible.]

The Will to Believe[64]
William James

THE WILL TO BELIEVE.[1]

In the recently published Life by Leslie Stephen of his brother, Fitz-James, there is an account of a school to which the latter went when he was a boy. The teacher, a certain Mr. Guest, used to converse with his pupils in this wise: "Gurney, what is the difference between justification and sanctification?--Stephen, prove the omnipotence of God!" etc. In the midst of our Harvard freethinking and indifference we are prone to imagine that here at your good old orthodox College conversation continues to be somewhat upon this order; and to show you that we at Harvard have not lost all interest in these vital subjects, I have brought with me to-night something like a sermon on justification by faith to read to you,--I mean an essay in justification of faith, a defence of our right to adopt a believing attitude in religious matters, in spite of the fact that our merely logical {2} intellect may not have been coerced. 'The Will to Believe,' accordingly, is the title of my paper.

I have long defended to my own students the lawfulness of voluntarily adopted faith; but as soon as they have got well imbued with the logical spirit, they have as a rule refused to admit my contention to be lawful philosophically, even though in point of fact they were personally all the time chock-full of some faith or other themselves. I am all the while, however, so profoundly convinced that my own position is correct, that your invitation has seemed to me a good occasion to make my statements more clear. Perhaps your minds will be more open than those with which I have hitherto had to deal. I will be as little technical as I can, though I must begin by setting up some technical distinctions that will help us in the end.

I.

Let us give the name of hypothesis to anything that may be proposed to our belief;

---

[64]http://www.booksshouldbefree.com/download/text/Will-to-Believe-and-Other-Essays-in-Popular.txt

and just as the electricians speak of live and dead wires, let us speak of any hypothesis as either live or dead. A live hypothesis is one which appeals as a real possibility to him to whom it is proposed. If I ask you to believe in the Mahdi, the notion makes no electric connection with your nature,--it refuses to scintillate with any credibility at all. As an hypothesis it is completely dead. To an Arab, however (even if he be not one of the Mahdi's followers), the hypothesis is among the mind's possibilities: it is alive. This shows that deadness and liveness in an hypothesis are not intrinsic properties, but relations to the {3} individual thinker. They are measured by his willingness to act. The maximum of liveness in an hypothesis means willingness to act irrevocably. Practically, that means belief; but there is some believing tendency wherever there is willingness to act at all.

Next, let us call the decision between two hypotheses an option. Options may be of several kinds. They may be--1, living or dead; 2, forced or avoidable; 3, momentous or trivial; and for our purposes we may call an option a genuine option when it is of the forced, living, and momentous kind.

1. A living option is one in which both hypotheses are live ones. If I say to you: "Be a theosophist or be a Mohammedan," it is probably a dead option, because for you neither hypothesis is likely to be alive. But if I say: "Be an agnostic or be a Christian," it is otherwise: trained as you are, each hypothesis makes some appeal, however small, to your belief.

2. Next, if I say to you: "Choose between going out with your umbrella or without it," I do not offer you a genuine option, for it is not forced. You can easily avoid it by not going out at all. Similarly, if I say, "Either love me or hate me," "Either call my theory true or call it false," your option is avoidable. You may remain indifferent to me, neither loving nor hating, and you may decline to offer any judgment as to my theory. But if I say, "Either accept this truth or go without it," I put on you a forced option, for there is no standing place outside of the alternative. Every dilemma based on a complete logical disjunction, with no possibility of not choosing, is an option of this forced kind.

{4}

3. Finally, if I were Dr. Nansen and proposed to you to join my North Pole expedition, your option would be momentous; for this would probably be your only similar opportunity, and your choice now would either exclude you from the North Pole sort of immortality altogether or put at least the chance of it into your hands. He who refuses to embrace a unique opportunity loses the prize as surely as if he tried and failed. Per contra, the option is trivial when the opportunity is not unique, when the stake is insignificant, or when the decision is reversible if it later prove unwise. Such trivial options abound in the scientific life. A chemist finds an hypothesis live enough to spend a year in its verification: he believes in it to that extent. But if his experiments prove inconclusive either way, he is quit for his loss of time, no vital harm being done.

It will facilitate our discussion if we keep all these distinctions well in mind.

II.

The next matter to consider is the actual psychology of human opinion. When we look at certain facts, it seems as if our passional and volitional nature lay at the root of all our convictions. When we look at others, it seems as if they could do nothing when the intellect had once said its say. Let us take the latter facts up first.

Does it not seem preposterous on the very face of it to talk of our opinions being modifiable at will? Can our will either help or hinder our intellect in its perceptions of truth? Can we, by just willing it, believe that Abraham Lincoln's existence is a myth, {5} and that the portraits of him in McClure's Magazine are all of some one else? Can we, by any effort of our will, or by any strength of wish that it were true, believe ourselves well and about when we are roaring with rheumatism in bed, or feel certain that the sum of the two one-dollar bills in our pocket must be a hundred dollars? We can say any of these things, but we are absolutely impotent to believe them; and of just such things is the whole fabric of the truths that we do believe in made up,-- matters of fact, immediate or remote, as Hume said, and relations between ideas, which are either there or not there for us if we see them so, and which if not there cannot be put there by any action of our own.

In Pascal's Thoughts there is a celebrated passage known in literature as Pascal's wager. In it he tries to force us into Christianity by reasoning as if our concern with truth resembled our concern with the stakes in a game of chance. Translated freely his words are these: You must either believe or not believe that God is--which will you do? Your human reason cannot say. A game is going on between you and the nature of things which at the day of judgment will bring out either heads or tails. Weigh what your gains and your losses would be if you should stake all you have on heads, or God's existence: if you win in such case, you gain eternal beatitude; if you lose, you lose nothing at all. If there were an infinity of chances, and only one for God in this wager, still you ought to stake your all on God; for though you surely risk a finite loss by this procedure, any finite loss is reasonable, even a certain one is reasonable, if there is but the possibility of {6} infinite gain. Go, then, and take holy water, and have masses said; belief will come and stupefy your scruples,--Cela vous fera croire et vous abêtira.[65] Why should you not? At bottom, what have you to lose?

You probably feel that when religious faith expresses itself thus, in the language of the gaming-table, it is put to its last trumps. Surely Pascal's own personal belief in masses and holy water had far other springs; and this celebrated page of his is but an argument for others, a last desperate snatch at a weapon against the hardness of the unbelieving heart. We feel that a faith in masses and holy water adopted wilfully after such a mechanical calculation would lack the inner soul of faith's reality; and if we were ourselves in the place of the Deity, we should probably take particular pleasure in cutting off believers of this pattern from their infinite reward. It is evident that unless there be some pre-existing tendency to believe in masses and holy water, the option offered to the will by Pascal is not a living option. Certainly no Turk ever took to masses and holy water on its account; and even to us Protestants these means of salvation seem such foregone impossibilities that Pascal's logic, invoked for them

---

[65] "That will make you believe and will stupefy you."

specifically, leaves us unmoved. As well might the Mahdi write to us, saying, "I am the Expected One whom God has created in his effulgence. You shall be infinitely happy if you confess me; otherwise you shall be cut off from the light of the sun. Weigh, then, your infinite gain if I am genuine against your finite sacrifice if I am not!" His logic would be that of Pascal; but he would vainly use it on us, for the hypothesis he offers us is dead. No tendency to act on it exists in us to any degree.

{7}

The talk of believing by our volition seems, then, from one point of view, simply silly. From another point of view it is worse than silly, it is vile. When one turns to the magnificent edifice of the physical sciences, and sees how it was reared; what thousands of disinterested moral lives of men lie buried in its mere foundations; what patience and postponement, what choking down of preference, what submission to the icy laws of outer fact are wrought into its very stones and mortar; how absolutely impersonal it stands in its vast augustness,--then how besotted and contemptible seems every little sentimentalist who comes blowing his voluntary smoke-wreaths, and pretending to decide things from out of his private dream! Can we wonder if those bred in the rugged and manly school of science should feel like spewing such subjectivism out of their mouths? The whole system of loyalties which grow up in the schools of science go dead against its toleration; so that it is only natural that those who have caught the scientific fever should pass over to the opposite extreme, and write sometimes as if the incorruptibly truthful intellect ought positively to prefer bitterness and unacceptableness to the heart in its cup.

It fortifies my soul to know
That, though I perish, Truth is so--

sings Clough, while Huxley exclaims: "My only consolation lies in the reflection that, however bad our posterity may become, so far as they hold by the plain rule of not pretending to believe what they have no reason to believe, because it may be to their advantage so to pretend [the word 'pretend' is surely here redundant], they will not have reached the {8} lowest depth of immorality." And that delicious enfant terrible Clifford writes; "Belief is desecrated when given to unproved and unquestioned statements for the solace and private pleasure of the believer,... Whoso would deserve well of his fellows in this matter will guard the purity of his belief with a very fanaticism of jealous care, lest at any time it should rest on an unworthy object, and catch a stain which can never be wiped away.... If [a] belief has been accepted on insufficient evidence [even though the belief be true, as Clifford on the same page explains] the pleasure is a stolen one.... It is sinful because it is stolen in defiance of our duty to mankind. That duty is to guard ourselves from such beliefs as from a pestilence which may shortly master our own body and then spread to the rest of the town.... It is wrong always, everywhere, and for every one, to believe anything upon insufficient evidence."

III.

All this strikes one as healthy, even when expressed, as by Clifford, with somewhat too much of robustious pathos in the voice. Free-will and simple wishing do seem, in the matter of our credences, to be only fifth wheels to the coach. Yet if any one should thereupon assume that intellectual insight is what remains after wish and will and sentimental preference have taken wing, or that pure reason is what then settles our opinions, he would fly quite as directly in the teeth of the facts.

It is only our already dead hypotheses that our willing nature is unable to bring to life again But what has made them dead for us is for the most part {9} a previous action of our willing nature of an antagonistic kind. When I say 'willing nature,' I do not mean only such deliberate volitions as may have set up habits of belief that we cannot now escape from,--I mean all such factors of belief as fear and hope, prejudice and passion, imitation and partisanship, the circumpressure of our caste and set. As a matter of fact we find ourselves believing, we hardly know how or why. Mr. Balfour gives the name of 'authority' to all those influences, born of the intellectual climate, that make hypotheses possible or impossible for us, alive or dead. Here in this room, we all of us believe in molecules and the conservation of energy, in democracy and necessary progress, in Protestant Christianity and the duty of fighting for 'the doctrine of the immortal Monroe,' all for no reasons worthy of the name. We see into these matters with no more inner clearness, and probably with much less, than any disbeliever in them might possess. His unconventionality would probably have some grounds to show for its conclusions; but for us, not insight, but the prestige of the opinions, is what makes the spark shoot from them and light up our sleeping magazines of faith. Our reason is quite satisfied, in nine hundred and ninety-nine cases out of every thousand of us, if it can find a few arguments that will do to recite in case our credulity is criticised by some one else. Our faith is faith in some one else's faith, and in the greatest matters this is most the case. Our belief in truth itself, for instance, that there is a truth, and that our minds and it are made for each other,-- what is it but a passionate affirmation of desire, in which our social system backs us up? We want to have a truth; we want to believe that our {10} experiments and studies and discussions must put us in a continually better and better position towards it; and on this line we agree to fight out our thinking lives. But if a pyrrhonistic sceptic asks us how we know all this, can our logic find a reply? No! certainly it cannot. It is just one volition against another,--we willing to go in for life upon a trust or assumption which he, for his part, does not care to make. [2]

As a rule we disbelieve all facts and theories for which we have no use. Clifford's cosmic emotions find no use for Christian feelings. Huxley belabors the bishops because there is no use for sacerdotalism in his scheme of life. Newman, on the contrary, goes over to Romanism, and finds all sorts of reasons good for staying there, because a priestly system is for him an organic need and delight. Why do so few 'scientists' even look at the evidence for telepathy, so called? Because they think, as a leading biologist, now dead, once said to me, that even if such a thing were true, scientists ought to band together to keep it suppressed and concealed. It would undo the uniformity of Nature and all sorts of other things without which scientists cannot carry on their pursuits. But if this very man had been shown something which as a scientist he might do with telepathy, he might not only have examined the evidence, but even have found it good enough. This very law which the logicians would impose upon us--if I may give the name of logicians to those who would rule out our willing nature here--is based on nothing but their own natural wish to exclude all elements for {11} which they, in their professional quality of logicians, can find no use.

Evidently, then, our non-intellectual nature does influence our convictions. There are passional tendencies and volitions which run before and others which come after belief, and it is only the latter that are too late for the fair; and they are not too late when the previous passional work has been already in their own direction. Pascal's argument, instead of being powerless, then seems a regular clincher, and is the last stroke needed to make our faith in masses and holy water complete. The state of things is evidently far from simple; and pure insight and logic, whatever they might do ideally, are not the only things that really do produce our creeds.

IV.

Our next duty, having recognized this mixed-up state of affairs, is to ask whether it be simply reprehensible and pathological, or whether, on the contrary, we must treat it as a normal element in making up our minds. The thesis I defend is, briefly stated, this: Our passional nature not only lawfully may, but must, decide an option between propositions, whenever it is a genuine option that cannot by its nature be decided on intellectual grounds; for to say, under such circumstances, "Do not decide, but leave the question open," is itself a passional decision,--just like deciding yes or no,--and is attended with the same risk of losing the truth. The thesis thus abstractly expressed will, I trust, soon become quite clear. But I must first indulge in a bit more of preliminary work.
{12}

V.

It will be observed that for the purposes of this discussion we are on 'dogmatic' ground,--ground, I mean, which leaves systematic philosophical scepticism altogether out of account. The postulate that there is truth, and that it is the destiny of our minds to attain it, we are deliberately resolving to make, though the sceptic will not make it. We part company with him, therefore, absolutely, at this point. But the faith that truth exists, and that our minds can find it, may be held in two ways. We may talk of the empiricist way and of the absolutist way of believing in truth. The absolutists in this matter say that we not only can attain to knowing truth, but we can know when we have attained to knowing it; while the empiricists think that although we may attain it, we cannot infallibly know when. To know is one thing, and to know for certain that we know is another. One may hold to the first being possible without the second; hence the empiricists and the absolutists, although neither of them is a sceptic in the usual philosophic sense of the term, show very different degrees of dogmatism in their lives.

If we look at the history of opinions, we see that the empiricist tendency has largely prevailed in science, while in philosophy the absolutist tendency has had everything its own way. The characteristic sort of happiness, indeed, which philosophies yield has mainly consisted in the conviction felt by each successive school or system that by it bottom-certitude had been attained. "Other philosophies are collections of opinions, mostly false; my philosophy {13} gives standing-ground forever,"--who does not recognize in this the key-note of every system worthy of the name? A system, to be a system at all, must come as a closed system, reversible in this or that detail, perchance, but in its essential features never!

Scholastic orthodoxy, to which one must always go when one wishes to find perfectly clear statement, has beautifully elaborated this absolutist conviction in a doctrine which it calls that of 'objective evidence.' If, for example, I am unable to doubt that I now exist before you, that two is less than three, or that if all men are mortal then I am mortal too, it is because these things illumine my intellect irresistibly. The final ground of this objective evidence possessed by

certain propositions is the adaequatio intellectûs nostri cum rê.[66] The certitude it brings involves an aptitudinem ad extorquendum certum assensum[67] on the part of the truth envisaged, and on the side of the subject a quietem in cognitione,[68] when once the object is mentally received, that leaves no possibility of doubt behind; and in the whole transaction nothing operates but the entitas ipsa[69] of the object and the entitas ipsa of the mind. We slouchy modern thinkers dislike to talk in Latin,--indeed, we dislike to talk in set terms at all; but at bottom our own state of mind is very much like this whenever we uncritically abandon ourselves: You believe in objective evidence, and I do. Of some things we feel that we are certain: we know, and we know that we do know. There is something that gives a click inside of us, a bell that strikes twelve, when the hands of our mental clock have swept the dial and meet over the meridian hour. The greatest empiricists among us are only empiricists on reflection: when {14} left to their instincts, they dogmatize like infallible popes. When the Cliffords tell us how sinful it is to be Christians on such 'insufficient evidence,' insufficiency is really the last thing they have in mind. For them the evidence is absolutely sufficient, only it makes the other way. They believe so completely in an anti-christian order of the universe that there is no living option: Christianity is a dead hypothesis from the start.

VI.

But now, since we are all such absolutists by instinct, what in our quality of students of philosophy ought we to do about the fact? Shall we espouse and indorse it? Or shall we treat it as a weakness of our nature from which we must free ourselves, if we can?

I sincerely believe that the latter course is the only one we can follow as reflective men. Objective evidence and certitude are doubtless very fine ideals to play with, but where on this moonlit and dream-visited planet are they found? I am, therefore, myself a complete empiricist so far as my theory of human knowledge goes. I live, to

---

[66] "Conformity of our minds to the fact."

[67] "A power to compel sure assent."

[68] "quiet rest in knowledge."

[69] "entity itself"

be sure, by the practical faith that we must go on experiencing and thinking over our experience, for only thus can our opinions grow more true; but to hold any one of them--I absolutely do not care which--as if it never could be reinterpretable or corrigible, I believe to be a tremendously mistaken attitude, and I think that the whole history of philosophy will bear me out. There is but one indefectibly certain truth, and that is the truth that pyrrhonistic scepticism itself leaves {15} standing,--the truth that the present phenomenon of consciousness exists. That, however, is the bare starting-point of knowledge, the mere admission of a stuff to be philosophized about. The various philosophies are but so many attempts at expressing what this stuff really is. And if we repair to our libraries what disagreement do we discover! Where is a certainly true answer found? Apart from abstract propositions of comparison (such as two and two are the same as four), propositions which tell us nothing by themselves about concrete reality, we find no proposition ever regarded by any one as evidently certain that has not either been called a falsehood, or at least had its truth sincerely questioned by some one else. The transcending of the axioms of geometry, not in play but in earnest, by certain of our contemporaries (as Zöllner and Charles H. Hinton), and the rejection of the whole Aristotelian logic by the Hegelians, are striking instances in point.

No concrete test of what is really true has ever been agreed upon. Some make the criterion external to the moment of perception, putting it either in revelation, the consensus gentium, the instincts of the heart, or the systematized experience of the race. Others make the perceptive moment its own test,--Descartes, for instance, with his clear and distinct ideas guaranteed by the veracity of God; Reid with his 'common-sense;' and Kant with his forms of synthetic judgment a priori. The inconceivability of the opposite; the capacity to be verified by sense; the possession of complete organic unity or self-relation, realized when a thing is its own other,--are standards which, in turn, have been used. The much {16} lauded objective evidence is never triumphantly there, it is a mere aspiration or Grenzbegriff, marking the infinitely remote ideal of our thinking life. To claim that certain truths now possess it, is simply to say that when you think them true and they are true, then their evidence is objective, otherwise it is not. But practically one's conviction that the evidence one goes by is of the real objective brand, is only one more subjective opinion added to the lot. For what a contradictory array of opinions have objective evidence and absolute certitude been claimed! The world is rational through and through,--its existence is an ultimate brute fact; there is a personal God,--a personal God is inconceivable; there is an extra-mental physical world immediately known,--the mind can only know its own ideas; a moral imperative exists,--obligation is only the resultant of desires; a permanent spiritual principle is in every one,--there are only shifting states of mind; there is an endless chain of causes,--there is an absolute first cause; an eternal necessity,--a freedom; a purpose,--no purpose; a primal One,--a primal Many; a universal continuity,--an essential discontinuity in things; an infinity,--no infinity. There is this,--there is that; there is indeed nothing which some one has not thought absolutely true, while his neighbor deemed it absolutely false; and not an absolutist among them seems ever to have considered that the trouble may all the time be essential, and that the intellect, even with truth directly in its grasp, may have no infallible signal for knowing whether it be truth or no. When, indeed, one remembers that the most striking practical application to life of the doctrine of objective certitude has been {17} the conscientious labors of the Holy Office of the Inquisition, one feels less tempted than ever to lend the doctrine a respectful ear.

But please observe, now, that when as empiricists we give up the doctrine of objective certitude, we do not thereby give up the quest or hope of truth itself. We still pin our faith on its existence, and still believe that we gain an ever better position towards it by systematically continuing to roll up experiences and think. Our great difference from the scholastic lies in the way we face. The strength of his system lies in the principles, the origin, the terminus a quo of his thought; for us the strength is in the outcome, the upshot, the terminus ad quem.[70] Not where it comes from but what it leads to is to decide. It matters not to an empiricist from what quarter an hypothesis may come to him: he may have acquired it by fair means or by foul; passion may have whispered or accident suggested it; but if the total drift of thinking continues to confirm it, that is what he means by its being true.

VII.

One more point, small but important, and our preliminaries are done. There are two ways of looking at our duty in the matter of opinion,--ways entirely different, and yet ways about whose difference the theory of knowledge seems hitherto to have shown very little concern. We must know the truth; and we must avoid error,--these are our first and great commandments as would-be knowers; but they are not two ways of stating an identical commandment, they are two separable laws. Although it may indeed happen that when we believe the truth A, we escape {18} as an incidental consequence from believing the falsehood B, it hardly ever happens that by merely disbelieving B we necessarily believe A. We may in escaping B fall into believing other falsehoods, C or D, just as bad as B; or we may escape B by not believing anything at all, not even A.

Believe truth! Shun error!--these, we see, are two materially different laws; and by choosing between them we may end by coloring differently our whole intellectual life. We may regard the chase for truth as paramount, and the avoidance of error as secondary; or we may, on the other hand, treat the avoidance of error as more imperative, and let truth take its chance. Clifford, in the instructive passage which I have quoted, exhorts us to the latter course. Believe nothing, he tells us, keep your mind in suspense forever, rather than by closing it on insufficient evidence incur the awful risk of believing lies. You, on the other hand, may think that the risk of being in error is a very small matter when compared with the blessings of real knowledge, and be ready to be duped many times in your investigation rather than postpone indefinitely the chance of guessing true. I myself find it impossible to go with Clifford. We must remember that these feelings of our duty about either truth or error are in any case only expressions of our passional life. Biologically considered, our minds are as ready to grind out falsehood as veracity, and he who says, "Better go without belief forever than believe a lie!" merely shows his own preponderant private horror of becoming a dupe. He may be critical of many of his desires and fears, but this fear he

---

[70] "Boundary at which"

slavishly obeys. He cannot imagine any one questioning its binding force. For my own part, I {19} have also a horror of being duped; but I can believe that worse things than being duped may happen to a man in this world: so Clifford's exhortation has to my ears a thoroughly fantastic sound. It is like a general informing his soldiers that it is better to keep out of battle forever than to risk a single wound. Not so are victories either over enemies or over nature gained. Our errors are surely not such awfully solemn things. In a world where we are so certain to incur them in spite of all our caution, a certain lightness of heart seems healthier than this excessive nervousness on their behalf. At any rate, it seems the fittest thing for the empiricist philosopher.

VIII.

And now, after all this introduction, let us go straight at our question. I have said, and now repeat it, that not only as a matter of fact do we find our passional nature influencing us in our opinions, but that there are some options between opinions in which this influence must be regarded both as an inevitable and as a lawful determinant of our choice.

I fear here that some of you my hearers will begin to scent danger, and lend an inhospitable ear. Two first steps of passion you have indeed had to admit as necessary,--we must think so as to avoid dupery, and we must think so as to gain truth; but the surest path to those ideal consummations, you will probably consider, is from now onwards to take no further passional step.

Well, of course, I agree as far as the facts will allow. Wherever the option between losing truth and gaining it is not momentous, we can throw the {20} chance of gaining truth away, and at any rate save ourselves from any chance of believing falsehood, by not making up our minds at all till objective evidence has come. In scientific questions, this is almost always the case; and even in human affairs in general, the need of acting is seldom so urgent that a false belief to act on is better than no belief at all. Law courts, indeed, have to decide on the best evidence attainable for the moment, because a judge's duty is to make law as well as to ascertain it, and (as a learned judge once said to me) few cases are worth spending much time over: the great thing is to have them decided on any acceptable principle, and got out of the way. But in our dealings with objective nature we obviously are recorders, not makers, of the truth; and decisions for the mere sake of deciding promptly and getting on to the next business would be wholly out of place. Throughout the breadth of physical nature facts are what they are quite independently of us, and seldom is there any such hurry about them that the risks of being duped by believing a premature theory need be faced. The questions here are always trivial options, the hypotheses are hardly living (at any rate not living for us spectators), the choice between believing truth or falsehood is seldom forced. The attitude of sceptical balance is therefore the absolutely wise one if we would escape mistakes. What difference, indeed, does it make to most of us whether we have or have not a theory of the Röntgen rays, whether we believe or not in mind-stuff, or have a conviction about the causality of conscious states? It makes no difference. Such options are not forced on us. On every account it is better not to make them, but still keep weighing reasons pro et contra with an indifferent hand.

{21}

I speak, of course, here of the purely judging mind. For purposes of discovery such indifference is to be less highly recommended, and science would be far less advanced than she is if the passionate desires of individuals to get their own faiths confirmed had been kept out of the game. See for example the sagacity which Spencer and Weismann now display. On the other hand, if you want an absolute duffer in an investigation, you must, after all, take the man who has no interest whatever in its results: he is the warranted incapable, the positive fool. The most useful investigator, because the most sensitive observer, is always he whose eager interest in one side of the question is balanced by an equally keen nervousness lest he become deceived. [3] Science has organized this nervousness into a regular technique, her so-called method of verification; and she has fallen so deeply in love with the method that one may even say she has ceased to care for truth by itself at all. It is only truth as technically verified that interests her. The truth of truths might come in merely affirmative form, and she would decline to touch it. Such truth as that, she might repeat with Clifford, would be stolen in defiance of her duty to mankind. Human passions, however, are stronger than technical rules. "Le coeur a ses raisons," as Pascal says, "que la raison ne connaît pas;"[71] and however indifferent to all but the bare rules of the game the umpire, the abstract intellect, may be, the concrete players who furnish him the materials to judge of are usually, each one of them, in love with some pet 'live hypothesis' of his own. Let us agree, however, that wherever there is no forced option, the {22} dispassionately judicial intellect with no pet hypothesis, saving us, as it does, from dupery at any rate, ought to be our ideal.

The question next arises: Are there not somewhere forced options in our speculative questions, and can we (as men who may be interested at least as much in positively gaining truth as in merely escaping dupery) always wait with impunity till the coercive evidence shall have arrived? It seems a priori improbable that the truth should be so nicely adjusted to our needs and powers as that. In the great boarding-house of nature, the cakes and the butter and the syrup seldom come out so even and leave the plates so clean. Indeed, we should view them with scientific suspicion if they did.

IX.

Moral questions immediately present themselves as questions whose solution cannot wait for sensible proof. A moral question is a question not of what sensibly exists, but of what is good, or would be good if it did exist. Science can tell us what exists; but to compare the worths, both of what exists and of what does not exist, we must consult not science, but what Pascal calls our heart. Science herself consults her heart when she lays it down that the infinite ascertainment of fact and correction of false belief are the supreme goods for man. Challenge the statement, and science can

---

71 "The heart has reasons that Reason doesn't know."

only repeat it oracularly, or else prove it by showing that such ascertainment and correction bring man all sorts of other goods which man's heart in turn declares. The question of having moral beliefs at all or not having them is decided by {23} our will. Are our moral preferences true or false, or are they only odd biological phenomena, making things good or bad for us, but in themselves indifferent? How can your pure intellect decide? If your heart does not want a world of moral reality, your head will assuredly never make you believe in one. Mephistophelian scepticism, indeed, will satisfy the head's play-instincts much better than any rigorous idealism can. Some men (even at the student age) are so naturally cool-hearted that the moralistic hypothesis never has for them any pungent life, and in their supercilious presence the hot young moralist always feels strangely ill at ease. The appearance of knowingness is on their side, of naïveté and gullibility on his. Yet, in the inarticulate heart of him, he clings to it that he is not a dupe, and that there is a realm in which (as Emerson says) all their wit and intellectual superiority is no better than the cunning of a fox. Moral scepticism can no more be refuted or proved by logic than intellectual scepticism can. When we stick to it that there is truth (be it of either kind), we do so with our whole nature, and resolve to stand or fall by the results. The sceptic with his whole nature adopts the doubting attitude; but which of us is the wiser, Omniscience only knows.

Turn now from these wide questions of good to a certain class of questions of fact, questions concerning personal relations, states of mind between one man and another. Do you like me or not?—for example. Whether you do or not depends, in countless instances, on whether I meet you half-way, am willing to assume that you must like me, and show you trust and expectation. The previous faith on my part in your liking's existence is in such cases what makes {24} your liking come. But if I stand aloof, and refuse to budge an inch until I have objective evidence, until you shall have done something apt, as the absolutists say, ad extorquendum assensum meum,[72] ten to one your liking never comes. How many women's hearts are vanquished by the mere sanguine insistence of some man that they must love him! he will not consent to the hypothesis that they cannot. The desire for a certain kind of truth here brings about that special truth's existence; and so it is in innumerable cases of other sorts. Who gains promotions, boons, appointments, but the man in whose life they are seen to play the part of live hypotheses, who discounts them, sacrifices other things for their sake before they have come, and takes risks for them in advance? His faith acts on the powers above him as a claim, and creates its own verification.

A social organism of any sort whatever, large or small, is what it is because each member proceeds to his own duty with a trust that the other members will simultaneously do theirs. Wherever a desired result is achieved by the co-operation of many independent persons, its existence as a fact is a pure consequence of the precursive faith in one another of those immediately concerned. A government, an army, a commercial system, a ship, a college, an athletic team, all exist on this condition, without which not only is nothing achieved, but nothing is even attempted. A whole train of passengers (individually brave enough) will be looted by a few highwaymen, simply because the latter can count on one another, while each

---

[72] "To force my unqualified assent"

passenger fears that if he makes a movement of resistance, he will be shot before any one else backs him up. If we believed that the whole car-full would rise {25} at once with us, we should each severally rise, and train-robbing would never even be attempted. There are, then, cases where a fact cannot come at all unless a preliminary faith exists in its coming. And where faith in a fact can help create the fact, that would be an insane logic which should say that faith running ahead of scientific evidence is the 'lowest kind of immorality' into which a thinking being can fall. Yet such is the logic by which our scientific absolutists pretend to regulate our lives!

X.

In truths dependent on our personal action, then, faith based on desire is certainly a lawful and possibly an indispensable thing.

But now, it will be said, these are all childish human cases, and have nothing to do with great cosmical matters, like the question of religious faith. Let us then pass on to that. Religions differ so much in their accidents that in discussing the religious question we must make it very generic and broad. What then do we now mean by the religious hypothesis? Science says things are; morality says some things are better than other things; and religion says essentially two things.

First, she says that the best things are the more eternal things, the overlapping things, the things in the universe that throw the last stone, so to speak, and say the final word. "Perfection is eternal,"--this phrase of Charles Secrétan seems a good way of putting this first affirmation of religion, an affirmation which obviously cannot yet be verified scientifically at all.

{26}

The second affirmation of religion is that we are better off even now if we believe her first affirmation to be true.

Now, let us consider what the logical elements of this situation are in case the religious hypothesis in both its branches be really true. (Of course, we must admit that possibility at the outset. If we are to discuss the question at all, it must involve a living option. If for any of you religion be a hypothesis that cannot, by any living possibility be true, then you need go no farther. I speak to the 'saving remnant' alone.) So proceeding, we see, first, that religion offers itself as a momentous option. We are supposed to gain, even now, by our belief, and to lose by our non-belief, a certain vital good. Secondly, religion is a forced option, so far as that good goes. We cannot escape the issue by remaining sceptical and waiting for more light, because, although we do avoid error in that way if religion be untrue, we lose the good, if it be true, just as certainly as if we positively chose to disbelieve. It is as if a man should hesitate indefinitely to ask a certain woman to marry him because he was not perfectly sure that she would prove an angel after he brought her home. Would he not cut himself off from that particular angel-possibility as decisively as if he went and married some one else? Scepticism, then, is not avoidance of option; it is option of a certain particular kind of risk. Better risk loss of truth than chance of error,--that is your faith-vetoer's exact position. He is actively playing his stake as much as the believer is; he is backing the field against the religious hypothesis, just as the believer is backing the religious hypothesis against the field. To preach scepticism to us as a duty until {27} 'sufficient evidence' for religion be found, is tantamount therefore to telling us, when in presence of the religious hypothesis, that to yield to our fear of its being error is wiser and better than to yield to our hope that it may be true. It is not intellect against all passions, then; it is only intellect with one passion laying down its law. And by what, forsooth, is the supreme wisdom of this passion warranted? Dupery for dupery, what proof is there that dupery through hope is so much worse than dupery through fear? I, for one, can see no proof; and I simply refuse obedience to the scientist's command to imitate his kind of option, in a case where my own stake is important enough to give me the right to choose my own form of risk. If religion be true and the evidence for it be still insufficient, I do not wish, by putting your extinguisher upon my nature (which feels to me as if it had after all some business in this matter), to forfeit my sole chance in life of getting upon the winning side,--that chance depending, of course, on my willingness to run the risk of acting as if my passional need of taking the world religiously might be prophetic and right.

All this is on the supposition that it really may be prophetic and right, and that, even to us who are discussing the matter, religion is a live hypothesis which may be true. Now, to most of us religion comes in a still further way that makes a veto on our active faith even more illogical. The more perfect and more eternal aspect of the universe is represented in our religions as having personal form. The universe is no longer a mere It to us, but a Thou, if we are religious; and any relation that may be possible from person to person might be possible {28} here. For instance, although in one sense we are passive portions of the universe, in another we show a curious autonomy, as if we were small active centres on our own account. We feel, too, as if the appeal of religion to us were made to our own active good-will, as if evidence might be forever withheld from us unless we met the hypothesis half-way. To take a trivial illustration: just as a man who in a company of gentlemen made no advances, asked a warrant for every concession, and believed no one's word without proof, would cut himself off by such churlishness from all the social rewards that a more trusting spirit would earn,--so here, one who should shut himself up in snarling logicality and try to make the gods extort his recognition willy-nilly, or not get it at all, might cut himself off forever from his only opportunity of making the gods' acquaintance. This feeling, forced on us we know not whence, that by obstinately believing that there are gods (although not to do so would be so easy both for our logic and our life) we are doing the universe the deepest service we can, seems part of the living essence of the religious hypothesis. If the hypothesis were true in all its parts, including this one, then pure intellectualism, with its veto on our making willing advances, would be an absurdity; and some participation of our sympathetic nature would be logically required. I, therefore, for one cannot see my way to accepting the agnostic rules for truth-seeking, or wilfully agree to keep my willing nature out of the game. I cannot do so for this plain reason, that a rule of thinking which would absolutely prevent me from acknowledging certain kinds of truth if those kinds of truth were really there, would be an irrational rule. That for me {29} is the long and short of the formal logic of the situation, no matter what the kinds of truth might materially be.

I confess I do not see how this logic can be escaped. But sad experience makes me fear that some of you may still shrink from radically saying with me, in abstracto,[73] that we have the right to believe at our own risk any hypothesis that is live enough to tempt our will. I suspect, however, that if this is so, it is because you have got away from the abstract logical point of view altogether, and are thinking (perhaps without realizing it) of some particular religious hypothesis which for you is dead. The freedom to 'believe what we will' you apply to the case of some patent superstition; and the faith you think of is the faith defined by the schoolboy when he said, "Faith is when you believe something that you know ain't true." I can only repeat that this is misapprehension. In concreto,[74] the freedom to believe can only cover living options which the intellect of the individual cannot by itself resolve; and living options never seem absurdities to him who has them to consider. When I look at the religious question as it really puts itself to concrete men, and when I think of all the possibilities which both practically and theoretically it involves, then this command that we shall put a stopper on our heart, instincts, and courage, and wait--acting of course meanwhile more or less as if religion were not true[4]--till {30} doomsday, or till such time as our intellect and senses working together may have raked in evidence enough,--this command, I say, seems to me the queerest idol ever manufactured in the philosophic cave. Were we scholastic absolutists, there might be more excuse. If we had an infallible intellect with its objective certitudes, we might feel ourselves disloyal to such a perfect organ of knowledge in not trusting to it exclusively, in not waiting for its releasing word. But if we are empiricists, if we believe that no bell in us tolls to let us know for certain when truth is in our grasp, then it seems a piece of idle fantasticality to preach so solemnly our duty of waiting for the bell. Indeed we may wait if we will,--I hope you do not think that I am denying that,--but if we do so, we do so at our peril as much as if we believed. In either case we act, taking our life in our hands. No one of us ought to issue vetoes to the other, nor should we bandy words of abuse. We ought, on the contrary, delicately and profoundly to respect one another's mental freedom: then only shall we bring about the intellectual republic; then only shall we have that spirit of inner tolerance without which all our outer tolerance is soulless, and which is empiricism's glory; then only shall we live and let live, in speculative as well as in practical things.

I began by a reference to Fitz James Stephen; let me end by a quotation from him. "What do you think {31} of yourself? What do you think of the world?... These are questions with which all must deal as it seems good to them. They are riddles of the Sphinx, and in some way or other we must deal with them.... In all important transactions of life we have to take a leap in the dark.... If we decide to leave the riddles unanswered, that is a choice; if we waver in our answer, that, too, is a choice: but whatever choice we make, we make it at our peril. If a man chooses to turn his back altogether on God and the future, no one can prevent him; no one can show beyond reasonable doubt that he is mistaken. If a man thinks otherwise and acts as he thinks, I do not see that any one can prove that he is mistaken. Each must act as he thinks best; and if he is wrong, so much the worse for him. We stand on a mountain pass in

---

[73] "in the abstract"
[74] "in concrete"

the midst of whirling snow and blinding mist, through which we get glimpses now and then of paths which may be deceptive. If we stand still we shall be frozen to death. If we take the wrong road we shall be dashed to pieces. We do not certainly know whether there is any right one. What must we do? 'Be strong and of a good courage.' Act for the best, hope for the best, and take what comes.... If death ends all, we cannot meet death better." [5]

[1] An Address to the Philosophical Clubs of Yale and Brown Universities. Published in the New World, June, 1896.

[2] Compare the admirable page 310 in S. H. Hodgson's "Time and Space," London, 1865.

[3] Compare Wilfrid Ward's Essay, "The Wish to Believe," in his Witnesses to the Unseen, Macmillan & Co., 1893.

[4] Since belief is measured by action, he who forbids us to believe religion to be true, necessarily also forbids us to act as we should if we did believe it to be true. The whole defence of religious faith hinges upon action. If the action required or inspired by the religious hypothesis is in no way different from that dictated by the naturalistic hypothesis, then religious faith is a pure superfluity, better pruned away, and controversy about its legitimacy is a piece of idle trifling, unworthy of serious minds. I myself believe, of course, that the religious hypothesis gives to the world an expression which specifically determines our reactions, and makes them in a large part unlike what they might be on a purely naturalistic scheme of belief.

[5] Liberty, Equality, Fraternity, p. 353, 2d edition. London, 1874.

Chapter 4: The Ontological Argument

> *Comprehension questions you should be able to answer after reading this chapter:*
>
> 1. What are "*a priori*" arguments? What are "*a posteriori*" arguments?
> 2. What is the "GCB?"
> 3. What does existence "*in re*" mean? Existence "*in intellectu?*"
> 4. Why does Anselm think the GCB must exist both "*in intellectu*" and "*in re?*"
> 5. What is Gaunilo's "greatest conceivable lost island" objection to the ontological argument?
> 6. What is a predicate, and how does this relate to Kant's criticism of the ontological argument?
> 7. What is Plantinga's version of the OA?
> 8. What is a "possible world"?
> 9. How is Plantinga's verion of the OA supposed to be "immune" to Kant's criticism?
> 10. Why does Plantinga think his own argument probably doesn't "work"?

The next several chapters will present several different TAs. The first few will be "positive" TAs—arguments that argue *for* God's existence. Along the way, we will consider some of the more common criticisms of those arguments as well. Then, we will turn to some "negative" TAs—arguments *against* God's existence. To be fair, we'll consider some common criticisms of those negative TAs as well.

There are many different types of arguments for God's existence. At its most basic level, an argument for God's existence is simply an attempt to prove God's existence, or at least justify belief in the existence of God. Some arguments rely explicitly on overtly "religious" pieces of evidence—the argument from the occurrence of miracles, for example. Such arguments, though interesting, are not usually addressed by philosophers of religion (though they might be terrific material for theologians). There is a simple explanation for this: it doesn't do us much good to assume the very thing we are trying to prove. If our question concerns whether there is a God, and if we are trying to explore this question in a way that will be satisfying to believers and skeptics alike, appealing to miracles will be controversial, to say the least. Since miracles are usually understood to be the supernatural suspension or overriding of the laws of nature, the existence of the supernatural is presupposed in a key premise of the argument. If I'm an atheist, and don't believe in the supernatural, I'm not going to believe in miracles either. The argument will go nowhere for me. Imagine the following conversation:

Theist: "Hey, Mr. Atheist! You should believe that God exists!"

Atheist: "Why?"

Theist: "Because of miracles. I've seen hundreds of people being miraculously healed by ministers on TV, and the Bible is filled with accounts of miracles. How can we explain the occurrence of those miracles if there isn't a God?"

Atheist: "What miracles? What you call 'biblical accounts of miracles,' I call myths and fairy tales. What you can 'miraculous healings on TV,' I call fraud, preying on people's hopes and fears for money, and the placebo effect."

Not very effective, is it? This is not to disparage miracles, or their possibility—it's simply to point out that if one is not already predisposed to accept accounts of the supernatural, appealing to miracles will not accomplish much. What most philosophers of religion will try to do, then, is appeal to premises that are much less controversial, and much more acceptable to skeptics.

TAs can be divided into two broad categories: "*a priori*" arguments and "*a posteriori*" arguments. *A priori* arguments operate by means of the very concepts involved, and do not require research or experience. Strawson describes an *a priori* claim, famously and amusingly, as follows: "you can see that it is true just lying on your couch. You don't have to get up off your couch and go outside and examine the way things are in the physical world. You don't have to do any science." An example of such a claim is that all bachelors are unmarried. If you know what a bachelor is in the first place, you already know, just by virtue of that concept, that bachelors are unmarried. *A posteriori* arguments (or claims), on the other hand, *do* involve or require research, data, investigation, etc. An example of an *a posteriori* claim is that some bachelors are obese. There is nothing about the concept of bachelor that entails that some are obese. In order to know that, you would actually have to "get up off your couch" and gather some information.

Most TAs are *a posteriori* arguments (i.e., they rely on observation, inference, experience, etc.), but the OA is a notable exception: it is an *a priori* argument.

The Ontological Argument

The Ontological argument for God's existence attempts to establish the existence of God by arguing that existence is part of God's essential "being" (ontology). That is, the very concept of God entails God's necessary existence. There have been several attempts to employ the ontological argument throughout the history of Western philosophy, involving such notables as Descartes and Alvin Plantinga (more recently), but the most famous version was advanced by St. Anselm. The following is an excerpt from Anselm's *Proslogion*:

> Therefore, Lord, you who give knowledge of the faith, give me as much knowledge as you know to be fitting for me, because you are as we believe and that which we believe. And indeed we believe you are something greater than

which cannot be thought. Or is there no such kind of thing, for "the fool said in his heart, 'there is no God'" (Ps. 13:1, 52:1)? But certainly that same fool, having heard what I just said, "something greater than which cannot be thought," understands what he heard, and what he understands is in his thought, even if he does not think it exists. For it is one thing for something to exist in a person's thought and quite another for the person to think that thing exists. For when a painter thinks ahead to what he will paint, he has that picture in his thought, but he does not yet think it exists, because he has not done it yet. Once he has painted it he has it in his thought and thinks it exists because he has done it. Thus even the fool is compelled to grant that something greater than which cannot be thought exists in thought, because he understands what he hears, and whatever is understood exists in thought. And certainly that greater than which cannot be understood cannot exist only in thought, for if it exists only in thought it could also be thought of as existing in reality as well, which is greater. If, therefore, that than which greater cannot be thought exists in thought alone, then that than which greater cannot be thought turns out to be that than which something greater actually can be thought, but that is obviously impossible.[75]

Therefore something than which greater cannot be thought undoubtedly exists both in thought and in reality.

Or, as a formal paraphrase:

1. By definition, God is a being "greater than which cannot be thought" (the greatest conceivable being, or GCB).
2. Something that exists both in reality (*in re*) and in imagination (*in intellectu*) is greater than something that exists solely in one's imagination.
3. God exists *in intellectu*.
4. If God did exist both *in re* and *in intellectu*, then God would not be a being "greater than which cannot be thought" (the GCB).
5. Therefore, God must exist in reality.

Before delving into the effectiveness of the OA, it's necessary to unpack some of its key components. The central assumption of the OA is that existence is a "great-making" property. What is a "great-making" property? There are any number of ways to answer that question, but I think the contemporary philosopher of religion, Steven Davis, says it best when he describes a great-making property in terms of "power, ability, freedom of action." In this very specific context, "greatness" refers to things like the ability to produce effects, to bring about change, to successfully exercise one's will, etc. I'm going to refer to this collection of terms as "power," from now on. If we accept this understanding of "great-making," then some properties would be considered great-making, and others wouldn't. Having a beard probably doesn't equate with having greater power, so "bearded" doesn't seem to be a great-making property (in this sense)—but being sentient (as opposed to being an inanimate object, for example) would seem to enhance a thing's "power." My cat has greater

---

[75] https://sourcebooks.fordham.edu/source/anselm.asp

ability to exert her will than does my office chair, and I have greater such ability than both of them. Therefore, sentience is a great-making property, and "higher" forms of sentience (e.g., intentionality, rationality, etc.) would be greater still.

With this understanding of "great-making" in mind, two questions need to addressed:

1. Is greatness (so defined) a comparative property that allows for a maximum (i.e., "the greatest")?
2. Is existence a great-making property?

Is greatness comparative, and such that it allows for a maximum? Well, if we're understanding greatness in terms of "power," then the answer is readily available. Certainly power is comparative, as we recognize that some things are more (or less) powerful than others. Is there a maximal case of power? Omnipotence (being "all-powerful") would be the obvious maximal case of power. So, unless you think that omnipotence (i.e., being capable of bringing about any logically possible state of affairs) is an incoherent concept, the answer to our first question appears to be "yes."

What about our second question? Is existence a great-making property? Anselm clearly believes it is, and this is implied in the second premise of his argument. To see why existence might be regarded as a great-making property, we need to understand his particular vocabulary. Anselm points out that things can exist in two different ways: "*in intellectu*," and "*in re*." To exist "*in intellectu*" is to exist "in the mind," as a mental object. To exist "*in re*" is to exist "out there," in "reality"—not merely "in the mind." Unicorns exist in my mind. I have a concept of a unicorn. I can think about unicorns and conjure up mental pictures of unicorns. Therefore, unicorns exist "*in intellectu*." I don't believe that they exist "*in re*," however. In other words, I don't think there are any actual horses with pretty horns coming out of their foreheads, running around in the world, munching on grass and looking majestic. My cat also exists "*in intellectu*." I have a mental concept of my cat. I can think about her, conjure up a mental image of her, etc. An important difference between my cat and a unicorn, though, is that my cat also exists "*in re*." That is, she doesn't exist only in my mind, but she's "out there" in the world as well—in fact, I'm looking at her right now. It's possible that there are things that exist "*in re*" but not "*in intellectu*." Perhaps there exists a chemical element not yet discovered or even imagined by us. Such a compound would exist "out there in the world" even though we have no concept of it just yet. To summarize, then: some things exist "*in intellectu*" only, some things might exist "*in re*" only, and some things exist both "*in intellectu*" and "*in re*."

Having distinguished these two forms of existence, Anselm claims that a thing that exists both "*in intellectu*" and "*in re*" is greater than something that exists "*in intellectu*" only. This might not be an obvious point, but I think it can be demonstrated without too much work if we keep in mind the concept of greatness we've been assuming. If we understand greatness in terms of "power," then there's a certain, obvious sense in which things that exist both "*in re*" as well as "*in intellectu*" have greater power. My cat has more power than the unicorn that exists only in my mind. My cat can exert her will and produce change in the world (e.g., eat bugs, shred curtains, warm up a bed, befoul a litter box, etc.). The unicorn in my mind can't do *anything* unless my mind makes it—which really indicates that it's my mind that has the power, and not the mental unicorn. Something that exists *"in re"* and not only *"in intellectu,"* therefore, has more "power" than something that exists only *"in intellectu."* Therefore, something that exists *"in re"* is *greater* than that which exists only *"in intellectu."*

Let us now turn from cats and unicorns, to the God that is the focus of the OA. Most atheists would grant that "God" exists *"in intellectu,"* at least.[76] Clearly, lots of people have an idea of "God" in their heads—but that's the problem, according to atheists: "God" exists *only* in their heads! "God" is no more "real" than unicorns or the tooth-fairy. Just as the tooth-fairy exists *"in intellectu,"* but not *"in re,"* so too does "God" (like other mythical creatures) exist *"in intellectu,"* but not *"in re."*

Anselm thinks that chain of reasoning is self-contradictory, and the following arguments attempts to demonstrate this.

1. The GCB exists *"in intellectu"* but not *"in re."*
2. Existence is greater *"in re"* than existence *"in intellectu"* alone.
3. The GCB's existence *"in re"* is conceivable.
4. If the GCB existed *"in re,"* then it would be greater.
5. It is conceivable that there is a being greater than the GCB.
6. It is false that the GCB exists *"in intellectu"* but not *"in re."*
7. Therefore, the GCB exists *"in re."*

This argument is an example of argument by contradiction, or a (formal) *"reductio ad absurdum"* argument. We start with the assumption that the GCB exists *only* in the mind. This assumption is then shown to generate a contradiction (occurring in line 5 above). This allows us to negate our starting assumption, thereby establishing that the GCB exists in "reality" as well as in the mind.

To reinforce this point, remember that Anselm thinks that a God that exists *"in re"* is greater than a God which exists only *"in intellectu."* This is probably obvious. A God that actually exists in the world has more power than an imaginary one existing only in our minds! But remember: God is defined as the greatest conceivable being (GCB), or, as Anselm words it, "something greater than which cannot be thought." A God which exists only *"in intellectu"* (the "God" that atheists have in mind (literally)), is not as great as one that exists *"in re"* as well. Therefore, that "God" is *not* the GCB, since a greater being than "God" *can* be conceived: namely, the one that exists *"in re"* as well. God, understood as the GCB, *must* exist *"in re"* as well as *"in intellectu"*—the very concept of God as the GCB entails it. But, if God exists *"in re"* as well as *"in intellectu,"* then God exists "out there," in the world, and not just in some people's heads. In other words, God exists.

---

[76] I say most, instead of all, because some atheists think that "God" is an incoherent concept, and therefore doesn't even exist in the mind. This is not the view of most atheists or agnostics, however.

Criticism of the OA

If this argument seems "fishy" to you, you're in good company. As famous as this argument is, its criticism is equally (if not more) famous. Criticism began in Anselm's own time, and one of the more famous critiques came from Gaunilo, who, in effect, offered a *reductio ad absurdum* objection to the OA.[77]

> For example: it is said that somewhere in the ocean is an island, which, because of the difficulty, or rather the impossibility, of discovering what does not exist, is called the lost island. And they say that this island has an inestimable wealth of all manner of riches and delicacies in greater abundance than is told of the Islands of the Blest; and that having no owner or inhabitant, it is more excellent than all other countries, which are inhabited by mankind, in the abundance with which it is stored.

> Now if some one should tell me that there is such an island, I should easily understand his words, in which there is no difficulty. But suppose that he went on to say, as if by a logical inference: "You can no longer doubt that this island which is more excellent than all lands exists somewhere, since you have no doubt that it is in your understanding. And since it is more excellent not to be in the understanding alone, but to exist both in the understanding and in reality, for this reason it must exist. For if it does not exist, any land which really exists will be more excellent than it; and so the island already understood by you to be more excellent will not be more excellent.

> If a man should try to prove to me by such reasoning that this island truly exists, and that its existence should no longer be doubted, either I should believe that he was jesting, or I know not which I ought to regard as the greater fool: myself, supposing that I should allow this proof; or him, if he should suppose that he had established with any certainty the existence of this island. For he ought to show first that the hypothetical excellence of this island exists as a real and indubitable fact, and in no wise as any unreal object, or one whose existence is uncertain, in my understanding.[78]

Gaunilo's criticism is sometimes called the "lost island" criticism, or the "greatest conceivable island" objection. His point is that if we allow the sort of reasoning employed in the OA, we can prove the existence of *anything*. Since we shouldn't be able to prove the existence of just anything, there must be something wrong with the OA.

---

[77] Gaunilo, it's worth pointing out, was a Christian monk. He is a perfect illustration that it is possible to agree with someone's conclusion, but find fault with their argument. As a monk, it's safe to assume that he agreed with St. Anselm that God exists. However, he didn't think that the OA *proved* it.

[78] Gaunilo, "In Behalf of the Fool," section 6. Available here: http://sourcebooks.fordham.edu/basis/anselm-gaunilo.asp

Gaunilo invites us to imagine the "greatest conceivable island." He proposes (in parody of the OA) that an island which exists "*in re*" is greater than one that exists "*in intellectu*" only. Therefore, such an island must actually exist out in the ocean somewhere, otherwise it wouldn't be the greatest conceivable island. You're supposed to think that there's something absurd about proving the existence of a hypothetical island in that fashion, so, therefore, there must also be something absurd about proving the existence of God with the OA.

Has Gaunilo succeeded? Supporters of Anselm think not—and neither did Anselm himself, though, to be honest, he doesn't really directly address the island argument except to repeat himself. Supporters of Anselm, though, have tackled the island objection head on, and their reply is based on the meaning of "greatness" that we had to establish earlier on. What does "greatness" mean with regard to an island? Well, according to Gaunilo, it means something like having an "inestimable wealth of all manner of riches and delicacies." Apparently, being uninhabited also makes an island great—at least according to his example. One problem with the island objection, thus far, is that "greatness" is clearly referring to different things in Gaunilo's example than in the OA. Greatness in the OA refers to "power," but obviously islands aren't the sorts of things that have "power," in the same sort of way. Moreover, the qualities Gaunilo has in mind don't seem to allow a maximum. What would be the "maximum" with regard to "riches and delicacies?" Presumably, we're dealing with things like mineral deposits, fruit trees, etc. What's the "maximum" ("greatest") with regard to fruit? An infinite amount of fruit? But, how could an infinite amount of fruit grow on an island which, by definition, must be a finite body bounded by water? The problem with Gaunilo's example seems to be that the "greatest conceivable island" doesn't seem to even exist, in any clear sort of way, "*in intellectu*"—and, since the notions of "greatness" being employed are different, Gaunilo and Anselm are basically talking past one another.

Does this mean that Gaunilo's style of objection is worthless, then? No. A variant of his objection claims that the OA could just as easily prove the existence of the "greatest conceivable evil being" as it could prove the existence of God. After all, the OA (at best) proves the existence of an omnipotent being. Nothing about the OA, by itself, demands that this being be the God that is described by Anselm's Christian faith.

That's correct.

Assuming that the OA works perfectly, it does seem "only" to establish the existence of an omnipotent being. By itself, it does not prove the existence of an omnipotent being who also spoke to Moses by means of a burning bush, or who became incarnate in the person of Jesus of Nazareth, etc. Like all the other major (philosophical) TAs, the "God" that is proved (best-case scenario) is a generic "God of the philosophers" who might, or might not, be the same God that is described in the various Western theistic traditions. If someone wanted to prove that *their* God exists, they would have to appeal to more than just the TAs we're going to consider in this book. But, that being granted, let's be fair: even if the OA *only* proves the existence of an omnipotent being, that's still a pretty big deal! But does the OA do even that?

Although criticism of the argument began with Anselm's contemporary, Gaunilo, it was made legendary by Immauel Kant. For those interested, Immanuel Kant (1724 –

1804) was an 18th-century German philosopher.[79] He is generally regarded as a terribly influential philosopher, certainly among the most important in the Western tradition.

If you ask philosophy majors, "what was Kant's criticism of the ontological argument?" many of them will be able to provide the answer: "existence isn't a predicate!" Fewer than many will actually be able to give a decent explanation of what that means.

A predicate is a fancy grammatical term that (roughly) means the same thing as "property" or "quality." A thing (e.g., an apple) will have various properties (e.g., being edible, being red, being a certain size, having a certain mass, etc.). Those properties are also its "predicates." The ontological argument asks us to compare two possible gods: one that exists in reality as well as in the mind, and one that exists only in the mind. The suggestion is that there is a qualitative difference in the properties (predicates) of these two gods.

God$_1$	**God$_2$**
Omniscient	Omniscient
Omnipotent	Omnipotent
Eternal	Eternal
Perfectly good	Perfectly good
Exists	Does not exist

If we compare these two "gods," it appears that one has the property of existence, and the other does not. Since Anselm claimed that existence was a "great making" property, the god that exists is greater than the god that does not, and, since God is the greatest conceivable being, it must be the case that God$_1$ (and not God$_2$) is God. Lo and behold, that just happens to be the one with existence as a property. Therefore, God exists.

Kant's complaint (as mentioned above) is that we can't treat existence as property/predicate like that.

"Being" is obviously not a real predicate; that is, it is not a concept of something which could be added to the concept of a thing. It is merely the positing of a thing, or of certain determinations, as existing in themselves. Logically, it is merely the copula of a judgment. The proposition "God is omnipotent" contains two concepts, each of which has its object -- God and omnipotence. The small word "is" adds no new predicate, but only serves to posit the predicate in its relation to the subject. If, now, we take the subject (God) with all its predicates (among which is omnipotence), and say "God is," or "There is a God," we attach no new predicate to the concept of God, but only posit it as an object that stands in relation to my concept. The content of both must be one and the same; nothing can have been added to the concept, which expresses merely what is possible, by my thinkings its object (through the expression "it is") as given

---

[79] Like Gaunilo, Kant believed that God exists as well—he just didn't think the OA could prove it.

absolutely. Otherwise stated, the real contains no more than the merely possible. A hundred real thalers does not contain the least coin more than a hundred possible thalers. For as the latter signify the concept and the former the object and the positing of the concept, should the former contain more than the latter, my concept would not, in that case, express the whole object, and would not therefore be an adequate concept of it. My financial position, however, is affected very differently by a hundred real thalers than it is by the mere concept of them (that is, of the possibility). For the object, as it actually exists, is not analytically contained in my concept, but is added to my concept (which is a determination of my state) synthetically; and yet the conceived hundred thalers are not themselves in the least increased through thus acquiring existence outside my concept.

By whatever and by however many predicates we may think a thing -- even if we completely determine it -- we do not make the least addition to the thing when we further declare that this thing is. Otherwise it would not be exactly the same thing that exists, but something more than we had thought in the concept: and we could not, therefore, say that the object of my concept exists. If we think in a thing every feature of reality except one, the missing reality is not added by my saying that this defective thing exists." [80]

According to Kant, existence doesn't "add" to the qualitative description of a thing in the way that redness does, or fragility does. Or, the way the complaint is usually expressed, "existence is not a 'real' predicate." A predicate (understood grammatically) is something that modifies a subject. Linguistically, any word whatsoever can be a "logical predicate"—which is just to say that the word can occupy the predicate slot in a sentence. Consider the following examples:

- The <u>horse</u> is *fast.*
- The <u>horse</u> is a *horse.*
- The <u>horse</u> is a *fish.*
- The <u>horse</u> is *flurbin.*

In each case, the underlined word (horse) is the subject, and the italicized word is the predicate. The first example actually makes sense and the predicate adds something meaningful to the subject. We now know that the horse is fast. The second example is coherent, but not terribly interesting. Nothing has been "added" to the subject. The third example is just plain weird. Self-contradictory, in fact. Given the concept of "horse," it can't be a fish. The last example is nonsense. "Flurbin" is a meaningless word I just made up. Needless to say, it doesn't "add" anything to its subject either.

The point of all of this is that while any word can stand, in a sentence, as a predicate, not every predicate is what Kant is calling a "real" predicate. A "real"

---

[80] Kant, Immanuel. *Critique of Pure Reason.* Section A599/B627.

predicate "adds" something to its subject. "Fast" is a real predicate for "horse," since it adds something to "horse." Existence, according to Kant, is not a "real" predicate.

According to this criticism, when someone says that God exists, they are not saying that there is a thing (God) and that God possesses the property of existence. If existence worked as a property like that, it would mean that atheists are claiming that there is a God who lacks the property of existence—but this is to both affirm God's existence ("there is a God. . . .") and *deny it* ("who lacks the property of existence") *at the same time*. Aside from being silly, this also violates a fundamental law of logic, the law of non-contradiction—and one doesn't want to do that.

So, if existence isn't a property/predicate, what *do* we mean when we say that something exists? To say that something exists is to say that it is exemplified, or instantiated, in the world. Existence doesn't tell us about the subject (e.g., an apple, or God), it tells us about the world—namely, that the world contains whatever that subject is. Try to follow this: when I say that an apple exists but that Santa Claus does not, I'm not describing the properties/ predicates of apples or Santa, I'm describing the properties/predicates of this world, namely, that *this world* has the property of including apples, but lacks the property of including Santa Claus.

If you're not convinced, yet, that existence is not a ("real") predicate of things, ask yourself, what does "existence" add to my qualitative description of a subject? Once I've described an apple's color, mass, size, and so on, what "more" is added if I toss "existence" onto the pile? The concept of the apple is the same (in terms of its color, size, mass, etc.) whether it exists or not—but the *world* is different based on whether or not the apple exists. To claim the apple exists says something about this world— that it contains something matching up to the qualitative description of the apple, but it doesn't tell us anything interesting about the apple itself.

Why is this so important? Remember, the ontological argument was driven by the comparison between the God that exists in reality, and the god that does not. The God with the property of existence is greater than the one which lacks that property. But, if Kant is right (and most philosophers and theologians believe he was), that kind of comparison is impossible, because existence can't be placed on the list of properties. After removing existence as a property/predicate, do the same comparison we tried before.

God₁
Omniscient
Omnipotent
Eternal
Perfectly good

God₂
Omniscient
Omnipotent
Eternal
Perfectly good

Which one is greater now? Obviously, the concepts are identical. We can compare the *world* in which there is a God with a *world* in which there is none, but we can't compare the *God* who exists with one who does not. Without that comparison, the ontological argument goes nowhere.

So, is the OA "dead?" Not necessarily. You might have noticed a few paragraphs ago when I said that *most* philosophers seem to think that Kant was right about existence not being a "real" predicate. Some argue that, in some contexts, existence *does* operate as a "real" predicate.

> *But what about those linguistic contexts in which the existence of the thing being discussed is not necessarily presupposed? To say that the thing exists may well, in those cases, expand our concept of it. I am quite sure that my concept of the Loch Ness Monster would change if someone were to convince me that the creature exists, that there really is (let's say) a reproducing colony of plesiosaurs in the loch left over from the Cretaceous period. Here 'exists' is a real predicate.*[81]

Even using Kant's own example of a hundred thalers, Davis points out that existence "adds" something to the concept in question: a hundred imaginary thalers have no purchasing power, whereas a hundred real thalers do. In fairness to Kant, he seems to recognize this ("My financial position, however, is affected very differently by a hundred real thalers than it is by the mere concept of them...") but nevertheless doesn't grant that existence operates as a real predicate. Davis simply disagrees, at least in certain contexts. If the subject is the Loch Ness Monster, Davis claims that "existence" does seem to "add" to our concept of Nessie.[82] If the subject is God, would "existence" add to our concept of God as well, or would it only add to our concept of the world?

The OA had largely become a historical curiosity amongst philosophers of religion, due to the efforts of Kant—largely, but not exclusively. More contemporary versions of the OA have emerged, including those that claim to avoid the "not a real predicate" critique of Kant altogether. One such version was made famous by Alvin Plantinga.

Plantinga's Modal OA

Plantinga's version of the OA is often referred to as a "modal" version of the OA due to it being based on the concepts of possibility and necessity. We will preview his argument, then explore some of its details, and finally consider how this version of the OA might evade Kant's criticism.

1. There is a possible world in which maximal greatness is instantiated.
2. Necessarily, maximal greatness is instantiated in a possible world only if maximal excellence is instantiated in every world.
3. Therefore, maximal greatness is instantiated in the actual world.

Don't read too much into this idea of "possible worlds." Some people import way too much metaphysical significance into the idea, and think that "possible worlds"

---

[81] Steven Davis, "God, Reason, and Theistic Proofs," p. 34.

[82] I imagine Kant might agree that a concept has indeed changed, but not in the way Davis claims. Our concept of the *world* would be changed in that it now includes "God" as a (rather significant) feature. This is just to reiterate his assertion that to say that a thing exists doesn't "add" to our concept of the thing, but only means that the thing is "instantiated" in the world.

refer to other universes that actually exist "out there" in reality, with fantastic (and exciting) implications. Maybe there is a "possible world" in which I never studied philosophy, and became a diplomat with the U.S. Foreign Service instead—and maybe I could somehow travel to that world and have a conversation with that alternate version of "me?"

That would indeed be fascinating, but this language of "possible worlds" entails no such thing—fascinating though it is to think about. To say that there is a possible world in which I became a diplomat is just a fancy way of saying that it's conceivable that I had become a diplomat instead of a philosopher. To say that there is a possible world in which the Nazis won World War Two is not to make some fantastic metaphysical claim that there exists an alternate universe of actual people where we all speak German! It is merely to say that the Nazis could have won the war. "The Nazis won the war" is a logically possible description of reality just like "it is raining today" is a logically possible description of reality even though it is not, in fact raining today (in Southern California, as of the time I am typing this sentence).

For those who are unfamiliar with the terminology of possible worlds, let me explain that by "a possible world" one doesn't mean a planet or even a universe, but rather a complete description of reality, or a way reality might be. Perhaps the best way to think of a possible world is a huge conjunction p & q & r & s..., whose individual conjuncts are the propositions p, q, r, s, ... A possible world is a conjunction which comprises every proposition or its contradictory, so that it yields a maximal description of reality—nothing is left out of such a description. By negating conjuncts in a maximal description we arrive at different possible worlds:

W_1: p & q & r & s...
W_2: p & ~q & r & ~s...
W_3: ~p & ~q & r & s...
W_4: p & q & ~r & s...

Only one of these descriptions will be composed of conjuncts all of which are true and so will be the way reality actually is, that is to say, the actual world.[83]

Although Craig's description might seem intimidating, the meaning is actually fairly simple. Suppose that the claim variable p refers to "Preston is a philosophy professor," q refers to "Dixon is a cabinet maker," r refers to "Jackson is a motivational speaker," and s refers to "Brutlag is a chauvinist." The different possible worlds that Craig enumerates above would translate as follows:

W_1: Preston is a philosophy professor, and Dixon is a cabinet maker, and Jackson-Preston is a public health professor, and Brutlag is a chauvinist....

W_2: Preston is a philosophy professor, and Dixon is a not cabinet maker, and

[83] Craig, William Lane. *Reasonable Faith*, 3rd edition. Crossway Books, 2008, 183.

Jackson-Preston is a public health professor, and Brutlag is not a chauvinist....

W_3: Preston is not a philosophy professor, and Dixon is not a cabinet maker, and Jackson-Preston is a public health professor, and Brutlag is a chauvinist....

W_4: Preston is a philosophy professor, and Dixon is a cabinet maker, and Jackson-Preston is not a public health professor, and Brutlag is a chauvinist....

Each of those conjunction is a possible description of reality, but only one of all the possible descriptions will be the one in which all the conjuncts are true—the one that accurately describes reality. The actual world is simply the logically possible "description" of reality that is, in fact, accurate, the one that "obtains" the one that is "instantied." All of that is a fancy way of saying the "real world."[84]

One more important feature of possible worlds: the propositions offered in the conjunctions must be capable of being true. For example, t: "Floyd is an even number" is not even possibly true, so no possible world W_x could include t as one of its conjuncts. Instead, its negation ($\sim t$) will be a conjunct of every possible world, since t is necessarily false—it's false in every possible world. Conversely, necessarily true propositions ("the sum of the interior angles of a triangle is 180 degrees") are true in every possible world, and exist as a conjunct in every possible world.

Let's review our vocabulary, and add a couple more terms.

- Possible world: a (logically) possible description of reality.

- Actual world: the world that actually exists, the description of reality that is actually instantiated.

- Maximal excellence: having the properties of omniscience, omnipotence, and moral perfection.

- Maximal greatness: having the property of maximal excellence instantiated in every world.

The two additional terms are both potentially controversial in that some might claim that they are conveniently arbitrary. A critic might complain that Plantinga is defining his terms in ways that will promote the conclusion he wishes to obtain (i.e., God exists), and we will address his own recognition of that complaint at the end of this chapter. For now, though, let us proceed to examine the argument.

1. There is a possible world in which maximal greatness is instantiated

Ask yourself: is it even *possible* that an all-powerful, all-knowing, perfectly good, and necessarily existing being could exist? Or, is that logically impossible? Is a possible world (W) where maximal greatness is instantiated an impossible description? Supposing that "maximal greatness is instantiated" is represented by z,

---

[84] In case you were curious, the "actual world" out of those four possible worlds is W_2.

is z a conjunct in *any* world (W)? Or, is z like the claim that Floyd is an even number? False is every possible world? It seems to be at least *possible* that there is a world (W) that could look like this:

> W₂: Preston is a philosophy professor, and Dixon is a not cabinet maker, and Jackson is a motivational speaker, and Brutlag is not a chauvinist, and maximal greatness is instantiated...

Therefore, in some possible world W maximal greatness is instantiated.

2.   Necessarily, maximal greatness is instantiated in a possible world only if maximal excellence is instantiated in every world.

This premise merely expounds on the definition of maximal greatness. If there is a possible world (W) in which "maximal greatness" is instantiated, then, because maximal greatness entails a maximally excellent being, (W) is a world in which maximal excellence is instantiated. However, maximal greatness entails maximal excellence in *every* world. By definition, the difference between maximal excellence and maximal greatness is that the latter requires the former to be instantiated in *every* world.

3.   Therefore, maximal greatness is instantiated in the actual world.

If (W) contains maximal greatness (i.e., a maximally excellent being that exists in every possible world), then maximal greatness is instantiated in *every* world—including the *actual* world, It is impossible for maximal greatness *not* to be instantiated in any possible world. The actual world is a possible world. Therefore, maximal greatness is instantiated in the actual world. That means that a maximally excellent being (i.e., one that is omnipotent, omniscient, and perfectly good) exists in the actual world. Does that sort of being sound familiar? Does it sound an awful lot like God, perhaps? By a quick application of the "matching strategy," we now have a philosophical argument for God's existence.

Earlier in this section, I suggested that this version of the OA might be immune to Kant's famous critique of the OA. We can now consider why that might be.

Remember, Kant's complaint is that existence is not a "real predicate." Existence doesn't "add" to our concept of a thing, but merely tells us whether that thing is instantiated in the world. Note that in Plantinga's version of the OA, existence is not being offered as a predicate of the GCB. Instead, the *property* of "maximal greatness" is claimed to be *instantiated* in the actual world. This is precisely the sort of existence claims that Kant thinks are legitimate. Since maximal greatness entails maximal excellence (omnipotence, omniscience, and perfect goodness), and since something can't have those properties unless it exists, that means there exists a being that is omnipotent/omniscient/perfectly good ("God"). The argument still asserts that "God exists," but not by treating existence as a predicate intrinsic to the concept of God. Therefore, Kant's criticism is inapplicable.

Does this mean that Plantinga's modal OA is immune to any criticism? Of course not. In fact, oddly enough, Plantinga himself acknowledges the limits of his own argument.

> But here we must be careful; we must ask whether this argument is a successful piece of natural theology, whether it proves the existence of God. And the answer must be, I think, that it does not. An argument for God's existence may be sound, after all, without in any useful sense proving God's existence. Since I believe in God, I think the following argument is sound:
>
> Either God exists or 7 + 5 = 14
> It is false that 7 + 5 = 14
> Therefore God exists.
>
> But obviously this isn't a proof; no one who didn't already accept the conclusion, would accept the first premise. The ontological argument we've been examining isn't just like this one, of course, but it must be conceded that not everyone who understands and reflects on its central premise -- that the existence of a maximally great being is possible -- will accept it. Still, it is evident, I think, that there is nothing contrary to reason or irrational in accepting this premise. What I claim for this argument, therefore, is that it establishes, not the truth of theism, but its rational acceptability. And hence it accomplishes at least one of the aims of the tradition of natural theology.

What does Plantinga mean, here? Consider the argument example he provides:

1. Either God exists or 7 + 5 = 14
2. It is false that 7 + 5 = 14
3. Therefore God exists.

This argument is a classic case of an application of "disjunctive syllogism:"

1. P v Q
2. ~Q
3. P

The argument is undeniably valid (according to the rules of propositional logic). So far, so good. Is the argument sound? Well, Plantinga thinks so. He certainly thinks that the second premise ("it is false that 7 + 5 = 14") is true—in other words, 7 + 5 does *not* equal 14. What about the first premise? Because Plantinga thinks that it is true that God exists, he accepts the disjunction that either God exists or 7 + 5 = 14 as a true claim. This probably requires some explanation. According to propositional logic, a disjunction (an "or" statement) is true so long as one of its disjuncts is true. Only if both disjuncts are false, is the disjunctive claim false. Consider the following example:

Either today is a holiday, or we have school.

In this example, the entire statement is the disjunction. The first disjunct is the first underlined portion (today is a holiday), and the second disjunct is the second underlined portion (we have school). That claim is true so long as at least one of the disjuncts is true—but if both are false then the entire disjunctive claim is also false. As it turns out, the claim is false, because it's possible for both disjuncts to be false. What if today is a Saturday? Neither a holiday, nor a day in which we have school?

Returning to Plantinga's example, the first premise (Either God exists or 7 + 5 = 14) is true so long as at least one of the disjuncts is true. It is false that 7 + 5 = 14, but Plantinga thinks it is true that God exists—therefore, the first premise is true. Since the second premise is also true, the argument is sound—or so Plantinga *believes*.

What would an atheist, think, though? An atheist would certainly agree that the second premise is true, but what about the first? The atheist would agree that 7 + 5 = 14 is false, but would *also* think that God exists is false. That means both disjuncts are false, and therefore the first premise is false. If the first premise is false, then, even though the argument is valid, it is not *sound*—or the so the atheist *believes*.

Reconsider Plantinga's actual argument, in light of all this.

1. There is a possible world in which maximal greatness is instantiated.
2. Necessarily, maximal greatness is instantiated in a possible world only if maximal excellence is instantiated in every world.
3. Therefore, maximal greatness is instantiated in the actual world.

The argument is valid, but is it sound? Plantinga thinks so—but that's because he believes both premises are true. He has *defined* maximal greatness as the instantiation of maximal excellence in every world, so of course he accepts that premise as true. However, a critic could reject that definition of maximal greatness. What if an atheist thinks that building "omnipotence, omniscience, and perfect goodness in every possible world" is just a sneaky way of defining the Western concept of God into existence? Or, what about the first premise? Plantinga thinks that "maximal greatness" being instantiated is possible, but what if someone thinks that there is something actually *impossible* about the instantiation of a being possessing the required properties? What if you think "perfect goodness" is incoherent, because it would require both prefect justice and perfect mercy, and you think those are mutually exclusive? Or what if you think omnipotence and omniscience are mutually exclusive, because (for example) an omniscient being would know how to do something beyond its power (omnipotence)? I'm not arguing for any of these examples, mind you—merely pointing out that it's possible that someone could have legitimate, reasonable concerns about the truth of either premise. In that case, they would reject the argument as unsound.

Plantinga cedes this point: "but it must be conceded that not everyone who understands and reflects on its central premise -- that the existence of a maximally great being is possible -- will accept it." The OA *might* be sound, and Plantinga thinks it is sound—but he acknowledges that he can't prove that it is sound, and therefore the OA can't *prove* that God exists. Is it useless then? Certainly not, according to Plantinga.

Still, it is evident, I think, that there is nothing contrary to reason or irrational in accepting this premise [premise 1]. What I claim for this argument, therefore, is that it establishes, not the truth of theism, but its rational acceptability. And hence it accomplishes at least one of the aims of the tradition of natural theology.

The OA is an ambitious TA. It purports to deduce God's existence simply by reflecting on the very concept of God itself. This is probably overly ambitious, if we expect that the OA can prove the truth of its conclusion, even to those who started out disagreeing with it. But, as stated in previous chapters, a TA can be effective in other respects: it can increase warrant for those who already accept its conclusion, and it can demonstrate the rationality of believing its conclusion to be true even to those who reject it. This is precisely what Plantinga thinks the OA accomplishes.

Chapter 5: The Cosmological Argument

> *Comprehension questions you should be able to answer after reading this chapter:*
>
> 1. What is Aquinas' argument from motion ("1st Way")?
> 2. What is Aquinas' argument from causation ("2nd Way")?
> 3. What is the "matching strategy?"
> 4. What is the difference between hierarchical causes (HCs) and linear causes (LCs)?
> 5. What is the difference between contingent beings (CBs) and necessary beings (NBs)?
> 6. What is Aquinas' argument from contingency and necessity ("3rd Way")?
> 7. What is the Kalam Cosmological Argument (KCA)?
> 8. Why does Craig think an "actual infinite" can only exist "*in intellectu*," but not "*in re*," and why is this important for the KCA?
> 9. What are the features of the "First Cause" that Craig believes can be revealed by philosophical conceptual analysis?

Why is there something, rather than nothing? What accounts for the existence of the universe? What is the original source of all motion and change in the universe?

The cosmological argument (CA) offers "God" as an answer to those profound questions. Made famous by St. Thomas Aquinas, and more recently by William Lane Craig, this argument attempts to establish the existence of God as an explanation for the existence of this universe, or for the motion or "effects" we see in the universe.

There are several versions of this argument. We will first consider the version of the CA offered by Aquinas, and then consider the more contemporary version offered by Craig: the "Kalam Cosmological Argument (KCA)."

Aquinas

First, note that the CA, unlike the OA, is an "*a posteriori*" argument. That is, it is based on and draws from experience. "Experience of what?" you might ask. Several different things, according to Aquinas. In the famous passage from his *Summa Theologica*, usually referred to as "the Five Ways," Aquinas offers three different variations of the CA. The "first way" concerns motion, the "second way" concerns causation, and the "third way" concerns contingency and necessity.

I answer that, The existence of God can be proved in five ways.

The first and more manifest way is the argument from motion. It is certain, and evident to our senses, that in the world some things are in motion. Now whatever is in motion is put in motion by another, for nothing can be in motion except it is in potentiality to that towards which it is in motion; whereas a thing moves inasmuch as it is in act. For motion is nothing else than the reduction of something from potentiality to actuality. But nothing can be reduced from potentiality to actuality, except by something in a state of actuality. Thus that which is actually hot, as fire, makes wood, which is potentially hot, to be actually hot, and thereby moves and changes it. Now it is not possible that the same thing should be at once in actuality and potentiality in the same respect, but only in different respects. For what is actually hot cannot simultaneously be potentially hot; but it is simultaneously potentially cold. It is therefore impossible that in the same respect and in the same way a thing should be both mover and moved, i.e. that it should move itself. Therefore, whatever is in motion must be put in motion by another. If that by which it is put in motion be itself put in motion, then this also must needs be put in motion by another, and that by another again. But this cannot go on to infinity, because then there would be no first mover, and, consequently, no other mover; seeing that subsequent movers move only inasmuch as they are put in motion by the first mover; as the staff moves only because it is put in motion by the hand. Therefore it is necessary to arrive at a first mover, put in motion by no other; and this everyone understands to be God.

The "first way," as mentioned, concerns motion. The intuition behind this version of the CA is fairly obvious, and can be presented formally as follows:

1. Everything that is in motion is moved by something else. ("Now whatever is in motion is put in motion by another")
2. Infinite regress is impossible. ("But this cannot go on to infinity, because then there would be no first mover, and, consequently, no other mover")
3. Therefore, there must be a first mover. ("Therefore it is necessary to arrive at a first mover, put in motion by no other")
4. ("and this everyone understands to be God")

I place the 4th premise in parentheses to indicate its special status in the argument. What you will discover about nearly every TA is that their conclusions don't (and typically can't) specify a specific "God" as understood from within a specific religious tradition. Instead, they will mention a "GCB" (as in the OA), or a "prime mover," "first cause," or "necessary being" (as in the CA), etc. Aquinas is no different in this respect, initially. The conclusion of the CA as described in the first way is simply that there must be a "first mover." As a point of clarification, he offers that "this everyone understands to be God." In other words, the first mover "proved" by the CA is identical to the God that is described by Aquinas' own faith tradition.

This *"matching strategy"* is quite common, and you will encounter it often. Anselm argued for the GCB, but he, of course, believed that the GCB was identical to his God. Paley argues that the universe is probably the product of intelligent design, but he, of course, believes the "designer" to be his God. Craig will argue that there must an objective, transcendent source of moral values, but he, of course, believes that source to be his God.

Note that the "match" has not been proven by these arguments, even if the arguments are thought to be persuasive arguments—but nor is that what they are trying to accomplish. Remember my point earlier about TAs serving best to establish warrant for beliefs. If, for example, someone believes in a God who created the universe and set it in motion, the CA does not prove the existence of that God, but the theist would likely (and understandably) consider a philosophical proof of a "first cause" to provide evidence for her belief in her God that she believes responsible for the very same thing.

Let us return to the first way. Again, the intuition is simple: everything that we observe in motion has been set into motion by something else. Either there is a "prime mover" that began this motion, or else we have an infinite regress of movers. But, on the assumption that such an infinite regress is impossible, there must be a "prime mover" instead—and some people (like Aquinas) identify this prime mover to be God. But why should we assume an infinite regress is impossible? Why couldn't motion just go on "forever," including forever backwards in time, such that no "first mover" is posited? The alleged impossibility of an infinite regress is critically important to every version of the CA of which I am aware. Accordingly, the reasons why some think such an infinite regress is impossible is important enough to deserve its own section later in this chapter.

You will see, for example, the appeal to the impossibility of an infinite regress in Aquinas' second way.

The second way is from the nature of the efficient cause. In the world of sense we find there is an order of efficient causes. There is no case known (neither is it, indeed, possible) in which a thing is found to be the efficient cause of itself; for so it would be prior to itself, which is impossible. Now in efficient causes it is not possible to go on to infinity, because in all efficient causes following in order, the first is the cause of the intermediate cause, and the intermediate is the cause of the ultimate cause, whether the intermediate cause be several, or only one. Now to take away the cause is to take away the effect. Therefore, if there be no first cause among efficient causes, there will be no ultimate, nor any intermediate cause. But if in efficient causes it is possible to go on to infinity, there will be no first efficient cause, neither will there be an ultimate effect, nor any intermediate efficient causes; all of which is plainly false. Therefore it is necessary to admit a first efficient cause, to which everyone gives the name of God."

1. Every effect has a cause. ("In the world of sense we find there is an order of efficient causes")
2. An effect cannot be self-caused ("There is no case known (neither is it, indeed, possible) in which a thing is found to be the efficient cause of itself")

3. An infinite regress of causes is impossible. ("Now in efficient causes it is not possible to go on to infinity")
4. Therefore, there must be a first cause. ("Therefore it is necessary to admit a first efficient cause")
5. ("to which everyone gives the name of God.")

Once again, note the matching strategy. This second version of the CA does not, strictly speaking, prove "God's" existence, even in the best of cases. At most, it proves the existence of a "first cause"—and Aquinas identifies this first cause as being God.

Also note the similarity with the first way. Aquinas is appealing to "efficient causes" rather than "motion," but the structure and strategy are basically the same. An "efficient cause" is an Aristotelian term—a philosopher to whom Aquinas owes much.[85] Aristotle actually describes four kinds of causes.

1. Material cause
2. Efficient cause
3. Formal cause
4. Final cause

A thing's Material cause is its matter, the raw materials of which it is made. Using the example of a statue, its Material cause is marble (or whatever kind of stone the sculptor used). An Efficient cause is a thing's origin—the process responsible for it being what it is. In the case of the statue, its Efficient cause is the sculptor and her tools. The Formal cause is a thing's essence, the governing idea giving it its structure and form. For the statue, its Formal cause is the vision of the completed sculpture entertained by the sculptor. Finally, we have the Final cause. The Final cause is the end or purpose ("telos") that the thing is to fulfill. With the statue, perhaps its Final cause is to depict the likeness of Aristotle.

Aquinas' second way focuses on the concept of an efficient cause. That is good news, for us, since when most of us (today) think about or speak of causes, we usually mean an efficient cause. My typing on a keyboard is the efficient cause of words appearing on the screen. My neighbor pressing a button is the efficient cause of my doorbell ringing, and so on. The basic idea behind the "second way" version of the CA is that every effect has an efficient cause. Things don't "just happen" from no cause whatsoever. Aquinas claims that for any effect, the cause of that effect must either be itself, or something else. However, an effect can't be "self-caused" (i.e., the cause of itself) "for so it would be prior to itself, which is impossible." Think of it this way: imagine that you asked me what caused my doorbell to ring, and I answered "itself." You would probably be puzzled by this answer. "Itself? What could Professor Preston mean? Does he mean that there is something faulty with the wiring, so that the doorbell sometimes rings without someone touching the button?" That would make sense, but then my answer would have been misleading. In that case, something like an electrical surge would have been the cause of the ringing. My claim (bizarre as it

85 Indeed, Aquinas so respected Aristotle that when he references him, he calls him simply "The Philosopher."

was) was that the ringing sound of the doorbell itself (the effect) was the cause of the ringing. The ringing caused the ringing. If you think that sounds silly, Aquinas would agree. What sense does it make to claim that the effect caused *itself*? Given that our *usual* experience of causation involves a temporal relationship in which the cause is (temporally) prior to the effect, to say that the effect caused itself would require the effect to have existed before it existed!

Not surprisingly, then, Aquinas rules out "self-causation" to account for the experience of efficient causation we all share. On the assumption that an infinite regress of causes is impossible (again: important enough to get its own section later), that leaves only a "first cause" to account for causation in general. Aquinas believes this "first cause" to be God.

We can't defer the discussion of an infinite regress any longer. The impossibility of such a regress has already played an important role in both the first and second way, and will play a role in the third way as well—in addition to being critical to Craig's KCA later on. Why would someone think that an infinite regress (of the types in question) would be impossible? Why could there not be motion going "infinitely" into the past, with no beginning, or infinite causes reaching back in time to no beginning?

One way to justify the claim that such an infinite regress is impossible first involves distinguishing "linear causes" (LC) from hierarchical causes" (HC). A LC is the kind of cause in which the effect continues to exist even if the cause stops exerting its causal influence. Probably most of the causes that we tend to think of when asked to imagine "causes" are LCs. For example, the cause of the words appearing on this page is my having pressed certain keys on my keyboard. The words remain on the page even though I'm no longer pressing the keys. Or, if you draw a picture of something, the drawing continues to exist, on its own, even after you're finished drawing it. It's not as if you have to keep drawing it "forever" in order for it to remain in existence! As a final example, when a row of dominoes fall against one another, causing the next in line to topple, we have linear causation. Once the first domino has struck the second, it has done its "job"—it's not as if it has to keep pushing on that second domino.

The situation is different, though, when we're talking about an HC. With an HC, the effect can't continue to exist unless its cause persists in its causal activity. If a musician plays a note with a trumpet, for example, the note (effect) only persists for as long as air is blown through the trumpet (cause). Stop blowing that horn, and the sound goes away. As another example, if you are holding an object up in the air, your act of holding it serves as an HC for the effect of it being suspended in the air. Let go, and the effect (being suspended in air) will disappear. As a final example, consider the rotating gears of a machine: if one gear stops moving, all the rest cease in their movement as well.

With this vocabulary in mind, two sorts of "infinite regress" have to be considered with respect to efficient cause: an infinite linear sequence, and an infinite hierarchical sequence. We will consider an argument for the impossibility of an infinite sequence of LCs later in the chapter when we review Craig's KCA. For now, we will focus on HCs.

Why an infinite (hierarchical) regress is (allegedly) impossible

The aforementioned Steven Davis does an exceptional job of formalizing an argument that purports to demonstrate the impossibility of an infinite (hierarchical) regress, and I will draw heavily from his work in my adaptation of the argument below. His argument is intimidating, at first glance, but we will work through it together, line by line (literally, one line at a time). First, though, it's important to identify some important terminology that appears in the argument.

Contingent being (CB): a being who can exist, or not; a being who depends on other things for its existence; a being with a finite "lifespan" Examples of CBs are endless: me you, the earth, i-phones, etc.

Necessary being (NB): a being who exists at all moments in time; a being who depends on no other beings for its existence. It remains to be established whether any NB exists. Certainly God, if God exists, would be considered a NB.

As a reminder, HC refers to "Hierarchical cause."

1. Every existing being is either a NB or a CB.
2. All existing CBs have HCs (hierarchical causes).
3. All CBs are such that they exist, at any given time t, only if all their HCs also exist at t.
4. All CBs are such that at some time they fail to exist, and one of the times they fail to exist is before they exist.
5. There is no first moment of time.
6. All existing beings are CBs.
7. A given CB, namely, x, exists now.
8. All of x's HCs exist now (3,4).
9. A given HC of x, namely, y, has existed for an infinite time (2,3,5,8)
10. Y is a CB (6).
11. All CBs begin to exist at some point in time (4,5).
12. At some past point in time y began to exist (10,11).
13. At some past point in time y did not exist (5, 12).
14. Y has not existed for an infinite time (13).
15. Y has both existed for an infinite time, and has not existed for an infinite time (9, 14).
16. (10), and thus (6), are false (6, 10, 15—by *reductio ad absurdum*)
17. Therefore, y is a NB (1, 16).
18. Therefore, at least one NB exists (17).

Just in case that didn't make perfect sense the first time through, we'll now consider it one line of the argument at a time.

1. *Every existing being is either a NB or a CB.* These options exhaust the logical possibilities. Thanks to Aristotle's law of excluded middle, we can safely

assume that it's either one, or the other. That is, for any being, it is either a CB, or a NB.

2. *All existing CBs have HCs* (hierarchical causes). This might not be obvious, at first glance, but it is a claim based on experience. The HC of a musical note is obvious: the blowing of the trumpet. Less obvious is the HC of myself, or of you. What is "sustaining" my existence, at this moment? An obvious answer would be God. According to Christian doctrine, God is the HC of all created things. This is supported in several Biblical verses (underlining added for emphasis). "For you love all things that exist, and detest none of the things that you have made; for you would not have made anything if you had hated it. How would anything have endured, if you had not willed it? Or how would anything not called forth by you have been preserved? You spare all things, for they are yours, O Lord, you who love the living (Wisdom 11: 26)." "My Father works until now and I work (John 5:17)." Also "He upholds all things by the word of his power (Hebrews 1:3)." Moreover, St. Augustine's commentary on John 5:17 is as follows: "Let us therefore believe that God works constantly, so that all created things would perish, if his working were withdrawn." And, the Catechism of the Catholic Church (paragraph 301) states: "With creation, God does not abandon his creatures to themselves. He not only gives them being and existence, but also, and at every moment, upholds and sustains them in being, enables them to act and brings them to their final end. Recognizing this utter dependence with respect to the Creator is a source of wisdom and freedom, of joy and confidence."

William Lane Craig explains Aquinas' view in relatively clear prose (perhaps clearer than my own): "On Aquinas's Aristotelian-inspired metaphysic, every existing finite thing is composed of essence and existence and is therefore radically contingent. A thing's essence is a set of properties which serve to define what that thing is. Now if an essence is to be instantiated or exemplified, there must be conjoined with that essence an act of being. This act of being involves a continual bestowal of being, or the thing would be annihilated. Essence is in potentiality to the act of being, and therefore without the bestowal of being the essence would not be exemplified. For the same reason no substance can actualize itself; for in order to bestow being upon itself it would have to be already actual. A pure potentiality cannot actualize itself but requires some external cause. Now although Aquinas argued that there cannot be an infinite regress of causes of being (because in such a series all the causes would be merely instrumental and so no being would be produced, just as no motion would be produced in a watch without a spring even if it had an infinite number of gears) and that therefore there must exist a First Uncaused Cause of being, his actual view was that there can be no intermediate causes of being at all, that any finite substance is sustained in existence immediately by the Ground of Being. This must be a being which is not composed of essence and existence and, hence, requires no sustaining cause. We cannot say that this being's essence includes existence as one of its properties, for existence is not a property, but an act, the instantiating of an essence. Therefore, we must conclude that this being's essence just is existence. In a sense, this being has no essence; rather it is the pure act of being, unconstrained by any essence. It is, as Thomas says, *ipsum esse subsistens*, the act of being itself subsisting. Thomas identifies this being with the God whose name was revealed to Moses as "I am" (Exod. 3.15)."[86]

Of course, to offer God as an example of all CBs having an HC would be question-begging! What other examples might we produce? As far as you or I, as CBs, are concerned, what about the Sun? If the Sun ceased to exist, we would cease to exist as well, and there is certainly a sense in which the Sun sustains our existence by virtue of the energy it provides. Is this precisely the same as the way a musician sustains a musical note? No. It is analogous, at best—and the aforementioned Craig has concerns about the strength of this analogy: "The difficulty with appeal to the Thomist argument, however, is that it is very difficult to show that things are, in fact, contingent in the special sense required by the argument. Certainly things are naturally contingent in that their continued existence is dependent upon a myriad of factors including particle masses and fundamental forces, temperature, pressure, entropy level, and so forth, but this natural contingency does not suffice to establish things' metaphysical contingency in the sense that being must continually be added to their essences lest they be spontaneously annihilated."[87] If you reject the implicit Aristotelian/Thomist metaphysics lurking in this premise, you are unlikely to find the argument persuasive, but let's continue for the sake of argument all the same.

3.   All CBs are such that they exist, at any given time *t*, only if all their HCs also exist at *t*. This premise is true, by definition. If something is an HC for a CB, the HC must exist at any time the CB exists.

4.   All CBs are such that at some time they fail to exist, and one of the times they fail to exist is before they exist. This is also true by definition. Any CB has a finite "lifespan," simply by virtue of being a CB.

5.   There is no first moment of time. This premise is simply a reflection of what Aquinas is assuming in his argument: that time is infinite.[88] Today, this is an admittedly controversial assumption, as there are many (myself included) who would deny that time is infinite. For those who disagree with this

86 William Lane Craig & J.P. Moreland, *Philosophical Foundations for a Christian Worldview*, pp. 465-466.

87 Ibid., 468.

88 To make this argument more confusing: Aquinas believed, by faith, that time was *not* infinite—but he didn't think he could prove it by reason alone. Therefore, for the sake of argument, he argues from the assumption that time is infinite, instead.

premise, Craig's Kalam Cosmological Argument will offer an argument against infinite regress that assumes that time is finite, instead.

6. All existing beings are CBs. A special argumentative maneuver begins with this premise. This is the beginning of what's known as a formal "*reductio ad absurdum.*" The way a *reductio* works is by beginning with a premise, then showing that "absurd" things (namely, contradictions) result from that premise. Therefore, we are entitled to reject (negate) the premise. The strategy in this case is to show that if we assume that all existing things are CBs, we will generate a contradiction—thereby demonstrating that it is *false* that all existing things are CBs.

7. A given CB, namely, x, exists now. This premise merely stipulates that some particular CB ("x") exists now. There is nothing controversial about this premise, as "x" can be any CB you like, such as yourself, myself, my cat, an oak tree, etc.

8. All of x's HCs exist now (3, 4). This is implied by premises 3 and 7. Recall that premise 3 states that "all CBs are such that they exist, at any given time *t*, only if all their HCs also exist at *t*," while premise 7 states that "a given CB, namely, x, exists now." So, if x exists now, all of x's HCs must also exist now.

9. A given HC of x, namely, y, has existed for an infinite time (2, 3, 5, 8). This premise is one of the more difficult to understand, at first glance. It might not immediately be obvious why an HC of x needs to have existed "forever." You might wonder, for example, why a chain of HCs, over time, couldn't produce x, without any link in that chain needing to have lasted "forever." A few points will help to clarify why that proposal couldn't work. First, it's important to note that a property of HCs is that they are "transitive." That is, if y is an HC of x, and z is an HC of y, then Z is also an HC of x. Why is this so? Remember that an HC is the kind of cause such that if the HC ceases its causal activity, its effect ceases as well. So, if z is an HC of y, and z ceases, then y ceases as well. And, if y was an HC of x, and y ceases, then x ceases as well. So, given that z is an HC of y, if z ceases, x ceases too. Therefore, z is also an HC of x. Remember also that according to premise 6, all existing things are CBs. That means that y (an HC of x) is itself a CB. Premise 2 claims that all CBs have HCs. This would mean that x has an HC (y, for example), but also that y has an HC (z, maybe?). Premise 3 implies that whenever x exists, its HCs must also exist. In the scenario we're imagining, that would mean that when x exists, y and z must also exist (etc.). Premise 8 makes this clear: all of x's HCs exist now (given that x exists now). Premise 5 claims that time is infinite. Since x exists now, any HCs of x must also exist. Since we're stipulating that time goes back "forever," some HC of x (y, in this case) must have existed "forever" as well. Otherwise, a link in the HC chain would have been broken, causing all the subsequent links to cease to exist—including x.

10. Y is a CB (6). This simply follows from premise 6. While y is an HC of x, it is also itself a CB.

11. CBs begin to exist at some point in time (4, 5). This follows from premise 4. Since any CB, by definition, has a finite lifespan, it must have a beginning of its lifespan. And, since time is infinite (premise 5), it's not possible that any CB began to exist simultaneously with time itself, so as to somehow avoid having a beginning *in* time.

12. At some past point in time y began to exist (10, 11). Given that y is a CB, and given that all CBs begin to exist at some point in time, it follows that y began to exist at some point in time.

13. At some past point in time y did not exist (5, 12). Given that y began to exist at some point in time, and given that time is "infinite," there must have been some portion of time (indeed, an infinite amount, it would seem!) prior to y's existence. All of that time prior to y beginning to exist is time in which y did not exist.

14. Y has not existed for an infinite time (13). Given that there has been time in which y has not existed, y has not existed "forever."

15. Y has both existed for an infinite time, and has not existed for an infinite time (9, 14). We now have exposed a contradiction. We inferred as of premise 14 that y has *not* existed for an infinite time, but premise 9 required that y *has* existed for an infinite time. According to the argument, then, y both has and has not existed for an infinite time—a clear contradiction.

16. (10), and thus (6), are false (6, 10, 15—by *reductio ad absurdum*). We began the attempted *"reductio"* in premise 6. Premise 6 claimed that all existing things are CBs, and y was just one example of a CB. However, by starting with those assumptions, we generated a contradiction. Logically, then, we're entitled to negate the premise that generated the contradiction. This suggests that premise 6 is false, as is premise 10 (since it was our assumptions about y that generated the contradiction). It is false that y is a CB, and also false that all existing things are CBs.

17. Therefore, y is a NB (1, 16). If y is not a CB, and all existing things are either CBs or NBs, then y must be a NB.

18. Therefore, at least one NB exists (17). Simply put: if y is a NB, there must exist at least one NB (namely, y!).

You shouldn't feel embarrassed about having to read, and re-read that argument (and its explanation) multiple times before it even *starts* to make sense. It is a difficult argument to understand—and even if you understand it, that doesn't entail that you must agree with it. Remember the context, though: some of Aquinas' variants of the CA depend (crucially) on the premise that an infinite regress (whether with regard to causation, or motion) is impossible. The beast of an argument above is meant to provide philosophical support for why an infinite series of HCs is impossible. A little later in this chapter, we will see an argument that attempts to show that an infinite series of LCs is also impossible. If both arguments "work," then infinite series of either type will be ruled out, indicating that there must be a "first" cause, a "first" mover— and proponents of the CA believe that to be God.

We're not yet done with Aquinas, though. We have one more version of the CA— one that doesn't rely on the impossibility of infinite series. It will, however, make use of the now-familiar vocabulary of NBs and CBs.

Aquinas' "3rd Way"

> The third way is taken from possibility and necessity, and runs thus. We find in nature things that are possible to be and not to be, since they are found to be generated, and to corrupt, and consequently, they are possible to be and not to be. But it is impossible for these always to exist, for that which is possible not to be at some time is not. Therefore, if everything is possible not to be, then at one time there could have been nothing in existence. Now if this were true, even now there would be nothing in existence, because that which does not exist only begins to exist by something already existing. Therefore, if at one time nothing was in existence, it would have been impossible for anything to have begun to exist; and thus even now nothing would be in existence---which is absurd. Therefore, not all beings are merely possible, but there must exist something the existence of which is necessary. But every necessary thing either has its necessity caused by another, or not. Now it is impossible to go on to infinity in necessary things which have their necessity caused by another, as has been already proved in regard to efficient causes. Therefore we cannot but postulate the existence of some being having of itself its own necessity, and not receiving it from another, but rather causing in others their necessity. This all men speak of as God.

We may formalize Aquinas' argument in the following way:

1. Some contingent beings (CBs) exist ("We find in nature things that are possible to be and not to be, since they are found to be generated, and to corrupt, and consequently, they are possible to be and not to be.").
2. If any contingent beings exist, then a necessary being (NB) exists ("not all beings are merely possible, but there must exist something the existence of which is necessary.").
3. Therefore, a NB exists ("Therefore we cannot but postulate the existence of some being having of itself its own necessity").
4. ("This all men speak of as God.")

What are we to make of this argument so far? It appears to be valid. That is, if both premise 1 and 2 are true, the conclusion must also be true. Is it sound? Premise

1 is hardly controversial. It seems pretty obvious that some CBs exist. I think I'm a decent example of one myself! So, if any part of this argument has the potential to be controversial, it's going to be premise 2. As support for premise 2, Davis suggests the following thought experiment/argument.

1. Suppose *only* CBs exist
2. Suppose 10^{100} CBs
3. Suppose no overlapping lifespans
4. Suppose the sum total of these lifespans is $10^{10^{100}}$ years
5. Suppose time is infinite
6. If time is infinite, then, if nothing else, there was nothing $10^{10^{100}}$ years ago
7. But, from nothing comes nothing (*"ex nihilo, nihilo fit"*)
8. Therefore, nothing would exist *now*
9. However, some CBs do exist now
10. Therefore, at least 1 NB exists.

Just as we did with the previous argument, we will dissect this argument one premise at a time.

1. Suppose *only* CBs exist. Our thought experiment stipulates that there are no NBs, only CBs.

2. Suppose 10^{100} CBs. We are to imagine that the total number of CBs in existence is equal to 10 to the hundredth power (i.e., one followed by 100 zeroes). You might think that it's arbitrary and speculative to suppose a certain number of CBs that exists, and it probably is. However, the intent with this number is to be breathtakingly generous, to assume far more CBs than is likely to exist. After all, the total number of atoms in the entire universe is estimated to be 10^{80}—a number that, while huge, is much smaller than 10^{100}. If anything, this premise supplies far too many CBs.

3. Suppose no overlapping lifespans. Suppose that none of these CBs overlap in their lifespans. This is not true, obviously, since every CB that exists right now is overlapping in lifespan—but, again, the point is to be overgenerous. By assuming that only one CB exists at a time, and that another CB only comes into existence as its predecessor completes its lifespan, we produce a total lifespan that is far larger in duration than would exist in real life.

4. Suppose the sum total of these lifespans is $10^{10^{100}}$ years. This is another one of those breathtakingly generous premises. The thought experiment proposes that the total sum of all the lifespans of those CBs is a "googolplex." Keep in mind that according to Big Bang cosmology, the universe is only 15 billion years old (roughly). Using scientific notation, that would be 15^9 years: 15, followed by 9 zeroes. Premise 4 is allowing that the total amount of time that has passed thus far is 1 followed by a googol (10^{100}) number of zeroes!

Honestly, that's a span of time so incomprehensibly vast as to be, well, incomprehensible!

5. Suppose time is infinite. This is admittedly a controversial premise, today, as it is by no means obvious that time is infinite. But, Aquinas seemed to think it was (for the sake of argument), and we're exploring Aquinas' argument.

6. If time is infinite, then, if nothing else, there was nothing $10^{10^{100}}$ years ago. As big a number as that is, it's still less than infinity. So, if time really does run "forever" into the past, then if the total lifespan (combined) of all CBs is $10^{10^{100}}$, then as we soon as get past that number (in the past), we will reach a point beyond the lifespans of all the CBs—in other words, a point at which no CBs exist.

7. But, from nothing comes nothing ("ex nihilo, nihilo fit"). This is basic philosophical principle that is admittedly impossible to prove, but is taken for granted and continually reinforced each and every day. Someone could argue, of course, that premise 7 is false, but they take upon themselves a heavy burden of proof, in that case.

8. Therefore, nothing would exist *now*. If at some really distant point in the past, no CBs existed, and if it's impossible for something (e.g., a CB) to come from "nothing," then that would entail that no CBs exist now.

9. However, some CBs do exist now. Common sense observation: some CBs (e.g., you, me, etc.) do exist right now.

10. Therefore (by *"reductio ad absurdum"*), at least 1 NB exists. Once again we have the result of a *"reductio."* If we start with the assumption that there exists only CBs, and that premise leads us to a contradiction, we are entitled to negate the offending premise. In this case, that entails that at least one NB exists (i.e., it is not the case that all existing things are CBs).

A basic assumption driving all variants of the CA is that "something" can't come from "nothing." Given that "something" exists now, "something" must have always existed—otherwise the first "something" would have had to come from "nothing." There are two ways we might account for the present existence of "something:"

i.   At least one (singular) thing has always existed (i.e., is an NB), and is the source of all the other "somethings" (CBs) that exist now.
ii. An infinite regress of "somethings" (CBs) stretch forever back in time, without any start to the series of CBs.

One of Aquinas' arguments is for the necessity of at least one NB, and his other two argue for the same conclusion but by demonstrating the impossibility of infinite regress. The specific kind of infinite regress he attempts to rule out is a hierarchical series. Now we will turn to another variant of the CA that attempts to rule out the possibility of an infinite linear series as well.

The Kalam Cosmological Argument (KCA)

The KCA is a variant of the CA, called the "Kalam" CA because it developed in the "Kalam" ("discursive") tradition of Islamic philosophy (notably by Al-Kindi and Al-Ghazali). The KCA owes its present popularity to the American philosopher of religion William Lane Craig. His version of the KCA is quite simple in its formulation.

1.   Everything that begins to exist has a cause.
2.   The universe began to exist.
3.   Therefore, the universe must have a cause.

The first premise is thought to be relatively uncontroversial. In our experience, everything that begins to exist has a cause. Objects don't spring forth from "nothing." Causality runs through every event that we've ever experienced. What's more, if it were possible for things to come to exist from (literally) *nothing*, why don't we observe such magical events occurring? The fact is that we don't. Quite the contrary. It's theoretically possible, of course, that there might be some things that begin to exist without any cause whatsoever, but we have no experience of that, and the burden of proof is presumably on those that would wish to deny premise one, rather than on those who assert it.

The second premise asserts that the universe began to exist. It's possible that the universe is, instead, eternal, and has always existed—but you won't find many astronomers today willing to make that claim. The dominant "big bang" model of the universe claims that the universe (including both space and time) came into existence roughly 14 billion years ago.[89] If we assume the big bang model is accurate (as Craig does), it does indeed indicate that the universe began to exist several billion years ago.

Must we rely on assumption only, though? Craig believes a variety of evidence exists to support the second premise of the KCA, both scientific and philosophical. We will begin with some of his philosophical evidence.

If the universe never began to exist, and is, instead, "eternal," then history is an infinite series of events stretching into the past. Craig thinks that such an infinite series is impossible to attain "*in re*," though we might have a perfectly decent abstract concept of such infinitude "*in intellectu*." The argument that attempts to show that an actually existing ("*in re*") infinite number of things (such as historical events stretching back infinitely into the past) cannot exist is as follows:

---

[89] Some astrophysicists propose that the big bang is part of an eternal cycle in which the universe expands from a singularity, then eventually contracts, then has another big bang, then another contraction, and so on for all eternity. This "oscillating" model does not claim that the universe began to exist, but it's also not a generally accepted model of our universe. Indeed, there are many arguments against this model.

1. The universe can be understood as either a finite series, or an infinite series.
2. If finite, then there is a "beginning."
3. If infinite, then the series of all past events is infinite, and there is no "beginning" to the series.
4. A beginning-less series of events in time entails an actually infinite number of things.
5. But, an actually infinite series of events can't exist.
6. Therefore, a beginning-less series of events in time cannot exist.
7. Therefore, the universe began to exist.

Premise 1 seems to be a statement of the logical possibilities: the universe consists of either a finite series of events, or an infinite series. Premise 2 acknowledges that if the series is finite, it necessarily has a beginning simply by virtue of our concept of "finite." If, however, the series is infinite, then there is no beginning (premise 3). Premise 4 claims that an infinite series entails an actually infinite number of things (e.g., moments in time, events, movements of particles, etc.). Here, it would be useful to distinguish "actual infinites" from "potential infinites." Since we're using these terms in the context of Craig's argument, we'll use the terms as he understands them.

An actual infinite is a collection of definite and discrete members whose number is greater than any natural number 0, 1, 2, 3 . . . This sort of infinity is used in set theory to designate sets that have an infinite number of members, such as {0, 1, 2, 3 . . .}. The symbol for this kind of infinity is the Hebrew letter aleph: ℵ. The number of members in the set of natural numbers is ℵ0. By contrast, a potential infinite is a collection that is increasing toward infinity as a limit but never gets there. The symbol for this kind of infinity is the lemniscate: ∞. Such a collection is really indefinite, not infinite. For example, any finite distance can be subdivided into potentially infinitely many parts. You can just keep on dividing parts in half forever, but you will never arrive at an actual "infinitieth" division or come up with an actually infinite number of parts.[90]

Premise 5 claims that an actually infinite series of events can't exist—and the rest of the argument follows from that, to the conclusion that the universe began to exist. This premise is the key to the KCA, and is the premise most likely to be challenged. As such, it requires justification. Why can't an "actual infinite" exist?

Technically, an actual infinite *can* exist (according to Craig), but (returning to our previous vocabulary), only "*in intellectu.*" That is, the concept of an actual infinite can be a meaningful and productive item in a particular "universe of discourse" (e.g,. set theory), but that doesn't mean that actual infinites exist "*in re*" as well. We can have conversations, and populate our "universe of discourse" with all sorts of things that make sense within the context of that conversation. I could, for example, have a

---

[90]Craig, *Reasonable Faith*, 116-117.

conversation with a friend about Darth Vader. Within the context of Star Wars, Darth Vader is Luke's Skywalker's father, and he was also a Sith Lord. Those words have meaning, and anyone familiar enough with the Star Wars "universe of discourse" can understand the conversation, participate in it, draw conclusions, make inferences, etc. None of that means there really is some guy named Darth Vader out there somewhere in space who can manipulate the dark side of the Force! Analogously, mathematicians can have meaningful conversations in which actual infinites are a useful part of a coherent conversation—but that doesn't mean that actual infinites exist "out there" ("*in re*"). To imagine they could (or do) is to invite absurdities, as Craig observes.

First, consider a simple demonstration involving sets. In an infinite set, a part of the set can be equal to the whole set. For example, the set of all whole numbers is infinite. The set of all even numbers is also infinite. Even though even numbers are a subset of whole numbers (seemingly equal to ½ of the set of whole numbers), even numbers can, nevertheless, be placed in a 1-to-1 correlation with whole numbers and are therefore equal in number. That's sort of dizzying, when you think about it. In fairness, if all we're doing is playing around with "math," then, dizzying though the exercise might be, we might think we can get away with it. After all, we're only manipulating abstract (mathematical) objects. But, what happens when we try to import actual infinitude into the real (physical) world?

Craig famously uses the example of "Hilbert's Hotel"[91] to demonstrate that absurd consequences result when we try to imagine actual infinites existing "*in re.*" What follows is a rough paraphrase of Craig's argument.

When we imagine a hotel with a finite number of rooms (i.e., any and every hotel of which we have any experience), we have a perfectly decent understanding of the consequences of there being no vacancies. If all the rooms are already occupied, there are no more rooms available. No one else can check in—at least not until someone else checks out. The math is simple, and easy to visualize. Suppose there are twenty rooms, each with only one occupant. That means there are twenty guests. Suppose one guest checks out. There are now nineteen guests, and one empty room. Suppose three more guests check out. There are now sixteen guests, and four empty rooms. Suppose four guests check in. There are now twenty guests (again), and no empty rooms. Easy, and obvious.

Now imagine a hotel with an infinite number of rooms. Keep in mind that this must be a physically-existing hotel; an actual "brick and mortar" building, occupying space, with features otherwise consistent with hotels. It will not do to imagine some sort of "mental" hotel, or a "non-spatial" hotel, since the very issue at stake is whether or not an actual infinite (in this case, a hotel with an actually infinite number of rooms) is possible "*in re.*" This hotel, as stated, has an infinite number of rooms. Each room is occupied by a single guest, indicating that each of the infinitely many rooms is occupied, and that there are no vacancies due to presence of the infinite number of guests already staying at the hotel.

Now imagine someone enters the lobby, hoping to stay at the hotel. The manager, eager to please, shifts the guest in room #1 into room #2, the guest in room #2 into room #3, and so on out to infinity. There is now an open room (#1), and the new guest

---

[91] Named after the German mathematician David Hilbert.

checks in. Even though every room was already occupied, a room was made vacant without anyone needing to check out or double-up—and the number of guests remains exactly the same (infinitely many).

Now imagine an infinite number of guests arrive in town for a conference on the absurdities of actual infinites, and they all wish to check in. The manager, eager to please, shifts the guest in room #1 into room #2, the guest in room #2 into room #4, the guest in room #3 into room #6, the guest in room #4 into room #8 (etc.—with each guest being placed into the room equal to twice the number of her original room number). As a result, every odd-numbered room is now vacant. There are an infinite number of odd-numbered rooms, which is just perfect for that infinite number of new guests! So, an infinite number of new guests have arrived and have been accommodated, even though every room was already occupied, no one had to check out, and the total number of guests remains the same (infinitely many) despite the addition of an infinite number of new guests.

If you're thinking to yourself "that doesn't make any sense," then you have grasped Craig's point. Actual infinitude, while perfectly at home and coherent within the context of a purely abstract, mathematical "universe of discourse," ceases to be coherent once transported into the physical world. If that is correct, then we have a philosophical demonstration that actual infinites cannot exist "*in re.*" If an eternal universe entails an actual infinite, then the universe can't be eternal (i.e., it must have begun to exist).[92]

In addition to philosophical arguments (of which we reviewed just one) demonstrating that the universe began to exist, Craig also points to a variety of scientific evidence that also supports that premise. Allow me a blunt disclaimer: I am a philosopher, not a physicist or astrophysicist. It is undoubtedly true that an astrophysicist could (and, one would hope, *would*) explain the following scientific evidence in more detail and greater sophistication. It should go without saying that we will only be scratching the surface, rather than plumbing the depths, of these fascinating ideas—but, for our purposes, that will have to do.

We will briefly consider two different lines of scientific evidence in support of the claim that the universe began to exist. The first concerns the expansion of the universe. Before the 20th century, astronomers assumed the universe was stationary and eternal, but in 1917 Einstein's General Theory of Relativity suggested that the universe could not be eternal and stationary. Shortly thereafter, Alexander Friedman and Georges Lemaître predicted an expanding universe. In 1929, Edwin Hubble's observation of the "red shift" of light from distant galaxies confirmed the expansion predicted by Friedman and Lemaître, and demanded by Einstein's theory. In brief, it demonstrated that the universe was expanding over time, and, if we "ran time backwards," the universe would shrink back down into a singularity of infinite

---

[92] It's worth noting, in connection to another version of the CA we examined earlier in this chapter, that the infinite series that the KCA is ruling out appears to be a linear series (i.e., one in which one event causes another event, which causes another event, which causes another event, etc.). Recall that the other CA ruled out an infinite hierarchical series. If both arguments "work," then both linear and hierarchical infinite series will have been established as impossible.

density at a finite point in the past (approximately 14 billion years ago). "Big Bang" cosmology had arrived. According to this model, all matter and energy, and even space and time themselves, came into existence from "nothing" by virtue of the Big Bang. The basic assumption of this Big Bang model (implied by the expansion of the universe) is that the universe came into existence at some point in the very distant past.

The second line of scientific evidence we will consider involves the 2nd law of thermodynamics. According to this 2nd law, within a closed system, processes will tend towards a state of equilibrium. Unless new energy is injected into the system, the system's processes will eventually run down and quit "processing". A practical application of this admittedly abstract principle is the fact that when you add hot water to a bath tub, the water disperses throughout the tub evenly, as opposed to some portions of the tub being hot, while others are cold. The application of this 2nd law to the universe is surprisingly similar to our bathtub example. On a purely naturalistic worldview, the universe is "everything." It is a closed system, comprising all matter and energy, and everything that exists. As a closed system, the 2nd law will apply to the universe. Over time, it will "run down" and achieve a state of equilibrium. Astrophysicists refer to this as "heat death." Oddly enough, there are two versions of this heat death: cold, and hot.

A "hot" heat death would occur if the universe's own gravitational pull is greater than the expansion force of the universe. In that case, the universe would expand (for a time), and then contract back on itself, crushing all matter and energy into a single, massive black hole from which the universe could not reemerge. But, if the universe has existed "forever," this should have already happened, and the current universe could not exist. Obviously, this event hasn't happened!

A "cold" heat death would occur if the force of expansion is greater than the gravitational force of the universe. In that case, the universe continues to expand, with all objects in the universe receding further and further apart from each other. Over time, the distances between objects will become incomprehensively vast. As Craig relates the data, "at 10^{30} years the universe will consist of 90 percent dead stars, and 9 percent supermassive black holes formed by the collapse of galaxies, and 1 percent atomic matter, mainly hydrogen. Elementary particle physics suggests that thereafter protons will decay into electrons and positrons, so that space will be filled with a rarefied gas so thin that the distance between an electron and a positron will be about the size of the present galaxy. At 10^{100} years, some scientists believe that the black holes themselves will dissipate by a strange effect predicted by quantum mechanics. The mass and energy associated with a black hole so warp space that they are said to create a 'tunnel' or 'worm-hole' through which the mass and energy are ejected in another region of space. As the mass of a black hole decreases, its energy loss accelerates, so that it is eventually dissipated into radiation and elementary particles. Eventually all black holes will completely evaporate and all the matter in the ever-expanding universe will be reduced to a thin gas of elementary particles and radiation. Equilibrium will prevail throughout, and the entire universe will be in its final state, from which no change will occur."[93]

---

[93] Craig, *Reasonable Faith*, 143.

At this point, the same question arises as was posed of the "hot" version of heat death: if the universe has existed "forever," why hasn't this already occurred? With respect to either version of heat death, the universe, over time, is "doomed" to either collapse in on itself, or else expand forever to a state of changeless, cold darkness. If an infinite amount of time has already passed, it would seem that either fate would have already occurred—but clearly this is not the case, thus suggesting that time is not infinite in the past. In other words, the universe began to exist. According to the KCA, if the universe began to exist, it must have had a cause....

Criticism of the CA

Like all TAs, the CA (including the KCA) has been subject to scrutiny and criticism. We will now consider some of the more common criticisms to have arisen over the centuries.

1. "What caused the First Cause (God)?"

All versions of the CA rely (among other things) on the assumption that "something" can't come from "nothing." The universe, therefore, must have come from "something." According to the KCA, because the universe began to exist, it must have a cause of its existence. It's understandable that a critic of the CA (or KCA) would wonder why the same demands shouldn't be placed on this First Cause (presumed to be God). Wouldn't it be the case that God would also need to have come from "something?" That God must have a cause of God's existence as well? Or, if not, then why can a theist accept God as a "brute fact" that doesn't require a cause, while the naturalist can't do the same for the universe itself?

In response to that criticism, let's first consider the sort of CA expounded by Davis. Recall that this version of the CA argued that there must be at least one NB in order to account for the existence of CBs. A NB, by its very nature, has always existed. It is eternal. It never came into existence, nor will it ever go out of existence. Questions of the form "what caused X?" can only apply to CBs, not NBs. Is this a case of special pleading? Not necessarily. This exemption from needing a causal explanation would apply to *any* NB, not just God. If someone could demonstrate that a NB is a logical impossibility, or an incoherent concept, then, of course, the argument falls apart. But, if one accepts the possibility of a NB, and if the CA proves the existence of at least one NB, then that NB does not require a cause of its existence, because *there could be no such cause.*

The same sort of reasoning is going to apply to the KCA. Recall that the KCA claims that whatever *begins to exist* has a cause. It makes no such claim about things that never began to exist. The cause of the universe is thought to be eternal, and therefore never began to exist—therefore, it doesn't have a cause of its own existence. Certainly, if the universe was eternal, and therefore never began to exist, it would not have a cause either—but the universe being eternal is contrary to both the philosophical arguments above as well as the Big Bang cosmology that dominates astrophysics.

2. All versions of the CA fail to prove *God's* existence.

This criticism is obviously true, up to a point. None of the versions of the CA (including the KCA) have "God" in their conclusion. Aquinas explicitly appeals to the "matching strategy" in his versions of the CA: "and this everyone understands to be God." To be sure, if the CA works, it proves the existence of a "first cause," or "prime mover unmoved," or "NB," and these philosophical concepts might or might not be the God described in the Western theistic traditions. Additional argument will need to be offered to provide some possible insight into the nature of that cause. Indeed, Craig believes that philosophical conceptual analysis reveals several intriguing features of this cause of the universe.

- Non-spatial (because it's the cause of space itself)
- Non-temporal (because it's the cause of time itself)
- Unchanging (because it's non-temporal, and time is, among other things, a measure of change)
- Non-physical/immaterial (because it's unchanging, and physical things are subject to change)
- Uncaused/beginningless (because it's the First Cause)
- One/singular (if we apply Ockham's razor, and resist "multiplying causes without necessity")
- Unimaginably powerful, even if not omnipotent (since it created the entire universe from "nothing," without any material cause)
- Personal (because, according to Craig, only persons/minds, and abstract objects, such as numbers, are timeless and material, and of the two, only persons can cause events to occur)

Craig's conceptual analysis is bold, and powerful (if successful). If his argument is correct, we have a philosophical reason to conclude that the universe had a cause of its existence. If his conceptual analysis is correct, we can deduce several fascinating features of this First Cause—all of which serve the "matching strategy," and imply that God is that First Cause.

Conclusion

Like most TAs, the CA attempts to start from publicly available, (relatively) non-controversial premises. Experience informs us all about motion, causality, and, with a bit more abstraction, necessity and contingency. The CA attempts to show that motion, causality (i.e., causal sequences), and CBs each require an "ultimate explanation." It attempts to show that our explanatory chain can't go on "forever," but must have a "stopping point" that is somehow an exception to that which it seeks to explain (i.e., unmoved, uncaused, NB). If the CA works, and it establishes the existence of a necessary, uncaused, unmoved being, this could provide warrant for the theists' belief in their God—even if the CA doesn't "prove" the existence of that God. This strategy of starting with publicly available evidence to infer the existence of something that "matches" with God will continue in our next chapter, as we consider variations of the Design Argument (DA).

St. Thomas Aquinas (1225 – 7 March 1274) was a Dominican priest and arguably the greatest theologian and philosopher the Catholic Church has ever produced. He is credited with incorporating Aristotle's philosophy into a Christian worldview (much as St. Augustine is credited with "Christianizing" Plato). This brief selection from his celebrated "Summa Theologica" includes his famous "five ways" (five arguments for God's existence). The first two arguments are variations of cosmological arguments, with one appealing to motion and the other to efficient causes. The third is a modal argument involving possibility and necessity. The fourth argument concerns "gradations" of qualities in things, and the implied ultimate source of qualities. Finally, he offers a teleological argument based on the seemingly "directed" features of Nature. Aside from the historical value of these arguments, they are important to consider in the context of contemporary philosophy of religion, as both cosmological and teleological arguments remain prominent, as are modal arguments to a lesser extent.

Summa Theologica[94]
St. Thomas Aquinas
Treatise on the One God

Question 2: The Existence of God (Three Articles)
Whether God exists?

Objection 1: It seems that God does not exist; because if one of two contraries be infinite, the other would be altogether destroyed. But the word "God" means that He is infinite goodness. If, therefore, God existed, there would be no evil discoverable; but there is evil in the world. Therefore God does not exist.

Objection 2: Further, it is superfluous to suppose that what can be accounted for by a few principles has been produced by many. But it seems that everything we see in the world can be accounted for by other principles, supposing God did not exist. For all natural things can be reduced to one principle which is nature; and all voluntary things can be reduced to one principle which is human reason, or will. Therefore there is no need to suppose God's existence.

On the contrary, It is said in the person of God: "I am Who am."

I answer that, The existence of God can be proved in five ways.

The first and more manifest way is the argument from motion. It is certain, and evident to our senses, that in the world some things are in motion. Now whatever is in motion is put in motion by another, for nothing can be in motion except it is in potentiality to that towards which it is in motion; whereas a thing moves inasmuch as it is in act. For motion is nothing else than the reduction of something from potentiality to actuality. But nothing can be reduced from potentiality to actuality,

---

[94]http://www.booksshouldbefree.com/download/text/Will-to-Believe-and-Other-Essays-in-Popular.txt

except by something in a state of actuality. Thus that which is actually hot, as fire, makes wood, which is potentially hot, to be actually hot, and thereby moves and changes it. Now it is not possible that the same thing should be at once in actuality and potentiality in the same respect, but only in different respects. For what is actually hot cannot simultaneously be potentially hot; but it is simultaneously potentially cold. It is therefore impossible that in the same respect and in the same way a thing should be both mover and moved, i.e. that it should move itself. Therefore, whatever is in motion must be put in motion by another. If that by which it is put in motion be itself put in motion, then this also must needs be put in motion by another, and that by another again. But this cannot go on to infinity, because then there would be no first mover, and, consequently, no other mover; seeing that subsequent movers move only inasmuch as they are put in motion by the first mover; as the staff moves only because it is put in motion by the hand. Therefore it is necessary to arrive at a first mover, put in motion by no other; and this everyone understands to be God.

The second way is from the nature of the efficient cause. In the world of sense we find there is an order of efficient causes. There is no case known (neither is it, indeed, possible) in which a thing is found to be the efficient cause of itself; for so it would be prior to itself, which is impossible. Now in efficient causes it is not possible to go on to infinity, because in all efficient causes following in order, the first is the cause of the intermediate cause, and the intermediate is the cause of the ultimate cause, whether the intermediate cause be several, or only one. Now to take away the cause is to take away the effect. Therefore, if there be no first cause among efficient causes, there will be no ultimate, nor any intermediate cause. But if in efficient causes it is possible to go on to infinity, there will be no first efficient cause, neither will there be an ultimate effect, nor any intermediate efficient causes; all of which is plainly false. Therefore it is necessary to admit a first efficient cause, to which everyone gives the name of God.

The third way is taken from possibility and necessity, and runs thus. We find in nature things that are possible to be and not to be, since they are found to be generated, and to corrupt, and consequently, they are possible to be and not to be. But it is impossible for these always to exist, for that which is possible not to be at some time is not. Therefore, if everything is possible not to be, then at one time there could have been nothing in existence. Now if this were true, even now there would be nothing in existence, because that which does not exist only begins to exist by something already existing. Therefore, if at one time nothing was in existence, it would have been impossible for anything to have begun to exist; and thus even now nothing would be in existence---which is absurd. Therefore, not all beings are merely possible, but there must exist something the existence of which is necessary. But every necessary thing either has its necessity caused by another, or not. Now it is impossible to go on to infinity in necessary things which have their necessity caused by another, as has been already proved in regard to efficient causes. Therefore we cannot but postulate the existence of some being having of itself its own necessity, and not receiving it from another, but rather causing in others their necessity. This all men speak of as God.

The fourth way is taken from the gradation to be found in things. Among beings there are some more and some less good, true, noble and the like. But "more" and "less" are predicated of different things, according as they resemble in their different ways something which is the maximum, as a thing is said to be hotter according as it more nearly resembles that which is hottest; so that there is something which is truest, something best, something noblest and, consequently, something which is uttermost being; for those things that are greatest in truth are greatest in being, as it is written in Metaph. ii. Now the maximum in any genus is the cause of all in that genus; as fire, which is the maximum heat, is the cause of all hot things. Therefore there must also be something which is to all beings the cause of their being, goodness, and every other perfection; and this we call God.

The fifth way is taken from the governance of the world. We see that things which lack intelligence, such as natural bodies, act for an end, and this is evident from their acting always, or nearly always, in the same way, so as to obtain the best result. Hence it is plain that not fortuitously, but designedly, do they achieve their end. Now whatever lacks intelligence cannot move towards an end, unless it be directed by some being endowed with knowledge and intelligence; as the arrow is shot to its mark by the archer. Therefore some intelligent being exists by whom all natural things are directed to their end; and this being we call God.

Reply to Objection 1: As Augustine says (Enchiridion xi): "Since God is the highest good, He would not allow any evil to exist in His works, unless His omnipotence and goodness were such as to bring good even out of evil." This is part of the infinite goodness of God, that He should allow evil to exist, and out of it produce good.

Reply to Objection 2: Since nature works for a determinate end under the direction of a higher agent, whatever is done by nature must needs be traced back to God, as to its first cause. So also whatever is done voluntarily must also be traced back to some higher cause other than human reason or will, since these can change or fail; for all things that are changeable and capable of defect must be traced back to an immovable and self-necessary first principle, as was shown in the body of the Article.

Chapter 6: The Design Argument

Comprehension questions you should be able to answer after reading this chapter:

1. What are some possible examples of "design" in the universe?

2. What is Paley's "watch argument?"

3. What is the fine-tuning version of the DA (in general)? What is Ross' version? What is the "privileged planet" version (Gonzalez & Richards)?

4. What is the "weak analogy" criticism of the DA?

5. How can evolution be seen as a threat to the DA?

6. What is the "multi-verse" criticism of the DA?

7. What is the "part to whole reasoning" criticism of the DA?

8. What is the "limited conclusion" criticism of the DA?

The Design Argument (DA), like the CA, is an ancient type of TA. Although what was being "proved" was, of course, not the same thing as with contemporary versions, we find examples of the DA from both Plato and Aristotle.

from the order of the motion of the stars, and of all things under the dominion of the mind that ordered the universe" (Plato, Laws, 12.966E, emphasis added).

When thus they would suddenly gain sight of the earth, seas, and the sky; when they should come to know the grandeur of the clouds and the might of the winds; when they should behold the sun and should learn its grandeur and beauty as well as its power to cause the day by shedding light over the sky; and again, when the night had darkened the lands and they should behold the whole of the sky spangled and adorned with stars; and when they should see the changing lights of the moon as it waxes and wanes, and the risings and settings of all these celestial bodies, their courses fixed and changeless throughout all eternity— when they should behold all these things, most certainly they would have judged both that there exist gods and that all these marvelous works are the handiwork of the gods."(Aristotle, Fragment, "On Philosophy," emphasis added)

We also find an implicit DA in the Psalms (19:1) of the Old Testament:

The heavens declare the glory of God;
    the skies proclaim the work of his hands.
Day after day they pour forth speech;

night after night they reveal knowledge.
They have no speech, they use no words;
   no sound is heard from them.
Yet their voice goes out into all the earth,
   their words to the ends of the world." (emphasis added)

And, in the New Testament, we find the following: "For what can be known about God is plain to them, because God has shown it to them. Ever since the creation of the world his eternal power and divine nature, invisible though they are, <u>have been understood and seen through the things he has made.</u>" (Romans 1:19-21, emphasis added).

Like the CA, the DA is also an "*a posteriori*" argument. The DA is driven by empirical observations of Nature and how it operates. Because it is empirically based, contemporary versions of the DA, especially, tend to make extensive use of scientific data. All versions of the DA will have in common not only that they are based on experience, observation, and inference, but also that their conclusions are probabilistic. These are inductive arguments that attempt to establish the likelihood of a certain kind of explanation for features we observe in the universe around us.

As a TA, the DA attempts to show (ultimately) the likelihood of God's existence as the best available explanation for the apparent "design" in Nature. If the argument works the way it is supposed to, it prods you into acknowledging that this world appears to have a certain order, structure, or apparent design to it, and then the argument offers two general possible explanations for that: intentional design, or random and unguided natural development. Between the two, the design argument will claim that intentional design seems most plausible—and this indicates the existence of some sort of "designer."

What sort of "apparent design" are we talking about? What follows are several kinds of candidates for "apparent design." It is possible that you might think that only some, or even none, of these candidates are actual indicators of design, but understand that these are the sorts of things that people using the DA tend to have in mind.

First, consider our own solar system. The orbits of all the planets around the sun are mathematically precise, elliptical, and predictable. Astronomers can tell us with staggering accuracy exactly where each planet will be on any given day of the year. You and I need not lose any sleep tonight worrying that Mars is going to crash into the Earth. It's just not going to happen. The mathematical structure and geometric precision of our solar system resembles (to some) a machine. Our solar system appears to be *designed* to function as it does.

For another possible example, consider ecosystems. Critics, and even average citizens, will sometimes express surprise, or even contempt, when environmental activists cry alarm when seemingly insignificant creatures are threatened. For example, many environmentally-oriented organizations are growing increasingly concerned about the toxicity of the Earth's oceans (as a result of pollution of various kinds, including fertilizer, among other products). The focus of this big problem might be smaller than you'd expect: krill. Krill are tiny shrimp-like invertebrates that fill the oceans. They consume phytoplankton and zooplankton (microscopic organisms), and are themselves eaten by many other creatures, including some kinds of whales. The problem is that certain kinds of pollutants inhibit the growth of invertebrate exoskeletons, and this means that krill might (ultimately) die out. "Who cares about krill?" you might wonder. Well, considering the concept of an ecosystem, we might all have a reason to care about the fate of krill. The fate of the krill is tied to the fate of everything that eats it (fish, whales, etc.). The fate of those things is tied to the fate of those who eat (or use, or care about) *them* (i.e., humans). The fate of the krill is even tied to oxygen-production in our atmosphere. In brief, these tiny shrimp-like creatures are pretty important to us.

What does any of this have to do with "design?" Some describe ecosystems as vast, intricate, biological machines, with each species serving as a gear or cog in that machine. Remove one of those gears, and the machine breaks down (or at least has to "adjust"). Suppose Nature is like a giant biological machine. What do we know about machines? They're *designed*.

Some marvel at the structure and operations of the human body. We can only go into the briefest of detail, but our heart is a pump, our kidneys are filters, and the skeleton and muscular system make up a system of pulleys and levers capable of brute force as well as intricate fine motor skills. Engineers, inspired by the "machinery" of our own anatomy, replicate it with robotics. If you look at a robot "arm," it's easy to see the "shoulder," "elbow," "wrist," "fingers," etc. Perhaps there's something to the analogy. We know that robots have the features they do because they were designed that way by engineers. Perhaps we have the features we do because we were "designed" that way as well.

There is another, common, example of the machinery of Nature: the laws of physics themselves. Briefly, as far as we know, the laws of physics are uniform, constant, the same throughout the whole universe, and mathematically simple. Our universe is not chaotic, it's ordered. Our universe's operations are understandable, and predictable, and can be expressed in surprisingly mathematically simple terms. There is math at the foundation of Nature, math that we can discover, understand, and put to our use. This order, simplicity, intelligibility, and predictability inspire some to see "design" behind these fundamental laws.

Finally, the emergence of life itself is sometimes taken as evidence of design. What we know is that our universe is extraordinarily hostile to life. So far as we know, the Earth is the only place in the entire universe capable of supporting life (as we know it). Everywhere else, the universe is deadly. What are the odds that life could emerge in our universe? We'll address this more when we get to the "fine-tuning" argument, but, for now, the answer is *really, really bad odds* that life could emerge by chance alone. If not by chance, then by what? "Design, perhaps?"

Although our treatment of Aquinas thus far focused on his variants of the CA, his "5th Way" is a version of the DA.

The fifth way is taken from the governance of the world. We see that things which lack intelligence, such as natural bodies, act for an end, and this is evident from their acting always, or nearly always, in the same way, so as to obtain the best result. Hence it is plain that not fortuitously, but designedly, do they achieve their end. Now whatever lacks intelligence cannot move towards an end, unless it be directed by some being endowed with knowledge and intelligence; as the arrow is shot to its mark by the archer. Therefore some intelligent being exists by whom all natural things are directed to their end; and this being we call God.[95]

Here, Aquinas appeals to observations of the operations of Nature indicating that they operate "designedly" to achieve their ends. Centuries later, William Paley would offer what is arguably the most famous version of the DA in the form of his "watch argument."

Paley

The argument is simple (on its surface). Paley invites us to imagine a scenario in which we are taking a country hike. We notice a stone upon the path. No big deal, right? No explanation needed—it's just a stone! Suppose, instead, that we spotted a watch?

All of the sudden, explanation is needed. The kind of answer that was permissible for the stone isn't permissible for the watch. Although we can get away with speculating that the stone has always been there, and was formed from natural processes, if we were to suggest the same of the watch, we would look foolish. Why? Because there are important and obvious differences between watches and stones. The watch has numerous features that indicate intentional design: geometric shapes, the interconnected (and moving) parts, the fact that there are *words* and *numbers* on the watch, etc. How are we confident that those are not the results of natural forces? Because, in our experience, Nature never (ever) produces, by itself, objects that look like that watch! When was the last time you saw a natural object (e.g., a rock, an orange, etc.) with numbers and letters on it (that hadn't been put there by a human)? Simply put, in our experience, although Nature often produces stone, it never produces watches. Humans do. So, when we encounter a watch, we naturally and confidently infer that someone, at some time, must have created it. Its features are taken to be such compelling evidence of design that we can't help but come to that conclusion. Indeed, he argues that it is a natural, inevitably, and unavoidable inference that the watch must have been designed.

The application of the watch story to the design argument is simply this: Paley claims that Nature has features similar to those of a watch, and that we should, therefore, infer a similar conclusion as to its origin.

1. Human artifacts (like watches) are products of intelligent design.
2. Nature resembles human artifacts.
3. Therefore, Nature is also a product of intelligent design.

The first premise should be uncontroversial. We know, from experience, that human artifacts (like watches) are products of intelligent design. Watches, or cars, or computers, or iPhones have the features they do because humans *designed* them that

---

[95] A larger section of this was provided at the end of the previous chapter.

way.

The second premise is the potentially controversial one. *How* Nature resemble human artifacts? In all those ways mentioned before in this chapter: the structure of the solar system, human anatomy, the laws of physics, ecosystems, etc. Paley's own preferred example is that of structure of the human eye.

WERE there no example in the world, of contrivance, except that of the eye, it would be alone sufficient to support the conclusion which we draw from it, as to the necessity of an intelligent Creator. It could never be got rid of; because it could not be accounted for by any other supposition, which did not contradict all the principles we possess of knowledge; the principles, according to which, things do, as often as they can be brought to the test of experience, turn out to be true or false. Its coats and humours, constructed, as the lenses of a telescope are constructed, for the refraction of rays of light to a point, which forms the proper action of the organ; the provision in its muscular tendons for turning its pupil to the object, similar to that which is given to the telescope by screws, and upon which power of direction in the eye, the exercise of its office as an optical instrument depends; the further provision for its defence, for its constant lubricity and moisture, which we see in its socket and its lids, in its gland for the secretion of the matter of tears, its outlet or communication with the nose for carrying off the liquid after the eye is washed with it; these provisions compose altogether an apparatus, a system of parts, a preparation of means, so manifest in their design, so exquisite in their contrivance, so successful in their issue, so precious, and so infinitely beneficial in their use, as, in my opinion, to bear down all doubt that can be raised upon the subject...."

Is it possible to believe that the eye was formed without any regard to vision; that it was the animal itself which found out that, although formed with no such intention, it would serve to see with?...There cannot be design without a designer, contrivance without a contriver...The marks of design are too strong to be got over. Design must have had a designer. That designer must have been a person. That person must have been God.[96]

Granting these examples of apparent design in Nature, how do we arrive at the conclusion from those premises? Here, there is some difference of opinion. Most interpreters of Paley tend to think that his argument parallels that of Hume's character "Cleanthes" (more on that later) and is therefore an argument by analogy. Other interpreters readily admit that Hume's version of the DA is analogical, but that Paley's version isn't technically, an argument by analogy. Rather than claiming "similar effects" observed in watches and Nature, this interpretation claims that it is

---

[96] Paley, William. *Natural Theology; Or, Evidences of the Existence and Attributes of the Deity. Collected from the Appearances of Nature.* 1809. Chapter VI. [A larger selection from this work is provided at the end of this chapter.]

identical effects (i.e., ordered arrangements) observed in each.[97] For our purposes, the subtleties of these distinctions (i.e., analogy v. inference) needn't be resolved, and can be left to specialists in both Paley and Hume. I personally think that the argument is analogical, in effect, even if it was not intended (strictly speaking) to be an argument by analogy—so we will continue as though it were an argument by analogy.

We engage in analogical reasoning all the time. It's indispensable to us on a daily basis. As a very simple example, suppose you look out a window right now and see smoke on the horizon. Any wild guesses as to what the cause of that smoke is? Fire, right? Did you know that it was fire? Probably not, but you'd still be pretty confident that it was. In your experience, every time you see smoke, there's a fire that caused it (or at least something burning, even if there are no visible flames). When you see smoke again, you draw upon your previous experiences with smoke and infer that the new case of smoke has a similar cause as all the previous cases: fire.

	Effect	**Cause**
Yesterday	Smoke	fire
Today	Smoke	?

All it takes to conclude that fire is (probably) responsible for today's smoke is previous experience with fire and smoke, and basic reasoning skills. Now let's apply this reasoning to the design argument.

	Effect	**Cause**
Watch	Structure/function/purpose	design
Universe	Structure/function/purpose	?

Paley is asking us to take a familiar object (a watch), and note the features that are evidence of design. Then, he invites us to notice similar features in the universe. If we know what causes those features in a watch (design), and we see those same kinds of features in the universe, we are led to infer that the cause is probably similar as well: design. Where there's smoke, there's fire....

Before considering any criticisms of this kind of argument, let us review a contemporary variation of the design argument known as the "fine-tuning" argument. This argument is also based on observation and inference, but the fine-tuning argument is based on probability calculations (both formal and informal). One of the virtues of this variation is that it is scientific. That is, it attempts to make use of the very latest findings of physics, astrophysics, and astronomy (not to mention statistics

---

[97] Indeed, some interpretations of Paley don't even agree that his argument is inductive. A deductive version of his argument is as follows: (1) We know that intelligent agents are capable of producing effects marked by the three properties of (i) relation to an end, (ii) relation of the parts to one another, and (iii) possession of a common purpose. (2) No other cause has ever been observed to produce effects possessing these three properties. (3) Therefore, if there are systems in Nature possessing these same properties, then the only cause adequate to account for these natural effects is an intelligent agent.

and probability). This is interesting because it flies in the face of the stereotype that science and religion must, for some reason, be "enemies." Another virtue of the fine-tuning argument is that it is contemporary. There are many philosophers, theologians, and scientists working on (and against) the fine-tuning argument right now.

"Fine-tuning" Argument

Older versions of the DA (e.g., those offered by Aquinas and Paley) tend to be arguments by analogy, or rely on biological examples of design, or both.[98] As we will see later in this chapter, either tendency can be vulnerable to certain sorts of criticism. More contemporary versions of the DA known as "fine-tuning" arguments (FT), on the other hand, operate differently, and are therefore immune to most of the older criticisms usually leveled at the DA. They will invite new criticism of their own, of course, but before addressing criticism (new or old), let's see how the FT arguments work.

To begin with, I can't resist pointing out what Paley had to say, centuries ago, on this topic:

> My opinion of Astronomy has always been, that it is not the best medium through which to prove the agency of an intelligent Creator; but that, this being proved, it shows, beyond all other sciences, the magnificence of his operations. The mind which is once convinced, it raises to sublimer views of the Deity than any other subject affords; but it is not so well adapted, as some other subjects are, to the purpose of argument. We are destitute of the means of examining the constitution of the heavenly bodies.... After all; the real subject of admiration is, that we understand so much of astronomy as we do. That an animal confined to the surface of one of the planets; bearing a less proportion to it than the smallest microscopic insect does to the plant it lives upon; that this little, busy, inquisitive creature, by the use of senses which were given to it for its domestic necessities, and by means of the assistance of those senses which it has had the art to procure, should have been enabled to observe the whole system of worlds to which its own belongs; the changes of place of the immense globes which compose it; and with such accuracy, as to mark out beforehand, the situation in the heavens in which they will be found at any future point of time; and that these bodies, after sailing through regions of void and trackless space, should arrive at the place where they were expected, not within a minute, but within a few seconds of a minute, of the time prefixed and predicted: all this is wonderful, whether we refer our admiration to the constancy of the heavenly motions themselves, or to the perspicacity and precision with which they have been noticed by mankind.[99]

---

[98] In what was perhaps an anticipation of these fine-tuning arguments, Paley's *Natural Theology* does include some non-biological examples, but his overwhelming focus (several hundred pages worth!) is biological examples of design.

[99] Paley, Ibid., Chapter XXII.

Paley clearly preferred biological examples, but this might have been largely due to the literal closeness and availability of biological specimens, in contrast to the limited observations of astronomical objects, available in his time. Astronomers today are much better equipped and much better informed.

As the name suggests, FT arguments appeal to apparent "fine-tuning" observed in Nature. There are several variants of FT arguments, each emphasizing different purposes for which the universe appears to be finely tuned. In terms of the tuning itself, however, there appears to be two kinds:

- Constants of Nature
- Arbitrary physical quantities

The "constants of Nature" refer to a variety of values exhibited by Nature, of which the following is a partial listing:

Speed of light c: 2.99792458·108 m/s
Fine structure constant: 1 / 137.0359895
Electron rest mass me: 9.1093897·10-31 kg
Proton rest mass mp: 1.6726231·10-27 kg
Neutron rest mass mn: 1.6749286·10-27 kg
Gravitational constant G: (6.673 +- 0.010)·10-11 m3/kg·s2
Acceleration due to gravity g: 9.80665 m/s2

These constants are *included* in natural laws, but are not *determined* by them. For example, the Law of Gravity is $F = G Ma Mb / r2$, where G = (6.673 +- 0.010)·10-11 m3/kg·s2. The gravitational force (F) between two objects is determined not only by their respective masses (Ma and Mb), and by the distance between them (r), but also by the value for G (above). This value for G is the same no matter what two bodies we're dealing with, and no matter the distance between them.

The claim offered by FT arguments is that these constants must be "finely tuned" for life to be possible. To provide a sense of scale, consider the following values.

- Number of seconds in the entire history of the universe: 10^{17} (1 followed by 17 zeroes)
- Number of subatomic particles in the known universe: 10^{80}
- If the weak force constant were altered by 1 part out of 10^{100}, no life would be possible
- If the cosmological constant were altered by 1 part out of 10^{120}, no life would be possible

The point, of course, is that these values seem to be calibrated with a precision that defies our comprehension—and this calibration begs for an explanation.

The other sort of fine-tuning involves various arbitrary physical quantities in the universe present as initial conditions of the universe, and on which the laws of nature operate. One of the more commonly cited such quantities is the amount of "entropy" present at the very beginning of the universe. Similar to the values cited for various constants of Nature, the amount of entropy needed for our universe to have existed as it does is also (and even more) staggering. The odds of the "low entropy" initial state of the universe (necessary for our universe to exist as it does): $10^{10^{123}}$. Stephen Hawking has estimated that a decrease or increase of even 1 part in a hundred thousand million million (one second after the Big Bang) would have prevented the formation of galaxies. In other words, the odds of our universe existing as it does, where even *matter* is possible (let alone life!), is staggeringly poor by chance alone. Instead, proponents of FT arguments will claim, the universe appears to have been finely tuned for that outcome.

Note that I mentioned the conditions needed for matter (let alone life). This is an important distinction, actually. Oftentimes, the argument is presented using the language of "life as we know it." If the initial low entropy conditions had not been met, "life as we know it" would not have been possible. An immediate and common response is to propose that life *"other* than as we know it" would have possible instead, and we're then invited to imagine a colorful host of science fiction aliens, or (more abstractly) silicon-based life (as opposed to carbon-based), or sentient energy, etc. The FT argument (if successful) is more powerful than that, however.

> By 'life' scientists mean the property of organisms to take in food, extract energy
> from it, grow, adapt to their environment, and reproduce. The point is that in
> order for the universe to permit life so-defined, whatever form organisms might
> take, the constants and quantities of the universe have to be incomprehensibly
> fine-tuned. In the absence of fine-tuning not even atomic matter or chemistry
> would exist, not to speak of planets where life might evolve.[100]

Variations of FT arguments are abundant. Here is one offered by Hugh Ross[101]:

Hugh Ross

1. The combination of physical constants (and range for variables) we observe in our universe is the only one capable of supporting life.
2. Numerous other combinations were possible.
3. Fine-tuning of the constants so as to support life is not improbable if there was a designer.
4. Such fine-tuning is highly improbable under chance alone [approximately much less than 1 chance in one hundred billion, trillion, trillion, trillion exists that even one such planet (capable of producing/sustaining life) would occur anywhere in the universe].
5. Therefore, the best available explanation for the fine tuning is a designer.

---

[100] Craig, *Reasonable* Faith, 159.

[101] Ross is a contemporary "apologist," seeking to defend belief in Christianity. It is noteworthy that he has a degree in physics, and a Ph.D. in astronomy. Thus, he approaches this issue as a believer *and* a scientist. For more on Ross and his work, review his website: www.reasons.org.

Let us (quickly) review the argument, one line at a time. The first premise appeals to the conditions necessary for life, as we know it. There are dozens and dozens of such conditions, ranging from the common-sense examples to those that only scientists are likely to understand. Take a common-sense example: our planet must reside within a limited band of distance from the sun in order for life, as we know it, to be possible. If our planet were outside of this "circumstellar habitable zone," we could not live. If the Earth were very much closer to the sun, the planet would be too hot for us to survive. Much further away, and it would be too gold. Instead, we live in what is sometimes jokingly referred to as the "Goldilocks Zone:" it is neither too hot, nor too cold; it is "just right."

As additional examples of the sorts of factors has in mind, consider this very brief list (there are 154 of these on some versions of Ross' list! For a full "appreciation" of these factors, explore Ross' website: www.reasons.org):

1. galaxy size
    * if too large: infusion of gas and stars would disturb sun's orbit and ignite too many galactic eruptions
    * if too small: insufficient infusion of gas to sustain star formation for long enough time
2. supernovae eruptions
    * if too close: life on the planet would be exterminated by radiation
    * if too far: not enough heavy element ashes would exist for the formation of rocky planets
    * if too infrequent: not enough heavy element ashes present for the formation of rocky planets
    * if too frequent: life on the planet would be exterminated
    * if too soon: heavy element ashes would be too dispersed for the formation of rocky planets at an early enough time in cosmic history
    * if too late: life on the planet would be exterminated by radiation
3. parent star distance from center of galaxy
    * if farther: quantity of heavy elements would be insufficient to make rocky planets; wrong abundances of silicon, sulfur, and magnesium relative to iron for appropriate planet core characteristics
    * if closer: galactic radiation would be too great; stellar density would disturb planetary orbits; wrong abundances of silicon, sulfur, and magnesium relative to iron for appropriate planet core characteristics
4. parent star color
    * if redder: photosynthetic response would be insufficient
    * if bluer: photosynthetic response would be insufficient
5. distance from parent star
    * if farther: planet would be too cool for a stable water cycle
    * if closer: planet would be too warm for a stable water cycle
6. thickness of crust
    * if thicker: too much oxygen would be transferred from the atmosphere to the crust

- if thinner: volcanic and tectonic activity would be too great

The second premise points out the obvious: for every one of these conditions, the outcome *could* have been different. Returning to our previous example, the Earth could have been slightly closer to the sun, or further, or a lot closer, or a lot further, or any number of locations in between. This premise serves to illustrate that there are a staggering number of possible universes we might have had. Remember, there is a wide range of what was possible for every single one of those approximately 100 conditions needed for life. Multiply all the possible outcomes for each one by the total number of conditions we're tracking and we end up with a really, really big number of possible universes.

The third premise encourages us to consider the possible explanations for the actual universe we have. The universe was either intentionally designed, or it wasn't. Logic and common sense combine with that statement of the obvious. *If* the universe were intentionally designed, there's nothing surprising about us having a universe capable of supporting life. In other words, *if* God exists, and if God created the universe, and *if* God wanted that universe to support life, it stands to reason we would have the kind of universe that we actually have (i.e., one in which life is possible!).

The fourth premise considers the other possibility, that the universe is not the product of intelligent design. If we can't appeal to intentional design, we must appeal to blind natural processes instead. That we have the universe we do, one capable of supporting life, is not anything planned, but is the product of really good luck. What are odds that we would be so lucky? According to Ross' math, there is less than one chance in a hundred billion, trillion, trillion, trillion that even one planet capable of supporting life would exist anywhere in the universe.

The conclusion? Given two possible explanations for the *fact* that we *do* live in a universe capable of supporting life, the best available explanation is intentional design. Is it possible that we just got lucky? Sure, but it's very *improbable*. Ross' strategy is to cause us to marvel at how many things have to line up just right in order for life to exist, recognize how unlikely that is by chance alone, and conclude that intentional design is the best available explanation instead.

The most recent version of the fine-tuning argument is worth mentioning due to its unique contribution to the design argument. I call this the "privileged planet" argument, after the book and video of the same name. As you'll see, the argument is almost identical to Ross', with one notable exception.

"The Privileged Planet" (as developed by Guillermo Gonzalez and Jay Richards)

1. Background conditions must be "finely tuned" for intelligent life to exist in our universe.
2. Background conditions must be "finely tuned" for intelligent life to be able observe and study the universe.
3. Therefore, the odds against intelligent life existing and situated so as to study the universe are staggeringly small (by chance alone).

4. The odds are quite good, if the universe was *intentionally* "fine-tuned" for such a result.
5. Intelligent life exists, and in such a place that permits tremendous knowledge acquisition.
6. Therefore, the best available explanation for this fact is *intentional* "fine-tuning."

The unique contribution of Gonzalez and Richards may be found starting in the second premise. Beyond the conditions needed for life, they also focus on the conditions needed for scientific study of the universe itself. They point out that not only must conditions be "just right" for life to exist, but they must also be "just right" for us to be able to study the universe in the manner we have. In many cases, the conditions needed for life, and those needed for scientific discovery will be the same (obviously, if I can't survive our atmosphere, I can't study it either!), but in many cases, the conditions needed for study are "extra." Their simplest and most memorable example involves a total solar eclipse.

A total solar eclipse occurs when the Moon passes between the Earth and the Sun. What makes a *total* eclipse possible is that the Moon and Sun appear to be exactly the same size, and therefore the moon can completely block the sun for a brief period of time. They're not the same size, of course. The sun is about 400 times larger than the moon, but it's also 400 times further away. This gives them the same *apparent* size. This is far more important than most realize. That we can experience a total eclipse does much more than present us with an opportunity to see something really pretty— it gives us an opportunity to study the chromosphere (the outer edge of the atmosphere) of the sun. The ratio of size and distance are critical here. If the moon were slightly larger, it would block too much of the sun; slightly smaller, and it would block too little. If it were slightly closer to the Earth, it would appear too large; slightly further away, and it would appear too small. Given the Earth, moon, and Sun being "just right" in terms of size and distance, just enough of the sun's light is blocked in order for scientists to study the sun's outer atmosphere. This allowed for the discovery of helium, and for an understanding of the composition of the sun. Since stars are simply other suns, this, in turn, opened up the field of astronomy and allowed scientists to learn about distant stars by comparing the properties of the light generated from those distant stars to that generated by our own. As a result, star types, age of stars, distances, and so on became available for study. What's more, a full solar eclipse allowed for a confirmation of Einstein's general theory of relativity. Notice that this goes beyond what's needed for life. Our moon could be slightly bigger or smaller, and we could still survive—but we couldn't make use of a total solar eclipse.

There are many more examples, but they go beyond the scope of our present project. Suffice it to say that Gonzalez and Richards will use these examples the same way that Ross did. Considering the conditions needed for a planet to permit both life and scientific discovery (a partial list includes the presence of liquid water, being located within the circumstellar habitable zone, having the right thickness of terrestrial crust, having a sufficient planetary magnetic field, having an oxygen-nitrogen atmosphere, having a large moon, orbiting a spectral type G2 dwarf main sequence star, being protected by gas giants, possessing a thin and transparent atmosphere, being located within a spiral galaxy, being located within the galactic habitable zone, having access to the visible light portion of the EM spectrum, having the right moon-planet-star relationship, etc.), they will ask us to consider the two possible explanations for the fact that we do have the conditions sufficient for both: intentional design, or chance. If the universe were intentionally designed, there would be nothing terribly surprising about the fact that our universe both supports life and is open to scientific study. If the universe were the product of lucky natural processes, though, the chances of our having a universe that not only meets the conditions needed for life but also for scientific study, are staggeringly bad: one in one thousandth of one trillionth, according to their conservative estimation. Just like Ross, they encourage us to conclude that the best available explanation for the universe we have is intentional design. In fact, Jay Richards cleverly claims that "the universe's features suggest conspiracy rather than coincidence"

Whichever version of an FT argument we consider, they have basic features in common. While older versions of the DA generally operate by analogy, FT variants are presented as inferences to the best explanation. If various constants and arbitrary quantities had to have particular values (or obtain values within a very narrow range) for our universe to exist as it does, and be life-permitting, what is the best explanation of the fact that the universe does exhibit those values? In general, we can present the core argument driving any FT argument in the following way:

1. The fine-tuning of the universe is due to physical necessity, chance, or design.
2. It is not due to physical necessity or chance.[102]
3. Therefore, it is due to design.

As we have done with other arguments, we'll consider this one each line at a time. The first premise claims that the apparent fine-tuning of the universe is due to one of the following: physical necessity, chance, or design. This premise is simply meant to exhaust the logical possibilities. Note that "fine-tuning" doesn't (and can't) mean "designed" without begging the question. So, fine-tuning, at this stage, just means that the features in question (i.e., the various constants and quantities) do, in fact, exhibit just the right values that they must exhibit in order for a life-possible universe to exist.

The second premise claims that this fine-tuning is not due to physical necessity or chance. With regard to physical necessity, this seems relatively uncontroversial. After all, why should we think that a life-prohibiting universe be physically impossible? Let alone logically impossible? Indeed, life-prohibiting universes seem far more *likely*—a point conceded by naturalists and theists alike. The far more plausible alternative to "design" is "chance." Admittedly, the odds of a universe like ours arising from unguided natural processes alone is breathtakingly poor—just consult any of the odds provided above! However, contemporary work involving multi-verse theories are summoned to provide support for precisely this alternative to design. We will get to that, and other objections, momentarily. For now, however,

---

[102] Where "chance" must refer to something like "unguided/unintentional natural processes."

let us acknowledge that *if* physical necessity and chance have been eliminated as the best explanations for the fine-tuning we observe in the universe, the only remaining explanation is design. In that case, the universe *appears* finely-tuned because it *is* finely-tuned.

As we have seen thus far, the DA is actually a collection of a variety of different kinds of arguments united by their general attempt to establish "design" as the best explanation for various features we observe in the universe. Older versions of the DA generally operate by analogy. FT arguments don't. Some versions of the DA employ biological examples, while others don't. Criticisms of the DA may be organized around which type of DA they address. We will begin with a criticism applying only to analogical versions of the DA, then consider a criticism applying only to DAs using biological examples of design, and conclude with several criticisms that could apply to any DA we've considered.

Paley and Hume

Before delving into criticism, I wish to engage in an act of personal/professional confession that I hope serves as a cautionary tale.

Paley published his *Natural Theology* in 1802. Hume's *Dialogues Concerning Natural Religion* was published three years after Hume's own death, in 1779. In case it wasn't obvious, Hume's criticism of the DA was published 23 years before Paley published his DA, and was written even earlier than that.

For years, I conveyed what I myself had been taught, and had read in numerous anthologies, about this unusual temporal relationship: "Paley seems to have been unaware of Hume's work and, therefore, unfortunately, didn't respond to his criticisms." Their non-encounter was taken to be one of the more glaring and unfortunate cases in the history of philosophy of "two ships passing in the night." If only Paley had been more well-read, he would have known that Hume offered numerous, "devastating" criticisms of the DA, and Paley, perhaps, could have tried to defend himself from them. What a shame, what a waste.

What a myth.

After years of teaching this story myself, I discovered, after reading more of Paley, and more carefully, the abject and undeniable *falsity* of this common view of the intellectual relationship between Paley and Hume. Paley mentions Hume, and the *Dialogues*, by name, in chapter 26 of *Natural Theology*.

> *Mr. Hume, in his posthumous dialogues, asserts, indeed, of idleness, or aversion to labour (which he states to lie at the root of a considerable part of the evils which mankind suffer), that it is simple and merely bad.*

Not only was Paley obviously aware not only of Hume's existence, but also that of the specific work in which the DA is criticized, Paley also addressed those criticisms, either implicitly, or, at times, explicitly. Indeed, one of Paley's chapter titles refers specifically to one of Hume's criticisms (as we'll see later).

I mention all this partly out of penance for my role in unwittingly perpetuating a falsehood about Paley, but also as a cautionary tale: just because something is repeated, from teacher to student, from one generation to another, doesn't necessarily mean that it's *true*.

Criticism

<u>Criticism of the Analogical DA: Weak Analogy (Hume)</u>

This criticism applies to any analogical version of the DA—including Paley's, if his version is indeed analogical. Any argument by analogy will only be as strong as the analogy itself. In other words, if the two things being compared are very similar, the argument has the potential to be quite strong. If the two things being compared are not very similar, the argument is weakened. We even have an expression in English to capture this idea: "that's like comparing apples and oranges." We use this expression when we think that things being compared just aren't sufficiently similar to make the desired point.

In reality, we engage in reasoning by analogy, or (more generally), inferential reasoning all the time. Many times, there is nothing faulty with this kind of reasoning at all. Indeed, without this kind of reasoning, much of what we reason about would be impossible. This kind of reasoning is problematic, however, when the analogy become strained.

For example, suppose that you are in class and you see me clutch my chest, complain of shortness of breath and chest pains, and then collapse onto the floor. Despite the fact that few (if any) of you are medical doctors, I'm sure you all have an educated hypothesis concerning what's wrong with me: a heart attack. How do you know this? Because you've seen (or heard about) other people with the same symptoms, and in those cases, it was a heart attack. What does that have to do with me? I'm a different person. Certainly, but I'm still a *person*. Different or not, I'm a human being just like all those other patients. Because human beings are all so biologically similar, it's reasonable for us to assume that our bodies operate and react in very similar ways. Since we all have the same kind of heart, it's reasonable for us to think that heart attacks will be experienced in very similar ways by any of us. If this kind of reasoning was faulty, medicine would be impossible. It is only because this kind of reasoning by analogy *does* work that we can accumulate theories of *human* health.

Continuing with the same example, suppose you come up with an amateur diagnosis of "heart attack." Suppose that there also happens to be a portable defibrillator in our classroom (don't ask why—just go with it).

Having seen enough television to know how this works, you leap into action, apply the shock paddles to my chest, shout "clear," and give me a good jolt. My heart starts beating again. Why would you think the paddles would help me in this situation? Because other human beings who were having heart attacks have been helped by the use of defibrillators—and I'm similar enough to other human beings for you to be confident it would work on me too.

Suppose that I return home, with a new appreciation for life, and having purchased my own portable defibrillator that I keep with me at all times (just in case). Upon returning home, I discover, to my horror, that my beloved cat Morgana is lying motionless, with her tiny paw clutching her chest. I freak out, then calm myself, and remember that wonderful defibrillator. I apply it to my cat's torso, and give her a good jolt. Any educated guesses as to how that's going to turn out? Probably nowhere near so well. Why? Because although my cat and I are both mammals, and both have hearts, we're not the same species, and not even close to the same size. The amount of voltage appropriate to shock me and that appropriate for a cat are likely to be pretty different. Because of some significant differences between myself and my cat, I should not be so confident that a medical intervention that worked on me will also work on my cat. One final example. Suppose I now look out on my balcony and notice that one of my cactus plants appears to be dead. My defibrillator battery still has some charge, so I head outside and give my cactus a good jolt. Pretty foolish, right? Why? Perhaps because my cactus is a plant? Because it doesn't even have a heart? Because the differences between humans and cacti are so great that very little medical information about one can be applied to the other?

What does any of this have to do with the design argument? Hume claims that the design argument is a weak analogy, that the two things being compared (the universe, and human artifacts, such as watches) are nowhere near similar enough to be able to draw compelling conclusions as to a similar origin.

> *If we see a house, Cleanthes, we conclude, with the greatest certainty, that it had an architect or builder; because this is precisely that species of effect which we have experienced to proceed from that species of cause. But surely you will not affirm, that the universe bears such a resemblance to a house, that we can with the same certainty infer a similar cause, or that the analogy is here entire and perfect. The dissimilitude is so striking, that the utmost you can here pretend to is a guess, a conjecture, a presumption concerning a similar cause; and how that pretension will be received in the world, I leave you to consider...[103]*

Moreover, the analogy is being driven by a unique sample (this is the one and only universe of which we have any experience), and a limited exposure to that unique sample at that (see the "part to whole reasoning" criticism later in this chapter)! An interesting feature of this criticism is that its success or failure depends entirely upon whether you think the analogy is weak, or strong, and our sample inadequate. That is, if you agree with Hume and believe that comparing watches and universes involves a hopeless analogy, and that the information we have at our disposal is insufficient to drive the analogy anyway, then you will agree with him that analogical versions of the design argument are weak. If, on the other hand, you think that the universe does resemble a watch in certain interesting ways, and that we have sufficient information on which to base that analogy, then you will disagree with Hume's criticism from the very start.

---

[103] Hume, David. *Dialogues Concerning Natural Religion*. 1779. Part 2. All of the quotations from Hume in this chapter come from his *Dialogues Concerning Natural Religions*, excerpts from which appear at the end of this chapter.

Criticism of Biologically-based DAs: Evolution

Although I believe the legendary conflict between evolution and theism to be exaggerated (in other words, there are interpretations of evolution and interpretations of theism that are not mutually exclusive, or even terribly antagonistic), there is a genuine sense in which evolution can be seen as a serious stumbling block for the design argument. Indeed, Richard Dawkins has claimed that "there has probably never been a more devastating rout of popular belief by clever reasoning than Charles Darwin's destruction of the argument from design."[104] In simple terms, the theory of evolution is a challenge to the design argument because the theory of evolution denies that there is any "design" in nature at all.

Remember, the design argument relies upon observing "design-like" features in nature, and inferring that the best explanation for this is that those features really are the result of intentional design. *If* one could demonstrate that the "design-like" features aren't really products of design, but can instead be explained by appealing to purely naturalistic processes in which design is not present, the design argument would be ruined. This is precisely what the theory of evolution threatens to do. First we must realize what the theory of evolution claims, and does not claim. This will be a scandalously brief treatment. Please bean in mind that I am a philosophy professor, not a professor of evolutionary biology, and that my Ph.D. is in philosophy, not evolutionary biology. If you're hoping for a nuanced and advanced exposition of evolutionary theory, you need to read someone else's book! But, for our purposes, we need only the basics.

"Evolution 101"

- Evolution: a change in the gene pool of a population over time.
- Gene pool: the set of all genes in a species or population.
- Species: all the individuals of a group that can exchange genes with one another
- Gene: hereditary unit that can be passed on (usually unaltered) for many generations.

Now that we have some core vocabulary in place, we can summarize the (general, basic) process of evolution:

1. Genes mutate.
2. Individuals are "selected," as a result of competition.
3. Populations evolve.

Mutation is a random process that increases genetic variation within a population. Mutations can be beneficial, harmful, or neither with respect to the organism in question—but most mutations are either neutral or harmful. Only a very

---

[104] Dawkins, Richard. *The God Delusion*, First Mariner Books edition, 2008, 103.

small percentage of mutations are somehow beneficial.

A simple way to think of mutation is as a copying error in which gene sequences are altered. When cells divide, they make copies of their DNA. Sometimes, the process is not executed perfectly, and the copy is not exactly the same. This deviance is a mutation. In movies and comic books, mutation occurs as the result of exposure to chemicals or radiation. Exposure to certain chemicals or radiation causes DNA to break down. Cells repair themselves, but sometimes the repairs are imperfect—resulting in a mutation. Although this is a "real thing," don't expect super-powered mutants to rampage through neighborhoods any time soon. Also, although environmental factors (such as radiation) might influence the rate of mutation, most evolutionary biologists believe that those factors don't influence the "direction" or mutation. In other words, living in an environment with high radiation levels might cause mutations to occur more often, but they won't cause mutations specifically pertaining to radiation, such as resistance to it. Mutation is capricious, and this is why it's called *random* genetic mutation. Whether or not a mutation occurs is independent of whether the mutation will actually be useful to the organism, let alone with respect to how, specifically, it might be useful.

The only sorts of mutations that matter on an evolutionary scale are those that will get passed on to offspring ("germ line mutations"). Such mutations can produce no perceivable effect on the phenotype (observable characteristics). In such cases, a mutation might occur in a portion of DNA that has no function, for example. Or, such mutations can produce a small change in the phenotype, such as a change in coloration, or ear shape, for example. Or, such mutations could produce a significant change in the phenotype, such as resistance to antibiotics in bacteria strains.

Random genetic mutation increases genetic variation within a gene pool, but natural selection *decreases* genetic variation by culling "unfit" variants from the pool. The ideas behind natural selection are pretty simple.

Some types of organisms within a population produce more offspring than others. Given time, this greater frequency will increase the numbers of this more prolific type within a population, and the population will change (evolve) to resemble that type. Living things are in competition with each other for food and reproductive access. Some members of each species are better (even if only slightly) at surviving and reproducing. This could be for any number of reasons. Perhaps they are stronger, or faster, or more clever, or blend in with their surroundings, or store fat more easily, or are resistant to a certain disease, etc. Survival is "sexy." To put it bluntly: dead creatures aren't very good at reproducing.

Arguably the most cited example of this process is work involves the "peppered moths" of England. Two major variants of this moth species occur in that area, and they are genetically identical except that one variant (a single gene) produces more melanin, causing it to be much darker in color. As a result, some moths within the population are white with black speckles, and others are just black. Historical records (such as records of moth specimen collections) reveal that the population has changed over time. Prior to the Industrial Revolution, and in rural areas far from industrial centers, the white speckled variants were more common, and the black variation quite rare. During and after the Industrial Revolution, when lots of coal was being burned, the population of moths shifted such that the black variant was much more prominent—up to 90%, in fact, although in rural areas the white speckled variation was still more numerous. What could account for these facts?

This species of moth spends much of its time perched on tree trunks. Before the Industrial Revolution, or in rural areas, such trees would grow lichen and the "speckled" moths would blend in very nicely against the trunks. This made them difficult to see, whereas the black variants were much more visible. As a result, the black ones got eaten more often, and therefore were less likely to reproduce. The population of moths favored the speckled variant. During the Industrial Revolution, however, urban areas were polluted by the soot of burning coal. This soot settled on tree trunks, killing the lichen and causing the trunks to appear black. In that context, the speckled moth is more visible, while the black variant blends in. The speckled moth gets eaten more often, the black variant reproduces more successfully, and the population of moths changed over time to favor the black variant. As a footnote to this story, with the imposition of environmental regulations since the 1950's, the air has gotten cleaner, soot has been reduced, and the tree trunks grow lichen again. The result? Once again, the speckled variant is favored, and the black variant has diminished within the population of moths.

To summarize this example: as a result of random genetic mutation, some moths are darker in color than their white/speckled peers. Given a particular environmental context ("sooty trees"), this mutation was advantageous and was therefore "selected" via natural selection. Over time, the population of moths changed (evolved) to reflect this.

Please note that the claim is that it is *populations* that evolve, not individual organisms (though natural selection occurs at the level of the individual). Continuing with that example, it's not as though a particular moth is growing darker over the span of its life, and seeing its chance for survival increase incrementally all the while. Rather, some moths reflect the mutation, and others don't. It just so happens that the mutation, in that case, is beneficial, and therefore gets passed down to new generations of moths. The population of moths, over a long span of time and many generations, changes to reflect this advantageous trait. As another example, *humans* have evolved, and continue to evolve, but individual human beings do not. In other words "Ted Preston" (I, the author) does not "evolve," but rather the species to which I belong evolves. To illustrate this, consider the uncomfortable example of obesity.

I have weighed various amounts over the span of my life thus far, sometimes "thinner," sometimes "heavier." The general explanation for why I weigh more or less at various times of my life (excluding obvious factors like being a tiny child as opposed to being a grown adult!) probably doesn't require much more insight than daily calorie intake and physical activity variations. My behavior contributes to my personal weight increases and losses, but it's not as if "humanity" is somehow being genetically altered to be fatter or thinner along with me.

That being said, a case can be made that humans, in general (at least in populations where food is abundant) *are* growing "heavier." Much talk is generated about the "obesity epidemic" in America, for example. Some medical doctors and nutritionists think there is an evolutionary explanation for this general trend of obesity. The idea is (roughly) this: *long* ago our human ancestors had far less reliable access to food. Hunting and gathering was not always successful, and sometimes humans starved. In that kind of environment, the tendency to store and retain fat would be advantageous. Those fat reserves could be used in "lean" times to allow the human to survive a bit longer, when food is scarce. Some humans were born, as a result of random genetic mutations, with a gene (or sequence of genes) that caused them to store fat more readily than other humans. That was advantageous to them. They were more likely to survive than their skinny, high metabolism neighbors. Because they were more likely to survive, they were more likely to reproduce, and they passed this "store fat" gene down to their children. Over time, this advantageous trait continued to be "selected for" and the population of humans changed, over a *long* span of time, such that the tendency to store fat became a common feature.

In those days, long ago, the tendency to store fat didn't entail that those early humans were all pleasantly plump, of course. There wasn't a surplus of food to make that possible, and there was plenty of physical activity with which to burn calories. Instead, it just meant that they didn't become "famine" skinny so easily, and were more likely to survive. Needless to say, times and circumstances have changed. In America, for example, you find very few "hunter/gatherers." We have an abundance of high calorie (processed) foods at our disposal, and many of us lead sedentary lives. Exercise is no longer a necessity for most of us, but a hobby, or a luxury pursued (often) for the sake of vanity. We still have our ancestors' disposition to retain fat, but we don't have our ancestors' food or lifestyle. The result? Many of us "retain" fat far more readily, and in excess, of what we would prefer, or is healthy.

On the assumption that this evolutionary account of our expanding waistlines is accurate, it reveals an important feature of natural selection: what is advantageous (selected for) is contingent upon the environmental circumstances at the time. The ability to retain fat might have promoted survival thousands of years ago, but might prove to impede survival now that our diets and lifestyles have changed.[105] Similarly, having a really long neck might be advantageous when there are tall plants to eat, but should all those plants die out, and the only plants that remain are low-lying shrubs, that long neck is no longer advantageous.

It is a very common *mis*understanding to believe that evolution "aims" at particular outcomes, or that the "goal" of evolution is survival, or reproductive fitness. In truth, classic evolutionary theory claims no such thing. Consider the following interpretations of a giraffe's long neck:

Design-minded theist: "The giraffe was designed to have a long neck. The reason it was designed that way was so that it could reach leaves on high branches."

Misguided wanna-be evolutionist: "The giraffe evolved to have a long neck, over time, in order to reach those leaves on the high branches."

Evolutionist who knows what she's talking about: "Long ago, some proto-giraffes were born pre-disposed to have slightly longer necks than their peers—perhaps

---

[105] Of course, strictly speaking, we need only to survive long enough to reproduce. So long as we delay our strokes and heart attacks long enough to have children, we've done the job our genes need us to do.

as a result of a random genetic mutation. This enabled them to reach higher branches, which gave them an advantage over others of their species. As a result, they had better reproductive success, and passed along that advantageous trait (i.e., a longer neck) to their offspring. Over a tremendous span of time, this trend continued and produced giraffes as we now know them."

The difference between the two understandings of evolution are subtle, at first glance, but terribly important. The *mistaken* view ascribes purpose, goals, aims, objectives, etc., to evolution—as if the proto-giraffe wanted to have a longer neck, and somehow made its offspring have longer necks as a result of its desire. The accurate view is that no one and no thing was trying to have a longer neck, or was supposed to have a longer neck. That some proto-giraffes had slightly longer necks was the result of a random genetic mutation. That mutation just so happened to prove beneficial. As a result, it was passed along to new generations of proto-giraffes, until, eventually, the species we know as giraffes came into being. Nature wasn't trying to make a giraffe. Nature doesn't "try" to do anything, in that sense (according to evolutionary theory). It's not the case that the giraffe grew a long neck in *order* to reach the leaves; it grew a long neck, and, as a result, was *able* to reach the leaves—and that gave it a reproductive advantage over its shorter-neck cousins.

Once we grasp this basic but important aspect of evolutionary theory, its challenge to the design argument should be clear. The design argument involves taking notice of various features in nature, detecting "design" in those features, and inferring that where there is design, there is likely a designer (or designers). For the strict evolutionist, what appears to be "design" to someone like Paley, is instead the result of natural selection in conjunction with random genetic mutation (and other factors serving to increase or decrease genetic diversity within a population). Instead of appealing to design, the evolutionist can appeal to natural selection. If there is no design, there is no need to posit a designer.

General Criticism: Who designed the "Designer?"

This criticism is similar to one we encountered when exploring the CA. As you might recall, some critics of the CA wonder why the universe must have a cause (and can't be a "brute" unexplained fact) if God is permitted to exist without a cause (as a "brute" fact)? Similarly, some critics of the DA, including such notable persons as Hume, and Richard Dawkins (echoing Hume in *The God Delusion*), raise the same sort of objection: "the designer hypothesis immediately raises the larger problem of who designed the designer." The objection seems to be that the design hypothesis doesn't actually accomplish anything since it merely pushes our explanation back one step. We appeal to a designer to account for the universe, but now we need something to account for the designer.

I don't editorialize often, but this is one of those rare occasions when I will. I have never understood why anyone has taken this to be a serious, credible objection. This is not to say that there are no serious, credible objections to the DA—indeed there are. This, however, is not one of them, in my opinion.

Explanations have "stopping points" based on what we're trying to explain. If I'm trying to explain why my car won't start, and I discover that the battery has no charge, I have an explanation for why my car won't start. It would be bizarre if someone then pointed out that because I don't know who made my battery, and under what circumstances it was made, I therefore have "accomplished nothing" with my explanation. If astronauts visit Mars and discover an ancient pyramid covered in what appears to be patterns of symbols, they would undoubtedly explain the existence of that pyramid by appealing to the historic presence of *some kind* of intelligent being or beings who constructed that pyramid. It would be absurd to deflate their discovery by pointing out that they don't know who those beings were, or what their ultimate origins are—and therefore the pyramid has no explanation. The explanatory process does not require an infinite regress of explanation, nor could it allow it. As Craig puts it, "in order to recognize an explanation as the best, you don't need to be able to explain the explanations. In fact, such a requirement would lead to an infinite regress of explanations, so that nothing could ever be explained and science would be destroyed."

While it is undoubtedly true that, even if the DA works, it has not provided an explanation for the existence of the "designer," nor particular features exhibited by the "designer," this is no serious objection to the DA itself. After all, it's not attempting to provide that information! *If* the DA provides the best explanation for the features of our universe, then it has "done its job" (in that context).

General Criticism: Weak Anthropic Principle

This criticism is based upon the recognition that "chance" is an alternative to design as a means to account for the fine-tuning of the universe necessary for life (or other purposes). A weak appeal to chance, sometimes invoked by critics of FT arguments, is simply a recognition that of the obscenely many possible configurations of the universe, *any* particular configuration is equally improbable, such that there is nothing especially improbable about our current (life-permitting) configuration. In other words, the universe had to turn out *somehow*, and any particular "somehow" is going to be unlikely, by chance alone. Therefore, a life-permitting "somehow" requires no special explanation.

This criticism overlooks a key point motivating the FT arguments, however. Consider a different example that should illustrate the point. Imagine that a computer program (or smartphone "app") is going to randomly generate a number between 1 and 100. Unless the number is 100, however, the computer (or phone) will explode, causing you great bodily harm. The odds of any particular number (1-100) being generated is the same: 1 in 100. So, it's true that the odds of any of those numbers being generated are the same. It's equally likely that you'll get 100 as that you'll get 23. There's nothing more shocking about getting 100 than getting 23, in terms of the odds.

This sort of observation is sometimes combined with what is known as the "weak anthropic principle" (WAP) to produce a criticism of the FT argument. Roughly, the WAP claims that conditions that are observed in the universe must allow the observer to exist. In other words, in order for there to even be observations about a universe in the first place, it has to be the sort of universe where observers could exist to make the observations! We shouldn't be surprised to discover that this universe is one where life is possible. If it weren't, we wouldn't be here to make any observations anyway.

In another (rare) editorial moment, allow me to say that this criticism, by itself, is silly—and I think it's easily shown to be so. The WAP sort of criticism relies upon a fundamental misunderstanding of what's being observed and explained in FT arguments.

Let's consider a different example. Imagine you have been kidnapped by a serial killer obsessed with Las Vegas games of chance. You are tied up in a chair, while the serial killer shuffles a deck of cards. He tells you that he's going to randomly deal you five cards from the deck, and that he is going to kill you—unless four of your cards happen to be aces. You are justifiably terrified. After all, the odds of being randomly dealt four aces in a five card hand is 1 in 54,145! Let's face it, you're doomed. . . He deals the cards, and you are shocked and relieved beyond description to discover that four of those five cards are, in fact aces. The serial killer notices the look of surprise on your face and asks, "why are you so surprised? After all, the odds of any particular hand are going to be terribly poor. It's just as likely that you would get four aces as that you would get four kings, for example. Nothing so interesting about what just happened...."

Although you probably wouldn't want to argue overly much with the serial killer, it's obvious that he has missed the point. It might be true that any particular hand is terribly unlikely, or even equally unlikely as any other hand, but that's not relevant to our example. The deck was stacked against you (pardon the pun). If *any* hand other than four aces was generated, you would be killed. The odds of getting those four aces was 1 in 54,145, but the odds of getting anything else (thereby resulting in your murder) was 54,144 in 54,145. To put it mildly, those odds are nowhere near the same. It was vastly more likely that you would get a lethal hand than the solitary life-saving hand that you, in fact, got dealt. Or, to return to our exploding cell phone example from above, while it is true that the odds of getting any particular number (1-100) are identical: 1 in 100—the odds of getting 100 and *any other number than 100* are *not* identical: 1 in 100 v. 99 in 100.

Proponents of the FT argument will point out the universe has dealt us a life-saving hand. Virtually any other hand would have been lethal. It's true that any particularly configuration is equally likely, but the odds of a life-possible configuration are way worse than a life-impossible configuration. That a life-possible universe is the one that we find ourselves in is, therefore, pretty darned surprising! And, while it's certainly true that we couldn't comment on the universe's features at all if the universe wasn't life-permitting, that fact doesn't make our universe's features any more likely. In our serial killer example, if you had been dealt anything other than those four aces, you wouldn't be around to comment on your lucky hand—but that doesn't make the hand any less extraordinary. In fact, in that scenario, you would probably suspect that the deal hadn't been truly random. Maybe the serial killer is trying to torture you with near-death experiences? The odds of getting four aces by chance alone are so poor that, although it is *possible*, you would probably suspect "cheating" in the event that it did occur. This is precisely the point of FT arguments: although it is *possible* that our universe's features could be the result of unguided processes alone, the odds of that are so poor that "cheating" is the better explanation.

General Criticism: The Multi-verse

The previous criticism (the WAP), by itself, doesn't accomplish much. However, if it is combined with another idea, a much more promising criticism emerges.

The driving force of the FT argument is the vast improbability of a life-possible universe existing by unguided natural processes alone. Given such long odds, and the fact that such a universe exists anyway, the better explanation is design—or so the argument claims. But what if there was a way to improve the odds?

Imagine the "shell game" employed by street hustlers around the world. In the standard version of the shell game, players bet money that they can find an object (e.g., marble, rock) that has been hidden under one of three shells (or cups, etc.), which have themselves been shuffled around in an attempt to make it difficult to know under which shell the object will be found. Assuming the object actually is under one of the shells (and that the hustler didn't hide it with some legerdemain instead!), the odds of finding it just by a chance guess alone is one in three. What if the game offered some very generous rules, though? What if, after your first guess, you get to guess again (with no further shuffling)? Your odds have improved to one in two. What if, after your second unlucky guess, you're allowed a third (with no further shuffling)? Your odds are now one in one. In other words, given enough tries, you *will* find the object—and this would be true no matter how many shells there were. If the marble was hidden under one of a thousand shells, you would still eventually, inevitably, find that marble if you got to keep trying until you found it! Even that improbable hand of four aces will eventually be dealt, by chance alone, if you're allowed to play approximately 54,145 times.

According to multi-verse cosmology (sometimes called "many-worlds," or "world-ensemble"), such impressive probabilistic resources are available to us—or at least they might be. This is not a textbook in astrophysics, so we're not going to delve into multi-verse theory in any significant detail, but the basic idea behind it is that this universe is not *the* universe, but rather *a* universe—just one universe in a larger multi-verse containing infinitely many other universes.

Suppose, for the sake of argument, that this were true: that there exists a multi-verse comprised of infinitely many randomly ordered universes. How would this be a threat to the FT argument? The FT argument claims that the odds of the universe having its features by chance alone is staggeringly poor. According to Ross' math, for example, the odds are less than one in a hundred billion, trillion, trillion, trillion. But, what if you got a hundred billion, trillion, trillion, trillion "tries?" What if you had an *infinite* number of "tries?" Given so many tries, you will have greatly increased your "probabilistic resources," and thereby have guaranteed the admittedly unlikely outcome, still by virtue of chance alone. In other words, if there exists an infinite number of randomly ordered universes, a life-possible universe *will* be generated, by chance alone, no matter how poor the odds of such a universe existing. And, when we recall that the WAP recognizes observable universes must have properties that permit observers to exist, we have an explanation for why we're in this universe rather than in one of those infinitely many other (life-impossible) universes.

The mulit-verse is supposed to serve as an alternative to intelligent design with regard to explaining the admittedly very poor odds of the universe existing, with the properties it has, by "luck" alone. The basic idea is simple: given enough probabilistic resources, any outcome *will* occur no matter how unlikely it is, so long as it's a possible outcome. Returning to the poker example, the odds of getting four aces in a hand of five card stud poker is one in 54,145, but if you play long enough (an infinite number of hands, for example), you *will* get that hand by luck alone—but notice what we have to be assuming in order for that to be true: the deck gets shuffled each time.

Suppose you get dealt a hand, and you don't get four aces. "No problem," you think, "since I'm going to play 'forever' and will eventually get those four aces anyway." The dealer takes back your five cards, and, rather than shuffling them back into the deck, simply places them right back on top of the deck in reverse order. You then get dealt your second hand. It should come as no surprise to you that you didn't get the four aces that time either. You got the exact same hand! You can play "forever," and you will never get those four aces *unless* the deck gets shuffled. Randomization is needed in order to provide the probabilistic resources necessary to get those four aces by luck alone.

With that in mind, reconsider the multi-verse as a means of providing the probabilistic resources necessary to generate a life possible universe by natural processes alone. In order for an infinite number of universes to provide a life-possible universe, the universes' features must be randomized. That is, the universes have to be "shuffled" each time they are formed. A multi-verse containing an infinite number of universes with the exact same properties does nothing to increase the odds of getting a life possible universe. Instead, you would just have an infinite number of "dead" universes. Each universe has to represent a new "shuffling," and a new "hand"—but why should we assume that the multi-verse randomizes universes? What mechanism could account for that? Why would it be necessary that the universes have randomly different features from each other? Why couldn't they all be the same, or at least similar?

Some critics of the multi-verse as an alternative to intelligent design claim that in order for universes to be randomized, the multiverse must be "fine-tuned" to make that happen. The fine-tuning of the multi-verse then needs an explanation. Is the multi-verse, then, a product of intelligent design (designed, it would seem, so as to randomly generate an infinite number of universes, in some of which life is possible)? Or, do we postulate a bigger multi-verse in which our own multi-verse is randomly generated, *ad infinitum*? In other words, the multi-verse just pushes back the need for design explanation one step, but without eliminating it—or so the critic of the multi-verse explanation claims.

General Criticism: The Problem of "Part-to-Whole Reasoning" (Hume)

"Part to Whole Reasoning" (hereafter, PTWR) occurs whenever we draw a conclusion about a large "body" based off of information gathered from a smaller part of that body. Science works in this way, as does statistics and surveying. Very often, there is nothing problematic with this sort of reasoning at all.

For example, beaches are sometimes closed because of water contamination. Certainly, those responsible for testing didn't empty the whole ocean and bring it back to their lab for testing! Instead, they took a sample of the water (a part), tested it, and then drew conclusions about the whole. When the sample of water shows contamination, this is taken to be a sufficient indicator that the water around that entire beach is contaminated. Is this hasty reasoning? No, because we know enough about water to know that soluble substances diffuse throughout a body of water. If the water is polluted at a particular point (A) along a beach, it's probably polluted a few feet from (A) as well.

PTWR goes wrong when our sample (the part) is not a representative sample of the whole. If the sample is too small, for example, we can't draw conclusions (with confidence) concerning the whole. If the water along Long Beach has a lot of oil in it, we can't infer that the entire ocean has a lot of oil in it. The ocean is really big, and sampling the water along one beach city just isn't enough. Similarly, if you survey one person and ask her who she's going to vote for in the next Presidential election, it would be wildly irresponsible to pronounce the next President as a result of your survey. A sample of one (out of over 200 million eligible voters in the U.S.!) is just not big enough to warrant that conclusion.

Again, what does any of this have to do with the design argument? Remember the structure of the analogical DA:

1. Human artifacts (like watches) are products of intelligent design.
2. Nature resembles human artifacts.
3. Therefore, Nature is also a product of intelligent design.

Premise two claims that Nature resembles human artifacts. Not only would Hume claim that this suffers from a weak analogy, he also claims that the information upon which this claim is based is far too small a sample to justify the conclusion. Premise two makes claims about all of Nature, the whole universe. Obviously, no one has "sampled" the whole universe, so that claim is based on a smaller sample, and the assumption that the rest of the universe is fairly similar to what we have already experienced. Perhaps it is, but do we know that it is? Design enthusiasts might suggest that we've already justified a similar example: water testing. We don't have to sample the whole ocean to know the beach should be closed, just like we don't need to sample the whole universe to know that it resembles human artifacts. Water sampled just of the beach is sufficient, just like the universe as viewed from our "beach" (Earth) is sufficient.

Or is it? Here, Hume would say that there is a very big difference between water and the universe: prior experience. The reason why we're confident in making claims about a large body of water based on a relatively small sample of water is because we know, *from experience*, that soluble substances diffuse throughout water. Try adding sugar to your coffee without that assumption! Whether we're dealing with water in a cup, or in a tub, or in a pool, or in the ocean, we have observed again and again the properties of water, and what happens when substances dissolve in it.

Perhaps our universe is similar to water in the sense that properties applicable to one portion of it will be applicable to all parts as well, but can we know this to be true? Our confidence in the case of water is based on previous experience with other bodies of water. How many universes have you experienced before this one? If we had somehow experienced several other, previous universes, and if in each one of them the qualities of the universe were uniform, and found to be the same throughout the whole cosmos, then we would have reason to be confident that this universe is also uniform in that respect. But, considering that this universe is unique, the only one with which we have any experience, we can't draw upon our prior experience to justify that assumption. We can *assume* that the universe is similar throughout, and that the "order" we observe in our own cosmic neighborhood really is representative of the universe in general, but an assumption is not at all the same thing as a proof. If Hume is right, and we aren't entitled to our claims about the universe, as a whole, this is a serious problem for that kind of design argument, as it threatens to destroy its second premise. Maybe the universe resembles human artifacts in our own part of the universe, but perhaps the rest of it is very different, chaotic, and not at all like a watch. Hume is not saying that the universe, and its laws and operations are *not* uniform, but he is saying that he just doesn't know (with confidence), one way or another. If we don't know that much, we should be careful about making analogies involving assumptions about the universe....

Paley flatly disagrees, claiming that:

> if other parts of nature were inaccessible to our inquiries, or even if other parts of nature presented nothing to our examination but disorder and confusion, the validity of this example would remain the same. If there were but one watch in the world, it would not be less certain that it had a maker. If we had never in our lives seen any but one single kind of hydraulic machine, yet if of that one kind we understood the mechanism and use, we should be as perfectly assured that it proceeded from the hand and thought and skill of a workman, as if we visited a museum of the arts, and saw collected there twenty different kinds of machines for drawing water, or a thousand different kinds for other purposes. Of this point each machine is a proof independently of all the rest. So it is with the evidences of a divine agency. The proof is not a conclusion which lies at the end of a chain of reasoning, of which chain each instance of contrivance is only a link, and of which, if one link fail, the whole falls; but it is an argument separately supplied by every separate example. An error in stating an example affects only that example. The argument is cumulative, in the fullest sense of that term. The eye proves it without the ear; the ear without the eye. The proof in each example is complete; for when the design of the part, and the conduciveness of its structure to that design is shown, the mind may set itself at rest; no future consideration can detract any thing from the force of the example.[106]

According to Paley, even a single example (such as a human eyeball) is sufficient to detect design in Nature just as only a single watch would invite the same conclusion.

---

[106] Paley, Ibid., Chapter VI.

The PTWR criticism boils down to a question of reasoning, and to a related empirical issue. The "reasoning" issue is whether it's problematic to infer (or deduce, as the case might be) design from a single sample. If you side with Paley, you'll answer "no." If you side with Hume, then we must face the empirical issue: just how much of the universe have we "sampled," and how well do we understand that sample? It's reasonable to think that Paley was much more vulnerable to this criticism, a couple centuries ago, than contemporary astro-physicists such as Hugh Ross are today. With the help of satellites, the Hubble telescope, and radio telescopes, astronomers today are likely to claim that their "sample" of the universe is pretty impressive—perhaps impressive enough to make general claims about the properties of the universe throughout. For this reason, although the problem of PTWR could apply to any version of the DA (and is therefore included as a "general" criticism), it is arguable that more contemporary FT arguments are less vulnerable to it due to their broader and more comprehensive empirical basis.

General Criticism: The Problem of the "Limited Conclusion" (Hume)

When we reach this criticism, Hume is willing to be generous for the sake of argument. Just for the sake of argument, suppose that the design argument works perfectly. What has it "proven?" Each version of the design argument that we've considered can establish, at best, the likelihood of intentional design. Notice that "intentional design" is consistent with every major (Western) religious tradition. Design implies "designer," but who is this designer? The God of Christianity? Islam? Judaism? The design argument works for all three. For that matter, why should we assume there is only one designer?

> *And what shadow of an argument, continued Philo, can you produce, from your hypothesis, to prove the unity of the Deity? A great number of men join in building a house or ship, in rearing a city, in framing a commonwealth; why may not several deities combine in contriving and framing a world? This is only so much greater similarity to human affairs. By sharing the work among several, we may so much further limit the attributes of each, and get rid of that extensive power and knowledge, which must be supposed in one deity, and which, according to you, can only serve to weaken the proof of his existence. And if such foolish, such vicious creatures as man, can yet often unite in framing and executing one plan, how much more those deities or demons, whom we may suppose several degrees more perfect![107]*

If we consult our own experience, we discover that the bigger the project, and the more complicated it is, the more people it takes to design and build it. I might be able to build, on my own, a tool shed given enough time and some instructions, but I could never, ever build an entire skyscraper all by myself. The bigger the project, the more builders are required. What could be bigger than the universe? Yet, instead of supposing that many designers are needed, theists usually appeal to a single designer

---

[107] Hume, Ibid.

instead?

"Because of Ockham's razor," you might reply.

"What now?" respond others of you, not knowing what on earth Ockham's razor refers to.... Ockham's razor refers to a principle of explanatory simplicity: *"entia non sunt multiplicanda praeter necessitatem."* In case your Latin is a bit rusty, this translates into "entities must not be multiplied beyond necessity." The much more common way of expressing this principle is this: all else being equal, the simpler the explanation, the better.

Applied to the design argument, one might think that, all else being equal, an explanation requiring one designer is more simple than an explanation requiring several. So, according to Ockham's razor, we should prefer a monotheistic version of the design argument. Hume was prepared for this.

> *To multiply causes without necessity, is indeed contrary to true philosophy: but this principle applies not to the present case. Were one deity antecedently proved by your theory, who were possessed of every attribute requisite to the production of the universe; it would be needless, I own, (though not absurd,) to suppose any other deity existent. But while it is still a question, whether all these attributes are united in one subject, or dispersed among several independent beings, by what phenomena in nature can we pretend to decide the controversy?[108]*

In other words, had we already established the existence of one designer capable of designing the whole universe, that one designer would indeed be a better explanation, all things considered—but the existence of that designer is the very thing in question, and can't be taken as an assumption at this stage. That means that several designers (polytheism) are as much a candidate as is monotheism.

Hume gets a bit playful with this criticism, and a bit irreverent.

> *In a word, Cleanthes, a man who follows your hypothesis is able perhaps to assert, or conjecture, that the universe, sometime, arose from something like design: but beyond that position he cannot ascertain one single circumstance; and is left afterwards to fix every point of his theology by the utmost license of fancy and hypothesis. This world, for aught he knows, is very faulty and imperfect, compared to a superior standard; and was only the first rude essay of some infant deity, who afterwards abandoned it, ashamed of his lame performance: it is the work only of some dependent, inferior deity; and is the object of derision to his superiors: it is the production of old age and dotage in some superannuated deity; and ever since his death, has run on at adventures, from the first impulse and active force which it received from him.[109]*

For all we know, this is a lousy "rough draft" of a universe. Maybe the designer(s) are ashamed of it. Maybe the designer(s) hate us, or couldn't care less? Hume isn't

---

[108] Ibid.
[109] Ibid.

saying any of these things are true, but he is saying they *could* be true, even if the design argument works just the way it's supposed to. In the best-case scenario, if the argument from design works, we can conclude that the universe is (probably) the product of intelligent design, but we can't determine the number of designers, or the properties of the designer(s), or the will of the designer(s), or any particular feature of any specific religious tradition.

This is why Hume grants (sarcastically) that (at best) the argument can conclude that "the universe, sometime, arose from something like design." But, what he gives in one sentence, he takes away just a few words later: "but beyond that position he cannot ascertain one single circumstance; and is left afterwards to fix every point of his theology by the utmost license of fancy and hypothesis."

Fancy and hypothesis? In other words, all of the particular elements of the major religious traditions of the West are feats of imagination. They're made up. No wonder he waited until he was dead to have his *Dialogues* published. In the 18th century, this would have been a very unpopular statement to make.

A major feature of the "Paley and Hume myth" to which I used to subscribe was that this criticism, in particular was undeniably true. The conclusion of the DA is necessarily vague, and can't demonstrate the existence of any particular deity as described in any particular religious tradition.

Hume is at least partially right about this.

That's correct. Hume is right, in one very important (but limited) way. If someone uses the design argument, all by itself, and thinks she can produce a conclusion specific to a particular religious tradition, such a person is guilty of the very thing Hume is here criticizing.

1. Human artifacts (like watches) are products of intelligent design.
2. The universe resembles human artifacts.
3. Therefore, Jesus is Lord.

Anyone who dares to present the design argument as above deserves Hume's criticism. The design argument can't produce that conclusion—it's simply not built to do so. However, even though Hume is right about the design argument not being capable of proving any particular religious tradition to be true, the design argument can still be seen as rather useful.

Suppose someone wants to convince an atheist friend that Jesus is, indeed, Lord. The design argument alone can't do it, but why accept the design argument all by itself? Suppose the design argument is effective in establishing its more modest conclusion: the universe is probably the product of intelligent (intentional) design. The atheist friend, if he or she has accepted the design argument, modest conclusion and all, has now accepted a *personal* explanation for the existence and properties of the universe. Atheism is now no longer an option. No particular religion has been established, but *something* "religious" is going to serve as the explanation for Nature. What's more, Paley argues that the DA, while not able to establish the specific truth of Christianity, is able to provide several features of the "designer" that facilitate the "matching strategy."

Chapter 24 of *Natural Theology* is dedicated to identifying features of the designer by means of conceptual analysis. Paley acknowledges the limitations of the DA, but claims:

> Nevertheless, if we be careful to imitate the documents of our religion, by confining our explanations to what concerns ourselves, and do not affect more precision in our ideas than the subject allows of, the several terms which are employed to denote the attributes of the Deity, may be made, even in natural religion, to bear a sense consistent with truth and reason, and not surpassing our comprehension.

> These terms are; Omnipotence, omniscience, omnipresence, eternity, self-existence, necessary existence, spirituality.

To address each of those properties would be too much of a tangent, for the purposes of this one section of but one chapter of this book, so we'll consider just one, as it directly addresses Hume's claim that the DA is problematic because, in our experience, all "designers" are embodied—rather unlike the God of Christianity.

> Contrivance, if established, appears to me to prove every thing which we wish to prove. Amongst other things, it proves the personality of the Deity, as distinguished from what is sometimes called nature, sometimes called a principle: which terms, in the mouths of those who use them philosophically, seem to be intended, to admit and to express an efficacy, but to exclude and to deny a personal agent. Now that which can contrive, which can design, must be a person. These capacities constitute personality, for they imply consciousness and thought. They require that which can perceive an end or purpose; as well as the power of providing means, and of directing them to their end. They require a centre in which perceptions unite, and from which volitions flow; which is mind. The acts of a mind prove the existence of a mind: and in whatever a mind resides, is a person. The seat of intellect is a person. We have no authority to limit the properties of mind to any particular corporeal form, or to any particular circumscription of space. These properties subsist, in created nature, under a great variety of sensible forms. Also every animated being has its sensorium, that is, a certain portion of space, within which perception and volition are exerted. This sphere may be enlarged to an indefinite extent; may comprehend the universe; and, being so imagined, may serve to furnish us with as good a notion, as we are capable of forming, of the immensity of the Divine Nature, i. e. of a Being, infinite, as well in essence as in power; yet nevertheless a person.... of this however we are certain, that whatever the Deity be, neither the universe, nor any part of it which we see, can be He. The universe itself is merely a collective name: its parts are all which are real; or which are things. Now inert matter is out of the question: and organized substances include marks of contrivance. But whatever includes marks of contrivance, whatever, in its constitution, testifies design, necessarily carries us to something beyond itself, to some other being, to a designer prior to, and out of, itself. No animal, for instance, can have contrived its own limbs and senses; can have been the

author to itself of the design with which they were constructed. That supposition involves all the absurdity of self-creation, i. e. of acting without existing. Nothing can be God, which is ordered by a wisdom and a will, which itself is void of; which is indebted for any of its properties to contrivance ab extra. The not having that in his nature which requires the exertion of another prior being (which property is sometimes called self-sufficiency, and sometimes self-comprehension), appertains to the Deity, as his essential distinction, and removes his nature from that of all things which we see. Which consideration contains the answer to a question that has sometimes been asked, namely, Why, since something or other must have existed from eternity, may not the present universe be that something? The contrivance perceived in it, proves that to be impossible. Nothing contrived, can, in a strict and proper sense, be eternal, forasmuch as the contriver must have existed before the contrivance.[110]

Here, Paley argues that the DA establishes that the designer is a "person," because design implies consciousness and thought. Moreover, every *embodied* person is limited to "a certain portion of space, within which perception and volition are exerted," but the "volition" exhibited in the design of Nature is co-extensive with Nature itself, and not confined to any particular body. Nor can we identify the designer with the whole "body" (i.e,. Nature) itself. "But whatever includes marks of contrivance, whatever, in its constitution, testifies design, necessarily carries us to something beyond itself, to some other being, to a designer prior to, and out of, itself." It is Nature that bears the marks of design, so something "beyond" Nature must be the source of that design. Since Nature exhausts the physical realm, the designer must be non-physical ("spiritual") and a person.

How could we presume just one designer? "what shadow of an argument, continued Philo, can you produce, from your hypothesis, to prove the unity of the Deity?" In the chapter entitled "Of the Unity of the Deity," Paley addresses this specific question.[111]

Of the "Unity of the Deity," the proof is, the uniformity of plan observable in the universe. The universe itself is a system; each part either depending upon other parts, or being connected with other parts by some common law of motion, or by the presence of some common substance. One principle of gravitation causes a stone to drop towards the earth, and the moon to wheel round it. One law of attraction carries all the different planets about the sun.... It may likewise be acknowledged, that no arguments which we are in possession of, exclude the ministry of subordinate agents. If such there be, they act under a presiding, a controlling will; because they act according to certain general restrictions, by certain common rules, and, as it should seem, upon a general plan: but still such agents, and different ranks, and classes, and degrees of them, may be

---

[110] Paley, Ibid. Chapter XXIII.

[111] Still more evidence that Paley was well aware of Hume's criticism, and responsive to it.

employed.[112]

That Nature exhibits uniformity in its "design" (e.g., one law of gravitation throughout the whole known universe) is evidence, for Paley, of one source of design, as opposed to several. He admits that this does not rule out "intermediary agents" (a pantheon of divine agents? Angels? Devils?), but even in that case they appear to be under the direction of one, commanding will. Even if there are many members of a divine construction crew, there appears to be a single architect....

Does the DA prove Christianity to be true, then? No. In that respect, at least, Hume is clearly right—but Paley concedes this fact, and readily acknowledges that revealed theology must take over where natural theology leaves off. The eager theist can now make use of other arguments to try to establish the truth of her own religion, specifically. The design argument can't succeed all by itself, but in the best of scenarios, it can open the door, or it could at least provide warrant for what the theist already believes.

Conclusion

The DA, like the CA, is both ancient and contemporary. It has its origins in philosophers and theologians from thousands of years ago, but has received contemporary "upgrades" and revision to keep pace with developing thought and emerging scientific understanding of the universe. Contemporary FT arguments, in particular, engage science to a degree far beyond what most TAs exhibit, and thereby has potential for appeal across worldviews. Like the other TAs we've reviewed thus far, the DA does not seem to offer definitive "proof" that the theistic worldview is correct, though it could certainly increase the warrant possessed by theists, if the DA withstands its critics.

In our next chapter, we will focus on a very different sort of TA, and it will be the last in our series. While the DA focuses on the "starry stars above," the moral argument (MA) will focus on the "moral law within."

---

[112] Paley, Ibid., Chapter XXV.

William Paley (July 1743 – 25 May 1805) was an important philosopher and Christian apologist. This excerpt from his "Natural Theology" includes one of the most famous arguments for God's existence from the Western tradition. He begins with a thought experiment in which we find a watch. He concludes that we would confidently infer that the watch had a creator and was designed, based on its features, despite several possible objections to this reasoning that could be produced. The point of this thought experiment is clear when he delivers his analogy: Nature is like a watch. As such, conclusions we draw from watches (i.e., that they are designed), can be applied to Nature (i.e., that it is probably designed as well). While more contemporary design arguments focus on "fine-tuning," some analogical arguments still exist, and remind us of Paley's famous argument.

Natural Theology; Or, Evidences of the Existence and Attributes of the Diety. Collected from the Appearances of Nature[113]
William Paley, D.D. – Late Archdeacon of Carlisle
The Twelfth Edition (1809)

CHAPTER I.
STATE OF THE ARGUMENT.

IN crossing a heath, suppose I pitched my foot against a *stone*, and were asked how the stone came to be there; I might possibly answer, that, for any thing I knew to the contrary, it had lain there for ever: nor would it perhaps be very easy to show the absurdity of this answer. But suppose I had found a *watch* upon the ground, and it should be inquired how the watch happened to be in that place; I should hardly think of the answer which I had before given, that, for any thing I knew, the watch might have always been there. Yet why should not this answer serve for the watch as well as for the stone? why is it not as admissible in the second case, as in the first? For this reason, and for no other, viz. that, when we come to inspect the watch, we perceive (what we could not discover in the stone) that its several parts are framed and put together for a purpose, e. g. that they are so formed and adjusted as to produce motion, and that motion so regulated as to point out the hour of the day; that, if the different parts had been differently shaped from what they are, of a different size from what they are, or placed after any other manner, or in any other order, than that in which they are placed, either no motion at all would have been carried on in the machine, or none which would have answered the use that is now served by it. To

---

[113] http://darwin-online.org.uk/content/frameset?itemID=A142&viewtype= text&pageseq=1

reckon up a few of the plainest of these parts, and of their offices, all tending to one result:-- We see a cylindrical box containing a coiled elastic spring, which, by its endeavour to relax itself, turns round the box. We next observe a flexible chain (artificially wrought for the sake of flexure), communicating the action of the spring from the box to the fusee. We then find a series of wheels, the teeth of which catch in, and apply to, each other, conducting the motion from the fusee to the balance, and from the balance to the pointer; and at the same time, by the size and shape of those wheels, so regulating that motion, as to terminate in causing an index, by an equable and measured progression, to pass over a given space in a given time. We take notice that the wheels are made of brass in order to keep them from rust; the springs of steel, no other metal being so elastic; that over the face of the watch there is placed a glass, a material employed in no other part of the work, but in the room of which, if there had been any other than a transparent substance, the hour could not be seen without opening the case. This mechanism being observed (it requires indeed an examination of the instrument, and perhaps some previous knowledge of the subject, to perceive and understand it; but being once, as we have said, observed and understood), the inference, we think, is inevitable, that the watch must have had a maker: that there must have existed, at some time, and at some place or other, an artificer or artificers who formed it for the purpose which we find it actually to answer; who comprehended its construction, and designed its use.

I. Nor would it, I apprehend, weaken the conclusion, that we had never seen a watch made; that we had never known an artist capable of making one; that we were altogether incapable of executing such a piece of workmanship ourselves, or of understanding in what manner it was performed; all this being no more than what is true of some exquisite remains of ancient art, of some lost arts, and, to the generality of mankind, of the more curious productions of modern manufacture. Does one man in a million know how oval frames are turned? Ignorance of this kind exalts our opinion of the unseen and unknown artist's skill, if he be unseen and unknown, but raises no doubt in our minds of the existence and agency of such an artist, at some former time, and in some place or other. Nor can I perceive that it varies at all the inference, whether the question arise concerning a human agent, or concerning an agent of a different species, or an agent possessing, in some respects, a different nature.

II. Neither, secondly, would it invalidate our conclusion, that the watch sometimes went wrong, or that it seldom went exactly right. The purpose of the machinery, the design, and the designer, might be evident, and in the case supposed would be evident, in whatever way we accounted for the irregularity of the movement, or whether we could account for it or not. It is not necessary that a machine be perfect, in order to show with what design it was made: still less necessary, where the only question is, whether it were made with any design at all.

III. Nor, thirdly, would it bring any uncertainty into the argument, if there were a few parts of the watch, concerning which we could not discover, or had not yet discovered, in what manner they conduced to the general effect; or even some parts, concerning which we could not ascertain, whether they conduced to that effect in any manner whatever. For, as to the first branch of the case; if by the loss, or disorder, or decay of the parts in question, the movement of the watch were found in fact to be stopped, or disturbed, or retarded, no doubt would remain in our minds as to the utility or intention of these parts, although we should be unable to investigate the manner according to which, or the connexion by which, the ultimate effect depended upon their action or assistance; and the more complex is the machine, the more likely is this obscurity to arise. Then, as to the second thing supposed, namely, that there were parts which might be spared, without prejudice to the movement of the watch, and that we had proved this by experiment,--these superfluous parts, even if we were completely assured that they were such, would not vacate the reasoning which we had instituted concerning other parts. The indication of contrivance remained, with respect to them, nearly as it was before.

IV. Nor, fourthly, would any man in his senses think the existence of the watch, with its various machinery, accounted for, by being told that it was one out of possible combinations of material forms; that whatever he had found in the place where he found the watch, must have contained some internal configuration or other; and that this configuration might be the structure now exhibited, viz. of the works of a watch, as well as a different structure.

V. Nor, fifthly, would it yield his inquiry more satisfaction to be answered, that there existed in things a principle of order, which had disposed the parts of the watch into their present form and situation. He never knew a watch made by the principle of order; nor can he even form to himself an idea of what is meant by a principle of order, distinct from the intelligence of the watch-maker.

VI. Sixthly, he would be surprised to hear that the mechanism of the watch was no proof of contrivance, only a motive to induce the mind to think so:

VII. And not less surprised to be informed, that the watch in his hand was nothing more than the result of the laws of *metallic* nature. It is a perversion of language to assign any law, as the efficient, operative cause of any thing. A law presupposes an agent; for it is only the mode, according to which an agent proceeds: it implies a power; for it is the order, according to which that power acts. Without this agent, without this power, which are both distinct from itself, the *law* does nothing; is nothing. The expression, "the law of metallic nature," may sound strange and harsh to a philosophic ear; but it seems quite as justifiable as some others which are more familiar to him, such as "the law of vegetable nature," "the law of animal nature," or indeed as "the law of nature" in general, when assigned as the cause of phænomena, in exclusion of agency and power; or when it is substituted into the place of these.

VIII. Neither, lastly, would our observer be driven out of his conclusion, or from his confidence in its truth, by being told that he knew nothing at all about the matter. He knows enough for his argument: he knows the utility of the end: he knows the subserviency and adaptation of the means to the end. These points being known, his ignorance of other points, his doubts concerning other points, affect not the certainty of his reasoning. The consciousness of knowing little, need not beget a distrust of that which he does know.

CHAPTER II.
STATE OF THE ARGUMENT CONTINUED.

SUPPOSE, in the next place, that the person who found the watch, should, after some time, discover that, in addition to all the properties which he had hitherto observed in it, it possessed the unexpected property of producing, in the course of its movement, another watch like itself (the thing is conceivable); that it contained within it a mechanism, a system of parts, a mould for instance, or a complex adjustment of lathes, files, and other tools, evidently and separately calculated for this purpose; let us inquire, what effect ought such a discovery to have upon his former conclusion.

I. The first effect would be to increase his admiration of the contrivance, and his conviction of the consummate skill of the contriver. Whether he regarded the object of the contrivance, the distinct apparatus, the intricate, yet in many parts intelligible mechanism, by which it was carried on, he would perceive, in this new observation, nothing but an additional reason for doing what he had already done,--for referring the construction of the watch to design, and to supreme art. If that construction *without* this property, or which is the same thing, before this property had been noticed, proved intention and art to have been employed about it; still more strong would the proof appear, when he came to the knowledge of this further property, the crown and perfection of all the rest.

II. He would reflect, that though the watch before him were, *in some sense*, the maker of the watch, which was fabricated in the course of its movements, yet it was in a very different sense from that, in which a carpenter, for instance, is the maker of a chair; the author of its contrivance, the cause of the relation of its parts to their use. With respect to these, the first watch was no cause at all to the second: in no such sense as this was it the author of the constitution and order, either of the parts which the new watch contained, or of the parts by the aid and instrumentality of which it was produced. We might possibly say, but with great latitude of expression, that a stream of water ground corn: but no latitude of expression would allow us to say, no stretch of conjecture could lead us to think, that the stream of water built the mill, though it were too ancient for us to know who the builder was. What the stream of water does in the affair, is neither more nor less than this; by the application of an unintelligent impulse to a mechanism previously arranged, arranged independently of it, and arranged by intelligence, an effect is produced, viz. the corn is ground. But the effect results from the arrangement. The force of the stream cannot be said to be the cause or author of the effect, still less of the arrangement. Understanding and plan in the formation of the mill were not the less necessary, for any share which the water has in grinding the corn: yet is this share the same, as that which the watch would have contributed to the production of the new watch, upon the supposition assumed in the last section. Therefore,

III. Though it be now no longer probable, that the individual watch, which our observer had found, was made immediately by the hand of an artificer, yet doth not this alteration in anywise affect the inference, that an artificer had been originally employed and concerned in the production. The argument from design remains as it was. Marks of design and contrivance are no more accounted for now, than they were before. In the same thing, we may ask for the cause of different properties. We may ask for the cause of the colour of a body, of its hardness, of its head; and these causes may be all different. We are now asking for the cause of that subserviency to a use, that relation to an end, which we have remarked in the watch before us. No answer is given to this question, by telling us that a preceding watch produced it. There cannot be design without a designer; contrivance without a contriver; order without choice; arrangement, without any thing capable of arranging; subserviency and relation to a purpose, without that which could intend a purpose; means suitable to an end, and executing their office, in accomplishing that end, without the end ever having been contemplated, or the means accommodated to it. Arrangement, disposition of parts, subserviency of means to an end, relation of instruments to a use, imply the presence of intelligence and mind. No one, therefore, can rationally believe, that the insensible, inanimate watch, from which the watch before us issued, was the proper cause of the mechanism we so much admire in it;--could be truly said to have constructed the instrument, disposed its parts, assigned their office, determined their order, action, and mutual dependency, combined their several motions into one result, and that also a result connected with the utilities of other beings. All these properties, therefore, are as much unaccounted for, as they were before.

IV. Nor is any thing gained by running the difficulty farther back, *i. e.* by supposing the watch before us to have been produced from another watch, that from a former, and so on indefinitely. Our going back ever so far, brings us no nearer to the least degree of satisfaction upon the subject. Contrivance is still unaccounted for. We still want a contriver. A designing mind is neither supplied by this supposition, nor dispensed with. If the difficulty were diminished the further we went back, by going back indefinitely we might exhaust it. And this is the only case to which this sort of reasoning applies. Where there is a tendency, or, as we increase the number of terms, a continual approach towards a limit, *there*, by supposing the number of terms to be what is called infinite, we may conceive the limit to be attained: but where there is no such tendency, or approach, nothing is effected by lengthening the series. There is no difference as to the point in question (whatever there may be as to many points), between one series and another; between a series which is finite, and a series which is infinite. A chain, composed of an infinite number of links, can no more support itself, than a chain composed of a finite number of links. And of this we are assured (though we never *can* have tried the experiment), because, by increasing the number of links, from ten for instance to a hundred, from a hundred to a thousand, &c. we make not the smallest approach, we observe not the smallest tendency, towards self-support. There is no difference in this respect (yet there may be a great difference in several respects) between a chain of a greater or less length, between one chain and another, between one that is finite and one that is infinite. This very much resembles the case before us. The machine which we are inspecting, demonstrates, by its construction, contrivance and design. Contrivance must have had a contriver; design, a designer; whether the machine immediately proceeded from another machine or not. That circumstance alters not the case. That other machine may, in like manner, have proceeded from a former machine: nor does that alter the case; contrivance must have had a contriver. That former one from one preceding it: no alteration still; a contriver is still necessary. No tendency is perceived, no approach towards a diminution of this necessity. It is the same with any and every succession of these machines; a succession of ten, of a hundred, of a thousand; with one series, as with another; a series which is finite, as with a series which is infinite. In whatever other respects they may differ, in this they do not. In all equally, contrivance and design are unaccounted for.

The question is not simply, How came the first watch into existence? which question, it may be pretended, is done away by supposing the series of watches thus produced from one another to have been infinite, and consequently to have had no-such *first*, for which it was necessary to provide a cause. This, perhaps, would have been nearly the state of the question, if no thing had been before us but an unorganized, unmechanized substance, without mark or indication of contrivance. It might be difficult to show that such substance could not have existed from eternity, either in succession (if it were possible, which I think it is not, for unorganized bodies to spring from one another), or by individual perpetuity. But that is not the question now. To suppose it to be so, is to suppose that it made no difference whether we had found a watch or a stone. As it is, the metaphysics of that question have no place; for, in the watch which we are examining, are seen contrivance, design; an end, a purpose; means for the end, adaptation to the purpose. And the question which irresistibly presses upon our thoughts, is, whence this contrivance and design? The thing required is the intending mind, the adapting hand, the intelligence by which that hand was directed. This question, this demand, is not shaken off, by increasing a number or succession of substances, destitute of these properties; nor the more, by increasing that number to infinity. If it be said, that, upon the supposition of one watch being produced from another in the course of that other's movements, and by means of the mechanism within it, we have a cause for the watch in my hand, viz. the watch from which it proceeded. I deny, that for the design, the contrivance, the suitableness of means to an end, the adaptation of instruments to a use (all which we discover in the watch), we have any cause whatever. It is in vain, therefore, to assign a series of such causes, or to allege that a series may be carried back to infinity; for I do not admit that we have yet any cause at all of the phænomena, still less any series of causes either finite or infinite. Here is contrivance, but no contriver; proofs of design, but no designer.

V. Our observer would further also reflect, that the maker of the watch before him, was, in truth and reality, the maker of every watch produced from it; there being no difference (except that the latter manifests a more exquisite skill) between the making of another watch with his own hands, by the mediation of files, lathes, chisels, &c. and the disposing, fixing, and inserting of these instruments, or of others equivalent to them, in the body of the watch already made in such a manner, as to form a new watch in the course of the movements which he had given to the old one. It is only working by one set of tools, instead of another.

The conclusion of which the *first* examination of the watch, of its works, construction, and movement, suggested, was, that it must have had, for the cause and author of that construction, an artificer, who understood its mechanism, and designed its use. This conclusion is invincible. A *second* examination presents us with a new discovery. The watch is found, in the course of its movement, to produce another watch, similar to itself; and not only so, but we perceive in it a system or organization, separately calculated for that purpose. What effect would this discovery have, or ought it to have, upon our former inference? What, as hath already been said, but to increase, beyond measure, our admiration of the skill, which had been employed in the formation of such a machine? Or shall it, instead of this, all at once turn us round to an opposite conclusion, viz. that no art or skill whatever has been concerned in the business, although all other evidences of art and skill remain as they were, and this last and supreme piece of art be now added to the rest? Can this be maintained without absurdity? Yet this is atheism.

CHAPTER III.
APPLICATION OF THE ARGUMENT.

THIS is atheism: for every indication of contrivance, every manifestation of design, which existed in the watch, exists in the works of nature; with the difference, on the side of nature, of being greater and more, and that in a degree which exceeds all computation. I mean that the contrivances of nature surpass the contrivances of art, in the complexity, subtility, and curiosity of the mechanism; and still more, if possible, do they go beyond them in number and variety; yet, in a multitude of cases, are not less evidently mechanical, not less evidently contrivances, not less evidently accommodated to their end, or suited to their office, than are the most perfect productions of human ingenuity.

I know no better method of introducing so large a subject, than that of comparing a single thing with a single thing; an eye, for example, with a telescope. As far as the examination of the instrument goes, there is precisely the same proof that the eye was made for vision, as there is that the telescope was made for assisting it. They are made upon the same principles; both being adjusted to the laws by which the transmission and refraction of rays of light are regulated. I speak not of the origin of the laws themselves; but such laws being fixed, the construction, in both cases, is adapted to them. For instance; these laws require, in order to produce the same effect, that the rays of light, in passing from water into the eye, should be refracted by a more convex surface, than when it passes out of air into the eye. Accordingly we find that the eye of a fish, in that part of it called the crystalline lens, is much rounder than the eye of terrestrial animals. What plainer manifestation of design can there be than this difference? What could a mathematical-instrument-maker have done more, to show his knowledge of his principle, his application of that knowledge, his suiting of his means to his end; I will not say to display the compass or excellence of his skill and art, for in these all comparison is indecorous, but to testify counsel, choice, consideration, purpose?...

CHAPTER VI.
THE ARGUMENT CUMULATIVE.

WERE there no example in the world, of contrivance, except that of the *eye*, it would be alone sufficient to support the conclusion which we draw from it, as to the necessity of an intelligent Creator. It could never be got rid of; because it could not be accounted for by any other supposition, which did not contradict all the principles we possess of knowledge; the principles, according to which, things do, as often as they can be brought to the test of experience, turn out to be true or false. Its coats and humours, constructed, as the lenses of a telescope are constructed, for the refraction of rays of light to a point, which forms the proper action of the organ; the provision in its muscular tendons for turning its pupil to the object, similar to that which is given to the telescope by screws, and upon which power of direction in the eye, the exercise of its office as an optical instrument depends; the further provision for its defence, for its constant lubricity and moisture, which we see in its socket and its lids, in its gland for the secretion of the matter of tears, its outlet or communication with the nose for carrying off the liquid after the eye is washed with it; these provisions compose altogether an apparatus, a system of parts, a preparation of means, so manifest in their design, so exquisite in their contrivance, so successful in their issue, so precious, and so infinitely beneficial in their use, as, in my opinion, to bear down all doubt that can be raised upon the subject. And what I wish, under the title of the present chapter, to observe is, that if other parts of nature were inaccessible to our inquiries, or even if other parts of nature presented nothing to our examination but disorder and confusion, the validity of this example would remain the same. If there were but one watch in the world, it would not be less certain that it had a maker. If we had never in our lives seen any but one single kind of hydraulic machine, yet, if of that one kind we understood the mechanism and use, we should be as perfectly assured that it proceeded from the hand, and thought, and skill of a workman, as if we visited a museum of the arts, and saw collected there twenty different kinds of machines for drawing water, or a thousand different kinds for other purposes. Of this point, each machine is a proof, independently of all the rest. So it is with the evidences of a Divine agency. The proof is not a conclusion which lies at the end of a chain of reasoning, of which chain each instance of contrivance is only a link, and of which, if one link fail, the whole falls; but it is an argument separately supplied by every separate example. An error in stating an example, affects only that example. The argument is cumulative, in the fullest sense of that term. The eye proves it without the ear; the ear without the eye. The proof in each example is complete; for when the design of the part, and the conduciveness of its structure to that design is shown, the mind may set itself at rest; no future consideration can detract any thing from the force of the example....

CHAPTER XXIV.
OF THE NATURAL ATTRIBUTES OF THE DEITY.

IT is an immense conclusion, that there is a GOD; a perceiving, intelligent, designing, Being; at the head of creation, and from whose will it proceeded. The *attributes* of such a Being, suppose his reality to be proved, must be adequate to the magnitude, extent, and multiplicity of his operations: which are not only vast beyond comparison with those performed by any other power, but, so far as respects our conceptions of them, infinite, because they are unlimited on all sides.

Yet the contemplation of a nature so exalted, however surely we arrive at the proof of its existence, overwhelms our faculties. The mind feels its powers sink under the subject. One consequence of which is, that from painful abstraction the thoughts seek relief in sensible images. Whence may be deduced the ancient, and almost universal propensity to idolatrous substitutions. They are the resources of a labouring imagination. False religions usually fall in with the natural propensity; true religions, or such as have derived themselves from the true, resist it.

It is one of the advantages of the revelations which we acknowledge, that, whilst they reject idolatry with its many pernicious accompaniments, they introduce the Deity to human apprehension, under an idea more personal, more determinate, more within its compass, than the theology of nature can do. And this they do by representing him exclusively under the relation in which he stands to ourselves; and, for the most part, under some precise character, resulting from that relation, or from the history of his providences. Which method suits the span of our intellects much better than the universality which enters into the idea of God, as deduced from the views of nature. When, therefore, these representations are well founded in point of authority (for all depends upon that), they afford a condescension to the state of our faculties, of which, they who have most reflected on the subject, will be the first to acknowledge the want and the value.

Nevertheless, if we be careful to imitate the documents of our religion, by confining our explanations to what concerns ourselves, and do not affect more precision in our ideas than the subject allows of, the several terms which are employed to denote the attributes of the Deity, may be made, even in natural religion, to bear a sense consistent with truth and reason, and not surpassing our comprehension.

These terms are; Omnipotence, omniscience, omnipresence, eternity, self-existence, necessary existence, spirituality.

"Omnipotence," "omniscience," "infinite" power, "infinite" knowledge, are *superlatives;* expressing our conception of these attributes in the strongest and most elevated terms which language supplies. We ascribe power to the Deity under the name of "omnipotence," the strict and correct conclusion being, that a power which could create such a world as this is, must be, beyond all comparison, greater than any which we experience in ourselves, than any which we observe in other visible agents; greater also than any which we can want, for our individual protection and preservation, in the Being upon whom we depend. It is a power, likewise, to which we are not authorized, by our observation or knowledge, to assign any limits of space or duration.

Very much of the same sort of remark is applicable to the term "omniscience," infinite knowledge, or infinite wisdom. In strictness of language, there is a difference between knowledge and wisdom; wisdom always supposing action, and action directed by it. With respect to the first, viz. *knowledge*, the Creator must know, intimately, the constitution and properties of the things which he created; which seems also to imply a foreknowledge of their action upon one another, and of their changes; at least, so far as the same result from trains of physical and necessary causes. His omniscience also, as far as respects things present, is deducible from his nature, as an intelligent being, joined with the extent, or rather the universality, of his operations. Where he acts, he is; and where he is, he perceives. The *wisdom* of the Deity, as testified in the works of creation, surpasses all idea we have of wisdom, drawn from the highest intellectual operations of the highest class of intelligent beings with whom we are acquainted; and, which is of the chief importance to us, whatever be its compass or extent, which it is evidently impossible that we should be able to determine, it must be adequate to the conduct of that order of things under which we live. And this is enough. It is of very inferior consequence, by what terms we express our notion, or rather our admiration, of this attribute. The terms, which the piety and the usage of language have rendered habitual to us, may be as proper as any other. We can trace this attribute much beyond what is necessary for any conclusion to which we have occasion to apply it. The degree of knowledge and power, requisite for the formation of created nature, cannot, with respect to us, be distinguished from infinite.

The Divine "omnipresence" stands, in natural theology, upon this foundation. In every part and place of the universe with which we are acquainted, we perceive the exertion of a power, which we believe, mediately or immediately, to proceed from the Deity. For instance; in what part or point of space, that has ever been explored, do we not discover attraction? In what regions do we not find light? In what accessible portion of our globe, do we not meet with gravity, magnetism, electricity; together with the properties also and powers of organized substances, of vegetable or of animated nature? Nay further, we may ask, What kingdom is there of nature, what corner of space, in which there is any thing that can be examined by us, where we do not fall upon contrivance and design? The only reflection perhaps which arises in our minds from this view of the world around us is, that the laws of nature every where prevail; that they are uniform and universal. But what do we mean by the laws of nature, or by any law? Effects are produced by power, not by laws. A law cannot execute itself. A law refers us to an agent. Now an agency so general, as that we cannot discover its absence, or assign the place in which some effect of its continued energy is not found, may, in popular language at least, and, perhaps, without much deviation from philosophical strictness, be called universal: and, with not quite the same, but with no inconsiderable propriety, the person, or Being, in whom that power resides, or from whom it is derived, may be taken to be *omnipresent*. He who upholds all things by his power, may be said to be every where present.

This is called a virtual presence. There is also what metaphysicians denominate an essential ubiquity; and which idea the language of Scripture seems to favour: but the former, I think, goes as far as natural theology carries us.

"Eternity" is a negative idea, clothed with a positive name. It supposes, in that to which it is applied, a present existence; and is the negation of a beginning or an end of that existence. As applied to the Deity, it has not been controverted by those who acknowledge a Deity at all. Most assuredly, there never was a time in which nothing existed, because that condition must have continued. The universal *blank* must have remained; nothing could rise up out of it; nothing could ever have existed since; nothing could exist now. In strictness, however, we have no concern with duration prior to that of the visible world. Upon this article therefore of theology, it is sufficient to know, that the contriver necessarily existed before the contrivance.

"Self-existence" is another negative idea, *viz.* the negation of a preceding cause, as of a progenitor, a maker, an author, a creator.

"Necessary existence" means demonstrable existence.

"Spirituality" expresses an idea, made up of a negative part, and of a positive part. The negative part consists in the exclusion of some of the known properties of matter, especially of solidity, of the *vis inertiæ*, and of gravitation. The positive part comprises perception, thought, will, power, *action*, by which last term is meant, the origination of motion; the quality, perhaps, in which resides the essential superiority of spirit over matter, "which cannot move, unless it be moved; and cannot but move, when impelled by another (*Note:* Bishop Wilkins's Principles of Natural Religion, p. 106.)." I apprehend that there can be no difficulty in applying to the Deity both parts of this idea.

CHAPTER XXV.
THE UNITY OF THE DEITY.

OF the "Unity of the Deity," the proof is, the *uniformity* of plan observable in the universe. The universe itself is a system; each part either depending upon other parts, or being connected with other parts by some common law of motion, or by the presence of some common substance. One principle of gravitation causes a stone to drop towards the earth, and the moon to wheel round it. One law of attraction carries all the different planets about the sun. This philosophers demonstrate. There are also other points of agreement amongst them, which may be considered as marks of the identity of their origin, and of their intelligent author. In all are found the conveniency and stability derived from gravitation. They all experience vicissitudes of days and nights, and changes of season. They all, at least Jupiter, Mars, and Venus, have the same advantages from their atmosphere as we have. In all the planets, the axes of rotation are permanent. Nothing is more probable than that the same attracting influence, acting according to the same rule, reaches to the fixed stars: but, if this be only probable, another thing is certain, *viz.* that the same element of light does. The light from a fixed star affects our eyes in the same manner, is refracted and reflected according to the same laws, as the light of a candle. The velocity of the light of the fixed stars is also the same, as the velocity of the light of the sun, reflected from the satellites of Jupiter. The heat of the sun, in kind, differs nothing from the heat of a coal fire.

In our own globe, the case is clearer. New countries are continually discovered, but the old laws of nature are always found in them: new plants perhaps, or animals, but always in company with plants and animals which we already know; and always possessing many of the same general properties. We never get amongst such original, or totally different, modes of existence, as to indicate, that we are come into the province of a different Creator, or under the direction of a different will. In truth, the same order of things attend us, wherever we go. The elements act upon one another, electricity operates, the tides rise and fall, the magnetic needle elects its position, in one region of the earth and sea, as well as in another. One atmosphere invests all parts of the globe, and connects all; one sun illuminates; one moon exerts its specific attraction upon all parts. If there be a variety in natural effects, as, *e. g.* in the tides of different seas, that very variety is the result of the same cause, acting under different circumstances. In many cases this is proved; in all, is probable.

The inspection and comparison of *living* forms, add to this argument examples without number. Of all large terrestrial animals, the structure is very much alike; their senses nearly the same; their natural functions and passions nearly the same; their viscera nearly the same, both in substance, shape, and office: digestion, nutrition, circulation, secretion, go on, in a similar manner, in all: the great circulating fluid is the same; for, I think, no difference has been discovered in the properties of *blood*, from whatever animal it be drawn. The experiment of transfusion proves, that the blood of one animal will serve for another. The *skeletons* also of the larger terrestrial animals, show particular varieties, but still under a great general affinity. The resemblance is somewhat less, yet sufficiently evident, between quadrupeds and birds. They are all alike in five respects, for one in which they differ.

In *fish*, which belong to another department, as it were, of nature, the points of comparison become fewer. But we never lose sight of our analogy, *e. g.* we still meet with a stomach, a liver, a spine; with bile and blood; with teeth; with eyes (which eyes are only slightly varied from our own, and which variation, in truth, demonstrates, not an interruption, but a continuance of the same exquisite plan; for it is the adaptation of the organ to the element, *viz.* to the different refraction of light passing into the eye out of a denser medium). The provinces, also, themselves of water and earth, are connected by the species of animals which inhabit both; and also by a large tribe of aquatic animals, which closely resemble the terrestrial in their internal structure; I mean the cetaceous tribe, which have hot blood, respiring lungs, bowels, and other essential parts, like those of land-animals. This similitude, surely, bespeaks the same creation and the same Creator.

Insects and *shell-fish* appear to me to differ from other classes of animals the most widely of any. Yet even here, beside many points of particular resemblance, there exists a general relation of a peculiar kind. It is the relation of inversion; the law of contrariety: namely, that, whereas, in other animals, the bones, to which the muscles are attached, lie *within* the body; in insects and shell-fish, they lie on the *outside* of it. The shell of a lobster performs to the animal the office of a *bone*, by furnishing to the tendons that fixed basis or immoveable fulcrum, without which, mechanically, they could not act. The crust of an insect is its shell, and answers the like purpose. The shell also of an oister stands in the place of a *bone;* the bases of the muscles being fixed to it, in the same manner, as, in other animals, they are fixed to the bones. All which (under wonderful varieties, indeed, and adaptations of form) confesses an imitation, a remembrance, a carrying on, of the same plan.

The observations here made, are equally applicable to plants; but, I think, unnecessary to be pursued. It is a very striking circumstance, and alone sufficient to prove all which we contend for, that, in this part likewise of organized nature, we perceive a continuation of the *sexual* system.

Certain however it is, that the whole argument for the divine unity, goes no further than to a unity of counsel.

It may likewise be acknowledged, that no arguments which we are in possession of, exclude the ministry of subordinate agents. If such there be, they act under a presiding, a controlling will; because they act according to certain general restrictions, by certain common rules, and, as it should seem, upon a general plan: but still such agents, and different ranks, and classes, and degrees of them, may be employed.

CHAPTER XXVI.
THE GOODNESS OF THE DEITY.

THE proof of the *divine goodness* rests upon two propositions; each, as we contend, capable of being made out by observations drawn from the appearances of nature.

The first is, "that, in a vast plurality of instances in which contrivance is perceived, the design of the contrivance is *beneficial.*"

The second, "that the Deity has superadded *pleasure* to animal sensations, beyond what was necessary for any other purpose, or when the purpose, so far as it was necessary," might have been effected by the operation of pain.

First, "in a vast plurality of instances in which contrivance is perceived, the design of the contrivance is *beneficial.*" . . .

Nor is the design abortive. It is a happy world after all. The air, the earth, the water, teem with delighted existence. In a spring noon, or a summer evening, on whichever side I turn my eyes, myriads of happy beings crowd upon my view. "The insect youth are on the wing." Swarms of newborn *flies* are trying their pinions in the air. Their sportive motions, their wanton mazes, their gratuitous activity, their continual change of place without use or purpose, testify their joy, and the exultation which they feel in their lately discovered faculties. A *bee* amongst the flowers in spring, is one of the most cheerful objects that can be looked upon. Its life appears to be all enjoyment; so busy, and so pleased: yet it is only a specimen of insect life, with which, by reason of the animal being half domesticated, we happen to be better acquainted than we are with that of others. The *whole winged* insect tribe, it is probable, are equally intent upon their proper employments, and, under every variety of constitution, gratified, and perhaps equally gratified, by the offices which the Author of their nature has assigned to them. But the atmosphere is not the only scene or enjoyment for the insect race. Plants are covered with aphides, greedily sucking their juices, and constantly, as it should seem, in the act of sucking. It cannot be doubted but that this is a state of gratification. What else should fix them so close to the operation, and so long? other species are *running about*, with an alacrity in their motions, which carries with it every mark of pleasure. Large patches of ground are sometimes half covered with these brisk and sprightly natures. If we look to what the *waters* produce, shoals of the fry of fish frequent the margins of rivers, of lakes, and of the sea itself. These are so happy, that they know not what to do with themselves. Their attitudes, their vivacity, their leaps out of the water, their frolics in it (which I have noticed a thousand times with equal attention and amusement), all conduce to show their excess of spirits, and are simply the effects of that excess. Walking by the sea-side, in a calm evening, upon a sandy shore, and with an ebbing tide, I have frequently remarked the appearance of a dark cloud, or, rather, very thick mist, hanging over the edge of the water, to the height, perhaps, of half a yard, and of the breadth of two or three yards, stretching along the coast as far as the eye could reach, and always retiring with the water. When this cloud came to be examined, it proved to be nothing else than so much space, filled with young *shrimps*, in the act of bounding into the air from the shallow margin of the water, or from the wet sand. If any motion of a mute animal could express delight, it was this: if they had meant to make signs of their happiness, they could not have done it more intelligibly. Suppose then, what I have no doubt of, each individual of this number to be in a state of positive enjoyment; what a sum, collectively, of gratification and pleasure have we here before our view!

The *young* of all animals appear to me to receive pleasure simply from the exercise of their limbs and bodily faculties, without reference to any end to be attained, or any use to be answered by the exertion. A child, without knowing any thing of the use of language, is in a high degree delighted with being able to speak. Its incessant repetition of a few articulate sounds, or, perhaps, of the single word which it has learned to pronounce, proves this point clearly. Nor is it less pleased with its first successful endeavours to walk, or rather to run (which precedes walking), although entirely ignorant of the importance of the attainment to its future life, and even without applying it to any present purpose. A child is delighted with speaking, without having any thing to say; and with walking, without knowing where to go. And, prior to both these, I am disposed to believe, that the waking hours of infancy are agreeably taken up with the exercise of vision, or perhaps, more properly speaking, with learning to see.

But it is not for youth alone that the great Parent of creation hath provided. Happiness is found with the purring cat, no less than with the playful kitten; in the armchair of dozing age, as well as in either the sprightliness of the dance, or the animation of the chase. To novelty, to acuteness of sensation, to hope, to ardour of pursuit, succeeds, what is, in no inconsiderable degree, an equivalent for them all, "perception of ease." Herein is the exact difference between the young and the old. The young are not happy, but when enjoying pleasure; the old are happy, when free from pain. And this constitution suits with the degrees of animal power which they respectively possess. The vigour of youth was to be stimulated to action by impatience of rest; whilst to the imbecility of age, quietness and repose become positive gratifications. In one important respect the advantage is with the old. A state of ease is, generally speaking, more attainable than a state of pleasure. A constitution, therefore, which can enjoy ease, is preferable to that which can taste only pleasure. This same perception of ease oftentimes renders old age a condition of great comfort; especially when riding at its anchor after a busy or tempestuous life. It is well described by Rousseau, to be the interval of repose and enjoyment, between the hurry and the end of life. How far the same cause extends to other animal natures, cannot be judged of with certainty. The appearance of satisfaction, with which most animals, as their activity subsides, seek and enjoy rest, affords reason to believe, that this source of gratification is appointed to advanced life, under all, or most, of its various forms. In the species with which we are best acquainted, namely our own, I am far, even as an observer of human life, from thinking that youth is its happiest season, much less the only happy one: as a Christian, I am willing to believe that there is a great deal of truth in the following representation given by a very pious writer, as well as excellent man(*Note:* Father's Instructions; by Dr. Percival of Manchester. p. 317): "To the intelligent and virtuous, old age presents a scene of tranquil enjoyments, of obedient appetite, of well-regulated affections, of maturity in knowledge, and of calm preparation for immortality. In this serene and dignified state, placed as it were on the confines of two worlds, the mind of a good man reviews what is past with the complacency of an approving conscience; and looks forward, with humble confidence in the mercy of God, and with devout aspirations towards his eternal and ever-increasing favour." ...

we contend, in the terms of our original proposition, that throughout the whole of life, as it is diffused in nature, and as far as we are acquainted with it, looking to the average of sensations, the plurality and the preponderancy is in favour of happiness by a vast excess. In our own species, in which perhaps the assertion may be more questionable than in any other, the prepollency of good over evil, of health, for example, and ease, over pain and distress, is evinced by the very notice which calamities excite. What inquiries does the sickness of our friends produce! what conversation their misfortunes! This shows that the common course of things is in favour of happiness: that happiness is the rule, misery the exception. Were the order reversed, our attention would be called to examples of health and competency, instead of disease and want....

Contrivance proves design: and the predominant tendency of the contrivance indicates the disposition of the designer. The world abounds with contrivances: and all the contrivances which we are acquainted with, are directed to beneficial purposes. Evil, no doubt, exists; but is never, that we can perceive, the *object* of contrivance. Teeth are contrived to eat, not to ache; their aching now and then is incidental to the contrivance, perhaps inseparable from it: or even, if you will, let it be called a defect in the contrivance: but it is not the object of it. This is a distinction which well deserves to be attended to. In describing implements of husbandry, you would hardly say of the sickle, that it is made to cut the reaper's hand; though, from the construction of the instrument, and the manner of using it, this mischief often follows. But if you had occasion to describe instruments of torture or execution; this engine you would say, is to extend the sinews: this to dislocate the joints; this to break the bones; this to scorch the soles of the feet. Here, pain and misery are the very objects of the contrivance. Now, nothing of this sort is to be found in the works of nature. We never discover a train of contrivance to bring about an evil purpose. No anatomist ever discovered a system of organization calculated to produce pain and disease; or, in explaining the parts of the human body, ever said, this is to irritate; this to inflame; this duct is to convey the gravel to the kidneys; this gland to secrete the humour which forms the gout; if by chance he come at a part of which he knows not the use, the most he can say is, that it is useless; no one ever suspects that it is put there to incommode, to annoy, or to torment....

The TWO CASES which appear to me to have the most of difficulty in them, as forming the most of the appearance of exception to the representation here given, are those of *venomous* animals, and of animals *preying* upon one another....

The SECOND CASE, *viz.* that of animals *devouring* one another, furnishes a consideration of much larger extent. To judge whether, as a general provision, this can be deemed an *evil*, even so far as we understand its consequences, which, probably, is a partial understanding, the following reflections are fit to be attended to.

1. Immortality upon this earth is out of the question. Without death there could be no generation, no sexes, no parental relation, *i. e.* as things are constituted, no animal happiness. The particular duration of life, assigned to different animals, can form no part of the objection; because, whatever that duration be, whilst it remains finite and limited, it may always be asked, why it is no longer. The natural age of different animals varies, from a single day to a century of years. No account can be given of this; nor could any be given, whatever other proportion of life had obtained amongst them.

The term then of life in different animals being the same as it is, the question is, what mode of taking it away is the best even for the animal itself.

Now, according to the established order of nature (which we must suppose to prevail, or we cannot reason at all upon the subject), the three methods by which life is usually put an end to, are acute diseases, decay, and violence. The simple and natural life of *brutes*, is not often visited by acute distempers; nor could it be deemed an improvement of their lot, if they were. Let it be considered, therefore, in what a condition of suffering and misery a brute animal is placed, which is left to perish by *decay*. In human sickness or infirmity, there is the assistance of man's rational fellow-creatures, if not to alleviate his pains, at least to minister to his necessities, and to supply the place of his own activity. A brute, in his wild and natural state, does every thing for himself. When his strength, therefore, or his speed, or his limbs, or his senses fail him, he is delivered over, either to absolute famine, or to the protracted wretchedness of a life slowly wasted by the scarcity of food. Is it then to see the world filled with drooping, superannuated, half-starved, helpless, and unhelped animals, that you would alter the present system, of pursuit and prey?

2. Which system is also to them the spring of motion and activity on both sides. The pursuit of its prey, forms the employment, and appears to constitute the pleasure, of a considerable part of the animal creation. The using of the means of defence, or flight, or precaution, forms also the business of another part. And even of this latter tribe, we have no reason to suppose, that their happiness is much molested by their fears. Their danger exists continually; and in some cases they seem to be so far sensible of it as to provide, in the best manner they can, against it; but it is only when the attack is actually made upon them, that they appear to suffer from it. To contemplate the insecurity of their condition with anxiety and dread, requires a degree of reflection, which (happily for themselves), they do not possess. A *hare*, notwithstanding the number of its dangers and its enemies, is as playful an animal as any other.

3. But, to do justice to the question, the system of animal *destruction* ought always to be considered in strict connexion with another property of animal nature, viz. *superfecundity*. They are countervailing qualities. One subsists by the correction of the other. In treating, therefore, of the subject under this view (which is, I believe, the true one), our business will be, first, to point out the advantages which are gained by the powers in nature of a superabundant multiplication; and, then, to show, that these advantages are so many reasons for appointing that system of national hostilities, which we are endeavouring to account for.

In almost all cases, nature produces her supplies with profusion. A single cod-fish spawns, in one season, a greater number of eggs, than all the inhabitants of England amount to. A thousand other instances of prolific generation might be stated, which, though not equal to this, would carry on the increase of the species with a rapidity which outruns calculation, and to an immeasurable extent. The advantages of such a constitution are two: first, that it tends to keep the world always full; whilst, secondly, it allows the proportion between the several species of animals to be differently modified, as different purposes require, or as different situations may afford for them room and food. Where this vast fecundity meets with a vacancy fitted to receive the species, there it operates with its whole effect: there it pours in its numbers, and replenishes the waste. We complain of what we call the exorbitant multiplication of some troublesome insects; not reflecting, that large portions of nature might be left void without it. If the accounts of travellers may be depended upon, immense tracts of forest in North America would be nearly lost to sensitive existence, if it were not for *gnats*. "In the thinly inhabited regions of America, in which the waters stagnate and the climate is warm, the whole air is filled with crowds of these insects." Thus it is, that where we looked for solitude and death-like silence, we meet with animation, activity, enjoyment; with a busy, a happy, and a peopled world. Again; hosts of *mice* are reckoned amongst the plagues of the north-east part of Europe; whereas vast plains in Siberia, as we learn from good authority, would be lifeless without them. The Caspian deserts are converted by their presence into crowded warrens. Between the Volga and the Yaik, and in the country of Hyrcania, the ground, says Pallas, is in many places *covered* with little hills, raised by the earth cast out in forming the burrows. Do we so envy these blissful abodes, as to pronounce the fecundity by which they are supplied with inhabitants, to be an evil; a subject of complaint, and not of praise? Further; by virtue of this same superfecundity, what we term destruction, becomes almost instantly the parent of life. What we call blights, are, oftentimes, legions of animated beings, claiming their portion in the bounty of nature. What corrupts the produce of the earth to us, prepares it for them. And it is by means of their rapid multiplication, that they take possession of their pasture; a slow propagation would not meet the opportunity.

But in conjunction with the occasional use of this fruitfulness, we observe, also, that it allows the proportion between the several species of animals to be differently modified, as different purposes of utility may require. When the forests of America come to be cleared, and the swamps drained, our gnats will give place to other inhabitants. If the population of Europe should spread to the north and the east, the mice will retire before the husbandman and the shepherd, and yield their station to herds and flocks. In what concerns the human species, it may be a part of the scheme of Providence, that the earth should be inhabited by a shifting, or perhaps a circulating population. In this œconomy, it is possible that there may be the following advantages: When old countries are become exceedingly corrupt, simpler modes of life, purer morals, and better institutions, may rise up in new ones, whilst fresh soils reward the cultivator with more plentiful returns. Thus the different portions of the globe come into use in succession as the residence of man; and, in his absence, entertain other guests, which, by their sudden multiplication, fill the chasm. In domesticated animals, we find the effect of their fecundity to be, that we can always command *numbers*; we can always have as many of any particular species as we please, or as we can support. Nor do we complain of its excess; it being much more easy to regulate abundance, than to supply scarcity.

But then this *superfecundity*, though of great occasional use and importance, exceeds the ordinary capacity of nature to receive or support its progeny. All superabundance supposes destruction, or must destroy itself. Perhaps there is no species of terrestrial animals whatever, which would not overrun the earth, if it were permitted to multiply in perfect safety; or of fish, which would not fill the ocean: at least, if any single species were left to their natural increase without disturbance or restraint, the food of other species would be exhausted by their maintenance. It is necessary, therefore, that the effects of such prolific faculties be curtailed. In con junction with other checks and limits, all subservient to the same purpose, are the *thinnings* which take place among animals, by their action upon one another. In some instances we ourselves experience, very directly, the use of these hostilities. One species of insects rids us of another species; or reduces their ranks. A third species, perhaps, keeps the second within bounds: and birds or lizards are a fence against the inordinate increase by which even these last might infest us. In other, more numerous, and possibly more important, instances, this disposition of things, although less necessary or useful to us, and of course less observed by us, may be necessary and useful to certain other species; or even for the preventing of the loss of certain species from the universe: a misfortune which seems to be studiously guarded against. Though there may be the appearance of failure in some of the details of Nature's works, in her great purposes there never are. Her species never fail. The provision which was originally made for continuing the replenishment of the world, has proved itself to be effectual through a long succession of ages.

What further shows, that the system of destruction amongst animals holds an express relation to the system of fecundity; that they are parts indeed of one compensatory scheme; is, that, in each species, the fecundity bears a proportion to the smallness of the animal, to the weakness, to the shortness of its natural term of life, and to the dangers and enemies by which it is surrounded. An elephant produces but one calf; a butterfly lays six hundred eggs. Birds of prey seldom produce more than two eggs: the sparrow tribe, and the duck tribe, frequently sit upon a dozen. In the rivers, we meet with a thousand minnows for one pike; in the sea, a million of herrings for a single shark. Compensation obtains throughout. Defencelessness and devastation are repaired by fecundity.

We have dwelt the longer on these considerations, because the subject to which they apply, namely, that of animals *devouring* one another, forms the chief, if not the only instance, in the works of the Deity, of an œconomy, stamped by marks of design, in which the character of utility can be called in question. The case of *venomous* animals is of much inferior consequence to the case of prey, and, in some degree, is also included under it. To both cases it is probable that many more reasons belong, than those of which we are in possession.

Our FIRST PROPOSITION, and that which we have hitherto been defending, was, "that, in a vast plurality of instances, in which *contrivance* is perceived, the design of the contrivance is beneficial."

Our SECOND PROPOSITION is, "that the Deity has added *pleasure* to animal sensations, beyond what was necessary for any other purpose, or when the purpose, so far as it was necessary, might have been effected by the operation of pain."

This proposition may be thus explained: The capacities, which, according to the established course of nature, are *necessary* to the support or preservation of an animal, however manifestly they may be the result of an organization contrived for the purpose, can only be deemed an act or a part of the same will, as that which decreed the existence of the animal itself; because, whether the creation proceeded from a benevolent of a malevolent being, these capacities must have been given, if the animal existed at all. Animal properties, therefore, which fall under this description, do not strictly prove the goodness of God: they may prove the existence of the Deity; they may prove a high degree of power and intelligence: but they do not prove his goodness; forasmuch as they must have been found in any creation which was capable of continuance, although it is possible to suppose, that such a creation might have been produced by a being whose views rested upon misery.

But there is a class of properties, which may be said to be superadded from an intention expressly directed to happiness; an intention to give a happy existence distinct from the general intention of providing the means of existence; and that is, of capacities for pleasure, in cases wherein, so far as the conservation of the individual or of the species is concerned, they were not wanted, or wherein the purpose might have been secured by the operation of pain. The provision which is made of a variety of objects, not necessary to life, and ministering only to our pleasures; and the properties given to the necessaries of life themselves, by which they contribute to pleasure as well as preservation; show a further design, than that of giving existence(Note: See this topic considered in Dr. Balguy's Treatise upon the Divine Benevolence. This excellent author first, I think, proposed it; and nearly in the terms in which it is here stated. Some other observations also under this head are taken from that treatise.).

A single instance will make all this clear. Assuming the necessity of food for the support of animal life; it is requisite, that the animal be provided with organs, fitted for the procuring, receiving, and digesting of its food. It may be also necessary, that the animal be impelled by its sensations to exert its organs. But the pain of hunger would do all this. Why add pleasure to the act of eating; sweetness and relish to food? why a new and appropriate sense for the perception of the pleasure? Why should the juice of a peach, applied to the palate, affect the part so differently from what it does when rubbed upon the palm of the hand? This is a constitution which, so far as appears to me, can be resolved into nothing but the pure benevolence of the Creator. Eating is necessary; but the pleasure attending it is not necessary: and that this pleasure depends, not only upon our being in possession of the sense of taste, which is different from every other, but upon a particular state of the organ in which it resides, a felicitous adaptation of the organ to the object, will be confessed by any one, who may happen to have experienced that vitiation of taste which frequently occurs in fevers, when every taste is irregular, and every one bad....

Rational natures also, as such, exhibit qualities which help to confirm the truth of our position. The degree of understanding found in mankind, is usually much greater than what is necessary for mere preservation. The pleasure of choosing for themselves, and of prosecuting the object of their choice, should seem to be an original source of enjoyment. The pleasures received from things, great, beautiful, or new, from imitation, or from the liberal arts, are, in some measure, not only superadded, but unmixed, gratifications, having no pains to balance them(Note: Balguy on the Divine Benevolence.).

I do not know whether our attachment to *property* be not something more than the mere dictate of reason, or even than the mere effect of association. Property communicates a charm to whatever is the object of it. It is the first of our abstract ideas; it cleaves to us the closest and the longest. It endears to the child its plaything, to the peasant his cottage, to the landholder his estate. It supplies the place of prospect and scenery. Instead of coveting the beauty of distant situations, it teaches every man to find it in his own. It gives boldness and grandeur to plains and fens, tinge and colouring to clays and fallows.

All these considerations come in aid of our *second* proposition. The reader will now bear in mind what our two propositions were. They were, firstly, that in a vast plurality of instances, in which contrivance is perceived, the design of the contrivance is beneficial: secondly, that the Deity has added pleasure to animal sensations beyond what was necessary for any other purpose; or when the purpose, so far as it was necessary, might have been effected by the operation of pain.

Whilst these propositions can be maintained, we are authorized to ascribe to the Deity the character of benevolence: and what is benevolence at all, must in him be *infinite* benevolence, by reason of the infinite, that is to say, the incalculably great, number of objects, upon which it is exercised....

CHAPTER XXVII.
CONCLUSION.

IN all cases, wherein the mind feels itself in danger of being confounded by variety, it is sure to rest upon a few strong points, or perhaps upon a single instance. Amongst a multitude of proofs, it is *one* that does the business. If we observe in any argument, that hardly two minds fix upon the same instance, the diversity of choice shows the strength of the argument, because it shows the number and competition of the examples. There is no subject in which the tendency to dwell upon select or single topics is so usual because there is no subject, of which, in its full extent, the latitude is so great, as that of natural history applied to the proof of an intelligent Creator. For my part, I take my stand in human anatomy: and the examples of mechanism I should be apt to draw out from the copious catalogue, which it supplies, are the pivot upon which the head turns, the ligament within the socket of the hip-joint, the pulley or trochlear muscles of the eye, the epiglottis, the bandages which tie down the tendons of the wrist and instep, the slit or perforated muscles at the hands and feet, the knitting of the intestines to the mesentery, the course of the chyle into the blood, and the constitution of the sexes as extended throughout the whole of the animal creation. To these instances, the reader's memory will go back, as they are severally set forth in their places; there is not one of the number which I do not think decisive; not one which is not strictly mechanical; nor have I read or heard of any solution of these appearances, which, in the smallest degree, shakes the conclusion that we build upon them.

But, of the greatest part of those, who, either in this book or any other, read arguments to prove the existence of a God, it will be said, that they leave off only where they began; that they were never ignorant of this great truth, never doubted of it; that it does not therefore appear, what is gained by researches from which no new opinion is learnt, and upon the subject of which no proofs were wanted. Now I answer that, by *investigation*, the following points are always gained, in favour of doctrines even the most generally acknowledged, (supposing them to be true), *viz.* stability and impression. Occasions will arise to try the firmness of our most habitual opinions. And upon these occasions, it is a matter of incalculable use to feel our foundation; to find a support in argument for what we had taken up upon authority. In the present case, the arguments upon which the conclusion rests, are exactly such, as a truth of universal concern ought to rest upon. "They are sufficiently open to the views and capacities of the unlearned, at the same time that they acquire new strength and lustre from the discoveries of the learned." If they had been altogether abstruse and recondite, they would not have found their way to the understandings of the mass of mankind; if they had been merely popular, they might have wanted solidity.

But, secondly, what is gained by research in the stability of our conclusion, is also gained from it in *impression*. Physicians tell us, that there is a great deal of difference between taking a medicine, and the medicine getting into the constitution. A difference not unlike which, obtains with respect to those great moral propositions, which ought to form the directing principles of human conduct. It is one thing to assent to a proposition of this sort; another, and a very different thing, to have properly imbibed its influence. I take the case to be this: perhaps almost every man living has a particular train of thought, into which his mind glides and falls, when at leisure from the impressions and ideas that occasionally excite it; perhaps, also, the train of thought here spoken of, more than any other thing, determines the character. It is of the utmost consequence, therefore, that this property of our constitution be well regulated. Now it is by frequent or continued meditation upon a subject, by placing a subject in different points of view, by induction of particulars, by variety of examples, by applying principles to the solution of phænomena, by dwelling upon proofs and consequences, that mental exercise is drawn into any particular channel. It is by these means, at least, that we have any power over it. The train of spontaneous thought, and the choice of that train, may be directed to different ends, and may appear to be more or less judiciously fixed, according to the purpose, in respect of which we consider it: but, in a *moral view*, I shall not, I believe, be contradicted when I say, that, if one train of thinking be more desirable than another, it is that which regards the phænomena of nature with a constant reference to a supreme intelligent Author. To have made this the ruling, the habitual sentiment of our minds, is to have laid the foundation of every thing which is religious. The world thenceforth becomes a temple, and life itself one continued act of adoration. The change is no less than this, that, whereas formerly God was seldom in our thoughts, we can now scarcely look upon any thing without perceiving its relation to him. Every organized natural body, in the provisions which it contains for its sustentation and propagation, testifies a care, on the part of the Creator, expressly directed to these purposes. We are on all sides surrounded by such bodies; examined in their parts, wonderfully curious; compared with one another, no less wonderfully diversified. So that the mind, as well as the eye, may either expatiate in variety and multitude, or fix itself down to the investigation of particular divisions of the science. And in either case it will rise up from its occupation, possessed by the subject, in a very different manner, and with a very different degree of influence, from what a mere assent to any verbal proposition which can be formed concerning the existence of the Deity, at least that merely complying assent with which those about us are satisfied, and with which we are too apt to satisfy ourselves, will or can produce upon the thoughts. More especially may this difference be perceived, in the degree of admiration and of awe, with which the Divinity is regarded, when represented to the understanding by its own remarks, its own reflections, and its own reasonings, compared with what is excited by any language that can be used by others. The works of nature want only to be contemplated. When contemplated, they have every thing in them which can astonish by their greatness: for, of the vast scale of operation, through which our discoveries carry us, at one end we see an intelligent Power arranging planetary systems, fixing, for instance, the trajectory of *Saturn*, or constructing a ring of two hundred thousand miles diameter, to surround his body, and be suspended like a magnificent arch over the heads of his inhabitants; and, at the other, bending a hooked tooth, concerting and providing an appropriate mechanism, for the clasping and reclasping of the filaments of the feather of the humming-bird. We have proof, not only of both these works proceeding from an intelligent agent, but of their proceeding from the same agent; for, in the first place, we can trace an identity of plan, a connexion of system, from Saturn to our own globe: and when arrived upon our globe, we can, in the second place, pursue the connexion through all the organized, especially the animated, bodies which it supports. We can observe marks of a common relation, as well to one another, as to the elements of which their habitation is composed. Therefore one mind hath planned, or at least hath prescribed, a general plan for all these productions. One Being has been concerned in all.

Under this stupendous Being we live. Our happiness, our existence, is in his hands. All we expect must come from him. Nor ought we to feel our situation insecure. In every nature, and in every portion of nature, which we can descry, we find attention bestowed upon even the minutest arts. The hinges in the wings of an *earwig*, and the joints of its antennæ, are as highly wrought, as if the Creator had nothing else to finish. We see no signs or diminution of care by multiplicity of objects, or of distraction of thought by variety. We have no reason to fear, therefore, our being forgotten, or overlooked, or neglected.

The existence and character of the Deity, is, in every view, the most interesting of all human speculations. In none, however, is it more so, than as it facilitates the belief of the fundamental articles of *Revelation.* It is a step to have it proved, that there must be something in the world more than what we see. It is a further step to know, that, amongst the invisible things of nature, there must be an intelligent mind, concerned in its production, order, and support. These points being assured to us by Natural Theology, we may well leave to Revelation the disclosure of many particulars, which our researches cannot reach, respecting either the nature of this Being as the original cause of all things, or his character and designs as a moral governor; and not only so, but the more full confirmation of other particulars, of which, though they do not lie altogether beyond our reasonings and our probabilities, the certainty is by no means equal to the importance. The true theist will be the first to listen to *any* credible communication of Divine knowledge. Nothing which he has learned from Natural Theology, will diminish his desire of further instruction, or his disposition to receive it with humility and thankfulness. He wishes for light: he rejoices in light. His inward veneration of this great Being, will incline him to attend with the utmost seriousness, not only to all that can be discovered concerning him by researches into nature, but to all that is taught by a revelation, which gives reasonable proof of having proceeded from him.

But, above every other article of revealed religion, does the anterior belief of a Deity bear with the strongest force upon that grand point, which gives indeed interest and importance to all the rest,--the resurrection of the human dead. The thing might appear hopeless, did we not see a power at work adequate to the effect, a power under the guidance of an intelligent will, and a power penetrating the inmost recesses of all substance. I am far from justifying the opinion of those, who "thought it a thing incredible, that God should raise the dead:" but I admit, that it is first necessary to be persuaded, that there *is* a God, to do so. This being thoroughly settled in our minds, there seems to be nothing in this process (concealed as we confess it to be) which need to shock our belief. They who have taken up the opinion, that the acts of the human mind depend upon *organization*, that the mind itself indeed consists in organization, are supposed to find a greater difficulty than others do, in admitting a transition by death to a new state of sentient existence, because the old organization is apparently dissolved. But I do not see that any impracticability need be apprehended even by these; or that the change, even upon their hypothesis, is far removed from the analogy of some other operations, which we know with certainty that the Deity is carrying on. In the ordinary derivation of plants and animals, from one another, a particle, in many cases, minuter than all assignable, all conceivable dimension; an aura, an effluvium, an infinitesimal; determines the organization of a future body: does no less than fix, whether that which is about to be produced, shall be a vegetable, a merely sentient, or a rational being: an oak, a frog, or a philosopher; makes all these differences; gives to the future body its qualities, and nature and species. And this particle, from which springs, and by which is determined a whole future nature, itself proceeds from, and owes its constitution to, a prior body: nevertheless, which is seen in plants most decisively, the incepted organization, though formed within, and through, and by a preceding organization, is not corrupted by its corruption, or destroyed by its dissolution: but, on the contrary, is sometimes extricated and developed by those very causes; survives and comes into action, when the purpose, for which it was prepared, requires its use. Now an œconomy which nature has adopted, when the purpose was to transfer an organization from one individual to another, may have something analogous to it, when the purpose is to transmit an organization from one state of being to another state: and they who found thought in organization, may see something in this analogy applicable to their difficulties; for, whatever can transmit a similarity of organization will answer their purpose, because, according even to their own theory, it may be the vehicle of consciousness, and because consciousness carries identity and individuality along with it through all changes of form or of visible qualities. In the most general case, that, as we have said, of the derivation of plants and animals from one another, the latent organization is either itself similar to the old organization, or has the power of communicating to new matter the old organic form. But it is not restricted to this rule. There are other cases, especially in the progress of insect life, in which the dormant organization does not much resemble that which encloses it, and still less suits with the situation in which the enclosing body is placed, but suits with a different situation to which it is destined. In the larva of the libellula, which lives constantly, and has still long to live, under water, are descried the wings of a fly, which two years afterwards is to mount into the air. Is there nothing in this analogy? It serves at least to show, that even in the observable course of nature, organizations are formed one beneath another; and, amongst a thousand other instances, it shows completely, that the Deity can mould and fashion the parts of material nature, so as to fulfil any purpose whatever which he is pleased to appoint.

They who refer the operations of mind to a substance totally and essentially different from matter, (as most certainly these operations, though affected by material causes, hold very little affinity to any properties of matter with which we are acquainted), adopt perhaps a juster reasoning and a better philosophy: and by these the considerations above suggested are not wanted, at least in the same degree. But to such as find, which some persons do find, an insuperable difficulty in shaking off an adherence to those analogies, which the corporeal world is continually suggesting to their thoughts; to such, I say, every consideration will be a relief, which manifests the extent of that intelligent power which is acting in nature, the fruitfulness of its resources, the variety, and aptness, and success of its means; most especially every consideration, which tends to show that, in the translation of a conscious existence, there is not, even in their own way of regarding it, any thing greatly beyond, or totally unlike, what takes place in such parts (probably small parts) of the order of nature, as are accessible to our observation.

Again; if there be those who think, that the contractedness and debility of the human faculties in our present state, seem ill to accord with the high destinies which the expectations of religion point out to us, I would only ask them, whether any one, who saw a child two hours after its birth, could suppose that it would ever come to understand *fluxions* (*Note:* See Search's Light of Nature, *passim.*); or who then shall say, what farther amplification of intellectual powers, what accession of knowledge, what advance and improvement, the rational faculty, be its constitution what it will, may not admit of, when placed amidst new objects, and endowed with a sensorium adapted, as it undoubtedly will be, and as our present senses are, to the perception of those substances, and of those properties of things, with which our concern may lie.

Upon the whole; in every thing which respects this awful, but, as we trust, glorious change, we have a wise and powerful Being, (the author, in nature, of infinitely various expedients for infinitely various ends), upon whom to rely for the choice and appointment of means, adequate to the execution of any plan which his goodness or his justice may have formed, for the moral and accountable part of his terrestrial creation. That great office rests with *him:* be it *ours* to hope and to prepare, under a firm and settled persuasion, that, living and dying, we are his; that life is passed in his constant presence, that death resigns us to his merciful disposal.

FINIS.

David Hume (7 May 1711 – 25 August 1776)is one of the most important and influential philosophers of the Western tradition. Considered a prominent figure of the Scottish Enlightenment, Hume was a consistent and serious skeptic with regard to the claims of religion. His Dialogues Concerning Natural Religion provides a critique of numerous arguments for God's existence, and the reliability of miracle testimony, among other things. The work was not published until after his death. The "Dialogues" features three characters: Demea, Cleanthes, and Philo. In our excerpt, Cleanthes offers a version of the design argument similar to the one Paley will provide several decades later. Philo then begins a systematic criticism of this argument, questioning the analogy itself, the sample on which it is based, and the scope and specificity of its conclusion even in the unlikely event that the argument survives the other criticisms. For these reasons, and others, Hume is often regarded as a philosophical mentor to those advocating skeptical philosophy in general, or agnosticism with regard to theism in particular.

Dialogues Concerning Natural Religion[114]
David Hume
Treatise on The One God – Part II

...Not to lose any time in circumlocutions, said Cleanthes, addressing himself to Demea, much less in replying to the pious declamations of Philo; I shall briefly explain how I conceive this matter. Look round the world: contemplate the whole and every part of it: you will find it to be nothing but one great machine, subdivided into an infinite number of lesser machines, which again admit of subdivisions to a degree beyond what human senses and faculties can trace and explain. All these various machines, and even their most minute parts, are adjusted to each other with an accuracy which ravishes into admiration all men who have ever contemplated them. The curious adapting of means to ends, throughout all nature, resembles exactly, though it much exceeds, the productions of human contrivance; of human designs, thought, wisdom, and intelligence. Since, therefore, the effects resemble each other, we are led to infer, by all the rules of analogy, that the causes also resemble; and that the Author of Nature is somewhat similar to the mind of man, though possessed of much larger faculties, proportioned to the grandeur of the work which he has executed. By this argument a posteriori, and by this argument alone, do we prove at once the existence of a Deity, and his similarity to human mind and intelligence.

I shall be so free, Cleanthes, said Demea, as to tell you, that from the beginning, I could not approve of your conclusion concerning the similarity of the Deity to men; still less can I approve of the mediums by which you endeavour to establish it. What! No demonstration of the Being of God! No abstract arguments! No proofs a priori! Are these, which have hitherto been so much insisted on by philosophers, all fallacy, all sophism? Can we reach no further in this subject than experience and probability? I will not say that this is betraying the cause of a Deity: but surely, by this affected

---

[114] https://people.rit.edu/wlrgsh/Dialogues.pdf

candour, you give advantages to Atheists, which they never could obtain by the mere dint of argument and reasoning.

What I chiefly scruple in this subject, said Philo, is not so much that all religious arguments are by Cleanthes reduced to experience, as that they appear not to be even the most certain and irrefragable of that inferior kind. That a stone will fall, that fire will burn, that the earth has solidity, we have observed a thousand and a thousand times; and when any new instance of this nature is presented, we draw without hesitation the accustomed inference. The exact similarity of the cases gives us a perfect assurance of a similar event; and a stronger evidence is never desired nor sought after. But wherever you depart, in the least, from the similarity of the cases, you diminish proportionably the evidence; and may at last bring it to a very weak analogy, which is confessedly liable to error and uncertainty. After having experienced the circulation of the blood in human creatures, we make no doubt that it takes place in Titius and Maevius. But from its circulation in frogs and fishes, it is only a presumption, though a strong one, from analogy, that it takes place in men and other animals. The analogical reasoning is much weaker, when we infer the circulation of the sap in vegetables from our experience that the blood circulates in animals; and those, who hastily followed that imperfect analogy, are found, by more accurate experiments, to have been mistaken.

If we see a house, Cleanthes, we conclude, with the greatest certainty, that it had an architect or builder; because this is precisely that species of effect which we have experienced to proceed from that species of cause. But surely you will not affirm, that the universe bears such a resemblance to a house that we can with the same certainty infer a similar cause, or that the analogy is here entire and perfect. The dissimilitude is so striking, that the utmost you can here pretend to is a guess, a conjecture, a presumption concerning a similar cause; and how that pretension will be received in the world, I leave you to consider.

It would surely be very ill received, replied Cleanthes; and I should be deservedly blamed and detested, did I allow, that the proofs of a Deity amounted to no more than a guess or conjecture. But is the whole adjustment of means to ends in a house and in the universe so slight a resemblance? The economy of final causes? The order, proportion, and arrangement of every part? Steps of a stair are plainly contrived, that human legs may use them in mounting; and this inference is certain and infallible. Human legs are also contrived for walking and mounting; and this inference, I allow, is not altogether so certain, because of the dissimilarity which you remark; but does it, therefore, deserve the name only of presumption or conjecture?

Good God! cried Demea, interrupting him, where are we? Zealous defenders of religion allow, that the proofs of a Deity fall short of perfect evidence! And you, Philo, on whose assistance I depended in proving the adorable mysteriousness of the Divine Nature, do you assent to all these extravagant opinions of Cleanthes? For what other name can I give them? or, why spare my censure, when such principles are advanced, supported by such an authority, before so young a man as Pamphilus?

You seem not to apprehend, replied Philo, that I argue with Cleanthes in his own way; and, by shewing him the dangerous consequences of his tenets, hope at last to reduce him to our opinion. But what sticks most with you, I observe, is the representation which Cleanthes has made of the argument a posteriori; and finding that that argument is likely to escape your hold and vanish into air, you think it so disguised, that you can scarcely believe it to be set in its true light. Now, however much I may dissent, in other respects, from the dangerous principles of Cleanthes, I must allow that he has fairly represented that argument; and I shall endeavour so to state the matter to you, that you will entertain no further scruples with regard to it.

Were a man to abstract from every thing which he knows or has seen, he would be altogether incapable, merely from his own ideas, to determine what kind of scene the universe must be, or to give the preference to one state or situation of things above another. For as nothing which he clearly conceives could be esteemed impossible or implying a contradiction, every chimera of his fancy would be upon an equal footing; nor could he assign any just reason why he adheres to one idea or system, and rejects the others which are equally possible.

Again; after he opens his eyes, and contemplates the world as it really is, it would be impossible for him at first to assign the cause of any one event, much less of the whole of things, or of the universe. He might set his fancy a rambling; and she might bring him in an infinite variety of reports and representations. These would all be possible; but being all equally possible, he would never of himself give a satisfactory account for his preferring one of them to the rest. Experience alone can point out to him the true cause of any phenomenon.

Now, according to this method of reasoning, Demea, it follows, (and is, indeed, tacitly allowed by Cleanthes himself,) that order, arrangement, or the adjustment of final causes, is not of itself any proof of design; but only so far as it has been experienced to proceed from that principle. For ought we can know a priori, matter may contain the source or spring of order originally within itself as well as mind does; and there is no more difficulty in conceiving, that the several elements, from an internal unknown cause, may fall into the most exquisite arrangement, than to conceive that their ideas, in the great universal mind, from a like internal unknown cause, fall into that arrangement. The equal possibility of both these suppositions is allowed. But, by experience, we find, (according to Cleanthes,) that there is a difference between them. Throw several pieces of steel together, without shape or form; they will never arrange themselves so as to compose a watch. Stone, and mortar, and wood, without an architect, never erect a house. But the ideas in a human mind, we see, by an unknown, inexplicable economy, arrange themselves so as to form the plan of a watch or house. Experience, therefore, proves, that there is an original principle of order in mind, not in matter. From similar effects we infer similar causes. The adjustment of means to ends is alike in the universe, as in a machine of human contrivance. The causes, therefore, must be resembling.

I was from the beginning scandalized, I must own, with this resemblance, which is asserted, between the Deity and human creatures; and must conceive it to imply such a degradation of the Supreme Being as no sound Theist could endure. With your assistance, therefore, Demea, I shall endeavour to defend what you justly call the adorable mysteriousness of the Divine Nature, and shall refute this reasoning of Cleanthes, provided he allows that I have made a fair representation of it.

When Cleanthes had assented, Philo, after a short pause, proceeded in the following manner.

That all inferences, Cleanthes, concerning fact, are founded on experience; and that all experimental reasonings are founded on the supposition that similar causes prove similar effects, and similar effects similar causes; I shall not at present much dispute with you. But observe, I entreat you, with what extreme caution all just reasoners proceed in the transferring of experiments to similar cases. Unless the cases be exactly similar, they repose no perfect confidence in applying their past observation to any particular phenomenon. Every alteration of circumstances occasions a doubt concerning the event; and it requires new experiments to prove certainly, that the new circumstances are of no moment or importance. A change in bulk, situation, arrangement, age, disposition of the air, or surrounding bodies; any of these particulars may be attended with the most unexpected consequences: and unless the objects be quite familiar to us, it is the highest temerity to expect with assurance, after any of these changes, an event similar to that which before fell under our observation. The slow and deliberate steps of philosophers here, if any where, are distinguished from the precipitate march of the vulgar, who, hurried on by the smallest similitude, are incapable of all discernment or consideration.

But can you think, Cleanthes, that your usual phlegm and philosophy have been preserved in so wide a step as you have taken, when you compared to the universe houses, ships, furniture, machines, and, from their similarity in some circumstances, inferred a similarity in their causes? Thought, design, intelligence, such as we discover in men and other animals, is no more than one of the springs and principles of the universe, as well as heat or cold, attraction or repulsion, and a hundred others, which fall under daily observation. It is an active cause, by which some particular parts of nature, we find, produce alterations on other parts. But can a conclusion, with any propriety, be transferred from parts to the whole? Does not the great disproportion bar all comparison and inference? From observing the growth of a hair, can we learn any thing concerning the generation of a man? Would the manner of a leaf's blowing, even though perfectly known, afford us any instruction concerning the vegetation of a tree?

But, allowing that we were to take the operations of one part of nature upon another, for the foundation of our judgment concerning the origin of the whole, (which never can be admitted,) yet why select so minute, so weak, so bounded a principle, as the reason and design of animals is found to be upon this planet? What peculiar privilege has this little agitation of the brain which we call thought, that we must thus make it the model of the whole universe? Our partiality in our own favour does indeed present it on all occasions; but sound philosophy ought carefully to guard against so natural an illusion.

So far from admitting, continued Philo, that the operations of a part can afford us any just conclusion concerning the origin of the whole, I will not allow any one part to form a rule for another part, if the latter be very remote from the former. Is there any reasonable ground to conclude, that the inhabitants of other planets possess thought, intelligence, reason, or any thing similar to these faculties in men? When nature has so extremely diversified her manner of operation in this small globe, can we imagine that she incessantly copies herself throughout so immense a universe? And if thought, as we may well suppose, be confined merely to this narrow corner, and has even there so limited a sphere of action, with what propriety can we assign it for the original cause of all things? The narrow views of a peasant, who makes his domestic economy the rule for the government of kingdoms, is in comparison a pardonable sophism.

But were we ever so much assured, that a thought and reason, resembling the human, were to be found throughout the whole universe, and were its activity elsewhere vastly greater and more commanding than it appears in this globe; yet I cannot see, why the operations of a world constituted, arranged, adjusted, can with any propriety be extended to a world which is in its embryo state, and is advancing towards that constitution and arrangement. By observation, we know somewhat of the economy, action, and nourishment of a finished animal; but we must transfer with great caution that observation to the growth of a foetus in the womb, and still more in the formation of an animalcule in the loins of its male parent. Nature, we find, even from our limited experience, possesses an infinite number of springs and principles, which incessantly discover themselves on every change of her position and situation. And what new and unknown principles would actuate her in so new and unknown a situation as that of the formation of a universe, we cannot, without the utmost temerity, pretend to determine.

A very small part of this great system, during a very short time, is very imperfectly discovered to us; and do we then pronounce decisively concerning the origin of the whole?

Admirable conclusion! Stone, wood, brick, iron, brass, have not, at this time, in this minute globe of earth, an order or arrangement without human art and contrivance; therefore the universe could not originally attain its order and arrangement, without something similar to human art.

But is a part of nature a rule for another part very wide of the former? Is it a rule for the whole? Is a very small part a rule for the universe? Is nature in one situation, a certain rule for nature in another situation vastly different from the former?

And can you blame me, Cleanthes, if I here imitate the prudent reserve of Simonides, who, according to the noted story, being asked by Hiero, What God was? desired a day to think of it, and then two days more; and after that manner continually prolonged the term, without ever bringing in his definition or description? Could you even blame me, if I answered at first, that I did not know, and was sensible that this subject lay vastly beyond the reach of my faculties? You might cry out sceptic and rallier, as much as you pleased: but having found, in so many other subjects much more familiar, the imperfections and even contradictions of human reason, I never should expect any success from its feeble conjectures, in a subject so sublime, and so remote from the sphere of our observation. When two species of objects have always been observed to be conjoined together, I can infer, by custom, the existence of one wherever I see the existence of the other; and this I call an argument from experience. But how this argument can have place, where the objects, as in the present case, are single, individual, without parallel, or specific resemblance, may be difficult to explain. And will any man tell me with a serious countenance, that an orderly universe must arise from some thought and art like the human, because we have experience of it? To ascertain this reasoning, it were requisite that we had experience of the origin of worlds; and it is not sufficient, surely, that we have seen ships and cities arise from human art and contrivance....

Part III

How he most absurd argument, replied Cleanthes, in the hands of a man of ingenuity and invention, may acquire an air of probability! Are you not aware, Philo, that it became necessary for Copernicus and his first disciples to prove the similarity of the terrestrial and celestial matter; because several philosophers, blinded by old systems, and supported by some sensible appearances, had denied that similarity? but that it is by no means necessary, that Theists should prove the similarity of the works of Nature to those of Art; because this similarity is self-evident and undeniable? The same matter, a like form; what more is requisite to shew an analogy between their causes, and to ascertain the origin of all things from a divine purpose and intention? Your objections, I must freely tell you, are no better than the abstruse cavils of those philosophers who denied motion; and ought to be refuted in the same manner, by illustrations, examples, and instances, rather than by serious argument and philosophy.

Suppose, therefore, that an articulate voice were heard in the clouds, much louder and more melodious than any which human art could ever reach: suppose, that this voice were extended in the same instant over all nations, and spoke to each nation in its own language and dialect: suppose, that the words delivered not only contain a just sense and meaning, but convey some instruction altogether worthy of a benevolent Being, superior to mankind: could you possibly hesitate a moment concerning the cause of this voice? and must you not instantly ascribe it to some design or purpose? Yet I cannot see but all the same objections (if they merit that appellation) which lie against the system of Theism, may also be produced against this inference.

Might you not say, that all conclusions concerning fact were founded on experience: that when we hear an articulate voice in the dark, and thence infer a man, it is only the resemblance of the effects which leads us to conclude that there is a like resemblance in the cause: but that this extraordinary voice, by its loudness, extent, and flexibility to all languages, bears so little analogy to any human voice, that we have no reason to suppose any analogy in their causes: and consequently, that a rational, wise, coherent speech proceeded, you know not whence, from some accidental whistling of the winds, not from any divine reason or intelligence? You see clearly your own objections in these cavils, and I hope too you see clearly, that they cannot possibly have more force in the one case than in the other.

But to bring the case still nearer the present one of the universe, I shall make two suppositions, which imply not any absurdity or impossibility. Suppose that there is a natural, universal, invariable language, common to every individual of human race; and that books are natural productions, which perpetuate themselves in the same manner with animals and vegetables, by descent and propagation. Several expressions of our passions contain a universal language: all brute animals have a natural speech, which, however limited, is very intelligible to their own species. And as there are infinitely fewer parts and less contrivance in the finest composition of eloquence, than in the coarsest organized body, the propagation of an Iliad or Aeneid is an easier supposition than that of any plant or animal.

Suppose, therefore, that you enter into your library, thus peopled by natural volumes, containing the most refined reason and most exquisite beauty; could you possibly open one of them, and doubt, that its original cause bore the strongest analogy to mind and intelligence? When it reasons and discourses; when it expostulates, argues, and enforces its views and topics; when it applies sometimes to the pure intellect, sometimes to the affections; when it collects, disposes, and adorns every consideration suited to the subject; could you persist in asserting, that all this, at the bottom, had really no meaning; and that the first formation of this volume in the loins of its original parent proceeded not from thought and design? Your obstinacy, I know, reaches not that degree of firmness: even your sceptical play and wantonness would be abashed at so glaring an absurdity.

But if there be any difference, Philo, between this supposed case and the real one of the universe, it is all to the advantage of the latter. The anatomy of an animal affords many stronger instances of design than the perusal of Livy or Tacitus; and any objection which you start in the former case, by carrying me back to so unusual and extraordinary a scene as the first formation of worlds, the same objection has place on the supposition of our vegetating library. Choose, then, your party, Philo, without ambiguity or evasion; assert either that a rational volume is no proof of a rational cause, or admit of a similar cause to all the works of nature.

Let me here observe too, continued Cleanthes, that this religious argument, instead of being weakened by that scepticism so much affected by you, rather acquires force from it, and becomes more firm and undisputed. To exclude all argument or reasoning of every kind, is either affectation or madness. The declared profession of every reasonable sceptic is only to reject abstruse, remote, and refined arguments; to adhere to common sense and the plain instincts of nature; and to assent, wherever any reasons strike him with so full a force that he cannot, without the greatest violence, prevent it. Now the arguments for Natural Religion are plainly of this kind; and nothing but the most perverse, obstinate metaphysics can reject them. Consider, anatomize the eye; survey its structure and contrivance; and tell me, from your own feeling, if the idea of a contriver does not immediately flow in upon you with a force like that of sensation. The most obvious conclusion, surely, is in favour of design; and it requires time, reflection, and study, to summon up those frivolous, though abstruse objections, which can support Infidelity. Who can behold the male and female of each species, the correspondence of their parts and instincts, their passions, and whole course of life before and after generation, but must be sensible, that the propagation of the species is intended by Nature? Millions and millions of such instances present themselves through every part of the universe; and no language can convey a more intelligible irresistible meaning, than the curious adjustment of final causes. To what degree, therefore, of blind dogmatism must one have attained, to reject such natural and such convincing arguments?...

Now, Cleanthes, said Philo, with an air of alacrity and triumph, mark the consequences. First, By this method of reasoning, you renounce all claim to infinity in any of the attributes of the Deity. For, as the cause ought only to be proportioned to the effect, and the effect, so far as it falls under our cognizance, is not infinite; what pretensions have we, upon your suppositions, to ascribe that attribute to the Divine Being? You will still insist, that, by removing him so much from all similarity to human creatures, we give in to the most arbitrary hypothesis, and at the same time weaken all proofs of his existence.

Secondly, You have no reason, on your theory, for ascribing perfection to the Deity, even in his finite capacity, or for supposing him free from every error, mistake, or incoherence, in his undertakings. There are many inexplicable difficulties in the works of Nature, which, if we allow a perfect author to be proved a priori, are easily solved, and become only seeming difficulties, from the narrow capacity of man, who cannot trace infinite relations. But according to your method of reasoning, these difficulties become all real; and perhaps will be insisted on, as new instances of likeness to human art and contrivance. At least, you must acknowledge, that it is impossible for us to tell, from our limited views, whether this system contains any great faults, or deserves any considerable praise, if compared to other possible, and even real systems. Could a peasant, if the Aeneid were read to him, pronounce that poem to be absolutely faultless, or even assign to it its proper rank among the productions of human wit, he, who had never seen any other production?

But were this world ever so perfect a production, it must still remain uncertain, whether all the excellences of the work can justly be ascribed to the workman. If we survey a ship, what an exalted idea must we form of the ingenuity of the carpenter who framed so complicated, useful, and beautiful a machine? And what surprize must we feel, when we find him a stupid mechanic, who imitated others, and copied an art, which, through a long succession of ages, after multiplied trials, mistakes, corrections, deliberations, and controversies, had been gradually improving?

Many worlds might have been botched and bungled, throughout an eternity, ere this system was struck out; much labour lost, many fruitless trials made; and a slow, but continued improvement carried on during infinite ages in the art of world-making. In such subjects, who can determine, where the truth; nay, who can conjecture where the probability lies, amidst a great number of hypotheses which may be proposed, and a still greater which may be imagined?

And what shadow of an argument, continued Philo, can you produce, from your hypothesis, to prove the unity of the Deity? A great number of men join in building a house or ship, in rearing a city, in framing a commonwealth; why may not several deities combine in contriving and framing a world? This is only so much greater similarity to human affairs. By sharing the work among several, we may so much further limit the attributes of each, and get rid of that extensive power and knowledge, which must be supposed in one deity, and which, according to you, can only serve to weaken the proof of his existence. And if such foolish, such vicious creatures as man, can yet often unite in framing and executing one plan, how much more those deities or demons, whom we may suppose several degrees more perfect!

To multiply causes without necessity, is indeed contrary to true philosophy: but this principle applies not to the present case. Were one deity antecedently proved by your theory, who were possessed of every attribute requisite to the production of the universe; it would be needless, I own, (though not absurd,) to suppose any other deity existent. But while it is still a question,

Whether all these attributes are united in one subject, or dispersed among several independent beings, by what phenomena in nature can we pretend to decide the controversy? Where we see a body raised in a scale, we are sure that there is in the opposite scale, however concealed from sight, some counterpoising weight equal to it; but it is still allowed to doubt, whether that weight be an aggregate of several distinct bodies, or one uniform united mass. And if the weight requisite very much exceeds any thing which we have ever seen conjoined in any single body, the former supposition becomes still more probable and natural. An intelligent being of such vast power and capacity as is necessary to produce the universe, or, to speak in the language of ancient philosophy, so prodigious an animal exceeds all analogy, and even comprehension.

But further, Cleanthes: men are mortal, and renew their species by generation; and this is common to all living creatures. The two great sexes of male and female, says Milton, animate the world. Why must this circumstance, so universal, so essential, be excluded from those numerous and limited deities? Behold, then, the theogony of ancient times brought back upon us.

And why not become a perfect Anthropomorphite? Why not assert the deity or deities to be corporeal, and to have eyes, a nose, mouth, ears, etc.? Epicurus maintained, that no man had ever seen reason but in a human figure; therefore the gods must have a human figure. And this argument, which is deservedly so much ridiculed by Cicero, becomes, according to you, solid and philosophical.

In a word, Cleanthes, a man who follows your hypothesis is able perhaps to assert, or conjecture, that the universe, sometime, arose from something like design: but beyond that position he cannot ascertain one single circumstance; and is left afterwards to fix every point of his theology by the utmost license of fancy and hypothesis. This world, for aught he knows, is very faulty and imperfect, compared to a superior standard; and was only the first rude essay of some infant deity, who afterwards abandoned it, ashamed of his lame performance: it is the work only of some dependent, inferior deity; and is the object of derision to his superiors: it is the production of old age and dotage in some superannuated deity; and ever since his death, has run on at adventures, from the first impulse and active force which it received from him. You justly give signs of horror, Demea, at these strange suppositions; but these, and a thousand more of the same kind, are Cleanthes's suppositions, not mine. From the moment the attributes of the Deity are supposed finite, all these have place. And I cannot, for my part, think that so wild and unsettled a system of theology is, in any respect, preferable to none at all.

Chapter 7: The Moral Argument

Comprehension questions you should be able to answer after reading this chapter:

1. What is the difference between objective and subjective claims?

2. What is Craig's version of the moral argument (MA)?

3. Why does Craig think that objective moral values/duties could not exist, unless God exists?

4. What is the "selfish gene?" What are the (4) behavioral patterns Dawkins proposes that would help promote the survival of the selfish gene? How could these be seen as an alternative to religiously-based explanations of ethics?

5. What is the "Euthyphro problem," and how is it seen as a threat to religiously-based explanations of ethics?

6. What is Craig's solution to the Euthyphro problem?

7. What is Craig's "perceptual analogy" with moral experience, and how is it supposed to support the second premise of the MA?

8. What is cultural relativism, and what are Lewis' (provided) reasons for rejecting it? How is his rejection of CR meant to be support for the second premise of the MA?

Two things fill the mind with ever new and increasing admiration and awe, the more often and steadily we reflect upon them: the starry heavens above me and the moral law within me

The above quotation comes from the great philosopher Immanuel Kant. It is found in his *Critique of Pure Reason*, and was engraved on his tombstone. I think it provides a perfect transition from our last chapter that dealt with the "starry heavens above" (the DA) to our current chapter dealing with the "moral law within" (MA).

The MA claims that the existence of (objective) moral values and duties entails the existence of a being capable of providing or "grounding" those objective values. This is somewhat analogous to some versions of the CA we've studied previously. The version concerning contingency and necessity argued that not all things can be contingent beings (CBs), but that some necessary being (NB) is needed to "ground" the existence of all those CBs. That NB is then identified as God via our "matching strategy." Similarly, the MA will argue that the source of (objective) moral values and duties cannot be something contingent or arbitrary, but must instead be an objective "ground" for those values and duties. The same matching strategy will identify this source/ground as God.

I have already indicated (parenthetically) that the moral values and duties of which we speak are objective. Before delving any further into the MA, then, it is important to clarify objective from subjective claims, and thereby distinguish objective moral values/duties from subjective moral values/duties.

First, let us delve into some epistemology.

As I hope you recall from our critical thinking chapter, a "claim" (in this context) is simply a statement, an assertion, a proposition. One of the features of claims is that they have a "truth value." This is just a fancy way of saying that a claim must be either true or false, even if we're not sure which one it is. For example, "Ted Preston is a philosophy professor" is a claim. That claim is either true, or it isn't. If you have no idea who Ted Preston is (or to which Ted Preston I refer), you might not be sure whether it is a true statement, but you can be confident that it's either true or it's false. If you have enough information, you might be confident as to which one of those two truth values is accurate. But, what is it that would make the claim true (or false)? How would we know? The answer depends upon the kinds of claims we're talking about.

We may divide claims into two basic categories: objective claims, and subjective claims. Objective claims concern facts, while subjective claims concern opinion. The typical view is that the truth or falsity of objective claims is *independent* of whatever I (or you) happen to think, or desire, or prefer. Facts don't discriminate. They apply equally to all people at all times. If it is a fact that 2 +2 = 4, then that fact applies just as much to me as it does to you—and if I happen to believe that 2 +2 = 17, I'm *wrong*. Error is possible when we're dealing with objective claims. In fact, one of the ways to figure out if a claim is objective is to ask yourself what it would mean if two or more people disagreed about the claim. If their disagreement indicates at least one of the people is mistaken, that's a pretty good sign that the claim is objective. If I think that 2 +2 = 17, and you think that it equals 4, that's an indicator that one of us mistaken (or maybe both of us are mistaken, and the correct answer is some third option that neither one of us came up with).

Subjective claims, in contrast, concern opinions and personal taste preferences. Disagreement does not indicate error. If I think a meal is delicious, and you think it's too spicy, it's not the case that one of us is "wrong" about the meal. If I love the band "Switchfoot," and you can't bear to listen to them, it's not the case that one of us is in error. Opinions are indexed to particular people, at particular times and places. The truth or falsity of a subjective claim is "up to me" in a meaningful sort of way—unlike the truth or falsity of objective (factual) claims.

One of the kinds of claims we make—indeed, one of the most important kinds of claims we can make—is a moral claim. Moral claims are simply assertions involving some moral issue. "Eating meat is wrong." "War is never justifiable." "Abortion is wrong." "Premarital sex is morally acceptable." These are all examples of moral claims.

According to a subjectivist approach to morality, moral claims are matters of personal opinion. As such, there is no "fact" that validates some opinions, but refutes others. Very simply, if I believe something is morally wrong, then, for me, it is morally wrong. If you believe differently, then it's not wrong for you. If you and I disagree, it's not the case that one of us is mistaken—we simply have different perspectives on the matter. A variant of this subjectivist approach claims that moral claims are no matters of individual opinion, but collective opinion. Each culture develops its own "taste" with regard to various traits and behaviors, and things are morally good or bad depending upon whether they conform to the "taste preferences" of that community. This is known as cultural relativism (or sometimes ethical relativism). In either case, however, moral claims are matters of opinion, rather than fact.

Does this seem correct? Do moral claims seem to be matter of opinion (only)? Are there no moral "facts" that apply to all people, at all times? Whether morality is purely subjective, or whether there are some objective moral claims, is a critical issue for the Moral Argument (MA) for God's existence.

William Lane Craig's version of the MA is as follows:

1. If God does not exist, objective moral values and duties do not exist.
2. <u>Objective moral values and duties do exist.</u>
3. Therefore, God exists.

We will consider each line of this argument, one at a time, but before we do, make note of that second premise. As mentioned above, whether or not moral claims are objective or subjective is critical to the MA. We will devote much attention to it later in this chapter.

1. If God does not exist, *objective* moral values and duties do not exist.

This premise asserts that unless God (as understood in the Western theistic traditions, specifically) exists, then objective moral values and duties can't exist either. This is not to say that subjective moral values and duties couldn't exist—but there would be no objective moral values/duties.

To see why Craig thinks this is so, ask yourself, "what would be the basis for moral value (worth) within a purely naturalistic worldview?" Most of us believe that persons, by default, share a baseline measure of moral worth, and upon this foundation we develop our notions of basic human rights, moral obligations to do (or refrain from doing) various things, etc. If there is no God, and humans have developed solely via unguided natural (evolutionary) processes, in the same fashion as every other animal on Earth, from where would we get the idea that persons have moral worth?

Certainly *I* regard my own life as having value, and I think others should (at the least) refrain from harming me, and I would like to think that my friends and family find my life to be of value as well, but of course the mere fact that I value my own life doesn't make my life *objectively* valuable. I also value certain photographs I've taken (or that have been taken of me) over the years, but it's rather obvious that those photos have their value solely because I have invested them with that value. In other words, their value is subjective, based solely upon my own whims. Should my feelings change, I can easily imagine discarding those photos as casually as I would discard an old newspaper. There is no independent basis for those photos having value. Is there an independent basis for my *life* having value? Clearly, my own feelings and preferences can't provide it, as nothing could be more subjective than my own feelings! What about the feelings and preferences of the friends and family who value my life? Aren't those just someone *else's* subjective preferences? Couldn't their affection for, and interest in, me dissipate just as it could for some old photographs? Does the worth of a person hinge on something as tenuous as subjective preferences? If my human rights are rooted in my moral worth, and my moral worth is subject to how I (and others) *feel* about me, then are my rights as contingent as the value of my old photos?

In the absence of the supra-natural, all that remains is the natural. In Nature, where do we find any notion of objective moral value, or rights, or duties? "A hawk that seizes a fish from the sea *kills* it, but does not *murder* it; and another hawk that seizes the fish from the talons of the first *takes* it, but does not *steal* it - for none of these things is forbidden. And exactly the same considerations apply to the people we are imagining.... the concept of moral obligation is unintelligible apart from the idea of God. The words remain but their meaning is gone."[115] Indeed, the utilitarian Jeremy Bentham went so far as to dismiss the notion of "natural rights" as "simple nonsense: natural and imprescriptible rights, rhetorical nonsense,—nonsense upon stilts."

Rights imply duties, of course. If you have a right to your life, I have a duty to refrain from killing you (at the least), and possibly even a duty to preserve your life (e.g., by providing you food if you're starving, etc.). But, within a purely naturalistic worldview, who or what has the legitimate authority to impose duties on us, or enforce them?

Certainly, in practice, parents have power to impose duties on their children, and rulers have power to impose duties on those they rule, but from where do they derive the authority to make those impositions? In the end, does it come down to nothing more (or less) than power? Rulers can compel the ruled to do (or refrain from doing) any number of things, but most of us believe that not all commands are just or legitimate. Is our complaint against unjust commands based on nothing more than our own personal preferences? A difference of tastes?

In response, some might propose that what makes values good or bad, and what makes duties morally legitimate (or not) isn't merely the taste preferences of those in power, but is based rather on something independent from those tastes: human flourishing.

Human flourishing as a foundation for objective moral values and duties requires us to take a side trip into an evolutionary interpretation of ethics. As we've already seen, one of the first, core differences of opinion arising in the study of morality is the ultimate origin and explanation for our concepts of good and evil, rightness and wrongness, duty, obligation, justice, fairness, etc. Some philosophers (such as Craig) will claim that these things could not exist given a purely naturalistic worldview, and that some "higher" source is needed—at least if our moral values and duties are to be objective.

Other thinkers believe that not only could such things arise within a purely naturalistic worldview, but that they did. According to this view, humans have evolved to be "moral" animals, to have a sense of moral requirements, and to be motivated (variously) to behave according to moral standards.

Research has been conducted for decades in the "Baby Lab" (formally known as

---

[115] Taylor, Richard. *Ethics, Faith, and Reason.* Prentice Hall, 1984, 14, 83-84

the "Infant Cognition Center") at Yale University, with the test subjects being babies under 24 months of age. The purpose of the research was to gauge how much (if at all) babies understood "good" and "bad" behavior. The details are somewhat complicated, but the basic elements of one of the experiments are not: show a baby a puppet show in which a puppet displays "helping" behavior, and a different puppet engages in "unhelpful" behavior, and then see which puppet the babies prefer. More than 80% of the babies preferred the "nice" puppet (controlling for various other factors that might contribute to the choice)—and the percentage rises to 87% by the age of three.

Paul Bloom (a psychology professor connected to the lab) concludes that the research shows that babies are born with a rudimentary (admittedly limited) sense of justice. Babies are born with a natural preference for "nice" behavior over "mean" behavior, but it takes development and instruction before they extend these moral notions outside their immediate circle of family. According to Bloom, "We are by nature indifferent, even hostile to strangers; we are prone towards parochialism and bigotry."

What could account for this astonishing indicator that even *babies* have at least a crude sense of morality? Evolutionary approaches to ethics claim that humans have evolved to possess and display a moral sense in much the same way that we have evolved to have and display sexual desire, or any other "selected for" adaptations. According to the evolutionary account of the development of the human animal, our sense of morality (like everything else about us) is the result of evolutionary forces, such as natural selection. Compassion, charity, justice, fairness, and any and every other moral notion exists because they met the test of natural selection, or are byproducts of something *else* that met that test.

Before delving deeper, it's important to note that to offer an evolutionary origin as the explanation for moral values is not to somehow deny the existence of those values, or denounce them as fake. To say, for example, that a mother's love for her child evolved because those creatures who cared for their young were more successful at passing along their genes than those who didn't doesn't somehow mean that mothers don't actually love their children! That would be like claiming that because sexual desire evolved for the sake of procreation, whenever anyone feels amorous that person is really, secretly, only trying to reproduce. That inference is hard to reconcile with the use of birth control, homosexual sex, masturbation, or any sexual activity other than unprotected vaginal intercourse. Just because sex evolved because it promoted the propagation of our genes doesn't mean that its only use is that propagation, nor that propagation is what we intend by it. Compassion might exist because the disposition to feel compassion, and respond accordingly, promoted the survival of those human communities in which it was found. That doesn't mean compassion is an illusion, or that when we feel compassion and act on it we are "really" only intending to promote our species' survival.

Another common assumption that must be addressed concerns the association of evolution with the doctrine of the "survival of the fittest." If evolutionary forces favor "survivors," then wouldn't we expect to find nature promoting selfish creatures, and selfish behaviors? If that were so, how could we explain the seeming existence of altruism? Cooperative behavior? Charity? Even self-sacrifice? This is the so-called "problem of altruism," for evolutionary approaches to ethics. How could a purely naturalistic (evolutionary) understanding of morality explain moral values and behaviors that seem to defy the "eat or be eaten" code of nature?

The Selfish Gene

One attempt to answer such questions comes from the famed evolutionary biologist Richard Dawkins. In his book, *The Selfish Gene*, he argues that natural selection does not work at the level of the individual organism, but rather at the level of the individual *gene*. When he refers to "the selfish gene," he makes explicitly clear that he's not imagining that a gene is *actually* selfish, or capable of any sort of motives or intentions at all. It is a metaphorical way of describing the behaviors that promote the gene's survival *as though the gene were "selfish."* He has since admitted that it was perhaps a poor and misleading choice of words—but there's nothing to be done about that now!

Natural selection operates at the level of the gene, according to Dawkins, because living creatures (such as humans) don't last long enough (historically) to be a proper unit of natural selection. If I have a child, that child will possess ½ of my genes. If that child has a child, my grandchild will possess ¼ of my genes, and so on. Within just a few generations, so much gene mixing has taken place that "I" (as a temporary aggregation of genes) am no longer present in any genetically meaningful capacity. "I" am not found in my descendants in any meaningful sense, but some of the particular genes that, at one point, comprised me, *are* found in my descendants. So, "I" don't survive long enough to participate much in evolution, but some of my genes might.

Consider an analogy with poker. Imagine that genes are the cards found in a deck. The deck is the gene pool. Some of those cards form a small collection (a "hand"). That hand represents an individual organism. Shuffling and reshuffling the deck represents the gene-mixing that takes place when we reproduce, resulting in new hands being dealt—new collections of genes. Notice that the cards survive the shuffling process, but specific hands do not. So, if I am symbolically represented by all four kings and the ace of spades, "I" am gone and used up as soon as the cards are shuffled again—but those specific cards (i.e., the kings and the ace of spades) might well find themselves in a new hand that has been dealt. It might not be glorious, but we could imagine ourselves as giant, complicated machines that exist, ultimately, to replicate the genes that comprise us. Once we serve that function, and have promoted those genes, we are cast aside, but the genes endure.

Still *metaphorically speaking*, genes "want" to survive. Genes are "selfish" (metaphorically speaking!) in that way. But, we must understand that the so-called "selfish gene" isn't just one particular occurrence of the gene, but *every* occurrence of that gene, every replica of it found in any organism anywhere in the world. If we go back to our card analogy, it's as though the ace of spades isn't just seeking its own promotion into future hands of cards, but that of every ace of spades in any deck anywhere in the world. So, imagine that there is a gene that is part of my DNA. We'll call it gene X. Gene X is "selfish" (metaphorically speaking) in that it "wants" (metaphorically speaking) to survive and continue through history. There are a variety of behaviors and traits that would help gene X to survive, and would therefore potentially pass the test of natural selection.

1. Individual selfishness

The first and most obvious way of promoting gene X's survival (which, like any other gene, is "the selfish gene") would be programming individual organisms, such as myself, to be selfish. After all, in a statement of the obvious, I share 100% of my genes with myself. The longer I live, the longer those genes (including gene X) lives. So, behaviors and dispositions to behave that cause me to put myself first, to look after my own needs (even at the expense of others'), and other such tendencies, would promote gene X, make it more likely that I survive long enough to pass gene X on to my children, and therefore promote the survival of the "selfish gene." Perhaps this can explain the fact that we humans are, admittedly, pretty self-centered a lot of the time? However, individual selfishness is not the only way to promote the survival of gene X.

2. Kin selection/Kin altruism

Recall that part of the logic of individual selfishness was that it kept the organism (me) alive longer, ultimately increasing my odds of passing along my genes. Passing along the gene is a terribly important part of the process. After all, if the only creature carrying around gene X is me, it doesn't help gene X all that much to keep just me alive for a 100 years. Gene X would die with me. But, if I have children, gene X gets to keep surviving.

Any biological child of mine will have 50% of my genes, including, possibly, gene X. So, a good strategy for keeping gene X alive would be to program me to take care of creatures that probably carry gene X as well—like my own children, for example. A possible evolutionary explanation for why living creatures, in general (certainly mammals, at least) instinctively care for their own offspring is that those offspring carry copies of "the selfish gene" (such as gene X) within them as well. If the ultimate unit of evolutionary interest is the gene, rather than the organism, this could explain self-sacrifice—a mother dying to protect her child, for example. The mother dies, but the genes live on.

Consider the math of biological family. I share 100% of my genes, so of course promoting my own well-being serves the selfish gene. But, any children of mine would carry 50% of my genes, so helping them makes sense too. My parents also have 50% of my genes each (they're the source of them, after all), so it makes sense that I would be concerned about their survival. Any siblings of mine also share 50% of my genes. Uncles and aunts and cousins have fewer genes in common, but there's still a decent chance that gene X is in them too. Same with grandkids, etc. Heck, given the genetic similarity between humans, complete strangers have a chance of sharing some genes with me—but this is less obvious, and less likely, so it might make sense if humans had been programmed to look after themselves and their kin first and foremost.

3. Reciprocal altruism

Obviously, when we observe human behavior (and that of other animals as well), we don't observe that humans only help their own biological family. We also engage in behaviors that help non-relatives. The notion of reciprocal altruism could be used to help explain some of those behaviors. Reciprocal altruism can be summed up by the slogan, "you scratch my back, and I'll scratch yours." In other species, these sorts of arrangements are common. In fact, sometimes the arrangement literally involves scratching each other's backs! Reciprocal grooming promotes the health and well-being of each participant (e.g., two monkeys, two birds, etc.). Each one is helping another organism, who is not necessarily a blood relative, but is helped in return, thereby promoting the survival of its own genes. Such arrangements can even cross species lines. If you've ever seen video footage of little birds riding around on wildebeests, for example, eating the insects crawling around on the wildebeests' hide, you have observed "reciprocal altruism." The wildebeest gets pesky and possibly-health-threatening insects removed, and the bird gets a meal. Bees get food, and the flower gets pollinated.

The flower and bee example should make it obvious that reciprocal altruism doesn't require an explicit "deal" to be made, or even the capacity to form intentions. It would be silly to suggest that a flower and a bee drew up a mutually beneficial contract, or that the flower even "wants" anything at all. Nevertheless, in a metaphorical sort of way, both the flower and the bee are getting what they "want," and each organism's survival (and therefore the selfish gene's survival) is promoted.

4. Altruism as a show of dominance

Finally, one more possible explanation of altruistic behavior involves cases of benevolence in which (seemingly) nothing is received in return. Allow me to use an admittedly cynical example. Suppose I walk into a bar, dressed in obviously expensive clothes, wearing a gold watch and some gold rings, and I buy myself a glass of top-shelf whiskey. Then, to the presumed delight of some of my fellow patrons, I announce that I'm buying a round of drinks for the house. Everyone gets a free drink at my expense. Let's assume that I have no good reason to think that any of those patrons is one of my blood relatives. Let's also assume that I have no good reason to think that any of them is going to buy me a drink (or the equivalent) in return. What could explain this seemingly gratuitous display of generosity? I'll give you a moment to become equally cynical and ponder the possibilities.

The Ladies. Maybe that's my angle? After all, I've just walked into this bar, sharply dressed, and now I'm throwing money around like I've got it to burn. I'm flaunting it. A reasonable inference is that I must be a pretty good provider, and therefore a good candidate for a mate. I'm so good at "survival" that I can "waste" my resources on others, expecting nothing in return, and still get along just fine. I just made myself look good—better than my "competition" who can't provide free drinks, at least. Ladies, you better snatch me up while you can. . .

I'm being facetious, of course—but, joking or not, this kind of explanation gets to the heart of the idea of altruism as a show of dominance. By "dominance" we don' have to mean something cruel, or oppressive. Treating someone to dinner, or giving money to charity, is hardly an oppressive act, after all. But, the effect is, nevertheless, that the giver ends up looking like a good, resourceful mate. This is by no means to suggest that people care only about how much money their prospective partners have, or their earning potential, but evolution provides an explanation for the common sense (anecdotal) observation that, all else being equal, most of us (male and female alike) would probably prefer that our partners be "rich" than "poor." Consider, too, how, for most of human history, women did not have the opportunity to be financially independent—this is a relatively recent phenomenon. Historically, women were first dependent upon their parents, and then upon a husband. There's a perfectly decent evolutionary explanation for why a woman (in that case) would prefer a capable provider over a deadbeat! A capable provider makes her own survival (individual selfishness) and that of her children (kin selection/kin altruism) more likely. Accordingly, it is advantageous for the provider (historically, men—though not necessarily so today) to display that potential to be a good provider. Altruistic displays of "giving" (without receiving something in return) are just such a display.

In summary, through a variety of mechanisms (individual selfishness, kin selection, reciprocal altruism, and altruism as a show of dominance), behaviors that manifest as altruistic at the level of the organism, and within communities, are "selfish" at the level of the gene (e.g., the hypothetical gene X).

Does this "selfish gene" explanation (and the four strategies we just discussed) account for all of our moral behaviors and tendencies? Probably not, even under the best of interpretations. However, Dawkins thinks that our generalized notions of morality can be understood as a "blessed, precious mistake" of evolution.

A mistake? Yes. But, do keep in mind that he called the mistake a "blessed, precious" one. In calling morality a mistake, he means the same sort of thing when an evolutionary biologist calls any number of other generalized tendencies a "mistake." Natural selection does not operate with laser precision. Rather, behavioral "rules of thumb" that prove advantageous get selected and passed on. A simple example of this is the fact that birds, as a "rule of thumb," feed chicks that are in their nests. Some gene or sequence of gene that produced that "rule of thumb" made survival of those chicks much more likely (obviously!), and was therefore passed along to future generations of chicks, and "nested" quite comfortably within the gene pools of birds. The rule of thumb that programs birds to feed chicks isn't precise and discriminating, though. We can imagine it (metaphorically) to be something like "feed noisy creatures in the nest." In the overwhelming majority of cases, that noisy creature in the nest is the bird's own chick. However, the Cuckoo is a species of bird that knocks the eggs of other birds from their own nests, and then places its own eggs in their place. When the eggs hatch, it's a cuckoo. The oblivious other bird (a robin, let's say) isn't savvy enough to recognize that the noisy creature isn't its own, and feeds it anyway. Technically, it is making a "mistake," since its behavior is not promoting its own genes—but you shouldn't expect nuanced behaviors from genes!

To return to our previous example of human sexuality, a good case can be made that sexual desire evolved because it caused us to seek out sex, and that tends to result in reproduction. The selfish gene survives into a new generation of humans. "Reproduction" might have been what made sexual desire and sexual satisfaction adaptive, but once Pandora's Box had been opened, we were hardly limited to reproduction only. Humans simply desire, and seek out, sex—and most of the time we're not trying to reproduce. From a certain perspective, any of our sexual activities that don't lead to reproduction are "mistakes" in that they don't promote the purpose for which they were "selected" in the first place. But, the disposition that got bred into us wasn't so precise as to specify "have intercourse, but only when reproduction can occur."

Dawkins suggests that morality operates in similar fashion.

Perhaps tendencies such as compassion, charity, self-sacrifice, mercy, fairness, and the like, were originally "selected" in the context of very small human communities in which most of the members were probably blood relatives. Altruistic behaviors towards members of that community could probably be explained in terms of kin selection, or reciprocal altruism, or altruism as a show of dominance—but the genes responsible for those tendencies couldn't specify precise behaviors like "feel compassion for distressed little creatures—but only if it's your own child." Instead, "compassion" got bred into the human gene pool. Maybe compassion originally served to motivate us to feed our babies, and care for those in need within our tiny (family) communities, but Pandora's Box has been opened. Disposed to feel compassion, we can now feel compassion not just towards our own babies, but towards "creatures in distress" in general. We can watch a commercial showing footage of a starving child on the other side of the world and feel compassion and be moved to help. We can even see a non-human suffer (e.g., a cat or dog) and feel compassion at that as well. As Dawkins puts it:

> *Sexual lust is the driving force behind a large proportion of human ambition and struggle, and much of it constitutes a misfiring. There is no reason why the same should not be true of the lust to be generous and compassionate, if this is the misfired consequence of ancestral village life. The best way for natural selection to build in both kinds of lust in ancestral times was to install rules of thumb in the brain. Those rules still influence us today, even where circumstances make them inappropriate to their original functions.*[116]

As a final note, Dawkins suggests that if this approach is correct, if our moral sense is "Darwinian" in origin, then we should expect species-level (i.e., "universal") trends in morality. We should observe some similarities in moral codes and intuitions, and researchers have indeed found the presence of cross-cultural, trans-religious, and trans-lingual moral "intuitions" that often defy our ability to articulate. Indeed, as indicated earlier in the chapter, some researchers claim that even babies possess this moral sense.

Richard Dawkins (the evolutionary biologist) has attempted to provide an evolutionary basis for our moral impulses, but James Rachels (the ethicist) will take this evolutionary foundation and attempt to develop a universal moral code. Rachels argues that there are some universal moral requirements in the sense that they are necessary for human community to exist and survive. These moral principles are

---

[116] Dawkins, *The God Delusion*, 254

"universal" in that they occur in every culture, and they exist in every culture because in order for a culture to persist over time these values must be honored.

As examples, Rachels offers honesty, caring for children, and forbidding murder. Let us start with what is, perhaps, the most obvious of the three: caring for children.

Try to imagine a culture in which no moral value was placed on caring for the young. There is no stigma, no shame, no pressure, no laws associated with child-rearing. How could such a culture persist? In order to survive, a culture must produce new members who will survive long enough to continue its traditions, and then create the next generation themselves. Although people care for children in a variety of formats, we struggle to even imagine a culture that does not care for them at all.

As another example, Rachels claims that no culture could survive if it did not have some prohibition against murder. Try to imagine what it would be like to live in a society in which no positive value was placed on innocent life, and in which there was nothing wrong with killing innocent people. What an anxiety-filled existence! How could such a culture avoid self-destruction?

As one final example, consider honesty. Rachels claims that all cultures, in order to survive as cultures, must endorse honesty and condemn deception. Why? Consider the alternative. If there was no stigma attached to deception, and no expectation of honesty, under normal circumstances, why would you ever believe what other people tell you? What you read? What you hear? Why would you assume the words you're reading right now are sincere and accurate? Why go to school, if it's just as likely that your instructors are lying as they are not? Why read the newspaper, if it's no worse for it to be filled with lies than the truth? Clearly, without an expectation of honesty, there's no basis for trust. Without trust, there's no basis for cooperation, and without cooperation, there is no society—not even family units can survive without trust-enabled cooperation. Obviously, people can and do lie, but this is the exception, rather than the rule. Imagine trying to get through your day if it was just as likely that everyone you met was lying to you as that they were telling the truth?

If Rachels is correct, then this might be a major accomplishment. Though we might bicker as to just which moral principles and values are necessary for any society to survive (and are, therefore, universal), it would appear that there are some that fit that description. That, at the very least, is a very important start for the rest of our process, in that it will allow us to operate on the assumption that morality is objective (to some degree, at least)—and this objectivity has been obtained without any appeal to (or need for) God. Therefore, objective values and duties can exist without God.

Craig, however, finds fault with this approach. In the first place, he regards Rachel's efforts as amounting to, at best, a socio-anthropological *description* of what is needed for group survival and cohesion. This doesn't entail that those requirements are (morally) "good," nor demonstrate that those who defy them are (objectively) "bad"—it just entails that those behaviors are needed for group survival and cohesion. That is a descriptive exercise, not prescriptive. He cites others who acknowledge the merely descriptive aspect of these evolutionary accounts: "Morality is just an aid to survival and reproduction,... and any deeper meaning is illusory."[117] Moreover, he suggests that this approach is arbitrary, and possibly "speciesist." Why would the conditions needed for human survival (or the cohesion of human communities) amount to *objective* moral values? If "survival value" is the standard for objective moral values, why not the conditions needed for mouse survival and flourishing? Or those conditions that promote bacterial survival? If humans are wrought from the same evolutionary forces as every other living thing, why would humans be "special," and why would our survival and group cohesion needs be the standard for (objective) morality in general?

In addition, Craig points out that these particular survival-based behaviors are utterly contingent on the particular path evolution took with regard to the human species. As a simple illustration, one of Rachels' "universal moral values" involves caring for children. He argued that you will find some sort of moral value placed on caring for children in any and every human community, because children must survive (or, at least the "replacement value" of children must survive) in order for the community to persist over time. Therefore, caring for children (e.g., a variety of nurturing behaviors), having been selected for via natural selection, is a universal moral value. But, imagine if humans hadn't evolved as primates, or even as mammals? If the dinosaurs had never faced an extinction event, and had never created a space for mammals to thrive, perhaps "humans" would be sophisticated reptiles instead? Rather than giving birth to live, vulnerable young, perhaps "humans" would just lay eggs and our offspring, once hatched, would "fend for themselves," as is the case with many reptile species? There would be no need to care for our young, or engage in nurturing behavior, in that case, so "caring for children" is merely contingent upon the fact that our offspring happen to helpless when born. Charles Darwin seemed to have grasped something similar to this idea. "If...men were reared under precisely the same conditions as hive-bees, there can hardly be a doubt that our unmarried females would, like the worker bees, think it a sacred duty to kill their brothers, and mothers would strive to kill their fertile daughters, and no one would think of interfering."[118]

There seems to be at least two lines of critique here:

1. The "values" described by Dawkins and Rachels aren't really (moral) values because they are descriptive, rather than prescriptive. Rather than telling us what is good, what we ought to be, they simply tell us what we must do in order for our genes to be promoted over time and for communities to be cohesive.
2. These "values" are contingent upon a particular evolutionary path, and therefore not *objective* values, even if they are values.

In fairness to Dawkins and Rachels, I imagine they would reply that morality *just*

[117] Ruse, Michae. "Evolutionary Theory and Darwinian Ethics," *The Darwinian Paradigm*. Routledge, 1989, 289.

[118] Darwin, Charles. *The Descent of Man*, Amherst, NY: Prometheus Books, 1998, 102.

s a description of those behaviors and dispositions that promote human flourishing. To expect something more from morality, something that isn't somehow tied to the natural forces that produced and govern us, is to beg the question against naturalism in the first place. "In a universe of electrons and selfish genes, blind physical forces and genetic replication, some people are going to get hurt, other people are going to get lucky, and you won't find any rhyme or reason in it, nor any justice. The universe that we observe has precisely the properties we should expect if there is, at bottom, no design, no purpose, no evil, no good, nothing but pitiless indifference."[119] There is, on this account, something that we call "morality," but, like everything else, it results from evolutionary forces because of its survival value.

With regard to the contingency concern, I have my own critique of Craig. It seems to me that Craig might be equivocating on "objective." Here are Craig's own words:

"Objective" means "independent of people's (including one's own) opinion."

"Subjective" means "just a matter of personal opinion." If we do have objective moral duties, then in the various circumstances in which we find ourselves we are obligated or forbidden to do various actions, regardless of what we think."[120]

Elsewhere, he writes: "I do take the word 'objective' to mean *mind-independent*. Lawrence Krauss once put it well: objective reality is what there still is when you quit thinking about it."[121]

"Objective," then (according to Craig), means "independent of people's opinion"—as opposed to being "just a matter of personal opinion." If that's all it means for a moral value or duty to be objective (i.e., not just a matter of personal opinion), then it's not clear how the "contingency" objection is really an objection. After all, if the (basic) evolutionary story is true, then the behaviors and disposition that promote gene survival and the cohesion of community are not merely matters of personal opinion. It is not an opinion that children (generally) must be cared for in order for human communities to survive, but a fact—indeed, Craig acknowledged that these are "merely" socio-anthropological descriptive *facts* (rather than values) in one of his other criticisms. Certainly it is true, on this account, that if humans had evolved in very different ways (e.g., as reptiles), then the behaviors that promote our flourishing would be different, and therefore those behaviors are contingent upon a particular evolutionary path—but this doesn't mean they are contingent in the sense of being merely personal opinion. My opinion is utterly irrelevant with regard to what conditions promote the survival of my genes. My opinion might be that being exposed to the vacuum of space will promote my genes' survival—but in that case my opinion is *false*.

If all "objective" means is "independent of personal opinion," or what is "there

---

[119] Richard Dawkins, "God's Utility Function," published in *Scientific American* November, 1995), p. 85.

[120] Question #347, answered 12-08-13, www.reasonablefaith.org

[121] www.reasonablefaith.org/theistic-ethics-and-mind-dependence

still when you quit thinking about it," then it seems that values arrived at via evolutionary would be "objective" in that sense. Granted, Craig can continue to claim that they aren't really "values" at all, in that they are merely descriptive (rather than prescriptive), and you can decide for yourself whether the account offered by Dawkins and Rachels actually provides "values."

"Equivocation" occurs when you mean one thing by a word at one point in an argument, and then you shift to a different meaning of that same word in another part of the argument. I suspect Craig might be equivocating on "objective" in that he defines objective as "independent of personal opinion" in one part of his argument, but seems to shift the meaning of objective to mean something like "not dependent upon human needs," or "transcending the human condition," or (frankly) "supernatural" when criticizing the naturalists' attempt to provide objective moral values and duties. It seems to me, then, that Craig's criticism of a purely naturalistic approach to ethics isn't (or shouldn't be) that it fails to produce values and duties that are independent of human opinion, but rather that the products of such a naturalistic approach fail to provide *values* at all, or any duties that have binding force behind them beyond the contingent, power-based threats that other humans might make in the event of failing to follow the "rules."

On the other hand, naturalists will often try to turn the tables on someone like Craig and counter that it is religiously-based systems of ethics that fail to provide objective moral values and duties. The most famous such objection is known as the "Euthyphro problem."

The Euthyphro Problem

Named for Plato's dialogue in which the argument is found, the Euthyphro problem explores the relationship between morality and the divine.

Socrates: And what do you say of piety, Euthyphro: is not piety, according to your definition, loved by all the gods?

Euthyphro: Yes.

Socrates: Because it is pious or holy, or for some other reason?

Euthyphro: No, that is the reason.

Socrates: It is loved because it is holy, not holy because it is loved?

Euthyphro: Yes.

Socrates: And that which is dear to the gods is loved by them, and is in a state to be loved of them because it is loved of them?

Euthyphro: Certainly.

Socrates: Then that which is dear to the gods, Euthyphro, is not holy, nor is that which is holy loved of God, as you affirm; but they are two different things. Euthyphro: How do you mean, Socrates?

Socrates: I mean to say that the holy has been acknowledge by us to be loved of God because it is holy, not to be holy because it is loved.

Euthyphro: Yes.

Socrates: But that which is dear to the gods is dear to them because it is loved by them, not loved by them because it is dear to them.

Euthyphro: True.

Socrates: But, friend Euthyphro, if that which is holy is the same with that which is dear to God, and is loved because it is holy, then that which is dear to God would have been loved as being dear to God; but if that which dear to God is dear to him because loved by him, then that which is holy would have been holy because loved by him. But now you see that the reverse is the case, and that they are quite different from one another. For one (theophiles) is of a kind to be loved cause it is loved, and the other (osion) is loved because it is of a kind to be loved. Thus you appear to me, Euthyphro, when I ask you what is the essence of holiness, to offer an attribute only, and not the essence-the attribute of being loved by all the gods. But you still refuse to explain to me the nature of holiness. And therefore, if you please, I will ask you not to hide your treasure, but to tell me once more what holiness or piety really is, whether dear to the gods or not (for that is a matter about which we will not quarrel) and what is impiety?

Euthyphro: I really do not know, Socrates, how to express what I mean. For somehow or other our arguments, on whatever ground we rest them, seem to turn round and walk away from us.

Is his usual clever and combative way, Socrates has teased out the tension in the Divine Command" approach to ethics. Is something morally good because it is willed by God? Or, is something willed by God because it is morally good? It might take a minute for the difference to become clear. Go ahead and take that minute.

If God commands something because it is morally good, then the command results from God's recognition of the act's goodness. In that case, the standard of goodness preceded God's command. The possible problem (for theistic approaches to ethics) with this interpretation is that this might be seen as placing a limit on God's power and authority. After all, if morality is independent of God and precedes God's commands, is it possible to know what is right, and do what is right, without God entering the picture at all? This would seem to undermine the first premise of the MA "If God does not exist, objective moral values and duties do not exist"). After all, it seems that these values could exist even if God does not.

On the other hand, if something is morally good because God commands it, then it is the act of God that makes it good in the first place. Whatever God commands is good, whatever God forbids is bad. The possible problem with this interpretation is that it appears to make morality a matter of God's whims—something too arbitrary for many to be comfortable with. If *anything* God commands, by definition, is the right thing to do, what if God were to command the slaughter of babies? Wouldn't that be, by definition, the morally right thing to do? If God's commands are arbitrary, then they don't appear to be "objective" anymore—but based on *God's* opinion instead of any of ours. In this case, God's existence fails to establish the existence of *objective* moral values/duties.

Some of you might be thinking, right now, "That's ridiculous. God would never order such a thing because God is perfectly good." Perhaps so, but Robert Solomon (a famous contemporary American philosopher) believes that such a reaction illustrates our powerful intuition that our conception of morality is that it does *not* depend wholly on God's will, and that a simple hypothetical example can demonstrate this. He invites us to imagine that what appears to be an authentic original manuscript from the Bible is discovered, one that appears to be older and more authentic than any other extant manuscripts. To the world's surprise, though, this manuscript provides a very different set of commandments, including the following:

Thou shalt kill.
Thou shalt steal.
Thou shalt commit adultery as much as thou wouldst.

Solomon is convinced that most believers, rather than undergoing a radical transformation in their values and practices, would instead reject the authenticity of the manuscript, in spite of all the evidence in its favor. Why? Because we are confident that God is a moral being, and such commandments would just not be the sorts of commandments issued by a moral being—let alone a perfect one. But, if we say that God would never do such a thing because God is good, what standard of goodness are we assuming here? If God *defines* goodness, then to say that God is good is simply to say that God does what God wants. It is only by presupposing an independent standard of goodness that someone could employ the defense that God wouldn't order anything "bad" because God is "good." If God defines goodness, then we beg the question when we say that God commands only good things.

This "Euthyphro problem" for divine command approaches is incredibly well known, and thought by many to be the death blow for divine command ethics—so much so that much of the time the divine command theory is offered in ethics courses only for the sake of thoroughness, or as an intellectual curiosity. However, we must keep in mind that the gods targeted by the "Euthyphro problem" (in its original historical context) were finite, anthropomorphic, and downright scandalous. For example, Zeus practiced incest (he had a daughter, Persephone, with his own sister, Demeter)—and his most famous wife, Hera, was another of his own sisters! He was also notorious for raping human women.

That the Euthyphro problem is used out of its original context should be obvious in that it would be pretty difficult to find anyone today who worships either the "gods" popular in ancient Greece (e.g., Zeus, Athena, Poseidon) or the non-personal "form of the good" that might be labeled "god" by Plato himself. Instead, the "problem" is always presented to particular religious traditions: usually Christianity, Judaism, or Islam. Each one of these traditions has its own concept of God, and its own understanding of the relationship between God and morality, but in none of these Western theistic traditions is God conceived as being very similar to Zeus, Ares, etc. To use the "Euthyphro problem" to attack the generic abstraction "god" is to attack a straw man (or, a straw deity, perhaps). That the *abstraction* fares poorly in the Euthyphro problem does not necessarily mean that any *actual* religious tradition, or any actual concept of God, is similarly imperiled.

To help illustrate this, William Lane Craig points out that for the Christian religious tradition; moral goodness is an aspect of God's very nature. If God's nature is to be (essentially) good, then goodness is neither something "separate" from God that God recognizes and endorses, nor is it something "arbitrary." Part of the Christian concept of God is that God's nature is eternal and unchanging. One aspect of God's nature is goodness. Being unchanging, that cannot and will not change.

Our moral duties are constituted by the commands of a just and loving God. For any action A and moral agent S, we can explicate the notions of moral requirement, permission, and forbiddenness of A for S as follows:

- *A is required of S if and only if a just and loving God commands S to do A.*
- *A is permitted for S if and only if a just and loving God does not command S not to do A.*
- *A is forbidden to S if and only if a just and loving God commands S not to do A.*

Since our moral duties are grounded in the divine commands, they are not independent of God....God may act naturally in ways which for us would be rule-following and so constitutive of goodness in the sense of fulfilling our moral duties, so that God can be said similarly to be good in an analogical way. This fact also supplies the key to the arbitrariness objection. For our duties are determined by the commands, not merely of a supreme potentate, but of a just and loving God. God is essentially compassionate, fair, kind, impartial, and so forth, and His commandments are reflections of His own character. Thus, they are not arbitrary, and we need not trouble ourselves about counterfactuals with impossible antecedents like 'If God were to command child abuse....' God may be said to be good in the sense that He possesses all these moral virtues--and He does so essentially and to the maximal degree![122]

In response, some critics have said this merely "pushes the problem back" one step. Now they can pose a differently formulated dilemma: is God's nature good because it is declared so or created so by God, or because it recognizes some other, external standard of goodness? Same dilemma, right? Not so, according to Craig. A

---

[122] Craig: http://www.bethinking.org/resources/the-coherence-of-theism---part-2.htm

"nature" is not the sort of thing that recognizes or declares or creates anything, including goodness. Persons recognize, or declare, or create, but properties (essential or otherwise) such as "goodness" aren't the sorts of things that can do any of that, any more than my own property of "male" can recognize, or create, or declare anything.

Craig reminds us that any notion of "goodness" must have a "stopping point." For the Christian, that stopping point is God, and the Euthyphro dilemma allegedly challenges that stopping point by asking whether God creates or merely recognizes what's good. The same alleged dilemma arises with any other possible source. Does "nature" create the good, and is therefore an arbitrary source, or does it merely recognize what's good and is therefore not necessary? Does the majority within a community create the good, and is therefore an arbitrary source, or does it merely recognize what's good and is therefore not necessary? For any "stopping point," for that which defines the good, for that which simply *is* "the good," it makes no sense to ask for the source of its own goodness. We either recognize the legitimacy of a "stopping point," a proper "ground" for goodness, or else we're stuck with an infinite regress. If we reject the infinite regress, we must then ask, of any proposed "stopping point," whether it is a plausible stopping point.

For Craig and other theists, God makes a very compelling "stopping point," as God is regarded as the metaphysical "ground" of all things, of all Creation. There is nothing "higher" or "greater" than God, as understood in the Western theistic traditions. Christians understand God to be the paradigm of goodness. "Eventually such questions must find a stopping point in the character of God. Kindness is good because that's the way God is; cruelty is evil because it is inconsistent with God's nature. Therefore He issues commands that forbid behavior which is cruel and prescribe behavior which is kind. Rape is cruel, not kind, and therefore it is forbidden by God and therefore wrong."

If this God exists, then God makes for a plausible and compelling "stopping point," to be sure. Any other "stopping point," however, based in something finite, such as "humanity," will seem arbitrary in comparison. Why stop there, rather than elsewhere? Why "humanity" rather than "my community," or "me?" If there is instead an appeal to some external, independent standard of "the good," then what could that be, or mean? The Platonist notion of "The Good" as an independently existing abstract object (like the number four, or the concept of a chair) hasn't been taken seriously for centuries. Goodness does not appear to be a thing existing unto itself, but rather a property borne by something else. In that case, paradoxically, "the good" could not itself be good. People can be good, but "the good" couldn't itself be morally good any more than the color blue could be morally good. Craig asserts that moral values are embodied in persons, not abstractions. God, therefore, is a proper candidate for goodness and is, indeed, the ultimate person, defining goodness by God's very nature.

Thus, when God wills something, it is not an arbitrary whim but a necessary expression of God's eternal and essential nature. The disturbing hypothetical scenario, then, of God suddenly deciding, on a whim, that raping children is now "good" works far better against an abstraction than the particular concept of God found in Christianity. The idea of the gods being whimsical was readily available at the time Plato was writing the Euthyphro. No wonder that Plato sought a source for goodness beyond these fickle deities, and questioned their legitimacy as a source for goodness!

The Christian concept of God is just plain different from those beings. In fact, early Jewish and Christian thinkers were quite sympathetic to Plato, recognizing their God as "the Good" referred to by Plato. What theism provides, according to Craig, "is a source of moral prohibition and moral obligation in the commands of a holy and loving God. God is not only the standard of moral goodness, but that standard issues in commandments, for us, that express God's nature, that are constitutive of our moral duties or obligations. And so, what theism gives you is not only a sound foundation for moral value, but it gives you a foundation for moral obligation and duty as well."

Even if Craig's response to the Euthyphro problem is effective, that doesn't mean that the Euthyphro no longer has any teeth—though it bites in a different spot now.

Having a concept of God whose eternal nature includes moral goodness solves the original dilemma, (or else shows that any moral framework suffers from the same "stopping point" issue) but the critic might now wonder whether it's plausible that such a concept of God actually matches up to the God actually described in Western religious traditions. In other words, the Euthyphro problem now targets the aforementioned "matching strategy" (by which one "matches" their God with the philosophical abstraction supported by effective TAs).

Consider the following from Deuteronomy 20:16-18: "However, in the cities of the nations the LORD your God is giving you as an inheritance, do not leave alive anything that breathes.   Completely destroy them—the Hittites, Amorites, Canaanites, Perizzites, Hivites and Jebusites—as the LORD your God has commanded you.   Otherwise, they will teach you to follow all the detestable things they do in worshiping their gods, and you will sin against the LORD your God."

Such "Old Testament challenges" have inspired some atheists to decry the God of Christianity as a "monster." "What makes my jaw drop is that people today should base their lives on such an appalling role model as Yahweh-and even worse, that they should bossily try to force the same evil monster (whether fact or fiction) on the rest of us."[123]

If the MA works and establishes the existence of an objective ground and source for our moral values and duties, and this objective ground is described as morally perfect by someone like Craig (to ward off "arbitrariness" concerns), then would such morally troubling examples as the one provided from Deuteronomy above prevent a successful matching strategy?

Craig seems to acknowledge this revised threat from the Euthyphro problem. He dismisses it as being no threat to the MA, in general, by pointing out that in order to condemn God (as recorded in the Bible), one must presuppose that objective moral value do exist (thereby affirming premise 2 of the MA). And, Biblical atrocities, even if truly atrocities, don't refute premise 1 either ("If God does not exist, then objective moral values and duties do not exist."). At best, this point would prove that certain Biblical accounts are mistaken in attributing to God certain actions, or that the Christian "God" isn't really God. At most, this would require an abandonment of belief in Biblical inerrancy, but not belief in God, nor even the Christian God (if one can

---

[123] Dawkins, The God Delusion, 248.

address the "atrocities" in a reasonable way).[124]

Having already engaged in a rather *long* (but important) diversion, it's probably useful to be reminded of the MA at this point:

1. If God does not exist, objective moral values and duties do not exist.
2. Objective moral values and duties do exist.
3. Therefore, God exists.

Thus far, we've been focused solely on premise 1, and Craig's defense of it, but what about premise 2? Are there any reasons to believe objective moral values and duties really do exist? Craig thinks so, and employs an analogy with sensory perception to demonstrate his point.

To begin with, we would presumably all acknowledge that perceptual experience exists. Although our senses are fallible, in the absence of specific reasons to distrust our senses, we have a general reason to trust their adequacy. That is, although we are perfectly aware that our senses are limited, and imperfect, and can sometimes be misleading or just plain mistaken, we don't therefore embrace a comprehensive and crippling skepticism and dismiss our sense testimony as useless. Instead, we proceed by living our lives, reliant on sense testimony, and trusting in the general accuracy of our senses despite their imperfections. On a related note, we are also confident that the perceptible world exists, though we technically can't *prove* it. Each of us tends to accept that a material world exists rather independently of our awareness of it, and perceiving of it, and it is that very world within which we operate, and with which our senses are engaged. Of course, you can't prove that the material world exists and isn't just a construction of your mind (for example), since any "proof" would also be dismissed as a mental construct. That being said, with the notable exception of discussions in philosophy classes, no one takes seriously the idea that all reality is merely their own mental construct. We believe the material world exists (though we can't prove it), and we believe that our senses perceive that world in a generally reliable sort of way.

Here comes the analogy.

Just as we all have perceptual experiences (e.g., seeing, hearing, tasting, etc.), we all also have moral experiences. We "perceive" that certain actions are wrong, and others are right, that some people are "good" and others "bad," that some traits are "virtues" and others "vices." We acknowledge that this moral sense is fallible. Each of

---

[124] An example of such a (possibly reasonable) way is offered by Craig: because all moral duties are ultimately grounded in divine commands which themselves issue from God's own nature, God is not bound by moral duties, since God does not issue commands to himself. Therefore, God may have prerogatives forbidden to us, and may issue morally righteous commands involving actions that would otherwise be morally forbidden in the absence of such a command" (in effect, "thou shalt not kill, unless God commands you to"). I (personally) think this approach is still problematic, and honest theists must grapple with the meaning of certain Biblical passages in an effort to harmonize God's perfectly good nature with actions or commandments attributed to God as recorded in the Bible.

us makes moral mistakes from time to time, and some people are morally "blind" to the point where we label them sociopaths. However, just as the existence of people who are vision or hearing impaired doesn't inspire the rest of us to doubt the existence of visible or audible things (or even to seriously question the general accuracy of our own vision and hearing), the existence of those who are morally impaired need not inspire us to doubt the existence and (general) accuracy of moral experience and moral perception. As Craig puts it, "in moral experience we apprehend a realm of moral values and duties that impose themselves upon us. There's no more reason to deny the objective reality of moral values than the objective reality of the physical world."

Just as it would require a compelling argument to get you to deny the general reliability of sense testimony, so too should it require a compelling argument to get you to override your default recognition of moral perception and experience.

Perhaps there are such moral perceptions, but they are merely subjective perceptions, rather than objective? After all, you might acknowledge that there really is an independently existing glass of wine that we're both tasting, but point out that our taste experience of that wine is going to be *subjective*. I might love the wine for being so "fruit-forward," while you might hate it for being a "fruit bomb." Similarly, one person's moral perception of the same act might result in a judgment of "evil" while another's judgment of that same act is "good."

Is my belief that it's wrong to torture babies for fun the same kind of claim as my belief that triple-cream brie is the best kind of cheese? Just a matter of perspective? Merely personal opinion? A matter of taste?

If you and I disagree about spicy food, we tend to think that's not a big deal. I'll eat spicy food, and you won't. Everyone's happy. But, what if I think it's OK for me to steal your identity and charge a bunch of merchandise in your name? I keep all the stuff, and you get stuck with the bill. You find out it was me, and you come complaining:

You: "Hey, Ted! What's wrong with you? Why did you steal my credit card and buy all that stuff for yourself? I just got a huge credit card bill in the mail?"

Me: "Um, I wanted the stuff, and I also didn't want to pay for it myself. Seemed like a pretty good way to handle that particular problem...."

You: "But you can't just steal my credit card because you want something and don't want to have to pay for it! That's wrong!"

Me: "No it's not...."

You: "What are you talking about? Of course it is!"

Me: "I don't think it is—and I would appreciate it if you would drop that self-righteous tone. The way you're speaking to me, it's as if you think your opinion concerning identity theft is somehow better, or more accurate, than mine. How arrogant...."

Professor Emeritus Harry Jaffa (from my own Alma Mater, Claremont McKenna College), penned a fictionalized account similar to this that is both more compelling and more wordy. Though I can't express enough how much I disagree with Professor Jaffa on certain subjects, he has managed to make the crux of a subjectivist understanding of morality clear in this dialogue that is presented as a transcript of an audio tape made by the infamous (and now executed) serial killer Ted Bundy. Jaffa has admitted, however, concerning the authenticity of the transcript, that it was "composed on the same principle as the speeches in Thucydides' History of the Peloponnesian War, attributing to each speaker the words that fit his character and the circumstances in which he spoke." In other words, he made it up—but in a way that he thought was at least consistent with the character of Bundy. A brief excerpt follows:

> Then I learned that all moral judgments are "value judgments," that all value judgments are subjective, and that none can be proved to be either "right" or "wrong." I even read somewhere that the Chief Justice of the United States had written that the American Constitution expressed nothing more than collective value judgments. Believe it or not, I figured out for myself what apparently the Chief Justice couldn't figure out for himself: that if the rationality of one value judgment was zero, multiplying it by millions would not make it one whit more rational. Nor is there any "reason" to obey the law for anyone, like myself, who has the boldness and daring — the strength of character — to throw off its shackles. I discovered that to become truly free, truly unfettered, I had to become truly uninhibited. And I quickly discovered that the greatest obstacle to my freedom, the greatest block and limitation to it, consists in the insupportable "value judgment" that I was bound to respect the rights of others. I asked myself, who were these "others"? Other human beings, with human rights? Why is it more wrong to kill a human animal than any other animal, a pig or a sheep or a steer? Is your life more to you than a hog's life to a hog? Why should I be willing to sacrifice my pleasure more for the one than for the other? Surely, you would not, in this age of scientific enlightenment, declare that God or nature has marked some pleasures as "moral" or "good" and others a "immoral" or "bad"? In any case, let me assure you, my dear young lady, that there is absolutely no comparison between the pleasure I might take in eating ham and the pleasure I anticipate in raping and murdering you. That is the honest conclusion to which my education has led me after the most conscientious examination of my spontaneous and uninhibited self.

Jaffa's point is pretty simple: if moral truth is relative to the individual, then, strictly speaking, Bundy isn't incorrect to believe that raping and murdering is a fine form of entertainment. I disagree with him, of course, and so do you (I hope!). But, if moral truths are subjective, then all that means is that we have a different opinion about rape and murder than he does. Our opinion is neither better, nor worse, than Bundy's—in much the same way that someone who dislikes spicy food isn't "wrong" (whatever I might believe about their taste preferences). Similarly, someone who believes it's acceptable to have sex with young children isn't "wrong" according to a subjectivist approach. Such a person's opinion is no doubt quite unpopular, but "unpopular" isn't the same thing as "wrong."

I have a friend who loves to eat cold, smoked oysters right from the can. Every other person I know finds them disgusting. Despite the extremely unpopular taste preference he exhibits, I wouldn't presume to say that he's "wrong" about smoked oysters. That's just what he likes. Is that true of pedophiles as well? Are we willing to think of "I like oysters" and "I like raping children" as the same kinds of claims? I'm being intentionally provocative here, because it's essential that we understand what it means if subjectivism is the proper way to understand morality.

From the standpoint of subjectivism, those of us who think it abhorrent to have sex with a child don't have "better" values than a pedophile. We're not "right." What we are, is more powerful, or more numerous. It just so happens that the no-sex-with-children crowd gained control at some point in our history, and has remained more populous and more powerful than the percentage of our population who think it acceptable to have sex with children. We have no moral advantage over them, but we can force them to follow our values rather than theirs. After all, if they refuse, we'll throw them in jail.

Craig (and other like-minded folks) regard this subjectivist approach to morality to be not only insufficient to provide any sort of serious and compelling moral system, but also, frankly, counter-intuitive. He's confident that our moral intuitions point to an objective basis for moral values and duties. Another famous Christian thinker, C.S. Lewis, agrees.

C.S. Lewis

Lewis starts from what he takes to be the universal recognition of objective moral "rights" and "wrongs." This is evident, he thinks, from the fact that we all tend to *judge* the behavior of others (and ourselves). We really do think that some actions are good, and others bad—and morally so, not merely so in terms of what's prudent. We really do think that some actions are virtuous, and others vile, and that some people are heroes, and others villains. Although our particular examples might vary, we all engage in this general behavior. In addition, we have behavioral expectations of others, and we are upset when people violate them. We all think there are certain things that people just shouldn't do, and we get upset with them if they do it anyway. Spouses shouldn't be unfaithful. Friends shouldn't lie to you. Politicians shouldn't accept (or expect) bribes. Your neighbor shouldn't steal from you. No one should molest your child. And so forth. We don't merely blithely announce our expectations, and then shrug when they're violated, as though it didn't matter. We are offended, indignant, outraged, betrayed, hurt. . . With respect to our own behavior, when someone else accuses *us* of violating moral norms, we usually try to make excuses for the behavior, if we don't outright confess—thereby implying the need for an explanation in the first place. Compare the following hypothetical exchanges:

You: "Hey! Don't cut in line in front of me."
Me: "My friend has been saving my spot."

You: "Hey! Don't cut in line in front of me."
Me: "I'll do whatever I want!"

While there certainly are some people who flout convention, and are unashamed to do so, we tend to judge those people very harshly—sometimes going so far as to label them sociopaths. Most of us play by the rules, try to justify our actions if we're caught "bending" them, get upset with others when they break them, and all the while at least implicitly acknowledge the existence of "the rules" in the first place. The implicit premise here seems to be that we all know that there exist certain (objective) moral principles.

Lewis is aware that not everyone would so readily agree to that claim, and he anticipates (and addresses) several possible objections. A first, obvious, objection is the theory of cultural relativism (sometimes called ethical relativism). If cultural relativism (hereafter, CR) is true, then there are no objective moral standards, but all moral principles are simply the dominant values and expectations of particular communities.

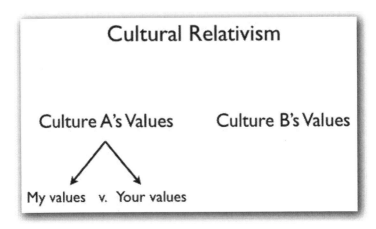

Consider the image above. It represents the kinds of judgments and comparisons possible according to CR. No such image was provided for subjectivism since, if subjectivism is true, no comparisons of values are possible anyway—at least not anything other than a "taste test." CR does allow some comparisons, some strong moral judgments, but it too is limited, and in very similar ways to subjectivism. Why?

Cultural relativism operates on just the same assumptions as subjectivism with one notable difference: whereas subjectivism claims that moral judgments are matters of personal opinion, and gain whatever legitimacy they have from the endorsement of the individual, CR claims that morality is a matter of collective judgment. What is right and wrong is determined by the prevailing values of a given community. You've probably heard the expression, "when in Rome, do as the Romans do." Assuming this is meant as more than just practical advice, this is an expression of CR.

What is morally right and morally wrong is established by the dominant values of a given culture. This allows for moral judgments and comparisons concerning individuals. The standard we would use for such judgments would be the dominant values of our culture. For example, in the United States, an adult male marrying a 9 year-old girl would not merely be considered morally wrong, he would be prosecuted for a sex crime. Thus, because the dominant cultural values of the U.S. frown upon such marriages, it is wrong to marry 9 year old girls in the U.S. Not so, elsewhere, however.

> *Tihun, a 9 year old Ethiopian girl, was arranged to marry a 19 year old Orthodox church deacon by her father. This is not an aberration. According to UN and Ethiopian statistics, in some parts of Ethiopia almost 90 percent of the local girls are married before age 15 (technically, it is against Ethiopian law to marry anyone under the age of 18, but the punishment is a $12 fine, is rarely enforced, and is generally ignored by the conservative population.). "'In truth, if a girl reaches 13, she is already too old to be married,' declares Nebiyu Melese, 54, Tihun's wiry farmer father. 'I know some people say this is uncivilized. But they don't live here. So how can they judge?'"[125]*

"How can they judge?" According to CR, we can't. Well, at least not with any special credibility. Because CR claims, like subjectivism, that there is no set of "true" moral values that apply to all people, everywhere, and at all times, there is no objective standard with which to judge the values of a culture. From *within* a given culture, one may (and should) employ the values of that culture, and individuals can (and should) be judged according to those standards. In the U.S., if you marry a 9 year old and I don't, I'm a morally superior person (on that one issue, at least) because my values and behavior are more in harmony with those prescribed by our culture. Outside of our own culture, however, we are in "no position to judge." Obviously, this interpretation of morality directly contradicts Lewis' claims about our perception of objective moral norms.

Why would anyone accept this view? One need not be especially well-traveled, or cosmopolitan to know that different cultures have different practices, and (seemingly) different values. Certain examples are obvious. Australian aborigines eat the "witchety grub" and consider it a welcome delicacy. Most Americans would only eat grubs if on a reality TV show. Americans eat meat with reckless abandon (200 pounds per person, in 2005, according to the U.S. Department of Agriculture), but Indian Hindus abstain from eating meat. "He who desires to augment his own flesh by eating the flesh of other creatures lives in misery in whatever species he may take his birth."[126]

It is not only our diets that vary, from one culture to the next. Marriage practices, sexual taboos, notions of masculinity and femininity, notions of "family," clothing practices, funerary practices, and many other activities vary. One need not be a world traveler to know this, just watch PBS or National Geographic.

Some cultural relativists, such as Ruth Benedict, observe these cultural

---

[125] As reported By Paul Salopek, Chicago Tribune foreign correspondent, published December 12, 2004.

[126] Mahabharat 115.47—for those unfamiliar, the Mahabharat is one of two major Sanskrit epics of ancient India. It is also an important part of Hindu mythology. Thus, quoting sections and verses from the Mahabarat is analogous to quoting from chapter and verse from the Christian Bible.

differences, and make something significant out of it. Benedict claims that standards of normalcy and deviance vary from one culture to the next.

The above picture shows former President George Herbert Walker Bush ("the Elder") (as well as former Vice President Dick Cheney and Secretary of State Colin Powell) walking hand-in-hand with Saudi King Abdullah. In the United States, this is an interesting event, because in the U.S. when two grown men walk around holding hands, it indicates something about their relationship. When we see two adult men holding hands, we assume they are homosexual. Even for straight allies, men holding hands is seen as a sub-cultural practice for homosexuals—there's been little, if any, infiltration of this practice into the (straight) mainstream culture. The practice, and its meaning, however, is quite different in Saudi culture. Men hold hands as a display of friendship, not as a display of a romantic relationship. "We" give a "high-five," "they" hold hands. Americans eat with forks, the Chinese eat with chopsticks. American men wear pants, traditional Scotsmen wear kilts. Different strokes for different folks....

Most of us are willing to acknowledge that certain practices vary from one culture to the next, and that each is a legitimate practice. That is, it's hard to find someone who would claim, in any serious tone, that it's wrong to eat with chop-sticks, Chinese or not, and that eating with a fork is the only morally legitimate means to transport food to one's mouth. Benedict goes quite a bit farther than this, though, by claiming not only that "normalcy" varies (legitimately) from one culture to the next, but also that normal and moral (goodness) are synonymous terms. In other words, when we say that something is morally good, what we're really saying is that the practice in question is what we consider "normal," and if we label something to be morally bad, that's just another way of saying it's "weird." A slight bit of logic allows us to see the implication of this.

1.   What is considered "normal" varies (legitimately) across cultures.

2. Therefore, there is no single standard of normalcy for humankind.
3. "Normal" and "morally good" are synonymous terms.
4. Therefore, there is no single standard of moral goodness for humankind.

A few points require immediate attention. First, it's far from obvious that "normalcy" and "morality" are, in fact, synonymous terms—at least not across the whole range of practices deemed either normal/deviant, or good/bad. For example, it's possible that there are practices deemed normal or abnormal that we don't regard as having any moral significance whatsoever. Talking to oneself in public is seen as "weird" in the U.S. culture, and is often assumed to be a sign of mental illness, but it's not obvious that it would also be considered morally wrong. Piercing one's face is still considered "extreme," despite the increasing popularity of body piercings, but it's not easy to find someone who would claim that those who do so have committed a moral offense.

Similarly, it's not obvious that we would all agree that certain practices, deemed immoral, are of the same type as those we also deem "abnormal." Child-rape is certainly considered deviant, and perceived as "weird," but the act seems to be more than just "weird." Intentionally urinating on oneself in public is weird. Very weird, in fact. Is raping a child just very, very weird? Very, very, very weird? Or, are some acts qualitatively different, such that they no longer fit into our categories or normalcy/deviancy, but require their own (distinct) category: good/evil?

In addition, as James Rachels has pointed out, the mere fact of difference does not mean that there are no values that apply to all people everywhere. The observation of cultural differences is consistent with both CR and objective approaches to ethics.

Rachels proposes that there is more "universality" across cultures than we might initially recognize. One reason for this is because cultures might manifest the same underlying value in different ways, given contingent historical, geographical, climatic, and other circumstances. For example, throughout most of the U.S., the dead are buried below ground, but in New Orleans, they are buried above ground. Why? New Orleans is below sea-level, and has a high water table. Graves fill with water, and caskets float, creating an unhealthy, as well as deeply disturbing, result. This is an example of how geography can influence the manifestation (burial below v. above ground) of the same underlying value (honor the dead). Other cultures cremate. Ancient Egyptians mummified their dead. All believed it right to honor the dead, but due to different circumstances, they demonstrated that belief in different ways. Indeed, Lewis makes this same point, claiming that there are fewer *actual* differences in moral values than might appear.

> *Think of a country where people were admired for running away in battle, or where a man felt proud of double-crossing all the people who had been kindest to him. You might just as well try to imagine a country where two and two made five. Men have differed as regards what people you ought to be unselfish to- whether it was only your own family, or your fellow countrymen, or everyone. But they have always agreed that you ought not to put yourself first. Selfishness has never been admired. Men have differed as to whether you should have one wife or four. But they have always agreed that you must not simply have any*

woman you liked.[127]

As another example, consider child-rearing. Some cultures adopt the so-called "nuclear family" (mom, dad, and 2.5 kids under the same roof). Others prefer extended families (multiple generations in the same home), and still others embrace communal child-rearing in which responsibility for caring for the young is shared by the larger community, including non-blood relatives. There are any number of explanations for why one culture might manifest its child-care in one fashion, while a different culture does so in another, but the allegation is that the underlying value is the same, even though the manifestation is different. The moral value that the young should be cared for is, in fact, one of a handful of values that Rachels claims that all cultures must have, if they are to survive as a culture. It is thus a universal (non-relative) value. If this point sounds familiar, that's a good thing: we considered Rachels' (evolutionarily-based) argument for some universal moral principles earlier in this chapter.

In cases of difference, a relativist will conclude that there are no universal values. Someone who believes morality is objective will look at those same differences and conclude that at least one of the cultures is mistaken. It might be difficult to discern who is in the right, but there is nothing logically inconsistent with looking at two cultures, one of which prosecutes the rapist when a woman is raped, the other of which stones the woman to death for adultery, noting the different responses, and concluding that one of them is in error. What's the point? Simply this: the fact of cultural differences, by itself, is not necessarily an indicator of the truth of CR.

Cultural differences alone do not require one to accept CR, but there might well be other reasons to do so. One reason is a general skepticism that a universal moral code could ever be agreed upon. After all, that there is deep division on numerous moral issues (e.g., abortion, the death penalty, homosexuality, etc.) is obvious. One might think that agreement will never be reached and take that as a sign that no such set of universal values could exist. That might be true, but it's a hasty conclusion.

Even if humanity never does come to consensus on the requirements of morality, that might say far more about our own limitations than about ethics. Humans might never fully understand the laws of Nature, or the true origin of the universe, but that doesn't mean that there is no explanation, no right answer—just none that we can reach. Moreover, even if it's true that we can never know, with certainty, the truth concerning our moral obligations, that doesn't mean that we can't progress towards the truth, that we can't come ever closer to a full and accurate ethical theory.

One more reason someone might embrace CR is a result of rejecting its perceived alternative (cynics might call this the "liberal guilt" argument for CR). The argument is presumably well-intentioned. It's rooted in recognition that, for most of recorded history, tribes have always assumed their own moral superiority over their neighbors.

In the West, we have a long and bloody history of European (and eventually, American) powers taking notice of a group of people, taking note of how different

---

[127] Lewis, C.S. "Mere Christianity," in *The Complete C.S. Lewis Signature Classics.* Harper One, 2002, Book 1, Chapter 1.

they are, judging that to be different is to be wrong and in need of correction, and then using that judgment to justify campaigns of invasion, colonization, exploitation, and even genocide.

If "savages" engage in morally inferior practices, then one is doing them a favor by correcting them. After all, they're being made "better." Since our way is the only "right" way, they should be made to dress like us, marry like us, speak like us, worship like us, govern like us, and so on.

The Argument From Tolerance

Many of us, looking back on history, and even on contemporary policies and practices, are repulsed by the cruelties and atrocities that were perpetrated by virtue of the self-righteous assumption of moral superiority. If the inspiration for such actions is the belief that there is one set of true moral values (undoubtedly, one's own!), then a rejection of such an assumption might prevent such actions. CR is seen as the tolerance-producing alternative to an objective ethics, and is, for that reason, embraced. The "argument from tolerance" may be formulated as follows:

1) If morality is relative to its culture, then there is no independent basis for criticizing the moral values of any other culture.
2) If there is no independent way of criticizing any other culture, then we ought to be tolerant of the moral values of other cultures.
3) Morality is relative to culture.
4) Therefore, (by 1-3) we ought to be tolerant of the moral values of other cultures.

Tolerance is a good thing, right? Not necessarily. Ask yourself this question: is there any limit as to what should be tolerated? And what does it even mean to be "tolerant?" Does it mean to let people do whatever they want? Does it allow for judgment, but not intervention? Does it just mean we have to be "polite" when judging others? Which of the following should be (or should have been) "tolerated?" What would it mean to "tolerate" such practices?

- South African apartheid.
- Nazi mass-extermination of Jews.
- The Armenian genocide perpetrated by Turkey?
- The Cherokee "Trail of Tears?"
- The thousands of African-Americans lynched in the American South?
- The internment of Japanese-Americans during WWII?
- Female Genital Mutilation that currently affects approximately 2 million girls each year?
- The harvesting of organs from executed criminals in China?
- Saddam Hussein's gassing of Kurdish villages?

(If you don't know what some of these examples refer to, look them up!)
Problem number one with the argument from tolerance is that it's not at all

obvious that tolerance is always a good thing. It certainly seems to be the case that some practices, and some values, should not be tolerated. Which values fit into that category will be subject to spirited debate, of course, but it does seem that such a category exists.

Problem number two with the argument from tolerance is a problem of internal consistency. Premise 1 seems uncontroversial, but premise 2 requires a close examination. Premise 2 claims that "we" ought to be tolerant. Two words are significant: "we," and "ought." Notice that "ought" is a value-term. To say that we ought to do something is to make a prescriptive claim. We should be tolerant. It's good to be tolerant. It's right to be tolerant. Who, exactly, are "we" who are being told that we ought to be tolerant? There are three possibilities:

1) "We" are all of humanity—all people, in all places, at all times.
2) "We" are people from the same culture as the person making the argument.
3) "We" are people from a different culture than that of the person making the argument.

No matter which is intended (1-3), a problem emerges. Let's work backwards. If (3), then we are from a different culture than that of the person urging us to be tolerant. Why should we listen to her? Her values might be right for her own people, but they don't apply to us. If CR is true, we should heed the moral requirements of our own culture, and if they differ from hers, so much the worse for her!

If (2), then she is speaking to us as a peer. Now we must figure out what the values of our (shared) culture happens to be. Is tolerance a dominant value in our culture? If so, then we should, in fact, be tolerant (whatever that means), but not because of her argument. We should be tolerant because that is what our cultural values prescribe. She's preaching to the choir.

On the other hand, what if our culture is not tolerant? What if we come from an imperialist culture that believes that other cultures' values are savage and wrong? In that case, according to CR, we should be intolerant! In fact, that tolerance-promoting troublemaker is actively encouraging us to be immoral by going against the values of our culture. What kind of a cultural relativist is she?

If (1), then she is claiming that there is at least one value (tolerance) that applies to all people, everywhere, at all times. That flatly contradicts a central feature of CR, namely, that there are no values that apply to all people, everywhere. She has contradicted herself and supplied the counter-example to her own theory. How embarrassing...

None of this means that a cultural relativist cannot, or will not, be tolerant. Instead, it simply demonstrates that tolerance is not a necessary consequence of CR. According to CR, one should be tolerant only if that is what one's culture demands, and if a culture is intolerant, that culture is not "wrong" for being so. Moreover, it seems implausible that unrestrained tolerance is even desirable, let alone morally required of us. If there is such a thing as "evil," certainly it should be resisted rather than accommodated.

Ultimately, CR is also vulnerable to the very same criticisms that were leveled against subjectivism, but adjusted to reflect CR's emphasis on collective values as opposed to personal opinion. Lewis participates in this criticism of CR by once again appealing to what he believes to be the actual (universal, consistent) practice of people in real-life.

In actual practice, people certainly speak and act as though they believe that certain actions are right, and others wrong; that certain policies or cultural practices are good, and others not. If CR is true, however, none of this can be done in any objective sense. Much as subjectivism does not allow comparisons of individuals (beyond expressions of our own personal opinions), CR is incapable of strong cross-cultural comparisons.

Consider the Taliban. Prior to the U.S. led overthrow of the Taliban (2001), the laws and practices of Afghanistan drew considerable international criticism. Here are a few examples:

- Public executions, including stonings, were common.
- Kite-flying (a "frivolous" activity) was outlawed.
- TV, music, and the internet were banned (to remove decadent Western influences).
- Men were required to wear beards.
- Girls were forbidden to attend school.
- Women could not be examined by male doctors.
- Women could no longer work as doctors (think about what these last two mean for women's health care under the Taliban).
- Women could not leave the home without a male escort.
- "Idolatrous" art was destroyed--such as the giant statues of Buddha (constructed 2nd and 3rd centuries A.D., destroyed in 2001).

If CR is true, then the practices of the Taliban were neither better nor worse than those of any other culture—just "different." Of course, the U.S. overthrow of the Taliban could not be condemned either, so long as it was consistent with the dominant values of U.S. culture, and neither the Taliban nor the U.S.-led overthrow could be judged by other cultures—after all, they have no privileged position from which to judge the U.S. any more than the U.S. has a privileged position from which to judge the Taliban.

Perhaps this is accurate, and no one is ever in a position to judge another. If so, though, we must face a radical revision of our common practices, since we do, in fact, tend to condemn cultures such as Nazi Germany, the Taliban, and apartheid-era South Africa. Are such acts of condemnation anything more than an expression of "our" opinion? Lewis' own experiences of the second World War, and the threat of the Nazis, is, for him, an example of a people and a cultural program gone *wrong*, and the mere fact that some Nazis might have thought differently doesn't change that fact. "People may be sometimes mistaken about [morals], just as people sometimes get their sums wrong; but they are not a matter of mere taste and opinion any more than the multiplication table."

A related objection is that, if CR is true, moral reformers are, paradoxically, always morally wrong. Remember, according to CR, the right thing to do is, by definition, whatever one's culture tells one to do. Since the dominant values of one's culture are the ultimate arbiter of morality (the "supreme court" as it were), there is nothing to which one can appeal higher than one's culture. One can never go "over the head" of one's culture in the event that one disagrees with the values of one's culture. So where does that leave reformers?

A reformer, by definition, is trying to change her culture. All reformers detect something about their culture that they think is wrong, and they try to change it. According to CR, though, it is not the individual's judgment that establishes what is right and wrong; it is the collective judgment of the entire culture as expressed in its dominant values. By definition, then, someone who is trying to change the values of the culture is trying to change what is right. That makes them wrong, doesn't it?

Both Martin Luther King Jr. and Rosa Parks were icons of the American Civil Rights era. Both fought against racism and segregation laws. Both were criminals, by definition, since they deliberately disobeyed segregation laws, and both were arrested for their "offenses." Both believed that the values of their culture, at the time, were wrong, and in need of correction. But who were they to challenge the values of their culture? By offering a set of values different from that of their culture, at the time, weren't they morally in the wrong, by definition? And yet, don't we tend to have precisely the opposite view of reformers, at least in retrospect?

When Rosa Parks died in 2005, her body was displayed in the Capital Rotunda. The tribute, which requires an act of Congress, has taken place only 30 times in this country's history. Those receiving this rare honor include President Ronald Reagan and several other presidents, eight members of Congress, and two Capitol police officers slain at their posts, among a handful of others. President Bill Clinton delivered a eulogy for her. In it, he said that she made us a "better people, and a better country."

If CR is true, what could it mean that she made us "better?" The segregationist values prior to the Civil Rights Movement were not "wrong," after all—just wrong given our current dominant values. There is, admittedly, an empirical issue here, as one could argue that the true dominant values of the U.S. were egalitarian, and that the segregationist and racist policies were in violation of the dominant values, and therefore wrong. If that's true, then Civil Rights activists were not "in the wrong," but were, instead, champions of the actual cultural values of the United States. Historians will be better prepared to address this issue, but it seems overly generous to think that racism and segregationism were not expressions of the dominant values at the time, considering how pervasive and enduring racism, and its legacy, has proven to be. Anti-"race-mixing" laws were not overturned by the Supreme Court until 1967. Lest one think such laws were regional only, found in the deep South alone, bear in mind that California's anti-miscegenation law was not overturned by a California Supreme Court until 1948, a mere seven years prior to the beginning of the Civil Rights movement. Much as individuals cannot get better or worse, in any strong sense, from a subjectivist perspective, neither can cultures get better or worse over time from the perspective of CR. Cultures become "different," but their former values were not wrong; they were right, at the time. This aspect is especially fascinating considering how often proponents of CR condemn the "imperialist" practices of their own culture. If CR is true, on what grounds can they complain about their own culture's values? And yet, as Lewis points out, people *do* argue that reform is possible, and desirable.

> *If no set of moral ideas were truer or better than any other, there would be no*
> *sense in preferring civilised morality to savage morality, or Christian morality*
> *to Nazi morality. In fact, of course, we all do believe that some moralities are*
> *better than others. We do believe that some of the people who tried to change*
> *the moral ideas of their own age were what we would call Reformers or*
> *Pioneers-people who understood morality better than their neighbours did.*[128]

In fairness, the advocate of CR could reply in the following way: "when we complain about our own culture, our complaint is that the practices of our culture are not consistent with its values. So, too, with reformers in general. What reformers do is appeal to the already existing values of their culture that are not being honored, to some extent."

Using the example of the Civil Rights movement, a relativist could say that King and others appealed to the values of equality, brotherhood, freedom, and dignity that were already found in Christianity and in the political philosophy that shaped our government and society. When King advocated equality, he was not introducing some new, alien value into the culture, but was simply pointing out that U.S. society was not living up to its very own ideals, by virtue of the rampant discrimination at the time. Indeed, the advocate could argue that had those basic values of equality, freedom, opportunity, and the like not already been present in the culture, the Movement could have never taken hold and been successful. This is a decent argument, and seems plausible, at least in the case of the Civil Rights Movement. It seems limited, however, in that it would appear that a culture could never undergo a radical transformation from within. Social change would always need to be somehow consistent with already existing and honored values. Any radical change would have to be understood in terms of an "invasion" of a foreign value, and in terms of that initially-wrong value "vanquishing" and ultimately replacing the native values, much as a foreign usurper may claim a throne. Small changes might be understood as a somewhat different application of an already dominant value, while major change must come from the outside. Major changes, at the least, and the advocates of major change, would have to be considered "wrong," at the time.

This produces a potentially counter-intuitive evaluation of moral reformers—at least those advocating significant change. In trying to change the "right" values of their culture, moral reformers are always wrong. If they succeed, and their own values become dominant later on, they will be hailed as moral visionaries, in retrospect. But, in their own time, they are moral villains.

Perhaps that's just "how it is." We must acknowledge the possibility that our own perception that a culture (including our own) has gotten morally better or worse over time is just an expression of the bias of our own time and place. We think segregation laws are wrong because in our own time, they are considered wrong. Had we been born (Caucasian) a half-century ago, though, we would have likely thought differently. Perhaps, at the time, we would have been "right." On the other hand, if you have any

---

[128]Ibid., Chapter 2.

strong intuition that cultures really do get better or worse over time, and that such judgments are not mere collective opinion, then you presumably have a hard time accepting the implications of CR. What is certain is that CR requires a radical revision of our everyday notions of cultural progress and regress—a revision that is less plausible, for Lewis, than is the recognition of objective moral values.

Another objection to the existence of objective moral values, very much in the spirit of CR, is that "morality" is merely social conditioning produced by our education and upbringing. Lewis, however, replies that *how* something is learned doesn't necessarily indicate its ultimate source or status (e.g., we learn the multiplication tables at school without this implying that math is merely a human convention). "But," the skeptic might wonder, "why think that morality is objective in a way analogous to math?" Because, says Lewis, the "Moral Law" is (generally, at its core) the same across cultures, whereas mere convention (e.g., which side of the road one drives on) is not. Returning to his arguments against CR, Lewis reiterates that we do, in actual practice, hold some cultural norms to be "better" or "worse" than others (e.g., Nazis are worse!), and alleged differences in values are often just differences in matters of fact. We have already rehearsed this point about alleged differences in values being just differences in local expressions of those values previously in this chapter, but Lewis uses an interesting example that's worth quoting: witch burning.

> *I have met people who exaggerate the differences, because they have not distinguished between differences of morality and differences of belief about facts. For example, one man said to me, 'Three hundred years ago people in England were putting witches to death. Was that what you call the Rule of Human Nature or Right Conduct?' But surely the reason we do not execute witches is that we do not believe there are such things. If we did-if we really thought that there were people going about who had sold themselves to the devil and received supernatural powers from him in return and were using these powers to kill their neighbours or drive them mad or bring bad weather, surely we would all agree that if anyone deserved the death penalty, then these filthy quislings did. There is no difference of moral principle here: the difference is simply about matter of fact. It may be a great advance in knowledge not to believe in witches: there is no moral advance in not executing them when you do not think they are there. You would not call a man humane for ceasing to set mousetraps if he did so because he believed there were no mice in the house.[129]*

A different sort of objection to the claim that morality is objective brings us back to the evolutionary understanding of morality previously considered by our appeals to Dawkins and Rachels. Perhaps "morality" is just our evolution-produced "herd instinct," just one instinctive drive amongst other instinctive drives? Lewis replies that desires are not identical to our sense of obligation with respect to those desires. For example, my awareness that I *ought* to be forgiving is not at all the same as a *desire* to be forgiving. Indeed, often our desires are in sharp contrast to our sense of obligation. Moreover, Lewis thinks that it makes little sense to understand moral

---

[129]Ibid.

prescriptions as impulses or desires amongst others, as he can identify no particular impulses or desires that the "Moral Law" tells us always to restrain or to pursue. Indeed, our sense of moral obligation seems to be a different sort of thing *by which we judge between* desires and impulses.

> *Supposing you hear a cry for help from a man in danger. You will probably feel two desires-one a desire to give help (due to your herd instinct), the other a desire to keep out of danger (due to the instinct for self-preservation). But you will find inside you, in addition to these two impulses, a third thing which tells you that you ought to follow the impulse to help, and suppress the impulse to run away. Now this thing that judges between two instincts, that decides which should be encouraged, cannot itself be either of them. You might as well say that the sheet of music which tells you, at a given moment, to play one note on the piano and not another, is itself one of the notes on the keyboard. The Moral Law tells us the tune we have to play: our instincts are merely the keys.*[130]

Nor does it seem plausible, according to Lewis, that morally good behavior is merely socially useful behavior (e.g., what's needed for community flourishing, as Rachels might argue). According to Lewis, morally good behavior *is* socially useful, but that doesn't explain its purpose (in a non-circular way), since being "socially useful" *is* of those behaviors we label "good."

> *If a man asked what was the point of playing football, it would not be much good saying 'in order to score goals,' for trying to score goals is the game itself, not the reason for the game, and you would really only be saying that football was football-which is true, but not worth saying. In the same way, if a man asks what is the point of behaving decently, it is no good replying, 'in order to benefit society,' for trying to benefit society, in other words being unselfish (for 'society' after all only means 'other people'), is one of the things decent behaviour consists in; all you are really saying is that decent behaviour is decent behaviour.*[131]

Suppose, for the sake of argument, that Lewis is right about the existence of an independent, objective Moral Law. Suppose also that we acknowledge that each one of us, seemingly without exception, violates it from time to time. This is just to say that none of us is morally perfect! Lewis thinks there are fascinating implications— implications that help us to decide between naturalistic and theistic worldviews.

At long last, we return to the ostensible point of this admittedly lengthy chapter: considering the MA as a TA. Given two basic worldviews, one purely naturalistic, and the other theistic, Lewis thinks that our experience of an objective Moral Law is more consistent with the theistic world view.

According to him, we observe a (binding) moral law that we did not create, and that we feel obliged to obey. *If* there were a "power" behind/beyond the universe,

---

[130] Ibid.
[131] Ibid.

then that power (whatever it is) couldn't exist as one of the observable "pieces" of the universe. By analogy, the architect of a house is not a particular piece of wood or bit of plaster, nor any part of the house at all. Instead, the architect is the mind responsible for the arrangement of all those parts in the first place. You might infer things about the architect by your observation of those parts, but you certainly couldn't expect to point to a fireplace and declare it to be the architect.

> *If there was a controlling power outside the universe, it could not show itself to us as one of the facts inside the universe- no more than the architect of a house could actually be a wall or staircase or fireplace in that house. The only way in which we could expect it to show itself would be inside ourselves as an influence or a command trying to get us to behave in a certain way. And that is just what we do find inside ourselves. Surely this ought to arouse our suspicions? In the only case where you can expect to get an answer, the answer turns out to be Yes; and in the other cases, where you do not get an answer, you see why you do not. Suppose someone asked me, when I see a man in a blue uniform going down the street leaving little paper packets at each house, why I suppose that they contain letters? I should reply, 'Because whenever he leaves a similar little packet for me I find it does contain a letter.' And if he then objected, 'But you've never seen all these letters which you think the other people are getting,' I should say, 'Of course not, and I shouldn't expect to, because they're not addressed to me. I'm explaining the packets I'm not allowed to open by the ones I am allowed to open.' It is the same about this question. The only packet I am allowed to open is Man. When I do, especially when I open that particular man called Myself, I find that I do not exist on my own, that I am under a law; that somebody or something wants me to behave in a certain way.*[132]

Lewis claims that our experience is almost universally of the "furniture" of the universe: all the particular objects, events, particles, and people we experience are "parts" of the universe analogous to the parts of a house, or objects within the house. Continuing with the architect analogy, if there were an "architect" of the universe, one way to detect that architect's existence would be by making inferences from what we observe about the house—and this is the sort of reasoning behind the DA, for example. But, another way to detect the "architect" involves our only, unique, "inside" experience: that of being a person. Our understanding of "people" is different from our understanding of everything else. Like everything else, we can observe people, just as we can observe comets, alligators, and blizzards. The unique difference between people and everything else we observe, is that *we are* people. "People" are not just another object of study, but the subjects that do the studying in the first place. My experience and understanding of people does involve observation of things going on around me, but it also includes, and starts with, my own first-person perspective from behind my own eyeballs. When we introspect, when we look "inside" our experience of personhood, we find the Moral Law—something we could never have inferred from only "external" observations of the operations of the universe.

---

[132] Ibid., Chapter 4.

Supposing science ever became complete so that it knew every single thing in the whole universe. Is it not plain that the questions, 'Why is there a universe?' 'Why does it go on as it does?' 'Has it any meaning?' would remain just as they were?

Now the position would be quite hopeless but for this. There is one thing, and only one, in the whole universe which we know more about than we could learn from external observation. That one thing is Man. We do not merely observe men, we are men. In this case we have, so to speak, inside information; we are in the know. And because of that, we know that men find themselves under a moral law, which they did not make, and cannot quite forget even when they try, and which they know they ought to obey. Notice the following point. Anyone studying Man from the outside as we study electricity or cabbages, not knowing our language and consequently not able to get any inside knowledge from us, but merely observing what we did, would never get the slightest evidence that we had this moral law. How could he? for his observations would only show what we did, and the moral law is about what we ought to do.[133]

If Lewis' argument works, it provides evidence, from the apparent existence of an objective Moral Law, of some sort of source of that Law. Lewis readily acknowledges that this is far from a proof of the Christian God.

Do not think I am going faster than I really am. I am not yet within a hundred miles of the God of Christian theology. All I have got to is a Something which is directing the universe, and which appears in me as a law urging me to do right and making me feel responsible and uncomfortable when I do wrong. I think we have to assume it is more like a mind than it is like anything else we know—because after all the only other thing we know is matter and you can hardly imagine a bit of matter giving instructions.[134]

Nevertheless, if the argument works, and points to some sort of mind-like source of objective moral values, then we need ask what sort of thing is a good candidate for that source, and once again the "matching strategy" comes into play. Both Craig and Lewis, then, think that there exists objective moral values, and the best explanation of this is the existence of a being (God) capable of grounding those values.

Conclusion

Like other TAs, the MA seeks to go from general, non-theistic observations and premises to a conclusion that points in a theistic direction. Proponents of the MA believe that if there are objective moral values and duties, the best explanation for those values and duties lies "outside" human opinion and experience, in which case

---

[133] Ibid.
[134] Ibid.

the existence of those values and duties would be evidence of something that could "match up" to God.

Like other TAs, the MA is subject to a variety of objections, not the least of which is one which questions the existence of objective moral values in the first place. Even given the existence of such values, some (like Rachels) argue that we needn't look beyond naturalistic explanations to account for them.

In our next chapter, we will encounter an interesting "twist." For one, we will explore a negative TA—that is, an argument *against* God's existence. The other twist is that it takes some of the assumptions of the MA and turns them on its head. While the MA takes the existence of (objective) good and evil to be evidence of God's existence, in the next chapter we will see how the existence of evil, at least, can be used as evidence *against* that God's existence.

Chapter 8: The Problem of Evil

Comprehension questions you should be able to answer after reading this chapter:

1. What is the "problem of evil (POE)?"

2. What is the difference between moral evil and natural evil?

3. What are the five claims that constitute an "inconsistent set," according to the POE?

4. What is the "free will defense?" Why do some believe that it is impossible for God to create humans with free will but without the risk of moral evil?

5. What is the "greater good defense?" What is the difference between a "general" and a "particular" greater good defense?

6. What is the "greater good" (chief purpose of life) according to Craig, Lewis, Hick, and Paley?

7. How does this greater good (#6) connect to the free will defense? The greater good defense?

8. How does Johnson criticize the free will defense? The greater good defense?

In the late Spring of 2008, a friend of mine died.

When it actually happened, I barely mourned for Shirley. I believe that's because I had already mourned for her, deeply and intensely some months prior, when we first learned of her cancer. Although no cancer is "kind," hers seemed especially cruel. The tumor in her throat closed it off, making it impossible for her to eat solid food for several months. She was fed through a tube inserted into her stomach, and could only suck on ice chips to keep her mouth and throat moist. Intensive chemotherapy caused the tumor in her throat to shrink down to the point where she was able to ingest tiny pieces of solid food, and I remember one day when she told me that had eaten a piece of buttered bread the night before, and how amazingly good it had tasted. Just buttered bread....

Chemotherapy or not, the cancer had spread to several internal organs, and all of us knew that Shirley had only months, at most, to live. As best she could, she remained active, until she was so weak and sickened from the cancer and the chemotherapy itself, that she became completely bedridden. I think it fortunate that she only lasted a few days in that state before one night, in the company of several friends, she simply closed her eyes and stopped breathing. About one week before, I had spoken with her on the phone, and she told me that her problem had to be "dealt with" in one way or another. I knew, then, what she meant: she had reached the point where death was being viewed as a welcome release.

Shirley's story has many elements of sadness to it, but I've not yet mentioned the triumphant elements. I have rarely, if ever, been so impressed by such courage. Her calm, valiant approach to her illness and her own death inspired me. I hope that when it's my turn to die, that I can do so with even a fraction of the dignity she displayed.

Another important feature of her story, not yet mentioned, is that she was a woman of faith. As death neared, her faith deepened and grew in ways that amazed me. Moreover, she testified to me (and others) that never in her life had she seen so clearly the power of love and friendship. Although the cancer had brought her body low, her spirit soared, borne up in part by her own courage, in part by the compassion and love of her friends, and perhaps even by Grace.

Shirley's story represents the antagonism behind the philosophical and theological problem known as the "Problem of Evil." The problem of evil (POE) is that it (viz., evil) seemingly should not exist—at least not if the God of the Western faith traditions exists. And yet, people like Shirley get cancer, suffer, and die.

Although this was not the case with Shirley, for many, the existence of (seemingly) unjustified suffering constitutes a challenge to theistic belief. The Christian writer and apologist C.S. Lewis wrote of his own experience and perspective as follows:

Not many years ago when I was an atheist, if anyone had asked me, 'Why do you not believe in God?' my reply would have run something like this:

"Look at the universe we live in. By far the greatest part of it consists of empty space, completely dark and unimaginably cold. The bodies which move in this space are so few and so small in comparison with the space itself that even if every one of them were known to be crowded as full as it could hold with perfectly happy creatures, it would still be difficult to believe that life and happiness were more than a byproduct to the power that made the universe. As it is, however, the scientists think it likely that very few of the suns of space— perhaps none of them except our own— have any planets; and in our own system it is improbable that any planet except the Earth sustains life. And Earth herself existed without life for millions of years and may exist for millions more when life has left her. And what is it like while it lasts? It is so arranged that all the forms of it can live only by preying upon one another. In the lower forms this process entails only death, but in the higher there appears a new quality called consciousness which enables it to be attended with pain. The creatures cause pain by being born, and live by inflicting pain, and in pain they mostly die. In the most complex of all the creatures, Man, yet another quality appears, which we call reason, whereby he is enabled to foresee his own pain which henceforth is preceded with acute mental suffering, and to foresee his own death while keenly desiring permanence. It also enables men by a hundred ingenious contrivances to inflict a great deal more pain than they otherwise could have done on one another and on the irrational creatures. This power they have exploited to the full. Their history is largely a record of crime, war, disease, and terror, with just

sufficient happiness interposed to give them, while it lasts, an agonised apprehension of losing it, and, when it is lost, the poignant misery of remembering. Every now and then they improve their condition a little and what we call a civilisation appears. But all civilisations pass away and, even while they remain, inflict peculiar sufferings of their own probably sufficient to outweigh what alleviations they may have brought to the normal pains of man. That our own civilisation has done so, no one will dispute; that it will pass away like all its predecessors is surely probable. Even if it should not, what then? The race is doomed. Every race that comes into being in any part of the universe is doomed; for the universe, they tell us, is running down, and will sometime be a uniform infinity of homogeneous matter at a low temperature. All stories will come to nothing: all life will turn out in the end to have been a transitory and senseless contortion upon the idiotic face of infinite matter. If you ask me to believe that this is the work of a benevolent and omnipotent spirit, I reply that all the evidence points in the opposite direction. Either there is no spirit behind the universe, or else a spirit indifferent to good and evil, or else an evil spirit."[135]

Sometimes the POE is offered as some sort of "proof" that God doesn't exist. Other times, it is offered as a way to undermine *warrant* (justification) for theistic belief. In real life, some people literally lose their faith when grappling with seemingly unjustified suffering. In this way, the POE constitutes a negative theistic argument (i.e., an argument *against* God's existence).

With regard to Shirley, suffering captures the first part of the POE. The virtue she displayed, and the faith she enjoyed, represents a possible response to the POE. We'll begin with some conceptual clarification, then proceed to outline the nature of the POE in greater detail. Finally, we'll consider the sorts of defenses theists have made in the face of the POE.

Evil

What is meant by "evil?" Oftentimes, what is meant by evil is something like "villainy" or "depravity." We associate evil with the deplorable acts of persons. But, for the purposes of the POE, evil is defined simply as "unjustified suffering." This is a more general usage of the term "evil," obviously, but it's a necessary broadening of the term in order to account for the different types of "evil" we encounter—not all unjustified suffering comes at the hands of bad people, after all.

1. **Natural evil**: *unjustified suffering attributed to "nature,"* as opposed to a moral agent.

2. **Moral evil**: *unjustified suffering inflicted by moral agents.*

Moral evil is fairly obvious: rape, murder, assault, abuse of all kinds—essentially, any of the many various horrible things humans can do to one another. If the

---

[135] C.S. Lewis, *The Problem of Pain*, Harper One, 1940/1996, pp. 1-3.

unjustified suffering can be traced back to a moral agent, it's an example of moral evil.

Natural evil is all the unjustified suffering that's left over, that can't be attributed to a moral agent. Natural disasters are good candidates, as well as disease, or naturally occurring droughts or famines. The inevitable frailty and decay of the body and mind could count as natural evil as well.

It's important to note that for both moral and natural evil, in order for them to count *as* evil, the suffering must be unjustified. If there is some sort of justification for the suffering, it is no longer "evil." A child might "suffer," for example, if you punish her for serious misbehavior, but so long as the punishment is fair and proportionate to the misbehavior (and aims at correcting that behavior), most of us would not regard the "time out" as "evil."

The possibility that there might be a justification to suffering leads to another important distinction: the logical POE v. the evidential POE.

The logical POE claims that there is something logically inconsistent between the existence of an all-powerful, all-knowing, morally perfect God, and the existence of evil. That is, if evil exists, that sort of God *can't* exist. The idea behind this is captured well by Lewis:

> "If God were good, He would wish to make His creatures perfectly happy, and if God were almighty He would be able to do what He wished. But the creatures are not happy. Therefore God lacks either goodness, or power, or both. This is the problem of pain, in its simplest form".[136]

To be honest, very few people take seriously the logical version of the POE, since all that is necessary to deflate it is the acknowledgment that it's *possible* that God could have a morally sufficient reason to allow suffering to occur. Given how difficult (if not impossible) it would be to somehow prove that it's not even *possible* that God (if God exists) could have a morally sufficient reason to allow suffering, most people concerned with the POE focus on the evidential version.

The evidential version of the POE does not claim that it's impossible for God to exist alongside evil, but merely that it's unlikely—that the existence of evil counts as evidence against God's existence. In this way, the POE serves to undermine confidence in the belief that God exists, it undermines *warrant*. For the remainder of this chapter, assume that any reference to the POE is a reference to the evidential version.

As a final point of clarification, it's important to note that the POE isn't some vague and sentimental notion that it's "sad" that bad things happen to good people nor is it (only) an intense, personally emotional response to an experience of suffering. The POE, understood in a philosophical context, is not a problem fit for counseling. This is not to disparage counseling, or minimize the significance of the "emotional" version of the POE—it's simply to point out that the emotional version of the POE is not an *argument*.

Sometimes, when confronted with tragedy and suffering, people of faith will have

---

[136] Ibid., 16. Note, what Lewis is calling the "problem of pain" is what we are calling the "problem of evil."

a "why God?" moment. Their pain and grief is real, and powerful—but they're not questioning God's *existence*. They might be questioning God's goodness, or faithfulness, or God's plan, or wondering (in general) why God would let such things happen to them, but they're not doubting the very existence of God, any more than a child who is upset with his parents for something is doubting his parents' existence. In those sorts of cases, what people need is a shoulder to cry on, some therapy, some support, and the like. They're not seeking a philosophical defense of the consistency of God's existence and the occurrence of suffering.

Within a philosophical context, the (evidential) POE is an *intellectual* problem, a problem of rationality and reasonableness. The problem only arises for theists. This is not to say that atheists don't suffer, of course, or that their suffering doesn't matter. Atheists and theists alike suffer, and die. The difference is that only theists might have any reason to be surprised by that fact.

If I am an atheist, I believe there is no God. Consequently, I believe that the origin and explanation for this universe is a naturalistic one. That we have *this* sort of universe is attributable to the laws of physics. That living things of various kinds and with various natures populate the Earth is explainable by appealing to evolution. There is no "plan" for the world, no way that the world is "supposed" to be.

If I believe that human beings are simply sophisticated animals, why should it surprise me when we sometimes turn against one another? As much as cancer or natural disasters might afflict me, why would I expect that the world would not have such things in it? Atheists might wish for a safer world with less suffering, but there should be no cause for surprise that we have a suffering-filled world in the first place. Why wouldn't we?

Theists, on the other hand, should have a different sort of problem with the POE. If one is a Christian, Jew, or Muslim, one believes (among other things) that there is an all-knowing, all-powerful, perfectly good God who created the entire universe. Given the presumed existence of such a God, the presence of unjustified suffering in the world poses an intellectual puzzle to be solved. Why would God permit such evil to exist and to occur?

The concern is this: if there is an all-knowing God, God knows about every instance of suffering in the entire world. God is never "surprised" by an occurrence of suffering. If God is all-powerful, God can do anything—including (it would seem) preventing any or all incidents of suffering. Finally, if God is perfectly good, it would seem that God would want there to be no unjustified suffering. So, if God is aware of suffering, and has the power to prevent it, and has the desire to prevent it, there should be no unjustified suffering. And yet, we find it all around us, including in our own lives.

Imagine that I told you that the Earth was flat, and that I appear to be serious. Imagine, also, that you care enough to debate with me on this issue. Imagine, too, that you present to me all the many pieces of evidence that would seemingly prove me wrong. Say, for example, that you show me photos of the Earth taken from space. Suppose, also, that you show me images of the shadow of the Earth that's cast on the moon, and point out its curvature.

Imagine if, after all the compelling evidence you've presented to me, I nevertheless shake my head, roll my eyes, and insist that the Earth is flat anyway.

Wouldn't I seem to be both irrational and unreasonable?

The threat behind the POE is that it might make theists appear to be irrational and unreasonable in the same sort of way. The fact of suffering is taken to be evidence against God's existence. If theists continue to claim God exists, in spite of this evidence, perhaps they're just as irrationally stubborn as those who insist that the Earth is flat, in spite of all the evidence to the contrary? Specifically, the concern is that you can't believe all five of the following claims to be true at the same time, and continue to be rational in your believing.

- God exists
- God is all-powerful (omnipotent)
- God is all-knowing (omniscient)
- God is morally perfect
- Evil exists

If we accept all of these claims, we appear to be accepting a contradiction—or at least a set of beliefs that are implausible, as a set. To resolve this problem and restore our rationality, we are supposed to deny the truth of at least one of those claims. In so doing, the intellectual puzzle is solved. Let us consider how denying each of these claims could "solve" the POE, and the consequences of each "solution."

- It is false that <u>God exists</u>

Atheism "solves" the POE. This is not to make the absurd claim that atheism somehow eliminates suffering, but merely to point out (as stated above) that the suffering is no longer puzzling if we eliminate the God that would (seemingly) not allow it to exist. Not surprisingly, this is not a popular strategy among theists! While atheism does eliminate the intellectual confusion concerning the existence of evil, it does so at the cost of one's faith.

- It is false that <u>God is all-powerful</u>

This "solves" the POE not by denying God's existence, but by denying one of the traditional properties of God thought to be inconsistent with the existence of evil. After all, if God is not powerful enough to prevent evil, it would explain why evil occurs even if God exists. The problem with this solution, however, is that this is certainly not the God of the Western theistic traditions! Even if there is room for legitimate theological debate as to whether God is truly *all*-powerful, God is clearly thought to be really, really powerful in all three Western theistic traditions. At the very least, God is powerful enough to create an entire universe without any material cause, and powerful enough to perform miracles from time to time. But, the God that is not powerful enough to prevent evil is, in some ways, not even as powerful as human beings. Human beings are powerful enough to prevent many cases of "evil." Human beings can be heroic and compassionate, can save lives, prevent bullying, heal wounds, etc. If God isn't even as powerful as a human fire fighter, or paramedic, how

; God worthy of worship?

- It is false that God is <u>all-knowing</u>

Similar to the previous "solution," if God is unaware of the occurrence of evil, or naware of how to stop it, it would explain why evil exists even if God exists. Also imilarly to the previous "solution," however, this strategy will not work for theists, ecause it requires a radical revision of their concept of God. Human beings can be ware of unjustified suffering, and even predict it, in cases like hurricanes. Weather >recasters can predict hurricanes, sometimes days ahead of time, and predict with enerally impressive accuracy where and when those hurricanes will strike—thereby iving residents sufficient warning to flee. Human law enforcement officers can rofile serial killers or sexual predators and predict (and thereby prevent) their iture crimes. What kind of God would God be if God didn't even know as much as a uman weather forecaster? The local weather person can predict a hurricane, but God an't?

It is false that <u>God is morally perfect</u>

If God is indifferent to our suffering, or perhaps even delights in it, it would xplain why evil occurs even if God exists. After all, the existence of evil is puzzling on 1e assumption that God is opposed to evil, but what if this assumption is false? While :chnically "solving" the POE, this, too, will not be a satisfying strategy for theists. /ithout God's perfect goodness, God is simply a cosmic dictator, worshipped out of :ar or awe rather than love. Perhaps this God exists, but if so, this is not the God of idaism, Christianity, or Islam—at least as understood by most adherents of those aditions.

- It is false that <u>evil exists</u>

If it will be unsatisfying to theists to deny God's existence, or any of God's essential) attributes, the only remaining option is to deny that "evil" exists. There are everal ways in which this might be done.

- All suffering is deserved

This approach eliminates "evil" by denying that the suffering is unjustified. 1stead, all suffering is deserved. There are no truly innocent people, no truly inocent "victims." Sometimes this strategy is explained by appealing to notions such s the doctrine of Original Sin. Perhaps all of us are born "sinful," and we all deserve ·hatever afflictions we face. Only by Grace alone are we spared from suffering. This iew is coherent, but terribly harsh. It requires us to believe even that newborn 1fants deserve to suffer. Childhood cancer? Deserved. A toddler kidnapped, raped, 1d murdered? Deserved. Not surprisingly, very few theists adopt this strategy.

- Suffering is not deserved, but is "justified."

Most theists will attempt to solve the POE by claiming that although there truly are many (tragic) cases of undeserved suffering, such suffering is nevertheless justified. That is, there is a good, morally sufficient reason that the suffering is allowed (by God) to take place. What that good reason is, remains to be seen, and will occupy our focus for the remainder of the chapter.

"Solving" the Problem of Evil

The POE is thought to make it difficult for a theist to remain a theist without suffering from some intellectual embarrassment. That is, the POE alleges that there is something irrational about believing in an all-knowing, all-powerful, perfectly good God in spite of the tremendous amount of (seemingly) unjustified suffering in the world. What can a theist say in response, and in defense of the rationality of her faith?

Any defense of theistic belief in the face of the POE (sometimes referred to as a "theodicy") will amount to a claim that there is a justification, or at least a possible justification, for the suffering to occur. In other words, there is a sufficient reason for God, if God exists, to permit the world to be as it is.

The sorts of reasons available to the theist will, not surprisingly, vary depending upon the particular faith tradition of that theist. There are certain "generic" resources available to virtually any adherent of the three major Western theistic traditions (i.e. Christianity, Islam, Judaism), but then each particular religion will also have its own "tool box," its own resources with which to confront the POE. We will consider a "generic" theodicy provided by William Paley, and then (briefly) consider the specifically (Protestant) Christian approach as provided by the prominent Christian philosopher and apologist William Lane Craig, as well as that of C.S. Lewis. In addition, we will consider the somewhat controversial "soul making" theodicy of John Hick.[13]

Most theodicies will address the evidential version of the POE by claiming that there is (or at least could be) a "morally sufficient justification" for God to have created (and sustained) a world such as this one. If that is true, then it is no longer inconsistent (or somehow intellectually embarrassing) to acknowledge our world as it is, and continue to believe in God. Most of these theodicies include a combination of what is known as the "free will defense" and the "greater good defense." Paley's, Craig's, and Lewis' versions are no exception.

---

[137] Why controversial? Although we will not go into these details in this chapter, part of Hick's theodicy involves some ideas that would not be considered mainstream Christian doctrine. For Hick, this is not a problem, since he is a "Universalist." We will consider the issue of universalism and pluralism in a later chapter. The potential controversy, however, concerns the "matching strategy" that I have mentioned in several chapters throughout this book. The concern is that if Hick's argument, in any of its essentials, is "heretical" then it would fail to "match up" with the actual religious worldview of people who might otherwise be tempted to embrace his argument. On the other hand, his approach is likely to match up rather well with self-identified Universalists/Unitarians.

The Free Will Defense

The mischiefs of which mankind are the occasion to one another, by their private wickednesses and cruelties; by tyrannical exercises of power; by rebellions against just authority; by wars; by national jealousies and competitions operating to the destruction of third countries; or by other instances of misconduct either in individuals or societies, are all to be resolved into the character of man as a free agent.[138]

Suppose that human beings have genuine free will. Suppose also that free will, in this context, is the "agency theorist" version of free will. That is, free will requires an "ability to do otherwise," genuine choice.[139] If I have free will, and if I am responsible for my actions, then, at the time of a given action, I must have had a genuine choice. I must have an "ability to do otherwise." If I am to be responsible for knocking someone to the ground, it must have been the result of my choice, and it must have been within my power to do something other than knock that person down. If I knock someone down as a result of having a seizure, or as a result of unintentionally stumbling into that person, or (more bizarrely) as a result of having been hypnotized or mind-controlled, then it wouldn't seem fair to say that I am responsible for what I did. On the other hand, if I could have knocked the person down, and could have refrained from doing so, but chose to knock the person down, then I am responsible for my action, because it was my choice, and because I could have done otherwise.

If humans have free will, then we can make good choices, or bad choices. Many of our bad choices introduce suffering into the world. This is what we referred to earlier as "moral evil," or what Paley refers to as "civil evil." Murder is a choice, as is rape, as is dishonesty, as is abuse of all kinds. To put it bluntly, if we are upset about moral evil, we shouldn't misplace the blame. Don't blame God for rape or murder, blame the rapist or murderer! Blame and righteous indignation are appropriate responses to moral evil, but we should direct them to the proper source: the person who actually did the evil deed.

The free will defense, by itself, is almost never recognized as "enough" of a defense for a variety of reasons. For one, it does nothing to address "natural evil" (what Paley refers to as "physical evil"). Human free will does nothing to account for natural disasters, for example (except on some very specific theological interpretations). A theodicy that included only a free will defense would leave unaddressed a significant source of suffering. Moreover, even if we confine ourselves only to the category of moral evil, there is still room to object.

Imagine a case of child molestation. A young child is being molested by his or her stepfather. Naturally, we are outraged and blame the stepfather for this terrible example of moral evil. Now imagine that we discover that the child's mother, while not a participant in the abuse, nevertheless knew that it was taking place, and did

---

[138] Paley, *Natural Theology*, chapter xxvi (selection included at the end of this chapter)

[139] Note: an extended explanation of free will is provided in the chapter of this book that addresses omniscience and free will.

nothing to stop it. It's possible to be sympathetic. After all, we might speculate, there might be any number of reasons why she didn't intervene? Maybe she was afraid. Maybe there's something we don't know. All the same, most of us, while we place the blame overwhelmingly on the shoulders of the abuser, still have some blame left over for the mother. She might not have been personally responsible for the abuse, but she knew about it and did nothing to stop it, and that's bad as well. We think it would be a terrible thing for a person to shove a child into a swimming pool, resulting in the child's drowning. We also think it a terrible thing if some other people witnessed the child drowning, and didn't even try to help.

We might call this the "bystander-problem." B.C. Johnson raises this problem with his hypothetical example of an infant trapped in a burning home, doomed to burn to death. Johnson asks, mostly rhetorically, "Could we possibly describe as "good" any person who had die power to save this child and yet refused to do so? God undoubtedly has this power and yet in many cases of this sort he has refused to help. Can we call God "good"? Are there adequate excuses for his behavior?"[140]

Note an important feature of this sort of example: it is not the arsonist who is being questioned, but the "innocent bystander" who, while not responsible for the fire, passively lets the infant die. Isn't such a bystander also, somehow, "responsible" for the death of the infant? If we would have concerns about the moral qualities of a person who wouldn't even *try* to save the infant, if she thought she could do so, shouldn't we have the same sorts of concerns about the moral qualities (or existence) of God?

This is a certainly a possible problem for Western theists. According to all three major Western religions, God is "everywhere" in the sense of being casually interactive with all points in space. God is also aware of what transpires in all places. God, then, is the perpetual "innocent bystander" who is there, and "does nothing" when any and every child is ever molested, when any and every child ever drowns. Indeed, for every occurrence of suffering, God is "right there" and does nothing to prevent the suffering from taking place. If we would hold a human being accountable for being an "innocent bystander" who refuses to help, why wouldn't we hold God accountable as well? Isn't it worse, actually, given the fact that, unlike a human being, God has nothing to fear from intervening? If I play the hero and intervene in a case of domestic violence, my own safety is endangered, but it's not as if God has to fear getting beat up, or shot, or stabbed—unlike me.

There are two basic ways to interpret this critique of the free will defense. The first is that it suggests that although humans do (and should) have free will, God shouldn't let us abuse it by making poor choices that cause harm to others. In the same way that a good parent presumably wouldn't let her child take a gun to school after he declared his intention to get revenge on some bullies, just for the sake of preserving his "autonomy," so too should God stop His "children" from harming one another as a result of poor free choices. Better yet, God should have created us so we never make such horrible choices in the first place!

Suppose that God is all-powerful, and can therefore do anything. God could have

140 Johnson, B.C. "The Problem of Good and Evil," *The Atheist Debater's Handbook*. Prometheus Books, 1983, 99-108.

created a world in which we have free will, and choose to abuse it and inflict suffering on each other (moral evil). Or, God could have created a world in which we have free will, but such that we never actually make any wrong decisions, and therefore never inflict moral evil on one another. The atheist philosopher poses the question: "if God has made men such that in their free choices they sometimes prefer what is good and sometimes what is evil, why could he not have made men such that they always freely choose the good?"[141]

If we compare two possible worlds (e.g., one with free will and moral evil, and one with free will but no moral evil), it seems that a perfectly good God would have created the one without moral evil—and yet, the world *with* moral evil is the one we got stuck with. How can a theist explain that?

One way is to dismiss the complaint as incoherent. That is, to say that God could have created us with free will, but in such a way that we would never abuse it, actually involves a contradiction. In fact, it is conceptually impossible that God create persons who are truly free, but who could never "sin."

> *To be a person is to be a finite center of freedom, a (relatively) free and self-directing agent responsible for one's own decisions. This involves being free to act wrongly as well as to act rightly. The idea of a person who can be infallibly guaranteed always to act rightly is self-contradictory. There can be no guarantee in advance that a genuinely free moral agent will never choose amiss. Consequently, the possibility of wrongdoing or sin is logically inseparable from the creation of finite persons, and to say that God should not have created beings who might sin amounts to saying he should not have created people.[142]*

Free will requires the *ability to do otherwise*. A guarantee never to abuse free will is to deny that "ability to do otherwise." Critics like Mackie, however, disagree—seeing no inherent impossibility of creating free creatures who always choose rightly, or, if there is one, then interpreting this limitation as evidence that God would not truly be omnipotent.

> *If there is no logical impossibility in a man's freely choosing the good on one, or on several, occasions, there cannot be a logical impossibility in his freely choosing the good on every occasion. God was not, then, faced with a choice between making innocent automata and making beings who, in acting freely, would sometimes go wrong: there was open to him the obviously better possibility of making beings who would act freely but always go right. Clearly, his failure to avail himself of this possibility is inconsistent with his being both omnipotent and wholly good.[143]*

---

141 Mackie, J.L. "Evil and Omnipotence," *Mind*, New Series, Vol. 64, No. 254. (Apr., 1955), 209.

142 Hick, John. "The Problem of Evil" in John Hick, *Philosophy of Religion* 4th. ed. (Upper Saddle Hill, N.J.: Prentice Hall, 1989. Chapter 3.

143 Mackie. Ibid.

Most theists, however, understand "omnipotence" as something like the ability to do all and anything that is *possible* to do. Classic conundrums like "Can God create a rock so heavy that He can't lift it?" are exposed as being meaningless questions, rather than theological pitfalls.

> *His Omnipotence means power to do all that is intrinsically possible, not to do the intrinsically impossible. You may attribute miracles to Him, but not nonsense. There is no limit to His power. If you choose to say, 'God can give a creature free will and at the same time withhold free will from it,' you have not succeeded in saying anything about God: meaningless combinations of words do not suddenly acquire meaning simply because we prefix to them the two other words, 'God can.' It remains true that all things are possible with God: the intrinsic impossibilities are not things but nonentities. It is no more possible for God than for the weakest of His creatures to carry out both of two mutually exclusive alternatives; not because His power meets an obstacle, but because nonsense remains nonsense even when we talk it about God.*[144]

While the application to free will and moral evil might be less obvious than the "create a rock too heavy to lift" demand, Lewis would allege they are of the same type: to propose that God create truly free persons who can be guaranteed never to choose to do wrong is akin to asking God to create a rock too heavy for God to lift, or to create a 4-sided triangle. In each case, the demand is for impossible, and omnipotence does not, and cannot, require the ability to do the intrinsically impossible—at least not without losing any coherent meaning.

How am I truly free if it is never within my power to choose to do something morally wrong? If it is not within my power to lie, how is it to my credit when I always tell the truth? To say that God should create persons who necessarily do no wrong is simply to say that God should not have created any persons at all!

"Agreed!" some of you might be thinking. "If moral evil is the price we have to pay for free will, then God shouldn't have created us with free will, and if people couldn't exists unless they had free will, then maybe there shouldn't be any people." This is the second way to interpret the critique of the free will defense. The theist must now explain why free will is "worth it," even though it comes at such a terrible price (moral evil).

The Greater Good Defense

Paley, Craig, Lewis, and Hick offer several reasons why God would not intervene to prevent suffering, most of which connect to a "greater good" defense. Any greater good defense is going to claim that a "greater good" is served by the occurrence of suffering than would have been possible without it. Some versions offer a "general justification" for suffering, while others offer a "particular justification" for suffering.

A general justification, or a general greater good defense, claims that a greater good is served by our living in a certain kind of world, namely, one in which we have free

---

[144] Lewis, Problem of Pain, 18.

will (and therefore run the risk of moral evil), and one in which natural evils can occur.
There is something so valuable about free will that it's "worth it" for humanity, even
if moral evil is the price we must pay for it. Similarly, living in a dangerous, challenging
environment is also worth it, despite the pains associated with natural evil. This
general justification does not claim that every single event in human history serves
this greater good, but merely that the basic conditions of this world do. As John Hick
describes such general justifications:

> *It does not claim to explain, nor to explain away, <u>every instance</u> of evil in human
> experience, but only to point to certain considerations which prevent the fact of
> evil…From constituting a final and insuperable bar to rational belief in God.*

> *It is not possible to show positively that <u>each item</u> of human pain serves the
> divine purpose of good, but, on the other hand, it does seem possible to show
> that the divine purpose as understood in Judaism and Christianity could not be
> forwarded in a world which was designed as a permanent hedonistic
> paradise.[145]*

As stated, a general greater good defense will claim that the general conditions of
this life and world serve a "greater good," and these general conditions include our
possessing free will, and living in an environment that includes natural evil. Let us
start with the possibly-bold assumption that God has a good reason to create people,
in general. If there are to be people, what follows from that?

Lewis proposes that for me (or you) to be a person (a self-conscious creature)
requires that others exist as well. After all, how can I understand "self" if there is no
"other" with which to contrast? And, if I am to be a *free* self, then choice must be
possible—and choice requires the existence of things from which to choose. "A
creature with no environment would have no choices to make: so that freedom, like
self-consciousness…again demands the presence to the self of something other than
the self."[146]

If two or more selves are to be able to meet and interact, they will require an
environment in which to do so—an "external world," as it were.

> *People often talk as if nothing were easier than for two naked minds to 'meet'
> or become aware of each other. But I see no possibility of their doing so except
> in a common medium which forms their 'external world' or environment. Even
> our vague attempt to imagine such a meeting between disembodied spirits
> usually slips in surreptitiously the idea of, at least, a common space and common
> time, to give the co- in co-existence a meaning: and space and time are already
> an environment. But more than this is required. If your thoughts and passions
> were directly present to me, like my own, without any mark of externality or
> otherness, how should I distinguish them from mine? And what thoughts or
> passions could we begin to have without objects to think and feel about? Nay,*

---

[145] Hick, Ibid.
[146] Lewis, Ibid., 20.

could I even begin to have the conception of 'external' and 'other' unless I had experience of an 'external world'?[147]

If there is to be an external world within which we will live and interact, what properties should this world have? The complaint against natural evil, of course, is that our actual world is filled with things that would not, or should not, exist if God exists. Our world shouldn't have diseases, natural disasters, droughts, famines, and the like. People shouldn't starve, or drown, or be crushed by earthquakes, or burned up in fires. Even if we can somehow account for moral evil by appealing to the free will defense, there is seemingly no justification for the dangerous and hostile world in which we live. Here, it is useful to quote Lewis' response at length.

If matter is to serve as a neutral field it must have a fixed nature of its own. If a "world" or material system had only a single inhabitant it might conform at every moment to his wishes — "trees for his sake would crowd into a shade." But if you were introduced into a world which thus varied at my every whim, you would be quite unable to act in it and would thus lose the exercise of your free will. Nor is it clear that you could make your presence known to me — all the matter by which you attempted to make signs to me being already in my control and therefore not capable of being manipulated by you.

Again, if matter has a fixed nature and obeys constant laws, not all states of matter will be equally agreeable to the wishes of a given soul, nor all equally beneficial for that particular aggregate of matter which he calls his body. If fire comforts that body at a certain distance, it will destroy it when the distance is reduced. Hence, even in a perfect world, the necessity for those danger signals which the pain-fibres in our nerves are apparently designed to transmit. Does this mean an inevitable element of evil (in the form of pain) in any possible world? I think not: for while it may be true that the least sin is an incalculable evil, the evil of pain depends on degree, and pains below a certain intensity are not feared or resented at all. No one minds the process "warm — beautifully hot — too hot — it stings" which warns him to withdraw his hand from exposure to the fire: and, if I may trust my own feeling, a slight aching in the legs as we climb into bed after a good day's walking is, in fact, pleasurable.

Yet again, if the fixed nature of matter prevents it from being always, and in all its dispositions, equally agreeable even to a single soul, much less is it possible for the matter of the universe at any moment to be distributed so that it is equally convenient and pleasurable to each member of a society. If a man traveling in one direction is having a journey down hill, a man going in the opposite direction must be going up hill. If even a pebble lies where I want it to lie, it cannot, except by a coincidence, be where you want it to lie. And this is very far from being an evil: on the contrary, it furnishes occasion for all those acts of courtesy, respect, and unselfishness by which love and good humor and modesty

---

[147] Ibid., 20-21.

express themselves. But it certainly leaves the way open to a great evil, that of competition and hostility. And if souls are free, they cannot be prevented from dealing with the problem by competition instead of courtesy. And once they have advanced to actual hostility, they can then exploit the fixed nature of matter to hurt one another. The permanent nature of wood which enables us to use it as a beam also enables us to use it for hitting our neighbor on the head. The permanent nature of matter in general means that when human beings fight, the victory ordinarily goes to those who have superior weapons, skill, and numbers, even if their cause is unjust.[148]

This "neutral" environment in which we actually find ourselves is objective. It does not favor my desires or thoughts over yours, or vice-versa. Fire is impartial: it is always hot! Sometimes, the heat is enjoyable, and sometimes it burns, but the fire, at least, is consistent. The very same feature of the world (e.g., fire's hotness) is agreeable or disagreeable to us relative to context. This allows for acts of kindness and hospitality (e.g., inviting you into my home to warm yourself by my fire), but also for acts of outright hostility (e.g., burning someone's house to the ground, or, worse, burning someone alive!). For God to miraculously prevent harm and spare us and others from pain or loss would either be to create a world in which free will was impossible (e.g., one in which I can't choose to use fire to hurt you), or else one with a miraculously fluctuating environment and no serious consequences for our actions (e.g., one in which the hotness of fire fluctuates depending on its application). The implications of such continuous "miraculous" interventions are both far-reaching, and mind boggling.

In a game of chess you can make certain arbitrary concessions to your opponent, which stand to the ordinary rules of the game as miracles stand to the laws of nature. You can deprive yourself of a castle, or allow the other man sometimes to take back a move made inadvertently. But if you conceded everything that at any moment happened to suit him — if all his moves were revocable and if all your pieces disappeared whenever their position on the board was not to his liking — then you could not have a game at all. So it is with the life of souls in a world: fixed laws, consequences unfolding by causal necessity, the whole natural order, are at once limits within which their common life is confined and also the sole condition under which any such life is possible. Try to exclude the possibility of suffering which the order of nature and the existence of free wills involve, and you find that you have excluded life itself.[149]

Later in this chapter, we will consider how such an unstable environment might (negatively) impact life's meaning and value, but here the claim is more blunt: a Nature not governed by predictable "rules" (e.g., fire is always hot) is not a "Nature" at all, and an environment in which life is immune to harm is one in which life is not actually possible. If there is to be life at all, it must exist in an environment at least

---

[148] Ibid., 22-24.
[149] Ibid., 25.

similar to the actual world—and this means the possibility of natural evil. If some of those living creatures are to be free, responsible, and self-conscious persons, then we run the risk of moral evil. The "general greater good defense" claims that these (general) conditions serve a greater good, and are therefore justified.

Recall, however, that there exist both "general" as well as "particular" justifications. *A particular justification will claim that every event that occurs is permitted to occur because it serves that greater good.* In Christianity, this is usually based on a belief in Providence—the view that God is in control of the unfolding of history, according to God's own perfect plan. If one believes in Providence, it is not merely that this general sort of world serves the "greater good," but that everything that occurs, though not necessarily willed by God (e.g., sin) is nevertheless permitted to occur because it serves the grander purpose of God's Providence.

> So when people ask, 'Why doesn't God just remove all the suffering from the world?', they really have no idea what they're asking for or what the consequences might be. The brutal murder of an innocent man or a child's dying of leukemia could send a ripple effect through history so that God's reason for permitting it might not emerge until centuries later or perhaps in another country. Only an omniscient mind could grasp the complexities of directing a world of free persons toward one's pre-visioned goals. You have only to think of the innumerable, incalculable contingencies involved in arriving at a single historical event, say, the Allied victory at D-day, in order to appreciate the point. We have no idea of the natural and moral evils that might be involved in order for God to arrange the circumstances and free agents in them necessary for some intended purpose, nor can we discern what reasons God might have in mind for permitting some instance of suffering to enter our lives. But He will have good reasons in light of the purposes of His Kingdom.[150]

In this passage from Craig, we find another of his arguments: *human beings are not in a good "epistemic position" to claim that it is unlikely that the world's suffering has a morally sufficient justification* (e.g,. by serving a greater good), let alone that it is impossible. We often find ourselves surprised by the unfolding of events over just a short span of time, and about which we think we have much understanding. Paley raised a similar point centuries prior:

> ...with many of these laws we are not acquainted at all, or we are totally unable to trace them in their branches, and in their operation; the effect of which ignorance is, that they cannot be of importance to us as measures by which to regulate our conduct. The conservation of them may be of importance in other respects, or to other beings, but we are uninformed of their value or use; uninformed, consequently, when, and how far, they may or may not be suspended, or their effects turned aside, by a presiding and benevolent will,

without incurring greater evils than those which would be avoided.[151]

I suspect many reading this chapter can think of events that, at the time, seemed disastrous, or at least very bad, but which, sometime later, turned out to have been "for the best." Many years ago, I applied for a full-time teaching position at a University where I had been teaching part-time, and was excited to get an interview. I was devastated when I didn't get the job and feared that it had been my "best shot" at being a tenured professor. Less than a year later I applied for the job I now have—a job I never would have applied for had I gotten the first one—and I am certain that I am much happier with the job I now have, than I would have been had I not been "devastated."

The chorus of a Garth Brooks song puts it this way:

Sometimes I thank God for unanswered prayers
Remember when you're talkin' to the man upstairs
That just because he doesn't answer doesn't mean he don't care
Some of God's greatest gifts are unanswered prayers

"But," an objector might say, "this will only be convincing for someone who already believes in God! That is, an appeal to Providence, and a faith that there is a 'greater good' being served even if I'm in no position to perceive it, presupposes that God exists and is good. Such an appeal will fall on deaf ears if presented to an atheist!" Indeed it does. The aforementioned B.C. Johnson dismisses such an appeal by observing that "this argument does not explain why God allowed the child to burn to death. It merely claims that there is some reason discoverable in the long run. But the belief that such a reason is within our grasp must rest upon the additional belief that God is good. This is just to counter evidence against such a belief by assuming the belief to be true."

Correct—but the POE isn't a problem for atheists. The POE is precisely a problem for those people who already believe in God, and are wondering if the POE should cause them to reconsider. But, if I already believe in God, and if I already believe that God has Providentially ordered the unfolding of history in ways I couldn't possibly hope to comprehend, why should those beliefs not factor into my evaluation of the POE?

Those promoting the POE claim that suffering renders God's existence unlikely. Unlikely relative to what context? Probability assessments are always made against a set of background considerations. For example, suppose we want to know what the probability is that a particular person has a Bachelor's degree. Is it likely, or unlikely? If your answer is "I have no idea, I need more information," then you've got the right idea. If, for example, we're talking about an average person over the age of 25 in the United States, the probability is roughly 30%, but if the context is the entire world, then the probability is roughly 7%. These numbers vary further of course by gender and other demographic variables. Imagine if the particular person were a student in a kindergarten class!

---

[151] Paley, Ibid., Chapter XXVI.

When someone claims suffering renders God's existence improbable, what is our context? Is suffering the only thing being considered? In that case, the case for God might look bad, but why should suffering be the only evidence being considered? What happens to that probability assessment if we add to it the notion of Providence? What if we add various arguments for God's existence, such as the design, cosmological, or ontological arguments? What if we add the argument from miracles, or an appeal to the internal witness of the Holy Spirit?

For a person of faith (in other words, for a person for whom the POE is a problem), there is likely more to consider than just suffering. *Craig claims that when we consider the full scope of the evidence it is by no means obvious that God's existence is improbable.*

Finally, as one more component of a "full scope of evidence/greater good" appeal, Craig recommends that we consider what assumption is being made about the purpose of life, when grappling with the POE. If we assume, for example, that the purpose of this life is pleasure, happiness, safety, or the like, then it will be challenging to perceive in what way many experiences of suffering serve those ends. If the "greater good" intended by life itself is happiness, then it might be difficult to discern in what way great suffering conduces to happiness. But why should we assume that the purpose of this life or this world is happiness? Paley, after considering various possible purposes for this world, instead concludes that this life is best understood as a place of "probation."

> *Now we assert the most probable supposition to be, that it is a state of moral probation; and that many things in it suit with this hypothesis, which suit no other. It is not a state of unmixed happiness, or of happiness simply: it is not a state of designed misery, or of misery simply: it is not a state of retribution: it is not a state of punishment. It suits with none of these suppositions. It accords much better with the idea of its being a condition calculated for the production, exercise, and improvement of moral qualities, with a view to a future state, in which these qualities, after being so produced, exercised, and improved, may, by a new and more favouring constitution of things, receive their reward, or become their own.*[152]

This proposal is echoed by John Hick centuries later. Hick motivates his theodicy by adopting a particular vision of Creation. He contrasts the understanding of creation as understood by St. Augustine (354-430 C.E.) with that offered by St. Irenaeus (2nd century C.E.-202 C.E.).

Augustine's account is familiar to most people, whether they accept it as the (gospel) truth, or as pure mythology, and is supported by a literal interpretation of the book of Genesis: God created Adam and Eve in the Garden of Eden. Creation was good. Eve was tempted by the Serpent, and (along with Adam), ate the apple from the tree of knowledge of good and evil. With that act of rebellion, sin and suffering entered the world, and humanity fell from Grace. Only through the divine intervention of Christ can humanity be restored to fellowship with God. The basic picture involves

---

[152] Paley, Ibid.

humanity starting in a state of perfection, than falling to depravity, and requiring a divine act of restoration.

The Irenaean account differs from Augustine's mainly because Irenaeus regards humanity to have been created in a state of spiritual immaturity. Rather than being created in a state of perfection, and (perhaps surprisingly) falling from that state into one of depravity, Irenaeus believed Adam and Eve were more like children who had some "growing up" to do.

Hick takes this Irenaean starting point, and adds to it. Hick believes that it is implausible that the Garden of Eden, or the literalist account of Adam and Eve, refer to factual, historical events. Instead, the account from Genesis is a powerful (symbolic) story of humanity's struggle with evil and our own moral failing. He believes Irenaeus had the right idea: "Adam" and "Eve" (humanity) were not created perfect, but in a state of spiritual immaturity—and they (we) are called by God to "grow up."

Growing up is precisely the point of this world. Hick envisions that Creation has been a two-stage process. The first stage occurred when God created the physical universe itself, including all living things. It might be important to note that Hick believes the development of living organisms (including humans) occurred by the long process of evolution—though he believes God used evolution to make this happen.

The second stage of Creation is the far more interesting part, from our perspective. This is the stage of "soul-making," as Hick calls it. Soul-making is the process by which we "grow up," the process by which we are supposed to craft our own moral and spiritual characters into the image of God. This is the primary purpose of the world in which we live. Understanding that this world is meant to be a place for soul-making is essential when trying to understand Hick's theodicy, and the role/necessity of free will and a "challenging" environment.

Consider an analogy. Imagine, for example, that we learn that a woman has dozens of cats, but keeps them in deplorable conditions. They don't have enough food. They live in filthy conditions, and many of them are injured or diseased and receive no medical care. Should we learn of a situation like that, as we sometimes do, we immediately infer several basic possible explanations.

- The woman can't afford to make things better.
- The woman doesn't know or understand how bad things are.
- The woman isn't actually there to take care of them (e.g., she has died, or moved away).
- The woman is cruel.

Now, apply this kind of reasoning to the POE. We are God's pets, and we're suffering. How can we explain this?

- [God] "can't afford" to make things better (i.e., God is not all-powerful).
- [God] doesn't know or understand how bad things are (i.e., God is not all-knowing).
- [God] isn't actually there to take care of them (i.e., God doesn't exist).

- [God] is cruel (i.e., God is not perfectly good).

You can see how this reasoning works. If we're God's pets, one might think we'd have a home that isn't so filled with danger and disease. One might think God wouldn't let so many of his pets starve, or hurt one another. Of course, this analogy is a bit problematic, since we "good and wise" humans often do things to and for our pets that are for their own good, but which, from their perspective, might seem "mean" or at least undesirable.

Lewis raises this analogy, using dogs as his specific example. Dogs are lovable, but humans interfere with the dog's nature to make them more so. We bathe dogs, house-train them, teach them not to steal food from the table, etc.—and in so doing enable ourselves to love the dog more completely. If the puppy could express its experience during the training phase, it might well question the goodness of humans, but (Lewis alleges), the fully-grown and well-trained dog who, by virtue of that, is healthier, longer-lived, and "admitted, as it were by Grace, to a whole world of affections, loyalties, interests, and comforts entirely beyond its animal destiny, would have no such doubts."[153] In my own case, I restrict my cat's access to food, and occasionally take her to the vet for check-ups, and she might well think that I am being "mean" (if such projections make any sense), but what I do is done out of love, and concern for her overall well-being.

Another, more significant problem, though, according to both Craig and Lewis, is that we shouldn't be thinking of ourselves as God's pets! If we think of ourselves as pets, we form certain expectations of what sort of world we think we should have, and, not finding that world in real life, we call God into question. The solution to this problem is to realize that we're not pets, but "children"—children of God, specifically.

My cat is brilliant and sweet, but I don't think she's ever going to be any "better" than she is now. That is, I think "nature" has provided her with all the tools she needs to survive thanks to her natural instincts. I like to think that she enjoys my company, but I'm sure that what she really enjoys is all the stuff I do for her, such as giving her food that she doesn't need to hunt! I monitor how many treats I give my cat, but not because I think she needs to learn any sort of lesson about temperance (as if she could learn such a lesson), but instead because I want to keep her from gaining too much weight at the expense of her health. Ultimately, I don't believe my cat is a "moral" creature. That is not to say that she's immoral, but rather amoral. She's just not capable of being morally responsible. It's not the sort of creature she is, or ever can be.

The same can't be said of human children, and that's why I don't employ the same principles with my niece and nephews as I do with my cat. I monitor what I give to them, and what I do for them, not merely for the sake of their health, but, to be blunt, because I don't want to have any part in turning them into spoiled brats. One day, my niece and nephews will be adults, and will have to tackle life's challenges on their own. Their childhood is the training ground in which they are learning how to do that. Part of being a responsible parent (or care-giver) is facilitating that training. A parent who indulges his child's every desire can, in some cases, be killing that child with

---

[153] Lewis, Ibid., 36.

indness. If the primary purpose of childhood, and the primary goal of childrearing, vas "happiness," then we should expect a certain sort of (generally indulgent) ehavior on the part of parents. But, if we switch the purpose and goal to something ke "facilitating the child's maturing into a responsible adult," then our expectations f parent behavior changes as well.

In 2014, a drunk driving case made national headlines because of a peculiar efense argument: "affluenza." The driver (16 year old Ethan Couch, who drove drunk nd caused an accident resulting in the deaths of four people) was defended in court y psychologist Dr. G. Dick Miller. Miller said the boy's parents gave him "freedoms o young person should have," that he was a product of "'affluenza"—which he escribed as his family thinking that wealth bought privilege, and not perceiving any ational link between behavior and consequences. As an example of this, Miller ointed out that Couch's parents allowed him to drive (illegally) starting at the age of 3, and that they did not punish him after police ticketed him (then 15) for being arked in a pickup truck with a naked, passed out, 14-year-old girl.[154]   The nplication, of course, legal defense strategy aside, is that we are not (ultimately) oing our children any favors if we fail to "set limits," or correct bad behavior.

> Love between father and son, in this symbol (Father to Christ), means essentially authoritative love on the one side, and obedient love on the other. The father uses his authority to make the son into the sort of human being he, rightly, and in his superior wisdom, wants him to be. Even in our own days, though a man might say it, he could mean noting by saying "I love my son but don't care how great a blackguard he is provided he has a good time.[155]

What kind of a parent is indifferent to what sort of person his or her child ecomes? How is it "love" to either not care whether your child is good or bad, or, if ou do care, to do nothing to promote the good? Indeed, Lewis argues, it is because of ve that we care, and the same is true of God.

> When Christianity says that God loves man, it means that God loves man: not that He has some "disinterested", because really indifferent, concern for our welfare, but that, in awful and surprising truth, we are the objects of His love. You asked for a loving God: you have one. The great spirit you so lightly invoked, the "lord of terrible aspect", is present: not a senile benevolence that drowsily wishes you to be happy in your own way, not the cold philanthropy of a conscientious magistrate, nor the care of a host who feels responsible for the comfort of his guests, but the consuming fire Himself, the Love that made the worlds, persistent as the artist's love for his work and despotic as a man's love for a dog, provident and venerable as a father's love for a child, jealous, inexorable, exacting as love between the sexes.[156]

---

[154] http://www.wfaa.com/story/local/2015/05/28/14140396/
[155] Lewis, Ibid., 37.
[156] Ibid., 39.

A basic principle that we all presumably recognize is that growth (the kind we most value, at least), requires resistance. We know that this is so with respect to growing in physical strength. If I join a gym, and I do one set of 5 curls with ½ pound weights, I'm just never going to grow bigger and stronger. In terms of fitness and strength, growth requires resistance to be overcome.

We also understand this principle with respect to intellectual growth. This might sound shocking, but you don't want this material, or this class, to be easy—at least not if you actually care about learning something. We only grow, intellectually, when we are presented with an intellectual challenge to overcome.

Can we also add moral and spiritual growth to this same pattern? To grow with respect to my moral character requires challenges to overcome as well. Children must be allowed to take risks, and make mistakes. Children must be allowed to experience disappointment and frustration. Only then will they be able to learn how to grapple with such things themselves. A child who never learns how to deal with fear, disappointment, frustration, or loss, as a child, will not be able to function as an adult member of society. This means that parents, including wise, morally decent parents, can be justified in allowing their children to suffer, if the purpose of that suffering is to allow opportunities for growth. Love is not always identical to kindness, or leniency.

By the goodness of God we mean nowadays almost exclusively His lovingness; and in this we may be right. And by Love, in this context, most of us mean kindness—the desire to see others than the self happy; not happy in this way or in that, but just happy. What would really satisfy us would be a God who said of anything we happened to like doing, 'What does it matter so long as they are contented?' We want, in fact, not so much a Father in Heaven as a grandfather in heaven—a senile benevolence who, as they say, 'liked to see young people enjoying themselves' and whose plan for the universe was simply that it might be truly said at the end of each day, 'a good time was had by all'. Not many people, I admit, would formulate a theology in precisely those terms: but a conception not very different lurks at the back of many minds. I do not claim to be an exception: I should very much like to live in a universe which was governed on such lines. But since it is abundantly clear that I don't, and since I have reason to believe, nevertheless, that, God is Love, I conclude that my conception of love needs correction.

I might, indeed, have learned, even from the poets, that Love is something more stern and splendid than mere kindness:...Kindness consents very readily to the removal of its object – we have all met people whose kindness to animals is constantly leading them to kill animals lest they should suffer. Kindness, merely as such, cares not whether its object becomes good or bad, provided only that it escapes suffering. As Scripture points out, it is bastards who are spoiled: the legitimate sons, who are to carry on the family tradition, are punished. (Hebrews 12:8) It is for people whom we care nothing about that we demand happiness on any terms: with our friends, our lovers, our children, we are exacting and would rather see them suffer much than be happy in contemptible and estranging modes. If God is Love, He is, by definition, something more than mere kindness. And it appears, from all the records, that though He has often rebuked us and condemned us, He has never regarded us with contempt. He has paid us the intolerable compliment of loving us, in the deepest, most tragic, most inexorable sense.[157]

If we believe the purpose of life is our own happiness, we might well expect a very pleasant environment in which to live, and question the qualities (or existence) of a God who failed to provide them. But, according to Lewis, Paley, Hick, and Craig, the chief purpose of life, according to Christianity, is not happiness, but knowledge of (and relation with) God. As Lewis puts it, "What we would here and now call our 'happiness' is not the end God chiefly has in view: but when we are such as He can love without impediment, we shall in fact be happy."[158]

According to Craig:

One reason that the problem of evil seems so puzzling is that we tend to think that if God exists, then His goal for human life is happiness in this world. God's role is to provide comfortable environment for His human pets. But on the Christian view this is false. We are not God's pets, and man's end is not happiness in this world, but the knowledge of God, which will ultimately bring true and everlasting human fulfillment. Many evils occur in life which may be utterly pointless with respect to the goal of producing human happiness in this world, but they may not be unjustified with respect to producing the knowledge of God. Innocent human suffering provides an occasion for deeper dependency and trust in God, either on the part of the sufferer or those around him. Of course, whether God's purpose is achieved through our suffering will depend on our response. Do we respond with anger and bitterness toward God, or do we turn to Him in faith for strength to endure?"[159]

In similar fashion (some centuries earlier), Paley points to the character-formation potential of the trials and tribulations of life (conceivable as the combination of natural/physical and moral/civic evils).

In the wide scale of human condition, there is not perhaps one of its manifold diversities, which does not bear upon the design here suggested. Virtue is infinitely various. There is no situation in which a rational being is placed, from that of the best-instructed Christian, down to the condition of the rudest barbarian, which affords not room for moral agency; for the acquisition, exercise, and display of voluntary qualities, good and bad. Health and sickness, enjoyment and suffering, riches and poverty, knowledge and ignorance, power and subjection, liberty and bondage, civilization and barbarity, have all their offices and duties, all serve for the formation of character: for when we speak of

---

157 Lewis, Ibid., 31-33.
158 Ibid., 41.
159 http://www.reasonablefaith.org/the-problem-of-evil

a state of trial, it must be remembered, that characters are not only tried, or proved, or detected, but that they are generated also, and formed, by circumstances.[160]

We can see the connection between this line of defense and the free will defense. According to the Christian tradition (as understood by Craig), God Providentially creates and orders a world that maximizes God's purposes. With respect to humans, this means a world best suited for bringing as many people as possible freely to knowledge of, and relationship with, God. To make it a genuine choice, we must have free will, and the possession of free will entails the risk of moral evil. What's more, one can imagine that a pain-free paradise (i.e., one without natural evil), while quite conducive to happiness, might not be as conducive to the purpose of bringing people to God. As Lewis describes:

> *My own experience is something like this. I am progressing along the path of life in my ordinary contentedly fallen and godless condition, absorbed in a merry meeting with my friends for the morrow or a bit of work that tickles my vanity today, a holiday or a new book, when suddenly a stab of abdominal pain that threatens serious disease, or a headline in the newspapers that threatens us all with destruction, sends this whole pack of cards tumbling down. At first I am overwhelmed, and all my little happinesses look like broken toys. Then, slowly and reluctantly, bit by bit, I try to bring myself into the frame of mind that I should be in at all times. I remind myself that all these toys were never intended to possess my heart, that my true good is in another world and my only real treasure is Christ. And perhaps, by God's grace, I succeed, and for a day or two become a creature consciously dependent on God and drawing its strength from the right sources. But the moment the threat is withdrawn, my whole nature leaps back to the toys: I am even anxious, God forgive me, to banish from my mind the only thing that supported me under the threat because it is now associated with the misery of those few days. Thus the terrible necessity of tribulation is only too clear. God has had me for but forty-eight hours and then only by dint of taking everything else away from me. Let Him but sheathe that sword for a moment and I behave like a puppy when the hated bath is over—I shake myself as dry as I can and race off to reacquire my comfortable dirtiness, if not in the nearest manure heap, at least in the nearest flower bed. And that is why tribulations cannot cease until God either sees us remade or sees that our remaking is now hopeless.*[161]

If the purpose of this life is to bring as many people as possible to a relationship with God, then a pain-free paradise might not serve that purpose well at all. Paley would add that such a paradise would likewise not be conducive to the formation of good character.

If life were a paradise free from pain, resistance, setbacks, struggle, or even toil,

---

[160] Paley, Ibid.
[161] Lewis, Ibid., 106-107.

ur "dependency upon supernatural aid" would produce undesirable results. No onger needing to "work" for anything, this would "introduce negligence, inactivity, nd disorder, into the most useful occupations of human life; and thereby deteriorate he condition of human life itself." Some of you might be thinking that such a deteriorated" condition sounds pretty good! No work? No struggle? No pain? No oss? But, according to Paley, such a life would lack numerous qualities that we deem aluable and important.

For one, virtue would be impossible. In the actual world, suffering is an occasion o develop and display virtue. "Again, one man's sufferings may be another man's trial. 'he family of a sick parent is a school of filial piety. . . . It is upon such sufferings alone hat benevolence can operate."[162] In other words, virtues require "the existence of vil, without which it would have no object, no material to work upon, . . ."[163] Courage equires danger. Compassion requires that others suffer. Charity requires need. .ıstice requires that things sometimes occur that shouldn't.

Moreover, Paley argues that even our enjoyment of life, and its meaning, would e imperiled in a world without pain.

Of other external evils (still confining ourselves to what are called physical or natural evils), a considerable part come within the scope of the following observation:--The great principle of human satisfaction is engagement. It is a most just distinction, which the late Mr. Tucker has dwelt upon so largely in his works, between pleasures in which we are passive, and pleasures in which we are active. And, I believe, every attentive observer of human life will assent to his position, that, however grateful the sensations may occasionally be in which we are passive, it is not these, but the latter class of our pleasures, which constitute satisfaction; which supply that regular stream of moderate and miscellaneous enjoyments, in which happiness, as distinguished from voluptuousness, consists. Now for rational occupation, which is, in other words, for the very material of contented existence, there would be no place left, if either the things with which we had to do were absolutely impracticable to our endeavours, or if they were too obedient to our uses. A world, furnished with advantages on one side, and beset with difficulties, wants, and inconveniences on the other, is the proper abode of free, rational, and active natures, being the fittest to stimulate and exercise their faculties. The very refractoriness of the objects they have to deal with, contributes to this purpose. A world in which nothing depended upon ourselves, however it might have suited an imaginary race of beings, would not have suited mankind. Their skill, prudence, industry; their various arts, and their best attainments, from the application of which they draw, if not their highest, their most permanent gratifications, would be insignificant, if things could be either moulded by our volitions, or, of their own accord, conformed themselves to our views and wishes.[164]

---

[162] Paley, Ibid.
[163] Paley, Ibid
[164] Paley, Ibid

Here Paley is claiming that, as much as we enjoy "passive" pleasures, we value "active" pleasures, requiring our deliberate engagement, more so. We can imagine a world in which I don't have to "do" anything in order to be pleased.

- Why bother getting out of bed? Nothing "bad" can happen to you if you stay in bed all the time instead.
- Why bother eating? You can't starve, or even feel hungry (since hunger is an experience of suffering). Of course, you can't overeat either....
- Why go to school? You can't suffer as a result of ignorance.
- Why go to work? You can't suffer as a result of not going to work. You can't lose your home, or your electricity, or anything else normally paid from your wages, since any of those outcomes would involve suffering. Of course, you don't need a house or electricity anyway, since being homeless and in the cold or dark can't produce any suffering....
- Why socialize with other people? You can't experience the suffering of loneliness. Of course, nothing bad can ever happen from any socializing that you might do anyway.
- Why *not* get drunk and then drive home? Nothing bad can happen to me, or anyone else. Hell, get drunk, put on a blindfold, and drive home backwards! No one can get injured. I can't even damage my car.
- Why not go to work with a gun and fire it at people as many times as you can squeeze the trigger? Nothing bad can happen to them, or you. No injuries, no deaths. You can't even be disappointed by your failure to hurt someone, since disappointment is also a form of suffering.
- Why do anything, in fact? After all, nothing bad can result from you doing absolutely nothing at all for your entire existence.

Contrast this bizarre world without consequences to the one in which we actually live. In this world, there *are* consequences for our actions. Real consequences. Permanent ones. If I get drunk and then drive home, it's not only my own life I place in danger, but the lives of everyone else on the road. My choice to drink and drive has profound significance because of the serious and lasting consequences that might result. If you choose to stay in bed all day, and never go to work or school, there will be consequences with respect to the overall quality of your life, and your life prospects. It makes a difference whether you get out of bed each day. It makes a difference what you do. A difference to you, and to others. A world without challenge (and, therefore, the risk of suffering) is a world empty of growth potential, and even meaning itself. That sort of world might be acceptable for a "pet," but not for a "child of God" engaged in the project of soul-making—and would we really desire such an existence? Isn't it possible that the conditions of our world, complete with natural and moral evils, actually serves a "greater good" (e.g., our character development)? If one can't imagine that to be so, Craig would remind us that we are not in a good epistemic position to assess whether the events and conditions of our world fail to serve such greater good.

But, the critic might ask, why do we have *so much* "evil" in the world? Perhaps some amount of suffering is needed for to make existence meaningful, and to give us opportunity for "growth," but surely we don't need *all* the suffering that we actually find in this world. For example, an environment in which the most "challenging" natural evil was mild rain and the common cold would still produce suffering, and therefore opportunities for growth. Why do we need natural disasters that kill thousands, or diseases like cancer that kill millions? Surely we have more suffering than is needed, and any suffering in excess of what is needed will be *unjustified*.

A possible theistic response to this is to challenge our ability to assess the amount of suffering needed in the first place. How do we *know* that we have "too much" suffering? How could we possibly know? Perhaps we have exactly as much suffering as is needed, and not a bit more. How could you, or I, be in a position to make that judgment? Moreover, isn't it the case that our perception of suffering is relative? That is, based upon one's life experiences and expectations, what is deemed "unbearable" to one person is a part of daily life to someone else. Spoiled, wealthy teens might groan from the injustice of having to make the bed in the morning, while another teen working in an Asian sweatshop on the other side of the world is grateful to have a 5 minute break to stretch and use the bathroom during her 10 hour shift. The muscle pain that might put me out of a game might be shrugged off by a more rugged athlete.

As a thought experiment, imagine a world in which the worst thing that could ever happen to someone, is a tooth-ache. Now, imagine that you awake one morning to find yourself with a tooth-ache. In that world, wouldn't you be crying out, "Why God? Why do you allow me to suffer so?" From our perspective, that seems silly, because we can imagine far worse things than a tooth-ache. We have to contend with cancer, and rape, genocide, and Alzheimer's disease. Certainly, those things are far worse. Or so it seems, to us. Try a different thought experiment.

What do you think is the worst thing that could ever happen to anyone? Identify it, whether it's having a certain disease, or a certain injury, or being the victim of a certain crime. *That* (whatever it is), is too much to bear. If God exists, God would never allow *that*. Now, suppose that God agrees, and eliminates that thing (whatever it was), from the world.

What's number two on your list? It just got promoted to number one, didn't it? Isn't that new thing (whatever *it* is), now "the worst thing in the world," that which "no one should ever have to endure?" Shouldn't God eliminate that new thing from the world? And if God does, what was number three? And then number four, and number five, and so on. You probably get the point by now. *Any* amount of suffering might seem like "too much." We don't like to suffer! But, if the only amount of suffering that we'll think is acceptable is "none at all," and if a world without suffering is a world without potential for meaning and growth, then we're just asking for a world in which the most basic project of our existence isn't possible. If there's a good reason for God to permit our suffering, than quibbling over the precise amount of suffering that's justifiable for God to allow won't get us anywhere.

Another possible complaint against this kind of greater good defense is that God could at least be more selective with respect to *who* He permits to suffer. Why does God let bad things happen to good people? Perhaps suffering is necessary. Perhaps we need free will and the consequent risk of moral evil. Perhaps we need a challenging environment, too, and therefore run the risk of natural evil. But, why doesn't God just cause natural and moral evil to afflict bad people only? Why should good people get cancer? Or get molested as a child? If those things are needed, why not be a little more discriminating and only allow people who *deserve* to suffer, to suffer?

As a reply, imagine that you lived in a world in which every time anyone told a lie of any kind, that person was immediately struck dead by a bolt of lightning. Imagine, also, that in that world, any time anyone refuses to help another person in need (when able to do so), the one who refuses to help grows a cancerous tumor instantly. I'd bet that this imaginary world is filled with honest and generous people! I'm confident that if I lived in that world, I would be scrupulously honest—boorishly so. I'm sure you would be as well. Why? Isn't the answer obvious? To avoid the deadly lightning! Or, in the case of helping others, to avoid the tumor. In such a world, we have an obvious ulterior motive when it comes to telling the truth and being charitable: our very lives are at stake. We're not being honest and generous because we deem it the right thing to do, but we're doing so out of fear of immediate and negative consequences if we refuse. Contrast that with the real world.

In the real world, being a good person is no guarantee that bad things will never happen to you. It's possible to be a wonderful, honest, kind, generous human being, and still get cancer, still become homeless, still get raped and murdered, still be killed by a natural disaster, etc. Being a good person is no insurance policy against suffering in this world. For that reason, we know that when people *do* choose to do the right thing, it's not because they think it will spare them from suffering. It must be for some other reason—perhaps simply because it's the right thing to do. A world where suffering can afflict any one of us is a world in which our motives can be more pure, more morally valuable—and therefore more conducive to character growth.

Ultimately, Paley argues that the kind of world in which we live, with all its attendant pains, is "worth it"—not only on the presumption that "Heaven" awaits those who pass their "probation," but even with respect to what we value in this life alone. As regards pain, Paley reminds us that it is "seldom the object of contrivance; that when it is so, the contrivance rests ultimately in good."[165] Pain serves as a warning against greater harms or dangers. Pain is also capable of relief, and although pain may be violent or frequent, "it is seldom both violent and long-continued: and its pauses and intermissions become positive pleasures."[166] Paley even goes so far as to claim that existence of pain causes pleasure to be all the more pleasurable, as moments of pain or sadness make joy all the more meaningful to us. Even death (and our fear of it), perhaps the most infamous of "pains," serves a positive function. Paley claims that the "horror of death proves the value of life."

Death implies separation: and the loss of those whom we love, must necessarily, so far as we can conceive, be accompanied with pain. To the brute creation, nature seems to have stepped in with some secret provision for their relief, under the rupture of their attachments. In their instincts towards their offspring, and of their offspring to them, I have often been surprised to observe

---

165 Paley, Ibid
166 Paley, Ibid

how ardently they love, and how soon they forget. The pertinacity of human sorrow (upon which, time also, at length, lays its softening hand) is probably, therefore, in some manner connected with the qualities of our rational or moral nature. One thing however is clear, viz. that it is better that we should possess affections, the sources of so many virtues, and so many joys, although they be exposed to the incidents of life, as well as the interruptions of mortality, than, by the want of them, be reduced to a state of selfishness, apathy, and quietism.[167]

Although this might be hard to accept in the depths of our grief, Paley claims that we are far better off being capable of all the depths of our emotions (including grief), necessitated by the kind of world in which we live, than if we were incapable of such feelings (including their depths, and contrasts) at all. Pain is "worth it." This world might not seem ideal from the standpoint of our comfort and pleasure, but Lewis suggests that it *shouldn't*.

The Christian doctrine of suffering explains, I believe, a very curious fact about the world we live in. The settled happiness and security which we all desire, God withholds from us by the nature of the world: but joy, pleasure, and merriment He has scattered broadcast...The security we crave would teach us to rest our hearts in this world and oppose an obstacle to our return to God...Our Father refreshes us on the journey with some pleasant inns, but will not encourage us to mistake them for home.[168]

B.C. Johnson takes issue with this general line of reasoning, of course. He attempts to show the perils of these sorts of arguments by means of a *"reductio ad absurdum"* technique. A *"reductio"* involves showing that an argument or claim, when pushed to its "inevitable conclusions" produces absurd results, and therefore there must be something faulty with the argument or claim itself.

How might this apply to the greater good strategy considered above? Johnson considers three variants of the greater good justification: that God doesn't intervene to prevent suffering because to do so would (1) cause us to become dependent creatures, (2) remove our sense of moral urgency, and (3) eliminate opportunities to develop and display virtue. Note that these represent the same basic points offered by Paley and Craig above. Johnson interprets these arguments as concluding that our suffering is justified because it maximizes our independence, sense of moral urgency, and opportunities to develop/display virtue. He then responds to these claims in the same way, by means of a *"reductio."*

1. If it is good to maximize X (independence/moral urgency/virtue building), then we ought to perform every action that promotes X.
2. We ought not to perform every action that promotes X.
3. Therefore, it is not good to maximize X

---

[167] Paley, Ibid
[168] Lewis, Ibid., 116.

The key to Johnson's argument is the second premise: we ought not to perform every action that promotes X. To see why this is so, Johnson considers several extreme (and absurd) examples of actions that promote "X (i.e., independence/moral urgency/virtue building)."

> *It is worthwhile to emphasize, however, that we encourage efforts to eliminate evils; we approve of efforts to promote peace, prevent famine, and wipe out disease. In other words, we do value a world with fewer or (if possible) no opportunities for the development of virtue (when "virtue" is understood to mean the reduction of suffering). If we produce such a world for succeeding generations, how will they develop virtues? Without war, disease, and famine, they will not be virtuous. Should we then cease our attempts to wipe out war, disease, and famine? If we do not believe that it is right to cease attempts at improving the world, then by implication we admit that virtue-building is not an excuse for God to permit disasters. For we admit that the development of virtue is no excuse for permitting disasters.[169]*

In other words, if we really believed that "we ought to perform every action that promotes X (independence/moral urgency/virtue building)," then rather than trying to eliminate sources of suffering in the world, we should be trying to *increase* suffering in the world. However, we all (presumably) think that is absurd. By implication, we don't *really* think that it is good to maximize "X (independence/moral urgency/virtue building)." Since the value of "maximizing X" was the force behind this version of the greater good defense, Johnson thinks the greater good defense fails.

Conclusion

The POE is a negative TA that can serve to undermine warrant for theistic belief. It is based on the claim that the sort of world in which we live (i.e., one filled with seemingly unjustified suffering) is unlikely to exist if there also exists a God who is all-knowing, all-powerful, and perfectly good. Given that our world *does* contain such suffering, that sort of God is unlikely to exist—and, even though the POE does not *refute* the existence of that God, it does (or can) serve to lessen the confidence that one might have that such a God really does exist.

The POE is a difficult problem, and not only for its intellectual properties, but also given the fact that the abstract observations about pain and suffering correspond to real-world occurrences. The POE hits people "at home." In their experiences of abuse. In their cancer. In their lost loved ones. For such reasons, the POE (literally) *feels* different than the "problem" posed by whether or not the universe had a cause of its existence, or whether the universe is actually infinite in the past.

For some, the POE is intractable, and they lose their faith from it, or never come to faith in the first place. It is, however, possible to offer "solutions" to the POE as we can see from Paley, Lewis, and Craig. Admittedly, these solutions threaten to be question-begging in that they are unlikely to be compelling except for those who

---

[169] Johnson, Ibid.

already believe in the existence of that sort of God. On the other hand, unlike with most of cases of begging the question, this is not necessarily a problem. After all, the POE arises as a problem only for those who already believe that God exists (and who are trying to make sense of evil given that belief). It only makes sense that efforts to understand evil in that context would make use of elements of the worldview that is imperiled by the POE in the first place.

Exercises for Wisdom and Growth

1. Do you believe that suffering serves a purpose? Does it always serve a purpose, or only sometimes? What is this purpose? If only sometimes, what makes the difference between "purposeful" suffering and suffering with no purpose?

2. If you believe in God, has there even been a time in your life when your belief or confidence in that God was shaken by a tragic event? How did you resolve your concerns? Do Craig's arguments help? Lewis'? Paley's?

3. If you do not believe in God, to what extent (if any) does the POE contribute to that?

4. In epistemology, there are what is known as "undercutting defeaters," and "rebutting defeaters." A "defeater" is simply a claim that counts against a belief that you have (i.e., it serves as evidence against it). Undercutting defeaters are bits of evidence that cause you to *lose confidence* that your belief is true. Rebutting defeaters serve to cause you to flatly reject your belief (i.e., to conclude that your belief is false). Do you find the POE to be a defeater for belief in God? If so, is it an "undercutting" defeater, or a "rebutting" defeater?

5. Some might claim that Craig's claim that we are no epistemic position to conclude that suffering could serve a greater good is just a fancier sounding version of the more commonly expressed claim that "God works in mysterious ways." Some might dismiss this as an appeal to ignorance. In effect, Craig can't identify the "greater good" being served, but merely assumes, on faith, perhaps, that there must be one anyway. Not surprisingly, Craig disagrees with this characterization of his argument. With whom do you agree? How much do you think your own faith (or lack thereof) contributes to your assessment?

We have another offering from Hume, from the same "Dialogues" we encountered in a previous chapter. In this section, Demea, Cleanthes, and Philo are continuing their discussion of religious arguments, though the discussion now focuses on human suffering. They catalog a variety of sources of such suffering, both "natural" and that inflicted by the actions of other humans. After the dramatic and sobering listing of these "evils," Philo delivers the punch line by appealing to the ancient philosopher Epicurus, and, in so doing, calls into question the properties, or existence, of God. This excerpt is doubly excellent for its capacity to provide a sense of history to the problem of evil. Considered by many to be the most compelling evidentiary threat against theism today, the problem of evil is here traced back not only to Hume, but thousands of years earlier to the pre-Christian philosopher Epicurus.

Dialogues Concerning Natural Religion[170]
David Hume

(This text of Dialogues Concerning Natural Religion is a corrected version of the 1854 Works. http://www.anselm.edu/homepage/dbanach/dnr.htm)

Part X

It is my opinion, I own, replied Demea, that each man feels, in a manner, the truth of religion within his own breast, and, from a consciousness of his imbecility and misery, rather than from any reasoning, is led to seek protection from that Being, on whom he and all nature is dependent. So anxious or so tedious are even the best scenes of life, that futurity is still the object of all our hopes and fears. We incessantly look forward, and endeavour, by prayers, adoration, and sacrifice, to appease those unknown powers, whom we find, by experience, so able to afflict and oppress us. Wretched creatures that we are! what resource for us amidst the innumerable ills of life, did not religion suggest some methods of atonement, and appease those terrors with which we are incessantly agitated and tormented?

I am indeed persuaded, said Philo, that the best, and indeed the only method of bringing every one to a due sense of religion, is by just representations of the misery and wickedness of men. And for that purpose a talent of eloquence and strong imagery is more requisite than that of reasoning and argument. For is it necessary to prove what every one feels within himself? It is only necessary to make us feel it, if possible, more intimately and sensibly.

The people, indeed, replied Demea, are sufficiently convinced of this great and melancholy truth. The miseries of life; the unhappiness of man; the general corruptions of our nature; the unsatisfactory enjoyment of pleasures, riches, honours; these phrases have become almost proverbial in all languages. And who can doubt of what all men declare from their own immediate feeling and experience?

In this point, said Philo, the learned are perfectly agreed with the vulgar; and in

---

[170] http://www.anselm.edu/homepage/dbanach/dnr.htm

all letters, sacred and profane, the topic of human misery has been insisted on with the most pathetic eloquence that sorrow and melancholy could inspire. The poets, who speak from sentiment, without a system, and whose testimony has therefore the more authority, abound in images of this nature. From Homer down to Dr. Young, the whole inspired tribe have ever been sensible, that no other representation of things would suit the feeling and observation of each individual.

As to authorities, replied Demea, you need not seek them. Look round this library of Cleanthes. I shall venture to affirm, that, except authors of particular sciences, such as chemistry or botany, who have no occasion to treat of human life, there is scarce one of those innumerable writers, from whom the sense of human misery has not, in some passage or other, extorted a complaint and confession of it. At least, the chance is entirely on that side; and no one author has ever, so far as I can recollect, been so extravagant as to deny it.

There you must excuse me, said Philo: Leibnitz has denied it; and is perhaps the first who ventured upon so bold and paradoxical an opinion; at least, the first who made it essential to his philosophical system.

And by being the first, replied Demea, might he not have been sensible of his error? For is this a subject in which philosophers can propose to make discoveries especially in so late an age? And can any man hope by a simple denial (for the subject scarcely admits of reasoning), to bear down the united testimony of mankind, founded on sense and consciousness?

And why should man, added he, pretend to an exemption from the lot of all other animals? The whole earth, believe me, Philo, is cursed and polluted. A perpetual war is kindled amongst all living creatures. Necessity, hunger, want, stimulate the strong and courageous: fear, anxiety, terror, agitate the weak and infirm. The first entrance into life gives anguish to the new-born infant and to its wretched parent: weakness, impotence, distress, attend each stage of that life: and it is at last finished in agony and horror.

Observe too, says Philo, the curious artifices of Nature, in order to embitter the life of every living being. The stronger prey upon the weaker, and keep them in perpetual terror and anxiety. The weaker too, in their turn, often prey upon the stronger, and vex and molest them without relaxation. Consider that innumerable race of insects, which either are bred on the body of each animal, or, flying about, infix their stings in him. These insects have others still less than themselves, which torment them. And thus on each hand, before and behind, above and below, every animal is surrounded with enemies, which incessantly seek his misery and distruction.

Man alone, said Demea, seems to be, in part, an exception to this rule. For by combination in society, he can easily master lions, tigers, and bears, whose greater strength and agility naturally enable them to prey upon him.

On the contrary, it is here chiefly, cried Philo, that the uniform and equal maxims of Nature are most apparent. Man, it is true, can, by combination, surmount all his real enemies, and become master of the whole animal creation: but does he not immediately raise up to himself imaginary enemies, the demons of his fancy, who haunt him with superstitious terrors, and blast every enjoyment of life? His pleasure, as he imagines, becomes, in their eyes, a crime: his food and repose give them umbrage and offence: his very sleep and dreams furnish new materials to anxious fear: and even death, his refuge from every other ill, presents only the dread of endless and innumerable woes. Nor does the wolf molest more the timid flock, than superstition does the anxious breast of wretched mortals.

Besides, consider, Demea: this very society, by which we surmount those wild beasts, our natural enemies; what new enemies does it not raise to us? What woe and misery does it not occasion? Man is the greatest enemy of man. Oppression, injustice, contempt, contumely, violence, sedition, war, calumny, treachery, fraud; by these they mutually torment each other; and they would soon dissolve that society which they had formed, were it not for the dread of still greater ills, which must attend their separation.

But though these external insults, said Demea, from animals, from men, from all the elements, which assault us, form a frightful catalogue of woes, they are nothing in comparison of those which arise within ourselves, from the distempered condition of our mind and body. How many lie under the lingering torment of diseases? Hear the pathetic enumeration of the great poet.

> Intestine stone and ulcer, colic-pangs,
> Demoniac frenzy, moping melancholy,
> And moon-struck madness, pining atrohy,
> Marasmus, and wide-wasting pestilence.
> Dire was the tossing, deep the groans: DESPAIR
> Tended the sick, busiest from couch to couch.
> And over them triumphant DEATH his dart
> Shook: but delay'd to strike, though oft invok'd
> With vows, as their chief good and final hope.

The disorders of the mind, continued Demea, though more secret, are not perhaps less dismal and vexatious. Remorse, shame, anguish, rage, disappointment, anxiety, fear, dejection, despair; who has ever passed through life without cruel inroads from these tormentors? How many have scarcely ever felt any better sensations? Labour and poverty, so abhorred by every one, are the certain lot of the far greater number; and those few privileged persons, who enjoy ease and opulence, never reach contentment or true felicity. All the goods of life united would not make a very happy man; but all the ills united would make a wretch indeed; and any one of them almost (and who can be free from every one?) nay often the absence of one good (and who can possess all?) is sufficient to render life ineligible.

Were a stranger to drop on a sudden into this world, I would shew him, as a specimen of its ills, an hospital full of diseases, a prison crowded with malefactors and debtors, a field of battle strewed with carcases, a fleet foundering in the ocean, a nation languishing under tyranny, famine, or pestilence. To turn the gay side of life to him and give him a notion of its pleasures; whither should I conduct him? to a ball, to an opera, to court? He might justly think, that I was only shewing him a diversity of distress and sorrow.

There is no evading such striking instances, said Philo, but by apologies, which still further aggravate the charge. Why have all men, I ask, in all ages, complained incessantly of the miseries of life? . . . . They have no just reason, says one: these complaints proceed only from their discontented, repining, anxious disposition....And can there possibly, I reply, be a more certain foundation of misery, than such a wretched temper?

But if they were really as unhappy as they pretend, says my antagonist, why do they remain in life?...

Not satisfied with life, afraid of death.

This is the secret chain, say I, that holds us. We are terrified, not bribed to the continuance of our existence....

And is it possible, Cleanthes, said Philo, that after all these reflections, and infinitely more, which might be suggested, you can still persevere in your Anthropomorphism, and assert the moral attributes of the Deity, his justice, benevolence, mercy, and rectitude, to be of the same nature with these virtues in human creatures? His power we allow is infinite: whatever he wills is executed: but neither man nor any other animal is happy: therefore he does not will their happiness. His wisdom is infinite: he is never mistaken in choosing the means to any end: but the course of Nature tends not to human or animal felicity: therefore it is not established for that purpose. Through the whole compass of human knowledge, there are no inferences more certain and infallible than these. In what respect, then, do his benevolence and mercy resemble the benevolence and mercy of men?

Epicurus's old questions are yet unanswered.

Is he willing to prevent evil, but not able? then is he impotent. Is he able, but not willing? then is he malevolent. Is he both able and willing? whence then is evil?...

Part XI
[204]
Did I shew you a house or palace, where there was not one apartment convenient or agreeable; where the windows, doors, fires, passages, stairs, and the whole economy of the building, were the source of noise, confusion, fatigue, darkness, and the extremes of heat and cold; you would certainly blame the contrivance, without any further examination. The architect would in vain display his subtilty, and prove to you, that if this door or that window were altered, greater ills would ensue. What he says may be strictly true: the alteration of one particular, while the other parts of the building remain, may only augment the inconveniences. But still you would assert in general, that, if the architect had had skill and good intentions, he might have formed such a plan of the whole, and might have adjusted the parts in such a manner, as would have remedied all or most of these inconveniences. His ignorance, or even your own ignorance of such a plan, will never convince you of the impossibility of it. If you find any inconveniences and deformities in the building, you will always, without entering into any detail, condemn the architect.

[205]
In short, I repeat the question: Is the world, considered in general, and as it appears to us in this life, different from what a man, or such a limited being, would, beforehand, expect from a very powerful, wise, and benevolent Deity? It must be strange prejudice to assert the contrary. And from thence I conclude, that however consistent the world may be, allowing certain suppositions and conjectures, with the

idea of such a Deity, it can never afford us an inference concerning his existence. The consistence is not absolutely denied, only the inference. Conjectures, especially where infinity is excluded from the Divine attributes, may perhaps be sufficient to prove a consistence, but can never be foundations for any inference.

There seems to be four circumstances, on which depend all, or the greatest part of the ills, that molest sensible creatures; and it is not impossible but all these circumstances may be necessary and unavoidable. We know so little beyond common life, or even of common life, that, with regard to the economy of a universe, there is no conjecture, however wild, which may not be just; nor any one, however plausible, which may not be erroneous. All that belongs to human understanding, in this deep ignorance and obscurity, is to be sceptical, or at least cautious, and not to admit of any hypothesis whatever, much less of any which is supported by no appearance of probability. Now, this I assert to be the case with regard to all the causes of evil, and the circumstances on which it depends. None of them appear to human reason in the least degree necessary or unavoidable; nor can we suppose them such, without the utmost license of imagination.

The first circumstance which introduces evil, is that contrivance or economy of the animal creation, by which pains, as well as pleasures, are employed to excite all creatures to action, and make them vigilant in the great work of self-preservation. Now pleasure alone, in its various degrees, seems to human understanding sufficient for this purpose. All animals might be constantly in a state of enjoyment: but when urged by any of the necessities of nature, such as thirst, hunger, weariness; instead of pain, they might feel a diminution of pleasure, by which they might be prompted to seek that object which is necessary to their subsistence. Men pursue pleasure as eagerly as they avoid pain; at least they might have been so constituted. It seems, therefore, plainly possible to carry on the business of life without any pain. Why then is any animal ever rendered susceptible of such a sensation? If animals can be free from it an hour, they might enjoy a perpetual exemption from it; and it required as particular a contrivance of their organs to produce that feeling, as to endow them with sight, hearing, or any of the senses. Shall we conjecture, that such a contrivance was necessary, without any appearance of reason? and shall we build on that conjecture as on the most certain truth?

[206]

But a capacity of pain would not alone produce pain, were it not for the second circumstance, viz. the conducting of the world by general laws; and this seems nowise necessary to a very perfect Being. It is true, if every thing were conducted by particular volitions, the course of nature would be perpetually broken, and no man could employ his reason in the conduct of life. But might not other particular volitions remedy this inconvenience? In short, might not the Deity exterminate all ill, wherever it were to be found; and produce all good, without any preparation, or long progress of causes and effects?

Besides, we must consider, that, according to the present economy of the world the course of nature, though supposed exactly regular, yet to us appears not so, and many events are uncertain, and many disappoint our expectations. Health and sickness, calm and tempest, with an infinite number of other accidents, whose causes are unknown and variable, have a great influence both on the fortunes of particular persons and on the prosperity of public societies; and indeed all human life, in a manner, depends on such accidents. A being, therefore, who knows the secret springs of the universe, might easily, by particular volitions, turn all these accidents to the good of mankind, and render the whole world happy, without discovering himself in any operation. A fleet, whose purposes were salutary to society, might always meet with a fair wind. Good princes enjoy sound health and long life. Persons born to power and authority, be framed with good tempers and virtuous dispositions. A few such events as these, regularly and wisely conducted, would change the face of the world; and yet would no more seem to disturb the course of nature, or confound human conduct, than the present economy of things, where the causes are secret, and variable, and compounded. Some small touches given to Caligula's brain in his infancy, might have converted him into a Trajan. One wave, a little higher than the rest, by burying Caesar and his fortune in the bottom of the ocean, might have restored liberty to a considerable part of mankind. There may, for aught we know, be good reasons why Providence interposes not in this manner; but they are unknown to us; and though the mere supposition, that such reasons exist, may be sufficient to save the conclusion concerning the Divine attributes, yet surely it can never be sufficient to establish that conclusion.

[207]

If every thing in the universe be conducted by general laws, and if animals be rendered susceptible of pain, it scarcely seems possible but some ill must arise in the various shocks of matter, and the various concurrence and opposition of general laws; but this ill would be very rare, were it not for the third circumstance, which I proposed to mention, viz. the great frugality with which all powers and faculties are distributed to every particular being. So well adjusted are the organs and capacities of all animals, and so well fitted to their preservation, that, as far as history or tradition reaches, there appears not to be any single species which has yet been extinguished in the universe. Every animal has the requisite endowments; but these endowments are bestowed with so scrupulous an economy, that any considerable diminution must entirely destroy the creature. Wherever one power is encreased, there is a proportional abatement in the others. Animals which excel in swiftness are commonly defective in force. Those which possess both are either imperfect in some of their senses, or are oppressed with the most craving wants. The human species, whose chief excellency is reason and sagacity, is of all others the most necessitous, and the most deficient in bodily advantages; without clothes, without arms, without food, without lodging, without any convenience of life, except what they owe to their own skill and industry. In short, nature seems to have formed an exact calculation of the necessities of her creatures; and, like a rigid master, has afforded them little more powers or endowments than what are strictly sufficient to supply those necessities. An indulgent parent would have bestowed a large stock, in order to guard against accidents, and secure the happiness and welfare of the creature in the most unfortunate concurrence of circumstances. Every course of life would not have been so surrounded with precipices, that the least departure from the true path, by mistake or necessity, must involve us in misery and ruin. Some reserve, some fund, would have been provided to insure happiness; nor would the powers and the necessities have been adjusted with so rigid an economy. The Author of Nature is inconceivably powerful: his force is supposed great, if not altogether inexhaustible: nor is there any reason, as far as we can judge, to make him observe this strict frugality in his dealings with his creatures. It would have been better, were his power extremely limited, to have created fewer animals, and to have endowed these with more faculties for their happiness and preservation. A builder is never esteemed prudent, who undertakes a plan beyond what his stock will enable him to finish.

[208]

In order to cure most of the ills of human life, I require not that man should have the wings of the eagle, the swiftness of the stag, the force of the ox, the arms of the lion, the scales of the crocodile or rhinoceros; much less do I demand the sagacity of an angel or cherubim. I am contented to take an increase in one single power or faculty of his soul. Let him be endowed with a greater propensity to industry and labour; a more vigorous spring and activity of mind; a more constant bent to business and application. Let the whole species possess naturally an equal diligence with that which many individuals are able to attain by habit and reflection; and the most beneficial consequences, without any alloy of ill, is the immediate and necessary result of this endowment. Almost all the moral, as well as natural evils of human life, arise from idleness; and were our species, by the original constitution of their frame, exempt from this vice or infirmity, the perfect cultivation of land, the improvement of arts and manufactures, the exact execution of every office and duty, immediately follow; and men at once may fully reach that state of society, which is so imperfectly attained by the best regulated government. But as industry is a power, and the most valuable of any, Nature seems determined, suitably to her usual maxims, to bestow it on men with a very sparing hand; and rather to punish him severely for his deficiency in it, than to reward him for his attainments. She has so contrived his frame, that nothing but the most violent necessity can oblige him to labour; and she employs all his other wants to overcome, at least in part, the want of diligence, and to endow him with some share of a faculty of which she has thought fit naturally to bereave him. Here our demands may be allowed very humble, and therefore the more reasonable. If we required the endowments of superior penetration and judgment, of a more delicate taste of beauty, of a nicer sensibility to benevolence and friendship; we might be told, that we impiously pretend to break the order of Nature; that we want to exalt ourselves into a higher rank of being; that the presents which we require, not being suitable to our state and condition, would only be pernicious to us. But it is hard; I dare to repeat it, it is hard, that being placed in a world so full of wants and necessities, where almost every being and element is either our foe or refuses its assistance . . . we should also have our own temper to struggle with, and should be deprived of that faculty which can alone fence against these multiplied evils.

[209]

The fourth circumstance, whence arises the misery and ill of the universe, is the inaccurate workmanship of all the springs and principles of the great machine of nature. It must be acknowledged, that there are few parts of the universe, which seem not to serve some purpose, and whose removal would not produce a visible defect and disorder in the whole. The parts hang all together; nor can one be touched without affecting the rest, in a greater or less degree. But at the same time, it must be observed, that none of these parts or principles, however useful, are so accurately adjusted, as to keep precisely within those bounds in which their utility consists; but they are, all of them, apt, on every occasion, to run into the one extreme or the other. One would imagine, that this grand production had not received the last hand of the maker; so little finished is every part, and so coarse are the strokes with which it is executed. Thus, the winds are requisite to convey the vapours along the surface of the globe, and to assist men in navigation: but how oft, rising up to tempests and hurricanes, do they become pernicious? Rains are necessary to nourish all the plants and animals of the earth: but how often are they defective? how often excessive? Heat is requisite to all life and vegetation; but is not always found in the due proportion. On the mixture and secretion of the humours and juices of the body depend the health and prosperity of the animal: but the parts perform not regularly their proper function. What more useful than all the passions of the mind, ambition, vanity, love, anger? But how oft do they break their bounds, and cause the greatest convulsions in society? There is nothing so advantageous in the universe, but what frequently becomes pernicious, by its excess or defect; nor has Nature guarded, with the requisite accuracy, against all disorder or confusion. The irregularity is never perhaps so great as to destroy any species; but is often sufficient to involve the individuals in ruin and misery.

[210]
On the concurrence, then, of these four circumstances, does all or the greatest part of natural evil depend. Were all living creatures incapable of pain, or were the world administered by particular volitions, evil never could have found access into the universe: and were animals endowed with a large stock of powers and faculties, beyond what strict necessity requires; or were the several springs and principles of the universe so accurately framed as to preserve always the just temperament and medium; there must have been very little ill in comparison of what we feel at present. What then shall we pronounce on this occasion? Shall we say that these circumstances are not necessary, and that they might easily have been altered in the contrivance of the universe? This decision seems too presumptuous for creatures so blind and ignorant. Let us be more modest in our conclusions. Let us allow, that, if the goodness of the Deity (I mean a goodness like the human) could be established on any tolerable reasons a priori, these phenomena, however untoward, would not be sufficient to subvert that principle; but might easily, in some unknown manner, be reconcilable to it. But let us still assert, that as this goodness is not antecedently established, but must be inferred from the phenomena, there can be no grounds for such an inference, while there are so many ills in the universe, and while these ills might so easily have been remedied, as far as human understanding can be allowed to judge on such a subject. I am Sceptic enough to allow, that the bad appearances, notwithstanding all my reasonings, may be compatible with such attributes as you suppose; but surely they can never prove these attributes. Such a conclusion cannot result from Scepticism, but must arise from the phenomena, and from our confidence in the reasonings which we deduce from these phenomena.

[211]
Look round this universe. What an immense profusion of beings, animated and organized, sensible and active! You admire this prodigious variety and fecundity. But inspect a little more narrowly these living existences, the only beings worth

regarding. How hostile and destructive to each other! How insufficient all of them for their own happiness! How contemptible or odious to the spectator! The whole presents nothing but the idea of a blind Nature, impregnated by a great vivifying principle, and pouring forth from her lap, without discernment or parental care, her maimed and abortive children!

Here the Manichaean system occurs as a proper hypothesis to solve the difficulty: and no doubt, in some respects, it is very specious, and has more probability than the common hypothesis, by giving a plausible account of the strange mixture of good and ill which appears in life. But if we consider, on the other hand, the perfect uniformity and agreement of the parts of the universe, we shall not discover in it any marks of the combat of a malevolent with a benevolent being. There is indeed an opposition of pains and pleasures in the feelings of sensible creatures: but are not all the operations of Nature carried on by an opposition of principles, of hot and cold, moist and dry, light and heavy? The true conclusion is, that the original Source of all things is entirely indifferent to all these principles; and has no more regard to good above ill, than to heat above cold, or to drought above moisture, or to light above heavy.

[212]

There may four hypotheses be framed concerning the first causes of the universe: that they are endowed with perfect goodness; that they have perfect malice; that they are opposite, and have both goodness and malice; that they have neither goodness nor malice. Mixed phenomena can never prove the two former unmixed principles; and the uniformity and steadiness of general laws seem to oppose the third. The fourth, therefore, seems by far the most probable.

What I have said concerning natural evil will apply to moral, with little or no variation; and we have no more reason to infer, that the rectitude of the Supreme Being resembles human rectitude, than that his benevolence resembles the human. Nay, it will be thought, that we have still greater cause to exclude from him moral sentiments, such as we feel them; since moral evil, in the opinion of many, is much more predominant above moral good than natural evil above natural good.

This is another selection from Paley's "Natural Theology." In this section, Paley attempts to respond to the problem of evil, considering possible justifications for both moral and natural evil.

Natural Theology; Or, Evidences of the Existence and Attributes of the Deity. Collected from the Appearances of Nature[171]

William Paley, D.D. –

Late Archdeacon of Carlisle

The Twelfth Edition (1809)

CHAPTER XXVI.
THE GOODNESS OF THE DEITY.

...

Of the ORIGIN OF EVIL, no universal solution has been discovered; I mean, no solution which reaches to all cases of complaint. The most comprehensive is that which arises from the consideration of *general rules.* We may, I think, without much difficulty, be brought to admit the four following points: first, that important advantages may accrue to the universe from the order of nature proceeding according to general laws: secondly, that general laws, however well set and constituted, often thwart and cross one another: thirdly, that from these thwartings and crossings, frequent particular inconveniencies will arise: and, fourthly, that it agrees with our observation to suppose, that some degree of these inconveniencies takes place in the works of nature. These points may be allowed; and it may also be asserted, that the general laws with which we are acquainted, are directed to beneficial ends. On the other hand, with many of these laws we are not acquainted at all, or we are totally unable to trace them in their branches, and in their operation; the effect of which ignorance is, that they cannot be of importance to us as measures by which to regulate our conduct. The conservation of them may be of importance in other respects, or to other beings, but we are uninformed of their value or use; uninformed, consequently, when, and how far, they may or may not be suspended, or their effects turned aside, by a presiding and benevolent will, without incurring greater evils than those which would be avoided. The consideration, therefore, of general laws, although it may concern the question of the origin of evil very nearly (which I think it does), rests in views disproportionate to our faculties, and in a knowledge which we do not possess. It serves rather to account for the obscurity of the subject, than to supply us with distinct answers to our difficulties. However, whilst we assent to the above-stated propositions as principles, whatever uncertainty we may find in the application, we lay a ground for believing, that cases of apparent evil, for which *we* can suggest no

---

[171] http://darwin-online.org.uk/content/frameset?itemID=A142&viewtype =text&pageseq=1

particular reason, are governed by reasons, which are more general, which lie deeper in the order of second causes, and which on that account, are removed to a greater distance from us....

Of *bodily pain*, the principal observation, no doubt, is that which we have already made, and already dwelt upon, *viz.* "that it is seldom the object of contrivance; that when it is so, the contrivance rests ultimately in good."

To which, however, may be added, that the annexing of pain to the means of destruction is a salutary provision; inasmuch as it teaches vigilance and caution; both gives notice of danger, and excites those endeavours which may be necessary to preservation. The evil consequence, which sometimes arises from the want of that timely intimation of danger which pain gives, is known to the inhabitants of cold countries by the example of frost-bitten limbs. I have conversed with patients who have lost toes and fingers by this cause. They have in general told me, that they were totally unconscious of any local uneasiness at the time. Some I have heard declare, that, whilst they were about their employment, neither their situation, nor the state of the air, was unpleasant. They felt no pain; they suspected no mischief; till, by the application of warmth, they discovered, too late, the fatal injury which some of their extremities had suffered. I say that this shows the use of pain, and that we stand in need of such a monitor. I believe also that the use extends further than we suppose, or can now trace; that to disagreeable sensations we, and all animals owe or have owed, many habits of action which are salutary, but which are become so familiar, as not easily to be referred to their origin.

PAIN also itself is not without its *alleviations*. It may be violent and frequent; but it is seldom both violent and long-continued: and its pauses and intermissions become positive pleasures. It has the power of shedding a satisfaction over intervals of ease, which, I believe, few enjoyments exceed. A man resting from a fit of the stone or gout, is, for the time, in possession of feelings which undisturbed health cannot impart. They may be dearly bought, but still they are to be set against the price. And, indeed, it depends upon the duration and urgency of the pain, whether they be dearly bought or not. I am far from being sure, that a man is not a gainer by suffering a moderate interruption of bodily ease for a couple of hours out of the four-and-twenty. Two very common observations favour this opinion: one is, that remissions of pain call forth, from those who experience them, stronger expressions of satisfaction and of gratitude towards both the author and the instruments of their relief, than are excited by advantages of any other kind; the second is, that the spirits of sick men do not sink in proportion to the acuteness of their sufferings; but rather appear to be roused and supported, not by pain, but by the high degree of comfort which they derive from its cessation, or even its subsidency, whenever that occurs: and which they taste with a relish, that diffuses some portion of mental complacency over the whole of that mixed state of sensations in which disease has placed them....

Of *mortal* diseases, the great use is to reconcile us to death. The horror of death proves the value of life. But it is in the power of disease to abate, or even extinguish, this horror; which it does in a wonderful manner, and, oftentimes, by a mild and imperceptible gradation. Every man who has been placed in a situation to observe it, is surprised with the change which has been wrought in himself, when he compares the view which he entertains of death upon a sick-bed, with the heart-sinking dismay with which he should some time ago have met it in health. There is no similitude between the sensations of a man led to execution, and the calm expiring of a patient at the close of his disease. Death to him is only the last of a long train of changes; in his progress through which, it is possible that he may experience no shocks or sudden transitions.

Death itself, as a mode of removal and of succession, is so connected with the whole order of our animal world, that almost every thing in that world must be changed, to be able to do without it. It may seem likewise impossible to separate the fear of death from the enjoyment of life, or the perception of that fear from rational natures. Brutes are in a great measure delivered from all anxiety on this account by the inferiority of their faculties; or rather they seem to be armed with the apprehension of death just sufficiently to put them upon the means of preservation, and no further. But would a human being wish to purchase this immunity at the expense of those mental powers which enable him to look forward to the future?

Death implies *separation:* and the loss of those whom we love, must necessarily, so far as we can conceive, be accompanied with pain. To the brute creation, nature seems to have stepped in with some secret provision for their relief, under the rupture of their attachments. In their instincts towards their offspring, and of their offspring to them, I have often been surprised to observe how ardently they love, and how soon they forget. The pertinacity of human sorrow (upon which, time also, at length, lays its softening hand) is probably, therefore, in some manner connected with the qualities of our rational or moral nature. One thing however is clear, *viz.* that it is better that we should possess affections, the sources of so many virtues, and so many joys, although they be exposed to the incidents of life, as well as the interruptions of mortality, than, by the want of them, be reduced to a state of selfishness, apathy, and quietism.

Of other external evils (still confining ourselves to what are called physical or natural evils), a considerable part come within the scope of the following observation:--The great principle of human satisfaction is *engagement*. It is a most just distinction, which the late Mr. Tucker has dwelt upon so largely in his works, between pleasures in which we are passive, and pleasures in which we are active. And, I believe, every attentive observer of human life will assent to his position, that, however grateful the sensations may occasionally be in which we are passive, it is not these, but the latter class of our pleasures, which constitute satisfaction; which supply that regular stream of moderate and miscellaneous enjoyments, in which happiness, as distinguished from voluptuousness, consists. Now for rational occupation, which is, in other words, for the very material of contented existence, there would be no place left, if either the things with which we had to do were absolutely impracticable to our endeavours, or if they were too obedient to our uses. A world, furnished with advantages on one side, and beset with difficulties, wants, and inconveniences on the other, is the proper abode of free, rational, and active natures, being the fittest to stimulate and exercise their faculties. The very *refractoriness* of the objects they have to deal with, contributes to this purpose. A world in which nothing depended upon ourselves, however it might have suited an imaginary race of beings, would not have suited mankind. Their skill, prudence, industry; their various arts, and their best attainments, from the application of which they draw, if not their highest, their most permanent gratifications, would be insignificant, if things could be either moulded by our volitions, or, of their own accord, conformed themselves to our views and wishes. Now it is in this refractoriness that we discern the seed and principle of *physical* evil, as far as it arises from that which is external to us.

Civil evils, or the evils of civil life, are much more easily disposed of, than physical evils: because they are, in truth, of much less magnitude, and also because they result, by a kind of necessity, not only from the constitution of our nature, but from a part of that constitution which no one would wish to see altered....

The mischiefs of which mankind are the occasion to one another, by their private wickednesses and cruelties; by tyrannical exercises of power; by rebellions against just authority; by wars; by national jealousies and competitions operating to the destruction of third countries; or by other instances of misconduct either in individuals or societies, are all to be resolved into the character of man as a *free agent*. Free agency in its very essence contains liability to abuse. Yet, if you deprive man of his free agency, you subvert his nature. You may have order from him and regularity, as you may from the tides or the trade-winds, but you put an end to his moral character, to virtue, to merit, to accountableness, to the use indeed of reason. To which must be added the observation, that even the bad qualities of mankind have an origin in their good ones. The case is this: human passions are either necessary to human welfare, or capable of being made, and, in a great majority of instances, in fact, made, conducive to its happiness. These passions are strong and general; and, perhaps, would not answer their purpose unless they were so. But strength and generality, when it is expedient that particular circumstances should be respected become, if left to themselves, excess and misdirection. From which excess and misdirection, the vices of mankind (the causes, no doubt, of much misery) appear to spring. This account, whilst it shows us the principle of vice, shows us, at the same time, the province of reason and of self-government: the want also of every support which can be procured to either from the aids of religion; and it shows this, without having recourse to any native, gratuitous malignity in the human constitution. Mr Hume, in his posthumous dialogues, asserts, indeed, of *idleness*, or aversion to labour (which he states to lie at the root of a considerable part of the evils which mankind suffer), that it is simple and merely bad. But how does he distinguish idleness from the love of ease? or is he sure, that the love of ease in individuals is not the chief foundation of social tranquillity? It will be found, I believe, to be true, that in every community there is a large class of its members, whose idleness is the best quality about them, being the corrective of other bad ones. If it were possible, in every instance, to give a right determination to industry, we could never have too much of it. But this is not possible, if men are to be free. And without this, nothing would be so dangerous, as an incessant, universal, indefatigable activity. In the civil world, as well as in the material, it is the *vis inertiæ* which keeps things in their places....

Of *sensible* interposition we may be permitted to remark, that a Providence always and certainly distinguishable, would be neither more nor less than miracles rendered frequent and common. It is difficult to judge of the state into which this would throw us. It is enough to say, that it would cast us upon a quite different dispensation from that under which we live. It would be a total and radical change And the change would deeply affect, or perhaps subvert, the whole conduct of human affairs. I can readily believe, that, other circumstances being adapted to it, such a state might be better than our present state. It may be the state of other beings; it may be ours hereafter. But the question with which we are now concerned is, how far it would be consistent with our condition, supposing it in other respects to remain as it is? And in this question there seem to be reasons of great moment on the negative side. For instance, so long as bodily labour continues, on so many accounts, to be necessary for the bulk of mankind, any dependency upon supernatural aid, by unfixing those motives which promote exertion, or by relaxing those habits which engender patient industry, might introduce negligence, inactivity, and disorder, into the most useful occupations of human life; and thereby deteriorate the condition of human life itself.

As moral agents, we should experience a still greater alteration; of which, more will be said under the next article.

Although therefore the Deity, who possesses the power of winding and turning, as he pleases, the course of causes which issue from himself, do in fact interpose to alter or intercept effects, which without such interposition would have taken place; yet it is by no means incredible, that his Providence, which always rests upon final good, may have made a *reserve* with respect to the manifestation of his interference, a part of the very plan which he has appointed for our terrestrial existence, and a part conformable with, or, in some sort, required by, other parts of the same plan. It is at any rate evident, that a large and ample province remains for the exercise of Providence, without its being naturally perceptible by us: because obscurity, when applied to the interruption of laws, bears a necessary proportion to the imperfection of our knowledge when applied to the laws themselves, or rather to the effects which these laws, under their various and incalculable combinations, would of their own accord produce. And if it be said, that the doctrine of Divine Providence, by reason of the ambiguity under which its exertions present themselves, can be attended with no *practical* influence upon our conduct; that, although we believe ever so firmly that there is a. Providence, we must prepare, and provide, and act, as if there were none; I answer, that this is admitted: and that we further allege, that so to prepare, and so to provide, is consistent with the most perfect assurance of the reality of a Providence: and not only so, but that it is, probably, one advantage of the present state of our information, that our provisions and preparations are not disturbed by it. Or if it be still asked, Of what use at all then is the doctrine, if it neither alter our measures nor regulate our conduct? I answer again, that it is of the greatest use, but that it is a doctrine of sentiment and piety, not (immediately at least) of action or conduct; that it applies to the consolation of men's minds, to their devotions, to the excitement of gratitude, the support of patience, the keeping alive and the strengthening of every motive for endeavouring to please our Maker; and that these are great uses.

OF ALL VIEWS under which human life has ever been considered, the most reasonable in my judgement is that, which regards it as a state of *probation.* If the course of the world was separated from the contrivances of nature, I do not know that it would be necessary to look for any other account of it, than what, if it may be called an account, is contained in the answer, that events rise up by chance. But since the contrivances of nature decidedly evince *intention;* and since the course of the world and the contrivances of nature have the same author; we are, by the force of this connexion, led to believe, that the appearance, under which events take place, is reconcileable with the supposition of design on the part of the Deity. It is enough that they be reconcileable with this supposition; and it is undoubtedly true, that they may be reconcileable, though we cannot reconcile them. The mind, however, which contemplates the works of nature, and, in those works, sees so much of means directed to ends, of beneficial effects brought about by wise expedients, of concerted trains of causes terminating in the happiest results; so much, in a word, of counsel, intention, and benevolence: a mind, I say, drawn into the habit of thought which these observations excite, can hardly turn its view to the condition of our own species, without endeavouring to suggest to itself some purpose, some design, for which the state in which we are placed is fitted, and which it is made to serve. Now we assert the most probable supposition to be, that it is a state of moral probation; and that many things in it suit with this hypothesis, which suit no other. It is not a state of unmixed happiness, or of happiness simply: it is not a state of designed misery, or of misery simply: it is not a state of retribution: it is not a state of punishment. It suits with none of these suppositions. It accords much better with the idea of its being a condition calculated for the production, exercise, and improvement of moral qualities, with a view to a future state, in which these qualities, after being so produced, exercised, and improved, may, by a new and more favouring constitution of things, receive their reward, or become their own. If it be said, that this is to enter upon a religious rather than a philosophical consideration, I answer, that the name of Religion ought to form no objection, if it shall turn out to be the case, that the more religious our views are, the more probability they contain. The degree of beneficence, of benevolent intention, and of power, exercised in the construction of sensitive beings, goes strongly in favour, not only of a creative, but of a continuing care, that is, of a ruling Providence. The degree of chance which appears to prevail in the world, requires to be reconciled with this hypothesis. Now it is one thing to maintain the doctrine of Providence along with that of a future state, and another thing without it. In my opinion, the two doctrines must stand or fall together. For although more of this apparent chance may perhaps, upon other principles, be accounted for, than is generally supposed, yet a future state alone rectifies all disorders: and if it can be shown, that the appearance of disorder is consistent with the uses of life as a *preparatory* state, or that in some respects it promotes these uses, then so far as this hypothesis may be accepted the ground of the difficulty is done away.

In the wide scale of human condition, there is not perhaps one of its manifold diversities, which does not bear upon the design here suggested. Virtue is infinitely various. There is no situation in which a rational being is placed, from that of the best-instructed Christian, down to the condition of the rudest barbarian, which affords not room for moral agency; for the acquisition, exercise, and display of voluntary qualities, good and bad. Health and sickness, enjoyment and suffering, riches and poverty, knowledge and ignorance, power and subjection, liberty and bondage, civilization and barbarity, have all their offices and duties, all serve for the *formation* of character: for when we speak of a state of trial, it must be remembered, that characters are not only tried, or proved, or detected, but that they are generated also, and *formed*, by circumstances. The best dispositions may subsist under the most depressed, the most afflicted fortunes. A West-Indian slave, who, amidst his wrongs, retains his benevolence, I for my part, look upon, as amongst the foremost of human candidates for the rewards of virtue. The kind master of such a slave, that is, he, who in the exercise of an inordinate authority, postpones, in any degree, his own interest to his slave's comfort, is likewise a meritorious character: but still he is inferior to his slave. All however which I contend for, is, that these destinies, opposite as they may be in every other view, are both *trials;* and equally such. The observation may be applied to every other condition; to the whole range of the scale, not excepting even its lowest extremity. *Savages* appear to us all alike; but it is owing to the distance at which we view savage life, that we perceive in it no discrimation of character. I make no doubt, but that moral qualities, both good and bad, are called into action as much, and that they subsist in as great variety, in these inartificial societies, as they are, or do, in polished life. Certain at least it is, that the good and ill treatment which each individual meets with, depends more upon the choice and voluntary conduct of those about him, than it does or ought to do, under regular civil institutions, and the coercion of public laws. So again, to turn our eyes to the other end of the scale, namely, that part of it which is occupied by mankind, enjoying the benefits of learning, together with the lights of revelation, there also, the advantage is all along *probationary*. Christianity itself, I mean the revelation of Christianity, is not only a blessing but a trial. It is one of the diversified means by which the character is exercised: and they who require of Christianity, that the revelation of it should be universal, may possibly be found to require, that one species of probation should be adopted, if not to the exclusion of others, at least to the narrowing of that variety which the wisdom of the Deity hath appointed to this part of his moral economy(*Note:* The reader will observe, that I speak of the revelation of Christianity as distinct from Christianity itself. The *dispensation* may already be universal. That part of mankind which never heard of CHRIST'S name, may nevertheless be redeemed, that is, be placed in a better condition, with respect to their future state, by his intervention; may be the objects of his benignity and intercession, as well as of the propitiatory virtue of his passion. But this is not "natural theology;" therefore I will not dwell longer upon it.)

Now if this supposition be well founded: that is, if it be true, that our ultimate, or our most permanent happiness, will depend, not upon the temporary condition into which we are cast, but upon our behaviour in it; then is it a much more fit subject of *chance* than we usually allow or apprehend it to be, in what manner, the variety of external circumstances, which subsist in the human world, is distributed amongst the individuals of the species. "This life being a state of probation, "it is immaterial, says Rousseau, "what kind of trials we experience in it, provided they produce their effects." Of two agents who stand indifferent to the moral Governor of the universe, one may be exercised by riches, the other by poverty. The treatment of these two shall appear to be very opposite, whilst in truth it is the same: for though, in many respects, there be great disparity between the conditions assigned, in one main article there may be none, *viz.* in that they are alike trials; have both their duties and temptations, not less arduous or less dangerous, in one case than the other; so that if the final reward follow the character, the original distribution of the circumstances under which that character is formed, may be defended upon principles not only of justice but of equality. What hinders therefore, but that mankind may draw lots for their condition? They take their portion of faculties and opportunities, as any unknown cause, or concourse of causes, or as causes acting for other purposes, may happen to set them out; but the event is governed by that which depends upon themselves, the application of what they have received. In dividing the talents, no rule was observed none was necessary: in rewarding the use of them, that of the most correct justice. The chief difference at last appears to be, that the right use of more talents, *i. e.* of a greater trust, will be more highly rewarded, than the right use of fewer talents, *i. e.* of a less trust. And since for other purposes, it is expedient, that there be an inequality of concredited talents here, as well, probably, as an inequality of conditions hereafter though all remuneratory, can any rule, adapted to that inequality, be more agreeable even to our apprehensions of distributive justice, than this is?

We have said, that the appearance of *casualty*, which attends the occurrences and events of life, not only does not interfere with its uses, as a state of probation, but that it promotes these uses.

Passive virtues, of all others the severest and the most sublime; of all others perhaps, the most acceptable to the Deity; would, it is evident, be excluded from a constitution, in which happiness and misery regularly followed virtue and vice. Patience and composure under distress, affliction, and pain; a steadfast keeping up of our confidence in God, and of our reliance upon his final goodness, at the time when every thing present is adverse and discouraging; and (what is no less difficult to retain) a cordial desire for the happiness of others, even when we are deprived of our own: these dispositions, which constitute, perhaps, the perfection of our moral nature, would not have found their proper office and object in a state of avowed retribution; and in which, consequently, endurance of evil would be only submission to punishment.

Again: one man's sufferings may be another man's trial. The family of a sick parent is a school of filial piety. The charities of domestic life, and not only these, but all the social virtues, are called out by distress. But then, misery, to be the proper object of mitigation, or of that benevolence which endeavours to relieve, must be really or apparently casual. It is upon such sufferings alone that benevolence can operate. For were there no evils in the world, but what were punishments, properly and intelligibly such, benevolence would only stand in the way of justice. Such evils consistently with the administration of moral government, could not be prevented or alleviated, that is to say, could not be remitted in whole or in part, except by the authority which inflicted them, or by an appellate or superior authority. This consideration, which is founded in our most acknowledged apprehensions of the nature of penal justice, may possess its weight in the Divine councils. Virtue perhaps is the greatest of all ends. In human beings, relative virtues form a large part of the whole. Now relative virtue presupposes, not only the existence of evil, without which it could have no object, no material to work upon, but that evils be, apparently at least *misfortunes;* that is, the effects of apparent chance. It may be in pursuance, therefore and in furtherance of the same scheme of probation, that the evils of life are made so to present themselves.

I have already observed, that, when we let in religious considerations, we often let in light upon the difficulties of nature. So in the fact now to be accounted for, the *degree* of happiness, which we usually enjoy in this life, may be better suited to a state of trial and probation, than a greater degree would be. The truth is, we are rather too much delighted with the world, than too little. Imperfect, broken, and precarious as our pleasures are, they are more than sufficient to attach us to the eager pursuit of them. A regard to a *future* state can hardly keep its place as it is. If we were designed therefore to be influenced by that regard, might not a more indulgent system, a higher, or more uninterrupted state of gratification, have interfered with the design? At least it seems expedient, that mankind should be susceptible of this influence, when presented to them: that the condition of the world should not be such, as to exclude its operation, or even to weaken it more than it does. In a religious view (however we may complain of them in every other) privation, disappointment, and satiety, are not without the most salutary tendencies.

Chapter 9: Divine Omniscience & Free Will

Comprehension questions you should be able to answer after reading this chapter:

1. What is a "reductionist materialist?"

2. What are the basic elements of "determinism?" How does it account for human behavior?

3. What is the one (important) difference between compatibilism and determinism?

4. Explain how compatibilists define "free will." What are "internal causes?" What are "external causes?"

5. Explain why there is no more "choice" ("ability to do otherwise") in compatibilism than there is in determinism.

6. Explain the agency theorist's criticism of the compatibilist definition of free will.

7. How do agency theorists define free will?

8. What is substance dualism? How would a dualistic understanding of human nature make "choice" possible?

9. What is Leibniz's Law of Identity, and how is it an argument in favor of substance dualism?

10. What is event causation? What is agent causation?

11. What is the definition of "omniscience" (as used in this chapter)?

12. What is the alleged tension between omniscience (that includes foreknowledge) and agency theorist free will?

13. In your own words, explain/paraphrase Nelson Pike's argument for the incompatibility of divine foreknowledge and agency theorist free will.

14. What does it mean to say that "future contingent claims" have an indeterminate truth value? How could this "solve" the problem of omniscience and free will?

15. According to Craig, what is the difference between "certainty" and "necessity?" Why does this mater in the context of omniscience and free will?

16. Explain what is meant by each of the following: (a) God's Natural Knowledge. (b) God's Free Knowledge. (c) God's Middle Knowledge.

17. How is Middle Knowledge supposed to "solve" the tension between divine foreknowledge and human free will?

18. What is the difference between logical priority and chronological priority?

Most of the chapters of this book have concerned arguments for (or against) God's existence. They have developed and criticized a variety of TA's in that regard. While that is the primary focus of this book, it is important to note that arguments for and against God's existence are not the sole task of philosophy of religion. We will briefly consider other activities within the philosophy of religion, beginning with this chapter, by considering the relationship between the concept of divine omniscience and human free will.

We might consider this issue to be a matter of "internal consistency" with respect to a (Western) theistic worldview. The beginning chapters of this book addressed the rationality of theistic belief, and the purpose and possible success of TA's. A central issue is whether or not a theistic worldview is rational to hold. One argument against the rationality of a theistic worldview would be to show that the implications of such a worldview contradict commonly (and persuasively) held beliefs. If we are confident that claim X is true, and a (Western) theistic worldview is inconsistent with X, that would be evidence against the truth of the theistic worldview – and by implication, it would seem irrational to continue to subscribe to that worldview.

One possible point of tension concerns a possible conflict between an aspect of human nature and an aspect of the divine nature. Although there are some important doctrinal differences between the major Western religious traditions (e.g., whether or not God is Trinitarian), there is a basic and core set of properties attributed to God shared by Islam, Judaism, and Christianity alike.

Without much controversy, we can say that the properties of omniscience, omnipotence, and omnibenevolence are attributed to God in the Western theistic traditions. With less consensus, other properties include:

- Necessity (i.e., God necessarily exists, as opposed to being a contingent being)
- Aseity (i.e., God is self-existent, independently of anything else)
- Incorporeal (i.e., God is a "spirit," nonphysical in nature)
- Omnipresence (i.e., God is not limited to any one particular physical location)
- Eternity (i.e., God has always existed and always will exist, having never come into, nor ever going out of, existence)
- Simplicity (i.e., God is undifferentiated, having no "parts")
- Immutability (i.e., God is unchanging – at least with regard to His essential properties)

For our limited purposes in this one chapter, we will focus on the property of omniscience. Specifically, we will consider whether or not an omniscient God is consistent with human free will. This will require several steps. We will need to establish an understanding of "omniscience." We will also need to establish an understanding of "free will." We then need to develop the alleged tension between these ideas, and finally consider possible "solutions." We will begin by considering the notion of free will.

Free Will

Before delving into any theories or vocabulary, before "biasing" your views with "official" philosophical positions, take a few minutes to reflect, using your own thoughts and your own vocabulary: Are you *free*? Think carefully before replying, as the issue is more complicated than it might first appear. In fact, take several minutes to reflect on the following questions, and even to jot down some notes.

1. What are ways in which you appear to be free? Why would you, or anyone, believe themselves to be free, to be in control of their own lives?
2. What are ways in which you appear to be unfree? Why would you, or anyone, believe themselves to not be in control of their own lives?
3. Finally, why does any of this matter? Aside from simple intellectual curiosity, why would someone (like your philosophy instructor by virtue of addressing this material, or me—possibly that same instructor—by virtue of writing about it) think this issue worthy of discussion? What's at stake?

If you followed instructions, you've spent a few minutes thinking about those questions, and have at least generated a mental list of answers and thoughts provoked by the exercise. If you did not follow instructions, take a few minutes a do so now. Seriously.

The reason why it's important to think through these questions yourself is because the responses we consider will make far more sense, and be much more meaningful to you, if you can see how they have connected with your own thoughts on these matters. Let's consider the first question: what are ways in which you appear to be free? Among numerous possibilities, you probably came up with reasons similar to the following (among others):

- You live in a "free country."
- You're able to make all kinds of choices, everyday, from trivial things like ordering off a restaurant menu, to pivotal decisions like whether or not to go to college.
- You have a powerful intuition of "spontaneity." That is, it seems like you can just "do something" without anything or anyone else having forced you to do it.
- You are confident that other people (and presumably yourself as well) are responsible for their actions, and you get angry or disappointed or pleased with people accordingly.

Why would you believe you are not free? You probably came up with reasons similar to the following:

- Your behavior is restricted by both laws and customs.
- Your choices are constrained by what's available to you, and, in some cases, such as when one has a serious disability, or is profoundly poor, what's available might be very little indeed.
- Your behavior might be influenced, or even fully determined, by circumstances rather than personal choices. The sort of person you are is probably very strongly influenced, maybe even established, by your life experiences—especially your childhood experiences.
- An all-knowing, all-powerful God might have "predestined" you to follow a certain path, and you, as a mere mortal, lack the ability to defy God.

Finally, why does any of this matter? You probably came up with reasons similar to the following:

- Self-concept: Your very sense of self will be impacted by whether or not you are in control of your life. Are you in control of your life, or are you simply playing out a script written by Nature, or perhaps God?
- Meaning: This is the so-called "existential" significance of freedom. If your life is not up to you in any significant way, you might wonder why it's worth living. Why bother to do anything, if it's not "you" who's responsible for whatever it is that you do?
- Responsibility: When we hold people responsible for their actions, we implicitly assume that their actions were, in some important way, of their own doing. In other words, I don't arrest you for murdering Ricky if I know that it was actually Samantha who did it. Similarly, if you are not free, if you are not in control of how your life turns out, it might not seem appropriate to think that you are responsible for your actions—even if it was clearly your own body that performed them. Without responsibility, there is no justification for praise or blame.
- Morality: Very much related to the issue of responsibility, when we make moral value judgments, and say that one should tell the truth, we are implying that one is capable of telling the truth, or telling a lie—but that telling the truth is what one *should* do. Clearly, if my life and my actions are not under my control, it makes little sense to tell me what I should or should not do. Without the ability to provide moral imperatives, what function does morality serve? The concern is that without freedom, there is no responsibility, and without responsibility, there is no (meaningful) notion of morality.
- Theology: related to both the issue of responsibility and morality, some religious worldviews (including many, if not most, of the denominations of the Western religious traditions) include a belief in Judgment. It is thought that persons are judged for their conduct and faith (or lack thereof) and receive eternal reward or punishment as a result. It is understandable to think that such judgment would

not be "fair" unless those persons are truly and meaningfully responsible for the conduct of their lives, truly and meaningfully "in control" of how they have lived.

If it wasn't obvious before, it should be obvious now: this topic is actually very important. The answers you come up with, and the position you ultimately take, has a tremendous impact on your sense of self, your view of personal responsibility, and your sense of morality itself. So, are you free? As with most philosophical questions, it depends on who you ask, and what is meant by "free."

Freedom

Before delving into any of the major philosophical theories, we should first distinguish between what we can call "political" freedom and "metaphysical" freedom. Believe it or not, grammar can help us articulate the difference.

Political Freedom	**Metaphysical Freedom**
Verb: May	Verb: Can
Focus: Permission	Focus: Ability

Political freedom refers to what we are *allowed* to do (without legal consequences) by our government (or, more generally, by whoever holds power over us). For example, in the United States, I am not free to kill my neighbor just because he's playing his radio too loud when I want to sleep. If I do, we call that murder, and I will be punished if I'm caught. I'm not permitted to kill people just because they annoy me. I'm not "free" to do so. In other countries, a person might not be free to criticize the government. They are not permitted to do so. If they do, they could get punished. In the United States, we *are* allowed to criticize the government. Political freedom varies depending on where you live. Some people have lots of political freedom, some people have very little. No one who lives in an organized community has *total* political freedom, since any community will impose some restrictions on behavior.

Political freedom is an interesting philosophical issue that gives rise to all sorts of important questions:

- How much freedom, if any, should persons enjoy?
- What sorts of restrictions on freedom are legitimate?
- When is it acceptable to limit freedom? If it's necessary to prevent a terrorist attack? If it's necessary to protect society from a "bad influence?"
- What sorts of actions are defensible in the name and pursuit of freedom? Protests? Armed revolution?

As interesting as political philosophy is, that is not our current focus. Our focus is on *metaphysical* freedom. The difference might appear subtle at first, but it's important. Consider our discussion of political freedom above. I am not free to commit murder (and neither are you). But, can't I do it anyway? Sure, I'll become a fugitive and likely suffer all kinds of negative consequences for my action, but (unfortunately) it's all too obvious that people *can* commit murder even though they are not *permitted* to do so.

When we ask if we have *free will*, we're not asking about what we *may* do, what we are *permitted* to do—we're asking about what is *possible* for us to do. For example, if it is legally permissible for me to be a famous, outgoing, beloved social superstar, but if I've inherited genes from my father that cause me to be shy, uncomfortable in public, and predisposed to introspection and seclusion, then even though I may (i.e., am allowed to) be a socialite, I can't become one. This is the sort of concern that arose before: that our lives are not under our control, that who we are, who we become, and what we do, is decided *for* us rather than *by* us.

To take a more serious example, what if serial killers truly can't help themselves? In the Showtime series Dexter that ran from 2006 until 2013, the main character is a serial killer. Dexter is an unusual sort of serial killer. He was mentored by a caring foster father and trained how to channel his murderous impulses in such a way that he only targeted rapists and murderers. His killing is still thought to be bad, but at least he only goes after those who "deserve it." Dexter has (seemingly) irresistible homicidal urges. Why? The explanation in the story is that he witnessed his own mother get murdered (with a chain saw!) before his very eyes when he was just a few years old. He was then left, unattended, for several days, sitting in a pool of his mother's blood, until he was eventually found and adopted by a police officer. The implication is clear: Dexter's traumatic childhood experience of blood and murder *caused* him to develop deviant homicidal desires that he otherwise would not have acquired. Why is Dexter a serial killer? Because of his childhood experiences over which he had no control.

Admittedly, Dexter is a fictional character, but similar sorts of psychological profiles are generated for real-life serial killers, serial rapists, child molesters, etc. Suppose, just for a moment, that there is something legitimate about such reasoning, and that people like that didn't *choose* to become serial killers, or child rapists, but found themselves to be such persons as a result of their DNA, or childhood experiences? If such a person truly can't control himself, and has no choice but to be a serial killer, does it make any sense to say that he is "free," that he is in control of his own life?

This is the sort of freedom that is at stake in the free will discussion: the freedom to be able to make one's own choices, as opposed to living out a life that is merely the product of one's DNA, or childhood, or any number of other causal influences; the freedom to be the author of your own life story, as opposed to merely being a character in a story "written" by outside forces.

With this clarified notion of metaphysical freedom in mind, go back over your responses to the reflection questions asked above, and see if anything has changed. Thinking specifically of metaphysical freedom (as opposed to political freedom), give a brief answer to those same three questions. Do you now believe you have "free will?"

Don't think that the answer to that question will be easy or obvious. The challenge posed by this question is that it appears *both* that we are free, *and* that we are not. We view the world, and our own lives, through two different perspectives—both of which seem accurate.

"Mechanistic" Perspective v. Perspective of Freedom

The first perspective we employ is the "scientific" perspective, the "mechanistic" perspective. This is the "cause-and-effect" perspective we employ all day, every day, to understand the world and its operations. According to this perspective, events are governed by the laws of physics, and if we simply understand the laws of physics well enough, and understand the antecedent conditions leading to the event well enough, we can predict with tremendous accuracy what will happen. Given sufficient information, Nature rarely surprises us. Try a simple experiment: pick up a small (non-fragile) object, such as a pencil. What will happen if you hold it up in the air, and then let it go? Have you made your prediction? Now, let it go. Let me guess: your object fell to the ground. Amazing....

Nature is orderly, reliable, predictable. This mechanistic perspective is convincing, reliable, and reinforced for us every day of our lives. We are very confident that this perspective is accurate. Now, the problem: human beings are a part of Nature. We are (ultimately) built of the very same sorts of particles (e.g., protons, neutrons, quarks, etc.) as is everything else in the universe.[172] If this perspective tells us that all objects in the universe are governed by the laws of physics, and that events are ultimately predictable, given enough information, then, if we are also objects in the universe, it would seem that we are also governed by those same laws of physics, and our actions are (in principle) equally predictable.

According to this perspective, events are the result of cause and effect relationships, not "free will." If we wouldn't describe the actions of your "small object" (e.g., a pencil) from the experiment above in terms of it "choosing" to fall to the ground, but would instead describe its actions in terms of gravitational forces, why shouldn't we use similar explanations for our own behavior, given that we are part of the same mechanistic universe?

If this were the only viewpoint, there would be no free will debate. But, we have a second perspective. This second perspective is a perspective of spontaneity and freedom. According to this perspective, I can and do make free, un-coerced choices all the time, and so do you. When I get up in the morning, go to my closet, and select which shirt to wear to work, it sure *feels* like it really was up to me, in a meaningful sense, which shirt I picked. It felt like I could have picked any one of several available shirts, but I *chose* a particular shirt. It didn't feel like a forced choice, or like I was compelled. It didn't feel like my DNA or childhood experiences caused me to pick a particular shirt. Presumably, your experience is much the same. Every day, it seems like you make free choices, like you freely choose one action rather than another.

This is the most powerful argument in favor of free will: our extraordinarily powerful and convincing intuition that we are in control of our actions (at least to a significant degree). According to this perspective, despite what we think we know about the laws of physics and how events are governed, we *appear* to be different from other things in the universe—we appear to be free to choose our actions even if other things in the universe are not.

---

[172] Note: the agency theorist will disagree with this, in an important way, as we will see later in this chapter.

What a dilemma! On the one hand, we are convinced that the mechanistic perspective is true—according to which we are *not* free, not in control of our lives. On the other hand, we are convinced that the spontaneous perspective is also true— according to which we *are* free, are in control of our lives. How do we reconcile this seemingly contradictory stance? As always, it depends on whom you ask....

Determinism

There are two broad types of determinist theories: theistic determinism, and materialist (causal) determinism.

Theistic determinism describes any theory that claims that all events that occur happen by virtue of God's design. According to this view, God has a plan for the universe and for history. God, being sovereign over all Creation, is in control. If your life turns out a certain way, it's because God willed that it be so. If taken seriously, one can see how theistic determinism (sometimes understood in terms of "destiny," "fate," or "predestination") can be seen as a threat to freedom.

If God has pre-ordained the course of your life, and you have no ability to do anything else, then wouldn't it seem like your life is not your own, that you're playing a role scripted by someone else? Granted, that someone else is God, and if your life has to be scripted by someone other than you, God's a pretty good choice—but isn't your freedom lost all the same?

Not surprisingly, theological perspectives that include predestination generate controversy with regard to personal responsibility, praise and blame, and punishment and reward. One famous example is the Calvinist notion of the "elect." The elect are those who have been predestined for salvation. Those who were not predestined for salvation will not be saved, and will go to hell. One's status (i.e., whether or not one is among the elect) is established long before one is born—and there is nothing one can do to change it. If you weren't born among the elect, you will never be among the elect. Not surprisingly, one of the most common criticisms of this aspect of Calvinist theology is that it's "unfair." Although Calvinists are certainly capable of defending their theological point of view, it seems as if a terribly important aspect of one's life (i.e., one's eternal destination) has already been established, and is outside of one's control.

Such fatalism is not restricted to theistic worldviews alone. Indeed, most so-called "determinists" tend to subscribe to purely naturalistic worldviews. If asked whether or not you have free will, the materialist determinist's (hereafter referred to as simply the determinist') answer is a resounding "no." Regarding our two competing perspectives (mechanistic, and spontaneous), the determinist claims that only the mechanistic perspective is accurate. The spontaneous perspective is an illusion. Why?

These sorts of determinists are almost invariably "*reductionist materialists.*" This means that they believe everything in the universe consists of matter (or energy), that everything is physical, and that all events are explainable solely in terms of physical processes. There is no room in the universe for non-physical things, such as minds, or souls, or spirits (or God, for that matter). Not surprisingly, such determinists are usually atheists, and will claim that our appeals to minds or souls are "folk psychological" appeals to events that would be better understood by referencing the brain instead. The "mind" is simply the brain. Our mental actions, including decision-making, are brain-events. The brain is a physical object, governed by physical laws. Therefore, the operations of the brain are just as causally determined as any other object in the universe. The formal version of this argument is as follows:

1. All physical events are entirely caused, and governed by the laws of nature.
2. Anything entirely caused, and governed by the laws of nature, is "determined."
3. Humans are purely physical things.
4. Therefore, human actions are entirely physical events.
5. Therefore, human actions are entirely caused, and governed by the laws of nature.
6. Therefore, human actions are determined.

To be "determined" in this sense is just to say that whatever it is that we do, whatever actions we take, are the products of cause and effect relationships governed by the immutable laws of physics. In the case of inanimate objects, such as comets, we recognize that their actions are not the product of anything like "choice," but are entirely determined by the past and the laws of physics. For example, if you tell an astronomer enough information about where a particular comet is right now, she can tell you where that comet will be five minutes from now, or even a hundred years from now. No one would suppose that the comet will occupy a particular portion of space because it "wants to," or because it "chooses to." Its location, its trajectory—everything about that comet and what it does—is simply a matter of the laws of physics.

We're generally fairly confident about making similar claims about non-human animals (most of them, at least). When we think about the behaviors of fish and lizards, horses and cats and dogs, and maybe even "higher" animals such as chimpanzees and gorillas, we tend to think that their behavior is governed by "instinct" as opposed to rational and intentional choice. As smart as I believe my cat to be, I imagine that much, if not all, of what she does is driven by fairly basic, hard-wired biological imperatives and drives. This is just to say that we don't hold animals to be responsible for their actions in the same sort of way that we hold humans responsible for their own. If my cat "misbehaves," I don't think she is willfully making bad "choices." At most, I think she has some behavioral patterns that need to be corrected, if possible—and I then proceed to try to condition her to behave differently.

What about humans? Well, if we're physical in the same sort of way as is everything else in the universe, then there's nothing "special" or significantly different about the human animal. We might be more sophisticated in our behavior, but we're animals all the same. Humans, too, behave as we do not by anything like "choice" but as a result of genetic programming, instinct, conditioning (experienced in childhood and throughout our lives), etc.—all of which occurs in accordance with, and as a result of, the laws of physics.

"But," you may wonder, "isn't it obvious that I have free will? If my own will, my own free choice, is not responsible for my actions, then what is?"

"Any number of things," says the determinist.

You have probably already heard of the so-called "nature v. nurture" debate. This debate focuses on whether our nature (i.e., our DNA and other important biological influences) or our nurture (i.e., our upbringing and social experiences) is more responsible for our character and behavior. Notice, by the way, that "choice" was not presented as an option in the debate! The "nature/nurture" debate, whether it intends to or nor, *already* gestures at "determinism" by implying that our behavior is the product of either our biological propensities, or our social condition, or both—neither of which is under our control, and neither of which is an expression of anything like "choice."

Let's start with "nature," and let's start simply. With non-human animals, we're usually pretty comfortable with claiming that most, if not all, of their behaviors are driven by instinct as opposed to something like rational choice. We recognize that non-human creatures, such as insects, fish, birds, and mammals all display useful behaviors that help them to survive, feed, reproduce, etc. We're probably comfortable believing that insects don't "choose" to make hives, or gather pollen, or sting large threatening creatures, but rather do such things "automatically." So, too, with birds building nests, or fish swimming in schools, or squirrels gathering and hiding food. We tend to assume that non-human animals don't run away when something surprising happens because they choose to, but instead because of an instinctive aversion to possible predators. From a purely physical perspective, a purely naturalistic perspective, aren't we just another (admittedly complicated) animal? *Homo sapiens*? Another primate? If all other animals are driven by instinct rather than rational choice, why wouldn't we draw the same conclusion about the human animal?

While scientists are a long way from proving that particular genes or gene sequences can or do determine all of our particular behaviors, it is widely believed that, at the very least, certain behavioral dispositions are linked to certain genes or gene sequences. If this is true, then whether you are shy or outgoing, friendly or aggressive, obedient or rebellious, is less a matter of how you "choose" to be than which genes you inherited from your biological parents. If there really are genes that determine certain kinds of behaviors, or simply certain kinds of personalities (which, themselves, then determine certain kinds of behaviors), then, since your genetic inheritance is in no way under your control, you would have reason to think that your behavior is *determined*.

From a purely physical perspective, we can delve deeper than DNA and consider the behavior of the sub-atomic particles of which your body is made. They bump into one another in accordance with the laws of physics, right? The effects of those collisions are likewise governed by the laws of physics. Imagine that your body is a pool table, and all the atoms of your body are pool balls (this is very abstract, I know, but bear with me). The pool balls only move if acted upon, right? One must be struck by another (or at least by *something*) before it will move. And, if we know enough about the impact, we can predict very well the outcome of the collision. In other words, we can predict which direction the struck ball will go, and with roughly what speed, and so on—and we can predict any other collisions that might result from the first. Well, can't we understand all the events and actions concerning your body, at the sub-atomic level, to be various collisions and interactions of sub-atomic particles, all of which are governed by the laws of physics? Wouldn't that imply that if we only knew enough about the circumstances just prior to, and during, the impact, we would be able to predict the outcome as well? And, if we can predict the outcome, aren't we predicting what your body is going to do? Finally, if I'm able to predict what your body is going to do, am I not predicting what *you* are going to do? If you are purely physical, as determinists believe, we have reason to think that our actions are, in principle, just as predictable as the movements of pool balls, because our own behavior is just as causally determined.

Even if we think that "nurture" is more responsible for our behavior than is "nature," we're not any better off in terms of personal choice and free will. Determinists claim that social experiences can also play a deterministic role in our actions. We respond very reliably to certain stimuli. Pain and pleasure are very predictable in how they influence what we do. Punishment and reward are simply applications of painful or pleasurable experiences for the sake of some desired behavior. This assumption governs our social institutions and family life, our personal relationships and our legal codes. We don't like to be assaulted, so we punish anyone who does so, and threaten punishment to everyone else. The threat of the painful experience of being punished for assaulting another causes most of us to play nicely with one another instead. When our children lie, or refuse to clean up their room, or speak to us disrespectfully, or anything else we might not want them to do, we punish them with a time out, or a spanking, or a stern talking-to, or by withholding a privilege such as playing video games. Our assumption is that such interventions will *cause* the child to behave differently in the future. We can "nurture" our children, as well as other adults, to behave in the ways we prefer.

The impact of social experience is especially obvious in the case of childhood experiences. Consider the following two hypothetical situations:

	Child A	**Child B**
Parents	Attentive, supportive, nurturing	Absent, critical, abusive
Home	Plenty of food, safety	Malnourishment, dangerous conditions
Education	Good schools, educational hobbies and activities	Inadequate schools, no extracurricular activities or stimulation
Other		Repeatedly molested and verbally and physically abused

Given these two hypothetical children and their imagined early childhood experiences, isn't it a reasonable assumption that their two lives are likely to turn out in very different ways? Doesn't it seem to make a difference whether or not one grows up with families dealing with addiction problems, or with poverty, or subject to abuse? Even the most zealous champions of free will must concede that such circumstances at least have an *influence* on personality and behavior. The determinist merely claims that the influence goes beyond mere inclination, and amounts to determination.

In summary, according to the theory of determinism, free will is an illusion. Choice is an illusion. Because we are composed of the same materials as everything else in the universe, we are governed by the same laws of physics as everything else in the universe. All events, without exception, are the products are cause and effect sequences—and human events are no different. Who we are, and what we do, is not "up to us" in any meaningful way, but is instead *determined* by forces outside of our control.

If the case for determinism is so compelling, why do so many people nevertheless believe in the existence of free will? One word explains it: ignorance.

Now, before you get upset, thinking that determinists are insulting you (or anyone else) who believes in free will, understand that "ignorance" is being used in its literal sense: lacking information.

Determinists will point out that humans have a long history of offering superstitious (and ultimately *false*) explanations for events during those periods of time when humans didn't truly understand the cause of those events. For example, some humans used to explain the existence of thunder by claiming that Thor, god of thunder (among other things) was banging an anvil with his hammer, *mjölnir*. Indeed, the legacy of this explanation still exists in the Swedish word for thunder: *tordön* (literally, "Thor's rumble," or "Thor's thunder"). However, I suspect very few people (if any) still think that Thor is the cause of thunder. Instead, we now understand that thunder is the sound caused by rapidly expanding waves of compressed air, which is itself caused by the heat of lightning increasing the pressure of the air along its path to many times the normal atmospheric pressure. "Magical" explanations such as the use of Thor to explain lightning is a mere placeholder until a real, scientific explanation is discovered.

Determinists think that using free will to explain human behavior is like using Thor to explain thunder: it is a superstitious non-explanation that is a mere placeholder until the actual, scientific explanation is realized.

Determinists are often sympathetic to this error. As Baron d'Holbach (a historically prominent (atheistic) determinist) puts it,

It is the great complication of motion in man, it is the variety of his action, it is the multiplicity of causes that move him, whether simultaneously or in continual succession, that persuades him he is a free agent: if all his motions were simple, if the causes that move him did not confound themselves with each other, if they were distinct, if his machine was less complicated, he would perceive that all his actions were necessary, because he would be enabled to recur instantly to the cause that made him act.[173]

In other words, given how complex a "machine" is a human being, it is very difficult for any of us to offer a precise and accurate causal explanation of every human action. Our inability to do so causes some people to infer that there is no causal explanation, and then appeal to "free will" to fill the explanatory void. But, understandable though this mistake might be, it is still a *mistake* according to determinists. On the assumption that we are built of the same fundamental particles as everything else in the universe, it would seem to follow that we are governed by the same laws of physics as everything else. If we acknowledge that cause and effect explains the operations of everything else in the universe, we should be consistent and recognize that cause and effect (and not "free will") explains everything that we do as well.

Compatibilism

If you think you understand determinism, this next theory should be pretty simple, as it's (basically) identical in every way but one. Take everything that you know about determinism, and "copy and paste" it into compatibilism—but leave out one thing: determinism's claim that we have no free will.

Compatibilists claim we *do* have free will. In fact, that's why the theory is called compatibilism: because it claims that determinism is *compatible* with free will. That's it. That's the only difference—though it's a big one.

Let's review what the two theories have in common. Most determinists believe that everything in the universe (including ourselves) is physical. So do most compatibilists. Accordingly, determinists believe that everything in the universe is subject to the laws of physics. So do compatibilists. Determinists believe that every event has a cause, and that the cause is the product of antecedent conditions as governed by the laws of physics. So do compatibilists. Determinists believe that everything that happens has been causally determined to happen and could not have turned out any other way. So do compatibilists. Determinists believe that human actions are determined, and that we lack an "ability to do otherwise." So do compatibilists. For this reason, determinists claim we have no free will. This is where the compatibilist stops agreeing.

There have been many famous compatibilists in the history of Western philosophy, including the ancient Stoics, David Hume, and Thomas Hobbes. More recently, a 20th century compatibilist, Walter Stace, introduced some helpful vocabulary.

To begin with, both Hume and Stace believe that the free will debate has arisen largely due to confusion. A sign that the free will problem is not a real problem is the fact that all of us, including self-professed determinists, live *as if* we have free will and treat other people *as if* they do as well. It's reasonable to assume that if a determinist is the victim of a crime, he or she will still get upset—*as if* the criminal is responsible for the crime, as opposed to being a mere puppet of causal determination. Ask a

---

[173] Paul Henri Thiery, Baron d'Holbach. *The System of Nature.* 1770, Chapter XI.

determinist what she'd like to drink with dinner, and watch her "choose"—*as if* it were "up to her" what she's going to pick. This all suggests that we have free will. However, if compatibilists agree with determinists that all events are causally determined, what does it mean to say that we have free will? Considering that this definition of free will amounts to the only and only significant difference between determinism and compatibilism, this definition is incredibly important.

"Common usage" will be the key to understanding how it's possible both that we have free will, *and* that determinism is true. Compatibilists like Stace believe that there are correct and incorrect definitions of terms, proper and improper uses of words. When a word is used improperly, all kinds of interesting (and ridiculous) conclusions can be produced.

1. Humans are five-legged primates.
2. There are no five-legged primates.
3. Therefore, there are no humans.

In terms of its logical structure (validity), this argument is flawless—and yet, I'm confident that not a single person reading that argument accepts the conclusion as true. What's the problem with the argument? Go for the obvious answer: humans are *not* five-legged primates! If humans were five-legged primates, then it would follow that there are no humans—but that's not the case. To challenge the conclusion of this argument, it's not necessary to prove that humans exist. All that's necessary is to point out that the definition of "human" being used is incorrect. "Incorrect according to who?" you might ask. Incorrect according to *"common usage."*

Although it's true that one can, in a certain sense, define a word however one pleases, that doesn't mean anyone else will take you seriously should you do so. Language, after all, is an essentially cooperative project. Words acquire and have their meaning in large part by how they are used within a community of people speaking the same language and using those same words. "Five-legged primate" doesn't correspond to the common usage of "human," so it's an incorrect definition. Stace believes that philosophers have created false problems by failing to comply with the common usage of certain terms. The solution to these problems will be to correct the definition so that it does conform to common usage.

How does this apply to the free will problem? Determinists have defined free actions as those that are *not* causally determined. Looking around the world, they find no actions that are not causally determined. As a result, they conclude that there are no free actions. Compatibilists claim that "not being causally determined" is an incorrect definition of free will. They will appeal to common usage to establish the correct definition of free will and, having done so, are confident that we will recognize both that determinism is true *and* that we have free will.

At the beginning of the chapter, you were asked to consider ways in which you are free, and also ways in which you are not. With those thoughts in mind, participate in this follow-up exercise.

1. Think of a time in your life when you thought that you were not free, or that your freedom had been reduced, or challenged. What were the

circumstances?

2. Think of the sorts of situations in which we say that people are not free. What are the properties of those situations?

3. Think of the sorts of circumstances in which we do not think people are responsible for their actions. What are the properties of those circumstances?

4. Think of a time in your life when you thought that you *were* free. What were the circumstances?

Understand that participating in this sort of exercise isn't "busy work." For Stace, it's an essential step in his argument. Remember, his definitional standard is common usage. How do *you* ("commonly") use the word "free?" If you're anything like Stace, your answers to questions 1-4 above will have a few things in common. Compatibilists believe that your examples and thoughts on freedom will probably look like the following:

Lack of freedom: being in jail, being held prisoner, not being allowed to engage in desirable activities—in essence, not being able to do what you want to do.

Freedom: no (or few) constraints on activities—in essence, being able to do what you want to do.

Responsible: when someone acts "on purpose," intentionally, from their own desires.

Not responsible: when someone acts unintentionally, "by accident," contrary to their own desires

Compatibilists would point out that there's nothing deeply philosophical, mysteriously metaphysical, or terribly complicated about this understanding of freedom and responsibility. When we are able to do what we *want* to do, we call that "freedom." When someone or something prevents us from doing what we want to do, or when someone or something forces us to do something we do not want to do, we call that not being free (or being oppressed, or forced, or coerced, etc.).

Let's look at a simple and timely example: are you free to stop reading this paragraph right now? Yes, or no? I would assume that almost anyone would say yes. After all, nothing is stopping you from stopping your reading, right? No one has immobilized your head, propped open your eyeballs, pointed them at the words you're reading, and prevented you from stopping, right? *Right?* (If your answer is "wrong," please call 911 as soon as possible) If you wanted to stop reading, you could, right?

In fairness, I can imagine someone might think "no," but what that person would mean by that is something like this: "It's possible for me to stop reading, but I 'must' keep reading or else I won't understand the material, I'll get behind in the work, and my grade will suffer." In other words, there are undesirable consequences for stopping. Those undesirable consequences inspire continued reading. Compatibilists wouldn't deny this, but they would point out that there's a big difference between someone physically preventing you from stopping your reading, and there being a good reason for you to continue. If you doubt that it's possible for you to stop, try this simple little experiment. STOP READING! For the next ten seconds, do something else. Go to the bathroom, get a drink, rest your eyes, whatever—but stop reading.

If you tried, I bet you were able to do it. This was just a long-winded way of demonstrating that you are reading right now because you *want* to.

I'm not naïve. I don't presume that you "want to" in the sense that you are eagerly soaking up every word and can't wait to get to the next page. But, at the very least, you want to read these words right now because doing so serves some other desire of yours (e.g., getting a good grade in a philosophy class, learning about compatibilism, etc.)—and for that reason you are still doing what you want to do. Clearly, if you wanted to do something else more, you would be doing that "something else" instead.

Putting all this together, a compatibilist would say that your reading right now is a "free action," because you are doing what you want to do. If someone snatches the book (or computer screen) away from you and won't give it back, you can no longer do what you want to do. You're no longer free to read.

In summary, we are free when we can do what we want to do, and we are unfree when we can't, or when we are forced to do something we don't want to do. We are free when there are no external constraints on our ability to act on our desires. This is our first, crude, compatibilist definition of freedom—and one that conforms to "common usage," it would seem.

The compatibilist definition of freedom is more complicated, of course. Remember, determinists believe that all events are causally determined, and for that reason there is no free will. Compatibilists agree with everything about determinism except the claim about there being no free will. That means that compatibilists *also* believe that all events are causally determined. Whether an action is free, or unfree, it will be the result of a causally determined sequence. Rather than distinguish free actions from unfree actions by saying that some actions are caused, and some are not, compatibilists will distinguish them on the basis of *what kind* of cause is the immediate (antecedent, or "proximate") cause of the event in question. To understand how this works, go back to the example of reading this section.

Let's suppose that you want to continue reading, and you do, in fact, continue to read. That sounds like being "free," right? You're able to do what you want: to continue reading. Is there a *cause* of your continuing to read? Of course there is. You continue to read because you want to. Is there a cause for you wanting to read? Of course there is. Maybe it's because you want to understand the material. Is there a cause for that? Maybe you want to get a good grade. Is there a cause for you wanting to get a good grade? Perhaps the cause is that you want to someday have a good job. Is there a cause for you wanting a good job? Perhaps its cause is a desire for financial security. Is there a cause for that desire? Maybe you grew up in a home where money was tight, and you learned the importance of being financially secure. Was there a cause for the money being "tight" in your home, growing up? Of course there was. This sequence goes on and on, far into the past long before you were born—in principle, all the way back to the very beginning of the universe. On this analysis, then, free actions certainly have causes—indeed, *every* event has a cause.

What about unfree actions? What would have to happen if we were to say you were *not* free to continue reading? Maybe you're reading this section on a computer, and the computer crashes, making it impossible for you to continue reading right now. Is there a cause for you being not free to read? Certainly: the computer crashed. Is there a cause for that? Maybe there was a power failure. Is there a cause for that? Maybe there was a lightning strike on a power line someplace. Is there a cause for the lightning strike? There was an electrical discharge from clouds. Is there a cause for that? Of course—and again, this sequence will go back far into the past, in principle to the very beginning of the universe. Unfree actions also have causes.

If this is so, then the difference between free and unfree actions isn't the difference between one kind of action being caused, and the other kind of action being uncaused. Instead, the difference will be the *kind* of cause.

The cause of your freely continuing to read was your own desire to read. Stace calls this kind of cause an "internal" cause because it's literally *internal* with respect to your body. Your desire is a product of some event in your brain. Your brain is inside your skull—hence, an "internal" cause.

What about when you were not free to continue reading? The cause, in that case, was "external." The computer crashing was an outside force (meaning, outside your body—unless you have an odd way of storing your computer!) that prevented you from acting on your desire.

The most common sorts of internal causes will be psychological states of various kinds: desires, motivations, beliefs, etc. External causes will include any causes that are external to your body, such as a power failure, a locked door, a car that won't start, handcuffs, a bouncer who is literally throwing you out of a bar, etc. If we want to know if an action is free or unfree, we can consult the following steps:

1. Identify the action under investigation
   - Example: falling off a bridge to one's watery death below
2. Identify the immediate/antecedent cause of the action
   - Example 1a: the deceased wanted to die
   - Example 1b: the deceased was knocked off balance by a gust of wind
3. Determine whether the immediate/antecedent cause was "internal" or "external"
   - Example 1a: internal cause (one's own suicidal desire)
   - Example 1b: external cause (gust of wind)
4. If the immediate cause is internal, the action was freely done. If the immediate cause was external, it was probably not freely done.
   - Example 1a: suicide (the deceased is responsible)
   - Example 1b: accidental death (not responsible)
5. Or, as a short cut that works most of the time, just ask yourself: did the person do "it" (whatever "it" is) because she *wanted* to? If yes, then the action was freely done, by definition. If no, then it was probably not freely done.

Notice how this evaluation produces results consistent with our common sense intuitions. If someone falls off a bridge because he wanted to die, we call that a suicide attempt. We recognize that the person did it on purpose, and, if the person survives, we'll probably try to convince them not to do that again. On the other hand, if the person falls off the bridge because of a gust of wind, we call that an accident. If the person survives, we probably wouldn't see any need for suicide counseling because we would recognize that they didn't go over the edge on purpose.

Given this understanding of freedom, we can now see why compatibilists believe we have free will: we act freely *all the time*. For most of us, our usual experience is that we do things because we want to. Even unpleasant things like going to the dentist are still things we "want" to do for the sake of avoiding future tooth pain. We exercise our free will countless times every single day. Every time you do something because you want to, that is a free act, according to compatibilism. Thankfully, few of us encounter serious or prolonged limitations of our freedom. Most of us don't get kidnapped, or get locked up in a cage, or are forced to do something against our will. When such things do happen, we say that we weren't free, and we tend to take those sorts of events very seriously!

Now it's time for the "tricky" part.

It's very important to always keep in mind that the *only* (significant) difference between determinism and compatibilism is that determinists say there is no free will, and compatibilists say that there is.

According to determinism, your actions are all the result of antecedent causes as governed by the laws of physics. In principle, we can know what will happen in the future if we only had enough information about the past, and a sufficient understanding of the laws of physics. With inanimate objects, this is easily illustrated. In fact, whether the writers intended to or not, this was illustrated in the 2006 Adam Sandler movie, "Click."

In "Click," Sandler's character (Michael Newman) acquires a fantastic "universal remote control" that allows him to manipulate reality as if it were a video or digital recording. He can fast forward, rewind, and "pause" reality (among other things). In one scene, he takes advantage of the pause feature to gain some vengeance on an older child who has been making fun of his own younger son. The two children are tossing a baseball back and forth. When his son throws it, and the older boy raises his glove to catch it, Michael pauses the flow of time. Somehow personally immune to the "pause," he walks over and pushes the older boy's glove down a few inches. He steps back to where he had been standing, presses pause again (so that time continues to "play"), and watches as the baseball strikes the boy in the face, as the glove is no longer in the way to catch it. The only way that this physical comedy makes any sense is by virtue of the fact that Michael was able to predict where the ball would be, thanks to his knowledge of where the ball had been, and his common-sense understanding of the laws of physics. Because the ball was governed entirely by causal forces, knowledge of the ball's past plus knowledge of the laws of physics at work on the ball at that instant provided an accurate prediction of the future.

Each one of us makes use of this common sense understanding and predictive ability every day. If you knock a glass off a counter, and your reflexes are quick enough to do something about it, you intuitively "calculate" where you need to put your hand in your attempt to catch the glass. As the glass falls towards the ground, you are very, very confident that in the next second or so that glass is going to move a little bit closer to the ground, along the same path it's following. You would never think that it might, instead, suddenly fly several feet straight out to one side or another. Because you can perceive where the glass is at one moment in time, and what it's doing, and because of your basic understanding of the laws of physics, you can predict with very reliable accuracy where that glass will be in the near future.

We can make this common sense understanding more sophisticated by adding some technical vocabulary. Imagine that it's possible to freeze time, like in that movie I mentioned. Imagine that that single frozen split second of time provides a picture of the entire universe at that precise moment—like a single frame of a film. Call this the "total world picture," or TWP. If the determinist worldview is accurate (and both determinists and compatibilists believe that it is), then *if* we had access to (and understanding of) the TWP at a particular instant in time (TWP_1), and we had an adequate understanding of the laws of physics, we would know just what the next instant in time (TWP_2) will look like (i.e., what will be happening at TWP_2). In other words, we would be able to predict the future. Of course, none of us has the ability to predict the future with perfect accuracy, but that's easy enough to explain: none of us has full knowledge of the TWP at any particular instant in time, nor (probably) a perfect understanding of the laws of physics.

Because the future is the inevitable product of the past and the laws of physics, the future is "fixed." Although you and I don't *know* what the future holds, that's a feature of our own (understandable) ignorance, not any indication that the future is somehow "open" or not determined. There is one (inevitable and unyielding) path that the future can take, and it was "determined" at the very moment the universe came into existence. There are no alternate paths, no forks in the road, no options. The future is "fixed"—and that includes your own future as well. It's worth repeating: everything claimed about the TWP and the predictability of future events is believed by *both* determinists and compatibilists.

Remember those free and unfree actions, as described by compatibilists? You're free if you stop reading because that's what you want to do. You're unfree when you stop reading because your computer crashes, despite your desire to continue. Recall that both free and unfree events have causes. In other words, both are part of the TWP, and both are the inevitable (and theoretically predictable) products of a prior TWP and the laws of physics.

At TWP_I, you stop reading because you wanted to stop. The immediate cause is internal, and it's a free action. At TWP_{I-1}, you formed the desire to stop reading because your eyes had become tired. If someone had access to the information in TWP_{I-1}, that person would have been able to predict your stopping reading at TWP_I. At TWP_{I-2}, your eyes became tired due to some biological cause (we don't have to know exactly what it is, for the sake of this discussion). If someone had known the contents of TWP_{I-2}, he would have been able to predict the formation of your desire to stop reading at TWP_{I-1}. At TWP_{I-3}, the cause of your eyes getting tired was itself caused by some other event. If someone had known the contents of TWP_{I-3}, he would have been able to predict your eyes getting tired. We could repeat this sequence a split second further into the past each time, until eventually (at who knows when,

TWP$_{I-1\text{ million}}$?) we would reach a TWP of a time before your birth. Theoretically, we could keep going backwards until we reached TWP$_1$—the very first split second of time after the Big Bang. That means that someone with knowledge of TWP$_1$ could predict TWP$_2$, TWP$_3$, TWP$_4$ (etc.), and could therefore ultimately predict TWP$_I$: the split second in which you stopped reading because you *wanted* to.

There is nothing else you could have done at TWP$_I$, given all those previous TWPs. It was causally necessitated that you stop reading, and your life (at that moment) could not have turned out any way. There is no possible way you could have done anything different (like, continue to read, for example). This very same analysis applies to actions coming from external causes as well. That computer crash is part of a TWP just like everything else, and we could run the same backwards analysis, or the same prediction sequence starting at the Big Bang, whether the cause of the event in question is external, or internal. In other words, whether the action was free, or unfree, it was causally necessitated and couldn't have turned out any other way.

It's absolutely critical to understand this point. Compatibilism is very easily misunderstood, and when (and if) it is misunderstood, it's always misunderstood in the same sort of way: by overestimating the difference between determinism and compatibilism, and by mistakenly believing that compatibilists believe that we have genuine "choice" as opposed to all our actions being the causally necessitated result of antecedent events/causes.

There is no "choice" in compatibilism. Unfortunately, some compatibilists misleadingly claim otherwise. They will say that one could have chosen otherwise if one had desired otherwise. In other words, you could have done something else if you had wanted to do something else.

"Could I have chosen to continue reading, instead of stopping?" Absolutely! So long as you had wanted to continue reading, instead of stopping. Recall, however, that your desires are just as causally determined, just as much a necessary product of a previous TWP, as anything else. Your desires couldn't have been any different, unless your past had been different. Pretty clearly, you have no control over your past. It's not as if you can reach back through time and change your childhood experiences so that you have different desires in the present.

Normally, when we say that we have a "choice," it means that we have an "ability to do otherwise"—it means there are multiple options, and it really is possible for us to exercise any of them.

We simply do *not* have "choice," in that sense, according to compatibilism.

In fairness, the compatibilist will say that this doesn't matter. According to common usage, we are free when we are able to do what we want to do (i.e., when we act from internal causes). An ability to do otherwise, an ability that requires that we have the power to resist the causal necessity that governs everything in nature, is not what we "commonly" mean by freedom—or so the compatibilist claims. According to compatibilists, when we say we acted "freely" (as opposed to under coercion), we're not suggesting that we somehow exercised some magical ability to ignore the laws of physics and the causal necessity that governs all reality. Instead, all we're saying is that we did something because we wanted to, on purpose, intentionally, of our own will, etc. That is the "common usage" of "freedom" in the context of free actions. If someone wants to understand "freedom" as the ability to be immune to the laws of physics, then that person will have effectively defined free will out of existence (as compatibilists claim the determinists have done)—but why should the rest of us accept that needlessly "metaphysical" definition of free will? Isn't it the case that our usage of words like "free" and "unfree," "voluntary" and "involuntary" just indicate the much simpler, much more common-sense, and much more *real* experience of sometimes doing things because we want to, and other times being prevented from acting on our desires?

Because the only difference between determinism and compatibilism is the definition of freedom, your evaluation of compatibilism will depend almost exclusively on what you think of that definition. What do *you* mean by freedom? Are you free so long as you are able to do what you want to do—even if your actions, and the desires that produce them, couldn't have turned out any other way? If your answer is yes, you just might be a compatibilist. If, on the other hand, you think that freedom requires genuine "choice," a genuine "ability to do otherwise," then compatibilism isn't going to satisfy your standards of freedom.

Agency Theory

If you believe that you *do* have free will, but you disagree with the compatibilist interpretation of freedom, you might be an "agency theorist." Indeed, I would guess that most people in the West are at least implicitly agency theorists (whether they realize it or not, and whether agency theory is *correct*, or not—and this is almost certainly the case with those who endorse a Western theistic worldview.).

Most, but not all, agency theorists embrace a dualistic understanding of human nature. This means that, unlike (most) determinists and (most) compatibilists, agency theorists do not believe that human beings are purely physical. There is something about persons that can't be reduced to purely physical explanations, that goes beyond physiology and physics. There are many different names for this "something-that-can't-be-reduced-to-purely-physical-explanation:'"soul," "mind," "spirit," "self," or "will."

Depending on who you ask, those terms could all have different meanings, but, for our purposes, each could capture that "something" that agency theorists have in mind.

Whatever "it" is, it is *non-physical*. Call it mental, or spiritual, or simply non-physical—in any case, it does not share the same properties as physical things, and is not subject to physical laws in the same manner as are bodies.

This exception is of profound importance. Because the mind (or whatever you prefer to call it) is not physical, it is not subject to the laws of physics. Because it is not subject to the laws of physics, it is not bound by causal determinism. Therefore, there is something about us—perhaps that which is most fundamental to us—that is outside the scope of determinism. This exception creates the space for a powerful version of free will.

Substance Dualism

Why should anyone believe in this dualistic understanding of human nature?

Although the idea that humans are non-physical souls (or minds) inhabiting physical bodies is a popular point of view, especially amongst people of faith, it is nevertheless an admittedly mysterious idea, and one that seemingly defies our experience of the world in terms of purely physical objects governed by the laws of nature.

The greatest challenge for, and criticism of, agency theorist accounts of free will is their reliance upon this dualistic understanding of human nature. We will therefore spend a small amount of time considering why anyone might accept this view, before returning to the particular issue of free will.

Anecdotally, and conventionally, for most people, their use of language betrays a dualistic understanding of human nature. Most of us do not identify ourselves with our bodies, either with particular parts nor even our body as a whole. We speak of our bodies (and their parts) as objects, as possessions. "*My* stomach hurts." "I *lost* a tooth." "*My* hair is too long." "You *have* a nice body."[174]

The two basic possible understandings of human nature we will consider in this section are the *reductionist materialist* understanding of human nature, and the *substance dualist* understanding of human nature.

According to *substance dualism*, the brain is a physical object with physical properties, but the mind (or soul) is a *mental substance with mental properties*. If we take a sensation, such as pain, that pain sensation will be understood both as a physical event, in terms of certain electro-chemical properties and events in the physical brain, as well as a mental event—the conscious awareness of pain—for the non-physical mind. If this view of human nature is accurate, then several interesting things might follow:

- Although the mind (somehow) interacts with the body, it is not identical to the body.
- The mind "transcends" the body and its experiences, and is identical to none of them in particular. Therefore, the same mind can persist through time and experience (and bodily change), thereby preserving personal identity.
- Because the mind is not the body, it is possible for the mind to continue to exist after the death/destruction of the body (i.e., an "afterlife" is possible).

On the reductionist materialist interpretation of human nature, in contrast, "mental things" (e.g., thoughts, desires, etc.) are nothing other than physical things (e.g., particular sequences of neurons activating in the brain), and "mental events" (e.g., believing, desiring, etc.) are also merely brain events.

If there are any exceptions to this pattern (i.e., that every "mental" event is merely

---

[174] In fairness, we shouldn't always read too much into the conventions of language. After all, we also still speak of the sun setting and rising, as though the sun were moving around the Earth, rather than the other way around. It's possible that language just hasn't caught up to a scientifically accurate understanding of human nature just yet.

a brain event); if some claim ("X") is true with respect to some mental state, but is not true with respect to a brain state, then it would establish that *not all* mental activity is reducible to brain activity, and this would be an argument *in favor* of substance dualism.

This reasoning relies upon a principle known as Leibniz's Law of Identity, and will be a central feature of the argument for substance dualism. *According to Lebiniz's Law of Identity, two things are the same if, and only if, they have all the same properties at the same time.*

If you prefer a fancier formulation, "*x* is identical to *y* if, and only if, for any property *p* attributable to *x* at time *t*, *p* is also attributable to *y* at time *t*."

For example, if Darth Vader is identical to Anakin Skywalker, then any property attributable to one (e.g., being the father of Luke and Leia) must also be attributable to the other. If *every* property attributable to one, is also attributable to the other, without exception, then they are identical. If, however, there are any properties attributable to one, but not the other (e.g., "being the smuggler who was frozen in carbonite"), then they are not identical. That is a fancy way of proving that Anakin Skywalker and Darth Vader are the same person, but Darth Vader and Han Solo are not the same person. While the properties of Star Wars characters are not particularly relevant to our topic, Leibniz's Law of Identity is.

The reductionist materialist claims that minds and brains are identical, that there is no distinct, non-physical mind or soul because we are all (and only) bodies. On a purely reductionist materialist understanding of human nature (i.e., the understanding employed by most determinists and compatibilists), "I" (along with everything else in the universe) am fully describable using the language of physics and chemistry. I am an object (a body) that is extended in a particular portion of space, with a certain shape, mass, size, etc. "I" am my body (in general), but probably especially my brain (and possibly my central nervous system).

If we apply Leibniz's Law of Identity, then, if minds are really just brains, then any property true of "minds" must also be true of brains (or at least of bodies, more generally). If, however, there are any properties that are true of minds but are *not* true of brains/bodies, then minds and brains are *not* identical—and the substance dualist can then argue that while bodies are physical, minds are non-physical.

Substance dualists usually offer several examples of mind-properties that are not also brain-properties (or vice versa). Two examples we will consider come from Rene Descartes.

...

> 4. But I do not yet know with sufficient clearness what I am, though assured that I am; and hence, in the next place, I must take care, lest perchance I inconsiderately substitute some other object in room of what is properly myself, and thus wander from truth, even in that knowledge (cognition) which I hold to be of all others the most certain and evident. For this reason, I will now consider anew what I formerly believed myself to be, before I entered on the present train of thought; and of my previous opinion I will retrench all that can in the least be invalidated by the grounds of doubt I have adduced, in order that there may at length remain nothing but what is certain and indubitable.
>
> 5. What then did I formerly think I was? Undoubtedly I judged that I was a

man. But what is a man? Shall I say a rational animal? Assuredly not; for it would be necessary forthwith to inquire into what is meant by animal, and what by rational, and thus, from a single question, I should insensibly glide into others, and these more difficult than the first; nor do I now possess enough of leisure to warrant me in wasting my time amid subtleties of this sort. I prefer here to attend to the thoughts that sprung up of themselves in my mind, and were inspired by my own nature alone, when I applied myself to the consideration of what I was. In the first place, then, I thought that I possessed a countenance, hands, arms, and all the fabric of members that appears in a corpse, and which I called by the name of body. It further occurred to me that I was nourished, that I walked, perceived, and thought, and all those actions I referred to the soul; but what the soul itself was I either did not stay to consider, or, if I did, I imagined that it was something extremely rare and subtile, like wind, or flame, or ether, spread through my grosser parts. As regarded the body, I did not even doubt of its nature, but thought I distinctly knew it, and if I had wished to describe it according to the notions I then entertained, I should have explained myself in this manner: By body I understand all that can be terminated by a certain figure; that can be comprised in a certain place, and so fill a certain space as therefrom to exclude every other body; that can be perceived either by touch, sight, hearing, taste, or smell; that can be moved in different ways, not indeed of itself, but by something foreign to it by which it is touched [and from which it receives the impression]; for the power of self-motion, as likewise that of perceiving and thinking, I held as by no means pertaining to the nature of body; on the contrary, I was somewhat astonished to find such faculties existing in some bodies.

6. But [as to myself, what can I now say that I am], since I suppose there exists an extremely powerful, and, if I may so speak, malignant being, whose whole endeavors are directed toward deceiving me? Can I affirm that I possess any one of all those attributes of which I have lately spoken as belonging to the nature of body? After attentively considering them in my own mind, I find none of them that can properly be said to belong to myself. To recount them were idle and tedious. Let us pass, then, to the attributes of the soul. The first mentioned were the powers of nutrition and walking; but, if it be true that I have no body, it is true likewise that I am capable neither of walking nor of being nourished. Perception is another attribute of the soul; but perception too is impossible without the body; besides, I have frequently, during sleep, believed that I perceived objects which I afterward observed I did not in reality perceive. Thinking is another attribute of the soul; and here I discover what properly belongs to myself. This alone is inseparable from me. I am--I exist: this is certain; but how often? As often as I think; for perhaps it would even happen, if I should wholly cease to think, that I should at the same time altogether cease to be. I now admit nothing that is not necessarily true. I am therefore, precisely speaking, only a thinking thing, that is, a mind (mens sive animus), understanding, or reason, terms whose signification was before unknown to me. I am, however, a real thing, and really existent; but what thing? The answer was, a thinking thing.

7. The question now arises, am I aught besides? I will stimulate my imagination with a view to discover whether I am not still something more than a thinking being. Now it is plain I am not the assemblage of members called the human body; I am not a thin and penetrating air diffused through all these members, or wind, or flame, or vapor, or breath, or any of all the things I can imagine; for I supposed that all these were not, and, without changing the supposition, I find that I still feel assured of my existence. But it is true, perhaps, that those very things which I suppose to be non-existent, because they are unknown to me, are not in truth different from myself whom I know. This is a point I cannot determine, and do not now enter into any dispute regarding it. I can only judge of things that are known to me: I am conscious that I exist, and I who know that I exist inquire into what I am. It is, however, perfectly certain that the knowledge of my existence, thus precisely taken, is not dependent on things, the existence of which is as yet unknown to me: and consequently it is not dependent on any of the things I can feign in imagination. Moreover, the phrase itself, I frame an image (efffingo), reminds me of my error; for I should in truth frame one if I were to imagine myself to be anything, since to imagine is nothing more than to contemplate the figure or image of a corporeal thing; but I already know that I exist, and that it is possible at the same time that all those images, and in general all that relates to the nature of body, are merely dreams [or chimeras]. From this I discover that it is not more reasonable to say, I will excite my imagination that I may know more distinctly what I am, than to express myself as follows: I am now awake, and perceive something real; but because my perception is not sufficiently clear, I will of express purpose go to sleep that my dreams may represent to me the object of my perception with more truth and clearness. And, therefore, I know that nothing of all that I can embrace in imagination belongs to the knowledge which I have of myself, and that there is need to recall with the utmost care the mind from this mode of thinking, that it may be able to know its own nature with perfect distinctness.

8. But what, then, am I? A thinking thing, it has been said. But what is a thinking thing? It is a thing that doubts, understands, [conceives], affirms, denies, wills, refuses; that imagines also, and perceives.[175]

1. Minds (unlike bodies) are "knowable."

Rene Descartes (pronounced: "ruh-nay day-cart") is one of the most famous and respected philosophers of the Western tradition. A true renaissance man, he was an accomplished philosopher, scientist, and mathematician. He was also, by all accounts, a pious Catholic. During his lifetime, academic skepticism experienced a resurgence of popularity. Skepticism was threatening for a man like Descartes. After all, skepticism claims that we can never know anything with certainty. This would include scientific claims, mathematical claims, and religious claims. One of Descartes primary aims, then, was to prove skepticism wrong, to establish that knowledge is, in fact, possible. To prove this point, he employed an interesting (and ironic) strategy: adopt skepticism.

Descartes was not entirely hostile to skepticism. He recognized the value of

---

[175] Descartes, Rene. *Meditations on First Philosophy.* 1641, meditation 2.

subjecting our beliefs to scrutiny, and not falling prey to naïve beliefs or unwarranted superstitions. Indeed, he went so far as to claim that everyone, at some point in his or her life, should question everything they had believed up to that point, put every belief to the test, and continue on only with those beliefs that had survived the trial.

To defeat skepticism, Descartes put all his own beliefs to the test, using the most potent skeptic techniques he could muster. His goal was to question everything, and see if anything survived that process. If anything did, it would establish that knowledge is possible, because it would show that there are some things (or some thing) that can't be doubted. Obviously, he couldn't doubt every one of his beliefs, one at a time. He would die long before he made any meaningful progress. Instead, he would subject his beliefs to doubt in broad categories, by employing a handful of skeptical arguments. It's important to remember, though, that although Descartes adopts skeptical techniques, his ultimate goal was to *defeat* skepticism.

His method of "radical doubt" is to call into question all of his beliefs, in large groups. He does so with a series of arguments meant to inspire doubt. One is rooted in the unreliability of the senses, another in the vivacity of dreams, another in the compelling nature of delusions, and the final argument even postulates the existence of an evil, deceptive demon! Each argument is presented below, in a formal fashion, with all claims numbered.

Descartes was no skeptic, but he did do a very convincing job of pretending to be one. By the end of his process of radical doubt, it's hard to see how we could be certain of *anything*—but Descartes thinks he can be. The one thing that survives the skeptic process is possibly the most famous slogan in Western philosophy—a quotation so famous that almost everyone has heard it (though few fully understand it): *Cogito Ergo Sum.*

Cogito ergo sum—I think, therefore I am (or, I think, therefore I exist). Try to doubt that the cogito is true. Seriously. As a thought experiment, right now, try to convince yourself that you do not exist.

You failed, didn't you? Of course you did. If it wasn't obvious why, ask yourself this: who was doing the convincing?

Obviously, in order to try to convince yourself of something, you have to exist at the time you're trying to convince yourself! Similarly, Descartes recognized that it was impossible for him to doubt the truth of the cogito, at least whenever he thought about it, because the very act of thinking about it proved that he was existing at that time. In other words, in order to believe anything, true or false, he has to exist at the time. He can't doubt his own existence (whenever he's thinking) because the very act of doubt establishes his existence. That he exists (when thinking) is something that he can't doubt, no matter how hard he tries. If he can't doubt it, he's *certain* that it's true.

Descartes then proceeds to analyze just *what* he is, this "self" that he knows to exist whenever it thinks. He does some conceptual analysis of himself, as that thing that exists whenever it exists. "But what then am I? A thing that thinks. What is that? A thing that doubts, understands, affirms, denies, wills, refuses, and which also imagines and senses." This "thing" he identifies as a mind. His essence, as a mind, is to think. To say that thinking is his essence is to say that if thinking were removed from his mind, as a property, it would cease to be a mind. As Descartes puts it:

[S]eeing that I could pretend that I had no body and that there was no world nor any place where I was, but that I could not pretend, on that account, that I did not exist; and that, on the contrary, from the very fact that I thought about doubting the truth of other things, it followed very evidently and very certainly that I existed....From this I knew that I was a substance the whole essence or nature of which was merely to think, and which, in order to exist, needed no place and depended on no material things. Thus this 'I,' that is, the soul through which I am what I am, is entirely distinct from the body...[176]

In summary, Descartes knows that at least one mind exists (namely, himself!). Therefore, he knows minds exist. Bodies, on the other hand, are not *known* to exist. So-called physical objects might just be figments of his imagination, hallucinations, dreams, or even the deception of an "evil demon." Descartes can't even be certain that his own body exists. Perhaps he is a disembodied soul that is only imagining that he has a physical body? Maybe the entire physical world, and even object within it, is simply an illusion, a projection of Descartes' own mind? These are all far-fetched possibilities, to be sure—but the point remains that they are *possible*. The existence of bodies can be doubted, but the existence of minds can't be doubted. Descartes knows minds exist, but he doesn't know bodies exist.

Recall Leibniz's Law of Identity: two things are the same if, and only if, they have all the same properties at the same time. One property of minds is "indubitability" (not capable of being doubted), but bodies lack this property—instead, one of their properties is the opposite: "dubitability." Some of the properties of bodies (including brains) don't seem to apply to minds, and vice versa. According to Leibniz's law, therefore, minds and bodies/brains are not identical.

2.   Minds and bodies have different essential properties.

This second example is very much related to our first. Descartes has analyzed himself as a mind, whose essence is to think. Bodies, in contrast, have a different essence. "Thinking" is certainly not essential to bodies, but "extension" (being extended in space) *is*. "I enumerate the [extended] thing's various parts. I ascribe to these parts certain sizes, shapes, positions, and movements from place to place; to these movements I ascribe various durations." Bodies, unlike minds, are describable in terms of properties that are quantifiable, and are therefore capable of being objects of scientific study.

Again, recall Leibniz's Law of Identity: two things are the same if, and only if, they have all the same properties at the same time. One property of minds (indeed, the *essential* property of minds) is thinking—but thinking is *not* an essential property of bodies, or even one of the properties of bodies at all (in most cases, to be sure, such as is the case with all inanimate, non-sentient bodies in the universe). Similarly, extension is a property of bodies (including brains)—indeed, it's the essential property of bodies—but being extended is *not* a property of minds. How much space does your mind fill? What part of space? What is the particular shape of your mind?

---

[176] Descartes, *Discourse on Method*. 1637, Part 4.

Some of the properties of bodies (including brains) don't seem to apply to minds, and vice versa. According to Leibniz's law, therefore, minds and bodies/brains are not identical.

In addition to these two "metaphysical" arguments, substance duelists can also appeal to intuition. With the possible exception of sociopaths, each one of us has a powerful set of intuitions concerning personal responsibility. We hold others responsible for their actions, as though they had a choice. When someone does something "bad," we get angry, or disappointed. This only makes sense, is only fair, if the person could have acted otherwise. Similarly, when we, ourselves, do something we think we shouldn't have, we feel guilty—but this only makes sense if we had a choice. Praise and blame each only make sense on the presupposition of choice, and personal responsibility. It makes no more sense to praise someone for doing something he could not help but do than it makes sense to praise me for having been born. In both cases, no choice was involved. The fact that we punish people for wrongdoing seems to presuppose personal responsibility. Otherwise, how is it fair to condemn people for actions they had no choice but to do? Finally, even the very notion of "right" and "wrong," good" and "bad" presupposes choice. A basic principle of ethics is that "ought implies can." That is, it only makes sense to say that someone ought to do something, if it is possible for that person to actually do it. Unless I have genuine choices in my life, it makes no sense to speak of what I "ought" to do.

All of these experiences of very powerful intuitions require that genuine choice is possible. But, on a purely reductionist materialist account of human nature, we have good reason to think that our behavior is causally determined—in which case, no choice is possible. So, either those intuitions concerning personal responsibility are all illusions, or else the reductionist materialist account of human nature is mistaken. If purely physical things are necessarily causally determined, but our intuitive experience suggests we are not causally determined, this might imply that we are not purely physical, and that we are not identical to our bodies.

Having now considered reasons why the dualist understanding of human nature might be true, let's return to the agency theorist interpretation of free will. Clearly, agency theorists reject the worldview shared by both determinists and compatibilists, as well as their specific views on freedom. What does "freedom" mean for an agency theorist?

Unlike compatibilists, who believe that to be free is to act from internal causes, agency theorists believe that freedom requires an ability to do otherwise. To put it differently, freedom requires genuine choice, genuine options.

According to this standard, I am free right now only if it truly is within my power to "do otherwise" than continue typing. That means it must truly be "up to me" in a meaningful sort of way, whether or not I continue typing. If I am compelled to continue by causal forces beyond my control, by my DNA, or childhood experiences— if stopping writing right now is not truly a live option for me, then I am not free. What's more, given the option of continuing to type or stopping, the deciding factor between those two choices must not be something about me, but me, myself. In other words, if my DNA causes me to continue, or if what I had for breakfast causes me to continue, then the act was not mine in any meaningful sort of way. But, if *I* (i.e., my "self," my mind, my soul, my will) am the deciding factor, then the act is truly *mine*.

Although the actual ways in which things like DNA, childhood experiences, daily events, and various other causal factors influence behavior is admittedly unclear according to agency theory, the idea is (roughly) that such things can *influence*, but they do not *cause*. A famous way of expressing this relationship is that it involves "inclination without necessitation."

Agency theorists are willing to acknowledge, of course, that how we are raised probably does exert a lot of influence over who we are, and how we behave. So, too, with our DNA, and our daily experiences. The difference between an agency theorist and a determinist (or compatibilist) is that the agency theorist believes that it is almost always possible, no matter how difficult, for us to override the influences of our childhood, or DNA, etc., and, by a sheer act of will, do something else, of our own choosing, instead. Only if we have this sort of freedom, this ability to choose our own path, are we truly free.

If this sounds like inspiring and awesome creative power, then your perception is correct. Indeed, this point of view gives to human beings so much power, and such special status in the universe, that some regard it as wishful thinking. The critic will find it implausible that human beings should be so different from everything else in the universe that we, somehow, have the power to defy causal determinism and the laws of physics, and create the future from our own free choices.

On the other hand, some find this image of humanity to be consistent with our own experience. After all, when we try to explain our actions, we can certainly talk about the physical aspects of our behavior, the muscles and tendons and neurons firing and so on—but what about the mysterious act that begins each action in the first place, what we might call "deciding" or "choosing" or "willing" to do something? For agency theorists, that component of human behavior is indispensable for providing a full account of human action, and that component does not admit of a purely physical description.

How are we to understand this special class of actions, those brought about not by causal determinism but by free choice? Some agency theorists distinguish two kinds of causes: event causes, and agent causes.

Event causation is the cause and effect relationship that governs all purely physical interactions. This causal relationship is something with which we are most familiar. One event causes another event, which causes another event, etc. The event of a pool cue striking a cue ball causes the event of the cue ball moving across the table at a certain trajectory, which causes the event of the cue ball striking the eight ball, which causes the event of the eight ball falling into the corner pocket. Determinists and compatibilists would say that event causation is the only causation that ever occurs.

Agent causation occurs when an event is caused not by another event, but by an "agent" (another term used to indicate that "something extra" otherwise referred to as soul, will, mind, etc.,). This "agent" is not an event, but a substance, and a non-physical substance at that. Therefore, we are dealing with a different sort of causal process altogether.

The critic will object that we have no good reason to believe that this "agent causation" exists, whereas event causation is well understood, and experienced continuously in our lives. The agency theorist will often claim, in response, that agent causation is actually *better* understood. Indeed, we understand event causation because we first experience agent causation. This can be explained by means of a story.

As very young children, we discover that have the ability to produce change in our environment. We can move objects around, we can summon large creatures that tend to our needs when we cry, etc. We understand this ability to produce change as causal power. Don't take this story too seriously. No one is suggesting that this is a conscious realization, as if, as a baby, I said to myself "hey, I can exert causal power and produce change in the world!" Instead, we should understand this as an intuitive awareness.

Continuing the story, we also discover that other things in our environment can exert causal power as well. I have the power to bring about change in the world by knocking the "sippy cup" from the high-chair to the floor, but so does my teddy bear. He, too, can knock the cup to the ground—and that large creature called "mommy" has the power to place the cup back on the table. The world is filled with things capable of bringing about change. Of course, my causal power and the teddy bear's causal power appear to be different. Teddy bear is passive. He never appears to act, only react. He can knock the cup over, but only after I have thrown him into the cup.

I, on the other hand, seem to have the power to bring about change without something first moving me. I appear to be active, and not merely passive. My causal power appears to be of a different kind, of a greater kind, than that of my teddy bear. This greater kind of causal power, the kind we come to understand first, is what agency theorists call agent causation. The other kind of causal power, the lesser kind employed by inanimate objects and other purely physical things, is what agency theorists call event causation. It is because we first recognize (agent) causal power in ourselves that we can recognize (event) causal power in the rest of nature.[177]

To be sure, agency theory is vulnerable to some criticisms and concerns, just like the other two theories. How exactly does agent causation work? If the "agent" (mind, soul, etc.) is non-physical, how does it interact with the (physical) body? What laws, or forces, are needed to explain causal interactions between minds and bodies, and why should we believe that such forces exist, aside from their necessity in explaining agent causation?

Another possible criticism concerns the curious vulnerability of the "mind" to *brain* injuries or conditions. If the mind is immaterial, and distinct from the brain, why would tumors, concussions, Alzheimer's disease, or even mere alcohol be able to impact our mental functioning? It seems, critics would argue, that such experiences are evidence that the "mind" just *is* the brain.

In response, the noted dualist William Lane Craig says: "A dualist-interactionist does not take the soul to operate independently of the brain like a ghost in a machine.

---

[177] In fairness, the determinist would claim that that story is profoundly misleading. It's simply not true (says the determinist) that, unlike my teddy bear, I was not first acted upon before acting. My actions, just the same as my teddy bear's, require some antecedent cause. The difference is that, in the case of the teddy bear knocking the cup over, the antecedent cause is obvious, whereas in the case of my own behavior, it's not easy to pinpoint the precise cause of my behavior (genetic influence? Childhood experience?).

Rather, as the Nobel Prize-winning neurologist Sir John Eccles emphasizes, the soul uses the brain as an instrument to think, just as a musician uses a piano as an instrument to make music. If his piano is out of tune or damaged, then the pianist's ability to produce music will be impaired or even nullified. In the same way, says Eccles, if the soul's instrument of thought, the brain, is damaged or adversely affected, then the soul's ability to think will be impaired or nullified."[178]

Given these challenges, why would anyone embrace agency theory? The short answer is that some believe that this theory, despite its problems and limitations, is the one that most closely conforms to our intuitions and experience. The fact is that even if we don't really exercise genuine choice, it often seems as if we do. Even if the future is fixed, it often seems as if there are many paths our lives might take.

It certainly *seems* as if we often can, and do, make choices that involve genuine options.

Whenever we have a conflict between our intuitions (e.g., the intuition of spontaneous choice) and the claims of a theory (e.g., the claims of determinism), we have to decide which is mistaken: the theory, or our intuition. Agency theorists fall on the side of favoring intuition, in this regard.

Having now developed the three major views concerning human agency and responsibility (i.e., determinism, compatibilism, agency theory), we can now turn our attention to the concept of omniscience.

Omniscience

It might come as some relief that this section is much simpler and much more brief than the previous section! At its simplest, to say that God is omniscient is to say that God knows "everything." To be more precise, we will use William Lane Craig's definition of omniscience:

> *Omniscience: for any person S, S is omniscient if and only if S knows every true proposition and believes no false proposition.*[179]

To be omniscient means that you know everything that it is possible to know (i.e., you have no "blind spots," and are ignorant of nothing), and that you are not mistaken about anything. If it is possible to know something, and S does not know it, then S is not omniscient. Similarly, if S is mistaken about anything, then S is not omniscient.

All of the major Western theistic traditions claim that God is omniscient. This is supported by philosophical/conceptual analysis, but perhaps more importantly in the context of actual religious traditions, it is supported by Scripture. The following references are very far from being exhaustive, but are merely meant to illustrate (with little discussion intended, given the limited focus of this chapter) that omniscience is both supported by Scriptural analysis and is important to the Western

---

[178] http://www.reasonablefaith.org/questions-about-body-soul-interaction#ixzz3du1u0hiO

[179] *Philosophical Foundations for a Christian Worldview*, by J.P. Moreland and William Lane Craig, InterVarsity press, 2003. p. 515.

concept of God.

Old Testament

General references to God's knowledge, including knowledge of human thoughts and actions:

- 1st Samuel 2:3
- Isaiah 40:28
- Psalms 147:5
- Psalms 139:17 – 18
- Job 28:24 ("for he looks to the ends of the earth, and sees everything under the heavens.")
- Psalms 147:4
- Job 38:31 – 33
- Isaiah 40:26
- Job 28:12 – 27
- Psalms 33:13 – 15 ("the Lord looks down from heaven, he sees all the sons of men; from where he sits enthroned he looks forth on all the inhabitants of the earth, he who fashions the hearts of them all, and observes all their deeds.")
- Job 24:23; 31:4; 34:21
- Psalms 119:168
- Jeremiah 16:17; 32:19
- Chronicles 16:9
- Jeremiah 17:9 – 10 ("the heart is deceitful above all things, and desperately corrupt; who can understand it? "I the Lord search the mind and try the heart, to give to every man according to his ways, according to the fruit of his doings."

References to God's knowledge of the future:

- Isaiah 46:9 – 10 ("I am God, and there is none like me, declaring the end of the beginning and from ancient times things not yet done, saying, "my counsel shall stand, and I will accomplish all my purpose.")
- Psalms and 139:1– 6 ("oh Lord, thou hast searched me and known me! Thou knowest when I sit down and when I rise up; thou discerneth my thoughts from afar. Thou searcheth out my path and my lying down, and art acquainted with all my ways. Even before a word is on my tongue, lo, O Lord, thou knowest it altogether. Thou dost beset me behind and before, and layest thy hand upon me. Such knowledge is too wonderful for me; it is high, I cannot attain it.)

References to prophecy (which presupposes knowledge of the future):

- Deuteronomy 18:22 ("when a prophet speaks in the name of the Lord, if the word does not come to pass or come true, that is a word of which the Lord has not spoken.")
- Genesis 15:13 – 14; 40:8
- Deuteronomy 31
- 1st Kings 13:2 – 3; 13:20 – 24
- 2nd Kings 8:7 – 15
- Daniel 2:36 – 43
- Isaiah 41:21-24 ("set forth your case, says the Lord; bring your proofs, says the king of Jacob. Let them bring them, and tell us what is to happen. Tell us the former things, what they are, that we may consider them, that we may know their outcome; or declare to us the things to come. Tell us what is to come hereafter, that we may know that you are gods; do good, or do harm, that we may be dismayed and terrified. Behold, you are nothing, and your work is not; an abomination is he who chooses you.")

New Testament

General references:
- Acts 1: 24; 2:23; 15:8
- 1 Peter 1:1 – 2; 19 – 20
- Mark 14:18, 30
- Matthew 10:29 – 30 (not a single sparrow dies without God knowing it); Luke 16:15 ("God knows your hearts.")
- Romans 8:27
- 1st Corinthians 4:5
- 1st John 3:19 – 20

References to God's knowledge of the future and/or Providence:
- Ephesians 3:9; 1:10; 3:11
- 2nd Timothy 1:9 – 10

References to the fulfillment of prophecy:
- 1st Peter 1:10 – 11
- Matthew 1:22; 2:15, 23; 4:14 – 16; 8:17; 12:17 – 21
- Mark 1:2 – 4; 9:9 – 13
- Luke 7:18 – 23, 18:31 – 33
- Acts 2:16 – 21; 3:18; 4:25 – 28; 7:52; 8:30 – 35; 10:43; 15:15 – 18
- John 12:38 – 41; 19

References to the foreknowledge of Jesus:
- Mark 8:31; 9:31; 10:32 – 34

- Matthew 17:27
- Mark 14:13 – 15 ("go into the city, and a man carrying a jar of water will meet you; follow him, and wherever he enters, say to the householder, "the teacher says, where is my guest room, where I am to eat the Passover with my disciples?" And he will show you a large upper room furnished and ready; there prepare for us."); 14:18 – 20.[180]

As a reminder, the point of providing those Scriptural references is that it shows the "matching strategy" that has been described and applied numerous times in previous chapters of this book. Omniscience is not merely a philosophical concept, but it "matches up" to a property attributed to the God of the Western Theistic traditions. If that God exists, that God is claimed to be omniscient. If there is a "tension" between omniscience and free will, then there is a "problem" not just for philosophers, but for actual people of faith, that requires a solution. Accordingly, we will now shift our focus to first establishing the nature of the so-called tension, and then consider possible solutions.

Omniscience v. Free Will?

The alleged tension between divine omniscience and human free will becomes apparent with only a little consideration. If God knows "everything," then God knows what each and every one of us will do in the future. For example, God knows what I will have for lunch later today. A philosopher no less significant (and no less a person of faith) than St. Augustine raised the resulting concern over 1500 years ago in book 3 of his work, "On the Free Choice of the Will."

> . . . It perplexes me beyond words how it could happen that [1] God has foreknowledge of everything that will happen, and yet [2] we do not sin by any necessity. Anyone who said that something can turn out otherwise than God previously foreknew would be trying to destroy God's foreknowledge with his senseless irreligiousness. Consequently, God foreknew that a good man was going to sin. Anyone who allows that God has foreknowledge of everything that will happen must grant me this. . . . Since God had foreknown that he was going to sin, it was necessary that what He foreknew would be the case would happen. So how is the will free where such unavoidable necessity is apparent? . . .

How is this, you might wonder, a "problem?" It might or might not be a problem depending upon what you think about God, foreknowledge, and free will.

- Question one: do you believe that the Western God exists?

---

[180] Credit goes to William Lane Craig for his thorough listing and description of these Scriptural references in chapter 1 of his book (Craig, William Lane: *The Only Wise God. The Compatibility Of Divine Foreknowledge And Human Freedom*. Wipf and Stock Publishers. 2000), pages 21 through 37.

- o   If your answer is "no," then there is no problem. Clearly, if you don't
      think that the (Western) God exists, there can be no tension between
      the concept of that God and human free will.
- o   If your answer is "yes," then proceed to question two.
- Question two: are you a determinist?
  - o   If your answer is "yes," then there is no problem. Clearly, if you don't
        think human beings have free will, there can be no tension between the
        concept of God and human free will.
  - o   If the answer is "no," then proceed to question three.
- Question three: are you a compatibilist?
  - o   If your answer is "yes," then there is no problem. As will soon be
        developed, the alleged problem is whether the concept of an omniscient
        God precludes the possibility of "an ability to do otherwise."
        Compatibilism endorses free will but denies that free will requires (or
        even allows) an ability to do otherwise.
  - o   If your answer is no," then proceed to question four.
- Question four: are you an agency theorist?
  - o   If your answer is "no," then you have chosen a view of human nature
        beyond what we have considered this chapter (since at this point you
        apparently haven't chosen determinism or compatibilism either). I'm
        not sure what to tell you. . . .
  - o   If your answer is yes," then there might be a problem. The alleged
        problem arises becomes the ability to do otherwise required by agency
        theory allegedly generates some unacceptable consequences when
        combined with a belief in divine omniscience that includes
        foreknowledge of future events. Contemporary philosopher Nelson
        Pike illustrates this tension by means of a formal argument.

Nelson Pike

For the sake of thoroughness, I have provided two versions of Pike's argument.
The first is more abstract and formal, and the second is made more "intuitive" by the
use of a specific example.

1. "God existed at T_1" entails "If Jones did X at T_2, God believed at T_1 that Jones
   would do X at T_2."
2. "God believes X" entails "'X' is true."
3. It is not within one's power at a given time to do something having a
   description that is logically contradictory.
4. It is not within one's power at a given time to do something that would
   bring it about that someone who held a certain belief prior to the time in
   question did not hold that belief at the time prior to the time in question.

5. If God existed at T_1, and if God believed at T_1 that Jones would do X at T_2, then if it was within Jones's power at T_2 to refrain from doing X, then (1) it was within Jones's power at T_2 to do something that would have brought it about that God held a false belief at T_1, or (2) it was within Jones's power at T_2 to do something that would have brought it about that God did not hold the belief He held at T_1.

6. Alternative (1) from item 5 (i.e. it was within Jones's power at T_2 to do something that would have brought it about that God held a false belief at $T_{1)}$ is false (from 2 and 3).

7. Alternative (2) from item 5 (i.e. it was within Jones's power at T_2 to do something that would have brought it about that God did not hold the belief He held at T_1) is false (from 4).

8. Therefore, if God existed at T_1, and if God believed at T_1 that Jones would do X at T_2, then it was not within Jones's power at T_2 to refrain from doing X (from 5 through 7).

9. Therefore, if God existed at T_1 and if Jones did X at T_2, it was not within Jones's power at T_2 to refrain from doing X (from 1 and 8).[181]

1. God's being omniscient necessarily implies that if Jones mows his lawn on Saturday afternoon, then God believes (at an earlier time) that Jones would mow his lawn on Saturday afternoon.

2. Necessarily, all of God's beliefs are true.

3. No one has the power to make a contradiction true.

4. No one has the power to erase someone's past beliefs, that is, to bring it about that something believed in the past by someone is not believed in the past by that person.

5. No one has the power to the erase someone's existence in the past, that is, to bring it about that someone who existed in the past did not exist in the past.

6. So if God believed that Jones would mow his lawn on Saturday afternoon, Jones can refrain from mowing his lawn only if one of the following alternatives is true:

   a. Jones has the power to make God's belief false;
   b. Jones has the power to erase God's past belief; or
   c. Jones has the power to erase God's past existence.

7. But alternative (a) is impossible. (This follows from steps 2 and 3.)

8. And alternative (b) is impossible. (This follows from step 4.)

9. And alternative (c) is impossible. (This follows from step 5.)

10. Therefore, if God believes that Jones would mow his lawn on Saturday afternoon, Jones does not have the power to refrain from mowing his lawn

---

[181]Nelson Pike, "Divine Omniscience and Voluntary Action," in *Philosophical Review* (June, 1965), 33-34.

on Saturday afternoon; that is to say, Jones is not free.

Once one has waded through the argument, it has much common-sense appeal. If we believe that God exists and that one of God's attributes is omniscience, and if we believe omniscience to mean (among other things) that God never holds false beliefs and that God knows—even into the future—all things and all sequences and consequences and courses of action, then it seems we believe that God has true beliefs about what we will do in the future. Thus, God knows, for example, what I will have for lunch tomorrow and at what time (in human terms) I will have lunch, and how much of the lunch I will ultimately eat, and so on. But, if God knows ahead of time all the details of my lunch, I must wonder how much (if any) of my lunch experience is under my control.

Assuming that God knows all things eternally, then at any time T_i prior to the lunch in question (for example, 2000 years ago), God knew the details of my lunch experience. That God *knew* the details means that His beliefs about them (e.g., what I would eat) were true. But if God *knows* on June 14th, 0001 CE. (for example) that I will have chicken and vegetable soup for lunch on June 14th, 2017 CE, then was it within my power to have had a bean and cheese burrito instead? If I could have chosen a different entrée, then it appears that I had it within my power to bring it about that God held a false belief at June 14th, 0001 CE as regards my lunch on June 14th, 2017 CE. This violates our assumptions concerning God's omniscience. On the other hand, if it was not within my power to choose another entrée—if I *must* have chicken and vegetables soup—then it appears that I was not free (in the sense of having had an ability to do otherwise) with respect to my lunch. What's more, there's nothing special about lunch. God's foreknowledge would seemingly apply to all acts and all decisions regarding anything whatsoever. In that case, if God knows what I will do (no matter how trivial) at all times throughout the course of my entire life, then it doesn't appear that I am free with respect to *anything* that I do. In this way, the conflict between divine omniscience and human freedom is intuitively clear. Or is it?

Solutions?

So, which is it? Do we have free will – in which case God does not have foreknowledge? Or, does God have foreknowledge, in which case we do not have free will? Or, is this a false dilemma? We have already seen that both determinism and compatibilism solve the problem by denying an ability to do otherwise, but those are certainly not the only possible solutions. Nor is it the case that the only other alternative is to deny God's omniscience, or even existence. In the remainder of the chapter we will consider two additional options: (1) that God's omniscience is not technically "foreknowledge," and (2) that God's foreknowledge is, in fact, genuinely compatible with an ability to do otherwise.[182]

---

[182] Please note that these additional options are very complicated and we will only scratch the surface. Also note that additional options are available even beyond these, but are beyond the scope of our purposes.

Future-indexed propositions have no truth value

A first possible solution is based on an interpretation about a property of claims that involve the future. This is a very old solution, going all the way back to Aristotle. Aristotle addresses this issue in Chapter 9 of his work, "On Interpretation."[183]

Clearly, therefore, not everything is or happens of necessity: some things happen as chance has it, and of the affirmation and the negation neither is true rather than the other; with other things it is one rather than the other and as a rule, but still it is possible for the other to happen instead.

What is, necessarily is, when it is; and what is not, necessarily is not, when it is not. But not everything that is, necessarily is; and not everything that is not, necessarily is not. For to say that everything that is, is of necessity, when it is, is not the same as saying unconditionally that it is of necessity. Similarly with what is not. And the same account holds for contradictories: everything necessarily is or is not, and will be or will not be; but one cannot divide and say that one or the other is necessary. I mean, for example: it is necessary for there to be or not be a sea battle tomorrow; but is not necessary for a sea-battle to take place tomorrow, nor for one not to take place – though it is necessary for one to take place or not to take place. So, since statements are true according to how the actual things are, it is clear that wherever these are such as to allow of contraries as chance has it, the same necessarily holds for the contradictories also. This happens with things that are not always so or are not always not so. With these it is necessary for one or the other of the contradictories to be true or false – not, however, this one or that one, but as chance has it; or for one to be true rather than the other, yet not already true or false.

Clearly, then, it is not necessary that of every affirmation and opposite negation one should be true and the other false. For what holds for things that are does not hold for things that are not but may possibly be or not be; with these it is as we have said.

The basic idea is that "future contingent propositions" have no truth value. That is, they are *neither* true *nor* false. For the sake of clarity, a future contingent proposition is just a claim made about some future state of affairs that is not *necessarily* true (or false). The future part is pretty simple. "I will take my parents to lunch later today" refers to the future (as opposed to claims such as "I had lunch with my parents yesterday," or "I am having lunch with my parents right now."). That claim is also "contingent" because nothing necessitates its truth or falsity. This is in contrast to a claim like "Next week, all bachelors will be unmarried men." Simply by virtue of the meaning of the word 'bachelor,' that claim is necessarily true.

Future contingent claims are thought to have no truth value because they haven't

---

[183] A slightly expanded version of this selection may be found at the end of the chapter.

happened yet, and neither is their truth value *necessary*. On a correspondence theorist interpretation of truth, there is no state of affairs (yet) to which the claim may correspond, or not. When the event occurs, it will correspond to the claim, or not, and at that point it will have a truth value. Until then, though, it is neither true nor false.

If future-indexed claims have no truth value, then they aren't anything that it is possible to "know." That means that future-indexed claims are not included in the set of claims that an omniscient God "knows." There is no tension between God knowing what I will do in the future and my freedom to do otherwise because God doesn't actually know what I will do in the future. This is thought to not come at the expense of God's knowledge, though, since the usual interpretation of God's properties is that they are limited to what is logically possible. For example, it is no threat to God's omnipotence that God can't create a square circle, since that is not anything that could be created! It's a literal contradiction in terms. Similarly, if the future is literally not anything that *can* be known, it is no deficiency for God that God does not know the future.

This solution has two immediate challenges, however: one philosophical, and one theological. The theological problem is that, as we have seen, the Western religions claim that God *does* know the future. This solution, therefore, doesn't "match up."

The philosophical problem concerns an interpretation of the correspondence theorist understanding of truth. According to Craig, the correspondence theorist understanding of truth does *not* require that the things or events which a true claim references must exist *except* when dealing with present tense statements. We recognize this in the context of past tense statements (e.g., we don't demand that Abraham Lincoln currently exist in order for it to be a true statement to say that Lincoln was assassinated while attending a play). In the context of future tense statements, to be true it is not required that the thing or event referenced in the claim currently exist, but only that it *will* exist.[184] "A future tense statement is true if matters turn out as the statement predicts, and false if matters fail to turn out as the statement predicts to – this is all the notion of truth as correspondence requires."[185] As an example, if "it is raining today" is presently true, how could "it will rain tomorrow" not have been true if asserted yesterday?

"Middle knowledge"

We have seen how Craig argues that denying a truth value to future-indexed contingent claims is not a workable solution to the alleged tension between omniscience and free will. Instead, he will claim, first, that some of the "tension" is based on confusion, and then he will offer an interpretation of God's knowledge that he thinks shows the compatibility of omniscience and libertarian free will.

To begin with, he claims that the "clear" tension between omniscience and free will is actually based on some semantic confusion. In everyday usage, the words 'certainty" and "necessity" (or "necessarily") are used interchangeably, as if they are

---

[184] Craig, William Lane: *The Only Wise God. The Compatibility Of Divine Foreknowledge And Human Freedom*. Wipf and Stock Publishers. 2000. 56 – 57.
[185] Ibid., 57 – 58.

synonyms. Indeed, this potentially confusing language is used in the aforementioned selection from Augustine: "For if God foreknows that someone is going to sin, you say, it is necessary that he sin; but if it is necessary, then there is no choice of the will in his sinning, but an unavoidable and fixed necessity instead." Notice the language here: God's foreknowledge renders it "necessary" that someone sin and this "fixed necessity" makes the action unavoidable and eliminates choice. In contrast to this use of language, Craig claims that the words certainty and necessary have different (though related) meanings.

In the context of logic and arguments, certainty is a property of *persons*, as opposed to truth. It is *people* who are certain, not propositions. I can be "certain" that today is Tuesday, and turn out to be mistaken. That is, I can be "certain" that today is Tuesday, despite the fact that "today is Tuesday" is (presently) a false claim. The "certainty" was a property of me, not of the claim. Similarly, "truth" (or falsity) is a property of the claim (as opposed to a property of me). I am not "true" (or false), but claims I make are.

Necessity is another property of some *claims* (or propositions). Necessity, too, is a property of claims rather than persons. A necessary claim is one that cannot have a different truth value. Its necessity has nothing to do with whether or not we know what that truth value is, let alone whether or not we are *certain* of that truth value.

The reason why this matters is that in the context of divine foreknowledge, God's knowledge of what a person will do in the future is *certain*. Some people interpret that certainty to mean necessity – that the person's action is causally necessitated, and could not have turned out any other way, and therefore conflicts with libertarian free will. However, God's certainty does not equate to the action's necessity. Craig proposes that premise 6 of Pike's argument (from the second version above) be expanded to include an additional option (d):

6) So if God believed that Jones would mow his lawn on Saturday afternoon, Jones can refrain from mowing his lawn only if one of the following alternatives is true:

a. Jones has the power to make God's belief false;
b. Jones has the power to erase God's past belief;
c. Jones has the power to erase God's past existence; *or*
d. *Jones has the power to act in a different way, and if he were to act in that way, God would have believed differently.*[186]

This alternative asserts "that if Jones *were* to refrain (as he is really able to do), then God *would have* always foreknown differently. Notice the mood of the italicized verbs in the preceding sentence: they are in the subjunctive mood, not the indicative mood. The subjunctive mood serves to indicate that what we have here is a contrary to fact hypothetical statement: if something *were* the case (which in fact it is not), then something else *would be* the case. Philosophers call such statements *counterfactual*

[186] Ibid., 70.

statements."[187] To clarify, "contrary to fact hypothetical statements" are statements about things that could happen, but do not (or did not) actually happen. For example, it could have been the case that I attended college at Georgetown University, but since that did not, in fact, happen, that would be a contrary to fact hypothetical.

Craig points out that it is important to recognize the distinction between the following sorts of arguments:

1. Necessarily, if God foreknows X, then X will happen.
2. God foreknows X.
3. Therefore, X will necessarily happen.

1. Necessarily, if God foreknows X, then X will happen.
2. God foreknows X.
3. Therefore, X will happen.

1. Necessarily, if Jones is a bachelor, Jones is unmarried.
2. Jones is a bachelor.
3. Therefore, Jones is necessarily unmarried.

1. Necessarily, if Jones is a bachelor, Jones is unmarried.
2. Jones is a bachelor.
3. Therefore, Jones is unmarried.

Is there any obvious difference between these sets of arguments? Only the wording is different in the conclusion, in each case—but that's a difference that makes a difference! Let's start with the argument about Jones and being a bachelor. There is nothing *necessary* about Jones being unmarried. Nothing forced him to not marry. He could have been married, or he could remain a bachelor. It just happens to be the case that he is not married. There is nothing impossible about Jones being married – though it would be impossible for him to be both married and a bachelor. Similarly, the fact that God foreknows that something will happen doesn't mean that it was necessary that the event happen. There is nothing impossible about a different event occurring – it just happens to be the case that since that event does occur, God had foreknowledge of that particular event (as opposed to a different event).[188]

Just as the real impossibility for the second set of arguments is that Jones be both married and a bachelor, in the first set of arguments the real impossibility is that God would foreknow an event and that event *not* occur. It would be impossible for God to have foreknowledge that Jones will mow the lawn, and for Jones to refrain from mowing the lawn – but this doesn't entail that Jones was somehow forced to mow the lawn, let alone that God somehow made him do so. What it does mean is that whatever it is that Jones freely chooses to do, that is what God will foreknow (in this case, mowing the lawn).

A simple way to put this is that "Jones does not mow the lawn because God foreknows; God foreknows because Jones will mow the lawn."[189] To make it a bit more sophisticated: "God's foreknowledge is *chronologically* prior to Jones mowing the

---

[187] Ibid., 71.

[188] Ibid., 72 – 73

[189] Ibid., 73.

lawn, but Jones mowing the lawn is *logically* prior to God's foreknowledge."[190]

At this point, it is important to explain the distinction between logical and chronological priority, since that terminology has been used several times in the last few paragraphs. Logical priority is not temporal priority. To say that something is logically prior to another thing is not to say that the logically prior thing occurs (in time) before the other thing. "Rather, logical priority means that something serves to explain something else. The one provides the grounds or basis for the other."[191] As an example, the premises in an argument are logically prior to the conclusion since the conclusion is based on the premises even though, temporally speaking, the premises and conclusion are all true simultaneously (in the case of a valid and sound argument). This distinction between logical and chronological priority brings us to Craig's proposed solution: an appeal to God's "Middle Knowledge."

Craig's inspiration for this solution that makes use of this logical/chronological distinction comes from the 16th century Spanish philosopher Luis de Molina (1535-1600). Molina was a Jesuit theologian who debated the Dominican order with regard to the nature of God's omniscience and human free will. His most famous work is "A Reconciliation Of Free Choice With The Gifts Of Grace, Divine Foreknowledge, Providence, Predestination And Reprobation," published in 1588. Key features of Molina's philosophical system include his endorsement of agency theorist free will ("that agent is called free who, with all the prerequisites for acting having been posited, is able to act and able not to act, or is able to do one thing in such a way that he is also able to do some contrary things."), and his delineation of different "moments" of God's knowledge: Natural Knowledge, Free Knowledge, and Middle Knowledge.

1. Logical moment one: Natural Knowledge: God knows the range of possible worlds
2. Logical moment two: Middle Knowledge: God knows the range of feasible worlds

[divine creative decree]

3. Logical moment three: Free Knowledge: God knows the actual world[192]

First (logical) moment: God's knowledge of all necessary truths (e.g., the laws of logic). Statements that are true in this logical moment are true by virtue of God's nature, as opposed to being dependent upon God's will. This first moment of divine knowledge is called "Natural Knowledge." This Natural Knowledge includes knowledge of all possibilities including all of the possible people that could be created, all of the possible circumstances in which they operate, all of their possible actions and responses, and all of the possible worlds that God could create. For example (and this is Craig's oft-used example), God knows that in some possible world Peter freely

---

[190] Ibid., 74.
[191] Ibid., 127.
[192] Ibid., 522.

denies Christ three times, but in other possible worlds Peter freely affirms Christ under identical circumstances. Both are possible. Neither is somehow logically contradictory. We're now going to skip ahead to the third logical moment because doing so helps with understanding.

Third (logical) moment: God's knowledge of the actual world which God created. This logical moment includes not only all necessary truths, but the truth value of all contingent claims (past, present, and future). This includes God's foreknowledge of everything that will in fact happen. Because this third logical moment is logically posterior (as opposed to prior) to God's decision to create the world in the first place God has control over which statements are true or false in this moment because whether or not they are true or false depends upon which world God, in fact, creates. As an example, if God had created a world in which I never existed, then it would not be true that I am writing this chapter in the summer of 2017. This moment of knowledge is called God's "Free Knowledge." Unlike God's Natural Knowledge, the content of this knowledge could be different, and would be different, if God had created a different world.

Second (logical) moment: God's Middle Knowledge, which is knowledge of contingently true counterfactual propositions, including propositions about the actions of free creatures. By actions of free creatures we just means the sorts of actions humans like us perform, in a context of "ability to otherwise," as described by agency theory. By "contingently true" we just mean that the claim isn't *necessarily* true, such as a claim like "bachelors are unmarried men." And, by a counterfactual proposition, we're just referring to claims describable in terms of "would" and "were." In this logical moment, God knows what every possible creature *would* do in every possible set of circumstances. To use Craig's example: logically prior to Creation, God knew that if Peter were in circumstances C he would freely deny Christ three times. This counterfactual knowledge actually limits the range of possible worlds that are feasible for God to create. If, for example, Peter were in circumstances C he would freely deny Christ three times, then though it is logically possible for Peter to do otherwise, he will not do otherwise in exactly the same circumstances. Therefore, a possible world in which Peter affirms Christ under exactly the same circumstances is not feasible for God to create. Of course, God could force Peter to affirm Christ, but that would change the circumstances – and therefore it would no longer be under exactly the same circumstances! As my own example, God knows what I *would* do were I offered a job in New York City (spoiler alert: I would turn it down). According to this view, this doesn't mean that I was causally determined/necessitated to turn down that job in New York. Instead, it holds that I am free to choose to accept it, or reject it, in the event that it were offered to me. God's knowledge is not of what I will *necessarily* do, but of what I will freely choose to do. This Middle Knowledge provides God with the range of possible worlds that God could create, given the free choices that free beings such as ourselves would make in them (on the assumption that free beings exist at all).

God's Middle Knowledge is similar to God's Natural Knowledge because it is logically prior to God's decision to create a world. It is similar to God's Free Knowledge because its content could be different given that free creatures could choose differently.

By virtue of what is possible (God's Natural Knowledge), and what is feasible (God's Middle Knowledge) God has a full understanding of what could, and *would* occur depending upon which possible world God creates. God then freely creates one of those possible worlds, and has foreknowledge of everything that *will* happen (Free Knowledge) in that now-actual world.

Recalling the distinction between logical and chronological priority, the application to God's omniscience and, ultimately, Middle Knowledge is as follows:

Logical order:	Chronological order:
1. Certain events occur.	1. Statements about certain future events are true or false, and of the statements God knows only and all those that are true.
2. Statements about these events are true or false.	
3. Of these statements God knows only and all those that are true.	2. The events occur.

Chronologically speaking, certain future tense statements are true from the beginning of time and known simultaneously by God – and later on the events that correspond to those claims actually occur. Logically speaking, God foreknows the events "because certain future tense statements about them are true, and such statements are true because the events will occur."[193]

The *means by which* God has Middle Knowledge is subject to debate. One interpretation is that God knows the individual essence of every possible creature so completely and well that God knows precisely what every free creature would do in every possible situation.[194] Alternatively, one could argue that a feature of omniscience is simply that one knows all (and only) truths, and counterfactual truths are among those truths. Here is a formal argument defending that claim:

1. If there are true counterfactuals about creaturely free choices, then God knows these truths.
2. There are true counterfactuals about creaturely free choices.
3. If God knows true counterfactuals about creaturely free choices, God knows them either logically prior to the divine creative decree or only logically posterior to the divine creative decree.
4. Counterfactuals about creaturely free choices cannot be known only logically posterior to the divine creative decree.
5. Therefore, God knows true counterfactuals about creaturely free choices. (Modus Ponens, 1, 2)
6. Therefore, God knows true counterfactuals about creaturely free choices

---

[193] Craig, William Lane: *The Only Wise God. The Compatibility Of Divine Foreknowledge And Human Freedom*. Wipf and Stock Publishers. 2000. 128.

[194] As an editorial note, I will say that this sounds more like compatibilism than agency theory to me. The claim seems to be that our behavior is somehow "determined" by our "essence." Nevertheless, there is some sense in which we are acting freely. This, to me, just sounds like another way of talking about acting from "internal causes."

either logically prior to the divine creative decree or only logically posterior to the divine creative decree. (Modus Ponens, 3, 5)

7.   Therefore, God knows true counterfactuals about creaturely free choices logically prior to the divine creative degree. (Disjunctive Syllogism, 4, 6)

Premise one is implied by the standard definition of omniscience, given that part of that definition involves knowing every true proposition.

Premise two is supported by our very actions and intuitions. We base very important decisions in our own lives off the assumption that counterfactual claims can be true. For example, "if I were given an opportunity to punch a baby, I would decline." That is a counterfactual claim, and I'm pretty confident that it is true.

Premise three simply exhausts the logical possibilities for an omniscient deity: if God knows true counterfactuals about our free choices, that God either knows them (logically) "before" or (logically) "after" God creates Nature.

Premise four is true, according to Craig, because if counterfactuals of creaturely freedom were known only (logically) posterior to the divine decree, then it would be God who determined what every creature would do in every circumstance. As stated above with regards to God's Free Knowledge, because this third logical moment is logically posterior (as opposed to prior) to God's decision to create the world in the first place God has control over which statements are true or false in this moment because whether or not they are true or false depends upon which world God, in fact, creates. The idea seems to be that if the truth of true counterfactuals about creaturely free choices was known by God logically *posterior* to Creation, then this would fall under Free Knowledge rather than Middle Knowledge. With respect to free knowledge, it is God that "makes" those claims true because it is God that created the world (from amongst options) that renders them true. In this sense, the "truth maker" of the claim is God, rather than the person and their free choice. However, this would mean that there really are no *actual* counterfactuals about creaturely *free* choices, and this contradicts premise two. If there are such things, they must be true logically prior to the divine decree.

Through a simple application of "modus ponens" we get premise five, and a second application gets us premise six.

Finally, our conclusion is derived using the technique of disjunctive syllogism from premises four and six. Either God knows true counterfactuals about creaturely free choices logically prior to the divine decree or logically posterior to that decree. Premise four rules out that they can be known logically posterior. Therefore, they are known logically prior to the creative decree. In effect, God's foreknowledge of what people will freely do in the future form the rational ground for the actual world God chooses to create.

If God has "Middle Knowledge," then there is a way that God can foreknow what a person will do without denying that person's ability to otherwise. If they *were* to do otherwise, God *would have* foreknown something different. Of course, all of this is merely a demonstration of the logical possibility of Middle Knowledge. What remains is a demonstration that such Middle Knowledge "matches up" with the God of the Western theistic tradition.

Old Testament "Matching":

> 6 (Now Abiathar son of Ahimelek had brought the ephod down with him when he fled to David at Keilah.)
>
> 7 Saul was told that David had gone to Keilah, and he said, "God has delivered him into my hands, for David has imprisoned himself by entering a town with gates and bars." 8 And Saul called up all his forces for battle, to go down to Keilah to besiege David and his men.
>
> 9 When David learned that Saul was plotting against him, he said to Abiathar the priest, "Bring the ephod." 10 David said, "Lord, God of Israel, your servant has heard definitely that Saul plans to come to Keilah and destroy the town on account of me. 11 Will the citizens of Keilah surrender me to him? Will Saul come down, as your servant has heard? Lord, God of Israel, tell your servant."
>
> And the Lord said, "He will."
>
> 12 Again David asked, "Will the citizens of Keilah surrender me and my men to Saul?"
>
> And the Lord said, "They will."
>
> 13 So David and his men, about six hundred in number, left Keilah and kept moving from place to place. When Saul was told that David had escaped from Keilah, he did not go there. (1st Samuel 23:6 – 13)

The "Middle Knowledge" interpretation of this story is that God knew that if David *were* to remain, then Saul *would* come to get him, and that if Saul *were* to come to get David, then the men of the city *would* hand him over. This example is a terrible illustration of *simple* foreknowledge given that the predicted events did not actually happen. The story works, however, as an illustration of a counterfactual: what *would* happen under certain circumstances.

New Testament "Matching":

> 20 Then Jesus began to denounce the towns in which most of his miracles had been performed, because they did not repent. 21 "Woe to you, Chorazin! Woe to you, Bethsaida! For if the miracles that were performed in you had been performed in Tyre and Sidon, they would have repented long ago in sackcloth and ashes. 22 But I tell you, it will be more bearable for Tyre and Sidon on the day of judgment than for you. 23 And you, Capernaum, will you be lifted to the heavens? No, you will go down to Hades.[a] For if the miracles that were performed in you had been performed in Sodom, it would have remained to this day. 24 But I tell you that it will be more bearable for Sodom on the day of judgment than for you." (Matthew 11:20 – 24)

The "Middle Knowledge" interpretation of this passage is that Jesus declares that *if* his miracles *had been* performed in certain cities which did not (in fact) repent, they *would have* repented. In other words, under certain circumstances certain people *would have* acted in a certain way.

A philosophical objection to Middle Knowledge is that counterfactual statements about what a person would have freely done under alternative circumstances can't be true, because they do not have a truth value. Craig's response is twofold: First, this criticism is counterintuitive because we make those sorts of statements often. For example, I can easily envision myself saying "had I known you were going to come over, I would have cleaned up my house." Not only do I make statements similar to that, I'm fairly confident that that particular statement is true. Other statements of similar form seem even more obviously true. "Had I known that there would be a terrorist attack, I wouldn't have gone to that place." If someone objects that these examples all seem to refer to the past, what about this one? "If I were to receive notice that my campus is closed, I would not go to work that day." That certainly looks like a true statement to me!

Basically, this objection boils down to the same sort of objection that claimed that future tense statements have no truth value because there is no "reality" that corresponds to them. As Craig already argued previously in this chapter, in order for a future tense statement to be true, it is not necessary that the event is presently occurring – in fact that would be impossible since it would no longer be referring to the future! It need only be the case that the event will occur in the future. Similarly, for a counterfactual to be true, "it is not required that the circumstances or actions referred to actually exist. The view of truth as correspondence requires only that such actions *would* be taken if the specified circumstances *were* to exist."[195]

Conclusion

The alleged conflict between omniscience that includes foreknowledge and (agency theorist) free will is a fascinating example of a multi-faceted philosophical issue. It addresses the properties of God, the properties of human beings, and the nature of knowledge and truth, at minimum. The topic can be further expanded into the nature of time, among other things.[196] It's an effective illustration of how your "metaphysical commitments" (i.e., your worldview) impact your options "downstream" (e.g., if you are a determinist, your "solution" to this issue will be very different than if you are an agency theorist). Finally, it's a nice example of the "matching strategy" that we have discussed throughout this book, revealing how both the problem of foreknowledge and free will arises in both philosophical and theological contexts, as well as how a possible philosophical solution (e.g., Middle Knowledge) "matches up" to an interpretation of an actual religious tradition.

Our next chapter will consider another multifaceted issue with not only philosophical implications, but direct theological significance: the epistemic status of miracle testimony.

---

[195] Ibid., 140.

[196] Indeed, God's relationship to time actually has a very important role to play in addressing the problem of foreknowledge and free will, but is beyond the scope of this chapter.

Aristotle (384 BCE – 322 BCE) is tremendously important in the history of Western philosophy, and seemed to study and be an expert on virtually everything, ranging from physics to poetry, to marine biology, to logic, and to ethics (to name just a few). Aristotle's thought shaped much of medieval philosophy and was so respected that Aquinas refers to him simply as "the philosopher." Below, you have a very brief selection from De Interpretatione (On Interpretation), one of the earliest surviving philosophical works in the Western tradition to deal with the relationship between language and logic in a formal way. This selection contains his famous "sea battle" argument with which he advocates for the indeterminate truth value of future contingent claims.

De Interpretatione, Chapter 9 Aristotle[197]

https://www.st-andrews.ac.uk/~mnat/~ball0888/salamis/interpretatione.html

With regard to what is and what has been it is necessary for the affirmation or the negation to be true or false. And with universals taken universally it is always necessary for one to be true and the other false, and with particulars too, as we have said; but with universals not spoken of universally it is not necessary. But with particulars that are going to be it is different.

For if every affirmation or negation is true or false it is necessary for everything either to be the case or not to be the case. For if one person says that something will be and another denies this same thing, it is clearly necessary for one of them to be saying what is true – if every affirmation is either true or false; for both will not be the case together under such circumstances. For if it is true to say that it is white or is not white, it is necessary for it to be white or not white; and if it is white or is not white, then it was true to say or deny this. If it is not the case it is false, if it is false it is not the case. So it is necessary for the affirmation or the negation to be true. It follows that nothing either is or is happening, or will be or will not be, by chance or as chance has it, but everything of necessity and not as chance has it (since either he who says or he who denies is saying what is true). For otherwise it might equally well happen or not happen, since what is as chance has it is no more thus than not thus, nor will it be.

Again, if it is white now it was true to say earlier that it would be white; so that it was always true to say of anything that has happened that it would be so. But if it was always true to say that it was so, or would be so, it could not be not so, or not be going to be so. But if something cannot not happen it is impossible for it not to happen; and

---

[197] http://darwin-online.org.uk/content/frameset?itemID=A142&viewtype=text&pageseq=1

f it is impossible for something not to happen it is necessary for it to happen. verything that will be, therefore, happens necessarily. So nothing will come about as hance has it or by chance; for if by chance, not of necessity.

Nor, however, can we say that neither is true – that it neither will be nor will not e so. For, firstly, though the affirmation is false the negation is not true, and though he negation is false the affirmation, on this view, is not true. Moreover, if it is true to ay that something is white and large, both have to hold of it, and if true that they will old tomorrow, they will have to hold tomorrow; and if it neither will be nor will not e the case tomorrow, then there is no 'as chance has it'. Take a sea-battle: it would ave neither to happen nor not to happen.

These and others like them are the absurdities that follow if it is necessary for very affirmation and negation either about universals spoken of universally or about articulars, that one of the opposites be true and the other false, and that nothing of vhat happens is as chance has it, but everything is and happens of necessity. So there ould be no need to deliberate or to take trouble (thinking that if we do this, this will appen, but if we do not, it will not). For there is nothing to prevent someone's having aid ten thousand years beforehand that this would be the case, and another's having enied it; so that whichever of the two was true to say then, will be the case of ecessity. Nor, of course, does it make any difference whether any people made the ontradictory statements or not. For clearly this is how the actual things are even if omeone did not affirm it and another deny it. For it is not because of the affirming or enying that it will be or will not be the case, nor is it a question of ten thousand years eforehand rather than any other time. Hence, if in the whole of time the state of iings the state of things was such that one or the other was true, it was necessary for iis to happen, and for the state of things always to be such that everything that appens happens of necessity. For what anyone has truly said would be the case annot not happen; and of what happens it was always true to say that it would be the ase.

But what if this is impossible? For we see that what will be has an origin both in eliberation and in action, and that, in general, in things that are not always actual iere is the possibility of being and not being; here both possibilities are open, both eing and not being, and consequently, both coming to be and not coming to be. Many iings are obviously like this. For example, it is possible for this cloak to be cut up, nd yet it will not be cut up but will wear out first. But equally, its not being cut up is lso possible, for it would not be the case that it wore out first unless its not being cut p were possible. So it is the same with all other events that are spoken of in terms of iis kind of possibility. Clearly, therefore, not everything is or happens of necessity: ome things happen as chance has it, and of the affirmation and the negation neither true rather than the other; with other things it is one rather than the other and as a ile, but still it is possible for the other to happen instead.

What is, necessarily is, when it is; and what is not, necessarily is not, when it is ot. But not everything that is, necessarily is; and not everything that is not, necessarily is not. For to say that everything that is, is of necessity, when it is, is not the same as saying unconditionally that it is of necessity. Similarly with what is not. And the same account holds for contradictories: everything necessarily is or is not, and will be or will not be; but one cannot divide and say that one or the other is necessary. I mean, for example: it is necessary for there to be or not be a sea battle tomorrow; but is not necessary for a sea-battle to take place tomorrow, nor for one not to take place – though it is necessary for one to take place or not to take place. So since statements are true according to how the actual things are, it is clear that wherever these are such as to allow of contraries as chance has it, the same necessarily holds for the contradictories also. This happens with things that are not always so or are not always not so. With these it is necessary for one or the other of the contradictories to be true or false – not, however, this one or that one, but as chance has it; or for one to be true rather than the other, yet not already true or false.

Clearly, then, it is not necessary that of every affirmation and opposite negation one should be true and the other false. For what holds for things that are does not hold for things that are not but may possibly be or not be; with these it is as we have said.

Augustine was born in 354 CE in Numidia—a North African province of the Roman Empire. At the age of 19, Augustine read Cicero's Hortensius and developed his love of philosophy. This led him to read, among many other things, the Bible—though he was not initially impressed! Instead, he drifted into Manichaeism and was associated with that school of thought for a decade.[198] Over this time, he also studied Skepticism and Neo-Platonism. Eventually, he began to study the Bible again, and was influenced by Bishop Ambrose of Milan. After experiencing a seemingly miraculous event [hearing what sounded like a child's voice repeating "tolle lege" ("pick it up and read it")], he opened the Epistles of Paul to a random page and was drawn to Romans 13:13-14 ("Let us walk honestly as in a day, not in revelry and drunkenness, not in debauchery and licentiousness, not in quarreling and jealousy."). He eventually converted to Christianity himself, and was baptized by Bishop Ambrose on Easter in 387.

Upon his conversion, Augustine abandoned his old life for the sake of his new life, breaking with Manichaean past and ultimately founding a monastery and school in Hippo (North Africa). He was ordained a priest in 391, an auxiliary bishop in 395, and was appointed Bishop of Hippo in 396—a position he would fill until his death, 34 years later.

He wrote book one of "On the Free Choice of the Will" around 387, shortly after his conversion. Books 2 and 3 were written after he was made a priest in 391, and the work was completed in 395. The work is written in the form of the dialogue featuring himself and his friend Evodius. In their conversation, of which you have a brief excerpt below, they explore the compatibility of divine foreknowledge and human free will, with Augustine affirming both.

On the Free Choice of the Will
St. Augustine of Hippo[199]

Book 3

Evodius:...there is nothing I sense as firmly and intimately as that I have a will and that I am moved by it to the enjoyment of something. Surely I find nothing I might call mine if the will – by which I am willing or unwilling – is not mine! Accordingly, if I do anything evil through it, to whom should it be attributed but me? Since the God who made me is good, and I do nothing good except through the will, it is clearly apparent that it was given to me by God, who is good, for this purpose. Yet if the movement by which the will is turned one way or another were not voluntary and placed in our

---

[198] A religion founded in the 3rd century, CE, by the Persian Mani that offered a thoroughly dualistic understanding of reality, including a vision of an eternal battle between (equal) forces of good and evil, light and darkness.

[199] http://darwin-online.org.uk/content/frameset?itemID=A142&viewtype =text&pageseq=1

power, a man should neither be praised for swinging with the hinge (so to speak) of his will to higher things, nor blamed for swinging with it to lower things. Nor should he ever be admonished to put these things aside and to will to acquire eternal things or to be unwilling to live badly and to will to live well. But anyone who holds that a person should not be so admonished should be expelled from human companionship!

Since these things are so, it perplexes me beyond words how it could happen that [1] God has foreknowledge of everything that will happen, and yet [2] we do not sin by any necessity. Anyone who said that something can turn out otherwise than God previously foreknew would be trying to destroy God's foreknowledge with his senseless irreligiousness. Consequently, God foreknew that a good man was going to sin. Anyone who allows that God has foreknowledge of everything that will happen must grant me this. Thus if this is the case, I do not say that God would not make him – for He made him good; nor could any sin of his harm God, Who made him good, instead, He showed His own goodness in making him, even showing His justice in punishing him and His mercy in redeeming him – I do not say, therefore, that God would not make him, but I do say this: Since God had foreknown that he was going to sin, it was necessary that what He foreknew would be the case would happen. So how is the will free where such unavoidable necessity is apparent? . . .

Augustine: Surely what perplexes and upsets you is how these two claims are not opposed and inconsistent:

> [1] God foreknows everything that will be
> [2] We sin not by necessity but by the will

For if God foreknows that someone is going to sin, you say, it is necessary that he sin but if it is necessary, then there is no choice of the will in his sinning, but an unavoidable and fixed necessity instead. You fear that by this train of reasoning we infer either the negation of [1], which is irreligious, or, if we cannot deny [1], we infer instead the negation of [2]. Does anything else bother you?

Evodius: Nothing else right now.

Augustine: Therefore, you think: [3] everything God foreknows happens not by will but by necessity. . . .
Therefore, if He knows your will of tomorrow, and He foresees the future wills of all people who either exist now or will exist, so much the more does He foresee what He is going to do with regard to the just and the irreligious.

Evodius: If I claim that God has foreknowledge of my deeds, surely I should say with much greater assurance that He foreknows with certainty His own deeds and foresee what He is going to do.

Augustine: Then are you not worried that someone might raise this objection to you

"Whatsoever God is going to do, He too is going to do not by will but by necessity, given that everything God foreknows happens by necessity and not by will"?. . . So although God has foreknowledge of your future happiness – and nothing could happen otherwise than He foreknew, since then it would not be foreknowledge – nevertheless, we are not forced to hold on these grounds something quite absurd and far from the truth, namely that you are not willing to be happy. God's foreknowledge of your future happiness (which is certain even today) does not take away your will for happiness at the time when you begin to be happy. Likewise, a blameworthy will, if anything of the sort is going to be in you, will not thereby not be your will, merely because God foreknows that it is going to be. See how great the blindness is with which the following objection is raised: "If God foreknew what my will is going to be, then, since nothing can happen otherwise than He foreknew, it is necessary that I will what He foreknew; yet if it is necessary, we admit that I do not will it by my will at that time but rather by necessity." What exceptional foolishness! How then can it not happen otherwise than God foreknew, unless there is the will that He foreknew to be your will? I shall pass over the equal monstrousness uttered by this objector that I mentioned a little while ago, namely "It is necessary that I so will. He tries to take away the will by assuming necessity. For if it is necessary that he will, on what grounds does he will when it is not his will?

Suppose the objector does not say this but instead says that, since it is necessary that he will, he does not have the will itself in his power. Then the same problem will arise that you yourself ran into when I asked whether you were going to be happy against your will. You answered that if you had the power you would already be happy, for you said that you lacked only the power, not the will. I then added that the truth cries out from within you. For we cannot deny that we ourselves have the power, except while what we will is not present to us. Yet when we will, if we lack the will itself, surely we do not will. But if it can happen that we do not will when we will, surely the will is present in those who will; nor is there anything in our power other than what is present to those who will. Hence our will would not be a will if it were not in our power. Quite the contrary: Since it is in our power, it is free in us. What we do not have in our power, or what can not be what we have, is not free in us.

Thus it turns out both that we do not deny that God has foreknowledge of everything that will be, and nevertheless that we do will what we will. For although He has foreknowledge of our will, it is the will of which He has foreknowledge. Therefore, it is going to be our will, since He has foreknowledge of our will. Nor could it be our will if it were not in our power. Therefore, He has foreknowledge of our power. Hence power is not taken away from me due to His foreknowledge – it is thus mine all the more certainly, since He whose foreknowledge does not err foreknew that it would be mine.

Chapter 10: The Status of Miracles

Comprehension questions you should be able to answer after reading this chapter:

1. Explain Hume's distinction between ordinary, marvelous, and miraculous events.

2. What is Hume's argument against the warrant of miracle stories?

3. What are the conditions that Hume thinks would need to be satisfied in order for belief in a miracle story to be warranted?

4. What does Swinburne mean by each of the following terms: detailed historical evidence, personal memories, witness testimony, physical traces, general background evidence?

5. What does Swinburne mean by a law of nature? A fundamental law of nature?

6. What is Swinburne's criticism of Hume's argument against the warrant for miracle stories?

ﬕiracles

A feature shared by all three of the major Western religious traditions is the ﬔresence of miracle stories. The Pentateuch (shared by Judaism, Christianity, and ﬖlam alike) tells of the miraculous parting of the Red Sea, the various plagues of ﬓgypt, miraculous military victories, and miraculous healings (and even ﬔsurrections) performed by prophets, among other examples. Christianity, in ﬑ddition, tells of miraculous feedings of the "multitudes," Jesus converting water to ﬖine, Jesus healing the sick and raising Lazarus from the dead, and, central to the ﬑ith, the miraculous resurrection of Jesus Himself. Islam, too, offers miracle stories ﬐ addition to those found in the Pentateuch, including Mohammed ascending to ﬑aradise to consult with past prophets, as well as his own miraculous healings and ﬔultiplying of food.

Christianity, especially, seems to not only include miracles in its worldview, but ﬐ founded, essentially, on a miracle. "And if Christ be not risen again, your faith is ﬑in: for you are yet in your sins (*1st Corinthians 17*)." Indeed, the Vatican went so far ﬕ to make the denial of miracles grounds for excommunication! "If anyone shall say ﬑ . That miracles can never be known for certain, or that the divine origin of the ﬒ristian religion cannot properly be proved by them: let him be cast out."[200]

Clearly, then, miracles are important to the Western theistic traditions. Indeed, ﬒ey play an obvious role with respect to warrant. If you are convinced that miracles, ﬐ fact, occur, you have good and obvious reason to be confident in the existence of

---

[200] 3rd session of the First Vatican Council, 1870.

the supernatural. On the other hand, if you are convinced that miracles have not occurred, or that they are even impossible, then you have good reason to doubt the truth of any religious tradition that includes miracle stories.

Whether or not you think miracles occur will depend, in part, on what you think a miracle is. Sometimes "miracle" is defined far too loosely, such that all sorts of ordinary events are considered "miraculous," and other times miracles are, in effect, defined out of existence by virtue of overly stringent standards.

David Hume did a good job of distinguishing types of events with regard to miracles. "Ordinary" events are events consistent with our experience, inspiring no special response from us nor requiring any special explanation. Water flowing downhill is hardly shocking, and we don't think it demands any special explanation beyond how we normally account for the flow of water. "Marvelous" events, in contrast, are unlikely to occur, given our experience of the world, and will often inspire surprise when they occur, but they do not flatly contradict our general understanding of the world and how it works. Years ago, I went on a trip to Italy and met someone on the tour who attended the same Graduate program as I did (a few years before me), and it turned out that we lived within blocks of each other back home in California, and knew several of the same people. It was profoundly unlikely that I would travel to Italy only to meet someone who lived a few blocks from my home, and with whom I had so many connections—but although it was unlikely, it was hardly *impossible*. It didn't challenge my basic understanding of the way the world operates. Similarly, if someone emerges from a devastating car accident with only minor injuries, their lack of serious injury is surprising, but not "miraculous." Someone being doused in gasoline and set on fire, and emerging with no burns at all, on the other hand, isn't merely "unlikely," but contradicts our basic understanding of what happens when flesh and fire meet. We might well consider such an event a "miracle."

By "miracle," Hume understands an event that violates the laws of Nature, and thereby violates our general background knowledge, our worldview. In our experience, if someone is set on fire, they get burned. If they don't get burned, something weird has happened. We might suspect that that person is a stunt person and was wearing a protective fire suit. If we can verify that they had no special protection, then something *really* weird has happened. Similarly, in our experience, the dead do not return to life—and certainly not after three days in a tomb! Therefore, if someone were to rise from the dead in such a manner, it would contradict our general understanding of the operations of Nature, and we would deem it "miraculous."

Miracle stories, interestingly enough, serve both theistic and atheistic arguments. A very crude version of an "Argument from Miracles" might be as follows:

1. If miracles occur, then God exists.
2. Miracles occur.
3. Therefore, God exists.

Anecdotally, someone who witnesses a miracle might well come to faith, and someone who believes miracles occur has warrant for her theistic beliefs.

Skepticism with regard to miracles, on the other hand, could serve to undermine warrant. To be fair, the negation of the second premise above does not entail the negation of the conclusion. That would be an invalid argument. A disproof of miracles is not a disproof of God--but given that all three Western theistic traditions claim miracle stories, a disproof of miracles could certainly threaten a person's confidence in the truth of those traditions, generally speaking.

Hume

Skepticism is precisely the stance David Hume thinks appropriate with regard to miracle stories. Hume, like many, believed that we should proportion confidence in our beliefs to the evidence in support of those beliefs. This seems reasonable. Beliefs for which we have lots of evidence have lots of warrant. Beliefs with little evidence have little warrant. So, if you are presented with a claim concerning a miracle, how confident should you be that the claim is true? According to Hume, not very confident at all....

> *A miracle is a violation of the laws of nature; and as a firm and unalterable experience has established these laws, the proof against a miracle, from the very nature of the fact, is as entire as any argument from experience can possibly be imagined. Why is it more than probable, that all men must die; that lead cannot, of itself, remain suspended in the air; that fire consumes wood, and is extinguished by water; unless it be, that these events are found agreeable to the laws of nature, and there is required a violation of these laws, or in other words, a miracle to prevent them? Nothing is esteemed a miracle, if it ever happen in the common course of nature. It is no miracle that a man, seemingly in good health, should die on a sudden: because such a kind of death, though more unusual than any other, has yet been frequently observed to happen. But it is a miracle, that a dead man should come to life; because that has never been observed in any age or country. There must, therefore, be a uniform experience against every miraculous event, otherwise the event would not merit that appellation. And as a uniform experience amounts to a proof, there is here a direct and full proof, from the nature of the fact, against the existence of any miracle; nor can such a proof be destroyed, or the miracle rendered credible, but by an opposite proof, which is superior.[201]*

We may formalize Hume's argument as follows:

1. The evidence from experience in support of a law of nature is extremely strong
2. A miracle is a violation of a law of nature
3. Therefore, the evidence *against* the occurrence of a miracle is extremely strong.

---

[201] Hume, *An Enquiry Concerning Human Understanding*, Section X, Part I.

A more casual way of putting the argument would be this: suppose someone tells you that they witnessed a miracle, specifically, they saw someone raise another person from the dead. What seems more likely to you, given your experience of the world and how it works? That a miraculous resurrection took place, or that something else happened (e.g., the person wasn't really dead but sleeping or faking being dead; the person had only just died and was revived as happens all the time thanks to CPR; you are being lied to; it was a hallucination, etc.)?

> *The plain consequence is (and it is a general maxim worthy of our attention),
> 'that no testimony is sufficient to establish a miracle, unless the testimony be of
> such a kind, that its falsehood would be more miraculous, than the fact, which
> it endeavors to establish; and even in that case there is a mutual destruction of
> arguments, and the superior only gives us an assurance suitable to that degree
> of force, which remains, after deducting the inferior.' When anyone tells me, that
> he saw a dead man restored to life, I immediately consider with myself, whether
> it be more probable, that this person should either deceive or be deceived, or
> that the fact, which he relates, should really have happened. I weigh the one
> miracle against the other; and according to the superiority, which I discover, I
> pronounce my decision, and always reject the greater miracle. If the falsehood
> of his testimony would be more miraculous, than the event which he relates;
> then, and not till then, can he pretend to command my belief or opinion.[202]*

Hume would claim that you would be inclined to offer any number of possible explanations before believing that a miracle took place, because *any* of those explanations is more likely than the dead returning to life.

This is not to say that miracles are impossible, nor that the miracle story is necessarily *false*. This is, however, to say that our *warrant* for the miracle story is going to be low, and insufficient to justify belief that the miracle really occurred. Our experience favors the regular, continued operation of the laws of Nature more than it favors miracle testimony. It's more common (in our experience) for people to be mistaken or deceptive, than for the laws of Nature to be suspended or contradicted.

In order for our confidence in the miracle to overpower our confidence in the laws of Nature, Hume thinks that the miracle testimony would need to satisfy several conditions.

> *For first, there is not to be found, in all history, any miracle attested by a
> sufficient number of men, of such unquestioned good-sense, education, and
> learning, as to secure us against all delusion in themselves; of such undoubted
> integrity, as to place them beyond all suspicion of any design to deceive others;
> of such credit and reputation in the eyes of mankind, as to have a great deal to
> lose in case of their being detected in any falsehood; and at the same time,
> attesting facts performed in such a public manner and in so celebrated a part of
> the world, as to render the detection unavoidable: all which circumstances are*

---

[202] Ibid.

requisite to give us a full assurance in the testimony of men.[203]
In summary, the conditions are as follows:

- There must be a "sufficient number" of witnesses

- The witnesses must have sufficient "good sense and education"

- The witnesses must have "sufficient integrity and reputation"

- The alleged incident must have been "public"

Surely Hume is tapping into some "common sense" standards for credibility here. Generally speaking, we are much more confident in the truth of testimony if numerous people testify to the same thing (as opposed to just one person), if those persons are well-regarded with respect to their intelligence and competency, when we are confident in their moral character (i.e., we don't think them to be liars and con artists), and when the incident described in the testimony is one that happened "out in the open" where others could have seen it too. If a lone person with a reputation for being both ignorant and deceitful claims to have witnessed something, in private, that doesn't mean his testimony is false, but we are probably going to be much more suspicious of it, and him.

A generous, interpretation, then, of Hume's standards is that, given our confidence in the regular operations of the laws of Nature, we shouldn't believe in miracle testimony unless credible witnesses are providing the testimony.

A more critical interpretation is that Hume is biasing the case against miracles by demanding that hopelessly vague standards be satisfied. Just how many people will be a "sufficient number" of witnesses, for example? If two people make the same claim, is that enough? Two hundred? Two thousand? Couldn't a skeptic always just demand more witnesses? At what point is that demand unreasonable? Similarly, what counts as "good sense and education?" Surely Hume can't mean that a certain sort of degree (e.g., a Ph.D.) is needed for a witness to be credible when she reports seeing a miracle. What sort of education is needed to be a reliable witness to a miraculous healing? Do you need to be a medical doctor? If you witness water being turned to wine, do you need to have a degree in chemistry? Or viticulture? What counts as "good sense?" One hopes that simply believing a miracle to have occurred doesn't instantly disqualify you from having good sense! How do we measure "sufficient integrity and reputation?" This is similarly vague, of course. Finally, just how "public" must the event have been? This presumably relates back to the number of witnesses needed.

Whether Hume's standards are common sense, or biased, his argument is far from exhausted. He points out that humans are, in general, naively susceptible to the "passion of surprise and wonder."

The passion of surprise and wonder, arising from miracles, being an agreeable emotion, gives a sensible tendency towards the belief of those events, from which it is derived. And this goes so far, that even those who cannot enjoy this pleasure

---

[203] Ibid., part II.

immediately, nor can believe those miraculous events, of which they are informed, yet love to partake of the satisfaction at second-hand or by rebound, and place a pride and delight in exciting the admiration of others.[204]

That is, humans like to experience and believe in fantastic things. We entertain conspiracy theories, and we want to believe that wondrous events occur. If true, we might be predisposed to see things that aren't really there, to attribute significance to events beyond what's due. Perhaps a perfectly natural remission of cancer is described as a miracle because it would be really neat if a miracle had taken place?[205]

Hume also observes that miracle stories tend to arise from "ignorant and barbarous nations" (his words, not mine), in "unenlightened" past ages, and, suspiciously, no longer seem to occur (or at least no longer with the same frequency and publicity).

It forms a strong presumption against all supernatural and miraculous relations, that they are observed chiefly to abound among ignorant and barbarous nations; or if a civilized people has ever given admission to any of them, that people will be found to have received them from ignorant and barbarous ancestors, who transmitted them with that inviolable sanction and authority, which always attend received opinions. When we peruse the first histories of all nations, we are apt to imagine ourselves transported into some new world; where the whole frame of nature is disjointed, and every element performs its operations in a different manner, from what it does at present. Battles, revolutions, pestilence, famine and death, are never the effect of those natural causes, which we experience. Prodigies, omens, oracles, judgements, quite obscure the few natural events, that are intermingled with them. But as the former grow thinner every page, in proportion as we advance nearer the enlightened ages, we soon learn, that there is nothing mysterious or supernatural in the case, but that all proceeds from the usual propensity of mankind towards the marvellous, and that, though this inclination may at intervals receive a check from sense and learning, it can never be thoroughly extirpated from human nature.[206]

A similar tension between common sense and possible bigotry arises again. One hopes that those "ignorant and barbarous nations" aren't deemed so solely by virtue of their offering miracle stories! If not, though, it's questionable on what basis they are deemed ignorant and barbarous. New Testament miracle stories emerged in the Roman Empire (the peak of Civilization in the West, at the time), and in Jerusalem, the capital of the Jewish nation at the time. If such locales don't qualify as civilized, then Hume must intend that only modern nations are civilized (a possibly ironic

---

[204] Ibid.

[205] In fairness, it's not clear how we could determine whether a witness' belief was formed on the basis of evidence, or from being susceptible to the passions of surprise and wonder.

[206] Ibid.

stance, given that, from our perspective, Hume's own culture is perhaps a few centuries too "ignorant and barbaric," given contemporary standards). This seems to be an unjustifiable bias. On the other hand, there does seem to be something interesting about the fact that ancient cultures offer numerous fantastic tales of monsters, demigods, and miracles occurring on a grand scale. The Red Sea just doesn't get parted these days. The dead don't seem to return to life anymore. There might be theological explanations for why miracles no longer occur (or, if they do occur, are less grand in scale), but one might think it suspicious, all the same. If miracles occurred then, why wouldn't they occur now? And, if they don't occur now, maybe they didn't occur then?

This leads to a final criticism along this theme raised by Hume. Miracles stories are abundant in a *variety* of "ignorant and barbarous nations."

> ... in matters of religion, whatever is different is contrary; and that it is impossible the religions of ancient Rome, of Turkey, of Siam, and of China should, all of them, be established on any solid foundation. Every miracle, therefore, pretended to have been wrought in any of these religions (and all of them abound in miracles), as its direct scope is to establish the particular system to which it is attributed; so has it the same force, though more indirectly, to overthrow every other system. In destroying a rival system, it likewise destroys the credit of those miracles, on which that system was established; so that all the prodigies of different religions are to be regarded as contrary facts, and the evidences of these prodigies, whether weak or strong, as opposite to each other.[207]

Centuries and millennia ago, Christians told of miracles, but so did Jews and later Muslims. So did Hindus. So did worshippers of Zeus, or Osiris, or Odin. If each religion claims their God (or gods) performed miracles, wouldn't these accounts, in effect, cancel each other out? If Yahweh parted the Red Sea, it seems improbable that Athena turned Ariadne into a spider—and if Athena polymorphed Ariadne, it seems implausible that Yahweh parted the Red Sea.

Hume summarizes his point in a "snarky" fashion (to use some informal contemporary phrasing):

> ...upon the whole, we may conclude, that the Christian Religion not only was at first attended with miracles, but even at this day cannot be believed by any reasonable person without one. Mere reason is insufficient to convince us of its veracity: and whoever is moved by Faith to assent to it, is conscious of a continued miracle in his own person, which subverts all the principles of his understanding, and gives him a determination to believe what is most contrary to custom and experience.[208]

This passage requires careful reading to fully detect Hume's subtlety. He observes

---

[207] Ibid.
[208] Ibid.

that Christianity is (allegedly) founded on a miracle (the resurrection of Christ), but today requires a "miracle" for any reasonable person to believe in its truth. Did you catch that? The claims of the religion are so implausible, so contrary to reason, that it requires a "miracle" for any reasonable person to take it seriously! He also observes that those who do believe (by faith, certainly not reason!), experience a continuous "miracle" within themselves that allows them to "subvert all the principles of his understanding" and continue to believe in something so contrary to reason, experience, common sense, etc. It would take a "miracle" that any sensible person would believe anything so preposterous as the occurrence of miracles![209]

For Hume, though, though it is logically possible that miracles could occur, it is never reasonable to believe that a miracle has occurred. Belief in miracles is never warranted.

We have already considered a handful of objections to Hume's view (e.g., that his standards for testimony are too vague, etc.), but some claim that his approach is fundamentally misguided by virtue of what he considers (and fails to consider) when assessing the probability of miracle stories being true, as opposed to being fabrications or misunderstandings.

Hume's focus (for our purposes) was exclusively on miracle testimony, and we will maintain that focus. After all, historic miracle stories (testimonies) are far more fundamental to theistic belief than are contemporary stories. Christianity would collapse if the Resurrection didn't happen, but the religion won't collapse or even be imperiled if it turns out that Benny Hinn doesn't really perform legitimate faith healing today.

Swinburne

Keeping with this emphasis on past miracle stories, Richard Swinburne claims that when we're assessing the credibility of accounts of past events we must consider "detailed historical evidence," including personal memories, witness testimony, and physical traces, and we must also consider "general background evidence." We'll briefly consider what each means.

---

[209] Ironically, some theists might say that Hume is actually correct about this, but not in the way that he thought. Hume is being sarcastic. He is skeptical that miracles occur, and thinks that reason overwhelmingly favors the laws of nature over miracle testimony. Therefore, to override reason and believe in miracles anyway would itself be "miraculous." Hume seems to think that some sort of human psychological or sociological force is overcoming reason in the case of belief in miracles. "Fideists" (in general), believe that knowledge of and about God is the product of faith and God's own efforts, and is not accessible by reason. When someone comes to believe in God, God (or perhaps, specifically, the Holy Spirit) has "overwhelmed reason" and supplied belief in (and ultimately knowledge of) God that reason would not have produced on its own. Therefore, they might agree with Hume that it takes a miracle to believe in God—but they would not be being sarcastic, and would claim that such (actual) miracles really do occur in the case of every person who comes to believe in God.

Under the heading of detailed historical evidence, we first have personal memories. This is just what it sounds like. Our confidence in whether or not past events occurred as we think they occurred sometimes relies upon our own memories. I remember what I had for breakfast this morning (i.e., the morning on which I wrote the first draft of this section). My own memories inform my account of "Preston's breakfast on 11-7-13." It is both necessary and inevitable that we (generally) trust our memories. Granted, we sometimes misremember things, and memories are far from infallible, but our general stance is that we trust the reliability of our memories unless we have specific reason to doubt them. Of course, in the case of miracle stories from the Bible, we're not relying upon our own memories! So, in the context of this chapter, we must turn to witness testimony.

Similar to memories, we rely on "witness testimony" as the basis for countless of our beliefs, and we (generally) trust testimony to be truthful unless we have specific reason to doubt it. Witness testimony includes not only the obvious examples of someone telling you what they observed, firsthand, but also includes less obvious examples of the "testimony" we acquire from books, lectures, the internet, the radio, etc. Scientists testify as to the nature of physics, and your physics professor testifies further in your physics class. The author of the textbook for that class testifies to you as well—and I'm "testifying" to you as regards Swinburne's account of testimony! As with memories, it is both necessary and inevitable that we generally trust testimony unless we have a reason to do otherwise. How could you possible operate under the alternative, under a radical and comprehensive skepticism? On what basis would you doubt the truth of testimony, except by virtue of some *testimony* claiming you should *doubt* testimony (which would, itself, be untrustworthy, then!). Obviously, some testimony is false. Witnesses can be mistaken. Witnesses can be liars. If we have good reason to believe contrary to a witness' testimony, then we have reason to doubt her. Or, if we know her to be a liar, we have reason to doubt her. But, in the absence of those sorts of considerations, we generally trust the testimony of others.

In the context of this chapter, the obvious issue here is going to be whether we have reason to doubt the testimony of those reporting miracles.

Finally, we sometimes consider physical trace evidence in evaluating past events. Forensic investigators are obvious illustrations of this process. They might consider fingerprints, shell casings, blood spray patterns, DNA evidence, and other such "physical traces" (as well as witness testimony, when available) in investigating a crime scene. Given our focus on miracles, we can imagine that physical traces might sometimes be relevant, but other times not. If someone is claiming a recent miraculous curing of his blindness, then medical records, or even an inspection of his eyes, might be relevant—but if the miracle in question is said to have occurred in the distant past (e,g., the Resurrection), then physical traces might be unavailable, even if they once existed.

Beyond memories, witness testimony, and physical traces, Swinburne also claims that we consider our "general background evidence" (hereafter, GBE). Your GBE is your basic understanding of the world and how it works. It's your understanding of "what normally happens." It includes our understanding of all subjects. It is nothing less than one's "worldview." When evaluating claims (as regards their truth or falsity), part of our consideration is the extent to which that claim is consistent with our GBE. Claims consistent with your GBE are usually accepted as true, unless you have specific reason to doubt them. Conversely, claims that are inconsistent with your GBE are usually regarded with skepticism, unless the weight of evidence (e.g., witness testimony, physical traces, etc.) is sufficient to overcome the strength of your GBE.

Consider, as an example, the claim that "there was an exam in your Philosophy of Religion course last week." How would you evaluate that claim? Supposing, for the sake of argument, that you are a student enrolled in such a course, you would consider the claim with regard to its historical and background evidence. If you're a student, it's consistent with your GBE that exams take place. That doesn't necessarily mean that an exam for that class took place last week, but there's nothing mind-blowing about the idea that an exam took place in such a course. What about historical evidence? Do you remember taking an exam? If so, you have good reason to think the claim is true. If not, you have reason to doubt it. Have other students commented ("testified") about the exam last week? If so, you would reason to believe the claim is true, perhaps even if you don't remember it yourself. Finally, are there any physical traces, such as a graded and returned exam dated from last week? Rather obviously, if you remember taking the test, can look at the actual exam in your hands, and can have a conversation with others who speak of the same exam, you have ample reason to believe that it is, in fact, true that there was an exam last week. Absent *any* of that kind of evidence, though, the belief would be unwarranted.

Clearly, when both GBE and specific historical evidence align (e.g., that test example), we have warrant for the claim in question, but what happens when they are in conflict? Take the alleged Resurrection of Jesus, for example. According to your (and my) GBE (I presume), humans don't return from the dead after three days. If someone were to return from the dead in such fashion, it would be "surprising," to put it mildly. This is consistent with Hume's general point: our GBE is such that the laws of nature are not violated, so any claim to the contrary (e.g., a miracle story) is going to be met with skepticism, and must present powerful and overriding evidence to conquer the default stance offered by our GBE. The witness testimony (as presented in the Gospels of the Bible, for example) claims that Jesus rose from the dead. Our GBE says that doesn't happen. According to Hume, the caliber of witness testimony is insufficient to overwhelm our GBE, so we are not warranted in believing the miracle happened.

Swinburne disagrees.

To understand why, we need to delve into some of Swinburne's philosophical assumptions. Swinburne defines a "law of nature" as a principle that determines what often happens. He defines a "fundamental law of nature" as a principle that determines what happens, when what happens is determined by laws at all. Finally, he understands a violation of natural law to involve events that are contrary to the predictions of fundamental laws. It is a proper generalization to say that fundamental natural laws determine what happens, but he would add that such laws may be violated by a being that has the power to set aside those principles that govern the (natural) behavior of things. In other words, if God exists, and if God put into place those natural laws, then certainly those laws *could* be suspended or violated *if* God chose to do so.

It is here that the crucial significance of your GBE becomes clear. If we are considering the Resurrection, we have no personal memories to consider, nor any direct physical traces. There is witness testimony, of course, as presented in the Bible. Does that testimony conflict with GBE? That depends on what you include in your GBE.

If you are an atheist, and your GBE does not include God, nor any other supernatural entity, then miracle testimony will most obviously conflict with your GBE, and any such testimony will be hard pressed to overwhelm your GBE. This is Hume's position, of course. But what if you're a theist? What if your GBE includes the existence of God, and specifically of a God that created the laws of Nature and has reasons to suspend them from time to time—to demonstrate the significance of the person of Jesus, for example? In that case, the Resurrection account will *not* conflict with your GBE, and you are likely to take the testimony to be more credible. All this illustrates the probably obvious point that whether or not you're inclined to accept a miracle story as true depends, at least in part (perhaps in large part), on whether or not your worldview includes a God capable of performing miracles!

Swinburne believes there are several good arguments for God's existence (many of which we have studied in previous chapters of this book), and for those reasons, as well as reasons provided by virtue of personal experiences, Swinburne believes that God exists. If God does exist, there might well be good reasons for God to (sometimes) perform miracles (e.g., to interact with certain persons, to provide direct instruction, to provide great goods such as the atonement of sins, to authenticate Jesus' teachings in the case of Christianity, specifically, etc.). If the content of this paragraph partially describes your own GBE, then it is by no means obvious that a miracle story is, by default, so implausible as to be unwarranted. Miracles are consistent with a theistic worldview, so they can't be ruled out from the start, but must instead be assessed in terms of the specific evidence in their favor, case by case. A theist might believe that some miracles really happened, but dismiss others as fraud or wishful thinking.

In summary, Swinburne accuses Hume as being myopic with regard to our evaluation of miracles. Hume focuses on testimony, but even that narrow focus doesn't take into account (according to Swinburne) the role that the content of your GBE plays in the assessment of that testimony. Hume seems to assume that the inviolability of natural laws is present and dominant in every person's GBE—but this is true only for naturalists/atheists. Theists, in contrast, would not assume that natural laws are never violated.

"But isn't that just begging the question? Of course people who believe in God are more likely to accept miracle stories! But that doesn't mean that miracles actually prove that God exists."

Correct—but that wasn't the concern. Hume's claim was that we can never have sufficient *warrant* for miracle stories. Remember, warrant and truth are not the same thing. To say that a miracle claim could be warranted doesn't entail that the claim is true, just as saying that belief in God can be warranted doesn't entail that God actually exists. Hume's claim was that our confidence in the laws of nature always outweighs the possible credibility of miracle testimony, so, even if the miracle really did happen, we're not justified in believing in it. In contrast, Swinburne claims that that stance presupposes a purely naturalistic GBE. If you are an atheist, then very probably miracle claims are unwarranted for you (even if they're true!). On the other hand, if you are a theist, such claims might well be warranted (even if they're false!). This simply recognizes that the initial plausibility assessment of miracle claims is going to depend on whether your GBE includes the existence of any sort of being capable of performing miracles in the first place.

Conclusion

Among theists, there is plenty of room for disagreement as to whether miracles (as commonly understood) occur in contemporary times, and the various reasons why they do (or do not). There is certainly room for debate, amongst theists, as to whether any particular alleged miracle (e.g., a case of faith healing) really is a miracle. Where there's less room for debate, amongst most theists, is whether miracles have *ever* occurred. To repeat the most obvious example, it doesn't seem possible to have Christianity if the Resurrection didn't occur. Miracles, to put it mildly, are important to (most) theistic worldviews.

This chapter didn't even attempt to address the issue of whether miracles actually occur, and didn't consider arguments either for or against their occurrence. Instead, we focused on the more modest (but still important) issue of the *epistemic status* of miracle claims.

A recurring theme of this book has been warrant for theistic beliefs. In our opening chapters, I argued that the primary and most feasible use of TAs is to provide warrant for theistic beliefs. I then acknowledged that these TAs, even if successful, don't "prove" any particular religious system, but at best provide warrant for a "philosophical abstraction" such as the "First Cause." Theists must then engage a "matching strategy" to link these philosophical abstractions with the God of their worldviews. This is where the epistemic status of miracle claims is relevant.

If we are never warranted in believing in miracle stories, the matching strategy is going to be much more difficult. Even if we conclude that there is a First Cause, why think that the God described in Christianity actually exists, and is identical to this First Cause? On the other hand, if such miracle stories *can* be warranted, then the matching strategy is much more likely to be successful. After all, if someone has good reason to be confident that the stories of Jesus' miracles are true (including, especially, Jesus' own Resurrection), then this would be a strong indicator that this Jesus just might be who He said He was: God. And, if the God described in this faith tradition also is claimed to be the Creator of the universe, then that sounds like it "matches up" with the First Cause.

In this final selection from David Hume, he offers his famous criticism of the epistemic status of miracle testimony, weighing the reliability of the laws of nature against the plausibility of miracle stories.[Editorial note: there are some Latin phrases in this selection. For your convenience, I have provided translations as footnotes, when possible.]

An Enquiry Concerning Human Understanding
David Hume

SECTION X - OF MIRACLES
PART I

THERE is, in Dr. Tillotson's writings, an argument against the real presence, which is as concise, and elegant, and strong as any argument can possibly be supposed against a doctrine, so little worthy of a serious refutation. It is acknowledged on all hands, says that learned prelate, that the authority, either of the scripture or of tradition, is founded merely in the testimony of the Apostles, who were eye-witnesses to those miracles of our Saviour, by which he proved his divine mission. Our evidence, then, for, the truth of the Christian religion is less than the evidence for the truth of our senses; because, even in the first authors of our religion, it was no greater; and it is evident it must diminish in passing from them to their disciples; nor can any one rest such confidence in their testimony, as in the immediate object of his senses. But a weaker evidence can never destroy a stronger; and therefore, were the doctrine of the real presence ever so clearly revealed in scripture, it were directly contrary to the rules of just reasoning to give our assent to it. It contradicts sense, though both the scripture and tradition, on which it is supposed to be built, carry not such evidence with them as sense; when they are considered merely as external evidences, and are not brought home to every one's breast, by the immediate operation of the Holy Spirit.

Nothing is so convenient as a decisive argument of this kind, which must at least silence the most arrogant bigotry and superstition, and free us from their impertinent solicitations. I flatter myself, that I have discovered an argument of a like nature, which, if just, will, with the wise and learned, be an everlasting check to all kinds of superstitious delusion, and consequently, will be useful as long as the world endures. For so long, I presume, will the accounts of miracles and prodigies be found in all history, sacred and profane.

Though experience be our only guide in reasoning concerning matters of fact; it must be acknowledged, that this guide is not altogether infallible, but in some cases is apt to lead us into errors. One, who in our climate, should expect better weather in any week of June than in one of December, would reason justly, and conformably to experience; but it is certain, that he may happen, in the event, to find himself mistaken. However, we may observe, that, in such a case, he would have no cause to complain of experience; because it commonly informs us beforehand of the uncertainty, by that contrariety of events, which we may learn from a diligent observation. All effects follow not with like certainty from their supposed causes.

Some events are found, in all countries and all ages, to have been constantly conjoined together: Others are found to have been more variable, and sometimes to disappoint our expectations; so that, in our reasonings concerning matter of fact, there are all imaginable degrees of assurance, from the highest certainty to the lowest species of moral evidence.

A wise man, therefore, proportions his belief to the evidence. In such conclusions as are founded on an infallible experience, he expects the event with the last degree of assurance, and regards his past experience as a full proof of the future existence of that event. In other cases, he proceeds with more caution: he weighs the opposite experiments: he considers which side is supported by the greater number of experiments: to that side he inclines, with doubt and hesitation; and when at last he fixes his judgement, the evidence exceeds not what we properly call probability. All probability, then, supposes an opposition of experiments and observations, where the one side is found to overbalance the other, and to produce a degree of evidence, proportioned to the superiority. A hundred instances or experiments on one side, and fifty on another, afford a doubtful expectation of any event; though a hundred uniform experiments, with only one that is contradictory, reasonably beget a pretty strong degree of assurance. In all cases, we must balance the opposite experiments, where they are opposite, and deduct the smaller number from the greater, in order to know the exact force of the superior evidence.

To apply these principles to a particular instance; we may observe, that there is no species of reasoning more common, more useful, and even necessary to human life, than that which is derived from the testimony of men, and the reports of eye-witnesses and spectators. This species of reasoning, perhaps, one may deny to be founded on the relation of cause and effect. I shall not dispute about a word. It will be sufficient to observe that our assurance in any argument of this kind is derived from no other principle than our observation of the veracity of human testimony, and of the usual conformity of facts to the reports of witnesses. It being a general maxim, that no objects have any discoverable connexion together, and that all the inferences, which we can draw from one to another, are founded merely on our experience of their constant and regular conjunction; it is evident, that we ought not to make an exception to this maxim in favour of human testimony, whose connexion with any event seems, in itself, as little necessary as any other. Were not the memory tenacious to a certain degree; had not men commonly an inclination to truth and a principle of probity; were they not sensible to shame, when detected in a falsehood: were not these, I say, discovered by experience to be qualities, inherent in human nature, we should never repose the least confidence in human testimony. A man delirious, or noted for falsehood and villainy, has no manner of authority with us.

And as the evidence, derived from witnesses and human testimony, is founded on past experience, so it varies with the experience, and is regarded either as a proof or a probability, according as the conjunction between any particular kind of report and any kind of object has been found to be constant or variable. There are a number of circumstances to be taken into consideration in all judgements of this kind; and the ultimate standard, by which we determine all disputes, that may arise concerning them, is always derived from experience and observation. Where this experience is not entirely uniform on any side, it is attended with an unavoidable contrariety in our judgements, and with the same opposition and mutual destruction of argument as in every other kind of evidence. We frequently hesitate concerning the reports of others. We balance the opposite circumstances, which cause any doubt or uncertainty; and when we discover a superiority on any side, we incline to it; but still with a diminution of assurance, in proportion to the force of its antagonist.

This contrariety of evidence, in the present case, may be derived from several different causes; from the opposition of contrary testimony; from the character or number of the witnesses; from the manner of their delivering their testimony; or from the union of all these circumstances. We entertain a suspicion concerning any matter of fact, when the witnesses contradict each other; when they are but few, or of a doubtful character; when they have an interest in what they affirm; when they deliver their testimony with hesitation, or on the contrary, with too violent asseverations. There are many other particulars of the same kind, which may diminish or destroy the force of any argument, derived from human testimony.

Suppose, for instance, that the fact, which the testimony endeavours to establish, partakes of the extraordinary and the marvellous; in that case, the evidence, resulting from the testimony, admits of a diminution, greater or less, in proportion as the fact is more or less unusual. The reason why we place any credit in witnesses and historians, is not derived from any connexion, which we perceive a priori, between testimony and reality, but because we are accustomed to find a conformity between them. But when the fact attested is such a one as has seldom fallen under our observation, here is a contest of two opposite experiences; of which the one destroys the other, as far as its force goes, and the superior can only operate on the mind by the force, which remains. The very same principle of experience, which gives us a certain degree of assurance in the testimony of witnesses, gives us also, in this case, another degree of assurance against the fact, which they endeavour to establish; from which contradiction there necessarily arises a counterpoize, and mutual destruction of belief and authority.

I should not believe such a story were it told me by Cato, was a proverbial saying in Rome, even during the lifetime of that philosophical patriot. [1] The incredibility of a fact, it was allowed, might invalidate so great an authority.

The Indian prince, who refused to believe the first relations concerning the effects of frost, reasoned justly; and it naturally required very strong testimony to engage his assent to facts, that arose from a state of nature, with which he was unacquainted, and which bore so little analogy to those events, of which he had had constant and uniform experience. Though they were not contrary to his experience, they were not conformable to it. [2]

But in order to encrease the probability against the testimony of witnesses, let us suppose, that the fact, which they affirm, instead of being only marvellous, is really miraculous; and suppose also, that the testimony considered apart and in itself, amounts to an entire proof; in that case, there is proof against proof, of which the strongest must prevail, but still with a diminution of its force, in proportion to that of its antagonist.

A miracle is a violation of the laws of nature; and as a firm and unalterable experience has established these laws, the proof against a miracle, from the very nature of the fact, is as entire as any argument from experience can possibly be imagined. Why is it more than probable, that all men must die; that lead cannot, of itself, remain suspended in the air; that fire consumes wood, and is extinguished by water; unless it be, that these events are found agreeable to the laws of nature, and there is required a violation of these laws, or in other words, a miracle to prevent them? Nothing is esteemed a miracle, if it ever happen in the common course of nature. It is no miracle that a man, seemingly in good health, should die on a sudden: because such a kind of death, though more unusual than any other, has yet been frequently observed to happen. But it is a miracle, that a dead man should come to life; because that has never been observed in any age or country. There must, therefore, be a uniform experience against every miraculous event, otherwise the event would not merit that appellation. And as a uniform experience amounts to a proof, there is here a direct and full proof, from the nature of the fact, against the existence of any miracle; nor can such a proof be destroyed, or the miracle rendered credible, but by an opposite proof, which is superior. [3]

The plain consequence is (and it is a general maxim worthy of our attention), 'that no testimony is sufficient to establish a miracle, unless the testimony be of such a kind, that its falsehood would be more miraculous, than the fact, which it endeavors to establish; and even in that case there is a mutual destruction of arguments, and the superior only gives us an assurance suitable to that degree of force, which remains after deducting the inferior.' When anyone tells me, that he saw a dead man restored to life, I immediately consider with myself, whether it be more probable, that this person should either deceive or be deceived, or that the fact, which he relates, should really have happened. I weigh the one miracle against the other; and according to the superiority, which I discover, I pronounce my decision, and always reject the greater miracle. If the falsehood of his testimony would be more miraculous, than the event which he relates; then, and not till then, can he pretend to command my belief or opinion.

PART II

IN the foregoing reasoning we have supposed, that the testimony, upon which a miracle is founded, may possibly amount to an entire proof, and that the falsehood of that testimony would be a real prodigy: but it is easy to shew, that we have been a great deal too liberal in our concession, and that there never was a miraculous event established on so full an evidence.

For first, there is not to be found, in all history, any miracle attested by a sufficient number of men, of such unquestioned good-sense, education, and learning, as to secure us against all delusion in themselves; of such undoubted integrity, as to place them beyond all suspicion of any design to deceive others; of such credit and reputation in the eyes of mankind, as to have a great deal to lose in case of their being detected in any falsehood; and at the same time, attesting facts performed in such a public manner and in so celebrated a part of the world, as to render the detection unavoidable: all which circumstances are requisite to give us a full assurance in the testimony of men.

Secondly. We may observe in human nature a principle which, if strictly examined, will be found to diminish extremely the assurance, which we might, from human testimony, have in any kind of prodigy. The maxim, by which we commonly conduct ourselves in our reasonings, is, that the objects, of which we have no experience, resembles those, of which we have; that what we have found to be most usual is always most probable; and that where there is an opposition of arguments, we ought to give the preference to such as are founded on the greatest number of past observations. But though, in proceeding by this rule, we readily reject any fact which is unusual and incredible in an ordinary degree; yet in advancing farther, the mind observes not always the same rule; but when anything is affirmed utterly absurd and miraculous, it rather the more readily admits of such a fact, upon account of that very circumstance, which ought to destroy all its authority. The passion of surprise and wonder, arising from miracles, being an agreeable emotion, gives a sensible tendency towards the belief of those events, from which it is derived. And this goes so far, that even those who cannot enjoy this pleasure immediately, nor can believe those miraculous events, of which they are informed, yet love to partake of the satisfaction at second-hand or by rebound, and place a pride and delight in exciting the admiration of others.

With what greediness are the miraculous accounts of travellers received, their descriptions of sea and land monsters, their relations of wonderful adventures, strange men, and uncouth manners? But if the spirit of religion join itself to the love of wonder, there is an end of common sense; and human testimony, in these circumstances, loses all pretensions to authority. A religionist may be an enthusiast, and imagine he sees what has no reality: he may know his narrative to be false, and yet persevere in it, with the best intentions in the world, for the sake of promoting so holy a cause: or even where this delusion has not place, vanity, excited by so strong a temptation, operates on him more powerfully than on the rest of mankind in any other circumstances; and self-interest with equal force. His auditors may not have, and commonly have not, sufficient judgement to canvass his evidence: what judgement they have, they renounce by principle, in these sublime and mysterious subjects: or if they were ever so willing to employ it, passion and a heated imagination disturb the regularity of its operations. their credulity increases his impudence: and his impudence overpowers their credulity.

Eloquence, when at its highest pitch, leaves little room for reason or reflection; but addressing itself entirely to the fancy or the affections, captivates the willing hearers, and subdues their understanding. Happily, this pitch it seldom attains. But what a Tully or a Demosthenes could scarcely effect over a Roman or Athenian audience, every Capuchin, every itinerant or stationary teacher can perform over the generality of mankind, and in a higher degree, by touching such gross and vulgar passions.

The many instances of forged miracles, and prophecies, and supernatural events, which, in all ages, have either been detected by contrary evidence, or which detect themselves by their absurdity, prove sufficiently the strong propensity of mankind to the extraordinary and the marvellous, and ought reasonably to beget a suspicion against all relations of this kind. This is our natural way of thinking, even with regard to the most common and most credible events. For instance: There is no kind of report which rises so easily, and spreads so quickly, especially in country places and provincial towns, as those concerning marriages; insomuch that two young persons of equal condition never see each other twice, but the whole neighbourhood immediately join them together. The pleasure of telling a piece of news so interesting, of propagating it, and of being the first reporters of it, spreads the intelligence. And this is so well known, that no man of sense gives attention to these reports, till he find them confirmed by some greater evidence. Do not the same passions, and others still stronger, incline the generality of mankind to believe and report, with the greatest vehemence and assurance, all religious miracles?

Thirdly. It forms a strong presumption against all supernatural and miraculous relations, that they are observed chiefly to abound among ignorant and barbarous nations; or if a civilized people has ever given admission to any of them, that people will be found to have received them from ignorant and barbarous ancestors, who transmitted them with that inviolable sanction and authority, which always attend received opinions. When we peruse the first histories of all nations, we are apt to imagine ourselves transported into some new world; where the whole frame of nature is disjointed, and every element performs its operations in a different manner, from what it does at present. Battles, revolutions, pestilence, famine and death, are never the effect of those natural causes, which we experience. Prodigies, omens, oracles, judgements, quite obscure the few natural events, that are intermingled with them. But as the former grow thinner every page, in proportion as we advance nearer the enlightened ages, we soon learn, that there is nothing mysterious or supernatural in the case, but that all proceeds from the usual propensity of mankind towards the marvellous, and that, though this inclination may at intervals receive a check from sense and learning, it can never be thoroughly extirpated from human nature.

It is strange, a judicious reader is apt to say, upon the perusal of these wonderful historians, that such prodigious events never happen in our days. But it is nothing strange, I hope, that men should lie in all ages. You must surely have seen instances enough of that frailty. You have yourself heard many such marvellous relations started, which, being treated with scorn by all the wise and judicious, have at last been abandoned even by the vulgar. Be assured, that those renowned lies, which have spread and flourished to such a monstrous height, arose from like beginnings; but being sown in a more proper soil, shot up at last into prodigies almost equal to those which they relate.

It was a wise policy in that false prophet, Alexander, who though now forgotten, was once so famous, to lay the first scene of his impostures in Paphlagonia, where, as Lucian tells us, the people were extremely ignorant and stupid, and ready to swallow even the grossest delusion. People at a distance, who are weak enough to think the matter at all worth enquiry, have no opportunity of receiving better information. The stories come magnified to them by a hundred circumstances. Fools are industrious in propagating the imposture; while the wise and learned are contented, in general, to deride its absurdity, without informing themselves of the particular facts, by which it may be distinctly refuted. And thus the impostor above mentioned was enabled to proceed, from his ignorant Paphlagonians, to the enlisting of votaries, even among the Grecian philosophers, and men of the most eminent rank and distinction in Rome; nay, could engage the attention of that sage emperor Marcus Aurelius; so far as to make him trust the success of a military expedition to his delusive prophecies.

The advantages are so great, of starting an imposture among an ignorant people, that, even though the delusion should be too gross to impose on the generality of them (which, though seldom, is sometimes the case) it has a much better chance for succeeding in remote countries, than if the first scene had been laid in a city renowned for arts and knowledge. The most ignorant and barbarous of these barbarians carry the report abroad. None of their countrymen have a large correspondence, or sufficient credit and authority to contradict and beat down the delusion. Men's inclination to the marvellous has full opportunity to display itself. And thus a story, which is universally exploded in the place where it was first started, shall pass for certain at a thousand miles distance. But had Alexander fixed his residence at Athens, the philosophers of that renowned mart of learning had immediately spread, throughout the whole Roman empire, their sense of the matter; which, being supported by so great authority, and displayed by all the force of reason and eloquence, had entirely opened the eyes of mankind. It is true; Lucian, passing by chance through Paphlagonia, had an opportunity of performing this good office. But, though much to be wished, it does not always happen, that every Alexander meets with a Lucian, ready to expose and detect his impostures.

I may add as a fourth reason, which diminishes the authority of prodigies, that there is no testimony for any, even those which have not been expressly detected, that is not opposed by an infinite number of witnesses; so that not only the miracle destroys the credit of testimony, but the testimony destroys itself. To make this the better understood, let us consider, that, in matters of religion, whatever is different is contrary; and that it is impossible the religions of ancient Rome, of Turkey, of Siam, and of China should, all of them, be established on any solid foundation. Every miracle, therefore, pretended to have been wrought in any of these religions (and all of them abound in miracles), as its direct scope is to establish the particular system to which it is attributed; so has it the same force, though more indirectly, to overthrow every other system. In destroying a rival system, it likewise destroys the credit of those miracles, on which that system was established; so that all the prodigies of different religions are to be regarded as contrary facts, and the evidences of these prodigies, whether weak or strong, as opposite to each other. According to this method of reasoning, when we believe any miracle of Mahomet or his successors, we have for our warrant the testimony of a few barbarous Arabians: and on the other hand, we are to regard the authority of Titus Livius, Plutarch, Tacitus, and, in short, of all the authors and witnesses, Grecian, Chinese, and Roman Catholic, who have related any miracle in their particular religion; I say, we are to regard their testimony in the same light as if they had mentioned that Mahometan miracle, and had in express terms contradicted it, with the same certainty as they have for the miracle they relate. This argument may appear over subtile and refined; but is not in reality different from the reasoning of a judge, who supposes, that the credit of two witnesses, maintaining a crime against any one, is destroyed by the testimony of two others, who affirm him to have been two hundred leagues distant, at the same instant when the crime is said to have been committed.

One of the best attested miracles in all profane history, is that which Tacitus reports of Vespasian, who cured a blind man in Alexandria, by means of his spittle, and a lame man by the mere touch of his foot; in obedience to a vision of the god Serapis, who had enjoined them to have recourse to the Emperor, for these miraculous cures. The story may be seen in that fine historian[4]; where every circumstance seems to add weight to the testimony, and might be displayed at large with all the force of argument and eloquence, if any one were now concerned to enforce the evidence of that exploded and idolatrous superstition. The gravity, solidity, age, and probity of so great an emperor, who, through the whole course of his life, conversed in a familiar manner with his friends and courtiers, and never affected those extraordinary airs of divinity assumed by Alexander and Demetrius. The historian, a contemporary writer, noted for candour and veracity, and withal, the greatest and most penetrating genius, perhaps, of all antiquity; and so free from any tendency to credulity, that he even lies under the contrary imputation, of atheism and profaneness: The persons, from whose authority he related the miracle, of established character for judgement and veracity, as we may well presume; eye-witnesses of the fact, and confirming their testimony, after the Flavian family was despoiled of the empire, and could no longer give any reward, as the price of a lie. Utrumque, qui interfuere, nunc quoque memorant, postquam nullum mendacio pretium.[210] To which if we add the public nature of the facts, as related, it will appear, that no evidence can well be supposed stronger for so gross and so palpable a falsehood.

There is also a memorable story related by Cardinal de Retz, which may well deserve our consideration. When that intriguing politician fled into Spain, to avoid the persecution of his enemies, he passed through Saragossa, the capital of Arragon, where he was shewn, in the cathedral, a man, who had served seven years as a doorkeeper, and was well known to every body in town, that had ever paid his devotions at that church. He had been seen, for so long a time, wanting a leg; but recovered that limb by the rubbing of holy oil upon the stump; and the cardinal assures us that he saw him with two legs. This miracle was vouched by all the canons of the church; and the whole company in town were appealed to for a confirmation of the fact; whom the cardinal found, by their zealous devotion, to be thorough believers of the miracle. Here the relater was also contemporary to the supposed prodigy, of an incredulous and libertine character, as well as of great genius; the miracle of so singular a nature as could scarcely admit of a counterfeit, and the witnesses very numerous, and all of them, in a manner, spectators of the fact, to which they gave their testimony. And what adds mightily to the force of the evidence, and may double our surprise on this occasion, is, that the cardinal himself, who relates the story, seems not to give any credit to it, and consequently cannot be suspected of any concurrence in the holy fraud. He considered justly, that it was not requisite, in order to reject a fact of this nature, to be able accurately to disprove the testimony, and to trace its falsehood, through all the circumstances of knavery and credulity which produced it. He knew, that, as this was commonly altogether impossible at any small distance of time and place; so was it extremely difficult, even where one was immediately present, by reason of the bigotry, ignorance, cunning, and roguery of a great part of mankind. He therefore concluded, like a just reasoner, that such an evidence carried falsehood upon the very face of it, and that a miracle, supported by any human testimony, was more properly a subject of derision than of argument.

There surely never was a greater number of miracles ascribed to one person, than

---

[210] Roughly: "Those who were present now also mention both, when no reward for a lie [can be given]."

those, which were lately said to have been wrought in France upon the tomb of Abbe Paris, the famous Jansenist, with whose sanctity the people were so long deluded. The curing of the sick, giving hearing to the deaf, and sight to the blind, were every where talked of as the usual effects of that holy sepulchre. But what is more extraordinary; many of the miracles were immediately proved upon the spot, before judges of unquestioned integrity, attested by witnesses of credit and distinction, in a learned age, and on the most eminent theatre that is now in the world. Nor is this all: a relation of them was published and dispersed everywhere; nor were the Jesuits, though a learned body supported by the civil magistrate, and determined enemies to those opinions, in whose favour the miracles were said to have been wrought, ever able distinctly to refute or detect them.[5] Where shall we find such a number of circumstances, agreeing to the corroboration of one fact? And what have we to oppose to such a cloud of witnesses, but the absolute impossibility or miraculous nature of the events, which they relate? And this surely, in the eyes of all reasonable people, will alone be regarded as a sufficient refutation.

Is the consequence just, because some human testimony has the utmost force and authority in some cases, when it relates the battle of Philippi or Pharsalia for instance; that therefore all kinds of testimony must, in all cases, have equal force and authority? Suppose that the Caesarean and Pompeian factions had, each of them, claimed the victory in these battles, and that the historians of each party had uniformly ascribed the advantage to their own side; how could mankind, at this distance, have been able to determine between them? The contrariety is equally strong between the miracles related by Herodotus or Plutarch, and those delivered by Mariana, Bede, or any monkish historian.

The wise lend a very academic faith to every report which favours the passion of the reporter; whether it magnifies his country, his family, or himself, or in any other way strikes in with his natural inclinations and propensities. But what greater temptation than to appear a missionary, a prophet, an ambassador from heaven? Who would not encounter many dangers and difficulties, in order to attain so sublime a character? Or if, by the help of vanity and a heated imagination, a man has first made a convert of himself, and entered seriously into the delusion; who ever scruples to make use of pious frauds, in support of so holy and meritorious a cause?

The smallest spark may here kindle into the greatest flame; because the materials are always prepared for it. The avidum genus auricularum[6][211], the gazing populace, receive greedily, without examination, whatever sooths superstition, and promotes wonder.

How many stories of this nature have, in all ages, been detected and exploded in their infancy? How many more have been celebrated for a time, and have afterwards sunk into neglect and oblivion? Where such reports, therefore, fly about, the solution of the phenomenon is obvious; and we judge in conformity to regular experience and observation, when we account for it by the known and natural principles of credulity and delusion. And shall we, rather than have a recourse to so natural a solution, allow of a miraculous violation of the most established laws of nature?

I need not mention the difficulty of detecting a falsehood in any private or even

---

[211] Roughly: "The tribe with an eager ear for gossip."

public history, at the place, where it is said to happen; much more when the scene is removed to ever so small a distance. Even a court of judicature, with all the authority, accuracy, and judgement, which they can employ, find themselves often at a loss to distinguish between truth and falsehood in the most recent actions. But the matter never comes to any issue, if trusted to the common method of altercations and debate and flying rumours; especially when men's passions have taken part on either side.

In the infancy of new religions, the wise and learned commonly esteem the matter too inconsiderable to deserve their attention or regard. And when afterwards they would willingly detect the cheat in order to undeceive the deluded multitude, the season is now past, and the records and witnesses, which might clear up the matter, have perished beyond recovery.

No means of detection remain, but those which must be drawn from the very testimony itself of the reporters: and these, though always sufficient with the judicious and knowing, are commonly too fine to fall under the comprehension of the vulgar.

Upon the whole, then, it appears, that no testimony for any kind of miracle has ever amounted to a probability, much less to a proof; and that, even supposing it amounted to a proof, it would be opposed by another proof; derived from the very nature of the fact, which it would endeavour to establish. It is experience only, which gives authority to human testimony; and it is the same experience, which assures us of the laws of nature. When, therefore, these two kinds of experience are contrary, we have nothing to do but subtract the one from the other, and embrace an opinion, either on one side or the other, with that assurance which arises from the remainder. But according to the principle here explained, this subtraction, with regard to all popular religions, amounts to an entire annihilation; and therefore we may establish it as a maxim, that no human testimony can have such force as to prove a miracle, and make it a just foundation for any such system of religion.

I beg the limitations here made may be remarked, when I say, that a miracle can never be proved, so as to be the foundation of a system of religion. For I own, that otherwise, there may possibly be miracles, or violations of the usual course of nature, of such a kind as to admit of proof from human testimony; though, perhaps, it will be impossible to find any such in all the records of history. Thus, suppose, all authors, in all languages, agree, that, from the first of January, 1600, there was a total darkness over the whole earth for eight days: suppose that the tradition of this extraordinary event is still strong and lively among the people: that all travellers, who return from foreign countries, bring us accounts of the same tradition, without the least variation or contradiction: it is evident, that our present philosophers, instead of doubting the fact, ought to receive it as certain, and ought to search for the causes whence it might be derived. The decay, corruption, and dissolution of nature, is an event rendered probable by so many analogies, that any phenomenon, which seems to have a tendency towards that catastrophe, comes within the reach of human testimony, if that testimony be very extensive and uniform.

But suppose, that all the historians who treat of England, should agree, that, on the first of January, 1600, Queen Elizabeth died; that both before and after her death she was seen by her physicians and the whole court, as is usual with persons of her rank; that her successor was acknowledged and proclaimed by the parliament; and that, after being interred a month, she again appeared, resumed the throne, and governed England for three years: I must confess that I should be surprised at the concurrence of so many odd circumstances, but should not have the least inclination to believe so miraculous an event. I should not doubt of her pretended death, and of those other public circumstances that followed it: I should only assert it to have been pretended, and that it neither was, nor possibly could be real. You would in vain object to me the difficulty, and almost impossibility of deceiving the world in an affair of such consequence; the wisdom and solid judgment of that renowned queen; with the little or no advantage which she could reap from so poor an artifice: all this might astonish me; but I would still reply, that the knavery and folly of men are such common phenomena, that I should rather believe the most extraordinary events to arise from their concurrence, than admit of so signal a violation of the laws of nature.

But should this miracle be ascribed to any new system of religion; men, in all ages, have been so much imposed on by ridiculous stories of that kind, that this very circumstance would be a full proof of a cheat, and sufficient, with all men of sense, not only to make them reject the fact, but even reject it without farther examination. Though the Being to whom the miracle is ascribed, be, in this case, Almighty, it does not, upon that account, become a whit more probable; since it is impossible for us to know the attributes or actions of such a Being, otherwise than from the experience which we have of his productions, in the usual course of nature. This still reduces us to past observation, and obliges us to compare the instances of the violation of truth in the testimony of men, with those of the violation of the laws of nature by miracles, in order to judge which of them is most likely and probable. As the violations of truth are more common in the testimony concerning religious miracles, than in that concerning any other matter of fact; this must diminish very much the authority of the former testimony, and make us form a general resolution, never to lend any attention to it, with whatever specious pretence it may be covered.

Lord Bacon seems to have embraced the same principles of reasoning. 'We ought,' says he, 'to make a collection or particular history of all monsters and prodigious births or productions, and in a word of every thing new, rare, and extraordinary in nature. But this must be done with the most severe scrutiny, lest we depart from truth. Above all, every relation must be considered as suspicious, which depends in any degree upon religion, as the prodigies of Livy: and no less so, everything that is to be found in the writers of natural magic or alchimy, or such authors, who seem, all of them, to have an unconquerable appetite for falsehood and fable. [7]

I am the better pleased with the method of reasoning here delivered, as I think it may serve to confound those dangerous friends or disguised enemies to the Christian religion, who have undertaken to defend it by the principles of human reason. Our most holy religion is founded on Faith, not on reason; and it is a sure method of exposing it to put it to such a trial as it is, by no means, fitted to endure. To make this more evident, let us examine those miracles, related in scripture; and not to lose ourselves in too wide a field, let us confine ourselves to such as we find in the Pentateuch, which we shall examine, according to the principles of these pretended Christians, not as the word or testimony of God himself, but as the production of a mere human writer and historian. Here then we are first to consider a book, presented to us by a barbarous and ignorant people, written in an age when they were still more barbarous, and in all probability long after the facts which it relates, corroborated by no concurring testimony, and resembling those fabulous accounts, which every nation gives of its origin. Upon reading this book, we find it full of prodigies and miracles. It gives an account of a state of the world and of human nature entirely different from the present: of our fall from that state: of the age of man, extended to near a thousand years: of the destruction of the world by a deluge: of the arbitrary choice of one people, as the favourites of heaven; and that people the countrymen of the author: of their deliverance from bondage by prodigies the most astonishing imaginable: I desire any one to lay his hand upon his heart, and after a serious consideration declare, whether he thinks that the falsehood of such a book, supported by such a testimony, would be more extraordinary and miraculous than all the miracles it relates; which is, however, necessary to make it be received, according to the measures of probability above established.

What we have said of miracles may be applied, without any variation, to prophecies; and indeed, all prophecies are real miracles, and as such only, can be admitted as proofs of any revelation. If it did not exceed the capacity of human nature to foretell future events, it would be absurd to employ any prophecy as an argument for a divine mission or authority from heaven. So that, upon the whole, we may conclude, that the Christian Religion not only was at first attended with miracles, but even at this day cannot be believed by any reasonable person without one. Mere reason is insufficient to convince us of its veracity: and whoever is moved by Faith to assent to it, is conscious of a continued miracle in his own person, which subverts all the principles of his understanding, and gives him a determination to believe what is most contrary to custom and experience.

[1] Plutarch, in vita Catonis.

[2] No Indian, it is evident, could have experience that water did not freeze in cold climates. This is placing nature in a situation quite unknown to him; and it is impossible for him to tell a priori what will result from it. It is making a new experiment, the consequence of which is always uncertain. One may sometimes conjecture from analogy what will follow; but still this is but conjecture. And it must be confessed, that, in the present case of freezing, the event follows contrary to the rules of analogy, and is such as a rational Indian would not look for. The operations of cold upon water are not gradual, according to the degrees of cold; but whenever it comes to the freezing point, the water passes in a moment, from the utmost liquidity to perfect hardness. Such an event, therefore, may be denominated extraordinary, and requires a pretty strong testimony, to render it credible to people in a warm climate: But still it is not miraculous, nor contrary to uniform experience of the course of nature in cases where all the circumstances are the same. The inhabitants of Sumatra have always seen water fluid in their own climate, and the freezing of their rivers ought to be deemed a prodigy: But they never saw water in Muscovy during the winter; and therefore they cannot reasonably be positive what would there be the consequence.

[3] Sometimes an event may not, in itself, seem to be contrary to the laws of nature, and yet, if it were real, it might, by reason of some circumstances, be denominated a miracle; because, in fact, it is contrary to these laws. Thus if a person claiming a divine authority, should command a sick person to be well, a healthful man

to fall down dead, the clouds to pour rain, the winds to blow, in short, should order many natural events, which immediately follow upon his command; these might justly be esteemed miracles, because they are really, in this case, contrary to the laws of nature. For if any suspicion remain, that the event and command concurred by accident there is no miracle and no transgression of the laws of nature. If this suspicion be removed, there is evidently a miracle, and a transgression of these laws; because nothing can be more contrary to nature than that the voice or command of a man should have such an influence. A miracle may be accurately defined, a transgression of a law of nature by a particular volition of the Deity, or by the interposition of some invisible agent. A miracle may either be discoverable by men or not. This alters not its nature and essence. The raising of a house or ship into the air is a visible miracle. The raising of a feather, when the wind wants ever so little of a force requisite for that purpose, is as real a miracle, though not so sensible with regard to us.

[4] Hist. lib. v. cap. 8, Suetonius gives nearly the same account in vita Vesp.

[5] By Mons. Montgeron, counsellor or judge of the Parliament of Paris.

[6] Lucret.

[7] Nov. Org. lib. ii. aph. 29.

Chapter 11: The Problem of Pluralism

Comprehension questions you should be able to answer after reading this chapter:

1. What are the laws of identity, non-contradiction, and excluded middle?

2. What is the "problem of pluralism" with regard to truth, and how do the laws identified in question #1 apply to it?

3. What is the "problem of pluralism" with regard to warrant?

4. What does each of the following mean in the context of this chapter: exclusivism, agnosticism, universalism?

5. Why does Plantinga think "everyone" is "arrogant," if exclusivism is to be charged with arrogance?

6. What is the difference between (ordinary) agnosticism and what Plantinga calls "abstemious pluralism?"

7. Why does Plantinga think that abstemious pluralism is self-referentially inconsistent?

8. What is the "contingency of birth" objection to warrant for theistic beliefs, and how does Plantinga respond to it?

9. What is a "defeater"? How could the fact of religious pluralism serve as a defeater?

10. What is the "elephant parable," and how does Hick use it to illustrate his universalism?

11. What does Hick mean by the following terms: the "real-in-itself;" the "real-as-it-is-experienced-by-us."

12. What basic, common moral theme does Hick think all the major religious traditions have in common?

13. How might someone criticize Hick's universalist view?

If you have read the chapters, and followed the arguments of this book, then you have probably detected one of its recurring themes: whether theistic beliefs can be warranted, and whether TAs can provide that warrant. At the same time, you have probably detected the admittedly subjective aspect of that warrant. Certain theistic beliefs can be warranted for certain people, under certain circumstances—but not warranted for other people (or even the same person) under different circumstances. And, importantly, warrant is distinct from truth. Even if a person is justified in believing that God exists, that doesn't mean that it's true that God exists—just that the person in question is rationally justified in so believing.

At the same time, atheism might be warranted as well. Someone for whom none of the positive TAs are compelling, and for whom the POE is compelling, as well as the alternatives offered by the multiverse theory and evolution, for example, might have lots of justification for his atheism—without this entailing that God does not, in fact, exist.

But, if a Christian can be warranted in her beliefs under the right circumstances, and an atheist can be warranted in her beliefs in the right circumstances, what about a Jew, or a Muslim? What about a Wiccan, or a "Heathen" follower of Ásatrú? Hindus? Sikhs? If some (let alone all) of these different and competing worldviews can be warranted, does this create a "problem?" Does the existence of so many different worldviews undermine warrant for some, or even all of them?

Warrant v. Truth

You might have noticed already that, for at least one more time, I have stressed the notion of *warrant*. Religious pluralism, the existence of a variety of different, competing religious worldviews (not to mention the existence of the naturalistic worldview) poses a different "problem" whether we are concerned with truth or with warrant. First, let us consider the issue with regard to truth.

We all implicitly recognize and abide by certain logical principles that structure language and even thought. We may dispense with these principles only at the cost of rationality itself. Perhaps the most fundamental of these principles are the laws of logic first detailed by Aristotle:

– The law of identity: A is A
 [Formally symbolized: $(P \rightarrow P)$]

> *Now 'why a thing is itself' is a meaningless inquiry (for—to give meaning to the question 'why'—the fact or the existence of the thing must already be evident— e.g., that the moon is eclipsed—but the fact that a thing is itself is the single reason and the single cause to be given in answer to all such questions as why the man is man, or the musician musical, unless one were to answer, 'because each thing is inseparable from itself, and its being one just meant this.' This, however, is common to all things and is a short and easy way with the question.*[212]

A commonsense interpretation of this is that a thing is what it is. A cat is a cat. Cold is cold. A horse is a horse (of course).[213] This might seem obvious, and I hope it is! That just shows how central to basic reasoning these laws are.

– The law of non-contradiction: not both A and not-A
 [Formally symbolized: $\sim(P \& \sim P)$]

---

[212] Aristotle's *Metaphysics,* Book VII, Part 17, 1041a (Some scholars credit this law of logic more to Parmenides).

[213] I wonder how many of you caught that reference? If not, google "Mr. Ed."

The most certain of all basic principles is that contradictory propositions are not true simultaneously.[214]

This law prohibits contradiction. It makes no sense to say that the horse is not a horse. The hot fire is not hot is an absurd statement. If you deny the law of non-contradiction, rationality and coherence are lost.

- The law of excluded middle: A or not-A
  [Formally symbolized: (P v ~P)]

  there cannot be an intermediate between contradictories, but of one subject we must either affirm or deny any one predicate[215]

Finally, the law of excluded middle rounds out the pack. If we take a particular creature, it is either a horse, or it isn't a horse. It can't be both (law of non-contradiction), and it can't be neither (law of excluded middle). It's one, or the other.

Now that we have a basic understanding of all three of these laws, we can apply them to our current topic: the problem of pluralism with regard to truth.

Christianity, Islam, and Judaism each claim that there is one god. Hindus claim that there are many. The divine is singular, according to the first three religions mentioned. The divine is plural (not-singular), according to Hindus. According to the law of non-contradiction, not both of these claims can be true, as they contradict each other. If God is one, God is *not* many. If God is many, God is *not* one.

Christianity says that Jesus is divine. Judaism and Islam say that Jesus is not divine. According to our laws of logic, Jesus is either divine, or not. He can't be neither, or both.[216] This would indicate that if Christian claims about Jesus are true, other religions' claims about Jesus are false (and vice versa).

Political correctness notwithstanding, it seems that if we take the notion of *truth* seriously, if we believe that there is such a thing as objective truth, factual claims, then the existence of a plurality of religious claims indicates the existence of numerous *false* claims.

A different (but related) issue concerns the problem of pluralism with regard to warrant. Given the implications of the laws of logic above, the fact that there exists a variety of (conflicting and contradictory) theistic beliefs indicates that some of them are false. Of course, each believer usually thinks that her own beliefs are the true ones, and it's the other faiths that are mistaken in their claims. The mere fact that there exist other religions does not, of course, entail that one's own beliefs are false, but it might cause one to lose *confidence* in those beliefs.

For example, suppose that you are taking a math class in which you have to deduce the value of a variable. You do the work, "solve for X," and conclude that X = 5.

---

[214] Aristotle's *Metaphysics* , Book IV, Part 6, 1011b.

[215] Ibid., Book IV, Part 7, 1011b.

[216] Admittedly, Christian doctrine has a subtle interpretation of this, claiming that Jesus is both *fully* human *and fully* divine.

The instructor goes around the room asking for answers, and you (and several others) respond that X = 5. However, several other students answer that X = 7. The fact that someone else answered 7 does not, of course, mean that your answer of 5 is false (or vice versa). However, do you think that you might be less sure of your answer, given that several others answered differently? Might not your warrant for your belief that X = 5 be diminished by the fact that others believe it is equal to 7?

This is no mere speculation about a hypothetical scenario. Solomon Asch conducted some now-famous experiments in the 1950s that concerned precisely this issue. In these "conformity" experiments, a test subject was asked to view some lines (see below) and determine which of A, B, or C was the same length as line X. Pretty obviously, X = B, right?

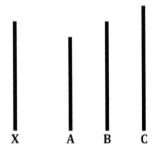

However, in these experiments, the test subject was placed in a room with seven "confederates" (actors who knew the purpose of the experiment). For a couple of rounds, things proceeded predictably: when lines were presented, each person provided the obviously correct answer. However, in the last round, one after another, the confederates each gave the same (wrong) answer to the question (e.g., X = C). When it came time for the test subject to answer, 75% of the test subjects gave the same incorrect answer. In that final round, the lines were no more subtle, no more difficult to discern. The correct answer was just as obvious. What differed was that everyone else gave the same wrong answer—and ¾ of the subjects conformed to that answer. When the subjects were interviewed as to why they answered as they did, some of them admitted that they were confident they were answering incorrectly, but they had succumbed to the peer pressure. The majority, however, exhibited what Asch called a "distortion of judgment" effect. These subjects were caused to lose confidence in their own answer, due to the competing answers of the confederates, and actually came to believe that they must have been mistaken!

Think about this is in the context of religion. Millions of people believe that Christianity is true (X = Christianity), but millions of others believe that Islam is true (X = Islam), and millions of others believe that Hinduism is true (X = Hinduism), and so on. The existence of Islam does not falsify the claims of Christianity (and vice versa), but might not the existence of these other worldviews (including atheism) diminish the warrant a believer has in her own? As in the Asch experiments, couldn't a Christian (for example) lose *confidence* in her own beliefs (that she believes to be true), given that other (presumably smart, well-meaning) people have sincerely answered "the question" differently? If so, warrant could be diminished—possibly to the point of coming to believe that the original belief was false.

We've seen how the existence of religious pluralism could be seen as problematic with regard to warrant, and its implications with regard to truth. A separate issue related to pluralism is another epistemic issue with possibly moral implications.

Some claim that, given the existence of so many varying religious traditions, it would be "arrogant" to believe that your own view is correct (and thereby competing views are false). Note the moral dimension to this. This is no longer a matter of the belief being less warranted by virtue of pluralism, but that persisting in the belief is, at best, "impolite," and, at worst, immoral. Arrogance, after all, is not usually regarded as a virtue.

"Exclusivism" is the position that some particular worldview X is correct, while other worldviews are incorrect to the extent that they contradict the (true) claims of X.[217] For example, someone is a (Christian) exclusivist if that person believes that their (Christian) worldview is generally accurate, and that any worldview that fundamentally disagrees is, to that extent, mistaken. Christian exclusivists would believe that the Hindu worldview is mistaken wherever it conflicts with the core claims of the Christian worldview (e.g., monotheism v. polytheism). I would like to point out, from the start, that atheism (naturalism) is *also* a worldview, and if one is an atheist exclusivist one believes that other worldviews (e.g., theistic worldviews) are mistaken whenever their claims clash with the core claims of naturalism (e.g., with regard to the existence of the supernatural).

Charges of "arrogance" are usually leveled at theistic exclusivists, if at anyone. "Who are you to think that your worldview is right, and people who believe otherwise are wrong?"

Plantinga and Exclusivism

In defense of exclusivism, Alvin Plantinga argues that exclusivism is unavoidable, regardless of worldview, and that if there's something "arrogant" about exclusivism, we are *all* (at least implicitly) equally arrogant!

In the context of (Western) theism, Plantinga defines an exclusivist as someone who satisfies the following conditions:

1. Believes something like "The world was created by an almighty, all-knowing, perfectly good, personal being."
2. Believe that any proposition incompatible with that belief is false.
3. Meets "condition C," which includes being fully aware of other religions, knowing that there appears to be genuine piety and devoutness in them, and believing that one knows no argument that would necessarily convince all or most honest and intelligent dissenters.

For the sake of clarity, "condition C" is just a fancy way to make sure we're talking

---

[217] Note that this is my own definition of exclusivism. I believe it to be consistent with most common usage of the term, but it might differ in some ways from the way others have defined the term.

about the "right kind" of exclusivist. One can imagine, for example, someone born in a time and place in which he is literally unaware of the existence of any other religion than the one practiced in his community. Such a person would, of course, believe that his worldview was the "one true faith," but this would perhaps only be by default: it's the "one true faith" because it's the only one that exists! Or, you could imagine someone who is aware of the mere existence of other faiths in a fuzzy sort of way, but who has never met any actual practitioners of those faiths, and perhaps he also entertains stereotypes of such "heathens" as primitive and barbaric. "They" believe otherwise, but that's only because they don't know any better.... Neither of these cases is the kind of exclusivist that Plantinga is seeking to defend. Instead, his focus is on an educated, intentional exclusivist. "Condition C" requires that the exclusivist be aware that other worldviews exist, be aware that some of the subscribers of those competing worldviews are intelligent, sincere, reasonable people (like himself), also be unaware of any argument that could necessarily convince those other people that they are mistaken, and maintain his exclusivism all the same. This is a bold exclusivism, where one says, in effect: "I am well aware that other intelligent people have a radically different point of view, and I'm aware that I cannot prove them wrong. Nevertheless, I still believe that my own view is the correct one."

Having focused on this specific sort of exclusivist, the criticism is that such exclusivism is morally deficient ("arrogant"), intellectually deficient (unwarranted), or both.

Plantinga observes that, given the fact of pluralism (i.e., the mere fact that other, competing worldviews exist), we have three general options:

1. Continue to believe in the truth of your own worldview and that, where other beliefs are in conflict, those beliefs are wrong (exclusivism)
2. Withhold judgment, and neither believe nor disbelieve in the truth of the core claims of your worldview (agnosticism)
3. Revise your beliefs such that they accommodate other worldviews (universalism)

Given these options, we will first consider Plantinga's response to the claim that exclusivism is morally problematic ("arrogant"). The complaint seems to be that when presented with religious diversity, the exclusivist is arrogant in continuing to believe as he does, because he believes himself to be in a superior epistemological state than those who disagree. We can perhaps imagine the critic: "Who do you think you are? What makes you think you're so smart, so special? You've figured out the truth, and anyone who disagrees with that truth must be mistaken. How arrogant!"

Plantinga's response to this charge is both simple and interesting, and will be a recurring theme for much of this section of this chapter: if such an attitude is arrogant, exclusivists are no more so than the alternatives.

The general structure of the complaint can be presented as follows:

•   You believe X.
•   Other (intelligent, educated, reasonable) people believe ~X.

- If other (intelligent, educated, reasonable) people believe ~X, and you persist in claiming that X is true, you are at least implicitly claiming that you are in a "superior epistemological state than those who disagree."
- To believe that you are in such a superior epistemological state is arrogant.

We can easily fill in the blanks to see how this applies to Plantinga's (Christian) exclusivism.

- You believe Christianity is correct.
- Other (intelligent, educated, reasonable) people believe that Christianity is not correct.
- If other (intelligent, educated, reasonable) people believe that Christianity is not correct, and you persist in claiming that Christianity is correct, you are at least implicitly claiming that you are in a "superior epistemological state than those who disagree."
- To believe that you are in such a superior epistemological state is arrogant.

Plantinga would now add, however, that the very same reasoning applies to the other available alternatives to exclusivism: agnosticism and universalism.

- You believe agnosticism is correct.
- Other (intelligent, educated, reasonable) people believe that agnosticism is not correct.
- If other (intelligent, educated, reasonable) people believe that agnosticism is not correct, and you persist in claiming that agnosticism is correct, you are at least implicitly claiming that you are in a "superior epistemological state than those who disagree."
- To believe that you are in such a superior epistemological state is arrogant.

Or:

- You believe universalism is correct.
- Other (intelligent, educated, reasonable) people believe that universalism is not correct.
- If other (intelligent, educated, reasonable) people believe that universalism is not correct, and you persist in claiming that universalism is correct, you are at least implicitly claiming that you are in a "superior epistemological state than those who disagree."
- To believe that you are in such a superior epistemological state is arrogant.

Notice that the structure of those claims is identical. Indeed, in writing those sections I literally just used the "replace all" feature of my word processor. If that structure entails arrogance on the part of the exclusivist, why wouldn't it also entail arrogance on the part of the agnostic or universalist?

As a general note, if you believe something to be true, it's difficult to see how you can avoid thinking that those who disagree are mistaken, unless you believe you are addressing a merely subjective issue. For example, if I complete a math problem, and I have double-checked my work, and I have a history of usually getting answers to math problems right, and I'm aware that someone else came up with a different answer, is it "arrogant" for me think that my own answer is correct, and that other person's answer is not? Certainly it's possible to *act* arrogantly in that situation. "You idiot! How could you possibly think your answer is correct? I'm the smartest person in the world!" Presumably, even Plantinga would admit that an exclusivist acting that way is being arrogant ("You idiot! How can you possibly think a worldview other than Christianity is correct? I'm the smartest person in the world!"). But, the complaint against exclusivism wasn't that particular exclusivists were parading around with their noses up and chests puffed out, sneering at their intellectual inferiors. Instead, the complaint was that *merely continuing to believe* that your worldview is correct, and competing worldviews are not, is arrogant. If so, Plantinga asks, aren't we all equally "arrogant?"

Christians (in general), believe that Christianity is true. If they didn't believe it was true, they wouldn't be Christians! If a Christian thought that Islam was true, she would be a Muslim instead. Or a Hindu. Or an atheist.

Muslims believe Islam is true. If they didn't, they wouldn't be Muslims, but would be "something else" instead.

Atheists believe atheism is true. If they didn't, they would be "something else."

If I think Christianity is true, I necessarily believe that atheism is false, just like if I believe atheism is true I necessarily believe that Christianity is false. What's more, on the assumption that my beliefs are warranted (i.e., I didn't just flip a coin to decide what worldview to adopt), I also believe that there are good reasons to believe my own worldview is true. Warranted Christians have good reason to believe that Christianity is true. Warranted atheists have good reason to believe that atheism is true.

If someone has good reasons to believe her worldview is true, and if believing that one worldview is true necessarily means believing that contradictory worldviews are false, then it seems that each one of us will believe our own view is correct, and others are not, regardless of what those particular views happen to be. Even agnosticism (of a certain kind) isn't a way out of this position.

Once again, we need to apply some precision to make sure we're talking about the "right kind" of agnostic.

Towards the end of 2013, the United States negotiated a preliminary agreement with Iran concerning Iran's production of nuclear materials. I (personally) don't claim to know whether the agreement is (ultimately) a good one or a bad one, whether it will succeed or fail—or even what would constitute success or failure. You could say I'm "agnostic" with respect to the ultimate value of that agreement. Agnosticism, in that sense, is just a suspension of belief due to a lack of relevant information. Some people are agnostics with respect to God's existence in that sense. They just aren't sure if there is a God, or not. It's a personal suspension of disbelief due to a lack of relevant information. Those aren't the agnostics Plantinga is talking about.

Abstemious Pluralism

Plantinga coins a special term for the agnostics he has in mind: "abstemious pluralists." This needlessly complicated term refers to people who, in the face of pluralism, not only (personally) abstain from believing that God exists, but who claim that *the only proper response* to pluralism is to abstain. I don't know how many such militant agnostics actually exist, but Plantinga argues that they are just as "arrogant" as the exclusivist in that they believe their own view ("abstention") is correct, and other views are not. What's worse, Plantinga argues that such "abstemious pluralism" is even self-referentially inconsistent. He attributes to abstemious pluralists the following claim:

(1) If S knows that others don't believe p and that he is in condition C with respect to p, then S should not believe p.

However, not everyone is an abstemious pluralist. In other words, many people do not believe (1) to be true. Suppose one realizes this, is aware of alternative positions, and believes one has no convincing argument for (1) (i.e,. one is in condition C with respect to (1)).[218] According to the demands presented in (1), wouldn't this mean that the right thing for the abstemious pluralist to do is to abstain from believing (1)? Or, to put it more succinctly: be agnostic about agnosticism? If the existence of a plurality of views on an issue demands abstention with regard to that issue, wouldn't the existence of a plurality of views on agnosticism/abstention itself demand agnosticism/abstention with regard to agnosticism/abstention?

The charge brought against exclusivism is that it was arrogant. Plantinga's basic position is that this is a hollow criticism in that there is no plausible way to avoid such "arrogance." We each, inevitably, believe various things for various reasons, and can't help but believe that those things are *true*. Unless you are a radical epistemic relativist, you believe that anything contradicting your beliefs is false. Even radical epistemic relativists believe their own relativism is true (in an ironic, likely-contradictory sort of way)! If everyone is "arrogant," arrogance has no sting. Certainly you can behave like a jerk when presenting your beliefs, but merely believing your beliefs to be true is no moral offense—or if it is, universalism and agnosticism are equally "offensive."

Plantinga thinks he has defused the moral objections to exclusivism, but what about the claim that it is irrational to be an exclusivist? Is it arbitrary to continue to believe in the truth of your own religious views in the face of so many seemingly sincere alternatives?

---

[218] Remember that "condition C," refers to being fully aware of other religions, knowing that there appears to be genuine piety and devoutness in them, and believing that one knows no argument that would necessarily convince all or most honest and intelligent dissenters.

Contingency of Birth

One argument used to support this complaint appeals to the apparent contingency of birth with regard to worldview. It seems obvious that the single greatest predictor of a person's worldview is the dominant worldview of her culture. This is just a fancy way of saying that if you are born and raised in a predominantly Christian community, you're more likely to be a Christian than anything else. If you are born and raised in Saudi Arabia, you're more likely to be a Muslim. And so on.

How is this an intellectual objection to exclusivism? The basic idea is that you believe as you do (e.g., Christianity) not on the basis of good reasons, but simply because of the contingent circumstances of your birth. Had you been raised elsewhere, you would have thought a different worldview was true instead. Plantinga believes Christianity is the "one true faith," but had he been born in Saudi Arabia, he would be endorsing Islam instead. Given the contingency of birth, your warrant for your own worldview is diminished, thereby undercutting any sort of confidence in exclusivism. Or so the argument goes.

Not surprisingly, Plantinga finds fault with this criticism, and deals with it in a now familiar theme: by turning it back on itself.

At a glance, dismissing someone's exclusivism as unwarranted just because of the circumstances of their birth looks like the genetic fallacy, but we needn't appeal to technical fallacy terms. Instead, Plantinga will simply point out that this "contingency" argument applies equally to naturalism/atheism, agnosticism, universalism, etc.

For example, naturalism has not always been a viable worldview, and it still isn't in many parts of the world. If you were born in Medieval France, you would likely be a Christian, not a naturalist. Therefore, your belief in naturalism is unwarranted. You only believe in naturalism because you happened to be born in the secular, post-modern West. Or, had you been born recently in Saudi Arabia you would more likely be a Muslim than a universalist, therefore your universalism is unwarranted. Once again, the theme is that we're all in the same boat. Presumably, the naturalist would retort "I'm a naturalist because there's good evidence for it, not just because I was born in the secular post-modern West!" In which case, Plantinga would cede that her naturalism is warranted, though not necessarily *true*. In just the same way, Plantinga believes he has good reasons to believe Christianity is true, and that he believes it on the basis of those reasons, not merely because he was born in a predominantly Christian community. If so, his own Christian exclusivism is likewise warranted, though not necessarily *true*. "But, what evidence could he have for his own view?" Review this entire book prior to this chapter. . . .

Does this mean that the existence of so many (competing) worldviews has no impact on the warrant of theistic belief, let alone exclusivist theistic belief, at all? No. Plantinga acknowledges that the fact of pluralism could work as a "defeater."

Defeaters

For many or most exclusivists, I think, an awareness of the enormous variety of human religious response serves as a defeater for such beliefs as (1) ["The world was created by an almighty, all-knowing, perfectly good, personal being."] and

(2) ["human beings require salvation, and God has provided a unique way of salvation through the incarnation, life, sacrificial death, and resurrection of his divine son"]—an undercutting defeater, as opposed to a rebutting defeater. It calls into question, to some degree or other, the sources of one's belief in (1) or (2). It doesn't or needn't do so by way of an argument; and indeed there isn't a very powerful argument from the proposition that many apparently devout people around the world dissent from (1) and (2) to the conclusion that (1) and (2) are false. Instead it works more directly; it directly reduces the level of confidence or degree of belief in the proposition in question. From a Christian perspective this situation of religious pluralism and our awareness of it is itself a manifestation of our miserable human condition; and it may deprive us of some of the comfort and peace the Lord has promised his followers. It can also deprive the exclusivist of the knowledge that (1) and (2) are true, even if they are true and he believes that they are. Since degree of warrant depends in part on degree of belief, it is possible, though not necessary, that knowledge of the facts of religious pluralism should reduce an exclusivist's degree of belief and hence of warrant for (1) and (2) in such a way as to deprive him of knowledge of (1) and (2). He might be such that if he hadn't known the facts of pluralism, then he would have known (1) and (2), but now that he does know those facts, he doesn't know (1) and (2). In this way he may come to know less by knowing more.[219]

Plantinga's wording is probably intentionally clever here: "he may come to know less by knowing more." Knowledge is standardly defined as "justified true belief," and this is the definition Plantinga is using as well. To *know* something, that "something" must not only be true, but you must believe it with a sufficient degree of warrant. The primary theme of this book has been how TAs can be used to provide warrant for theistic beliefs. Given enough warrant, one might not merely believe that God exists, but know it. If one *loses* warrant, on the other hand; if your confidence in the belief diminishes, it might "downgrade" from knowledge to mere belief.

Recall the Asch conformity experiments from earlier in the chapter. When it came for the test subject to answer, 75% of the test subjects gave the same incorrect answer. When the subjects were interviewed as to why they answered as they did, the majority exhibited what Asch called a "distortion of judgment" effect. These subjects were caused to lose confidence in their own answer, due to the competing answers of the confederates, and actually came to believe that they must have been mistaken. Initially, they probably not only believed that that line X was equal in length to line B, but had so much confidence that they *knew* it. But, when one person after another gave a different answer, their confidence fell to the point where they no longer knew line X was equal to line B—in fact, many no longer even *believed* it!

This is how pluralism could impact theistic beliefs. Maria might start out believing that God exists, and that God is the one that is described in her own religious

[219] Plantinga, Alvin. "A Defense of Religious Exclusivism." In Kevin Meeker & Philip Quinn (eds.), *The Philosophical Challenge of Religious Diversity*. New York: Oxford University Press. 1999.

tradition. Maria could have warrant for that belief, perhaps even to the point of *knowing* that God exists (on the assumption that the belief is true, of course), and is the God detailed in her religion. But then Maria becomes exposed to the wider world, and discovers that other faiths exist, and that millions and millions of sincere, intelligent people believe differently. Her confidence diminishes. What had once been knowledge now slides into mere belief, and possibly into a different sort of worldview altogether.

This seems to be just what happened to John Hick, ultimately resulting in his rejection of exclusivism in favor of "universalism."

John Hick

> *I myself became a Christian by evangelical conversion . . . and it was part of the package of belief that I accepted wholeheartedly that Christianity is uniquely superior to all others and the world in process of being converted to Christian faith. But that was some sixty years ago. In those days, like most of my generation, I had never met anyone of another faith and knew virtually nothing about the other world religions -and the little that I thought I knew has turned out to be largely caricature. But the present generation is generally much better informed. And today we all know, when we stop to think about it, that people of the other world religions have exactly the same view of their own faith as we do of ours.[220]*

Like many Christians, Hick started as an exclusivist, but his exposure to other world religions, over time, caused him to reject it. Troubled by the seeming contingency of birth, and its influence on the worldview to which one subscribes, Hick began to notice common themes within the major world religions. In meeting people of various faiths, and in visiting various houses of worship, he noticed a common moral core: a movement from self-centered egotism to an other-directedness, a movement out/up/beyond the narrow confines of the self to something higher/greater/other. He found common themes of love, charity, forgiveness, and compassion. One common and well-known example of such a common theme is found in the "golden rule."

Christianity	*All things whatsoever ye would that men should do to you, do ye so to them; for this is the law and the prophets.* Matthew 7:1
Confucianism	*Do not do to others what you would not like yourself. Then there will be no resentment against you, either in the family or in the state.* Analects 12:2
Buddhism	*Hurt not others in ways that you yourself would find hurtful.* Udana-Varga 5,1

---

[220] Hick, "Is Christianity the One True Religion, or One among Others?" Available here: http://www.johnhick.org.uk/article2.html

Hinduism	*This is the sum of duty; do naught onto others what you would not have them do unto you.*
	Mahabharata 5,1517
Islam	*No one of you is a believer until he desires for his brother that which he desires for himself.*
	Sunnah
Judaism	*What is hateful to you, do not do to your fellowman. This is the entire Law; all the rest is commentary.*
	Talmud, Shabbat 3id
Taoism	*Regard your neighbor's gain as your gain, and your neighbor's loss as your own loss.*
	Tai Shang Kan Yin P'ien
Zoroastrianism	*That nature alone is good which refrains from doing another whatsoever is not good for itself.*
	Dadisten-I-dinik, 94,5

Moreover, Hick didn't detect, anecdotally or historically, that Christians seem to have any special "edge" with respect to those traits or the behaviors that stem from them. These observations caused him to question not only Christian exclusivism, but the more "liberal" Christian "inclusivism" as well.[221]

It no longer seemed plausible to Hick that Christianity was the "one true faith," or even especially insightful in comparison to other major faiths. Given that all the major world religions had common moral themes, what could explain this commonality? Hick proposed universalism as a hypothesis to account for those common themes.

there is not just one and only one point of salvific contact between the divine reality and humanity, namely in the person of Jesus Christ, but that there is a plurality of independently valid contacts, and independently authentic spheres of salvation, which include both Christianity and the other great world faiths.[222]

Hick argues that *each* of the major world faiths describes a legitimate encounter with the divine, each is tapping into the same underlying divine reality, but each world faith is the result of the varied and culturally-historically contingent intersection of particular human cultures and the divine. "Religion is our human response to a transcendent reality, the reality that we call God. And as a *human* response there is always an inescapably *human* element within it." All the major religious traditions are simply different finite perceptions of the transcendent, infinite God. Hick quotes both Rumi and Aquinas to support this claim.

---

[221] Roughly, "inclusivism" is the view that Salvation is possible for good-hearted non-Christians as well, but that Christianity nevertheless provides special, clearer understanding of God and the means of Salvation.

[222]Ibid.

The lamps are different, but the Light is the same: it comes from Beyond[223]

Things known are in the knower according to the mode of the knower[224]

To further illustrate this idea, Hick makes use of the ancient and famous "elephant parable." Often attributed to the Buddha, the parable actually has versions not only in Buddhist sources, but in Jain, Sufi, and Hindu sources as well. According to this story, Buddha tells the story of a raja who had six blind men gathered together to examine the elephant.

When the blind men had felt the elephant, the raja went to each of them and said to each, 'Well, blind man, have you seen the elephant? Tell me, what sort of thing is an elephant?'

The blind men claim, variously, that the elephant is like a pot (head), winnowing basket (ear), ploughshare (tusk), plough (trunk), granary (body), pillar (foot), mortar (back), pestle (tail), or brush (tip of the tail), depending on which part they had grasped. Their disagreement is so great that they come to blows, at which time the raja says:

O how they cling and wrangle, some who claim
For preacher and monk the honored name!
For, quarreling, each to his view they cling.
Such folk see only one side of a thing.[225]

The basic idea behind the parable is easily paraphrased. Several blind men are each holding a part of an elephant, and asked to describe what the elephant is like. The one grasping the ear says that elephants are like fans. The one grasping a leg says that elephants are like columns. The one grasping the tail claims elephants are like braided rope. The one grasping a tusk claims elephants are like spears. The one grasping the trunk says elephants are like snakes. Each one of them is correct, but none is entirely correct, or exclusively correct. The elephant *is* like a snake, but it's *also* like a rope, and so on. The moral of the story is probably obvious: each of the major world religions is represented by one of the men,  the divine is the elephant, and each religious tradition is analogous to the interpretation of the elephant. One group of people experience the divine as Christianity, while another experiences Buddhism, and yet another Hinduism. Each

---

223 *Rumi, Poet and Mystic,* trans. R.A. Nicholson, 1978, p. 166.
224 Aquinas, *Summa Theologica,* II/II, Q.1, art 2.
225 Udana 68-69: Parable of the Blind Men and the Elephant

one of those experiences is a legitimate experience of the divine, but none exclusively or exhaustively manages to describe the "elephant."

In Hick's own words:

> ...between ourselves and God as God is in God's ultimate transcendent being there is a screen of varied and changing human images of God - not graven images but mental images, or pictures, or concepts of God. And our awareness of God is always through and in terms of these human images. We worship God through our own images of God, to which our human ideas and cultural assumptions have inevitably contributed.[226]

Hick distinguishes this transcendent divine reality as the "real-in-itself," with each religious tradition being only the "real-as-it-is-experienced-by-us." Necessarily limited by our human, mortal minds, necessarily limited by the constraints of human concepts and language, and necessarily constrained by cultural influences, we experience the divine through "filters." We shouldn't mistake the filtered *idea* for the transcendent "Other" that inspired the idea in the first place.

Does this mean that *every* "religion" is "right?" Can I just make something up, claiming that "the Force" binds all things together in the universe, and that various holy persons, some good, and some evil (known respectively as "Jedi" and "Sith") can tap into this power to perform miracles? Is my Star Wars inspired worldview now, conveniently, one of the "major world faiths" and on the same epistemic footing as Christianity and Islam (etc.)? Not exactly. Hick limits his universalism to only those faiths that have come out of a great revelatory religious experience, been tested through a long tradition of worship, and have sustained human faith over centuries of time and in millions of lives. These possibly vague criteria are presumably supplemented by his claims about the common moral core that inspired his endorsement of universalism in the first place (i.e., the faith in question must presumably exhibit that same movement from self-centeredness to other-directedness, etc.).

Many people find the elephant parable compelling, and Hick's application of it convincing. Not everyone agrees, though (not surprisingly). One possible problem with the elephant parable involves the need for a non-blind observer. Recall that everyone touching the elephant was blind, and what they didn't realize (but that we did) is that they were actually experiencing and describing the same animal. Of course, the only way the moral of that story can be conveyed is if at least one person can actually see the elephant! There needs to be a sighted observer who can make note of the fact that the blind men are all touching the same creature. If there were no such observer, we couldn't know that they weren't all touching different creatures. Analogously, Hick's application to universalism seems to presuppose that he is in the position of the sighted observer, able to discern that Christians are touching one part of the "elephant," while Hindus are touching another (etc.)—but if none of us ever perceives the "real-in-itself," how can Hick know that each world faith is "touching the same elephant?" If Hick is just as "blind" as the rest of us, how could he know that

---

[226]Hick, Ibid.

these world faiths aren't actually experiencing entirely different "creatures" altogether?

Hick grants this problem, and acknowledges that universalism is a hypothesis used to account for the fact that all the major religious traditions have in common a *movement from self-centeredness to divine-centeredness*. In other words, the observed common moral themes imply a common object responsible for that shared theme— but now we have another (different) possible problem.

Hick has labeled the transcendent Being (behind all the interpretations of God in the religious traditions) the "real-in-itself," while the gods and forces of specific religions are the "real-as-it-is-experienced-by-us." Given the inherent limitations of our filters, what can be said of the "real-in-itself?" "Nothing," admits Hick. Whatever we say about our experience of the Real only pertains to that experience—not to the real-in-itself.

> *Thus it [the Real as it is in itself] cannot be said to be one or many, person or thing, conscious or unconscious, purposive or non-purposive, substance or process, good or evil, loving or hating. None of the descriptive terms that apply within the realm of human experience can apply literally to the unexperienceable reality that underlies that realm.*[227]

If *none* of our concepts are applicable to the "real-in-itself," if none of our ideas or language can represent this transcendent divine reality, in what sense can we attribute "goodness" or "love" to the real-in-itself? It seems that Hick is acknowledging that, technically speaking, the "real-in-itself" is no more loving than hateful, no more forgiving than grudging. Neither love nor hate (human concepts that they are) can apply to the real-in-itself. Why, then, would the real-in-itself be manifested as good, loving, compassionate, charitable, forgiving (etc.) as allegedly indicated in that shared moral core that inspired the universalist hypothesis in the first place? Is there a tension here? If certain common moral traits in various world faiths are what inspire the idea that each faith is experiencing the same underlying divine reality, then wouldn't that indicate that the divine *really is* loving, forgiving, etc.? In that case, wouldn't it be the case that we actually *can* speak, with some clarity, about the real-in-itself? And, if that's true, wouldn't that mean that some interpretations are correct, and others incorrect (e.g., those interpretations that do *not* inspire love, charity, etc.)? Or, if Hick is right and we really are incapable of attributing any properties to the real-in-itself, how can we say that the real-in-itself is "loving?" Why wouldn't "hateful" worldviews be equally legitimate experiences of the divine? And, if any and every interpretation (loving, hateful, indifferent, or otherwise) is equally legitimate, have we devolved into a radical subjectivism that makes any meaningful conversation about "God" impossible?

Perhaps we draw some boundaries and acknowledge that some interpretations are somehow "more true" than others? There do seem to be some rather obvious contradictory claims between certain religious traditions, after all. Hinduism is polytheistic, whereas Islam is monotheistic. Christianity has a personal deity

---

[227] Hick, *An Interpretation of Religion*, Yale University Press. 1989, 350.

whereas Buddhism does not. In the "East" souls are reincarnated, in the "West" they are not. Do these contradictions indicate that some interpretations are "wrong?" Hick doesn't want to accept that implication.

> *Well, if we accept the distinction between the divine reality as it is in itself and as variously imaged by us, then our Christian doctrines are about the ultimate divine reality as conceived by us, in distinction from that reality as it is in itself. And the different truth-claims of the different religions are claims about different manifestations of the Ultimate to different human mentalities formed within different human cultures and different streams of religious history. As such, they do not contradict one another. That Muslims, for example, think of the divine, and experience the divine, as the Qur'anic Allah is not incompatible with the fact that Christians think of the divine, and experience the divine, as the heavenly Father of Jesus' teaching, or more theologically as the Holy Trinity. In other words, what are called the conflicting truth-claims of the religions do not in fact conflict, because they are claims about different human awarenesses of the divine, made possible by the fact that, to quote Aquinas again, things known are in the knower according to the mode of the knower.[228]*

We're back to the "real-in-itself" v. the "real-as-it-is-experienced-by-us" again. Consider a quick analogy: imagine my cat Morgana. What does she look like? Some of you will claim "I have no idea." But suppose I demand that you form a mental picture anyway. What color is she? "Black," some will say. "Calico," others will say. "Gray," say some others. Does that mean that my cat is literally changing colors from one moment to the next, based on whoever is describing her? Of course not! There is no contradiction or conflict in her *actual* color. The contradiction arises only in your various descriptions of her color. The conflict arises not in her, but in your ideas about her. So too with regard to the real-in-itself, according to Hick. There is no contradiction at the level of the real-in-itself. It is only our various filtered interpretations that contradict. It is no more the case that the real-in-itself is fluctuating in its actual properties than was the case with my cat—but none of our properties actually apply to the real-in-itself, unlike with my cat. Those of you imagined a black cat were right. My cat is black. If you imagined a white cat you were (forgivably) mistaken. According to Hick, if I imagine God is "personal," I am *not* mistaken. If a Buddhist experiences something non-personal, she is not mistaken either. If a Muslim conceives God as One, he is right. If a Hindu imagines God as Many, he is also right. Or, if someone who has studied too much philosophy says "neither one nor many, and both one and many," she is also right. Is the atheist who conceives God as "non-existent" also right? Do we any longer make any sense?

What are we to conclude from our exploration of pluralism, then? It depends, at least in part, on what you think of "truth." If you have a robust, objective understanding of truth, and if you think that our claims, expressed in human language and concepts, can at least partially "correspond" with reality as it really is, including God (if God exists), then the existence of a plurality of faiths could indicate that some

---

[228] Hick, "Is Christianity the only true religion, or one among others?" Ibid.

of them are mistaken, and *might* cause a loss of warrant for any particular set of religious beliefs. I say "might" because Plantinga, of course, thinks that exclusivist beliefs can be warranted, despite pluralism, under the right conditions. On the other hand, if you are skeptical of our ability to perceive and understand God (if God exists), then the conflict between belief systems might just be a conflict about necessarily limited concepts, and you might find universalism to be appealing—in which case warrant for exclusivism might be diminished.

Conclusion

This admittedly brief and limited examination of the philosophy of religion has, ultimately, focused on one particular theme: warrant. We examined a variety of theistic arguments, both positive and negative, recognizing that none of them is likely to succeed as a "proof." That is, no argument either for or against God's existence is likely to be irresistibly and irrefutably convincing. Instead, at best, such arguments can manipulate the warrant one has for theistic beliefs. Positive TAs, if successful, might increase warrant, whereas negative TAs, if successful, might diminish it.

In the end, we all find ourselves in a similar epistemic position. We each subscribe to a worldview, our basic understanding of the world and how it works. For some of us, that worldview is theistic. For others, it is purely naturalistic. In either case, we subscribe to that worldview because we find it to be more convincing than other available alternatives, and to the extent that we subscribe to one, we reject the others. We are all "exclusivists," in that sense, at least.

I claim that neither theistic worldviews (in general), nor naturalistic worldviews (in general) can be *proven* to be true or false, though I do believe that both kinds of worldviews can't be equally true. This is just a fancy way of saying that if God (somehow defined) exists, then the naturalistic worldview is mistaken, while if there is not any sort of God, then all the theistic worldviews are mistaken.

Most of us like to think that we believe what we do for good reasons, that we're not gullible, naïve consumers of popular thought who have never bothered to question what matters most. Your worldview (and mine), whether theistic or naturalistic, can be warranted, or not. By carefully considering the arguments and issues raised in this book (and others like it), we are, in effect, performing our "due diligence"—and that's the best any of us can do, and the least any of us should do.

Notes

Notes

Notes

Notes

Notes

Made in the USA
Columbia, SC
26 July 2022